Qualitative Research in Practice

Examples for Discussion and Analysis

Sharan B. Merriam and Associates

JOSSEY-BASS
A Wiley Company
www.josseybass.com

Published by

 JOSSEY-BASS
A Wiley Company
989 Market Street
San Francisco, CA 94103-1741

www.josseybass.com

Jossey-Bass books and products are available through most bookstores. To contact Jossey-Bass directly, call (888) 378-2537, fax to (800) 605-2665, or visit our website at www.josseybass.com.

Substantial discounts on bulk quantities of Jossey-Bass books are available to corporations, professional associations, and other organizations. For details and discount information, contact the special sales department at Jossey-Bass.

Library of Congress Cataloging-in-Publication Data

Merriam, Sharan B.
    Qualitative research in practice : examples for discussion and analysis / Sharan B. Merriam and associates.— 1st ed.
        p. cm. — (The Jossey-Bass higher and adult education series)
Includes bibliographical references (p.   ) and index.
    ISBN 0-7879-5895-6 (alk. paper)
    1. Social sciences—Research—Methodology. 2. Qualitative research. I. Title. II. Series.
    H62 .M4228 2002
    001.4'2—dc21   2001008201

FIRST EDITION
PB Printing 10 9 8 7 6 5 4 3 2

The Jossey-Bass
Higher and Adult Education Series

CONTENTS

Part One
The Nature of Qualitative Inquiry

Sharan B. Merriam
This chapter explains what qualitative research is, how it differs from positivist or quantitative research, what variations exist within the qualitative paradigm itself, and how one goes about designing and conducting a qualitative study.

Sharan B. Merriam
This chapter presents a framework for evaluating and assessing the quality and trustworthiness of a qualitative research study. It includes strategies to assess internal validity, reliability, and external validity or generalizability, as well as ethical considerations.

Part Two

Examples of Qualitative Research for Discussion and Analysis

ology to study in-depth the lived experience of in-church worship. It uses descriptions provided by participants in interviews to develop emergent themes and an interpretation of in-church worship. Finally, it uses these themes and interpretation to compare the experiences of worshipping in-church with worshipping by television.

This study explored the experience of "good" supervision events from the perspective of supervisees using a qualitative phenomenological research methodology. Eight intermediate- to advanced-level trainees participated in tape-recorded interviews in which they described a recent good supervision experience. Identification of themes reflective of good supervision events within the general meaning structure resulted in four distinct supervision phases: (1) existential baseline; (2) setting the stage; (3) good supervision experience; and (4) outcomes of good supervision.

This grounded theory study contributes to an understanding of school counselors' professional identity development. It explores and conceptualizes school counselors' professional interactions as defining experiences in the development of a professional identity. The research design included interviewing ten school counselors who were selected to represent diverse perspectives. The substantive theory generated from the study describes the context, conditions, and phases for a process identified as the "blending of influences."

   Susan R. Jones, Marylu K. McEwen
   *This study presents a conceptual model of multiple dimensions of
   identity. The model evolved from a grounded theory study of a group
   of ten women college students, aged twenty to twenty-four and of diverse racial-ethnic backgrounds. In the model, a core sense of self or
   one's personal identity is surrounded by intersecting circles which represent significant identity dimensions (e.g., race, sexual orientation,
   and religion) and contextual influences (e.g., family background and
   life experiences).*

   Susan R. Jones

   Ernestine K. Enomoto, Mary Antony Bair
   *In this sociological study, the tension between those educators who be-
   lieve in schooling for assimilation and those who favor cultural pluralism is explored by examining the school's role in the assimilation
   process. The study focused on a large comprehensive high school, which
   reflected a multi-ethnic student population, largely from recently immigrated families. The findings support the reproduction theory assumption that the school reflects and maintains the social stratification
   present in society.*

   Ernestine K. Enomoto, Mary Antony Bair

    Thomas P. Hébert, Teresa M. Beardsley
    *In this account of a gifted Black child living in an impoverished rural
    environment, a university researcher and a classroom teacher collab-
    orate to describe his creativity, his resilience, his struggle to find a place
    for himself in his community, and the significant factors that influ-
    enced the early formation of a strong self-identity. The findings offer
    educators helpful suggestions for identifying and addressing the edu-
    cational needs of gifted Black children living in rural poverty.*

Preface

Qualitative research is a powerful tool for learning more about our lives and the sociohistorical context in which we live. Though it has a long history in anthropology and sociology, qualitative research is no longer limited to these disciplines but is an accepted methodology in all the social sciences and applied fields of practice. The growing legitimacy of doing qualitative research has been accompanied by a surge of books, journals, Web sites, and international conferences devoted to this form of inquiry. The variety of topics, journals, and fields from which selections for this book were drawn in itself attests to the growing popularity of qualitative research in fields as diverse as counseling, public health, management, and education.

The myriad of resources available to novice researchers to learn about the method is both affirming, in that there is help available, and daunting, because there is *so much* help out there. Fortunately, a growing number of graduate programs include courses in qualitative research in addition to the usual array of research design and statistics courses. Courses in qualitative research methods introduce students to this form of research, as well as guide them in the experience of designing and implementing a qualitative study. There are practitioners in many fields, however, who have had no training in this method but who have questions about their practice that are best approached from a qualitative rather than quantitative perspective. Understanding a phenomenon from the participants' perspectives—the meanings people derive from a situation or understanding a process—requires asking important questions, questions that lend themselves to qualitative inquiry. This book has been compiled for both students and practitioners who wish to learn more about qualitative research through reading and studying articles that report on qualitative research. It is important to note where this book is positioned with regard to major, overarching, philosophical orientations to research in general, including the familiar positivist perspective. As explained in "Introduction to Qualitative Research," qualitative research can include interpretive, critical, postmodern-poststructural, feminist, Marxist, and participatory action research. This book, including the majority of article selections, reflects an *interpretive* orientation to research.

Qualitative Research in Practice: Examples for Discussion and Analysis is not by itself a textbook on qualitative research; rather, it is designed to be used along with standard texts in the field. It is primarily a collection of articles (sixteen in Part Two) exemplifying different types of qualitative research. A unique feature of the book is that each article is followed by a short reflection piece by the article's author commenting on his or her experience engaging in this type of research. Some of these reflections are written by novice researchers who describe how they made their way through the study, learning as they went; others are by more seasoned researchers who have some very insightful things to say about conducting a qualitative study. Readers will be able to resonate with the trial-and-error tenor of doing qualitative research regardless of whether one has had years of experience or is new to the methodology.

This book is intended for all those interested in qualitative research regardless of discipline or experience with this kind of study. Although researchers in fields such as education, nursing, social work, or urban studies may ask different questions of their practice, the *process* of interpretive qualitative inquiry is the same. First, the question needs to be shaped in a manner congruent with the philosophical underpinnings of this form of research; a particular qualitative design is then selected, followed by sample selection, data collection, and analysis. Finally, the interpretation of the data (the findings) is presented in a format compatible with the particular qualitative design. The introductory chapters of this volume present the "basics" of doing qualitative research, the different types of qualitative inquiry, and how to evaluate and assess studies conducted in this paradigm. Readers can then approach the sixteen examples of qualitative research knowing what to look for. It will be a particularly useful resource for understanding the variety of qualitative research and what differentiates one form from another. It is my intention that this volume be used as a resource for studying and discussing the nature of qualitative research, and that the authors' reflections, in particular, will both encourage more effort in this area and demystify the process.

Oveview of the Contents

Qualitative Research in Practice: Examples for Discussion and Analysis is divided into two main parts. Part One presents two overview chapters; Part Two offers sixteen articles—each exemplifying a particular type of qualitative research—along with authors' reflections. The last chapter pulls together advice and observations from the sixteen author reflection pieces.

Chapter One, "Introduction to Qualitative Research," explains what qualitative research is and how it differs from the more familiar positivist research. This chapter also describes the variations within the qualitative paradigm itself, focusing on eight of the most common forms: basic interpretive, phenomenology, grounded theory, case study, ethnography, narrative analysis, critical research, and postmodern research. The last section of the chapter is a brief overview of the process of conducting a qualitative study. Chapter Two is on assessing and evaluating qualitative research. Determining the "quality" and "trustworthiness" of this type of research involves consideration of what qualitative research is designed to do and criteria for assessing its validity and reliability—criteria that are congruent with the philosophical assumptions underlying this paradigm. Chapter Two contains both a general checklist of points to be considered when reading the articles in the volume and a table of strategies researchers might employ to enhance the study's validity and reliability.

The sixteen articles in Part Two are organized into eight sections, each representing a particular qualitative research design. Twelve of the sixteen selections are representative of an interpretive qualitative stance. From an interpretive qualitative orientation there are two examples each of basic interpretive studies, phenomenological research, grounded theory, and narrative analysis, and two examples each of ethnography and case study. The last four articles consist of two critical qualitative research studies and two postmodern studies. It should be noted here that several articles could have been categorized several ways. For example, Krenske and McKay's (2000) study of a heavy metal music club, is illustrative of ethnography because the analysis is a sociocultural interpretation of the phenomenon. However, it could have just as easily been categorized as a case study or as an example of critical research. Further, although there is no separate section for "feminist" research, several of the studies draw from feminist theory for their theoretical framework. The convergence of critical and feminist theory is briefly discussed in the introduction to critical research.

The sixteen articles and sixteen author reflections of Part Two make up the heart of this book. The two introductory chapters in Part One are meant to inform readers about this type of research, with guidelines as to how to approach a study which claims to be qualitative. Those guidelines can be used to assess the quality and value of the articles in Part Two. Finally, from the author reflection pieces I have included a postscript in Chapter Nineteen where I have drawn some generalities about engaging in qualitative research.

Acknowledgments

First to be acknowledged are the authors of the articles included in this volume. You were all wonderfully responsive to having your piece included and to writing your reflections on doing qualitative research. Your contribution will be appreciated by students, novices, and experienced researchers alike. I would also like to thank Diane Vreeland and Anita Sledge, doctoral students in the Department of Adult Education at the University of Georgia, for their invaluable assistance in tracking authors and publishers and in handling the myriad details associated with an undertaking such as this. Finally, I'd like to personally thank David Brightman, editor at Jossey-Bass, who is every author's "dream" editor—responsive, reasonable, and caring—for his help in bringing this project to fruition.

January 2002   Sharan B. Merriam
Athens, Georgia

The Editor

SHARAN B. MERRIAM is professor of adult and continuing education at the University of Georgia in Athens, where her responsibilities include teaching graduate courses in adult education and qualitative research methods and supervising graduate student research. She received her B.A. degree (1965) in English literature from Drew University, her M.Ed. degree (1971) in English education from Ohio University, and her Ed.D. degree (1978) in adult education from Rutgers University. Before coming to the University of Georgia, she served on the faculties of Northern Illinois University and Virginia Polytechnic Institute and State University.

Merriam's research and writing activities have focused on the foundations of adult education, adult development, adult learning, and qualitative research methods. She has served on steering committees for the annual North American Adult Education Research Conference, the Qualitative Research in Education Conference held annually at the University of Georgia, and the Commission of Professors of Adult Education. For five years she was coeditor of *Adult Education Quarterly*, the major research and theory journal in adult education. She has conducted workshops and seminars on adult learning and qualitative research throughout North America and internationally, including countries in southern Africa, Southeast Asia, the Middle East, and Europe. In 1998 she was a Fulbright Scholar to Malaysia. She is a three-time winner of the prestigious Cyril O. Houle World Award for Literature in Adult Education for books published in 1982, 1997, and 1999.

Merriam's recent books include *Philosophical Foundations of Adult Education* (with J. Elias, 1994), *The Profession and Practice of Adult Education: An Introduction* (with R. Brockett, 1997), *Qualitative Research and Case Study Applications in Education* (1998, second edition), *Learning in Adulthood* (with R. S. Caffarella, 1999), *A Guide to Research for Educators and Trainers of Adults* (with E. L. Simpson, 2000, updated second edition), and *Adult Learning and Development: Multicultural Stories* (with L. Baumgartner, 2000).

The Contributors

Leslie Rebecca Bloom is associate professor in curriculum and instruction, educational leadership and policy studies, and women's studies at Iowa State University in Ames. She received her B.A. degree (1979) in English literature and art history from Boston University, her M.A. degree (1985) in English literature from the University of Delaware, and her Ph.D. degree (1993) in curriculum and instruction from Indiana University. Her research interests and publishing focus on qualitative and feminist methodologies, feminism and education, and recently, she has been doing ethnographic research on educational and grassroots programs for women in poverty.

Pamelia E. Brott is an assistant professor with the counselor education program at Virginia Polytechnic Institute and State University at the Northern Virginia Center in Falls Church, Virginia. Previously, she was a faculty member at the University of Houston, Clear Lake, in the counseling program. She received her doctorate from the University of North Carolina at Greensboro in 1997. Dr. Brott's research interests include professional identity development of school counselors, comprehensive school counseling programs, and constructivist career counseling.

Nicholas C. Burbules is professor of educational policy studies at the University of Illinois, Urbana-Champaign. His primary areas of scholarship include philosophy of education, critical social and political theory, and educational technology. His most recent books include *Watch IT: The Risks and Promises of New Information Technologies for Education* (Westview), with Thomas A. Callister, Jr., and *Education and Globalization: Critical Perspectives* (Routledge) edited with Carlos Torres. He is also the current editor of *Educational Theory*.

SHELLEY J. CORRELL is assistant professor of sociology at the University of Wisconsin, Madison. She recently received her Ph.D. in sociology from Stanford University. Her research interests are in gender and social psychology, trying to explicate how various social psychological processes reproduce structures of gender inequality.

ERNESTINE K. ENOMOTO is an associate professor in the Department of Educational Administration at the University of Hawaii, Manoa. Her research interests include educational leadership, and organizational culture and contexts, especially those serving multi-ethnic student populations. Her most recent publications on school communities are in *Urban Education* and *Educational Administration Quarterly.*

THOMAS P. HÉBERT is associate professor of educational psychology in the College of Education at the University of Georgia in Athens, Georgia. Dr. Hébert teaches graduate courses in gifted education and qualitative research methods. His research interests include underachievement in high ability students, culturally diverse gifted students, and counseling issues faced by gifted young men.

JUANITA JOHNSON-BAILEY is an associate professor at the University of Georgia in the Department of Adult Education and the Women's Studies Program. She is the author of *Sistahs in College: Making a Way Out of No Way* (Krieger Press, 2001) and the coeditor of *Flat-Footed Truths: Telling Black Women's Lives* (Henry Holt, 1998), a collection of narratives. Dr. Johnson-Bailey specializes in narrative methodology and in researching race and gender in educational and workplace settings.

SUSAN R. JONES is assistant professor in higher education and student affairs and director of the Student Personnel Assistantship Program in the School of Educational Policy and Leadership at The Ohio State University in Columbus. She received her B.A. degree (1978) in sociology from Saint Lawrence University, her M.Ed. degree (1981) in higher education and student affairs from the University of Vermont, and her Ph.D. degree (1995) in college student personnel from the University of Maryland. Her research interests and publishing focus on identity development, student affairs administration, qualitative methodology, and service-learning in higher education.

LEIGH KRENSKE is about to complete her Ph.D. dissertation at the School of Social Sciences at the University of Queensland, Australia. She received her B.A. honours in 1995 from the same institution and has ongoing research interests in youth subcultures, gender, and identity.

WANDA S. PILLOW is an assistant professor in educational policy studies at the University of Illinois at Urbana-Champaign where she teaches courses in qualitative research methodology, policy analysis, and feminist theory. She is completing research on the provision of school-based programs for teen mothers and beginning research on the work of historical and present day representations of Sacajawea, the Lemhi-Shoshone woman now on the United States' one dollar coin.

JENNIFER A. SANDLIN works with the Texas Center for Adult Literacy and Learning based at Texas A&M University in College Station, Texas. Her research interests include critical literacy, workforce education, and curriculum in adult education. Dr. Sandlin received her M.A. in anthropology from the University of New Mexico and her Ph.D. in adult education from the University of Georgia.

ELIZABETH A. ST. PIERRE is associate professor of language education and affiliated professor of both the Qualitative Research Program in the College of Education and of the Women's Studies Department at the University of Georgia. Her research interests focus on the work of language in the construction of subjectivity in women and on troubling the traditional categories of qualitative inquiry during her investigations.

ELIZABETH J. TISDELL is associate professor in the Department of Adult and Continuing Education at National-Louis University in Chicago. Her research interests are in spirituality and cultural issues in adult and higher education.

RICHARD F. WOLFF is assistant professor and chair of speech in the Communication Arts program at Dowling College on Long Island, New York. He holds a master's degree from the Lutheran School of Theology at Chicago and a doctorate in mass communication from the College of Communication at Ohio University. His research interests include media history and the representation of the church in American popular television and radio.

VAUGHN E. WORTHEN is associate clinical professor of student development in the Counseling and Career Center at Brigham Young University. His research interests include psychotherapy supervision, therapy process and outcomes, career development and choice, and meaning making.

Part One

The Nature of
Qualitative Inquiry

Introduction to
Qualitative Research

Sharan B. Merriam

Drawing from a long tradition in anthropology, sociology, and clinical psychology, qualitative research has, in the last twenty years, achieved status and visibility in the social sciences and helping professions. Reports of qualitative research studies can be found at conferences, on the World Wide Web, and in journals in social work, nursing, counseling, family relations, administration, health, community services, management, all subfields of education, and even medicine. In addition, there are numerous methodological texts on qualitative research available in fields as disparate as gerontology (Reinharz & Rowles, 1988) and organizational science and management (Lee, 1999).

What is the nature of qualitative inquiry that it has captured the attention of so many? The purpose of this chapter is to explain what qualitative research is, how it differs from the more familiar positivist or quantitative research, what variations exist within the qualitative paradigm itself, and how one goes about conducting a qualitative study. This chapter and the following chapter on evaluating and assessing qualitative research offer the backdrop for exploring the collection of qualitative studies and author commentaries that follow.

The Nature of Qualitative Research

The key to understanding qualitative research lies with the idea that meaning is socially constructed by individuals in interaction with their world. The world, or reality, is not the fixed, single, agreed upon, or measurable phenomenon that it is assumed to be in positivist, quantitative research. Instead, there are multiple constructions and interpretations of reality that are in flux and that change over time. Qualitative researchers are interested in understanding what those interpretations are at a particular point in time and in a particular context. Learning how individuals experience and interact with their social world, the meaning it has for them, is considered an *interpretive* qualitative approach. If you were interested in studying the placement of a child in foster care, for example, you might focus on understanding the experience from the perspective of the child, the foster family, the agency involved, or all three.

Drawing from critical social theory, you might also investigate how the social and political aspects of the situation shape the reality; that is, how larger contextual factors affect the ways in which individuals construct reality. This would be a *critical* qualitative approach. Using the same example of placement of a child in foster care, from a critical qualitative perspective you would be interested in how the social institution of the placement agency, or the foster family, is structured such that the interests of some members and classes of society are served and perpetuated at the expense of others. Whose interests are being served by this placement? How do power, privilege, and oppression play out? Critical social science research has its own variations. Much of feminist research draws from critical theory, as does participatory or participatory action research, a form of research that involves participants in the design and implementation of a study. Some critical research incorporates a strong emancipatory agenda along with critique; that is, the overall objective is to empower participants in the process of conducting the investigation.

Another, more recent, philosophical stance is called *postmodern* or *poststructural.* Here researchers question all aspects of the construction of reality, what it is and what it is not, how it is organized, and so on. As Bruner (1993, p. 1) writes, meaning is "radically plural, always open, and . . . politics [is] in every account." For example, a poststructural inquiry would question and "disrupt" the dichotomies (for example foster-nonfoster family, child-adult) inherent in the research problem above. Lather (1992) lays out these three overarching theoretical perspectives in terms of *understanding* (interpretive), *emancipation* (critical and feminist are included here), and *deconstruction* (postmodern). Although I have included examples of critical and postmodern studies in this volume, the emphasis is on *interpretive* qualitative research studies.

As a qualitative researcher, you can approach an investigation from any of the philosophical or theoretical stances outlined above. Your particular stance will determine the specific research design that you employ for actually carrying out your study. If your primary interest is in understanding a phenomenon, you have many options, the most common being grounded theory, phenomenology, narrative, ethnography, case study, or just a basic interpretive study. Critical, feminist, postmodern, and participatory studies all have goals that include but go beyond understanding.

Several key characteristics cut across the various *interpretive* qualitative research designs (also called forms, types, or genres by various authors). The first characteristic is that researchers strive to *understand the meaning* people have constructed about their world and their experiences; that is, how do people make sense of their experience? As Patton (1985, p. 1) explains: Qualitative research "is an effort to understand situations in their uniqueness as part of a particular context and the interactions there. This understanding is an end in itself, so that it is not attempting to predict what may happen in the future necessarily, but to understand the nature of that setting—what it means for participants to be in that setting, what their lives are like, what's going on for them, what their meanings are, what the world looks like in that particular setting. . . . The analysis strives for depth of understanding."

A second characteristic of all forms of qualitative research is that *the researcher is the primary instrument* for data collection and data analysis. Since understanding is the goal of this research, the human instrument, which is able to be immediately responsive and adaptive, would seem to be the ideal means of collecting and analyzing data. Other advantages are that the researcher can expand his or her understanding through nonverbal as well as verbal communication, process information (data) immediately, clarify and summarize material, check with respondents for accuracy of interpretation, and explore unusual or unanticipated responses.

However, the human instrument has shortcomings and biases that might have an impact on the study. Rather than trying to eliminate these biases or "subjectivities," it is important to identify them and monitor them as to how they may be shaping the collection and interpretation of data. Peshkin (1988, p. 18) goes so far as to make the case that one's subjectivities "can be seen as virtuous, for it is the basis of researchers making a distinctive contribution, one that results from the unique configuration of their personal qualities joined to the data they have collected."

Often qualitative researchers undertake a qualitative study because there is a lack of theory or an existing theory fails to adequately explain a phenomenon. Therefore, another important characteristic of qualitative research is that the process is *inductive*; that is, researchers gather data to build concepts, hypotheses, or theories rather than deductively deriving postulates or hypotheses to be tested (as in positivist research). In attempting to understand the meaning a phenomenon has for those involved, qualitative researchers build toward theory from observations and intuitive understandings gleaned from being in the field. Typically, findings inductively derived from the data in a qualitative study are in the form of themes, categories, typologies, concepts, tentative hypotheses, and even substantive theory.

Finally, the product of a qualitative inquiry is *richly descriptive*. Words and pictures rather than numbers are used to convey what the researcher has learned about a phenomenon. There are likely to be descriptions of the context, the participants involved, the activities of interest. In addition, data in the form of quotes from documents, field notes, and participant interviews, excerpts from videotapes, electronic communication, or a combination thereof are always included in support of the findings of the study. These quotes and excerpts contribute to the descriptive nature of qualitative research.

In summary, qualitative research attempts to understand and make sense of phenomena from the participant's perspective. The researcher can approach the phenomenon from an interpretive, critical, or postmodern stance. All qualitative research is characterized by the search for meaning and understanding, the researcher as the primary instrument of data collection and analysis, an inductive investigative strategy, and a richly descriptive end product.

Distinguishing Among Types of Qualitative Research

From education to anthropology to management science, researchers, students, and practitioners are conducting qualitative studies. It is not surprising, then, that different disciplines and fields ask different questions and have evolved somewhat different strategies and procedures. Writers of qualitative texts have organized the diversity of forms of qualitative research in various ways. Patton (1990), for example, presents ten orientations to qualitative research according to the different kinds of questions researchers from different disciplines might ask. Creswell (1998) has identified five "traditions"—biography, phenomenology, grounded theory, ethnography, and case study. Tesch (1990) lists forty-five approaches divided into designs (for example, case study), data analysis techniques (for example, discourse analysis), and disciplinary orientation (for example, ethnography). Denzin and Lincoln (2000) identify eight research strategies of case study, ethnography, phenomenology, grounded theory, biographical, historical, participatory, and clinical. They write that qualitative research "does not belong to a single discipline. Nor does qualitative research have a distinct set of methods that are entirely its own" (p. 6).

Given the variety of qualitative research designs or strategies, I have chosen to organize this resource book around eight of the more commonly used approaches to doing qualitative research: basic interpretive, phenomenology, grounded theory, case study, ethnography, narrative analysis, critical, and postmodern-poststructural. These and other types of qualitative research do have some attributes in common that result in their falling under the umbrella concept of "qualitative." However, they each have a somewhat different focus, resulting in variations in how the research question might be asked, sample selection, data collection and analysis, and write-up. Following is a short description of each of the eight types. More thorough discussions of each type of qualitative research, along with examples and author commentaries, can be found in Part Two.

Basic Interpretive Qualitative Study. A basic interpretive and descriptive qualitative study exemplifies all the characteristics of qualitative research discussed above; that is, the researcher is interested in understanding how participants make meaning of a situation or phenomenon, this meaning is mediated through the researcher as instrument, the strategy is inductive, and the outcome is descriptive. In conducting a basic qualitative study, you seek to discover and understand a phenomenon, a process, the perspectives and worldviews of the people involved, or a combination of these. Data are collected through interviews, observations, or document analysis. These data are inductively analyzed to identify the recurring patterns or common themes that cut across the data. A rich, descriptive account of the findings is presented and discussed, using references to the literature that framed the study in the first place. For example, Levinson and Levinson's (1996) study of women's development is situated in the literature on adult growth and development. The authors interviewed fifteen homemakers, fifteen corporate businesswomen, and fifteen academics. Findings of women's developmental patterns parallel their earlier study of male development in which forty men in midlife were interviewed. Levinson and Levinson found that the basic structure or underlying pattern of a woman's life evolves through periods of tumultuous, structure-building phases alternating with stable periods of development.

Phenomenology. Because phenomenology as a school of philosophical thought underpins all qualitative research, some assume that all qualitative research is phenomenological, and certainly in one sense it is. However, even though the phenomenological notions of experience and understanding run through all qualitative research, one could also engage in a phenomenological study using its own "tools" or inquiry techniques that differentiate it from other types of qualitative inquiry.

In the same way that ethnography focuses on culture, a phenomenological study focuses on the essence or structure of an experience. Phenomenologists are interested in showing how complex meanings are built out of simple units of direct experience. This form of inquiry is an attempt to deal with inner experiences unprobed in everyday life. According to Patton (1990), this type of research is based on "the assumption that *there is an essence or essences to shared experience*. . . . The experiences of different people are bracketed, analyzed, and compared to identify the essences of the phenomenon, for example, the essences of loneliness, the essence of being a mother, or the essence of being a participant in a particular program" (p. 70, emphasis in original).

In order to understand the essence or structure of an experience, the researcher temporarily has to put aside, or "bracket," personal attitudes or beliefs about the phenomenon. With belief temporarily suspended, consciousness itself becomes heightened, allowing the researcher to intuit or see the essence of the phenomenon. Examples of phenomenological studies include Howard's (1994) study of the experience of first-time computer users and Healy's (2001) recent study of insight meditation as a transformational learning experience.

Grounded Theory. It can be argued that Glaser and Strauss' 1967 book, *The Discovery of Grounded Theory,* launched, or at least was key in the development of qualitative research as a viable research paradigm. The goal of this type of qualitative study is to derive inductively from data a theory that is "grounded" in the data—hence, grounded theory. Grounded theory research emphasizes discovery with description and verification as secondary concerns. Researchers in this mode build substantive theory, which is distinguished from grand or formal theory. Substantive theory is localized, dealing with particular real-world situations such as how adults manage school, family, and work life, or what constitutes an effective counseling program for teen mothers, or how a community allocates its resources.

Data gathered for a grounded theory study are analyzed via the constant comparative method of data analysis. Other qualitative researchers have adopted this method, which involves continually comparing one unit of data with another in order to derive conceptual elements of the theory, even though they may not be developing theory. This has resulted in some claiming they are doing a grounded theory study when in fact there is no substantive theory as an outcome of the inquiry. A grounded theory consists of categories, properties, and hypotheses that state relationships among categories and properties. Unlike hypotheses in experimental studies, grounded theory hypotheses are tentative and suggestive rather than tested.

Case Study. The case study is an intensive description and analysis of a phenomenon or social unit such as an individual, group, institution, or community. The case is a bounded, integrated system (Stake, 1995, Merriam, 1998). By concentrating upon a single phenomenon or entity (the case), this approach seeks to describe the phenomenon in depth. The unit of analysis, not the topic of investigation, characterizes a case study. For example, a study of women's experiences in welfare-to-work training programs could be a qualitative study but not a case study; the unit of analysis would be the women's experiences, and there could be an indefinite number of women selected for the study. For it to be a case study, one particular program (a bounded system), selected because it was typical, unique, experimental, or highly successful, etc., would be the unit of analysis. A case study could also be conducted of the experiences of a single woman.

Since it is the unit of analysis that determines whether a study is a case study, this type of qualitative research stands apart from the other types defined here. And in fact, since it is the unit of analysis that defines the case, other types of studies can be and sometimes are combined with case study. Ethnographic case studies are quite common, for example, wherein the culture of a particular social group is studied in depth. In addition, one could build grounded theory within a case study, or analyze the data from a case study from a critical science perspective, or obtain one person's "story," hence combining narrative with case study, and so on. The examples of case study in Part Two of this book illustrate how the case study is a vehicle for in-depth description and analysis.

Ethnographic Study. This form of qualitative research has a long tradition in the field of anthropology. It was developed by anthropologists specifically to study human society and culture. Although culture has been variously defined, it usually refers to the beliefs, values, and attitudes that shape the behavior of a particular group of people. D'Andrade (1992) writes that culture is something behaviorally and cognitively shared by an identifiable group of people and that it has "the potential of being passed on to new group members, to exist with some permanency through time and across space" (p. 230).

Confusion results when the term *ethnography* is used interchangeably with fieldwork, participant observation, case study, and so on. For a qualitative study to be an *ethnography*, it must present a sociocultural interpretation of the data. Therefore, ethnography is not defined by how data are collected, but rather by the lens through which the data are interpreted. As LeCompte and Preissle (1993) point out, "ethnographies re-create for the reader the shared beliefs, practices, artifacts, folk knowledge, and behaviors of some group of people" (pp. 2–3). Most people are familiar with ethnographies of foreign and exotic cultures such as Margaret Mead's *Coming of Age in Samoa* (1973). There are also many ethnographies of various social groups within a larger culture, such as Cordeiro and Carspecken's (1993) ethnographic account of twenty successful Hispanic high school achievers.

Narrative Analysis. The narrative analysis of lives, or life narratives, is currently a popular form of qualitative research. The key to this type of qualitative research is the use of stories as data, and more specifically, first-person accounts of experience told in story form. Other terms for this type of research include biography, autobiography, life history, oral history, autoethnography, and life narratives. Manning and Cullum-Swan (1994, p. 465) write that "narrative analysis typically takes the perspective of the teller, rather than that of the society." Context is important, however, for "if one defines narrative as a story with a beginning, middle, and end that reveals someone's experiences, narratives take many forms, are told in many settings, before many audiences, and with various degrees of connection to actual events or persons" (p. 465).

There are several strategies one can use to do the actual analysis of narratives or people's stories. The three most common are psychological, biographical, and discourse analysis. In the psychological approach, the story is analyzed in terms of internal thoughts and motivations. A more biographical approach attends to the person in relation to society and takes into account the influences of gender, class, and "family beginnings" (Denzin, 1989, p. 17). Discourse analysis examines the written text of the story for its component parts or assesses the spoken words by looking for intonation, pitch, and pauses as lens to the meaning of the text (Gee, 1991). Whatever the approach to analyzing the data, the central defining feature of this type of qualitative research is that the data are in the form of a story. Part Two contains two examples of narrative analysis.

Critical Qualitative Research. Drawing from critical social science and in particular Habermas' (1972) theory of knowledge, critical qualitative research uncovers, examines, and critiques the social, cultural, and psychological assumptions that structure and limit our ways of thinking and being in the world. The ultimate objective of this type of critique is to free ourselves from these constraints, to become empowered to change our social context and ourselves.

Critical research focuses less on individuals than on context. Critical educational research, for example, queries the context where learning takes place, including the larger systems of society, the culture and institutions that shape educational practice, the structural and historical conditions framing practice. Questions are asked regarding whose interests are being served by the way the educational system is organized, who really has access to particular programs, who has the power to make changes, and what are the outcomes of the way in which education is structured. Critical qualitative research, then, raises questions about the influence of race, class, and gender (and their intersections), how power relations advance the interests of one group while oppressing those of other groups, and the nature of truth and the construction of knowledge.

A critical perspective informs other types of research, most commonly participatory action research (PAR) and some feminist research. PAR focuses upon the political empowerment of people through group participation in the search for and acquisition of knowledge and subsequent action to change the status quo. Critical feminist research questions and critiques the societal, historical, and cultural assumptions about women that have resulted in their marginal status compared to men.

Postmodern Research. The most recent development in qualitative research is the infusion of a postmodern or poststructural perspective. In contrast to the "modern" world, where reality is predictable, research is scientific, and there are assumed to be universal norms for truth and morality, the postmodern world is one of uncertainty, fragmentation, diversity, and plurality. There are many truths, and all generalizations, hierarchies, typologies, and binaries (good/bad, right/wrong, male/female, etc.) are "contested," "troubled," or challenged.

Postmodern research thus challenges the form and categories of traditional qualitative research. A postmodern research report does not follow a specific format; each has its own rhythm and structure. Data analysis also differs from traditional qualitative research. This has created what Denzin and Lincoln (2000) call a "triple crisis." The first crisis has to do with representation—postmodern researchers question whether the lived experience of someone else can be captured; "such experience, it is now argued, is created in the social text written by the researcher" (p. 17). The second crisis has to do with being able to evaluate postmodern research. What makes a study valid and reliable if traditional qualitative criteria are inadequate? Because postmodern research is so experimental and each study unique, there are few if any guidelines about how to do this type of study, or how to assess its trustworthiness. The third crisis has to do with social action. "If society is only and always a text" (p. 17), how can participatory action research, for example, bring about change?

❧

To summarize this brief overview of the different designs or types of qualitative research, we see that the eight chosen for review vary widely in form and purpose. Not all qualitative research is the same; neither can terms such as "grounded theory," "ethnography," "narrative analysis," and so on be used interchangeably.

However, because of the underlying view of reality and the focus on understanding and meaning, the forms of qualitative research reviewed here have some characteristics in common that allow them to be categorized as "qualitative." A more detailed discussion of these types can be found in Part Two, along with examples and author commentaries.

The Design of a Qualitative Study

The design of a qualitative study focused on interpretation includes shaping a problem for this type of study, selecting a sample, collecting and analyzing data, and writing up the findings. An understanding of this process is important for assessing the rigor and value of individual reports of research (see Chapter Two for more discussion on evaluating and assessing qualitative research). Presented here is a brief overview of the component parts of the process of conducting a qualitative research study.

The Research Problem and Sample Selection. A research study begins with your being curious about something, and that "something" is usually related to your work, your family, your community, or yourself. A research problem can also come from social and political issues of the day or from the literature. Often these spheres intersect. For example, perhaps you work for a social service agency that assists the homeless in becoming stabilized in their housing needs. Your work is very much about a pressing social problem. Or you might have observed how comfortable your children are with computers and you wonder how people *your* age are learning to function in this technological age. In any case, the place to "look" for a research problem is in your everyday experience—ask questions about it, be curious as to why things are as they are or how they might be better.

The types of questions that you ask are key to doing a qualitative study. Marshall and Rossman (1995) suggest that qualitative research is designed to (1) understand processes, (2) describe poorly understood phenomena, (3) understand differences between stated and implemented policies or theories, and (4) discover thus far unspecified contextual variables. If you want to understand a phenomenon, uncover the meaning a situation has for those involved, or delineate process (how things happen), then a qualitative design would be most appropriate. For example, with regard to the first topic above, you might ask what the experience of being homeless is *really* like, or you might ask what the necessary steps or stages are in the transition process of moving from homelessness to stable housing. Or from a more critical perspective, you could ask how the social service agency for which you work reinforces, challenges, or mediates the problem of homelessness. Does it further oppress the homeless with its rules and regulations, or does it empower individuals to act on their behalf?

The basic question of your study is set within what is called the problem statement. In crafting the research problem, you move from general interest, curiosity, or doubt about a situation to a specific statement of the research problem. In effect, you have to translate your general curiosity into a problem that can be addressed through research. The structure of a problem statement moves from the general topic of interest, including key concepts, what has already been studied, why it's an important topic, to the specific question that you have. This specific question is most often written as a purpose statement and addresses some gap in the knowledge base on that topic (if previous research has already provided an answer to your question, there is no need to do the study). Using the homeless topic above, one purpose statement might read: "The purpose of this study is to understand the experience of being homeless," or "The purpose of this study is to identify the process of moving from homelessness to stable housing," or, "The purpose of this study is to uncover how a social service agency both reinforces and challenges the state of homelessness of its clients." (For more on problem formation, see Merriam, 1998; Merriam & Simpson, 2000).

The next step in the design of a qualitative study is to select a sample from which you will collect data. For nearly every study there exist sites that could be visited, people who could be interviewed, documents that could be read and analyzed. How do you select *which* sites, people, and documents to be included in your study? To begin with, since you are not interested in "how much" or "how often," random sampling makes little sense. Instead, since qualitative inquiry seeks to understand the meaning of a phenomenon from the perspectives of the participants, it is important to select a sample from which the most can be learned. This is called a purposive or purposeful sample. Patton (1990) argues that it is important to select "*information-rich cases* for study in depth. Information-rich cases are those from which one can learn a great deal about issues of central importance to the purpose of the research, thus the term *purposeful* sampling" (p. 169, emphasis in original). To begin purposive sampling, you first determine what criteria are essential in choosing who is to be interviewed or what sites are to be observed. In the study of the experience of homelessness, for example, you would first decide whether men and women would be included, what age range would be important, the length of homelessness, and so on.

Data Collection and Analysis. There are three major sources of data for a qualitative research study—interviews, observations, and documents. The data collection strategy used is determined by the question of the study and by determining which source(s) of data will yield the best information with which to answer the question. Often there is a primary method of collecting data with support from another. Sometimes only one method is used. For example, in studying how a social service agency both reinforces and challenges the status quo of the homeless, you might interview both homeless people and staff of the agency, conduct observations of the daily operation of the agency, and study internal and external agency documents. However, if you were most interested in the experience of homelessness, interviews with those who are or have been homeless would yield the most relevant information. If at all possible, researchers are encouraged to use more than one method of data collection as multiple methods enhance the validity of the findings.

Interviews range from highly structured, where specific questions and the order in which they are asked are determined ahead of time, to unstructured, where one has topic areas to explore but neither the questions nor the order are predetermined. Most interviews fall somewhere in between. The semistructured interview contains a mix of more and less structured questions. Usually, specific information is desired from all the participants; this forms the highly structured section of the interview. The largest part of the interview is guided by a list of questions or issues to be explored, and neither the exact wording nor the order of the questions is determined ahead of time.

A second major means of collecting data is through observation. Observational data represent a firsthand encounter with the phenomenon of interest rather than a secondhand account obtained in an interview. Like interviewing, there is a range here also from being a complete observer to being an active participant. A complete observer is unknown to those being observed, such as from behind a one-way mirror or in an open, public place. A very active participant observer might be someone who is a member of the group or organization who is thus participating while observing. When observation is used in conjunction with interviewing, the term *fieldwork* or *field study* is sometimes used. Observation is the best technique when an activity, event, or situation can be observed firsthand, when a fresh perspective is desired, or when participants are not able or willing to discuss the phenomenon under study.

The third major source of data is documents. These can be written, oral, visual (such as photographs), or cultural artifacts. Public records, personal documents, and physical material are types of documents available to the researcher for analysis. The strength of documents as a data source lies with the fact that they already exist in the situation; they do not intrude upon or alter the setting in ways that the presence of the investigator might. Nor are they dependent upon the whims of human beings whose cooperation is essential for collecting data through interviews and observations. Entire studies can be built around documents. For example, Abramson's (1992) case study of Russian Jewish emigration is based solely on his grandfather's diaries written over a twelve-year period. In contrast to documents already present in the research setting, researcher-generated documents are prepared at the request of the researcher after the study has begun. Participants might be asked to keep a diary or a log of their activities relevant to the phenomenon being studied, take pictures, write a life history, and so on. Whether preexisting or researcher-generated, documents often contain insights and clues into the phenomenon, and most researchers find them well worth the effort to locate and examine.

Interviews, observations, and documents are the three traditional sources of data in a qualitative research study. With the advent of computer technology and the World Wide Web, data can also be collected on-line. Web pages, papers available on-line, and so on can be considered documents simply accessed on-line; artifacts in the form of illustrations and games can be downloaded; interviews can be conducted by e-mail; and researchers can "observe" on-line chat rooms and other forms of interaction. On-line data collection to some extent offers an electronic extension of familiar data-gathering techniques. However, the medium affects the nature of the data collected (an on-line interview will be different from an in-person interview). As with any form of data collection, researchers need to be cognizant of the characteristics of each strategy and how those characteristics shape the nature of the data collected.

In qualitative research, data analysis is *simultaneous* with data collection. That is, one begins analyzing data with the first interview, the first observation, the first document accessed in the study. Simultaneous data collection and analysis allows the researcher to make adjustments along the way, even to the point of redirecting data collection, and to "test" emerging concepts, themes, and categories against subsequent data. To wait until all data are collected is to lose the opportunity to gather more reliable and valid data; to wait until the end is also to court disaster, as many a qualitative researcher has found himself or herself facing hundreds of pages of transcripts or field notes without a clue where to begin.

With that caveat in mind, data analysis is essentially an inductive strategy. One begins with a unit of data (any meaningful word, phrase, narrative, etc.) and compares it to another unit of data, and so on, all the while looking for common patterns across the data. These patterns are given names (codes) and are refined and adjusted as the analysis proceeds.

Although all qualitative data analysis is inductive, different theoretical stances and different disciplines have evolved particular strategies for data analysis. In an ethnographic study, for example, an organizing scheme or typology of categories might be used such as Lofland and Lofland's (1995) four broad categories for organizing aspects of society (economy, demographics, social structures, the environment). Narrative analysis might employ psychological, literary, or sociolinguistic data analysis strategies. Many qualitative researchers have adopted the constant comparative method, originally used for developing grounded theory, whether or not they are seeking to build substantive theory. In a phenomenological study, specific techniques such as epoche, bracketing, imaginative variation, and so on are used to analyze experience. In a postmodern-poststructural study, new forms of data analysis are being developed such as deconstruction, rhizoanalysis, genealogy, archaeology, and schizoanalyses (Elizabeth St. Pierre, personal communication, February 2001). These and other data analysis strategies are addressed in a bit more detail under the appropriate sections of Part Two. However, for more detailed discussions, readers are encouraged to refer to some of the resources listed here and in Part Two.

Writing Up Qualitative Research. There is no standard format for reporting qualitative research. Rather, as can be seen from a quick glance at the sixteen reports of qualitative research in Part Two of this book, there is a diversity of styles, some of which are quite creative. Although not addressed in this book, the presentation of qualitative findings can be through media other than print (for example, drama, dance, film).

In any write-up of qualitative research, what does need to be considered is the audience for the report. A funding agency or the general public may want an executive summary of the findings and will probably not be interested in how the study was conducted. But colleagues and other researchers will want a detailed description of the methodology in order to assess the study's contribution to the field.

Although the relative emphasis given each section as well as the overall form of the report can vary widely, *all* write-ups of qualitative research contain at the very minimum a discussion of the research problem, the way the investigation was conducted, and the findings, including a discussion of their importance or relevance to theory and practice. Since findings are in the form of words rather than numbers, reports vary widely with regard to the ratio of supporting "raw" data included versus interpretation and analysis. The best guideline is whether enough data in the form of quotes from interviews, episodes from field observations, or documentary evidence are presented to support adequately and convincingly the study's findings. In qualitative research, it is the rich, thick descriptions, the words (not numbers) that persuade the reader of the trustworthiness of the findings. Nevertheless, in any report, there is tension between having the right amount of supporting data versus analysis and interpretation. Another problem is finding the right voice to present the findings. Write-ups can vary from intimate, first-person accounts to more formal presentations to creative experimentation wherein the text is divided by perspective. For example, Lather and Smithies (1997) use a split-text format wherein the participants' words are presented on the same page parallel to the researchers' interpretation. In another example, Wolf (1992) presents the same tale of a woman shaman in Taiwan as a short story, as field notes, and as an academic journal article.

Summary

This chapter has presented an introductory overview of qualitative research. *Qualitative research* is an umbrella term that encompasses several philosophical or theoretical orientations, the most common being interpretive, critical, and postmodern. There are also several designs, types, or genres of qualitative research, including a basic interpretive study, phenomenology, grounded theory, case study, narrative analysis, ethnography, critical qualitative research, and postmodern or poststructural research. All these types of qualitative research have in common the search for meaning and understanding, the researcher as the primary instrument of data collection and analysis, an inductive analysis process, and a product that is a rich description of the phenomenon.

Also reviewed in this chapter are the phases of a qualitative research process. One must first shape a research problem that is appropriate for qualitative inquiry. Next, a purposeful sample is chosen from which data are collected. The three primary sources of data are interviews, observations, and documents. As data are being collected, data analysis is ongoing and simultaneous. There are a variety of data analysis strategies that can be employed, depending upon the type of qualitative study. Finally, it is important to present the findings of the study in a format appropriate to the audience. It is only through the presentation and dissemination of the study's findings that a contribution can be made to the knowledge base of a field and to practice.

References

Abramson, P. R. (1992). *A case for case studies*. Thousand Oaks, CA: Sage.

Bruner, E. M. (1993). Introduction: The ethnographic self and the personal self. In P. Benson (Ed.), *Anthropology and literature* (pp. 1–26). Urbana: University of Illinois Press.

Cordeiro, P. A., & Carspecken, P. F. (1993). How a minority of the minority succeed: A case study of twenty hispanic achievers. *Qualitative Studies in Education, 6*(4), 277–290.

Creswell, J. W. (1998). *Qualitative inquiry and research design*. Thousand Oaks, CA: Sage.

D'Andrade, R. G. (1992). Afterword. In R. G. D'Andrade & C. Strauss (Eds.), *Human motives and cultural models*. Cambridge, England: Cambridge University Press.

Denzin, N. K. (1989). *Interpretive biography*. Newbury Park, CA: Sage.

Denzin, N. K., & Lincoln, Y. S. (2000). Introduction: The discipline and practice of qualitative research. In N. K. Denzin & Y. S. Lincoln (Eds.), *Handbook of qualitative research* (pp. 1–28). Thousand Oaks, CA: Sage.

Gee, J. P. (1991). A linguistic approach to narrative. *Journal of Narrative and Life History, 1*(1), 15–39.

Glaser, B. G., & Strauss, A. L. (1967). *The discovery of grounded theory*. Chicago: Aldine.

Habermas, J. (1972). *Knowledge and human interests*. Portsmouth, N.H.: Heinemann Educational Books.

Healy, M. F. (2001). The transformational learning process within insight (vipassana) meditation: A phenomenological study. Unpublished doctoral dissertation, Department of Adult Education, The University of Georgia, Athens.

Howard, D.C.P. (1994). Human-computer interactions: a phenomenological examination of the adult first-time computer experience. *Qualitative Studies in Education, 7*(1), 33–49.

Lather, P. (1992, Spring). Critical frames in educational research: Feminist and post-structural perspectives. *Theory into Practice, 31*(2), 87–99.

Lather, P., & Smithies, C. (1997). *Troubling the angels: Women living with HIV/AIDS*. Boulder, CO: Westview.

LeCompte, M. D., & Preissle, J., with Tesch, R. (1993). *Ethnography and qualitative design in educational research*. (2nd ed.) Orlando, FL: Academic Press.

Lee, T. W. (1999). *Using qualitative methods in organizational research*. Thousand Oaks, CA: Sage.

Levinson, D. J., & Levinson, J. D. (1996). *The seasons of a woman's life*. New York: Ballantine.

Lofland, J., & Lofland, L. H. (1995). *Analyzing social settings: A guide to qualitative observation and analysis*. (3rd ed.) Belmont, CA: Wadsworth.

Manning, P. K., & Cullum-Swan, B. (1994). Narrative, content, and semiotic analysis. In N. K. Denzin & Y. S. Lincoln (Eds.), *Handbook of qualitative research* (pp. 463–477). Thousand Oaks, CA: Sage.

Marshall, C., & Rossman, G. B. (1995). *Designing qualitative research.* (2nd ed.) Thousand Oaks, CA: Sage.

Mead, M. (1973). *Coming of age in samoa.* (6th ed.) New York: Morrow Hill.

Merriam, S. B. (1998). *Qualitative research and case study applications in education.* (2nd ed.) San Francisco: Jossey-Bass.

Merriam, S. B., & Simpson, E. L. (2000). *A guide to research for educators and trainers of adults.* (2nd ed., updated) Malabar, FL: Krieger Publishing Company.

Patton, M. Q. (1985, April). Quality in qualitative research: Methodological principles and recent developments. Invited address to Division J of the American Educational Research Association, Chicago.

Patton, M. Q. (1990). *Qualitative evaluation methods.* (2nd ed.) Thousand Oaks, CA: Sage.

Peshkin, A. (1988). In search of subjectivity—one's own. *Educational Researcher, 17*(7), 17–22.

Reinharz, S., & Rowles, G. D. (Eds.) (1988). *Qualitative gerontology.* New York: Springer.

Stake, R. E. (1995). *The art of case study research.* Thousand Oaks, CA: Sage.

Tesch, R. (1990). *Qualitative research: Analysis types and software tools.* New York: Falmer Press.

Wolf, M. A. (1992). *A thrice-told tale: Feminism, postmodernism, and ethnographic responsibility.* Stanford, CA: Stanford University Press.

2

Assessing and Evaluating Qualitative Research

Sharan B. Merriam

A ssume for a moment that you are the director of human resource development for your company and you notice that men seem to get promoted more readily than women. Or that you are the principal of a high school with a diverse student body and you have data showing that minority students have a higher dropout rate than white, middle-class students. For either of these questions you could turn to research studies to better understand the problem and to get ideas for what you might do to change the situation. However, before you implement any changes based on what you discover in the research, you want to be certain that the changes will help, not exacerbate the situation. How will you know which research results are trustworthy? Which studies were done well? Which changes to implement? These questions are especially important to professionals in applied fields such as education and training where practitioners intervene in people's lives. Lincoln and Guba (2000, p. 178) underscore this point by asking whether a study's findings are "sufficiently authentic . . . that I may trust myself in acting on their implications? More to the point, would I feel sufficiently secure about these findings to construct social policy or legislation based on them?"

In other words, what constitutes a "good" or "quality" qualitative study, one that can be trusted should we want to make use of the knowledge generated by the study? This chapter outlines what to look for in general terms in evaluating and assessing a qualitative research study. This section is followed by a more specific discussion on assessing the validity and reliability of qualitative research, including how ethical issues are inextricably intertwined with the trustworthiness of the findings.

What to Look for When Evaluating Qualitative Research

"It is impossible to imagine a person leading a life without making judgments or without making discriminations," write Smith and Deemer (2000, p. 888). They go on to point out that "in our roles as inquirers, educators, evaluators, we are always making judgments about papers for publication, presentations, books, dissertations, student papers, and so on. As we approach judgment in any given case, we have in mind or bring to the task a list . . . of characteristics that we use to judge the quality of that production" (p. 888). Systematically evaluating or critiquing a qualitative study involves considering the overall design of the study, as well as the rigor with which the study was conducted. Drawing from material presented in Chapter One, the following discussion presents "characteristics" or factors to consider in evaluating specific studies, emphasizing qualitative studies that are interpretive rather than critical or postmodern. It is important to note that not all factors will apply equally to all studies.

The first question to ask is whether the problem is appropriate for qualitative inquiry. Recall that this type of research is designed to uncover or discover the meanings people have constructed about a particular phenomenon. The researcher wants to obtain an in-depth understanding of a phenomenon, an individual, a situation. Qualitative researchers are not interested in people's surface opinions as in survey research, or in cause and effect as in experimental research; rather, they want to know *how* people do things, and what meaning they give to their lives. Questions of meaning, understanding, and process are appropriate for qualitative research. One should look for a clear statement of the purpose of the study. This is often found in the introductory material or in a section identified as the problem statement.

The problem of the study also needs to be situated in the literature. What research and theory does this study draw upon? What is the theoretical framework where the topic is anchored? What theory or literature does it seek to extend and inform? What do we already know about the phenomenon, and what is the gap in our knowledge?

A second question one could ask is how significant the problem is. The author needs to make a case that there is some gap in our knowledge about a particular phenomenon, and it is important to answer the questions raised by the study. This is done by informing the reader of what *is* known, usually through a review of previous literature and research. Then a case has to be made for the importance of this particular research. How will this knowledge make a contribution in the world? Who will benefit and in what ways? There should be some sense of urgency surrounding the issue. The mere fact that this topic has not been investigated before does not in and of itself justify doing the research; maybe there's no need to know the answers. In applied fields like education and management, for example, research is often undertaken for the expressed purpose of improving practice. How might someone make use of the findings of the study? Who in particular would be most interested? Will this research help someone make better decisions, plan programs, teach, develop policies, engage in social action, empower others?

In setting up the problem of the study, some authors also identify their particular interest in the topic, their assumptions and biases. In qualitative research reports it is becoming accepted practice for the researcher to explain his or her perspective on and relationship to the problem. This is sometimes embedded in the introduction and problem statement, and sometimes it is found in the methods section discussed below.

Moving beyond the problem and significance of the study, we can take a close look at the methods section of the report. Does the author identify which *type* of qualitative research design being used? Is this a basic interpretive study? An ethnography? Grounded theory? Narrative analysis? Each of these genres has its own purpose and strategies. Is this really the type of qualitative study it purports to be? Qualitative studies are commonly mislabeled in the literature. Some are labeled case studies when in fact they are not really an in-depth investigation of a bounded system; a study is called "grounded theory" because the researcher has used the constant comparative method but does not build theory; a study is labeled "critical" because there is some analysis, but not of race, class, and gender, power and oppression, and so on. Mislabeling signals a superficial understanding of qualitative research.

Sample selection should be clearly explained. In qualitative research a sample is selected on purpose to yield the most information about the phenomenon of interest. There are usually criteria specified for selection. In a qualitative study (Courtenay, Merriam, & Reeves, 1998) of the transformational learning process of young adults diagnosed HIV-positive, for example, the following criteria were used in selecting a purposive sample: racially diverse men and women under the age of forty-five with a t-cell count of five hundred or less (at the time of the study before protease inhibitors, this measure signaled medical intervention). Not only should we know how the sample was selected, and the rationale for various selection criteria, we should be given a description of the final study participants. This description is sometimes placed at the beginning of the findings section. Depending on the number of participants, the description can be presented in summary form (that is, "ten men and eight women ranging in age from eighteen to forty-five"), or as short portraits or biographies of each participant. In narrative analysis studies, each participant's "story" can be quite lengthy and is part of the findings.

In the methods section we should also be told something about how the data were collected, managed, and analyzed. It might be recalled that the three primary sources of data are interviews, observations, and documents. If interviews were used, how were they arranged, where were they held, how long did they take, and what kind of interview schedule was used? What areas related to the topic did the interviewer probe? Observations also need to be described. Where and when were these scheduled? Did the researcher videotape or audiotape as part of the observation? Was a standardized check sheet used? With regard to documents, we need to know how the researcher accessed them and what type of documents they were. For public or official documents, the researcher should explain the original purpose of the documents.

Another source of data is from on-line interaction. While on-line data collection offers an electronic extension of familiar research techniques (one can interview on-line, observe groups, access documents), the medium itself makes for some important differences. For example, research suggests that there can be major discrepancies between real and on-line personalities (Phillips & Barnes, 1995). If data were collected on-line, it is important for the researcher to address its validity and reliability relative to the study's purpose.

Not only how the data were collected, but the system for managing the data as well as how they were analyzed need to be presented in the methods section. If a computer software program such as *The Ethnograph, NUDIST,* or *Atlas-ti* was used to manage the data, its use needs to be briefly described as well as any unique adaptations the author might have designed. It is commonly understood that these software programs manage and may facilitate data analysis, but the researcher's analytical strategies are still central to deriving categories, themes, or "regularities" across the data set. Just how researchers do this is highly idiosyncratic and intuitive. Nevertheless, some explanation of how the researcher proceeded, with maybe an accompanying example, will be helpful to the reader. Further, different types of qualitative research use different data analysis strategies. For example, in a phenomenological study, "bracketing" and "phenomenological reduction" are strategies; in grounded theory, there is "theoretical sampling" and a "core category."

Related to evaluating the methodology of the study, a reader can note whether any of the strategies for enhancing internal validity, reliability, and external validity were employed (see the next section of this chapter). Do we know anything about the researcher's assumptions, biases, or connection to the phenomenon or participants of the study? Was there any form of triangulation, if appropriate? Member checks? Peer examination? Do any of the procedures or the conduct of the study raise ethical questions in the mind of the reader? Are these addressed?

The explanation of the methods of the study, how the sample was selected, how the data were collected and analyzed, and how validity and reliability were addressed constitutes an audit trail. This audit trail or transparency of method is one strategy for enhancing the study's reliability. How detailed this trail is, how transparent the methodology is, is also one basis for assessing the value of the study.

Traditional qualitative studies present the findings of the inquiry as a mix of rich, thick description and interpretation. It should be noted that the field is currently experimenting with innovative and creative presentations of research findings, a situation that complicates how one assesses the persuasiveness of presentations of qualitative research. Open to debate and yet to be developed are appropriate criteria for evaluating poetic, fictional, dramatic, musical, artistic, and mixed media presentations of qualitative research findings. However, in more traditional qualitative research, it is general practice to present enough data to adequately and convincingly support the findings of the study. Firestone (1987) notes that a quantitative and qualitative research paradigm each employs different "rhetoric" to convince readers of its trustworthiness. "The quantitative study must convince the reader that procedures have been followed faithfully because very little concrete description of what anyone does is provided. The qualitative study provides the reader with a depiction in enough detail to show that the author's conclusion 'makes sense'" (p. 19). Further, "the quantitative study portrays a world of variables and static states. . . . By contrast the qualitative study describes people acting in events" (p. 19).

Just how much is "enough" detail and description and how to present it are open to debate. At the very least, each finding must be supported by the "raw" data from which the finding was derived. These data are in the form of exact quotes from people interviewed, episodes from field observations, and references from supporting documents. On one hand, a major or unique insight or discovery needs more than one quote from a participant to substantiate its presence in the data. On the other hand, presentations of supporting data should not be so long or so dense that the reader loses interest.

Erickson (1986) has made a helpful distinction among description that is particular or general, and interpretive commentary. Particular description consists of exact quotes from the raw data, general description includes comments to the reader as to whether the quotes and vignettes are typical of the data as a whole, and interpretive commentary guides "the reader to see the analytic type of which the instance is a concrete token. . . . Interpretative commentary thus points the reader to those details that are salient for the author, and to the meaning-interpretations of the author" (p. 152).

Since there are no agreed-upon guidelines as to the right balance between the particular and the general, between description and analysis, the reader makes the judgment as to whether there is "enough" data to support the author's interpretation. The bottom line is whether the reader is persuaded that the findings make sense in light of the data presented.

By way of summarizing this section on "what to look for when evaluating qualitative research," Table 2.1 provides a check sheet of the points discussed. This should be used with caution, however, as no single study is likely to meet all of the expectations. Further, all such evaluation forms reflect the author's orientation to the phenomenon being assessed—in this case, my constructivist and interpretive stance to qualitative research. As Smith and Deemer (2000) point out, "a list of characteristics must be seen as always open-ended, in part unarticulated, and, even when a characteristic is more or less articulated, it is always and ever subject to constant reinterpretation" (p. 888).

Ensuring for "Quality" in Qualitative Research

All researchers aspire to produce valid and reliable knowledge in an ethical manner. And both producers and consumers of research want to be assured that the findings of an investigation are to be believed and trusted. In qualitative research as in other kinds of research, there are ways to ensure for rigor in the conduct of

Table 2.1. Assessing the "Quality" of Qualitative Research.

A. Problem	1. Is the problem appropriate for qualitative inquiry? Is the question one of meaning, understanding, or process?
	2. Is the problem clearly stated?
	3. Is the problem situated in the literature? That is, is the literature used to put the problem in context?
	4. Is the relationship of the problem to previous research made clear?
	5. Is the researcher's perspective and relationship to the problem discussed? Are assumptions and biases revealed?
	6. Is a convincing argument explicitly or implicitly made for the importance or significance of this research? Do we know how it will contribute to the knowledge base and practice?
B. Methods	1. Is the particular qualitative research design identified and described (basic interpretive, grounded theory, phenomenology, ethnography, and so on)?
	2. Is sample selection described including rationale for criteria used in the selection?
	3. Are data collection methods described and are they congruent with the problem being investigated and the type of qualitative design?
	4. How were the data managed and analyzed?
	5. What strategies were used to ensure for validity and reliability? (See Table 2.2.)
	6. What ethical considerations are discussed?
C. Findings	1. Are the participants of the study described? (This may be in Methods.)
	2. Are the findings clearly organized and easy to follow?
	3. Are the findings directly responsive to the problem of the study? That is, do they "answer" the question(s) raised by the study?
	4. Do the data presented in support of the findings (quotations from interviews, incidents from field notes, material from documents, and so on) provide adequate and convincing evidence for the findings?
D. Discussion	1. Are the findings "positioned" and discussed in terms of the literature and previous research?
	2. Are the study's insights and contributions to the larger body of knowledge clearly stated and discussed?
	3. Are implications for practice discussed?
	4. Do the study's implications follow from the data?
	5. Are there suggestions for future research?

the study. An understanding of these strategies is important for assessing the value of a particular qualitative study. First discussed are the concepts of validity and reliability and the strategies that can be employed to ensure each. Since trustworthiness very much hinges on the *ethical* conduct of research, ethical issues particularly relevant to qualitative research are also mentioned in this section.

It is not uncommon to hear people ask whether a particular study is a "good" study. "Good" is of course a relative term open to interpretation, but what people usually mean by that question is whether the study was conducted in a rigorous, systematic, and ethical manner, such that the results can be trusted. Measures to ensure validity and reliability in positivist research (for example, surveys or experiments) are well developed and accepted by the scientific community. All graduate students are well acquainted with Campbell and Stanley's (1963) classic discussion of "threats" to validity and reliability such as survivor bias, testing effects, and selective sampling, for example. Qualitative research also has strategies for establishing validity and reliability, strategies based on the different worldview and different questions congruent with the philosophical assumptions underlying this perspective.

Currently, there is much debate and discussion in the literature and at conferences as to how to think about validity and reliability in qualitative research. In particular, writers from postmodern, poststructural, and critical perspectives are challenging interpretive/constructivist notions of validity and reliability. Denzin and Lincoln (2000) consider the postmodern turn in qualitative research, for example, as problematic for evaluating qualitative research. "This is the legitimation crisis. It involves a serious rethinking of such terms as *validity, generalizability,* and *reliability,* terms already retheorized in" other types of qualitative research (p. 17, emphasis in original). Kvale (1996) proposes thinking of validity as (1) craftsmanship in which the researcher adopts a critical outlook during data analysis, (2) communication where validity is determined in dialogue with others, and (3) pragmatic validity, which goes beyond an argument's persuasiveness to assessing validity in terms of real-world changes brought about as a result of the research. Even within an interpretive orientation, Connelly and Clandinin (1990), in speaking of narrative inquiry for example, write that the criteria for judging narratives will be different from other qualitative genres, and that at the time of their writing, these criteria were not yet agreed upon.

Nevertheless, most producers and consumers of research do not want to wait for the scholars of qualitative research to develop a consensus as to the appropriate criteria for assessing validity and reliability, if indeed that is even possible (see Hammersley, 1990, for example). While the theoretical debate goes on, there are immediate needs to be met regarding these issues. As Stake (2000) notes, knowledge gained in an investigation "faces hazardous passage from the writer to reader. The writer needs ways of safeguarding the trip" (p. 443). Further, qualitative researchers need to respond to the concerns of outsiders, many of whom may be unfamiliar with or blatantly challenging of the credibility of qualitative research. With these concerns in mind, the following sections address dealing with internal validity, reliability, external validity, and ethics in interpretive qualitative research.

Internal Validity

Internal validity asks the question, How congruent are one's findings with reality? In quantitative research this question is usually construed as, Are we observing or measuring what we think we are observing or measuring? The question hinges on what we think constitutes reality. As was discussed in Chapter One, reality in qualitative inquiry assumes that there are multiple, changing realities and that individuals have their own unique constructions of reality. In fact, no matter which paradigm one is working from, reality is always interpreted through symbolic representations such as numbers and words. In qualitative research, the understanding of reality is really the researcher's interpretation of participants' interpretations or understandings of the phenomenon of interest. For example, it is well known that eyewitnesses to a crime can have widely varying accounts of what actually happened. So too, of course, when you ask people how they have experienced a particular phenomenon, how they have made meaning of their lives, or how they understand certain processes. In qualitative research we are not interested in how many or the distribution of predefined variables. Rather, it is important to understand the perspectives of those involved, uncover the complexity of human behavior in context, and present a holistic interpretation of what is happening.

Because qualitative researchers are the primary instruments for data collection and analysis, interpretations of reality are accessed directly through observations and interviews. We are "closer" to reality than if an instrument with predefined items had been interjected between the researcher and the phenomenon being studied. Most agree that when reality is viewed in this manner—that it is always interpreted—internal validity is considered a strength of qualitative research.

There are a number of strategies that qualitative researchers can employ to shore up the internal validity of a study. Probably the most well known of these is *triangulation*. Foreman (1948) first cited this procedure more than fifty years ago. He recommended using independent investigators "to establish validity through pooled judgment" and using outside sources to validate case study materials (p. 413). Denzin (1970) presented an extended discussion of triangulation, identifying four types: multiple investigators, multiple theories, multiple sources of data, or multiple methods to confirm emerging findings. Triangulating multiple theories is rare, but the other three forms, especially using multiple data collection methods, are commonly found in qualitative studies. In this triangulation strategy the researcher collects data through a combination of interviews, observations, and document analysis. For example, what someone tells you in an interview can be checked against what you observe in a field visit or what you read or see in documents or artifacts relevant to the investigation. The use of multiple researchers also strengthens the internal validity of a study. This notion of multiple researchers has been discussed in other contexts as collaborative or team research. In participatory research, where the goal of the research is political empowerment, the participants along with the researcher collectively define the problem to be addressed, conduct the study, and engage in collective action to bring about change.

It should be noted that as with other strategies for ensuring validity and relia-bility, triangulation is being revisited in the literature from a postmodern perspec-tive. Richardson (2000) points out that triangulation assumes a "'fixed point' or 'object' that can be triangulated." But in postmodern research, "we do not trian-gulate; we *crystallize*. We recognize that there are far more than three sides from which to approach the world" (p. 934). However, from an interpretive perspective, triangulation remains a principal strategy to ensure for validity and reliability.

A second common strategy for ensuring validity in qualitative research is *mem-ber checks*. Here you ask the participants to comment on your interpretation of the data. That is, you take your tentative findings back to some of the participants (from whom you derived the raw data through interviews or observations) and ask whether your interpretation "rings true." While you may have used different words, participants should be able to recognize their experience in your inter-pretation or suggest some fine-tuning to better capture their perspectives. Some writers suggest doing member checks throughout the course of the study.

Peer review is yet another strategy. In one sense, all graduate students have a peer review process built into their thesis or dissertation committee—as each member reads and comments on the findings. Peer review or peer examination can be conducted by a colleague either familiar with the research or one new to the topic. There are advantages to both, but either way, a thorough peer ex-amination would involve asking a colleague to scan some of the raw data and assess whether the findings are plausible based on the data.

The relationship between the researcher and what and who are being studied has been the topic of much scholarly writing in the last decade. Lincoln (1995) in fact suggests that the emerging criteria for quality in interpretive inquiry be based on considering the relational aspects of the research process (for example, the knower and the known). In so doing, the distinction between quality or rigor and ethics "collapses" (p. 275). In any case, even in journal articles researchers are being called upon to articulate and clarify their assumptions, experiences, worldview, and theoretical orientation to the study. Investigators should explain their position vis-à-vis the topic being studied, the basis for selecting participants, the context of the study, and what values or assumptions might affect data col-lection and analysis. This strategy is sometimes labeled "researcher's position" and more recently, "reflexivity"—"the process of reflecting critically on the self as researcher, the 'human as instrument'" (Lincoln and Guba, 2000, p. 183). Such a clarification allows the reader to better understand how the individual researcher might have arrived at the particular interpretation of the data.

Finally, it is recommended that the researcher be submerged or engaged in the data collection phase over a long enough period to ensure an in-depth un-derstanding of the phenomenon. How long one needs to observe or how many people need to be interviewed are always difficult questions to answer ahead of time. The best rule of thumb is that the data and emerging findings must feel saturated; that is, you begin to see or hear the same things over and over again, and no new information surfaces as you collect more data.

Adequate time in the field should also be coupled with purposefully looking for variation in the understanding of the phenomenon. Some writers even suggest that you should purposefully seek cases that might disconfirm or challenge your expectations or emerging findings. This strategy has been labeled negative or discrepant case analysis (Lincoln & Guba, 1985; Silverman, 1993).

Reliability

As many have pointed out, there is no point in considering reliability without validity. That is, you could have a highly reliable instrument, a thermometer for instance, that records boiling water at 85 degrees Fahrenheit each and every time it is placed in boiling water, but it is not at all valid. *Reliability* refers to the extent to which research findings can be replicated. In other words, if the study were repeated would it yield the same results? Reliability is problematic in the social sciences simply because human behavior is never static, nor is what many experience necessarily more reliable than what one person experiences. Consider the magician who can fool the audience of hundreds but not the stagehand watching from the wings. Replication of a qualitative study will not yield the same results, but this does not discredit the results of any particular study; there can be numerous interpretations of the same data. The more important question for qualitative researchers is *whether the results are consistent with the data collected.* Lincoln and Guba (1985, p. 288) were the first to conceptualize reliability in qualitative research as "dependability" or "consistency." That is, rather than insisting that others get the same results as the original researcher, reliability lies in others' concurring that given the data collected, the results make sense—they are consistent and dependable.

Further, since reliability most often has to do with the instrumentation of the study, and since the researcher is the primary instrument of data collection and analysis in qualitative research, the researcher can become a more reliable instrument through training and practice. Also, the reliability of documents and personal accounts can be assessed through various techniques of analysis and triangulation.

Strategies that a qualitative researcher can use to ensure for consistency and dependability or reliability are triangulation, peer examination, investigator's position, and the audit trail. The first three have been discussed under internal validity. The use of multiple methods of collecting data, for example, can be seen as a strategy for obtaining consistent and dependable data as well as data that are most congruent with reality as understood by the participants. The *audit trail* is a method suggested by Guba and Lincoln (1981). Just as an auditor authenticates the accounts of a business, independent readers can authenticate the findings of a study by following the trail of the researcher. While "we cannot expect others to replicate our account," Dey (1993, p. 251) writes, "the best we can do is explain how we arrived at our results." An audit trail in a qualitative study describes in detail how data were collected, how categories were derived, and how decisions were made throughout the inquiry. The audit trail is dependent upon the researcher keeping a research journal or recording memos throughout the conduct of the study. What go into this journal are your reflections, questions, and decisions on the problems, issues, ideas you encounter in collecting data. A running record of your interaction with the data as you engage in analysis and interpretation is also recommended. However this journaling is set up, it is important to capture reflections and thoughts about you as a researcher, about data collection issues, and about interpretations of the data. In a book-length or thesis-length report of the research, the audit trail is really a detailed account of how the study was conducted and how the data were analyzed. Due to space limitations, journal articles tend to have a very abbreviated audit trail, if any at all.

External Validity or Generalizability

More than internal validity or reliability, the issue of external validity or generalizability in qualitative research has stimulated substantial discussion and debate. It is also a major challenge for novice qualitative researchers to justify their qualitative inquiry in terms of generalizability. Part of the problem lies with the common perception of generalizability derived from positivist-oriented research wherein one can generalize in a statistical sense from a random sample to a population. The basic question even for qualitative research is the extent to which the findings of one study can be applied to other situations. But since small, nonrandom samples are selected purposefully in qualitative research, it is not possible to generalize statistically. A small sample is selected precisely because the researcher wishes to understand the particular in depth, not to find out what is generally true of the many.

Because qualitative research draws from different assumptions about reality, generalizability needs to be thought of differently from quantitative research. There are a number of understandings of generalizability that are more congruent with the worldview of qualitative research. Some argue that empirical generalizations are too lofty a goal for social science; instead we should think in terms of what Cronbach (1975) calls working hypotheses—hypotheses that reflect situation-specific conditions in a particular context. Working hypotheses that take account of local conditions can offer practitioners some guidance in making choices—the results of which can be monitored and evaluated in order to make better decisions in the future. Patton (1990) also promotes thinking of "context-bound extrapolations rather than generalizations" (p. 491).

If one thinks of what can be learned from an in-depth analysis of a particular situation or incident and how that knowledge can be transferred to another situation, generalizability in qualitative research becomes possible. Erickson (1986) writes that rather than abstract universals arrived at through statistical analysis, what we have in qualitative research are concrete universals. The general lies in the particular; what we learn in a particular situation we can transfer to similar situations subsequently encountered. Eisner (1991) points out that more than abstractions can be generalized—skills and images can also. For example, we learn a skill in one situation and transfer it to another. Images also generalize. "For qualitative research, this means that the creation of an image—a vivid portrait of excellent teaching, for example—can become a prototype that can be used in the education of teachers or for the appraisal of teaching" (Eisner, 1991, p. 199).

Probably the most common way generalizability has been conceptualized in qualitative research is as reader or user generalizability. In this view, readers themselves determine the extent to which findings from a study can be applied to their context. Called case-to-case transfer by Firestone (1993), "It is the reader who has to ask, what is there in this study that I can apply to my own situation, and what clearly does not apply?" (Walker, 1980, p. 34). Case-to-case or user generalizability is common practice in law and medicine, where the practitioner decides whether a previous case is applicable to the present situation. In order to facilitate the reader (not the researcher) transferring findings from one study to his or her present situation, the researcher must provide enough detail of the study's context so that comparisons can be made.

Providing *rich, thick description* is a major strategy to ensure for external validity or generalizability in the qualitative sense. This involves providing an adequate database, that is, enough description and information that readers will be able to determine how closely their situations match, and thus whether findings can be transferred. Multisite designs or *maximizing variation* in the purposely selected sample is another strategy. The logic behind this strategy is that if there is some diversity in the nature of the sites selected (an urban and a rural school, for example) or in participants interviewed, or times and places of field visits, results can be applied to a greater range of situations by readers or consumers of the research.

Ethical Issues

A "good" qualitative study is one that has been conducted in an ethical manner. To a large extent, the validity and reliability of a study depend upon the ethics of the researcher. Suppose, for example, that you are studying an adult literacy program reputed to have an unusually high retention rate. You interview teachers, administrators, and students and begin to identify the factors that might account for the high retention rate. Then you stumble upon some records that appear to have been tampered with, inflating attendance and graduation rates. Your decision as to how to handle this discovery will have a direct impact on the trustworthiness of your entire study. While some sense of the researchers' values can be inferred from the statement of their assumptions and biases or from the audit trail, readers of course are likely never to know what ethical dilemmas were confronted and how they were dealt with. It is ultimately up to the individual researcher to proceed in as ethically a manner as possible.

In qualitative research, ethical dilemmas are likely to emerge with regard to the collection of data and in the dissemination of findings. Overlaying both the collection of data and the dissemination of findings is the researcher-participant relationship. For example, this relationship and the focus of the research determine how much the researcher reveals about the actual purpose of the study—how informed the consent can actually be—and how much privacy and protection from harm is afforded the participants. Ethical considerations regarding the researcher's relationship to participants are becoming a major source of discussion and debate in qualitative research, especially with the growing interest in critical, participatory, feminist, and postmodern research. When the research is highly collaborative, participatory, and/or political, ethical issues become prominent. Lincoln (1995), in particular, aligns ethical considerations with the researcher's relationship with research participants and considers validity to be an ethical question. She suggests seven "standards" for validity, such as the extent to which the research allows all voices to be heard, the extent of reciprocity in the research relationship, and so on.

Although qualitative researchers can turn to guidelines, others' experiences, and government regulations for dealing with some of the ethical concerns likely to arise, the burden of producing a study that has been conducted and disseminated in an ethical manner lies with the individual investigator. No regulation can tell a researcher when the questioning of a participant becomes an interrogation rather than an interview, when to intervene in abusive or illegal situations, or how to ensure that the study's findings will not be used to the detriment of those involved. As Punch (1994, p. 84) points out, "Acute moral and ethical dilemmas . . . often have to be resolved *situationally,* even spontaneously." All possibilities cannot be anticipated, nor can one's reaction. Examining the assumptions one carries into the research process—assumptions about the context, participants, data, and the dissemination of knowledge gained through the study—is at least a starting point for conducting an ethical study.

❧

In summary, there is no simple answer as to what makes a "good" qualitative study. Researchers and consumers alike want to be able to trust the results of any research study, especially in applied fields where we intervene in human lives. To be trustworthy, a study needs to be valid and reliable and conducted in an ethical manner. There are strategies that researchers can employ that will enhance the trustworthiness of their research, such as triangulation, member checks, use of rich, thick description, and so on. Used in conjunction with an awareness of ethical issues, these strategies can build confidence in the validity and reliability of the study. Table 2.2 summarizes the strategies for enhancing validity and reliability in interpretive qualitative research.

Summary

This chapter has addressed two questions: What should you look for when evaluating qualitative research? and, What makes a good qualitative study? The two are of course highly interrelated. Evaluating a qualitative study means raising questions about all aspects of the process and write-up, beginning with whether the topic is appropriate for qualitative inquiry and whether it is an important enough question to spend time, money, and other resources on answering. Methodology questions are also important, including sample selection and description, data collection and analysis, validity and reliability safeguards, and presentation and discussion of findings. Table 2.1 provides a check sheet for assessing these points.

What makes a good qualitative study is whether it has been systematically and ethically carried out and whether the findings are trustworthy. The question of

Table 2.2. Strategies for Promoting Validity and Reliability.

Strategy	Description
Triangulation	Using multiple investigators, sources of data, or data collection methods to confirm emerging findings
Member checks	Taking data and tentative interpretations back to the people from whom they were derived and asking if they were plausible
Peer review/examination	Discussions with colleagues regarding the process of study, the congruency of emerging findings with the raw data, and tentative interpretations
Researcher's position or reflexivity	Critical self-reflection by the researcher regarding assumptions, worldview, biases, theoretical orientation, and relationship to the study that may affect the investigation
Adequate engagement in data collection	Adequate time spent collecting data such that the data become "saturated"; this may involve seeking *discrepant* or *negative* cases of the phenomenon
Maximum variation	Purposefully seeking variation or diversity in sample selection to allow for a greater range of application of the findings by consumers of the research
Audit trail	A detailed account of the methods, procedures, and decision points in carrying out the study
Rich, thick descriptions	Providing enough description to contextualize the study such that readers will be able to determine the extent to which their situation matches the research context, and hence, whether findings can be transferred

trustworthiness has to do with issues of internal validity, reliability, and external validity or generalizability. Strategies ensuring for adequate treatment of each of these issues include triangulation, member checks, peer examination, investigator position, audit trail, and rich, thick description. The sixteen articles in Part Two can be approached using the guidelines summarized in Tables 2.1 and 2.2.

References

Campbell, D., & Stanley, J. (1963). Experimental and quasi-experimental designs for research on teaching. In N. Gage (Ed.), *Handbook for research on teaching* (pp. 171–246). Chicago: Rand McNally.

Connelly, F. M., & Clandinin, D. J. (1990). Stories of experience and narrative inquiry. *Educational Researcher, 9*(5), 2–14.

Courtenay, B. C., Merriam, S. B., & Reeves, T. (1998). The centrality of meaning-making in transformational learning: How HIV-positive adults make sense of their lives. *Adult Education Quarterly, 48*(2), 65–84.

Cronbach, L. J. (1975). Beyond the two disciplines of scientific psychology. *American Psychologist, 30,* 116–127.

Denzin, N. K. (1970). *The research act: A theoretical introduction to sociological methods.* Chicago: Aldine.

Denzin, N. K., & Lincoln, Y. S. (2000). Introduction: The discipline and practice of qualitative research. In N. K. Denzin & Y. S. Lincoln (Eds.), *Handbook of qualitative research.* (pp. 1–28). Thousand Oaks, CA: Sage.

Dey, I. (1993). *Qualitative data analysis.* London: Routledge.

Eisner, E. W. (1991). *The enlightened eye: Qualitative inquiry and the enhancement of educational practice.* Old Tappan, NJ: Macmillan.

Erickson, F. (1986). Qualitative methods in research on teaching. In M. C. Whittrock (Ed.), *Handbook of research on teaching.* (3rd ed.) Old Tappan, NJ: Macmillan.

Firestone, W. A. (1987). Meaning in method: The rhetoric of quantitative and qualitative research. *Educational Researcher, 16*(7), 16–21.

Firestone, W. A. (1993). Alternative arguments for generalizing from data as applied to qualitative research. *Educational Researcher, 22*(4), 16–23.

Foreman, P. B. (1948). The theory of case studies. *Social Forces, 26*(4), 408–419.

Guba, E. G., & Lincoln, Y. S. (1981). *Effective evaluation.* San Francisco: Jossey-Bass.

Hammersley, M. (1990). *Reading ethnographic research: A critical guide.* London: Longman.

Kvale, S. (1996). *InterViews: An introduction to qualitative research methodology.* Thousand Oaks, CA: Sage.

Lincoln, Y. S. (1995). Emerging criteria for quality in qualitative and interpretive research. *Qualitative Inquiry, 1*(1), 275–289.

Lincoln, Y. S., & Guba, E. G. (1985). *Naturalistic inquiry.* Thousand Oaks, CA: Sage.

Lincoln, Y. S., & Guba, E. G. (2000). Paradigmatic controversies, contradictions, and emerging confluences. In N. K. Denzin & Y. S. Lincoln (Eds.), *Handbook of qualitative research.* (2nd ed.) (pp. 163–188). Thousand Oaks, CA: Sage.

Patton, M. Q. (1990). *Qualitative evaluation methods.* (2nd ed.) Thousand Oaks, CA: Sage.

Phillips, G. M., & Barnes, S. B. (1995). Is your epal an ax-murderer? *Interpersonal Computing and Technology, 3*(4), 12–41.

Punch, M. (1994). Politics and ethics in qualitative research. In N. K. Denzin & Y. S. Lincoln (Eds.), *Handbook of qualitative research.* (pp. 83–97). Thousand Oaks, CA: Sage.

Richardson, L. (2000). Writing: A method of inquiry. In N. K. Denzin & Y. S. Lincoln (Eds.), *Handbook of qualitative research.* (2nd ed.) (pp. 923–948). Thousand Oaks, CA: Sage.

Silverman, D. (1993). *Interpreting qualitative data.* London: Sage.

Smith, J. K., & Deemer, D. K. (2000). The problem of criteria in the age of relativism. In N. K. Denzin & Y. S. Lincoln (Eds.), *Handbook of qualitative research.* (2nd ed.) (pp. 877–896). Thousand Oaks, CA: Sage.

Stake, R. E. (2000). Case studies. In N. K. Denzin & Y. S. Lincoln (Eds.), *Handbook of qualitative research.* (2nd ed.) (pp. 435–454). Thousand Oaks, CA: Sage.

Walker, R. (1980). The conduct of educational case studies: Ethics, theory and procedures. In W. B. Dockerell & D. Hamilton (Eds.), *Rethinking educational research.* London: Hodder & Stoughton.

Part Two

Examples of
Qualitative Research
for Discussion and Analysis

Basic Interpretive
Qualitative Research

A central characteristic of qualitative research is that individuals construct reality in interaction with their social worlds. Constructionism thus underlies what I am calling a basic interpretive qualitative study. Here the researcher is interested in understanding the meaning a phenomenon has for those involved. Meaning however, "is not discovered but constructed. Meaning does not inhere in the object, merely waiting for someone to come upon it. . . . Meanings are constructed by human beings as they engage with the world they are interpreting" (Crotty, 1998, pp. 42–43).

Phenomenology and symbolic interactionism also inform interpretive qualitative research. From phenomenology comes the idea that people interpret everyday experiences from the perspective of the meaning it has for them. "What phenomenologists emphasize, then, is the subjective aspects of people's behavior. They attempt to gain entry into the conceptual world of their subjects (Geertz, 1973) in order to understand how and what meaning they construct around events in their daily lives" (Bogdan & Biklen, 1992, p. 34). Symbolic interaction also focuses on interpretation but within the context of the larger society; that is, the meaning of an experience is constructed by an individual interacting with other people; meaning is formed as the person intersects with society. From a research perspective, "the emphasis [is] on putting oneself in the place of the other and seeing things from the perspective of others" (Crotty, 1998, p. 76). Even the self is a social construction, a self-definition generated through interaction with other people. Since the self in interaction with others is an ongoing process, people can "change and grow as they learn more about themselves through this interactive process" (Bogdan & Biklen, 1992, p. 37).

Thus drawing from phenomenology and symbolic interaction in particular, qualitative researchers conducting a basic interpretive study would be interested in (1) how people interpret their experiences, (2) how they construct their worlds, and (3) what meaning they attribute to their experiences. The overall purpose is to *understand* how people make sense of their lives and their experiences. While this understanding characterizes all of qualitative research, other types of qualitative studies have an *additional* purpose. For example, a grounded theory study seeks not to just understand, but to build a substantive theory about the phenomenon of interest. A phenomenological study seeks understanding about the essence and the underlying structure of the phenomenon. Narrative analysis uses the stories people tell, analyzing them in various ways, to understand the meaning of the experience as revealed in the story. Ethnography strives to understand the interaction of individuals not just with others, but with the *culture* of the society in which they live. Qualitative case studies, while interpretive, endeavor to present a holistic, in-depth description of the total system or case. Finally, with reference to the other types of qualitative research presented in this volume, both critical and postmodern studies interpret phenomena through the additional lenses of critical, feminist, and postmodern theory.

Basic interpretive qualitative studies can be found throughout the disciplines and in applied fields of practice. They are probably the most common form of qualitative research found in education, for example. In an interpretive study of educational practice, a researcher might draw upon concepts, models, and theories in educational psychology, developmental psychology, cognitive psychology, or sociology to frame the study. Data are collected through interviews, observations, or document analysis. What questions are asked, what is observed, and what documents are deemed relevant will depend on the disciplinary theoretical framework of the study. An educational psychologist for example, might be interested in understanding the teaching-learning transaction in a classroom, while someone with a sociological frame would be more interested in questions of social roles and social interaction patterns in the same classroom. The analysis of the data involves identifying recurring patterns (presented as categories, factors, variables, themes) that cut through the data. Findings are a mix of these recurring patterns supported by the data from which they were derived. The overall interpretation will be the researcher's understanding, mediated by his or her particular disciplinary perspective, of the participants' understanding of the phenomenon of interest.

There are two examples of basic interpretive research studies included in this collection of qualitative articles. Merriam and Muhamad's (2000) goal is to understand the nature of learning for older adults in the non-Western society of Malaysia. Some might assume, because this study was conducted in a different culture and the concept of cultural values was used to frame the study and interpret the data, that this is an ethnography. Certainly there are elements of ethnography embedded in this study, but there was no extended stay at the research site, nor was there a full sociocultural interpretation of the data as would be common in an ethnography. Rather, we were interested in how older adults understood learning at this stage of their lives, and how those understandings were shaped by their interactions with others in the society in which they live.

The second selection by Tisdell (2000) reports on a study of the link between spirituality and social action of women adult educators. Tisdell wanted to *understand* how "women perceive and carry out their work as emancipatory educators." Tisdell framed her study from a developmental perspective, but one that takes into account the sociocultural context in which the development occurs. With her interest in social action, women, and culture, there are aspects of critical and emancipatory theory, feminist theory, and ethnography present in her study; however, it is still primarily a basic interpretive study. Tisdell speaks to this in her reflection immediately following the article: "What began as a largely interpretive study in its first phase as reported here, has now developed into an ongoing participatory action research study."

In summary, all qualitative research is interested in how meaning is constructed, how people make sense of their lives and their worlds. The *primary* goal of a basic qualitative study is to uncover and interpret these meanings. The inquiry is always framed by some disciplinary-based concepts, model, or theory (as, for example, cultural values and spiritual development in the above studies).

References

Bogdan, R. C., & Biklen, S. K. (1992). *Qualitative research for education: An introduction to theory and methods.* (2nd ed.) Boston: Allyn and Bacon.

Crotty, M. (1998). *The foundations of social research: Meaning and perspective in the research process.* Thousand Oaks, Calif.: Sage.

Geertz, C. (1973). *The interpretation of cultures.* New York: Basic Books.

3

How Cultural Values Shape
Learning in Older Adulthood
The Case of Malaysia

Sharan B. Merriam, Mazanah Muhamad

Although there is no single understanding of culture, most definitions center on the notion of shared beliefs, values, customs, and meanings that distinguish one group of people from another (Hofstede, 1991). Manifest in patterns of language and thought and in forms of activity and behaviors, culture is transmitted through symbols, artifacts, rituals, heroes, and values. The culture of a society is "the glue that holds its members together through a common language, dressing, food, religion, beliefs, aspirations, and challenges. It is a set of learned behavior patterns so deeply ingrained" that we act them out in "unconscious and involuntary" ways (Abdullah, 1996, p. 3). Indeed, culture shapes the meaning people make of their lives and defines how people experience movement through the life course: "Social and cultural factors shape the way people make a living, the social units in which they live and work, and the meanings they assign to their lives" (Fry, 1990, p. 129). Cultural constructions of the meaning of old age may even determine how well an aging person adapts to changing life circumstances, for a "group's cultural heritage represents the accumulation of its tried and tested methods for adapting to life" (Giordano, 1992, p. 23). It is a premise of this study that the nature of learning engaged in by older adults will also reflect the particular cultural context in which it takes place.

Perhaps because most of the research on aging has been conducted in the West (Bee, 2000), it is not surprising that a Western cultural bias characterizes models

Sharran B. Merriam & Mazanah Muhamad. (2000). "How Cultural Values Shape Learning in Older Adulthood: The Case of Malaysia." *Adult Education Quarterly, 51,* (1), 45–63. Reprinted with permission.

of development and learning. For both aging and learning, self-reliance, personal achievement, and autonomy underlie attitudes, behavior, and activities at any particular life stage. In an Eastern context, however, collective and interdependent behavior is valued. The purpose of this study was to understand the nature of learning in older adulthood in a non-Western culture. The Southeast Asian country of Malaysia was deemed a particularly rich setting for this study, as the culture itself is a blend of three Asian cultures—Malay, Chinese, and Indian. It was assumed that participants' learning would reflect, at least partially, if not wholly, the cultural values inherent in this Asian society.

Cultural Values, Aging, and Learning

The study of culture is indeed a complex undertaking. Competing concepts of culture together with postmodern or poststructural critiques "of a commonsensical, usually materialist notion of the social" (Bonnell & Hunt, 1999, p. 8) have made it desirable for researchers to identify their perspective. We align ourselves with the notion of culture as defined by cognitive anthropologists; that is, culture is acquired knowledge, including beliefs, concepts, and standards, organized by cognitive structures that people use to function properly in a cultural context (Quinn & Holland, 1987). Cultural values are emotion-laden, internalized assumptions, beliefs, or standards that shape how we interpret our life experiences. We have chosen to investigate older adult learning in Malaysia through the framework of cultural values.

A number of writers have compared Western and Eastern or Asian cultural values, and this seemed like a place to begin. We do recognize that these values are in flux and "do not correspond in any neat way with national or societal [and we would add regional] boundaries" (Sewell, 1999, p. 55). Furthermore, because Malaysia is fast becoming a modern, postindustrial nation with multinational and global interests, we would expect cultural values of *both* the East and the West to be influencing Malaysian society today.

Western cultural values favor controlling nature and focusing on the individual over the group, that is, being task oriented rather than relationship oriented and being independent and competitive. Control of nature or the environment manifests itself in Western media-based narratives of aging that reflect "a battle against the decay of human nature in the form of wrinkles, loss of energy, and memory," whereas political narratives "are dominated by discussions about the costs of care required by the aging society" (Baars, 1997, p. 294). Cultural values of autonomy, control, and production are implicit in Western models of development that focus on "successful" and "productive" aging. Successful aging involves optimizing gains and compensating for losses so that "a given individual continues to perform life tasks that are important to him or her despite decreases in skills, ability, memory, and performance" (VandenBos, 1998, p. 12). Riley and Riley (1994), although they recognize that their orientation is "frankly and perhaps inevitably American," still argue that "all older people, everywhere," want to remain contributing, *productive* members of society and will be able to do so if social norms and structures allow for their participation (p. 19).

For American, if not most Western cultures, remaining independent as one ages is valued above all else. Fry (1990) explains: "Americans emphasize rugged individualism and self-reliance. As an ideal, it reflects an economic organization that emphasizes the immediacy of reciprocity and participants as mobile, unconnected entities. Individuals are responsible for themselves. Also, affluence has made it possible for many individuals to achieve most of the ideal by maintaining separate households. . . .The value of independence is by no means universal. . . .Where social units are more cohesive and life more collective, the value of interdependence, not independence, is accentuated" (p. 138).

Because the meaning of aging shapes values of productivity, independence, self-sufficiency, and control over the physical manifestations of aging, it follows that what older adults choose to learn and how they go about their learning will also reflect these values. In a recent review of the literature on the learning needs of older adults in the United States, Wolf (1998) offers the following summary. Note how the learning needs reflect Western values associated with aging: "*Self-sufficiency, the ability to remain in control of one's life,* is a prime motivation for adults of all ages. Interestingly, older individuals who become deprived of this 'locus of control' have been found to be especially vulnerable to illness and passive behaviors (Beatty & Wolf, 1996; Langer & Rodin, 1977; Rodin & Langer, 1977). Learning for exercise and health maintenance is essential (Deobil, 1989; Hasselkus, 1983; Peterson, Valliant, & Seligman, 1988; Rowe & Kahn, 1987). *Education for continued self-sufficiency,* for community living, for vocational, retirement, health, housing, and for other concerns is ongoing (Reingold & Werby, 1990). Indeed, new ways of approaching aging, known as 'successful aging' in medical gerontology and '*productive aging*' in political gerontology, are a part of understanding the changing role of the older adult (Rowe & Kahn, 1987). *Education for autonomy* for older cohorts will be essential" (p. 20, italics added).

In contrast to Western cultural values associated with aging and learning, Eastern or Asian cultural values emphasize being in harmony with nature, relationships, and cooperation rather than competition and interdependence. Spiritual well-being is of more concern than material well-being. Cultural values can shape how something as fundamental as physical aging is viewed. In a youth-oriented culture, every effort is made to slow the aging process, cover it up, or deny it. In other cultures, efforts are made to act and look older to accrue the prestige and authority associated with that stage of life (Fry, 1990). Retirement presents another example. In Western societies, there is "a premium on overt and evident active involvement in life, on doing, going, belonging, making. Passivity, contemplation, withdrawal, introspection or even the giving of sage advice are disvalued as styles of life" (Antonovsky & Sagy, 1990, p. 364). One has to legitimize retirement by maintaining an active, "working" lifestyle. In contrast, Thomas's (1991) study of three religious renunciates in India found these wise men to be socially disengaged, detached from the concerns of life including their own physical welfare, living a life of meditation and reflection. Thomas makes the point that this was totally acceptable to their wives, extended families, and communities: "Unlike the ethos of Western society, which in popular culture and gerontic advice. . .extol[s] the virtues of the active mode of aging, elderly Indians are provided with cultural support to engage in reflection and contemplation in old age" (p. 226).

Studies with Asian older adults suggest that although there are some commonalities in the issues and concerns during this life stage, there are also differences. Most older adults, whether Asian or Western, are concerned with health matters and, to some extent, the security of their living situation. But even issues of health and security can be culturally defined as noted above. Certainly family relationships, the community, and spiritual life appear much more prominently in studies with Eastern elderly, reflecting Eastern cultural values of the collective, harmony, and spirituality. In Japan, for example, intergenerational interaction is based on the traditional belief that "the souls of the elderly and of children were thought to be deeply connected. Thirty-three years after the death of an old person, the soul was thought to be reborn as the soul of a child" (Yamazaki, 1994, p. 454). Likewise, in a comparative study of moral development of American and Japanese adults of all ages, Americans tended "to emphasize the autonomy of individual human life separated from the rest of the world, while Japanese. . .tend[ed] to see human life embedded in a human network" (Iwasa, 1992, p. 8). For the Japanese, "it was more moral. . .to pursue a way to achieve harmony between individual and society" (p. 8).

In another study, native Hawaiian female elders were interviewed to identify life themes and cultural values. Three major themes were found to be central to their lives: (a) relationships with people, (b) relationships with nature, and (c) spiritual and religious beliefs (Mokuau & Browne, 1994). In yet another study, adequate social relationships were found to be the key contributor to successful aging and mental health of elderly Vietnamese refugees (Yee, 1992).

Although no studies could be found that focused specifically on older adult learning in Eastern societies, it can be assumed that just as studies of Western older adult learning reflect Western cultural values, the same will hold true with regard to Eastern societies. The purpose of the study was to understand how culture defined the nature of learning for older adults in Malaysia.

Malaysia and Malaysian Values

The setting of this study is the Southeast Asian country of Malaysia. Two regions make up the country of Malaysia in Southeast Asia. West Malaysia, where the capital city of Kuala Lumpur is located, borders Thailand to the north and Singapore to the south. East Malaysia, made up of two states on either side of Brunei, occupies the northern part of Borneo. This study was conducted in East, or Peninsular, Malaysia. The population is approximately twenty-two million and of that, 6 percent are senior citizens. Islam is the official religion, but freedom of worship is guaranteed by the constitution. Peninsula Malaysia has been colonized by the Portuguese, Dutch, and British (from 1854 to 1957), and by the Japanese during World War II.

Perhaps the most striking characteristic of Malaysian society is its cultural diversity. In addition to numerous ethnic minorities, there are three main groups: Malays, constituting about 60 percent of the population; Chinese, 30 percent; and Indians, 10 percent. Malays predominate in rural areas and in government jobs, whereas Chinese are recognized as wielding economic power; Malay Indians often work in large estates and in public works. Each group has maintained its cultural heritage, including language, dress, food, religion, and customs. Following racial strife in the late 1960s, legislative policies enacted beginning in the early 1970s have been aimed at building a unified multiracial nation. Today, each group retains its own cultural identity while living and working side by side in forging a strong, modern Malaysia.

Although each ethnic group retains its own identity, certain values appear to be common to all Malaysian ethnic groups. Abdullah (1996) has identified the following five values. First, Malaysians are *collectivistic;* identity is determined by the collectivity or group to which one belongs, not by individual characteristics. Second, Malaysians are *hierarchical* in that power and wealth are distributed unequally; this inequality manifests itself in respect for the elders and "is considered normal as manifested in the way homage is paid to those who are senior in age and position" (p. 105). Third, Malaysians *are relationship oriented.* Their lives are embedded in a complex web of ties to family, village, country, and social group, where mutual and reciprocal obligations are clearly understood and acted upon. Fourth, *face,* or "maintaining a person's dignity by not embarrassing or humiliating him in front of others," is key to preserving social harmony and personal relationships (p. 106). Fifth, Malaysians are *religious.* Happiness comes "from suppressing self-interests for the good of others or discovering it from within oneself through prayers and meditations" (p. 106). It was anticipated that these cultural values would, to some extent, be reflected in the learning engaged in by older adults in Malaysia.

Method

To understand how culture shapes the nature of learning in older adulthood in Malaysia, a qualitative research design was employed. Qualitative research is descriptive and inductive, focusing on uncovering meaning from the perspective of participants (Bogdan & Biklen, 1998; Merriam, 1998; Patton, 1990). As a cross-cultural team conducting the research, we embodied both Western and Eastern values. An American, Sharan B. Merriam has traveled extensively in Asia and lived for two years in Afghanistan; she has been to Malaysia four times, most recently as a Fulbright scholar for a six-month period (during which this research was conducted). Mazanah Muhamad is a Malay Moslem and professor of adult education. She received her doctorate from North Carolina State University and has traveled throughout Asia, Europe, and North America. (For an extensive methodological discussion of our insider and outsider statuses in conducting this study, see Merriam and Muhamad, 2000.)

The sample consists of nineteen Malaysian adults older than age sixty. The minimum age of sixty was set as a criterion for inclusion in the sample for several reasons. First, retirement age for civil servants in Malaysia is fifty-five. Second, life expectancy is seventy-two for women and sixty-nine for men, somewhat lower than that of Western industrial nations. Maximum variation was used in an effort to include men and women from the three major ethnic groups of Malay, Chinese, and Indian in proportion to their presence in the population and to draw from both rural and urban areas of the country. Participants were located through the researchers' professional, academic networks; none were known personally to the researchers.

Of the nineteen participants, ten are Malays, five are Chinese Malaysians, and four are Indian Malaysians. There are twelve men and seven women distributed across the three ethnic groups. The youngest participant is sixty years old, and the oldest is eighty-three; the average age of the sample is sixty-eight. Level of education ranges from three participants with no formal education to one who has a Ph.D. Participants also represent a range of work experiences from business, agricultural, and educational settings. Seventeen of the nineteen respondents characterized their health as good. Table 3.1 presents a summary of participant characteristics.

Data were collected through interviews of approximately one hour in length. Eleven of the nineteen interviews were conducted in English. Six were conducted primarily in Malay and translated simultaneously from Malay to English by the bilingual research team member, Dr. Mazanah. Two interviews were conducted in Tamil and translated into English by a bilingual (English and Tamil) assistant. All interviews were audiotaped and transcribed. The interview schedule consisted of open-ended questions regarding the issues, concerns, and learning activities of this stage in life.

Informal observations of the setting in which the interview was conducted (village, home, workplace) provided confirmatory data. For example, an interview with an Indian barber was held in his shop. While his assistant conducted business as usual, the barber "advised" clients and others who strolled in regarding community events and activities, thus underscoring his view of learning for community service. Interviews, however, were the primary source of data. Data were analyzed by using the constant comparative method as presented by Glaser and Strauss (1967). First, each researcher analyzed the transcripts and coded data that appeared to address the research questions, comparing segments of data with each other *within* each interview transcript. Next, themes and concepts were compared *across* interviews. The two researchers then met and compared coding and analyses. From this process, a set of themes was inductively derived that characterized the nature of learning in older adulthood from the perspectives of these participants. These themes were informed by our understanding of Malaysian cultural values as defined above by Malaysian author Abdullah (1996), as well as our knowledge of the largely Western research base on aging and learning.

Table 3.1. Demographic Profile of Participants.

Name	Ethnic Group	Age	Sex	Work Experience	Education
Manan	Malay	75	Male	Governor and educator	B.A.
Ismail	Malay	65	Male	Farmer	Grade 5
Karimah	Malay	66	Female	Housewife	Grade 2
Ramli	Malay	61	Male	University dean	M.A.
Rokiah	Malay	81	Female	Housewife	No formal education
Shahkan	Malay	62	Male	Teacher and businessman	Grade 6
Shafie	Malay	60	Male	Tobacco farmer	Grade 9
Ali	Malay	67	Male	CEO and consultant	Ph.D.
Jafar	Malay	71	Male	Farmer	Grade 5
Aziza	Malay	61	Female	Businesswoman	Grade 3
Daniel	Chinese	70	Male	Military	Diploma[a]
Yin	Chinese	61	Male	Radio technician	Grade 11
Amy	Chinese	60	Female	Teacher	Diploma[a]
Grady	Chinese	80	Female	Housekeeper	Grade 6
Mary	Chinese	70	Female	Housekeeper	No formal education
William	Indian	69	Male	Military, educator	Diploma[a]
Velu	Indian	83	Male	Rubber tapper	No formal education
Gopal	Indian	68	Male	Barber	Grade 4
Devi	Indian	70	Female	Housewife	Grade 3

[a]Two or three years study beyond high school.

Findings

Three themes capture the nature of learning for the older Malaysian adults in this study. First, learning is nonformal and embedded in the concerns and activities of everyday life. Second, learning is communal. Third, learning is driven by spiritual or religious concerns.

Learning Is Nonformal and Experiential

Malaysia is a young country that gained its independence from England in 1957. Only within the past couple of decades has education been a priority; the first university was established in 1965. Consequently, the older cohort of Malaysians has had minimal formal schooling. In our sample, for example, three participants had no formal education, and seven had less than grade 6. For this cohort, grade 6 was considered highly educated; one could become a teacher with a grade 6 education. The lack of experience with formal education is coupled with the lack of educational programs for older adults. In a country that is concentrating on educating its youth, there are no senior centers, Universities of the Third Age, Elderhostels, or Learning-in-Retirement Institutes. Only a few designated programs for seniors exist sponsored by institutions or community agencies.

Older adult learning in Malaysia is thus characterized by its nonformal and incidental nature. "School" is not seen as a place for learning once one has become an adult, let alone an older adult. Religious classes at the local mosque are the closest thing to a formal learning setting mentioned by the participants. Although these classes are open to all ages, the classes tend to be composed mostly of older adults who have time to attend them. Learning is not only nonformal but is experientially based, embedded in respondents' everyday lives. There appears to be very little learning for leisure activity.

Participants mentioned a number of nonformal mechanisms for learning. Devi, a seventy-year-old Indian housewife, listens to a Tamil radio program where she learns songs and poetry; she is also learning English informally from her children and grandchildren. Yin, a Chinese retired radio technician, enjoys cooking and teaches himself new recipes through experimentation.

Although he has only a grade 4 education, Gopal, a sixty-eight-year-old barber, reads widely in Tamil textbooks on medicine, science, and philosophy. Ali, the only participant with a doctoral degree, reads motivational books, has learned to fly an airplane, and stays connected to his grown children through electronic mail. Ramli, who is a trained linguist, is perfecting his Thai, since he now lives in northern Malaysia near the border of Thailand. He also plans to learn Japanese in the future. Much of Ramli's learning is through reading and the Internet: "Before I went to the States I took some courses on speed reading. . . . When you have that skill—speed reading—I can read, say, one or two books a day and I can finish early in the morning. Before coming to work, I open the Internet, to see all the newspapers in the world—Malaysia, CNN, Short Channel Morning Post, Hindu Media, Indonesian newspapers, the Kopang Post from Timor, Bajo Maskin Post from Suawesi. Open those newspapers and read. . . .Scanning everything about the world."

Shafie, a tobacco farmer, has learned and continues to learn from experience and from community-based agricultural extension classes. He feels he has something to add to these classes: "I have my own experience. . . .The LTN [tobacco training institute] says, 'This tobacco died because you use this, this and this.' And I say, 'No, death is a natural part of life.' So I always kind of argue back because I have experience, they have the book learning. I always enjoy the dialogue."

Even Ari, with both an earned doctorate and an honorary doctorate to his credit, says he learns the most from "the average farmer" who has worked out basic concepts in commonsense ways.

What the study participants are learning is embedded in their everyday lives. As a function of normal aging, maintaining health has become a focus of informal learning for several. Yin walks two miles each day to stay fit and reads about health and nutrition. Ali has learned about hormone injections in chicken and has stopped eating it. Daniel and Amy have become vegetarian and are now learning about organic gardening. They have taken a short course and are experimenting with a small "kitchen garden" on their property. "We are still learning [with the garden]," Amy says, "because we are not learning in school, you know. And now we are learning about herbs." She recounts how their garden of vegetables and indigenous herbs has become something of a model for the neighborhood children and their parents.

For the Muslim Malays, religious instruction is also a part of their everyday lives. From Rokiah, with no formal education, to the most educated, reading the Qur'an and/or attending religious instruction, usually at the mosque, are daily activities. Ismail, a rural farmer and village elder, receives religious instruction at the mosque on a daily basis and also meets once a week with a religious teacher. Businesswoman Aziza, whose formal education was grade 3, goes to a religious center for instruction once a week for two hours. She also reports having more time for learning now that she is semiretired.

Learning is also integrally related to the respondents' work life. Aziza, for example, whose business is batik (hand-drawn wax designs on silk), is a member of an association that takes trips in the region and abroad to learn about different batik techniques and patterns. William, retired military but now working as marketing director for a private college, has had to learn computer skills for his job. Manan, a respected politician and educator, told us how at the age of seventy-five he was learning what he needed to know to start new businesses in Thailand and China. All four farmers, Shahkan, Safie, Ismail, and Jafar, reported learning new farming techniques to improve crop yield through a combination of experimentation and advice from local extension agents. Amy, a retired schoolteacher who now finds herself teaching exercise classes to older adults, had to first learn the exercises herself.

Thus, learning for these Malaysian older adults is nonformal, experiential, a function of their life circumstances. For those still working, some of their learning is directly related to what they have been doing, whether it is farming, teaching, or business. Other learning is also embedded in the concerns and issues of daily living. There is a seamlessness about their learning, in that the nature of the learning is congruent with past and present life circumstances.

Learning Is Communal

The group or community is a common Eastern cultural value. From this perspective, relationships with one's family, community, and country take precedence over individual needs and interests. The Malaysian older adults in this study expressed this communal orientation to learning in two ways. First, much of the learning was in the context of a community; learning was seen as a social activity that provided a vehicle for interacting with others. Second, informants engaged in learning to be able to better contribute to the well-being of others.

The Community Context. For most of the adults in the study, learning activities were seen as social activities. Aziza, who owns a batik shop, participates in association functions as much for the social interaction as for learning different batik techniques. She particularly enjoys the association-sponsored trips because of the friends she has made. She has no desire to expand her business as she just does it "to pass the time and not be lonely." Aziza wants to be seen as "a friendly businesswoman" to whose shop you can come, not to buy, but just to visit. Amy and Daniel joined a very educational "environmental walk" recently. "We decided to walk," she says, as "it was for a fund raising cause, to get funds. And there again . . . we got to meet people of all ages, very young people, and people from all walks of life. And some were really impressive, and they invited us in."

Yin also likes to travel to sightsee and "meet some friends." Sisters Grady and Mary who live in a retirement home spoke of their prized possession, a television set. This private set allows them to watch television away from the men and in the company of their women friends. Asked what makes them happy, Grady replied that it is their friends, "people who talk and love, and tell stories—friends." For Manan, learning and education are synonymous with personal relationships. Ramli observes that in a changing society such as Malaysia's, "the world is getting smaller," and although "mobility may be less when you get older, communication will be more and more." He will be able to keep up with his "wide circle of friends" through the Internet.

For others such as Devi, learning is intertwined with family relationships. For Devi, learning some English has more to do with the accompanying pleasure of interacting with her grandson, in particular, than how much English she will actually learn. Shahkan, a retired schoolteacher who currently runs a tobacco-curing business, was motivated to learn to use a computer to communicate with his daughter, who is studying in England. William finds his harmonica and piano playing a good means of linking with his seven-year-old granddaughter whom he "seduces" into playing the piano when he goes for a visit.

Attending study groups is a socially important activity for those who are learning more about their religion. For some, especially the women, it may be their only social outlet outside family activities. Rokiah, who had no formal schooling, learned to read in religious classes and became a leader of a women's Islamic study group. Until a year ago when she turned eighty-one, Rokiah participated in these classes on a regular basis. Karima, a wife of a rural farmer with a grade 2 education, attended religious classes at the *surau* (prayer room for women) after all of her eight children had left home; only recently has she been confined to the farm due to a major health problem. For a number of the men in the study, attending religious classes was also a social activity, sometimes involving the discussion of political and community civic issues.

Contributing to Others' Well-Being. Besides the social interaction of much of the participants' learning, learning was also seen as a responsibility or obligation. That is, many spoke of the necessity of learning so that they could be better prepared to help others. Ari echoed several respondents when he observed that "I am what I am today because somebody gave me a break." They in turn want to be prepared to help someone else. As Manan said, "Some of the things that are seen to come my way are given to me. Some I have created myself and developed myself. So it is a combination of what is given and what is developmental. So I have developed this very. . .beautiful experience that I live, not so much for myself, but for people [who have] trained and educated me. . . .And therefore I believe I owe. . .those that helped me grow up."

Shafie, a tobacco farmer, studies religious books so he can teach at the mosque. Ramli, a university dean, also recognizes that "in order to teach I have to learn a lot." He speaks of being "challenged" by his students: "The more they challenge me, the more I have to learn, and the better I am. In Malaysia you have the Chinese, the Indians, the Eurasian Malays. Everyone who comes to me I consider as a special case." He feels that because he is continuously learning, he has "something to offer." This something is not just book learning; it's what he has learned from "the big book [of life]." Both Daniel and Amy are learning Tai Chi for their own benefit but also so that they can teach older adults. Amy recounts how in the home for the aged where she volunteers, flowers are a luxury that few can afford. She has learned how to make plastic flower arrangements so that the home now has flowers. She even convinced a local florist to teach her free, since it was "for the old people and for charity."

The barber Gopal has an extensive learning program going on, not only to satisfy his own curiosity but also to be of help to others. He reads newspapers and books about medicine, politics, physical science; he writes poetry but says most of his learning "comes through meeting people." He wants to be a good example to young people. As a member of the Malaysian Dravidian Association, a social action group dedicated to uplifting the community, he tries to get scholarships for students to attend higher education. He himself speaks to community groups fostering self-help and development of the community. "He likes people to be cooperative," translated our research assistant. "He likes people to be in good situations. . . .He is happy if people are helping each other in good spirit. He has no self-interest." Gopal is particularly concerned about the Malaysian Indians: "There are three major races in this country—the Malays, the Chinese, and the Indians. Among these three races, the most unprogressive race is the Indian race. The other two races have already gone up—they have progressed, they are involved in business, in politics, and all these things. They are developed. But the Indians, they are progressing but very slow, very slow. This is the reason for the Dravidians. . .to bring the Indian race equal to the other two races."

To summarize this second theme, the communal dimension of learning, older adults in Malaysia see learning as embedded in social interaction, whether it is with their families or with the larger community. Learning is communal in another sense also. Participants felt that their own learning was something to be used for the benefit of others and for improving community. This responsibility was carried out through being good role models, through volunteering, and through engaging in social-action agendas.

Learning Is Spiritually and Philosophically Driven

Whether Moslem, Christian, Hindu, or Buddhist, the participants in this study spoke of learning in philosophical and spiritual terms. Personal or material gain did not appear to motivate these older adults. To a person, they are content with their lives as they are. Asked what guides their life and learning at their present age, most spoke about being open to new ideas, being tolerant of other races and religions, helping others, and generally leading a good life.

Yin, a Buddhist, had this to say: "To me, if you got the straight heart, you don't have to worry. . . .Do straight and do no harm to others. Don't hurt anybody and don't be too greedy." He does volunteer work at the temple and says, "I don't care whether he is a Malay, a Chinese, or Indian, you know. If they need my help, I help them. That's my policy." He says people should try their best to improve, so they "can do something for the country. . . .Don't be too selfish about life." William, a Christian, says only the fellow "who is lying in the grave has completed his education. Until that time you got to learn. And learning is a focus that goes throughout our life." Health and other things are only possible if "your God is with you. . . .My philosophy is, God, King, and country, in that order." Through learning and a belief in God, anything is possible: "I think God has really been good to me. I cannot thank God enough, you know, because I never suffered hardship. The only time I suffered hardship was during the Japanese occupation. . . .But fortunately, again, two strong hands, healthy body, and. . .hard work. You know, if you have been used to hard work, nothing is difficult. With God, everything is possible."

William sees learning as integral to living. We should be "eager to learn," and "even in a dark tomb, there's always light." He quotes a proverb that says, "zeal without knowledge is fire without light. I want to learn all things and ideas."

At eighty-three, Velu is our oldest participant. He is Indian Malay, a Hindu, and worked as a rubber tree tapper on a plantation all his life. He has no formal education. His philosophy is to "help others, don't do harm, don't rob, don't rogue, and don't visit others' wives." He works in his garden for exercise because he wants to stay healthy so as not to be a burden on others. He is at peace and comments that unlike Europeans who "would like to live up to ninety or a hundred," Asians are ready to die, as he is, at fifty-five, sixty-five, or seventy.

The Moslem participants spoke of their religious-based responsibility to keep learning for their spiritual health as well as to give back to others as discussed above. Ismail, a farmer and village elder, goes to the mosque for instruction because he is preparing for the afterlife. He has no concern about material things as he did when he was younger. Religious instruction is very important because at age sixty-five, he has already lived two years beyond when the prophet Muhammad died; one should begin preparing for the afterlife early (as he did at age forty-five), because "how do you know when you will leave [this world]?" Likewise, Karimah, the sixty-six-year-old housewife with eight children, says she has no concerns about this life. Rather, she is "making preparation" for when she leaves this world. Shahkan, a rural businessman and former headmaster who has learned how to use a computer for his business and for e-mailing his daughter, is also studying religious books, "because as a Muslim we have to focus ourselves on the next world." He reads the Qur'an "at least twenty or thirty minutes every day. . . and the book of knowledge of our religion." The best thing about this stage of life, he says, is that he is "closer and closer to my God. That is the good thing."

The spiritual dimension to these participants' learning was further underscored when we asked them whether they had a role model for this stage of life. Four identified someone whose philosophy they admired, but these role models were for living a good life in general, rather than a model for aging. Velu, for example, named a politician in the state of Madras, India, who was a philosopher and lecturer. Velu, himself poor and illiterate, admires all that this man did to raise the standard of living—"he built a lot of schools, a lot of roads and houses for the poor." The most important thing this man did was to build schools and provide free education until grade 6. Jafar, who at seventy-one feels he is living on bonus years because the Prophet died at sixty-three, seeks out a man in his village for religious education who is older than eighty. Gopal mentions an Indian who models the social justice philosophy that he lives by. This man "was known to set the first justice society in India. He is known as the Eastern Socrates." Gopal admires his philosophy and "the truth in his speech. He was an independent thinker."

The older adults in this study are also aware of the role they play as mentors, advisers, and wise elders, a role that inspires them to continue learning. Most respondents agreed that being elderly and experienced brought with them a favored position and status in their family and community. Ismail, a village elder, explains it this way: "Town people have a saying that you go back to the village to the older one, the one who has taken lots of salt [meaning had lots of experience, which in Malaysian culture equates to wisdom] to learn." Rokiah, an eighty-one-year-old widow living with her children, recounted how she is consulted when major decisions are made with regard to children and grandchildren. Finally, our contact person for Gopal, who is himself a well-educated engineer, told us how he regularly visits Gopal (who has very little formal education) at his shop to learn the "way of life" from the older man.

In summary, learning in older adulthood is characterized by a spiritual or philosophical overlay that most participants were aware of and could articulate. This quality permeates their view of aging as well as learning.

Discussion

The purpose of this study was to understand how culture shapes the nature of learning in older adulthood. From interviews with nineteen Malaysian older adults, it was discovered that learning is nonformal and experiential, that it is communal, and that much of it is spiritual or religious in nature. These findings are discussed in terms of what we know about older adults and learning and the Malaysian cultural values of collectivism, hierarchy, relationships, face, and religion (Abdullah, 1996).

That older adult learning in Malaysia is nonformal and embedded in the context of everyday life is hardly surprising, given what we know about adult learning in general. Throughout human history, learning has been firmly linked to living; indeed, humans had to learn to survive. The association of learning with formal institutions such as schools is a twentieth-century phenomenon. So firmly established is the link between learning and schooling that adults have a difficult time identifying the learning that is part of their everyday lives. Only through careful probing and attentive listening can this embedded learning be surfaced. Nearly thirty years ago, just such a study by Tough (1971, 1979) brought this type of learning to the attention of adult educators. He discovered that 90 percent of adults were engaged in learning projects, most of which were self-directed. Subsequent studies, including one with older adult learners (Sears, 1989), have substantiated the prevalence of self-directed learning projects among adult learners.

Participants in our study learned through experience and sometimes in combination with nonformal programs such as agricultural extension workshops, association meetings, and religious institutions. They also learned through *informal* adult education activities—those activities that occur naturally within the context of people's lives. Coombs (1985) defines informal learning as "the spontaneous, unstructured learning that goes on daily in the home and neighborhood, behind the school and on the playing field, in the workplace, marketplace, library and museum, and through the various mass media" (p. 92). Coombs also observes that because so much of adult learning takes place this way, nations should attend to enriching their informal learning environments especially through the availability of print materials, radio, television, and computers. Indeed, a number of our participants told us how they used radio, books, newspapers, and the Internet for learning.

Although the majority of adult learning, including learning by older adults, in all cultures is through nonformal and informal means (Merriam & Brockett, 1997), there are also some contextual factors that help explain its prevalence in Malaysia. The country's priority is on formally educating its youth. Even middle-aged adults have little opportunity to pursue formal education; for older adults there are no policies, resources, or support for education. Access to higher education and programs such as Elderhostel, Learning-in-Retirement Institutes, Universities of the Third Age, senior centers, and retirement communities with educational programs are nonexistent in Malaysia. Even if opportunities existed, the level of education of this generation of older adults would mitigate against participation (as the level of previous education is the best predictor of current participation). Nor is participating in formal education later in life a culturally accepted practice as it is in North America. For example, since 1976, when the Department of Professional Development and Continuing Education at University Putra Malaysia was established, only one student older than sixty years has attended (in 1999).

The second finding of our study on the collective nature of older adult learning in Malaysia is congruent with the cultural values (Abdullah, 1996) of this Asian society. Elders talked of learning as a highly social activity where they enjoyed being in a group and relating to other learners as much, if not more, than what they were actually learning. Socialized from birth "to maintain harmonious relationships in a social setting of mutual interdependence as found in the village. . . . family, friends, and the community take precedence over self-centered interests such as profit and materialism" (Abdullah, 1996, p. 26). This orientation helps explain why Aziza cares more for making her batik shop a place to socialize than for increasing her profits. For a number of our participants, attending religious study groups was as much for the social interaction as for learning. Even for those who were learning on their own, their projects involved interacting with other people. For example, Devi was learning English from her grandson, and Ramli and Ali were learning computers to be in touch with family members. As Abdullah explains, "The notion of a concept of self as an individual and maintaining privacy or solitude is neither well-known nor desirable. [A Malaysian] is affectively related to the others and gains from them satisfaction and a sense of being" (p. 26).

Malaysian older adults also see learning as a responsibility and a means of giving back to their communities. Several spoke of learning to be better mentors to younger people, and several were learning so that they could be more effective as social activists in their communities. Amy and Daniel, for example, first learned Tai Chi themselves so they could teach it to other elders. They are currently learning about organic gardening and have made their own "kitchen garden" accessible to interested visitors from the community. Triandis (1995) points out that "in collectivist cultures helping is a moral obligation, thus, obligatory, not voluntary [as it is in individualistic cultures]. In many collectivist cultures doing one's duty is realizing one's nature, and individual happiness is not important" (p. 120). In Malaysian culture, a priority is placed on making others happy. Personal happiness is secondary.

Motivational studies of participation in formal adult learning activities in the West have uncovered a complex picture of why adults participate. A number of studies have identified six factors that explain participation. Two of those factors—social relationships and social welfare—appear similar to what we are calling the communal nature of older adult learning in Malaysia. People say at least part of their motivation to participate is to make new friends or because they want to serve others or their community. These motives are in conjunction with motives related to external expectations, professional advancement, escape or stimulation, and cognitive interest (Merriam & Caffarella, 1998). Studies focusing just on *older* adults and their reasons for learning have also found social contact to be a major motivator (Fisher, 1998). However, the social dimension of learning in these studies is but one factor among many, whereas in our study it appears to be a major characteristic of older adult learning in Malaysia.

Our third finding, that learning is religiously or philosophically oriented, can be explained from a Malaysian cultural perspective. Malaysia is officially a Muslim country and approximately 60 percent of the population are Moslems. Other Malaysians are Buddhist, Hindu, Christian, Taoist, and so on. Malaysians are quite conscious of the diversity of religious practices and customs in their country and make an effort to be informed and tolerant of others' religious perspectives. This factor, combined with the service and learning orientation of these religions, shapes much of older adult learning in this setting. Islam, for example, "looks at education as a form of worship. . . .'To seek knowledge is a sacred duty of every Muslim, male and female'" (Abdullah, 1996, p. 33). According to the Qur'an, learning is an obligation for every Muslim to meet individual needs (for example, how to pray) and community needs (as in learning to prepare the dead for burial). This focus on learning extends into adulthood; Muslims are reminded that the first word from God to the forty-year-old illiterate prophet Muhammad was, "Read! In the name of your Lord, who has created all that exists" (Al Qur'an, surah 96, verse 1). Furthermore, the companions of the prophet studied despite being old.

This religious-philosophical orientation was further underscored by respondents' answers to our question about role models or mentors for aging. Those who mentioned someone were clear that these role models were not for aging alone but rather for leading a good life, doing good works, and exhibiting high moral authority throughout life. Finally, religious motivations could be seen in their desire to help others and their communities. In Islam, this can be explained by the obligation to learn to meet community or societal needs. Christianity calls for similar attention to the less privileged of society, evidenced in our study by Daniel and Amy's fervor in contributing to the old-folks home run by a Christian missionary. Hindu principles and culture also emphasize education in the service of society. This is evidenced by the exalted position given to the largely learned Brahmin caste. Hindus also believe in a selfless self. It is a duty for a Hindu to help others. This philosophy prompts Hindus like Gopal to be charitable. To be able to make meaningful contributions to society, one needs to continuously learn. Buddhists also see learning contributing toward life happiness for self and others. The close association between religion and learning in Malaysia is reflected in the role of the places of worship. The Muslim mosque, Christian church, and Hindu and Buddhist temples all double as places of learning and as community centers.

The philosophical orientation of several of the participants can also perhaps be linked to the developmental literature on late life. Erikson (1982) in particular has written about this stage of life and how people make meaning when their lives are nearly over. The developmental task for this stage is to be able to achieve a sense of ego integrity through reviewing one's life, through care taking, through feeling at peace with one's life as it has been lived. Of this stage in life, he writes, "What is the last ritualization built into the style of old age? I think it is philosophical: for in maintaining some order and meaning in the disintegration of body and mind, it can also advocate a durable hope in wisdom" (p. 64).

In summary, Eastern cultural values contributed to shaping the learning of older adults in this ethnically (Malay, Chinese, Indian) and religiously (Islam, Buddhist, Hindu, Taoist) diverse Asian country. But like other countries in the region, Malaysia is changing. And although we found the learning of the *current* generation of older adults in Malaysia to be a function of the cultural context and the values discussed above, we would expect to see a somewhat different scenario with the next generation of elders. For example, the current retirement age of fifty-five is based on life expectancy rates of the 1950s. Little, if any, attention is given to older, retired persons in terms of formal learning programs. As a result, the nature of learning for older adults in Malaysia is nonformal, experiential, and embedded in their everyday lives. With longer life expectancy and the rising cost of living, many will need to work longer. Improved health and living conditions are creating an experienced resource that would be to the country's advantage to tap. Thus, we would expect to see more attention given to formal learning programs for older adults focusing on both leisure activities and training for continued employment. At the same time, we would expect the collectivist orientation where family, friends, and community are priorities, as well as philosophical and spiritual values, to remain important in shaping older adult learning. This study has underscored the importance of considering cultural context and cultural values in mapping the learning activities of any particular group of adults. In applying a "cultural" lens to future research in adult learning, we might better describe the nature of adult learning, as well as shed light on the field's crucial issues of access and opportunity.

References

Abdullah, A. (1996). *Going glocal: Cultural dimensions in Malaysian management.* Kuala Lumpur, Malaysia: Malaysian Institute of Management.

Antonovsky, A., & Sagy, S. (1990). Confronting developmental tasks in the retirement transition. *The Gerontologist, 30*(3), 362–368.

Baars, J. (1997). Concepts of time and narrative temporality in the study of aging. *Journal of Aging Studies, 11*(4), 283–295.

Bee, H. (2000). *The journey of adulthood* (4th ed.). Princeton, NJ: Prentice Hall.

Bogdan, R., & Biklen, S. (1998). *Qualitative research for education.* Needham Heights, MA: Allyn & Bacon.

Bonnell, V. E., & Hunt, L. (1999). Introduction. In V. E. Bonnell & L. Hunt (Eds.), *Beyond the cultural turn* (pp. 1–34). Berkeley: University of California Press.

Coombs, P. H. (1985). *The world crisis in education: The view from the eighties.* New York: Oxford University Press.

Erikson, E. H. (1982). *The life cycle completed* (2nd ed.). New York: Norton.

Fisher, J. C. (1998). Major streams of research probing older adult learning. In J. C. Fisher & M. A. Wolf (Eds.), *Using learning to meet the challenges of older adulthood* (pp. 27–40). New Directions for Adult and Continuing Education, No. 77. San Francisco: Jossey-Bass.

Fry, C. L. (1990). Cross-cultural comparisons of aging. In K. F. Ferraro (Ed.), *Gerontology: Perspectives and issues* (pp. 129–146). New York: Springer.

Giordano, J. (1992). Ethnicity and aging. *Journal of Gerontological Social Work, 18,* 23–37.

Glaser, B. G., & Strauss, A. L. (1967). *The discovery of grounded theory.* Chicago: Aldine.

Hofstede, G. (1991). *Culture and organization.* London: McGraw-Hill.

Iwasa, N. (1992). Postconventional reasoning and moral education in Japan. *Journal of Moral Education, 21*(1), 3–16.

Merriam, S. B. (1998). *Qualitative research and case study applications in education.* San Francisco: Jossey-Bass.

Merriam, S. B., & Brockett, R. G. (1997). *The profession and practice of adult education.* San Francisco: Jossey-Bass.

Merriam, S. B., & Caffarella, R. S. (1998). *Learning in adulthood* (2nd ed.). San Francisco: Jossey-Bass.

Merriam, S. B., & Muhamad, M. (2000). Insider/outsider status: Reflections on cross-cultural interviewing. *Inquiry: Critical Thinking Across the Disciplines, 19*(3), 34–43.

Mokuau, N., & Browne, C. (1994). Life themes of native Hawaiian female elders: Resources for cultural preservation. *Social Work, 39*(1), 43–49.

Patton, M. Q. (1990). *Qualitative evaluation methods.* Newbury Park, CA: Sage.

Quinn, N., & Holland, D. (1987). Culture and cognition. In D. Holland & N. Quinn (Eds.), *Cultural models in language and thought* (pp. 3–40). New York: Cambridge University Press.

Riley, J. W., Jr., & Riley, M. W. (1994). Beyond productive aging. *Aging International, 21*(2), 15–19.

Sears, E.J.B. (1989). *Self-directed learning projects of older adults.* Unpublished doctoral dissertation, University of North Texas, Denton, TX.

Sewell, W. H., Jr. (1999). The concept(s) of culture. In V. E. Bonnell & L. Hunt (Eds.), *Beyond the cultural turn* (pp. 35–61). Berkeley: University of California Press.

Thomas, L. E. (1991). Dialogues with three religious renunciates and reflections on wisdom and maturity. *International Journal of Aging and Human Development, 32*(3), 211–227.

Tough, A. (1971, 1979). *The adult's learning projects: A fresh approach to theory and practice in adult learning.* Toronto: Ontario Institute for Studies in Education.

Triandis, H. C. (1995). *Individualism & collectivism.* Boulder, CO: Westview.

VandenBos, G. R. (1998). Life-span developmental perspectives on aging: An introductory overview. In I. H. Nordhus, G. R. VandeBos, S. Berg, & P. Fromholt (Eds.), *Clinical geropsychology* (pp. 3–14). Washington, DC: American Psychological Association.

Wolf, M. A. (1998). New approaches to the education of older adults. In J. C. Fisher & M. A. Wolf (Eds.), *Using learning to meet the challenges of older adulthood* (pp. 15–26). New Directions for Adult and Continuing Education, No. 77. San Francisco: Jossey-Bass.

Yamazaki, T. (1994). Intergenerational interaction outside the family. *Educational Gerontology, 20*(5), 453–462.

Yee, B.W.K. (1992). Markers of successful aging among Vietnamese refugee women. *Women and therapy, 13*(3), 221–238.

"Do All These People Have To Be Here?" Reflections on Collecting Data in Another Culture

Sharan B. Merriam
University of Georgia, Athens

The driver took us to the warehouse doubling as an office where we were scheduled to interview a semi-retired tobacco curer, and later, a tobacco farmer. Upon arrival both interviewees and the local extension agent met us. As we pulled out our materials, the driver, the extension agent, the two men, and three others lingering nearby all sat around the picnic table, ready for us to begin. I whispered to Mazanah, my co-researcher, "Do all these people have to be here?"

So began my experience doing research in Malaysia, a multi-ethnic, multi-religious society in Southeast Asia. Mazanah, a university professor in the department where I was on a Fulbright assignment, and I decided to pursue our common interests in adult learning and development by conducting a small-scale study of older adult learners in Malaysia. We have written elsewhere about being a cross-cultural team (Merriam & Muhamad, 2000); in this piece I focus on some of the things I learned while collecting data in another culture.

First, from previous experience doing qualitative research in the United States I had come to internalize some practices and assumptions that were challenged by the Malaysian setting. In the past I had conducted most interviews on a one-to-one basis in a quiet setting. However, as the above scenario illustrates, the Malaysian context is quite different but congruent with the collective, group-oriented culture of Malaysia (Mazanah terms it a "busybody culture"). Everyone knows everyone else's business, there are no secrets and very little privacy, and nearly all activities involve extended family or community. With the exception of two interviews conducted in a private office in the workplace, a similar pattern of numerous others—spouse, children, relatives, neighbors, even animals—being present characterized our interviews. In one village, the elder who was interviewed first accompanied us, along with the contact person, to two subsequent interviews, sitting through three interviews altogether. The most amusing example of the communal interview was an interview with an elderly Indian barber held in his shop while less than five feet away his assistant cut hair, shaved, and chatted with customers. The barber's cousin and the cousin's son, who was our contact person and occasional interpreter, were also present.

Equally surprising to me was the candor, in the presence of family members and others, with which participants answered questions and shared some thoughts—thoughts that in our culture would be considered private or at least sensitive. This seemed to underscore the communal orientation and the lack of a need for privacy. Though our questions for the most part were benign, having to do with activities, interests, and learning in older adulthood, participants also shared their disappointments, hopes, and fears. One elderly Indian woman, for example, spoke of being prepared to die, that she had no fear whatsoever, and that she was glad her adult daughter, who was present at the interview, knew this.

Though initially disconcerting to me, over time I came to expect others to be present and activities to be going on simultaneously with the interview. Also, I discovered that Malaysians find this communal atmosphere natural, normal, and comforting. For example, the tobacco farmer in the opening scenario shared with us the fact that by "sitting in" on the first interview, he overcame his reluctance to participate in the study. Nor did his hearing the first man's responses seem to influence his views.

There were other logistics in conducting interviews in this culture that I had to come to terms with. Since Malaysians typically arrange their furniture along opposite walls of a room, we had to first figure out how to sit so everyone could hear, and so that the tape recorder could pick up both questions and answers. Other distractions were sudden rainstorms pelting tin roofs, drainage ditches to traverse, mosquitoes, and ubiquitous side discussions among observers of the interview and comments to the interviewee.

In addition to this research experience leading me to examine some of my own research practices, I came to realize that the research process itself enabled me to learn much about Malaysian culture. For example, relationships are crucial in Malaysian culture because they define who has access to whom and whether or not certain tasks get done. An interview could not be set up without the intervention of a third party on our behalf. Further, it was important to attend to the relative status of both the contact person and the participant. For example, it would not have been possible to interview villagers without the contact person first going through a village elder (and our interviewing him first). Even when arranging an interview in the capital, Kuala Lumpur, with an educated, Westernized businessman, we had to first pay a courtesy call on his superior, who then wanted to be interviewed. So while we had particular criteria in mind for selecting our sample, there were occasions when we had to interview others to satisfy social expectations based on status.

This relationship orientation also played out in our interviews by our spending a leisurely amount of time in small talk before any formal interview could begin. Mazanah especially was called upon to connect with our respondents by exploring her work, her relationship to the contact person, where she was from in Malaysia, her family network, and so on. I was often asked how many children I had and how frequently I saw them. The focus on relationships was invariably underscored by the sharing of refreshments, even in the poorest home. Eating together is a sign of trust and friendship in Malaysian culture; if you refused someone's offer for food, you'd be rejecting their friendship. My Western, task-oriented mindset had to be adjusted to this more leisurely social orientation.

Malaysians are nonconfrontational, sensitive, indirect, and concerned with preserving face. Rather than refuse to be interviewed, a respondent might fall ill just before our scheduled meeting. Of course we never knew whether this was their way of saying no, or if they were really ill. Likewise, if in the course of an interview we overlapped with one of the five daily Muslim prayer times, respondents would become anxious and distracted rather than end the interview directly.

The experience of collecting data in another culture also rather dramatically highlighted the interrelated notions of positionality, power, and knowledge construction. My position as outsider to the culture meant I could ask questions to which Mazanah, as an insider, was presumed to know the answers. But our positions were not fixed. I became more comfortable in the culture, and Mazanah's status as insider was less central when we interviewed Chinese and Indian Malaysians.

Power intersected with our insider-outsider positionalities in a number of ways. On one hand, my outsider status enabled us to recruit some participants because they were curious about a "white lady." Also, we soon discovered that I needed to ask the questions (whether or not they spoke English) initially, because participants would explain to me what they assumed Mazanah already knew. On the other hand, Mazanah had power as an insider as well as a Western-educated professor to access participants and to understand their perspectives much more readily than I could as an outsider. Those we interviewed also subtly negotiated the power dynamics by determining where and when the interview was held, who else was present, and of course what information was shared.

Issues around knowledge construction also became quite real to me in the process of this study. To begin with, the very concepts that formed the heart of our inquiry, aging and learning of older adults, were most challenging to operationalize in terms of questions to participants, partly because our study was informed by Western models of aging and learning unfamiliar to this culture. Our question about what it meant to age "successfully" was quickly dropped as being incomprehensible to respondents. We also found that asking what they valued at this time in their lives did not translate into Malay, in which the word for *value* means how much something is worth. Further, multiple levels of translation complicated the process. The older generation of Malaysians has had little formal education, and the Indian and Chinese elderly more often than not have lived within their ethnic communities speaking their native language. Thus, on occasion, for example, I would ask a question in English, Mazanah would translate into Malay, and our interpreter would translate into Tamil or Chinese. Of course we worried about whether the translation to the respondent and then the answer back to us expressed what the respondent actually meant. Our strategy became to ask the same question in as many forms and variations as possible and to debrief with our interpreter immediately following the interview. The knowledge constructed by our participants and interpreted by us was very much defined by our positionality vis-à-vis the interview.

In summary, collecting data in another culture resulted in my learning at least as much about qualitative research as I did about Malaysians' perspectives on older adulthood. The experience afforded me the opportunity to understand how the methods employed shape what one learns about the phenomenon being studied. Much of the qualitative research that we engage in is with people or phenomena outside of our own experience. This can be a vehicle for learning about ourselves and about doing this kind of research as well as the topic of investigation. And my experience would suggest that the more different the research setting, the greater the opportunity for learning.

Reference

Merriam, S. B., & Muhamad, M. (2000). Insider/outsider status: Reflections on cross-cultural interviewing. *Inquiry: Critical Thinking Across the Disciplines, 19*(3), 34–43.

4

Spirituality and Emancipatory Adult Education in Women Adult Educators for Social Change

Elizabeth J. Tisdell

Teaching for social change is a work of passion for many adult emancipatory educators—a passion fueled by a deep underlying ethical, social, and often a spiritual commitment on the part of the adult educator. It is important work, and at the dawn of the new millennium, many adult educators are attempting to teach across borders of race, gender, class, national origin, and sexual orientation to increase cross-border understanding and to work toward greater equity between dominant and oppressed groups. Some educators are doing this by teaching classes in higher education that explicitly deal with these topics, whereas others are working with grassroots communities on projects aimed at social change.

How adult educators might respond to the educational needs of a multicultural society has been a subject of some discussion in feminist and critical pedagogy in the past few years and in considerations of how adult educators can challenge systems of power, privilege, oppression, and colonization and cross borders of race, gender, class, and national origin in this era of globalization (Brookfield & Preskill, 1999; Giroux, 1992; Hayes & Colin, 1994; Johnson-Bailey & Cervero, 1998; Tisdell, 1998; Walters & Manicom, 1996). Teaching across these borders for social change is difficult, requiring a willingness to deal with conflict, resistance, and strong emotions as groups engage in critical dialogue and, hopefully, move to social action. What has been missing from the literature is attention to what drives this underlying commitment or how spirituality informs the work of such emancipatory adult educators working from these critical, feminist, or antiracist educational frames.

Elizabeth J. Tisdell. (2000). "Spirituality and Emancipatory Adult Education in Adult Women Educators for Social Change." *Adult Education Quarterly, (50)* 4, 308–335. Reprinted by permission.

This is somewhat surprising because almost all of those who write about education for social change cite the important influence of educator and activist Paulo Freire, who was a deeply spiritual man strongly informed by the liberation theology movement of Latin America (Freire, 1997). With the exception of the recent study on community and commitment by Daloz, Keene, Keene, and Parks (1996), in which the connection between spiritual commitment and social action is implied, empirical research on how spirituality relates to a commitment to do social justice work is extremely limited. Clearly, there are both male and female adult educators and activists teaching for social change who are motivated to do so partly because of their spiritual commitments; but many are women of different race and class backgrounds guided by critical, feminist, or antiracist educational perspectives who have also had to renegotiate their adult spirituality in light of having been raised in patriarchal religious traditions. How has their spirituality changed over time, and how does it motivate and influence their adult education practice for social justice? In light of the lack of adult education literature that deals with women, spirituality, and social justice, the purpose of this study was to examine how spirituality influences the motivations and practices of a multicultural group of women adult educators who are teaching for social change, who were strongly informed by a particular religious tradition as a child, and have renegotiated a more relevant adult spirituality. This study suggests implications for how adult educators may draw on spirituality in their own emancipatory adult education practices, and it also offers beginning insight into women's spiritual development in the often ignored (by developmental theorists) sociocultural context.

Related Literature

With the exception of the subfield of adult religious education, spirituality has been given little attention in mainstream academic adult education, and its connection to discussions of emancipatory adult education efforts is even more limited. This may simply be because *spirituality* is difficult to define. It is a relatively elusive topic that can sometimes be confused with religion. Indeed, for many of us, our adult spirituality is clearly informed by how we were socialized both religiously and culturally. Yet spirituality is not the same as religion; religion is an organized community of faith that has written codes of regulatory behavior, whereas spirituality is more about one's personal belief and experience of a higher power or higher purpose. In seeking to give *spirituality* (as opposed to *religion*) a definition, Hamilton and Jackson (1998) conducted a qualitative study of women in the helping professions' conceptions of spirituality. Participants' definitions centered on the following three main themes: further development of self-awareness, a sense of interconnectedness, and a relationship to a higher power. Although this definition does give a sense of the psychological aspects of spirituality as broadly related to meaning making, it does not get at the potential relationship of cultural experience and spirituality, nor does it get at the connection between spirituality and a commitment to social justice, which is the focus of this article.

Nevertheless, these three themes of spirituality—greater self-awareness, a sense of interconnectedness, and an experience of a perceived higher power—appear to be common aspects of what spirituality is about for most who consider it an important meaning-making aspect of their life.

Spirituality in Adult and Higher Education

Despite the fact that there is relatively little direct discussion of spirituality in academic adult education, recently the recognition of the spiritual dimension has begun to creep into some adult and higher education discussions, and this is likely to be an area of some future discussion. Most of these references focus on spirituality more generally in teaching and learning, and this is the focus of the newly released sourcebook on spirituality edited by English and Gillen (2000). Dirkx (1997) has also noted that attention to "soul" in adult learning is important, particularly in attending to group process. He suggests that our interest is not so much to teach soul work or spirituality but rather to nurture soul; that is, "to recognize what is already inherent within our relationships and experiences, to acknowledge its presence with the teaching and learning environment, to respect its sacred message" (Dirkx, 1997, p. 83). In a similar vein, Palmer (1998) discusses the importance of attending to paradox, sacredness, and graced moments in teaching and learning in developing a spirituality of education. Similarly, Young (1997) describes spirituality as the underpinning of our values in higher education. English (2000) discusses very directly the focus on meaning making in adult learning as intricately related to the spiritual quest of adults, whereas Vella (2000), in her discussion of a spirited epistemology, suggests that attending to the spiritual dimension of adult learning is part of honoring the learner as "subject," and thus the author of his or her own life in the quest for meaning making. Indeed, the subject of spirituality is currently a hot topic in human resources development (HRD) and some of the workplace-related literature. However, as Fenwick and Lange (1998) suggest in their critique of the spirituality in the workplace literature in the field, most of these discussions have little or nothing to do with the connection of spirituality to social justice or emancipatory education. There are, of course, a few (not specifically connected to HRD or workplace adult education) who more specifically discuss the connection of work, spirituality, and the creation of a more just global economy. For example, Fox (1995) discusses the connection between spirituality as "inner work" and the revisioning of our "outer work" and the importance of ritual and celebration in the creation of a new cosmology as the great paradigm shift of our time.

Not surprisingly, in most references in adult education, spirituality is dealt with only from an individual, psychological perspective and from the standpoint of what is present in the learning environment in how individual participants construct meaning through image, symbol, and graced moments about the purpose of their life journey. Most discussions of spirituality end here; yet for many adult educators, their perceived purpose in the world relates directly to their emancipatory education efforts. Few adult education writers have discussed this, although the very well-known activist-educators Horton and Freire (1990) were clear about the influence of spirituality on their own work. Hart and Holton (1993) have suggested that spirituality offers hope to emancipatory adult education efforts; Walters and Manicom (1996) discuss the importance of spirituality among grassroots emancipatory adult educators working with women in an international context. They note that spirituality "is a theme that is increasingly significant in popular education practice as culturally distinct groups, women recovering 'womanist' traditions and ethnic collectives, draw on cultural and spiritual symbols in healing and transformative education" (Walters & Manicom, 1996, p. 13). Other than these instances, the field of adult education has been relatively silent about the connection between spirituality and emancipatory education efforts. Yet more recently and more in discussions of education in general, educators and cultural critics are beginning to discuss the importance of spirituality antiracist and emancipatory education efforts. In her own education efforts, hooks (1994, 1999) very directly discusses the importance of spirituality, and Simmer-Brown (1999) discusses both commitment and openness in education for cultural diversity and pluralism. These emancipatory education discussions hint at the importance of attending to spirituality in social justice efforts; yet there is little data-based research that focuses on how it informs the thinking or practices of educators. This study is one effort to get at these issues.

Spiritual Development

This study is primarily about how spirituality informs the work of a multicultural group of feminist or antiracist women emancipatory adult educators. To make sense of how these women perceive and carry out their work as emancipatory educators, it was necessary to understand some of their life history—some of their spiritual journeys or spiritual development as related to their cultural and life experiences. Thus, the literature on spiritual development also informs this study. Weibust and Thomas (1994), in their discussion of learning and spiritual development in adulthood, note that attention to "unity consciousness as knowing" (p. 124) and how adults seek wisdom through spiritual learning and openness to paradox is an important unexplored area of adult development and learning. As I have discussed elsewhere (Tisdell, 1999), so, too, is the area of how culture informs spiritual experience. There is, in fact, a paucity of literature that specifically discusses spiritual development as change over time or that attends to the sociocultural context. Taylor (1998) makes the observation that some have used Mezirow's theory of transformative learning as a jumping-off point to examine ways adults transform thought processes and develop through other ways of knowing, including through spirituality. However, as Taylor (1998) notes, Mezirow's theory is primarily driven by rationality; he does not discuss transformation as spirituality and neglects the role of unconscious thought processes in learning. The spiritual development literature that does exist tends to cite the landmark Fowler (1981) study of faith development, which resulted in a stage theory (six stages) of faith development based on a sample that was 97 percent white and Judeo-Christian. Although he draws on the work of Piaget and Kohlberg, he takes issue with them for "their restrictive understanding of the role of imagination in knowing, their neglect of symbolic processes generally and the related lack of attention to unconscious structuring processes other than those constituting reasoning" (Fowler, 1981, p. 103).

Despite some of the limitations to Fowler's study, it contributes to our understanding of how people construct knowledge through image and symbol, an area that has been ignored by most development and learning theorists. Clearly, there are other authors (mostly from the holistic health movement or in the popular press) who have discussed the power of image and symbol in constructing knowledge and in accessing forms of spiritual knowledge. For example, Myss (1996) provides ways of working with and using images and symbols over time to enhance spiritual development, and both Bolen (1994) and Borysenko (1996) specifically discuss women's biological and spiritual development by drawing on myth, metaphor, and symbol. But nearly all authors who discuss spiritual development as change over time tend to ignore the importance of the sociocultural context in development, and in so doing, they tend to privilege a white, middle-class experience primarily informed by the Judeo-Christian tradition. This is why Merriam and Caffarella (1999) are calling for more direct attention to sociocultural issues and more integrative perspectives on all aspects of adult development.

Spirituality and Development in a Sociocultural Context

Wuthnow (1999) recently conducted a study, from more of a sociological perspective, of two hundred adults who grew up in religious homes to see what patterns their spirituality has taken since childhood. He gives a bit more attention to the sociocultural context than have other researchers in the past. Although the majority of the sample was white and from the Judeo-Christian tradition, his sample was more diverse than Fowler's, with 20 percent being people of color, and 13 percent being Hindu, Muslim, or other non-Judeo-Christian traditions. The study suggests some developmental patterns for those who grew up and were socialized into religious traditions. For example, the spiritual path of the more mature participants required a deep questioning of their childhood traditions and, often, specific points of departure from it. Maintaining the identity-affirming parts, however, in addition to insights from a more broadened and inclusive perspective, often led to a renewed and more developed spiritual practice. In fact, it often led to an increased appreciation of diversity not only of spiritual perspectives but also of interest and desire to work against religious and racial bigotry and for their particular traditions to be more culturally inclusive. Thus, Wuthnow's (1999) study suggests the beginnings of attending to sociocultural issues in religion and spirituality.

There is clearly a lack of research-based literature about spiritual development in general. What literature that does exist gives almost no attention to cultural issues, so there is precious little about the spiritual development of women of color. Thus, the best source of knowledge about this is probably women writers of color who allude to spiritual issues. In regard to her own work as an educator, hooks (1994, 1999) very clearly addresses this, attempting to teach to challenge systems of oppression based on race, gender, and class. Hill Collins (1998), speaking a bit more generally, notes that "spirituality provides an important way that many African-American women are moved to struggle for justice. . . .Spirituality remains deeply intertwined with justice in black women's intellectual history. . . and thus influences black women's critical social theory in particular ways" (p. 244). Similarly, Gunn Allen (1992) speaks to the connection among culture, spiritual symbol, and the "personal choice-community responsibility" dialectic in American Indian communities. Chicana feminist writers Anzaldua (1987) and Castillo (1996), in discussing identity and political issues of Chicana feminists, discuss the significance of the psychological, spiritual, and political symbol of La Virgen de Guadalupe in Chicano culture. They suggest that Chicana feminists frame La Virgen as the Aztec mother/goddess and two-in-one-culture liberator in a way that creates a meaningful, life-enhancing, woman-positive spirituality that informs working for justice in the world. None of these writers are writing about spiritual development or even emancipatory education efforts per se. They are, however, writing about the larger experience of women of their own cultural group and how spirituality relates to their identity and to their working for social justice in the world. Their work, in addition to the work of feminist theologians as discussed in such edited works as Ruether (1996) and King (1996) (who discuss women's social action efforts grounded in feminist theology), offers insights both from a sociocultural perspective on spiritual development as well as how spirituality informs women's teaching for social change.

Method

This was a qualitative research study, and the purpose was to determine how spirituality influences the motivations and practices of a multicultural group of women adult educators who are teaching for social change, were strongly informed by a specific religious tradition as a child, and have renegotiated a more relevant adult spirituality. In this case, women teaching for social change included the following two groups of women: (a) women working in higher education either teaching classes that were specifically about gender, race, class, sexual orientation, or disability issues, or working in programs aimed at meeting the education needs of a specific marginalized group; and (b) women working as educators (in the broad sense) as community activists. There were a total of sixteen participants: four African American, two Latina, two Asian American, one Native American, and seven European American. (See Table 4.1 for more information on the participants.) The participants were well-educated (all had bachelor's degrees, most also had master's degrees, and nine participants had doctoral degrees), and many participants were strongly informed by the critical, feminist, or antiracist education literature cited earlier. Criteria for participant selection were that they (a) be women adult educators teaching across borders for social change either in higher education or as community activists in the ways noted above, (b) had grown up or were strongly informed by a specific religious tradition as a child, and (c) note that their adult spirituality (either based on a reappropriation of the religious tradition of their childhood or a different spirituality) strongly motivated them to do their social justice work. With the exception of Lisa (a pseudonym), all of the participants were strongly socialized in a specific religious tradition as a child. Lisa's growing up was informed by the Unitarian tradition in the sense that her mother was a Unitarian, although Lisa was never required to attend the Unitarian church. Although it may be that Lisa only loosely fit the "growing up in a religious tradition" criterion for selection, she was kept in the study because she offered some very interesting insights about spirituality as a social activist and educator whose spirituality informed her work.

Theoretical Framework

In general, qualitative research attempts to find out how people make meaning or interpret a phenomenon (Merriam, 1998). Some forms are strictly interpretive and only want to know how participants make meaning of their life experience. Other forms, with critical, feminist, or cultural theoretical underpinnings, are concerned

Table 4.1. The Participants.

Pseudonym	Age	Race, Ethnicity	Childhood Religious Background	Work Context
Afua	44	African American	Protestant, Catholic	Higher education
Anna	53	African American	Presbyterian, Baptist, Catholic	Higher education
Ava	37	Creole, Latina	Catholic	Higher education, CBO
Beverly	55	Native American	Catholic	Higher education, CBO
Elise	48	African American	Congregational	Higher education
Greta	51	White	Catholic	Higher education
Harriet	44	White	Pentecostal	CBO
Julia	46	Chicana	Catholic	CBO
Lisa	40	White	Unitarian[a]	CBO, nonprofit
Mariposa	50	Chinese American	Baptist	CBO, nonprofit
Maureen	56	White	Methodist	Higher education
Nancy	50	White	Jewish	Higher education
Patricia	40	White	Presbyterian	Higher education
Rachael	50	White	Jewish	CBO, nonprofit
Shirley	50	African American	Baptist	Higher education
Sue	69	Korean American	Presbyterian	Higher education

Note: CBO = community-based organization.
[a]Lisa only very loosely grew up influenced by the Unitarian tradition.

with giving voice to those who have been silenced or marginalized (McLaughlin & Tierney, 1993; Vaz, 1997) and with the emancipatory possibility for those participating in the research (Kincheloe & McLaren, 1999; Lather, 1991). This study was informed by a critical poststructural feminist theoretical frame that is concerned with giving voice to participants whose perspectives have been marginalized or ignored. Such a framework suggests that the positionality (race, gender, class, etc.) of researchers, teachers, participants, and students affects how one gathers and accesses data and how one constructs and views knowledge as well as how one deals with crossing borders in research and teaching (Denzin & Lincoln, 1998; Fine, 1998; Tisdell, 1998). Thus, my own positionality as a white, middle-class woman who grew up Catholic and has tried to negotiate a more relevant adult spirituality in addition to the fact that I teach classes specifically about race, class, and gender issues were factors that affected the data collection and analysis processes (see below). Furthermore, this study was about a multicultural group of women adult educators, in which more than half of the participants were women of color. My primary purpose was to find out how these women interpret how their spirituality influences their work in their attempts to teach for social change and how their spirituality has changed over time since their childhood. I was attempting not only to provide some data-based information about how their spirituality informs their work but I was also trying to examine the cultural aspects of spirituality. In essence, I was interested in looking at the often ignored sociocultural dimensions of spirituality and to explicitly make visible the spiritual experience of women of color as well as the experience of white, Anglo women.

Data Collection and Analysis

The primary means of data collection were audiotaped (and transcribed), semi-structured interviews that lasted from one and a half to three hours. To explain why I was interested in the topic, I did share with all of the participants some of my own background (in roughly five to ten minutes) prior to the data collection process. I gave participants a snippet of my own attempts as a white woman at antiracist and gender-inclusive adult education in addition to the general way in which my background and current spirituality inform my work. Due to time constraints, this was kept to a minimum, although I did tell participants that I would be happy to share more about that at a later time, and I also asked participants if they had questions prior to the interview. I believe this provided a context for why I was doing this work, helped create a rapport with participants, and made the interviews a shared conversation in which specific topics were pursued as they arose naturally. Furthermore, I was attempting to avoid what Fine (1998) and others refer to as "othering" the participants: gathering very personal data from participants while giving none about myself. Thus, I gave participants the opportunity to ask me questions if they so desired. Interviews focused on participants' definitions of spirituality, the sharing of three significant spiritual experiences, how their spirituality has changed over the years and motivates and informs their adult education practice, and how their spirituality relates to their own race, ethnicity, and cultural background. Many participants also provided written documents of their own writing that addressed some of their involvement in social action pursuits and/or issues directly related to their spirituality, or they sent e-mails offering further clarification on issues we had discussed. Thus, the multiple sources of data collection methods of interviews and documents was a means of triangulation.

Data were analyzed throughout the study. At the suggestion of Merriam (1998), a preliminary analysis was done after each interview. Data were coded and recoded according to the constant comparative method until themes began to emerge. At this point, member checks were conducted with several of the participants to increase dependability of findings. In six instances, a summary vignette was written up and sent to the participants for their feedback and for further detailed member checks, and corrections were made and any omissions were added. These six participants were chosen specifically because their cultural and class backgrounds were the most different from my own, and I wanted to ensure that I was accurately portraying the central points of their stories. This was particularly important because there were times when I had misunderstood some of the nuances of what they had shared during the interview. This was not only another way of member checking but it was also a way of ensuring what Fine (1998) refers to as "writing against 'othering'"—a way of guarding against inadvertently projecting my own experience onto these women while missing the real salient points of their own race, cultural, or class experiences from their perspectives.

Findings

As an introduction to the findings, it is interesting to note some significant commonalities among participants that were not specific to the criteria for sample selection. First, although all of these women were socialized very specifically in a specific faith tradition as a child (with the possible exception of Lisa), only one is currently an active participant in her childhood religion. Second, all of these women have personal experiences of marginalization. Obviously, the 9 women of color experience this based on their race or ethnicity, but of the seven white women, three are lesbians, two are Jewish, and four are from working-class backgrounds. Patricia, the only white, heterosexual, upper-middle-class background participant, had been married to a Muslim North African man for fifteen years and had spent time living in North Africa, so she also had personal experiences of marginalization. Perhaps because of their experiences of marginalization, these participants have a greater interest in teaching across the borders of race, gender, and culture. Third, these women range in age between thirty-seven and sixty-nine years, most of whom were strongly influenced by the civil rights movements and other social movements of the 1960s and 1970s. Thus, there may be strong cohort effects in light of this sample. There were five overlapping themes of spiritual experience that focus on the interconnection of spirituality, culture, and social justice education that emerged from the data.

A Spiral Process of Moving Beyond and "Re-Membering"

Broadly speaking, the spiritual experiences and development of the participants are characterized by a spiral process of moving beyond the religious tradition of their childhood and then, later, "re-membering" in the sense of reconsidering and reframing the life-enhancing elements of their religious tradition and their culture of origin while developing a more meaningful adult spirituality. In this sense, *re-membering* is different from simply remembering and connotes a reevaluation process of reworking of such childhood symbols and traditions and re-shaping them to be more relevant to an adult spirituality.

Moving Away. The early adulthood of most of these participants was character-ized by questioning their childhood religious understanding. For most, the initial moving away was largely a result of what they perceived as their institutionalized religion's hypocrisy, sexism, heterosexism, lack of personal or cultural support, or general irrelevance in relation to liberation politics. For example, Julia, a Chi-cana, noted that "I went away to college [in the early 1970s], and I stopped going to church. It was those rebellious times, the church, an institution. . .and the con-tradictions, the sexism, I started to question all of it." Julia more or less drifted away during those times, whereas Shirley, an African American woman and civil rights activist, noted that at about the same age, her move away was even more intentional: "I became convinced Christianity was a trick—the oppressor to keep us humble and in bondage. . .Even the terminology *Lord, Master, Father, God*—I had serious issue with it and stopped going to church." Greta's move away was also more intentional and occurred while she was developing a political con-sciousness. She notes, "This was the 1960s, and I renounced my Catholicism and became officially an atheist. It was like a liberation. At first I thought, 'I am go-ing to die in hell,' and then I became interested in all the events that were going on. . .1960s stuff was happening and it was very political. This was the begin-ning of my Marxist phase, not very spiritual."

"Re-Membering." Despite this move away, all of the participants reported going back and re-membering in the sense of reframing and reconfiguring the mean-ing aspects of their childhood faith culture that were important and life giving, and then reshaping them and applying such meaning perspectives to an adult context. For example, although Greta still feels largely negative toward the Catholicism of her upbringing, she notes,

> It took me decades to realize that it's the ritualistic aspect of my religious up-
> bringing I really cherished. Easter. I just *loved* Easter Saturday when we went to
> church and it's all quiet, and it's all dark, and there's no sound, no music, and
> when the resurrection moment came then all the lights turned on and there was
> music. . . and I think that has really profoundly affected me. That Easter—
> there's always some resurrection. You go to hell, you die, and you're really at
> the bottom of mystery, but then you get resurrected. Often I think about when
> I'm in bad shape—that resurrection.

For Greta, this concept of resurrection, or new life after a dark night of the soul, continues to be an important spiritual concept, although she has never had any desire to reconnect with the Catholic Church.

For many of the participants, the reframing of their faith of origin was related to an understanding of their core values. The white women tended to center more on the genesis of their values. Maureen, who had been heavily involved in the social action movements sponsored by the Methodist Church in the 1960s, noted that "it was from this crucible of spirituality and social action that my own sense of identity and core beliefs were formed." Similarly, Patricia reported that she came from a long line of preachers, teachers, and farmers that valued ethics, fairness, and justice, which continued to inform her social justice work. Others, particularly the women of color, described an ancestral connection that was also present in their faith of origin. For example, Anna, an African American woman, described the music of Aretha Franklin and its connection to the church of her ancestors as particularly significant and as also related to her earlier church experiences. She states,

> The way that Aretha sings is very old, so when I go back to my childhood, it's really connected to my parents' childhood, and so on, and so on, so she takes me back to places I don't even know that I know about. There are ancient roots that are beyond my memory of this time ad place. . .When I listen to Aretha— all of those songs are songs of struggle. . .about how to survive, how to resist oppression, and I got to thinking about other spirituals that I know, and they're all at that level.

Similarly, Afua, who leads trips to Africa, discussed at length the spiritual connection to ancestors as a significant part of her spirituality that is renewed in such trips and that it is always present with her in her daily meditation.

Julia also discussed this ancestral connection and, in critically reflecting on her Latino-Catholic roots, she discussed her current connection to her grandmother and *La Virgen de Guadalupe.*

> I think part of my journey is going back to my heritage, my Aztec and indigenous roots. . . . .Ana Castillo gives a different picture of what La Virgen could represent in terms of powerful women. . . .But there's another side to it. . . . .I don't always just go with "this is the way that it is" because I do question, was that a way for the Spaniards to. . .convert the Aztecs into Catholicism? Or is it really an Aztec goddess?. . .But I do believe it's a spirit—a spirit that kind of watches over me.

In addition to the ancestral connection and reexamining their core values, the participants also re-membered their culture of origin by looking for specific feminine examples of spiritual power and wisdom both from within and beyond their culture of origin and applied this to their adult spiritual lives. We see evidence of this in the importance of *La Virgin de Guadalupe* to Julia and with Aretha Franklin to Anna as noted above. Harriet, a white lesbian activist, takes inspiration in the work of Harriet Tubman, and Rachael, a social activist, notes, "It took nearly thirty years of my life for me to embrace my Jewishness in a deep emotional way, and so to claim my Jewishness as a significant part of my heritage and identity. My reading. . .along with my mentoring friendships with Jewish women activists— filled me with stories I related to, helping me access my own cultural background through women I identified with."

In sum, although these women needed to move beyond their childhood religious tradition to develop a meaningful adult spirituality, they often spiraled back to reconnect with and redefine important aspects of that culture that affirmed their gender and cultural identity.

Spirituality as Life Force, Interconnectedness, and Wholeness

All of the participants struggled to give *spirituality* concrete definition, noting that somehow language was inadequate to describe spiritual experience. As Lisa notes, "You're just in two different paradigms. For me it's an experience, which is why it's hard to translate. It has to do with the experience of the life-force. . . . Spirituality is some kind of aware honoring of that life-force that is happening through everything."

Like Lisa, most participants discussed spirituality as related to a sense of wholeness, interconnectedness, and order to all of creation as well as related to life force or a higher power. As Anna said, "I think of [spirituality] in terms of connections to all things, not just things here, but also things in the past, and things in the future. . . .Spirituality to me is not something that you can hold down. . . .It's something that's intuitive, and intuitive things are hard to express; it's something that's felt, and sensed, and not necessarily 'thought.'"

Furthermore, many of the participants discussed the fact that the more one has a sense of spirituality as connection, the more one's behavior is affected. In reflecting on this, Afua notes, "The more you're connected to that notion of spirit and spiritness, the more you will do what you're supposed to do. . . .If you believe that you are connected to other beings and other things and you share divinity, then you know if you harm somebody else, you're really harming yourself and vice-versa, and so you are going to be less likely to harm them because you know that's a part of you."

Although some participants discussed the sense of connection and oneness of all things more conceptually, most gave concrete examples of how they experienced spiritual experience as providing a sense of wholeness. For example, Julia noted, "We have this ritual in my family—every time I go home, and when I'm getting ready to leave, I ask for my parents' blessing, and so they'll take me into their room, and each one of them will bless me. . . .And I don't feel complete if I don't do that. . . .So my father will bless me, 'te encomiendo a Dios Padre. . .y a la Virgen de Guadalupe,' and ask my grandmother and La Virgen to watch over me, and so I feel like my grandmother's watching over me!"

For Julia, this sense of completeness or wholeness was ritualized in her parent's blessing that connected her with her grandmother and the important spiritual symbol of *La Virgen de Guadalupe*. Most participants also experienced it in the interconnectedness of all things, sometimes in a sense of synchronicity and in uncanny connections to other people. Many participants reported synchronous events such as when someone from long ago had been on their minds and that person would suddenly call, or the synchronistic meeting of specific people at various points in their lives. Others discussed a sense of spiritual connectedness both in personal significant love relationships and more broadly to others. Elise, an African American woman who had grown up in a largely white northern community, discussed the significance of living in a southern city as a young adult and experiencing a cultural interconnectedness to others of African descent as a spiritual connection. She noted that "in Atlanta, my beauty was affirmed. I could walk down the street and see myself; there was a sense of connectedness. . .that I would consider a spiritual connection."

For many of these participants, this wholeness or life force that is, as Lisa says, "happening through everything" was manifested in experiences beyond the cognitive that brought together the physical, the emotional, and the wholeness of creation and one's being. One participant described the three most significant spiritual experiences in her life as being related to the physical and the life force, which provided a sense of oneness and affirmation of life. These included giving birth, a deeply significant sexual and spiritual experience making love that gave her a new sense of identity, and a serious accident that left her near death and in a coma. Greta also described the significance of the physical in spiritual experience, such as experience in the marital arts and meditation practices that are part of them, that put her in touch with a source within and that resulted in a greater sense of spiritual connectedness with a life force within and beyond herself. Lisa, a white woman who grew up in Alaska and who also spent significant time living and working with Native people there, also described experiencing and witnessing a sense of oneness in watching a two-year-old do the Raven dance: "And she *got it*. She *was* Raven, and that's what the dance was teaching—sort of a mystical spirituality where you *are* coyote or you *are* whatever this is, and it transforms the way you are—your consciousness is different. And it was a *wonderful* moment, seeing this little tiny being who was already there."

The sense of the physical embodying of Raven in the dance of the two-year-old and her sense of the oneness to the point that she became Raven in that moment was key for Lisa. Like Lisa and Greta, many participants described spiritual experiences of becoming and witnessing a sense of wholeness and interconnectedness of all things: in nature, in relationship with others, and in connection with one's self. Beverly, an Alaska Native woman, talked specifically about her spiritual connection to nature as a runner in the woods of Alaska, where she has to negotiate the reality of moose and bear. She also connects this to some of her own cultural background and notes, "I really am not [afraid], because as I have seen these animals, I respect them, and I actually talk to them when we've bumped into each other. It's an acknowledgment and awareness, because *we're* animals. We're all on this earth together, and we just go about it in a different way. And because [I'm] Tlinket. . .there is a real kinship and a dependency on animals."

Like Beverly, Lisa also spoke of this relationship with the wilderness as a spiritual reminder of the connectedness of all creation.

Pivotal Experience of a Perceived Higher Power That Facilitates Healing

All of the participants discussed at length significant experiences related to a perceived higher power that specifically facilitated healing. In several cases, these experiences resulted in the courage to take new action in their personal lives. Most of these experiences were quite emotional and also were connected to a sense of wonder and mystery. Harriet, who grew up Pentecostal in a working-class community in the rural South, described an extremely significant spiritual experience that helped her come to terms with being a lesbian.

> I got hurt playing softball and I tore my quadriceps so bad I passed out. I went to the best orthopedist in town, who put a splint on it which hurt really bad. I also believed in faith healing, and one night I went to the altar I felt this real coldness go into my leg, and then [it] got really hot, and I thought "wow" and the minister told me—I took the splint off, and the big lump that was on my leg, it was gone!. . .Well that was a turning point for me, because I thought, "Why would God heal me, if I was this person that was condemned to hell?" God wouldn't do that for me, and I thought, "OK, this is my sign" that it's OK for me to be a lesbian.

From that day forward, she worked on behalf of women's rights, lesbian and gay rights, and on social issues of all kinds and also had a renewed appreciation for the mysterious and healing power of connecting to what was perceived as a divine presence.

Some of the participants reported experiences that were related to grief and new life. For example, Anna described an experience immediately after her mother died, when she was traveling on a train to her mother's funeral. She notes, "I was watching the telephone poles go by, and a black bird flew past the window and came real close, and in my ear, I heard my mother's voice say 'I'm free!' and it was like a major relief because I'd been grieving and crying and as soon as I heard that voice say 'I'm free,' it was OK."

Elise described a similar experience of the grief associated with having a miscarriage and a troubled relationship with her own mother. She described going to a meditation service led by a woman in the Siddha Yoga tradition, shortly after her miscarriage, and explains,

> Well I closed my eyes and everything was silent, and for the first time there is no internal dialogue. . . .And all of a sudden there's a voice in my head that is not my voice that says, "Why are you upset with your mother? I am the mother. Why blame her?". . .After the program was over. . .I went up and when I did this woman said to me "You've been working very hard," and immediately I broke out into tears. . .and I was just weeping and weeping and weeping, and at that moment my life changed.

Elise then went on to describe how she went about the healing of her relationship with her mother. Patricia described some significant dream experiences in the aftermath of her divorce that were seen as "graced moments" as offering a path for healing that helped her move on with her life. In short, all the participants described significant moments in which they had a strong sense of a divine presence that facilitated healing and the courage to take new action in their personal lives.

Facilitation of the Development of Authentic Identity

Virtually all of the participants discussed spiritual experiences such as those noted above as experiences that facilitated the development of what many referred to as their authentic identity. Furthermore, for many participants, their ongoing personal identity development could not be separated from their spirituality. Ava, who grew up in Central America, after describing parts of her mixed cultural heritage along with some of her Mayan ancestry, noted, "I think that spirituality is to know who you are, and to be able to define who you are, wherever you are, despite the changing conditions of your life." Harriet's experience of her physical healing also assured her of the authenticity of her own lesbian identity, and Elise's spiritual experience helped her deal more proactively and more maturely with her own relationship with her mother. Furthermore, for Elise, the fact that her healing was facilitated by a woman was significant, and in explaining the incident noted above, she noted, "I needed that woman energy. I needed it. I needed a mother. I didn't need a tangible mother. I needed to know and experience that love energy, that nurturing energy that my mother could not give, so I could forgive my mother. The actual quotation [she used] was 'I am God the father and the mother' but the part that was for me—the mother part. And that's the part I latched onto because I really needed a mother and I didn't have it. So to be able to have that experience was part of my personal development."

Some of the participants described experiences of moving away from their childhood religious traditions to develop other parts of themselves as an important part of both their spiritual development and the development of their identity. Patricia, a white woman and psychology professor, described recognizing a need when she was in her early twenties to develop the cognitive aspects of her identity and forego some of her involvements in a quasi-fundamentalist Christian community to develop both intellectually and spiritually. Anna also described her move away from her childhood religion at about the same age in addition to her involvement in neo-Marxist social movements as facilitating a greater understanding of spirituality and her own identity. She notes,

> I think Marxism is a form of spirituality because it really is about connections with other people; it's a rather earthly bound nature of connections, but it's still about looking back and looking forward, and taking care of each other. . . .So I guess it began in my Marxist period, which lasted until I was in my thirties; it was a transformation of God being outside of me who controlled all things [to] an inside internal controlling force—that human, or that life-on-the-planet work was involved in making change, involved in creating reality, taking care of each

other. . . that those connections happen here because of what we do as opposed to some other something outside of you doing something, and so I think in retrospect, my spirituality was still there.

Thus, Anna's ongoing cognitive development and understanding of her identity that included communal responsibility was related to her personal and her spiritual identity development. Similarly, Greta and Shirley also described their foray into neo-Marxist political literature and social movements in addition to their "atheist phase" as related to their overall spiritual development.

Some of the participants discussed their spirituality in conjunction with their identity development as in the case of those cited above. Others described it more as a source of support in their own identity development. For example, Beverly noted, "It certainly got me through a lot when I was going through my divorce, because I did spend a lot of time addressing issues that I had never addressed in my adult life." In essence, Beverly described the fact that her spirituality gave her the courage to face her own issues with the help and spiritual support of a couple of friends. Nancy, who grew up Jewish but now practices in the Siddha Yoga tradition, reported that her current spirituality and meditation practice help her stay focused on what is important in her life and who she is as a person rather than being focused on her own ambition and ego, which she says was a trap she fell into earlier in her career as an academic. Sue, an Asian American woman, described living for a time overseas away from her husband and finding a more solid independent identity apart from her husband as a spiritual experience that facilitated her authentic identity. Furthermore, she noted that her spirituality also helped her accept her daughter's lesbian identity. All of the participants viewed their spiritual development as related to a more authentic identity and, consequently, to also be more accepting of the identities of others.

A Way of Life Requiring Inner Reflection and Action for Social Change

Perhaps somewhat a function of the criteria for participant selection, yet extremely significant, was the participants' commitment to work for social change in light of their spirituality. Participants saw this not only as an ethical responsibility but also as a way of life that affected their emancipatory educational practices.

An Integrated Approach to Living. All of the participants discussed the importance of trying to create an integrated and balanced approach to living that was grounded in their spirituality. All of them also discussed struggling to try to actually do this while maintaining a commitment to the importance of a holistic spiritual grounding place. In considering how this integrated approach manifests itself in her work and personal life, Shirley noted, "I am always teaching whether I'm at [the community college] or not." In essence, this sense of nurturing a way of life required inner reflection and connecting to one's center or life force, the realm of mystery, or perceived higher power. Greta speaks specifically to this point and notes that there is an "ethical underpinning" to why she values spiritual practice.

"One of the things I've learned over the years is that if you practice a certain way it's like you become *one*—you don't have the mind-body split anymore; there's kind of a sense of oneness; and the sense of oneness for me translates into or is strongly related to [living] in the world. Everybody is separated, split, fragmented, except in bits and pieces—to try to translate a sense of oneness that's more like a mental-spiritual-emotional. . .[the point is] to live that out when you're not in a meditative state." She goes on to elaborate that spirituality is about cherishing as opposed to extracting life and is also core to one's deepest identity. Life "is there to maintain, to nurture. . . .And people are split and at war with each other because they don't cherish life the way it should be. So I guess it's kind of the spiritual foundation of the kind of calmness; if you want to meditate you have to have a sense of how important calmness is, and how important it is to be clear about the way you are, and who you are with that work; otherwise, you don't see what's going on."

Thus, for Greta and most of the participants, having a spirituality was foundational both to their core identities and to their social justice work. As Anna noted, "It is the reason really I am here, on a spiritual plane, but on a real plane, I have no alternative. There is really no alternative to doing this work because of the devastation, I mean what else do you do? It is my responsibility, my duty, my reason, my history, my spirit, my soul."

Although their spirituality was foundational to both their social justice work and their core identities, it also moved participants beyond themselves to develop more of a global consciousness. As Julia remarks, "It's bigger than just being Chicana. I'm also a member of a global community—it encompasses more. . . . For me, working for social justice isn't just done five days a week; it's in every part of my life. . .it's a way of living. I call it spirituality."

For many, this greater sense of having a global consciousness was also oriented to trying to build community. Mariposa, a Chinese American educator and activist, notes that spirituality for her is about "building community. I try to do that wherever I am; I know [it's] what helps me stay grounded." This sense of orientation toward community included a global community, but for many, it also included a historical community and legacy. As Shirley explains, "I think my responsibility is great because I know what people went through so that I could have the freedom and the power to move forward in the world, so I must get up! And I must dig deep! And I must do good! And to not do that would be an affront to my ancestors who stayed alive, and stayed strong, and stayed spiritually connected through centuries of brutality and everything, beyond slavery. That's what it is for me."

That is what it is for the participants in this study: a way of life that requires attention to the inner world through centering and meditation, but it also requires action in the world.

Spirituality as a Noncoercive Presence in Emancipatory Educational Practice. Part of what the action in the world for these women included was a commitment to teach or work with community groups in a way that challenged power relations. Participants indicated that spirituality indeed informed their educational practices, although most participants were somewhat tentative in how they discussed it or drew on it in educational settings. None of the participants wanted to be seen as doing anything coercive or in any way as pushing a spiritual or religious agenda. All of the participants were comfortable drawing on it in more subtle ways, noting that it was often present in learning environments in the lives of the learners as well as themselves. For example, many participants reported that in discussions of crossing borders of race, class, or culture, classroom or workshop participants will often bring representations from their cultural background that are also spiritual symbols. Most of the participants also noted that spiritual experience itself is not primarily a rational experience. Rachael reflected on this in relationship to culture. "They [culture and spirituality] are not separate, because what's culture? It's music, it's singing; it's dancing; it's storytelling; it's presentational knowing. . . .They're both less about what's happening in my head; they're more about what's happening in my body and my heart. . . .Culture is a way to express spirituality; they're very interwoven."

As Nancy noted in describing her experience with Siddha Yoga in meditating and chanting, spirituality was partially about learning to listen with her heart: "For me, being an intellectual academic person, I have to suspend my academic intellectual beliefs, and that it's really all about faith in your heart. So I really listen with my heart. That's what was transforming."

Perhaps because spiritual experience is not primarily about rational processes, there was a difference between the higher educators (nine participants) and the community-based educators (seven participants) in how directly participants discussed or drew on spirituality in educational activities. Of the higher educators, Afua, a psychology professor, was most direct in her use of it in her classes, but she noted that she rarely uses the word *spirituality* but, rather, would draw on it and make connections to cultural aspects of symbol when appropriate. For example, she begins many of her classes with a centering exercise, and when she teaches classes in psychology from an Africentric perspective, she may begin with a libation because she sees this as grounded in the cultural she's studying with students. In general, the higher educators tended to draw on spirituality more in preparation for classes (through meditation and centering exercises) or in less formal work with colleagues or students, such as in advising sessions where it may be directly discussed. Elise noted that she needed to pray to get through teaching classes about racism when she has to teach in the suburbs, and Nancy discussed the chanting and centering activities she uses in preparation to teach classes about social justice. Most of the higher educators reported that in actual classroom activities, spiritual issues would be acknowledged as they arose and would be drawn on implicitly, such as in the use of music, symbols, art forms, or in an occasional or one-time activity that might suggest a spiritual connection that moves beyond conflict. But many educators were hesitant to discuss it too directly or obviously so that, as one participant noted, "people don't feel coerced."

On the other hand, those who worked in nonprofit or community-based organizations reported that issues of spirituality come up more often in their work with communities; it is brought up and drawn on by community members themselves. For example, Mariposa reported that in her social justice work with a Latino community, the participants cocreated an educational activity done in the context of a Mass, and in her work with a Native American community, a ritual ceremony was created by participants as empowerment of the group. Harriet, who co-runs an adult popular education center in the South, reported that, as part of their social justice work, they host monthly spirituality circles that are made available to the community in which prayer, meditation, and ritual are used both to affirm people's identity and move them to action.

In general, those who work in community-based or nonprofit settings seemed to feel less confined by the rationalistic structures of higher education, so they felt freer to use different modalities to provide different kinds of experience for people. Spirituality was more or less accepted as a dimension of human experience that needed to be attended to on some level in potentially educating for social change. Lisa, who does antiracism workshops and is a singer-songwriter whose music and concerts focus on social justice issues, discusses the fact that spirituality is very much a part of her work as both a performer and an educator. In speaking broadly of spirituality and its connection to how she attempts to educate about justice issues, she emphasized the importance of setting a tone and notes,

> Music, of course, is evocative of the soul and of the emotions, so I'm modeling I think to a lot of people that really in fact it is not only safe, but *it's great* to put this stuff out there. That's what I mean partly by tone—I have a great deal of confidence in my perspective drawing as it does from the larger wild community, and a lot of people have lost that confidence, particularly urban or raised urban—or just to have somebody who sort of looks like them, they can "phew," be there, be safe, be connected. I totally get that we should be and are grieving for what's happening on the planet. Of course we are!. . .When I'm structuring experience for people, I'm very aware of the effect of tone so that the deeper the material, the lighter you have to have something else happening so that most people cannot sink. . .it allows people to stay with me.

Lisa's concern, like many of those who are doing educational work in community-based or nonprofit settings, was creating an atmosphere that helps people be more present and open to new kinds of learning that included an affective component with the hope of facilitating social change. Educators in these settings were not concerned that such learning experiences necessarily be explained in rational terms.

Although spirituality was the grounding place for the participants' social justice work, nearly all of them expressed the desire to more directly draw on it a bit more consciously in their educational practices. Most of the participants reported that there has been little direct or intentional discussion of it among their colleagues but that, more often, people are spontaneously bringing up what could be conceived of as spiritual issues, particularly in relation to teaching for social justice. Julia, who works with an educational consulting group on diversity issues, notes,

> I find there is a dimension of spirituality in the way we relate to each other and in the way we collectively approach the work of social change. Because we are each from a different cultural background, we express our spirituality in different ways: Hawaiian chants, prayers to the four directions, Christian prayer. . . .The interesting thing though, as I think more about it, I suspect that there are also atheists among the group, yet we somehow seem to delve into spirit. It might be striving to be human. . .I don't know. But we all believe in the goodness of people and the possibility of change while trying to live a life of community.

Although all of the participants drew on their spirituality in their practice, they expressed a desire to perhaps do this more directly but were struggling to find a way to do it in a way that would not be coercive.

Discussion and Conclusions

The findings of the study offer some interesting insights about the relationship between spirituality and emancipatory adult education efforts and potentially about the broader area of adult learning and development. They do need to be interpreted with caution because these findings are related to a particularly purposeful sample of women adult educators chosen specifically because of their involvement in social action efforts and because of their spiritual commitments; thus, these findings are not intended to be generalizable to all adult educators.

A primary finding of this study is that these participants saw their spirituality and their social justice efforts as an integrated way of life and as a way of thinking and being in the world. They had a strong sense of mission, fueled by their spirituality, of challenging systems of oppression based on race, class, gender, ability, and sexual orientation in their adult education practices. But their involvement in social action efforts also called them back to their spirituality. Such an integrated view of their work as a way of life was reminiscent of Fox's (1995) discussion of the reinvention of work as related to what he refers to as the interconnection of inner work (through centering, meditation, and experience of the realm of mystery) and outer work (working for greater balance in the world). Furthermore, the participants saw these integrated modes of work both in the paid and not-for-pay workforce as part of their life purpose and were also integrated with their personal and cultural history and, in many cases, an ancestral connection as well. There was a strong desire both to give back to their own communities and to create a more equitable society. This notion of creating community in a larger, more global sense was significant to most of them. In this respect, their stories are similar to some of the participants in the Daloz et al. (1996) study on community and commitment.

Although the notion of community was important, it was initially perplexing to me that only one of the participants (Sue) was still active as a regular attendee at services in the religion of her childhood. Given that spirituality was extremely important for all of them and strongly informed their social justice work, one might expect that more might have a desire to be involved with a spiritual community through organized religion. This was not the case for most participants; furthermore, most were quite personally leery of organized religion. Given that they are teaching classes or working in programs in which they are problemetizing and trying to change structural power relations based on gender, race, class, sexual orientation, and disability, it is perhaps no surprise that these women would also have trouble with similar structural oppression in aspects of organized religion. Class issues were alluded to by several of the participants, but most often, what was specifically mentioned as problematic aspects of their childhood religious tradition was the sexism and, for many, the heterosexism as well, particularly for participants who grew up Catholic or in the more conservative Protestant denominations. Many participants did discuss feeling a need for an occasional communal experience of spirituality, but not of organized religion. In some cases, this need for a spiritual communal experience was filled through the use of ritual and symbol built into their activist activities with specific groups and communities.

Despite having serious issues with structural systems of oppression in their faiths of origin, most of the participants were strongly attached to the symbols, music, and some of the rituals from their childhood religious traditions and the conceptual meanings attached to them. For example, although Greta has long since moved away from Catholicism, the symbolic meaning of Resurrection (the promise of new life after a dark night of the soul) continues to be an important metaphor for her. Similarly, although these women had moved beyond their childhood religious tradition, they often spiraled back and re-membered those aspects of it that were life giving at the same time that they integrated and were exposed to new ideas and new spiritual traditions and had further spiritual experiences as an adult. This aspect of the study is similar to what Wuthnow (1999) found in his study of people who grew up religious. However, what the women in this study seemed to be most attentive to as they re-membered their faith of origin was related to symbolic forms of knowing and unconscious processes: the music, aspects of ritual, and particular symbols. This was reminiscent of Fowler's (1981) remarks in his critiquing of Piaget and Kohlberg for "their restrictive understanding of the role of imagination in knowing, their neglect of symbolic processes generally, and the related lack of attention to unconscious structuring processes other than those constituting reasoning" (p. 103).

It is important also to note that the aspects of their childhood tradition that they were particularly attached to were also deeply rooted in a cultural identity. For example, we see evidence of this in the cultural and spiritual significance for Julia as Chicana of *La Virgen de Guadalupe,* in what the music of Aretha Franklin brought up for Anna of the African American experience, the significance of the wilderness for both Beverly, an Alaska Native woman, and for Lisa, who also grew up in Alaska. This aspect of the cultural significance of spirituality may also be in part why Sue continued to attend services in the Korean Presbyterian church; although there were aspects she found problematic, it was affirming of her cultural identity as a Korean American. In any event, this aspect of the study offers some beginning insights to the relation between cultural and spiritual significance that has been little discussed in the spiritual development or the adult development literature. Furthermore, what was most often mentioned as an important spiritual symbol for these women was a feminine symbol, embodied in one reminiscent of their culture or in whom participants had framed as an important current spiritual symbol for them. (Some of the spiritual figures mentioned in addition to Aretha Franklin and *La Virgen de Guadalupe* were Harriet Tubman, the feminine Buddhist wisdom figure Kuan Yin, female ancestors, and Sojourner Truth, to name a few.) It is interesting to note that currently, three of the participants (Maureen, Nancy, and Elise) now identify largely with the Siddha Yoga tradition, which is led by a woman. Although only a couple of participants noted that feminine figures were important spiritual figures for them specifically because they were women, it may be that on an unconscious level these spiritual figures are important in affirming their gender identity and their spirituality as women.

The primary purpose of this study was to examine how spirituality influences the motivations and practices of these women activist adult educators; it was not initially about their spiritual development. However, in sharing significant aspects of their own spiritual journeys and how their spirituality unfolded over time in relationship to their activism and emancipatory adult education efforts, they actually did discuss how their spirituality has changed over time. Thus, the findings have some strong implications for our understanding of spiritual development, although such implications need to be interpreted with caution. One cannot assume, based on the findings of this study, that spiritual commitment necessarily leads to working for social action or that involvement in social action necessarily presumes a spiritual commitment. Indeed, there are many adults whose spirituality is important in their lives, but they are not involved in social action efforts, and there are many activists who are atheists or who otherwise find spirituality irrelevant to their lives. Fowler's (1981) answer to why only some adults whose spirituality is important to them are involved in social action efforts whereas others are not would be that they are at different stages of spiritual development. The fact that these women did indeed have a spiritual commitment that required social action that directly challenged structural systems of oppression was a specific criterion for participant selection. This criterion was chosen to understand how spirituality informs their emancipatory education efforts, not consciously to choose people at a particular stage of spiritual development or of a particular age. Nevertheless, the fact that these participants were women at midlife, in their forties and fifties, may suggest that the development of their spirituality in consort with their activism is somewhat age related. Virtually all of the participants reported that reframing their social justice work from a spiritual perspective has become more important with age, but cohort effects are also likely at play here as well; most of these women were strongly affected by the civil rights movement and the women's movement of the 1960s and 1970s, which did influence their involvement in and attitudes about the importance of social action. Although the data does not suggest that there is a cause-effect relationship between spiritual commitment and social action work as part of spiritual development, they do suggest that there may be a relationship in many cases. However, this would need to be the subject of further study.

From a developmental perspective, it is also interesting to note that in many cases, what was described as significant spiritual experiences did result in participants' courage to take new action first in their personal lives. For example, Harriet's healing experience that helped her come to terms with being a lesbian, Elise's experience that facilitated her working on her relationship with her mother, and Lisa's experience of watching the two-year-old do the Raven dance and her resultant belief in the oneness and unity of all things resulted in their decisions to live differently and more proactively. Although many of the experiences described led to action in their personal lives, and not necessarily immediately to social action in the sense of directly challenging structural systems of privilege and oppression, it may be that the significant spiritual experiences that changed their personal lives were a necessary part of their development, which may also have been pivotal in eventually leading them to more structural social action.

As many participants discussed, spiritual experience is not primarily about rationality. For the participants, spirituality was about experiences of a perceived higher power or a life force, about an understanding of the wholeness of all of creation, and about making ultimate meaning out of one's life purpose, which, for these participants, was partly working for social justice. Spirituality was also about an experience of the realm of mystery. In Fowler's (1981) terms, spirituality is largely about symbolic processes that are not rational. As Lisa and others noted, it is difficult to put language around spiritual experience because language, in many ways, forces people to map rational processes around what is experienced outside of rationality. Yet at the same time, none of the participants suspended their rationality in the process of describing their own spiritual journey. Part of what their spiritual development seemed to be about was having spiritual experiences and critically and rationally analyzing some of what those experiences were about while continuing to be open to new spiritual experiences. The move away from their childhood spirituality was partly a result of rational thinking processes—thinking rationally about aspects of their childhood traditions and finding some of what was taught problematic. Furthermore, integrating new insights from different paradigms and new spiritual traditions was an important part of spiritual development. For example, Greta, Anna, and Shirley went through an atheist phase that was influenced partly by a foray into Marxism, the Black Power movement, and other social movements on an intellectual level. Yet similar to Freire (1997), who discusses the similarities between Marxism and Christianity, they eventually were able to integrate the aspects of Marxism that focus on challenging structural oppression with their spiritual beliefs to develop new aspects of their spirituality. However, these aspects of rationally thinking about these ideas or their spiritual experience was not a substitute for spiritual experience itself, which was viewed as being outside the realm of the rational. Thus, what may fuel spiritual development is the integration of symbolic knowing and spiritual experience with the rational process of thinking about those experiences. This potentially includes attending to the cultural and gendered nature of those experiences.

What do these insights about the relationship between spirituality and emancipatory education efforts suggest for the practice of emancipatory education? It is probably not surprising that the community-based educators felt a bit more free than the higher educators to discuss and draw on their own and the participants' spirituality in educating for social change, particularly when it arose from learners themselves. People in higher education were indeed aware of the almost exclusive focus on rationality that has been the tradition of higher education, which made them hesitant to discuss or draw on spirituality too overtly. However, all of the participants recognized that the work of social transformation cannot be accomplished entirely through rational processes. As hooks (1999) notes in her discussion of spirituality and liberatory education, people need to be inspired and have their affective, spiritual, and physical selves involved in order for emancipatory education around challenging systems of structural oppression to happen. Although the participants in this study agree, they also felt that attention to the spiritual needs to be handled carefully so that they are not seen as pushing a religious or spiritual agenda. Nevertheless, a few suggestions for practice can be gleaned from this study.

First, it is important to remember that adult learners bring their whole selves, including their spirituality, with them when they enter the learning environment. Dirkx (1997) suggests that adult educators do not necessarily need to "teach soul work" or spirituality but, rather, "to recognize its presence and to respect its sacred message" (p. 83). Mariposa referred to this phenomenon in her popular education work with grassroots communities. Spirituality is often present in learning communities because learners bring it up, refer to spiritual issues, and/or create rituals and celebrations that help ground their own social change work. When spirituality arises from participants, it is less likely to be impositional.

Second, given that spirituality is about the wholeness of life and is often related, as Fowler (1981) suggests, to knowledge constructed through image and symbol or manifested through story and music, occasional use of art forms, symbol, music, drama, and dance can perhaps be a way of touching on the spiritual in educational activities. Although this may be appropriate only in occasional settings, often educators can, as Lisa says, create a tone or a space in which such an activity can facilitate new learning, new insight, or perhaps a move to action. One participant had learners create a readers' theater based on a particularly provocative piece used in a multicultural class on manifestations of various forms of structural oppression. Because it involved the affective and physical, many reported back to her that there was a spiritual dimension to what they had done rather spontaneously. Such venues may touch on the spiritual dimension for people and, at the same time, the term *spirituality* may never be used.

Finally, in considering the relationship between spirituality and emancipatory education efforts, it is important to remember that rationality and spirituality are not complete opposites to each other. In fact, the study suggests that spiritual development appears to require a rational component; it is important to think critically about one's spiritual experience not as a substitute for the spiritual experience itself, but because critically analyzing messages from the larger culture, including one's religion of origin, is an important part of claiming one's own identity. Such critical analysis is clearly an important component of emancipatory education. Yet it may also be that having a sense of one's life's mission and drawing regularly on what gives one sustenance to do that social change work, which for many is related to the spiritual, is a needed component of efforts in emancipatory education. Clearly, more research is needed in this area, but so also are more collective opportunities for emancipatory adult educators to both experience and discuss the nature of spirituality in social change work. Indeed, this is something that the participants in this study, as well as many other adult educators, long for.

In sum, *spirituality* is an elusive term and an elusive concept, but perhaps this is so because it is all-encompassing and cannot be torn from other aspects of one's life, including one's cultural experience, one's further development, or one's social change work in the world. For many, it is a term that connotes wholeness and what gives meaning and coherence to life. It connects and encompasses everything from the creativity of artists and poets to our connections with loved ones to the way that we act as cultural workers and actors for justice in the world and to our understanding of a higher power or life force. It is difficult to discuss what is so elusive and at the same time so personal and so encompassing, and it was indeed an honor to listen to these women's spiritual experiences of this life force and their thoughts on how their spirituality informs their work for social justice. I found myself often inspired by their stories and uplifted by their efforts, and I felt a sense of wholeness and connection with them in this soul work that was part of our shared dialogue that bridged our similarities and differences. It gave me a renewed sense of my own, ongoing life work. Although this study is limited, it offers a beginning to a dialogue that has barely begun about the connection between spirituality and emancipatory education practice and the sociocultural context that informs spiritual development.

References

Anzaldua, G. (1987). *Borderlands/La frontera: The new mestiza.* San Francisco: Aunt Lute.

Bolen, J. (1994). *Crossing to Avalon: A women's midlife pilgrimage.* San Francisco: Harper.

Borysenko, J. (1996). *A woman's book of life: The biology, psychology, and spirituality of the feminine life cycle.* New York: Riverhead Books.

Brookfield, S., & Preskill, S. (1999). *Discussion as a way of teaching.* San Francisco: Jossey-Bass.

Castillo, A. (1996). *Massacre of the dreamers: Essays on xicanisma.* Albuquerque: University of New Mexico Press.

Daloz, L., Keene, C., Keene, J., & Parks, S. (1996). *Common fire: Lives of commitment in a complex world.* Boston: Beacon.

Denzin, N., & Lincoln, Y. (1998). *The landscape of qualitative research.* Newbury Park, CA: Sage.

Dirkx, J. (1997). Nurturing soul in adult learning. In P. Cranton (Ed.), *Transformative learning in action: Insights from practice* (pp. 79–88). San Francisco: Jossey-Bass.

English, L. (2000). Spiritual dimensions of informal learning. In L. English & M. Gillen (Eds.), *Addressing the spiritual dimensions of adult learning: What educators can do* (pp. 29–38). San Francisco: Jossey-Bass.

English, L., & Gillen, M. (Eds.). (2000). *Addressing the spiritual dimensions of adult learning: What educators can do.* San Francisco: Jossey-Bass.

Fenwick, T. J., & Lange, E. (1998). Spirituality in the workplace: The new frontier of HRD. *Canadian Journal for the Study of Adult Education, 12*(1), 63–87.

Fine, M. (1998). Working the hyphens. In N. Denzin & Y. Lincoln (Eds.), *The landscape of qualitative research* (pp. 130–155). Thousand Oaks, CA: Sage.

Fowler, J. (1981). *Stages of faith: The psychology of human development and the quest for meaning.* San Francisco: Harper & Row.

Fox, M. (1995). *The reinvention of work.* San Francisco: HarperCollins.

Freire, P. (1997). *Letters to Christina.* New York: Routledge.

Giroux, H. (1992). *Border crossings.* New York: Routledge.

Gunn Allen, P. (1992). *The sacred hoop.* Boston: Beacon.

Hamilton, D., & Jackson, M. (1998). Spiritual development: Paths and processes. *Journal of Instructional Psychology, 25*(4), 262–270.

Hart, M., & Holton, D. (1993). Beyond God the father and mother: Adult education and spirituality. In P. Jarvis & N. Walters (Eds.), *Adult education and theological interpretations* (pp. 237–258). Malabar, FL: Krieger.

Hayes, E., & Colin, S. (Eds.). (1994). *Confronting racism and sexism in adult education.* San Francisco: Jossey-Bass.

Hill Collins, P. (1998). *Fighting words: Black women and the search for justice.* Minneapolis: University of Minnesota Press.

hooks, b. (1994). *Teaching to transgress.* New York: Routledge.

hooks, b. (1999). Embracing freedom: Spirituality and liberation. In S. Glazer (Ed.), *The heart of learning: Spirituality in education* (pp. 113–129). New York: Putnum.

Horton, M., & Freire, P. (1990). *We make the road by walking: Conversations on education and social change.* Philadelphia, PA: Temple University Press.

Johnson-Bailey, J., & Cervero, R. (1998). Power dynamics in teaching and learning practices: An examination of two adult education classrooms. *International Journal of Lifelong Education, 17*(6), 389–399.

Kincheloe, J., & McLaren, P. (1999). Rethinking critical theory and qualitative research. In N. Denzin & Y. Lincoln (Eds.), *The landscape of qualitative research* (pp. 260–399). Newbury Park, CA: Sage.

King, U. (Ed.). (1996). *Feminist theology from the third world.* Maryknoll, NY: Orbis.

Lather, P. (1991). *Getting smart.* New York: Routledge.

McLaughlin, D., & Tierney, W. (Eds.). (1993). *Naming silenced lives.* New York: Routledge.

Merriam, S. B. (1998). *Qualitative research and case study applications in education.* San Francisco: Jossey-Bass.

Merriam, S. B., & Caffarella, R. (1999). *Learning in adulthood.* San Francisco: Jossey-Bass.

Myss, C. (1996). *Anatomy of the spirit: The seven stages of power and healing.* New York: Random House.

Palmer, P. (1998). *The courage to teach.* San Francisco: Jossey-Bass.

Ruether, R. (Ed.). (1996). *Women healing earth.* Maryknoll, NY: Orbis.

Simmer-Brown, J. (1999). Commitment and openness: A contemplative approach to pluralism. In S. Glazer (Ed.), *The heart of learning: Spirituality in education* (pp. 97–112). New York: Putnum.

Taylor, E. (1998). *The theory and practice of transformative learning: A critical review* (Information Series No. 374). Columbus, OH: ERIC Clearinghouse on Adult, Career and Vocational Education.

Tisdell, E. (1998). Poststructural feminist pedagogies: The possibilities and limitations of a feminist emancipatory adult learning theory and practice. *Adult Education Quarterly, 48*(3), 139–156.

Tisdell, E. (1999). The spiritual dimension of adult development. In M. C. Clark & R. Caffarella (Eds.), *An update on adult development theory* (pp. 87–96). San Francisco: Jossey-Bass.

Vaz, K. (Ed.). (1997). *Oral narrative research with black women.* Thousand Oaks, CA: Sage.

Vella, J. (2000). A spirited epistemology: Honoring the adult learner as subject. In L. English & M. Gillen (Eds.), *Addressing the spiritual dimensions of adult learning: What educators can do.* San Francisco: Jossey-Bass.

Walters, S., & Manicom, L. (Eds.). (1996). *Gender in popular education.* London: Zed Press.

Weibust, P., & Thomas, L. E. (1994). Learning and spirituality in adulthood. In J. Sinnott (Ed.), *Interdisciplinary handbook of adult lifespan learning.* Westport, CT: Greenwood.

Wuthnow, R. (1999). *Growing up religious.* Boston: Beacon.

Young, R. (1997). *No neutral ground.* San Francisco: Jossey-Bass.

Researching One's Passions: The Perils and Possibilities

Elizabeth J. Tisdell
National-Louis University, Chicago, Illinois

Conducting this qualitative research study was a joy for me, as it had been germinating for a long time. It emerged out of my own passion and interests and arose largely from my own experience of teaching higher education classes that deal with gender, race, class, and culture. I was motivated to teach such classes, not only because of a general concern for equity issues, but my own spiritual commitment almost required that I do so.

How the Study Came to Be: A Little Background

My own spirituality is informed, in part, by my cultural background of growing up in an Irish-Catholic family, having a master's degree in religion, and working for ten years as a Catholic campus minister (from 1979 to 1989), and being strongly influenced by the liberation theology movement of Latin America that emphasized equity and justice. It is also informed by the grounding that was part of my training and work in the healing arts of therapeutic massage, which I began in 1985. Although I left my formal work in an organized religious institution to do my doctoral work, I did not leave my spirituality behind, or its roots relating to equity and justice, or its connection to healing and wholeness. Further, in teaching diversity classes since 1994, during times of conflict that would inevitably arise or to put closure on a class, I found that I would occasionally incorporate exercises that I had done years before in my campus ministry days that were designed to resolve conflict or create unity. Though I never directly referred to "spirituality" per se in these classes, these occasional exercises, for me, were rooted in spirituality. They incorporated symbolic, somatic, or intuitive forms of knowledge construction that seemed to move participants out of their heads and beyond their emotions and incorporated another dimension of their humanity. This study emerged out of my wondering how women of different cultural backgrounds who were doing cultural work in higher education or in communities drew on their own (or participants') spirituality to facilitate greater understanding while challenging power relations, and what their spiritual journeys had been. Although I wasn't fully conscious of this when I began the study, I was trying to further my own spiritual development and to find new ways of drawing on the connection between spirituality and culture in my own educational practice. In hearing these women's stories, I too was spiraling back.

Insider-Outsider Issues in Collecting and Analyzing Data

The research process itself cannot be separated from the critical feminist poststructural theoretical framework on which this study rests, which brings to the foreground how positionality shapes research (and teaching). I conducted these interviews as a middle-class white woman, with many whose cultural, class, and religious backgrounds were very different from mine. Prior to the interviews I knew about half of these women casually, although I knew Julia, Anna, and Patricia very well from multicultural education circles. Those that I didn't know at all prior to the interview were recommended by other participants who created a context and made my access relatively easy, even with those of very different cultural backgrounds from my own. Nevertheless, I suspect that if I had been a woman of their race or ethnicity, the conversation would have been slightly different, as they would have spoken to me as an insider. With a couple of exceptions, the richest data came from those with whom I had some sort of prior relationship. Indeed, spirituality is an intimate subject, and participants seemed less inhibited if they knew me better.

In conducting research, in spite of best attempts to do otherwise, we tend unconsciously to project our own experience or knowledge onto others' stories. While the potential of coming to inaccurate conclusions is always there, even with those who are quite similar to ourselves, it is particularly possible when interviewing women of different cultural or class groups. My experience interviewing Anna, an African American woman, serves as an example.

Anna had told a story of going to college in the early 1960s and being one of eighty African American students on a campus of 22,000. After emphasizing that she was the only black Catholic on campus, she explained an incident at the campus Catholic Church. Prior to when Mass began, if one intended to go to communion, one would put a host in the chalice so that when the priest distributed communion he would come out evenly. So Anna put the host in the chalice. In the middle of the Mass, Anna realized she had eaten within the three hours of the required communion fast, so explained that she didn't go to communion, and had the feeling that everyone knew that she "left the Body of Christ on the altar." She left the Catholic Church that day and never went back.

In listening to this story, and having grown up Catholic, the story seemed a familiar one; to me it was a story of Catholic guilt. But much later in the interview, when I asked Anna a clarifying question about that particular story, she noted, "That wasn't about guilt! That was about being black in an all-white space!" Indeed, at the beginning of the story, Anna had emphasized that she was the only black Catholic. There was perhaps a small element of Catholic guilt in the story; but I had totally missed her main point of telling the story—a landmark turning point where she realized that she needed to find a space that was affirming of her cultural self. If I had been an insider, another African American woman, I probably would have instantly understood her main point. But being an outsider, I unconsciously grabbed onto the part of the story that I related to and initially completely missed that this was a story about culture and being black in an all-white space. This is one of the difficulties of researching across borders: the danger of misinterpretation. In the case of Anna, I was able to catch the potential error of my analysis. Indeed, this experience made me far more vigilant about the importance of member checks, and is why I did intense member checks in the form of summary vignettes with six of the participants who were the most different from myself by class, race, or culture.

Moving On: Critical Research Means Taking Action

As noted, this study was informed by a critical feminist, poststructural theoretical frame. Typically, the term *critical* means two things in research: (1) dealing with and challenging power relations (as in "critical theory" or "critical pedagogy"), and (2) facilitating some sort of action among participants while the study is going on. This study was critical in the sense that to some extent it dealt with power relations. But it was not a participatory or critical action research study in that I didn't do anything to try to make anything happen while the research was going on. Yet part of the larger purpose of the study was that I was hoping to make something happen *as a result of* the study. Most obviously, I was trying to open up the discussion about the place of spirituality in emancipatory education. I believe the study has made a contribution to that end. Less obviously, but more important, I was hoping ultimately to connect with a multicultural group of women interested in creating programs that deal with spirituality and culture in emancipatory education. I met some incredible women in conducting the study who have enriched my own spiritual development and have helped me understand the interplay between spirituality and culture in my own life in new ways, an understanding that has affected my own educational practice. Furthermore, shortly after completing the study, I began collaborating with one of the participants ("Afua"), Derise Tolliver, who teaches at neighboring DePaul University here in Chicago. I had never met Derise prior to our interview, yet we connected on many levels. In the nearly two years since then, we have not only become good friends, we have made presentations at conferences, conducted workshops, and have developed and taught a course together, "Spirituality and Culture in Adult Education." As women of different race and cultural backgrounds informed by different spiritual traditions, our collaboration as educators and researchers is enriched by each other's involvement and creates the possibility of far greater explorations of spirituality and culture in the adult learning environment than either of us could do alone. So was this a critical action research study? Not exactly, but together we're beginning to make something happen as a result of the study. Thus, what began as a largely interpretive study in its first phase, as reported here, has now developed into an ongoing participatory action research study. Further, it may lead to many possibilities in the future for the further development of emancipatory education and participatory research across borders of race, class, and culture.

Phenomenological Research

Phenomenology is both a twentieth century school of philosophy associated with Husserl (1970) and a type of qualitative research. With its roots in philosophy and psychology, phenomenology focuses on the subjective experience of the individual. Although all qualitative research is phenomenological in the sense that there is a focus on people's experience, a phenomenological study seeks to understand the *essence* or *structure* of a phenomenon. This approach rejects the notion of a dichotomy between subject and object; that is, "the reality of an object is only perceived within the meaning of the experience of an individual" (Creswell, 1998, p. 53). The person and his or her world are interrelated and interdependent. The researcher's focus is thus on neither the human subject nor the human world but on the essence of the meaning of this interaction. It is thus the researcher's task "to enter that dialogue, and eavesdrop, as it were; to listen in, and capture the essence of what is perceived by the subject" (van der Mescht, 1999, p. 3).

Phenomenological research addresses questions about common, everyday human experiences (for example, love), experiences believed to be important sociological or psychological phenomena of our time or typical of a group of people (for example, being a cancer patient), and transitions that are common or of contemporary interest (such as becoming a parent or changing gender roles) (Tesch, 1984). The defining characteristic of phenomenological research is its focus on describing the "essence" of a phenomenon from the perspectives of those who have experienced it.

Although documents can be a source of data, the phenomenological interview is the primary method of data collection wherein one attempts to uncover the essence, the invariant structure, of the meaning of the experience. Prior to interviewing others, phenomenological researchers usually explore their own experiences, in part to examine dimensions of the experience and in part to become aware of their own prejudices, viewpoints, and assumptions. These prejudices and assumptions are then *bracketed,* or set aside, so as not to influence the process. Bracketing is explained by Ashworth (1999):

> The procedure has the purpose of allowing the life-world of the participant in the research to emerge in clarity so as to allow a study of some specific phenomenon within the life-world to be carried out. The researcher must suspend presuppositions *in order to enter the life-world.* . . . Two main categories of presuppositions should be bracketed: those to do with the temptation to impose on the investigation of the life-world claims emanating from objective science or other authoritative sources, and those to do with the imposition of criteria of validity arising outside the life-world itself. [pp. 708–709]

Bracketing, or the process of *epoche,* allows the experience of the phenomenon to be explained in terms of its own intrinsic system of meaning, not one imposed on it from without.

In addition to bracketing, when conducting a phenomenological study, one engages in phenomenological reduction, horizontalization, and imaginative variation. *Phenomenological reduction* is the process of continually returning to the essence of the experience to derive the inner structure or meaning in and of itself. We focus on the phenomenon in order to comprehend its essence. *Horizontalization* is the process of laying out all the data and treating the data as having equal weight; that is, all aspects of data have equal value at the initial data analysis stage. Data are then clustered into themes, and repetitious statements are removed. Moustakas (1994, p. 96) explains that in horizontalization, "there is an interweaving of person, conscious experience, and phenomenon. In the process of explicating the phenomenon, qualities are recognized and described; every perception is granted equal value, nonrepetitive constituents of experience are linked thematically, and a full description is derived." *Imaginative variation* involves examining the data from divergent perspectives and varying frames of reference (Moustakas, 1994). The final step in a phenomenological study is to construct a synthesis of textual and structural descriptions (the *what* and *how*) of the phenomenon being studied.

The two articles in this section illustrate the nature of phenomenological research. Wolff's (1999) phenomenological study of in-church and televised worship employs semiotics, the analysis of language, in trying to capture the "lived experience" of both types of worship. Wolff employs most of the techniques of phenomenology listed above and provides an excellent description of their use in relation to the phenomenon of interest: worship. Worthen and McNeill's (1996) focus is on the experience of "good" supervision. In their description of procedures, they capture what a phenomenological study attempts to do. They ask, "What is absolutely essential for this experience of good psychotherapy supervision?" Their findings include a structural description of good supervision.

References

Ashworth, P. (1999). "Bracketing" in phenomenology: Renouncing assumptions in hearing about student cheating." *Qualitative Studies in Education, 12*(6), 707–721.

Creswell, J. W. (1998). *Qualitative inquiry and research design.* Thousand Oaks, Calif.: Sage.

Husserl, E. (1970). *The crisis of european sciences and transcendental phenomenology.* Evanston, Ind.: North University Press.

Moustakas, C. (1994). *Phenomenological research.* Thousand Oaks, Calif.: Sage.

Tesch, R. (1984, April 23–27). Phenomenological studies: A critical analysis of their nature and procedures. Paper presented at the 68th annual meeting of the American Educational Research Association, New Orleans, La. (ERIC Report No. ED 268 122).

Van der Mescht, H. (1999, July 5–8). Poetry, phenomenology, and "reality." Paper presented at the Conference on Qualitative Research, Rand Africaans University, Johannesburg, South Africa.

5

A Phenomenological Study
of In-Church and Televised Worship

Richard F. Wolff

The importance of worship to the life of the believer is universally recognized. Both liturgical theologians and churchgoers alike note the importance of worshipping in church. While it is valuable to understand the theological reasons for the importance of worship, it is likewise important to understand the perspective of the worshippers themselves and to interpret how they describe the experience. The interpretation of first-hand descriptions of worship is a contribution that qualitative research in general and phenomenological research in particular may make to understanding the importance of worship. The interest of the present study is not only to understand the importance of worship from first-hand descriptions but also to consider how the experience of in-church worship compares to that of televised worship.

Televised worship programs have become a significant subgenre of religious television. From slick nationwide televised services to local services recorded on camcorders, television audiences and churchgoers have the opportunity to experience worship services via television. But does the medium make possible a true appreciation of worship experience? Existing studies of religious television shed light on various genres (such as religious news, talk, variety, children's, testimonial, and worship programs) from the perspectives of sociology, political science, psychology, behaviorism, statistical audience analysis, content analysis, cultural studies, and ethnography. All of these studies provide important insights into the phenomenon of religious television; yet studies using an existential phenomenological approach are needed. This study seeks to add to

Richard F. Wolff. (1999). "A Phenomenological Study of In-Church and Televised Worship." *Journal for the Scientific Study of Religion, 38* (2), 219–235. Reprinted with permission.

the critical literature by using semiotic phenomenology to study one subgenre of religious television—televised worship.

Inasmuch as research studies using semiotic phenomenological methodology have burgeoned largely over the past decade, studies of in-church worship like-wise are needed. How do people experience worship in church? In existential terms, why do worshippers value the experience? Finally, how does worship-ping in church compare with experiencing televised worship, and are the dif-ferences significant? To answer these questions, this study develops a semiotic phenomenology of in-church worship and then compares the lived experience of in-church worship with televised worship.

Methodology and Research Design

Given my interest in researching lived experience, semiotic phenomenology is the research theory I used to guide my study (Lanigan, 1992, 1988). Phenomenology focuses on lived experience. It looks at people's everyday experiences of phenom-ena and how these experiences are structured, focusing the analysis on the per-spective of the individual experiencing the phenomenon. Phenomenology thus attends to how people experience phenomena existentially. The aim is to describe and interpret how the situated body makes sense of a phenomenon. People ex-press their experience of phenomena in language. Semiotics focuses on language as a medium of expression and how meaning and experience are captured in signs. In semiotic phenomenology, lived-significance and speech-as-signification are in-tertwined; the meaning *is* the phenomenon, and the focus on language as signi-fier is intertwined with the significance of lived meaning; the two structures are reversible (Merleau-Ponty, 1968). Semiotic phenomenology thus constitutes a methodology for analyzing conscious experience and the existential meaning re-vealed by speech in the description of a phenomenon (Lanigan, 1988, pp. 8–10, 144–52). (For the purposes of this research I make no esoteric distinctions among semiotic, existential, and hermeneutic phenomenology. Inasmuch as semiotic phe-nomenology posits that symbols and their meanings are inextricably bound with lived experience, semiotic phenomenology is existential; and inasmuch as the final phase of semiotic phenomenology involves an interpretation of the lived meaning of a phenomenon, the research is also hermeneutic.)

Using semiotic phenomenological procedure, a researcher may interpret per-sons' conscious experience of a phenomenon by using the methodological schema of description-reduction-interpretation (Lanigan, 1988, p. 148). Generally speak-ing, the initial procedure consists in the description (interviews), followed by reduction (thematizations) and interpretation (hermeneutic reflection). The de-scription is the explication of conscious experience; that is, the basic signs. Here, the description is the transcribed interviews with respondents. Description is taken through phenomenological reduction—finding emergent themes in the descrip-tions of the phenomenon. For example, in each respondent's descriptions I look for clusters of statements that coalesce around a central theme, such as "Church as Unity," and list these themes together with the research participant's comments, in this case church as "blending," "bringing together," an "experience of oneness." A similar procedure reveals themes across respondents' descriptions—that is, finding themes supported by comments from several participants.

Reduced elements are then interpreted to explicate what is signified, what the meaningful directedness points to (Lanigan, 1988, p. 148). This involves finding further thematizations, which bring together initial themes into more all-encompassing ones. For example, "Hierarchy" as a theme emerges from initial clusters concerning seeing and being seen; intersubjective relations among God, the pastor, congregation, and self; experiences of being controlled. In the interpretation, I explicate the structures of experience revealed in these thematizations and how they interrelate with each other.

This coalescence of themes into more encompassing themes leads to the discovery of one or two phrases that capture(s) the experience in a revealing manner. Such phrases may not at first seem particularly evocative of the phenomenal complexity of an experience until one examines how they express the essence of an experience in some revealing manner. These phrases will be densely layered with emergent themes and are therefore revelatory of persons' conscious experience of church. The interpretation involves an explication of how one or two phrases are so revelatory and the elucidation of a definition of the phenomenon which ties the themes together. Ultimately, I compare the structures of ecclesiastic and televisual experience, including televised worship.

In order to provide me with a description of the phenomena under study, I chose research participants from whom I could receive first-hand descriptions of ecclesiastic and televisual experience. The descriptions provided by these respondents reveal the lived meanings of the phenomena and provide a discursive means by which these experiences may be unveiled, examined, and understood in the coming phases of phenomenological procedure (Nelson, 1989b, p. 224). In all, I interviewed a dozen churchgoers and focused my analysis on the transcripts of the six most richly descriptive of these.

I used three strategies for selecting respondents. Since I was specifically seeking people who have experience with both television and in-church services I engaged in purposeful sampling, a technique which seeks information-rich cases (Patton, 1990, p. 169). In addition, I used homogeneous and typical case sampling (Patton, 1990, pp. 173–174). Homogeneous sampling provides focus and reduced variation while nonetheless encouraging descriptions from persons' unique perspectives. In keeping with this strategy, I interviewed members of a small, predominantly white Lutheran congregation in Athens, Ohio, who also meet the purposeful sampling criteria; just over half of those interviewed were female, and ages ranged from late twenties to late sixties. I also used typical case sampling, a strategy I chose to highlight experiences many people have in common. Notably, any selection strategy involves limitations, which are best recognized; for example, another study might look at devoted viewers of televised worship to compare their experiences with those chosen herein, or might look at members of church traditions which differ significantly from that used in this study. Nonetheless, if one bears in mind the specific strategies used for any particular study one may understand its relevance in context and use this to provide ideas and comparisons for further research.

To conduct my conversations, I selected the interview guide approach (Patton, 1990, pp. 283–284). This interview type allows the researcher to select a general list of topics to be covered, without formalizing a specific sequence or wording of questions. To provide the framework for the discussions, I developed a topical protocol—a list of topics of interest which I hoped to cover in whatever sequence seemed appropriate in the given interview situation. The interviews were conducted as a discussion, and participants guided the discussion from point to point as befit their situation. They spontaneously introduced whatever descriptions/interpretations they found appropriate. Flexibility, situational sensitivity, and open-ended responses are the features defining this interview type (Patton, 1990, pp. 283–284). The topical protocol I used for the interviews encouraged descriptions of a church, a worship service (in detail), God, congregation members, nonecclesiastic religious experience, and televised worship.

Once interviews were completed and transcribed I began the phenomenological reduction by looking for emergent themes, both of individual research participants (paradigmatic reduction) and across participants' responses (syntagmatic reduction). These thematic categories emerged from individual utterances of respondents, and I collected respondents' phrases under appropriate thematic headings. (Note: numbers appear parenthetically after quotations from the transcripts to identify which respondent offered that description.) For example, some emergent themes are Church as Dependable/Familiar ("you can depend on what's going to happen at what time," "everything is predictable," "it's very comforting to hear the same words") and Church as Public Acknowledgment ("it means something to say it, it means something to hear it," "even though you know all the words already, it's really good to hear them spoken," "I feel like I'm lending my presence in support of the prayers"). I continued the phenomenological reduction until I found three thematic categories which are the essential constituent elements of ecclesiastic experience. The essential thematic categories which emerged from this process are hierarchy, immersion, and freedom. These elements were themselves reduced in the phenomenological interpretation to a definition—a statement by which I attempt to explicate how these themes reveal the lived complexity of ecclesiastic experience.

Church and "Everyday" Experiences

Ecclesiastic experience consistently emerged among research participants' descriptions as a contrast to "everyday" experiences. A number of subthemes appear; these include church as distinct from work, everyday conflicts, and ordinary experiences of time. Church is experienced as distinct from everyday chaos: "You can go and be away from all the hubbub, and the phones, and the this and the that that goes on in your everyday life" (1). In contrast to such "hubbub," church provides a well-structured and peaceful environment: "The rest of the week is crazy. That's one point in time that's structured and peaceful and I look forward to that, kind of a renewing time of the week" (2). The formality of church experience provides an ordered contrast to less-ordered weekday experiences: in church, "you can depend on what's going to happen at what time" (2).

The experience of church as apart from everyday conflict, nonetheless, has an important influence on the everyday; church experience renews congregants and makes their everyday experiences more bearable:

I have a lot of stress, a lot of goals to meet at work and a lot of pressure, and I'm the only one in my office, my division, so I don't have anyone else I can go give anything to, it's all on my shoulders, and that's probably why I feel like the whole world is against me, even though I have everything going for me. But if I've gone to church on Sunday I feel better about the week and I think God's gonna give me enough time to get what's necessary done, and if I do not always get everything done, so what. (6)

At work there are always going to be conflicts coming up, problems and weariness of the day and the pacing, which the day goes through, and in church you don't usually have that. I can't say I ever go to work and get renewed, it's just a different emphasis. (1)

The rest of the week is crazy. That's one point in time that's structured and peaceful and I look forward to that, kind of a renewing time of the week. (2)

Church provides renewal for the week because of differing expectations: "At church I'm not expected to be a wonderful person, I'm expected to be a sinner who's going to be forgiven and somebody who's going to go out and try to be a better Christian and live out their faith in a better life, where at work you don't have that ability to necessarily fail and be readily forgiven, you're expected to do the best and not fail, and people don't necessarily forgive you if you do fail" (1).

The principal orientation is to past conflicts, although anxiety about the future is also present. One respondent notes that she experiences church as "peaceful" and "quiet" and in direct contrast to her everyday experience, particularly when her mind wanders in church and she starts thinking about everyday problems; she thinks of "something that's happened to me through the week that I haven't been able to shake off, or maybe even something I'm going to do" (3). Church emerges therefore as a temporal point of reference, a present experience from which worshippers reflect on the past and find renewal for the future.

The experience of church as a temporal point of reference emerges in all respondents' discussions. Church is experienced as either the end (orientation toward the past) or beginning (orientation toward the future) of a week:

It's the stopping point of the week for me. The rest of the week is crazy. That's one point in time that's structured and peaceful and I look forward to that, kind of a renewing time of the week. (2)

That's part of the letting down process, the end of the week syndrome, you know you race like crazy through the week then all of a sudden you're relaxed. (2)

[After church] I'm ready to face the week. (6)

I do a lot of bad things during the week, a lot of bad things, so I just feel a lot better when I've gone to church and it helps me start the week again, to try again. (6)

Now my sins are forgiven and now I can start another week. (6)

Then when you get to the communion part, it kind of completes the cleansing process and gives you added strength and food for going on in life and starting the week and doing things better this time. (1)

[The blessing] closes the service and begins my week right. (5)

I can touch base and go into the week. (4)

Although respondents report being aware of the passage of time during weekday experiences, time goes unnoticed at church: "This is one place where I don't pay much attention to time, at least during the service" (3); "I can't say that I'm aware of time passing or not as the case may be" (1); "it's sort of a suspension of time" (5); "I don't think I'm usually really aware" of the passage of time in a church service, "usually I don't notice" (4). Church is therefore distinguished from the everyday in that persons are not as aware of the passage of time during a worship service as they are during other experiences.

Ecclesiastic Modes of Corporeal Experience

While ecclesiastic experience involves a defocusing on the passage of time it also involves a heightened focus on sense. At different portions of a service, moreover, different senses are highlighted. Senses are "foregrounded" in relation to what is experienced as a neutral horizon forming the background. Thus, silence is the background against which speech is foregrounded; seatedness is the visual background against which a person standing commands attention; nearness is the tangible background against which touching is foregrounded.

Hearing. A predominant element of the sensual ensemble involved in the ecclesiastic setting emerges among interviewees' descriptions of hearing/listening. What most distracts worshippers from engagement in worship is aberrant sound: children speaking or crying (1, 2, 3, 4, 5), people talking when they should not be (4, 5), sounds coming from other parts of the building (5). Aberrant sound is distracting because it diverts worshippers from the intentional directedness, which they experience as appropriate. For example, the prelude is described as a time to be quiet (all respondents), "ponder" (1), and "meditate" (3), particularly on oneself; music is appropriate; self-examination is appropriate, verbal communication is a distraction. The structure of the service begins with a quiet focus on self such that that which worshippers offer to the group (their selves) is foregrounded. Before immersing oneself in the group identity/expression, an awareness of what one is immersing—the self—is the appropriate focus. Quietness and self-focus are therefore intertwined.

By means of the auditory, group identity is quickly forged. Against this beginning background of silence/self-focus a speech/group-focus emerges. After a brief order for confession and forgiveness (which participants report "frees them up" [1]), the congregation sings an opening hymn and acts as a whole: singing with other people is "a kind of a group expression and it's kind of like bringing everybody together and focused on one thing, and yeah, I think that does have meaning for me, 'cuz everybody has their own way of expressing that, but it comes into a whole" (4).

Hymn singing is a group expression in which voices intertwine or "blend" (3), forming an auditory unity. One's own voice blends with that of others such that shortcomings in one's vocal ability will be of no concern since individual voices get "drowned out" (6).

Throughout the descriptions of ecclesiastic experience, listening is the principal mode of engagement: listening to the sermon, prayers, Scripture readings, etc. It is implicit in many of the paradigmatic thematizations discussed above. For example, one research participant describes church as dependable, an experience which is intertwined with the auditory: "It's very comforting to hear the same words" (2). The intertwining is likewise present for another respondent, who explicates the auditory as central to her experience of church as public expression: "It means something to say it, it means something to hear it," and "sometimes it's really good to hear, even though you know all the words already, it's really good to hear them spoken" (5).

Seeing. Looking and listening is important in Scripture reading, yet "pure" listening is preferred for prayers. In the sensual ensemble of ecclesiastic experience, sight is at times experienced as a threat to what respondents experience as the more important intentional directness toward sound. Closing one's eyes during prayers is important, so that the visual will not distract one from the auditory. Participants explicate this intentional directedness toward listening as "concentration": when bowing one's head and closing one's eyes in prayer, "you're not concentrating on anything else for one thing, it helps you to keep your thoughts on the prayers" (3); likewise, "I really don't open my eyes at all, I keep my eyes shut and concentrate" (6). Note that respondents say that their concentration comes about by a conscious effort to be intentionally directed toward sound, the voice of one reading the prayers, and by bracketing the visual by not looking at the printed word, the reader, or other congregants.

The disengagement of the visual seems most often experienced during directedness toward God. How does one direct oneself "toward" something that is "around us and with us" (3)? Toward God, whom "no one's seen" (6)? While God's presence is symbolically visualized (3), attempts to address God necessitate disengaging from a visual orientation in order to be directed toward an auditory one. In the in-church setting, God is experienced as an essentially auditory phenomenon.

Touching. This discussion leads to the matter of tactility and bodily presence in church. There is a sense in which worshippers experience God as concretely present and touchable. After going to church, one respondent says, "I feel better that I'm back in touch with God" (6). This suggests Godly contact is lost during everyday activity and is restored in church. Sensing God's presence is connected to sensing the presence of other worshippers:

> I feel God's presence in the communion with the congregation, the caring and the friendly open feeling of the congregation to me speaks to God's presence, because you can be in another gathering for other reasons and the feeling of the group is totally different, so I think that you can feel God's presence in the mood, in the feeling of the people worshipping with you. (1)

> I think sometimes I just have to remind myself that He's there, and other times, I think that it helps me to remember by my relationships with this community. And there I can know that there's a presence, just because there's all these presences. . . .I guess it's different when I'm aware [of God's presence] because then I'm aware of the connection, and I can feel more connected, grounded. . .[connected] to God, or to, that somehow I'm connected to what's kind of underneath it all that gives it meaning and substance. . .just all, I guess it all, the universe. (4)

The presence of others directing their awareness to what connects them all serves metonymically to connect all things and all people. Central to this awareness is physical proximity and tangibility, as captured in the phrase, "you can get a feel for people" (1), which suggests a "feel" for others' moods and personas, and an actual tangible "feel" of others' corporeal presence: "I think that I tend to like closeness. . . .I think that you can feel probably the mood of people" (1). Going to church to "make" this contact is important; one participant notes that this contact is lost during everyday experiences when he "loses touch" with "the things that are important to me within the church service and also within my own emotional and spiritual ramblings" (4). The physical presence of others is necessary to "make" contact: "I feel better that I'm back in touch with God, that obviously I can't make it on my own" (6).

The necessity of physical presence and the ability to touch other worshippers for authentic ecclesiastic experience emerges most clearly when this is contrasted with watching a televised church service. TV worship lacks an essential physical presence and touchability:

> I wouldn't get that feeling. I might bow my head for the Lord's Prayer. . . .but it wouldn't be the same. A church to me is a fellowship with the believers, it's a fellowship. (3)

> The TV cuts me off too much, I don't feel like I'm a member or that I'm belonging to the congregation that's in the TV service, I'd rather be a part of the congregation. (1)

> It felt like you were just a spectator. (4)

> I'm not really feeling the elements and stuff, I don't know, it just seems like I am on the outside looking in. (3)

With in-church experience, respondents explicate the body as being "in" an experience, one that is separate from the everyday, as when a congregant notes that participating in church is "kind of like you're there in that sacred moment. And then you take that and then you can go on out into the world again, into your life" (4). This comment makes explicit a separation of planes which one may be "in," the church and the everyday, adding that although the churchly plane is apart from the everyday it affects life "in" the everyday.

Ecclesiastic Modalities of Intersubjective Awareness

Consociates (Congregants and Pastor). At times the service opens to a mutual, interactive dialogue in which some congregants are active. For example, portions of the service are flexible, explicitly designed to be contextually sensitive to contemporary time and concerns. Participants say these points occur when congregants other than themselves (consociates) are actively engaged in creating a personal expression for the ritual, such as writing one's own prayers or a sermon. These portions of the service are expressly capable of incorporating concerns relevant to a particular time and community. Such portions of the service are described as involving a passive stance by congregants, yet also yield a sense of being more personally addressed as during the pastor's sermon:

> On a personal level, she's a real warm and supportive person, and she's a very good pastor on a personal level. But when she goes up, to preach her sermon, then she's on a, it's as though she's stepped up to another level, and she's got something a little bit different to say to us. It's related to what she says to us any other time of the week that we see her, but it's got a different kind of significance somehow, it's coming from a different direction. (4)

> I guess I kind of think of her as a very good friend, and when she's preaching the sermon, I'm trying to be very receptive and open to a friend to see what they have to say to me. . . .Yeah, it's different probably because at other times of the week when I am with her it's more of a relationship of just another person, a good friend, where during a service and a sermon, she's acting more as a spokesperson for God. (1)

The pastor's everyday interaction with congregants forms a background, which contrasts with her role in the worship service, but which also influences congregants' relationships with her during a service. During this time, congregants describe themselves as more passive in their relationship with the pastor, but also confident that her interactions with them during the week make her sensitive to their needs during the service. Her role in the liturgy is to embody a site of interaction among herself, her congregational consociates, and various others: between congregants and biblical predecessors (whose lives and writings she is expected to make relevant to congregants today); between congregants and the institutionalized other—the service itself (whose institutionalized voice needs her embodiment to be present); and between congregants and God (for whom she is serving as "spokesperson").

Self. In the context of the ecclesiastic setting, the self emerges as the site of entwined modes of intersubjective awareness. In a process of transformation during a worship service, respondents describe the self as willingly separated from itself: "With a church service I hope that I'm a different person when I come out, because I've been forgiven, I've been renewed, and I am ready to start out again" (1). The self is renewed, and is different from the self who entered the service: the "bad" (6), "weak person" (3) who entered is a different person by the end of the service, one who is good and strong. The service transforms congregants from what they were into what they now are—until they will need renewal once again. The self therefore emerges as in continual reestablishment, the site where one is both transformed and stabilized; one must constantly be changed into another—perhaps more accurately, changed into a continuing sequence of others. One may look back, then, to the old self, or forward to the self that one will become by the end of the worship service. The "I" serves as a constant—that which holds despite being transformed into a different person: "With a church service I hope that I'm a different person when I come out, because I've been forgiven, I've been renewed, and I am ready to start out again" (1).

Contemporaries. Those capable of being transformed are not only those present at the same time and place of the worship service, but also others intended by worshippers to experience transformation even though they are in a different place at the time of the service. Contemporaries are those on whom one may have some potential influence, or be influenced by, should one be able to establish contact (Schutz, 1967, pp. 176–177). Contemporaries are incorporated into the service by congregants' hearing their names spoken or by thinking about them quietly. Contemporaries are most often intended during the more flexible and contextually sensitive portions of the service. One congregant often thinks of others during sermons and "wishes so and so could be hearing this too" because the pastor is addressing "something they've been questioning" (3). In a similar manner, all respondents think of contemporaries during the prayers, both family and friends, and others with whom they have never had contact (such as people of other countries). The means which establish the possibility of influence on these others are the congregation, the prayer, and God: "I'm thinking about each and every one we're praying for, there's some I don't know, but I assume God knows and I just hope that we're sending up these things, that God can really hear us and in some little way, you know, it's touching me" (3). Thus, others living in the world at the same time as congregants, but not present in the church, may also be influenced by the intentional directedness of the congregation to their contemporaries' needs.

God. God is in one sense apart from congregants and, in another, always together with them. The divine and human planes are layered, in one way distinguishable, in another entirely interrelated. Thus, God is exclusive of congregants: "It's as though God's always out there and we're in here worshipping Him" (4); "it's kind of an intonation for God to acknowledge that we're here. . .asking Him to pay attention to us" (1). Nonetheless, God is also present, and in a way that interconnects congregants with each other, predecessors, the world—everything.

One research participant, who experiences God as "out there," also experiences God as present in other congregants: "I can know that there's a presence, just because there's all these presences. . .that's another time when we're singing and going back and forth. . .that's the part where I really. . .start to recognize that God is there" (4). God is "always out there" but also present in this respondent's relationship with other congregants. A similar expression is made by another respondent, for whom God is both "around us and with us" (3). Likewise, another research participant says that God is "personally involved every minute of the day" and yet is someone that she must get "back in touch with" on Sunday mornings (6).

God is both separate and connected. God, in fact, is that which provides the means for a connection of all things to each other. God is unity. In prayer to God one may "touch" others, present or not (3). Listening to God's role in the lives of one's predecessors one finds God's relevance to oneself today. In God, one anticipates the reuniting of oneself with the dead (3). This experience of God is summarized well by a respondent who notes that at those times when he is most aware of God, "It's different. . .because then I'm aware of the connection, and I can feel more connected, grounded, to God, or to, that somehow I'm connected to what's kind of underneath it all that gives it meaning and substance; just all, I guess it all, the universe" (4).

This sense of unity is hard to express, as anything that would unite "the universe" is hard to conceive, let alone articulate. God thus emerges as necessarily ambiguous: respondents do not have a particular image of God and resist attempts to resolve Godly ambiguity by trying to find an image:

> It [God] defies description. I think that if you tried to make a picture of it, you cover it in ways that it shouldn't be, because you tend to put some kind of sex on it, in our thinking, my thinking, you can't put a body, if you're going to put a body on somebody, you can't put a body on somebody without making it some form of sex because even if you claim it's sexless, you still have to have some kind of face and hair and things, and that itself is going to speak to one sex or the other, and I think that's dangerous. (1)

God remains imageless (exclusive), so that all images (inclusive) may be experienced as God; hence when one respondent "recognizes" congregants around her during the greeting, what she recognizes is God's presence, and the unity of all persons established in their relation to God (2). God and these others are reversible structures ("by the congregation showing that it cares about one another we're showing that we care about God" [2]). God is thus both concrete and particular; ambiguous and limitless.

Thematizing Ecclesiastic Experience: Hierarchy, Immersion, and Freedom

Hierarchy. In ecclesiastic experience, hierarchical relationships present themselves in a number of ways: between God and humanity, pastor and congregation, old self and new self, church time and everyday time. Hierarchy presupposes heterogeneity—elements must be separate and different enough to allow a valuing of some elements over others. In a religious context, the experience of hierarchical relationships is essential, since the intentional orientation in worship assumes an orientation that sets apart that which worships from that which is worshipped. The intentional orientation of a worshipper, then, entails something worthy of her or his worship; something that she or he values as more powerful than the self.

In the context of the church service, these hierarchical relations are explicit. As one respondent says about going to church, "it puts things in better perspective" (6). The visual metaphor here is instructive, as it is sight that allows for the perception of separation and distance. Visual metaphors reveal an experience of containment and, as such, define boundaries. Sight emphasizes separation and heterogeneity (Straus, 1966, p. 7); thus, in "putting things in better perspective," one becomes more aware of differences and relative value than one is during the week. During the week, respondents "lose sight" of what is important to them (4). In "putting things in better perspective" the relative valuing of things is placed in sharper focus so that one becomes aware of what one values more as distinct from what one values less.

One phenomenon that is put in better perspective is temporal field relations. Ecclesiastic time is experienced as a temporal point of demarcation, a time which sets apart that which came before from that which comes after. This temporal positioning affords church a value over the everyday. Church is the ending of one week and the beginning of another, and the experience of the service occasions this temporal transformation. The significance of church time is determined by its relationship with nonchurch time, which comes before and after. Respondents "look forward to" church, and on leaving church "begin" their week "right" (5). This "looking forward" sets an orientation, one which sets apart and values ecclesiastic time for its powers of renewal. Church is a time wherein time's ordinary way of passing is bracketed ("it's sort of a suspension of time" [2]), thus differentiating this time from others. Church time is positioned hierarchically to everyday time. It is valued expressly in relation to the everyday for the powers it has—church is "taking special time out" (1).

Within the context of church, the pastor is hierarchically positioned over congregants. This, too, involves an emphasis on visual relationship. During a service, the pastor "steps up to another level" (4): "She's got something a little bit different to say to us, it's related to what she says to us any other time of the week that we see her, but it's got a different kind of significance somehow, it's coming from a different direction."

Recognizing the distinction between the localization of sound (it surrounds persons, making them its center) and the localization of a sound's source (which entails a more visual relationship [Straus, 1966, p. 5]) bespeaks of a visual spatiality, one which orients this respondent differently in church from during the week. What the pastor says comes from "another level." In church, the pastor is valued in relation to the congregation, which faces her. The pastor does things the congregation does not—for example, she stands while they sit for the sermon. Her body posture is a reflection of the congregation's. For example, she and the congregation face each other when she says prayers or exchanges petitions with the congregation. When she walks into the midst of the congregation to read the Gospel, the congregation alters its bodily orientation in order to remain facing her:

"We stand and turn and face the pastor when she goes down in the middle or the congregation, so that makes it seem a little different, but I'm not sure that I hear it that much different" (4). While the localization of the sound has not changed ("I'm not sure I hear it that different"), that of its source has (so "we stand and turn and face" the pastor, in the direction of the sound's source).

The pastor is an "authority figure" (6), a "spokesperson for God" (1), on "another [higher] level" (4). The congregation's gestures in relation to her are accordingly respectful—turning to face her, remaining quiet when she addresses them. She "leads" them in prayer and provides a mutually shared point of visual orientation for all congregants: the opening exchange is a time "for her to lead us in like a prayer, and also to get us on track, this is where we're going" (4).

Ultimately congregants are going away from the old self, the self of the past week, toward the new self, the self that will emerge from the service. The new self is valued over the old. The old self is that which has "lost touch" with God and must be renewed by "getting back in touch with God" (6). God is experienced as separate from and connected to congregants. The sense of separation from God involves a particularly visual spatiality, the visual emphasizing separation. What affords God ultimate power and authority is God's formlessness, invisibility, and exclusiveness. Congregants refuse to picture God with any particular features or constant form. God's high status is "protected through invisibility" (Meyrowitz, 1985, p. 67), an invisibility which makes a person unable to see God, but to be seen by God every moment of every day. God is "out there," is "other" (4), is that other that is "all around" (3). Since God is that other that is all around, God's hierarchical relation with respondents is particularly powerful: God is that outside power that frees the new self from bad things.

Immersion. In a church service, persons become explicitly aware of their separation from God, others, the everyday, and self. Visual metaphors reveal this in particular, foremost among these being that the service "puts things in perspective." This separation, however, is the background against which immersion becomes foreground. Against the backgrounds of separation, exclusivity, and hierarchy emerge experiences of immersion, inclusion, and equality. The self as isolated disappears and is freed from its limitedness by an immersion in community. It is no small matter that respondents use "I" most often when describing the beginning and ending of a service, and "we" and "us" when describing the central portions. After "I" reflect on the self in the act of confession and forgiveness at the beginning of a service, "we" sing a hymn, "we" exchange a greeting with the pastor, "we" listen and recite and stand and ask. This new community stands finally in relation to the hierarchic structures, particularly God and God's spokesperson, the pastor.

The emergence of community coincides with an intentional shift from the visual to the auditory. Whereas the visual emphasizes separation, difference, and hierarchy, the auditory emphasizes a bringing together, a filling of gaps, a homogenization (Straus, 1966, p. 7). Sound surrounds and is present to all persons in a way that makes each of them its center. Sound binds (Ong, 1967, p. 125), filling space between persons, thereby unifying all within its invisible presence (Idhe, 1973, p. 44). The auditory unifies congregants into a community, and they experience a belonging to the sound that surrounds and enfolds them, and to the community. Congregants may not see things from the same perspective but they are all immersed in the same sounds—the speaking of the prayers, which "links us up" (4), the singing of hymns in which individual voices get "drowned out" (6) and "blend" together (3).

At other times, when the congregation is less active as a group, such as when sitting and listening to the sermon, the gaze of others is perceived as a distraction. In the absence of any active community gesture (such as standing, speaking, or singing), the community identity is more easily broken by the gaze of another. It is then that the visual may overpower the auditory and suddenly reestablish an awareness of isolation and distance among congregants. At such moments, another's gaze reestablishes intentional awareness of separation by reinforcing the visual intentionality of distance. Looking at another both distances the congregants involved and breaks the community's common gesture. Without such distracting behavior the sense of community is maintained and congregants gain an identity beyond that of the self in isolation. The community is "isolated together" (Meyrowitz, 1985, p. 56). A church service is an in between period between old self and new self wherein a communal self is established, particularly in relation to hearing the spoken word.

At a point in the service immersion is taken a step further, and group identity becomes a tangible unity, an interwoven corporeality. The transformation is from immersion to coextension, a sense of connection. Church experience has this potential throughout: "You can get a feel for people" (1). But at some point, the potential ("can") is actualized. Nearness is transformed to coextension. This is not only when congregants touch others—the greeting and the communion—but also during the prayers. The prayer "links up" (4) the needs of the person, community, world—all things, and brings them to God in the word spoken in communal gesture: "[In church] I can know that there's a presence, just because there's all these presences. . . . I guess it's different when I'm aware [of God's presence] because then I'm aware of the connection, and I can feel more connected, grounded. . .connected to God, or to, that somehow I'm connected to what's kind of underneath it all that gives it meaning and substance. . .just all, I guess it all, the universe" (4).

What "gives it meaning" is God, the interconnection of all things. Connection to the transcendent relates people to everything and affords all a sense of the whole in which each entity participates. Congregants go to church specifically to "make that connection" (4, 6) with all things, since the liturgy "covers most everything" (2). One needs the presence of others to "make" a connection to all things and to God, something which is not possible to make alone: "I feel better that I'm back in touch with God, that obviously I can't make it on my own" (6). In church, one is immersed in community through which eventually one feels connected to all things, and this connection is experienced as freeing.

Freedom. Respondents experience immersion as freedom from their ordinary experience of self, time, world. They are freed from that which is limiting and are able to experience that which is all encompassing. Coming into the service the self is experienced as limited and this sets the background for freedom—that from which one seeks to be freed. Consequently, that which one is freed to is the situation one finds at a service's end. At a service's beginning the self is tainted by everyday conflict: "[Church is] a definite need in my life. It helps me get through life. It helps me to leave things that I don't need to hold onto anymore and move on with my life, to realize when there are conflicts that I can be freed of them" (1). Explicit discussion of freedom emerges particularly in discussing the confession (the service's beginning) and the communion (the service's end), and the hierarchical experience that values new self over old is also most explicit when discussing these points in the service.

At the beginning (confession) respondents focus on self, since no sense of community has yet emerged. Description of the confession is noteworthy for the changes it reveals in temporal intentionality, which shift among past, present, and future:

> [I'm] thinking over things that happened in the past week that I'm either not
> happy with, or things that I wish could be different, and really get ready to get rid
> of those things and let them go. And that's looking forward to the confession,
> which is what we usually start our service with, and that's really a big point for
> me because it really does free me up and let me move on and try to do things
> again and do them better, or at least not waste my time over wishful things that
> can't happen anymore. . . . [The confession] frees me from continuing to feel bad
> about things that I haven't done in the way I wished I could have done them. . .
> I can say, well this is the way it is, this is the way it happened, and that with the
> help of God who forgives me for making mistakes, I can move on and say, now
> we're going to try harder and do things better this week. (1)

The movement is from an intentionality of anxiety—where one "continually reopens the past, translates it into possibility [future], and keeps alive its disturbing relevance for the present"—to an intentionality of hope where "the present is lived in light of what the future might bring. In the deepest depths of despair hope can be nourished and kept alive through the envisagement of the transcending and redeeming power of the future" (Schrag, 1969, p. 97). This shift separates and values the new week, to which respondents look forward in hope, from the old, to which respondents look back upon in despair and anxiety.

If the confessional part of the service "frees" worshippers, and the communion/benediction defines when the new week starts, what of the time between? The church service seems to render an ambiguous experience of time, one free from both old and new weeks. The time therein is different from respondents' ordinary experience of time: congregants look back in anxiety, and forward in hope, from a center which draws these intentional structures together, and from which these structures radiate. Church involves "special time out" (1), a "suspension of time" (5). It is also a time during which identity is transformed from "I" to "we." The immersion in group, sound, and meaning is intertwined with the experience of connecting to all and "that seems to be the main focus of being there, is to make that connection" (4).

Hermeneutic Reflection. The themes of hierarchy, freedom, and immersion must now be further reduced to a phenomenological definition of in-church worship, and this definition is explicitly related to one or two of the participants' phrases that help reveal the complexities of this experience. Just as the previous reductions have encompassed themes that emerged from the participants' full-length descriptions, so too the definition now is a final reduction that brings together the bulk of the themes which have preceded. Explicating how previous themes relate to this phenomenological definition of in-church experience is the final stage of the process.

As discussed, in-church experience orients participants to hierarchical value relations, where a new time, world, and self are valued more than the old. Participants come to church to bring about the *transformation* of old to new. In order to achieve this renewal, participants are freed from the normal restraints of time (which is "suspended") and of an individuated experience of self. They become one expressive body, a body sharing *one center* which is stronger than any individual self because the whole stands in relation to God. By immersing themselves in group expression and identity, they become one communally expressive self, *conforming* their actions with that of the group; further, by their connection with God, the ground of all being, participants are made one with everything—they are one form with the world.

Ecclesiastic experience thus involves *a conformation (making one form, complying with a group expression) and concentration (making one center, making stronger) involved in an act of transformation (of self, time, world).* This meaning is captured in the revelatory phrases, church is a "suspension of time" which "puts things in better perspective." In church, persons assent to what is expected of them, to what is appropriate; hence, they conform. Persons also are united with others in a single communal expression—one form (con-form) becoming one expressive body. Church also "puts things in better perspective," so that once one is freed from ordinary restraints, such as when time is "suspended," one may be oriented differently, immersed in an identity beyond that of the limited self in order to be aware of what holds all things together. One is therefore made stronger by ecclesiastic experience, a strengthening which is captured in the word "concentration" (to make stronger). This strengthening emerges in part from immersing oneself in the auditory, particularly listening to God, which both makes congregants the center (of sound) and stronger (interconnected with others and God).

In sum, what emerges from ecclesiastic experience is a self valued more than the self that entered and a time valued more than the time that ended at the service's beginning. Both time and self are renewed by their connection with God, since God is what holds all things, all meaning together. God is the center of all existence, from which all things radiate. Ecclesiastic experience is similarly at the center of experience, as time and self flow into and emerge from church. Church brings about the transformation of self and time by means of conformity and concentration.

Comparing Ecclesiastic and Televisual Experience

Participants in the present study note that their experience of televised worship is significantly different from their experience of in-church worship, and that the different structures of the two experiences make worshipping by television less satisfying. The final segment of this study compares the structures of the two experiences in order to explicate how they are different and specifically why these participants find in-church worship more satisfying. To accomplish the comparison, this section relies on comments about televised worship made by the research participants, as well as existing phenomenological studies of televisual experience itself, since it is the structure of televisual experience that makes possible the experience of anything by television, including worship.

To begin, televisual experience is in many ways a contrast with in-church religious experience. Whereas church is apart from the everyday, televisual experience is integrated into everyday life: physically, TV is located in the home; temporally, it is watched daily. In addition, church is experienced as an opportunity to remember conflicts with others and personal failings that occurred during the week so that a person may be renewed for the following week. Church is transformative. Television, on the other hand, is revealed as a "divergence" that helps a person "to forget temporarily about stressful situations over which she or he has little control" (Nelson, 1989a, p. 394). TV as divergence is a temporary escape from thinking about one's problems; church as transformative is an experience which transfigures the person who enters church into another self. In a similar manner, television as divergence implies a temporary activity which disrupts a course of action. It is a momentary stepping aside between some beginning and some ending point. Perhaps this is why watching television often elicits guilt (Nelson, 1989a, p. 395), as diverting persons from accomplishing other tasks. Church, however, often induces guilt if one does not go (4, 6). The ecclesiastic is experienced as a more valued activity than the televisual, one that is not a diversion but a transformation.

Typically, televisual experience is not engaged exclusively, but combined with other activities: sewing, cooking, reading, eating. This is part of how TV is integrated into daily life and often results in a lack of intentional focus on the television. How and when one will focus on the television or other things is given to a number of factors: whether other persons are present in the room, whether one is engaged in other activities, and so on. These factors tend to occur randomly in the everyday home environment; that is, typically there is not a predicable pattern to when one will turn one's attention to what. In church, however, there are patterns of intentional directedness that are predictable. These patterns were set by predecessors and exist as the institutional other which controls the congregants. One defines one's focus in relation to what is considered appropriate for a given point in a service. Thus, even if one is distracted, one knows on what one should be focusing. In its patterning, church is predictable.

The church service is experienced as a familiar, dependable other, one which makes congregants feel "secure" (3). Television does not make respondents feel secure (3). This contrast applies not only to the form of televisual and ecclesiastic experience (unpatterned/controllable versus patterned/controlled) but also to their content. This is clear from comparing how respondents speak about stories involved in each setting: "The stories that we hear in church are the ones basically that teach us a lesson, that have some sort of moral value behind them, where the stories you hear on soaps are one story after the other of persons doing the wrong thing and messing up their lives. . . . I mean, how can you do all those things and not end up in utter despair? If—and TV might be responsible for some of the young persons totally destroying themselves, relationships wise" (2). Whereas church provides security, television is perceived as dangerous.

Some participants note feeling embarrassed when watching worship programs on TV. In describing his response to one program, a respondent notes: "Sometimes I was almost embarrassed about it. . . .It was kind of like opening to the world feelings that I felt should be private" (4). Other respondents also note feeling embarrassed watching televised worship. The distinction between public and private feelings in the above respondent's remark may help explicate the reason for this embarrassment. As Meyrowitz (1985, p. 287) explains: "Television takes already public events and makes them more public. Perhaps we should distinguish between 'private-public' events and 'public-public' events. By 'private-public,' I mean those events that involve public actions, but are still isolated in a particular time-space frame, and, therefore, are largely inaccessible to those not physically present. By 'public-public,' I mean those events that are carried beyond the time-space frame by electronic media, and therefore are accessible to almost everyone."

The respondent's comment suggests that he perceives ecclesiastic experience as best kept as a "private-public" event, such as when he is in church with a congregation. The televising of worship makes that which should be "private-public" "public-public." Thus, in opening to the world what he feels should be private, he gets embarrassed.

The presence of others in both televisual and ecclesiastic settings may at times be disruptive. In church, babies crying and people staring are distracting; in TV viewing, other persons' presence, movements, or comments may disturb the intentional directedness toward the television. In ecclesiastic experience, however, intersubjective awareness is at times specifically engaged, and perceived as essential. In televisual experience, persons often "turn to television in order to withdraw from being with other people" (Nelson, 1989a, p. 394). While watching television, one feels uncomfortable in the presence of another person who may monitor and critically assess one's responses. In televisual experience, viewers interact with the television as other, by talking back, crying, laughing, etc. When one does so alone, one is free to make whatever gestures occur naturally; if other persons are present, one monitors oneself (Nelson, 1989a).

Since expressive gestures in church are made together with others in a group, a person's gestures are less likely to be scrutinized. Intentional focus is ideally directed to the group expression as a whole, not to individual efforts. For example, one respondent notes that she will not sing anywhere but in church because there her off-key singing blends with that of others who are just as discordant. By immersing oneself in group expression, concern with others' critical focus is deflected. If one is made to feel under another's control in ecclesiastic experience, the institutional other or God is revealed to control respondents. Control by these others is actually appreciated: "Thank you, God, for making me come" (6).

Coming to church is important to ecclesiastic experience—taking the time and effort to actually move one's body to the church setting. Respondents feel obliged to attend; since God has done so much for them, they should make the effort to be present. Being bodily present allows them to "lend their presence" (5) to the community gesture. The actual bodily presence participants experience in church is what is most missing in televised worship for respondents. The respondents note: "I wouldn't get that feeling" (3); "The TV cuts me off too much, I don't feel like I'm a member or that I'm belonging to the congregation that's in the TV service" (1); "You're not there, you're not a part of it, you're on the outside looking in" (3). Respondents need to feel as a tangible part of the community, to be able to touch others, to co-inhabit the same space with other congregants, to conform/con-form, with the group. Televised worship is not able to give them that "feeling" (ability to touch/sense) that is so important in the ecclesiastic setting.

In church, interaction is essential—facing others and having them face you, touching others and having them touch you, hearing others and having them hear you. Far from an explicit attempt to remove oneself from others, church is an effort to be in community, to be able to "get a feel" for other persons (1), to be corporeally present and immersed in what becomes the unified body of the group. With television, interaction is either discouraged, in the case of other persons present ("you don't actually face other people" [6]), or unattainable, in the case of the others present via the television. As one participant says in regard to watching religious television, "You don't have any response that registers with them" (5). There is a sense of being outside of one's body, of "feeling like you were just a spectator" (4). One researcher has observed televisual experience is like having one's "eyes out of your head" (Nelson, 1989a, p. 398–401). Whereas church involves a corporeal immersion, television viewing ideally involves a bracketing of the body. In televisual experience, persons have a sense of being freed from the captive body. Persons may escape from themselves, their problems, and others, in a "pleasurable lethargy" (Nelson, 1989a, p. 395). When televisual experience achieves this freeing, people feel "immersed" in "another world" (Nelson, 1989a, pp. 393, 399).

Feeling freed and immersed is thematically similar to ecclesiastic experience. Nonetheless, the particular sense of freedom and immersion involved in ecclesiastic and televisual experience is different. As noted above, immersion may be disturbed by the presence of other bodies in the television viewing situation.

Televisual experience is often an escape from others. In church, the presence of others is essential to the experience. A congregant's ability to achieve a sense of freedom from self in the in-church setting is dependent on the presence of a community into which one may dissolve, with which one may conform (con-form).

Recall the above respondent's comment that watching television "does not make you feel secure." Although one's body remains in place, the televisually captivated self is moved from place to place; one may be sitting on a couch in a living room, but the environment that is perceived as nearest is the televisual one, in which the self is moved from place to place (Nelson, 1989a). Having forgotten the body, the freed self is moved by the succeeding images from here to there. The freed self lacks security while captivated in televisual experience, away from the forgotten body. The same respondent says she feels secure in church. The freedom she feels in this setting is a coextension of her body with others and the world. In the presence of God one feels "in touch" with the "ground" of all being, "connected. . .to the universe" (6). One's body is secure, and ecclesiastic freedom is experienced as an awareness of one's body extending to all other things, the body's corporeal intertwining with God, what "connects. . .it all" (6).

The directedness of freedom is distinguishable in both situations. Televisual experience is an immersion in another world. As one respondent says regarding religious television, "Their views are not my worldviews" (1), a phrase which distinguishes between two worlds. Yet despite the closeness of this world, in televisual experience one can't "get that feeling" (3), a feeling that is so integral to ecclesiastic experience. While televisual experience may, like church, expand one's horizon of awareness, one is not physically coextensive with the horizon opened up. Televisual experience immerses persons in another world, whereas ecclesiastic experience grounds one in the present world, with which one's body is coextensive. In ecclesiastic experience, the world in which one participates one coinhabits with others, in the same world. In church, one con-forms with those present and with the world on which one is grounded. God, the "ground" of everything (6), is that which connects all things together. In short, while televisual experience brings the distant close (or brings one close to the distant), ecclesiastic experience transforms the world, making all things new and interconnected; there is no distance to be brought close, since all things are one.

References

Idhe, D. (1973). *Sense and significance.* Pittsburgh, PA: Duquesne University Press.

Lanigan, R. L. (1988). *Phenomenology of communication: Merleau-Ponty's thematics in communicology and semiology.* Pittsburgh, PA: Duquesne University Press.

Lanigan, R. L. (1992). *The human science of communicology: A phenomenology of discourse in Foucault and Merleau-Ponty.* Pittsburgh, PA: Duquesne University Press.

Merleau-Ponty, M. (1968). *The visible and the invisible.* Translated by A. Lingis. Evanston: Northwestern University Press. (Original work published 1964.)

Meyrowitz, J. (1985). *No sense of place: The impact of electronic media on social behavior.* New York: Oxford University Press.

Nelson, J. L. (1989a). Eyes out of your head: On televisual experience. *Critical Studies in Mass Communication* 6: 387–403.

Nelson, J. L. (1989b). Phenomenology as feminist methodology: Explicating interviews. In K. Carter and C. Spitzak (Eds.), *Doing research on women's communication,* (pp. 221–410). Norwood, NJ: Ablex.

Ong, W. J. (1967). *The presence of the word: Some prolegomena for cultural and religious history.* Minneapolis: University of Minnesota Press.

Patton, M. Q. (1990). *Qualitative evaluation and research methods* (2nd ed.). Newbury Park, CA: Sage.

Schrag, C. O. (1969). *Experience and being.* Evanston, IL: Northwestern University Press.

Schutz, A. (1967). *The phenomenology of the social world,* G. Walsh and F. Lehnert (Eds.). Evanston, IL: Northwestern University Press. (Original work published 1932.)

Straus, E. W. (1966). *Phenomenological psychology* (E. Eng, Trans.). New York: Basic Books.

Self-Reflection:
An Essential Quality for Phenomenological Researchers

Richard F. Wolff
Dowling College, Oakdale, New York

Phenomenological research emphasizes the lived experience not only of the re-search participants but also that of the researcher. For the research participants, the lived experience is that of the phenomenon being studied—in this case of my study, ecclesiastic experience. For the researcher, the lived experience is the pro-cess of phenomenological procedure itself—the methodological movement among description, reduction, and interpretation. This, I believe, is one of the trickiest as-pects of semiotic-phenomenological research for beginning researchers to mas-ter—I know it was for me. It involves fully comprehending and practicing the ways in which phenomenological methodology is an embodied process.

For example, one practical matter concerns knowing how many interviews to complete. First-time phenomenological researchers may be uncertain as to how many interviews should be conducted before "beginning" the thematizations. In phenomenological terms, at what point does the description end and reduction begin? The answer lies not in some externally sanctioned number, but inside the one who embodies the research process. If there were an ideal number, knowing when to stop would be easy. Since there is not, this creates an uneasy, problem-atic situation for phenomenological researchers—particularly for first-timers. I found that one must have sensitivity, self-awareness, and confidence. Since phe-nomenological methodology is an embodied process, the researcher must engage in self-reflection to understand how the process is unfolding. The operative dis-tinction is between *decision* and *recognition*. A researcher comes to understand that one does not "decide" when the description is over and the reduction is about to begin; rather, one *recognizes* that the reduction *has already begun* and that the description is in the process of ending.

In conducting my interviews on the lived experience of in-church and televised worship, I found myself looking for some officially sanctioned number of interviews that would be approved by current mentors and future critics. This was a mistake. The proper place to look was at the process I was embodying. Thus, after conducting several interviews with research participants, I found myself awash in description. After a few more, I recognized some themes emerging in my own reflections. Finally, when I found myself less awash in description and more awash in emerging themes, I knew the reduction had begun, and that I ought to conduct the remaining interviews I had scheduled and begin formally to analyze the interview transcripts. In the case of my study of worshippers' experience, I perceived that the reduction had begun after about eight discussions with research participants; ultimately I completed a dozen interviews.

Another challenge for the beginning researcher is to know how to conduct the research interviews. Where does one draw the line between emphasizing one's own topical protocol and allowing the participants themselves to guide the discussion? Also, which items will receive the most attention in the interviews? Will the researcher try to spend equal time on all items on the protocol or emphasize particular items? Here once again I learned to balance sensitivity and self-assurance. During my first formal interview, I realized how much one should be guided by one's research participants. Proceeding through the items on my protocol, I came to the request for the churchgoer to describe a worship service. I was unprepared for two things: how much time this first interviewee devoted to describing every aspect of a worship service, and how essential gaining this rich, detailed description was going to be to my study. I learned how important it is to come prepared *and* open-minded for the first few interviews. The way these early discussions emerge gives the researcher insight into how best to conduct subsequent interviews.

Finally, I learned to accept that all research has its limitations, and that one should be ready to accept critical responses to one's research while also using that criticism to strengthen further research. One limitation of my study, for example, is that it reflects the lived experience of a particular kind of churchgoer. How might the experience of a worshipper in the free-church tradition, or the Baptist tradition, or the Catholic tradition differ in their descriptions of ecclesiastic experience? What insight would be gained by comparing these experiences? How might studies of churchgoers in these traditions unveil areas of my interpretation that are unique to the experience and description provided by members of the predominantly white Lutheran church I interviewed? Even more fascinating would be an awareness of which aspects of the interpretation would *not* change.

For example, one interesting revelation occurred to me while interviewing one member of a church tradition outside of Lutheranism. Curious about potential differences, I conducted one interview with a woman from a predominantly African-American Baptist congregation. When she described her church experience, she emphasized the free-form call-and-response style of interaction, where the congregation members vocalize their responses to the worship leaders. I realized how her experience differed from that of those in my study, where silence and conformity were more the model of behavior. I then realized that although the descriptions/experiences of these congregants were different, the interpretation would remain the same. The churchgoers in my study emphasized how conformity to the group expression was an important aspect of their patterned responses and periods of silence—those not remaining silent were a distraction. The Baptist woman I interviewed noted that all members of her congregation felt inspired and compelled to respond to the preacher, and that those not responding were not full participants in the group expression—those remaining silent were a distraction. I realized then that although the descriptions of these worship experiences differed (silence-as-conformity to group expression and speech-as-conformity with group expression), the interpretations of the experiences were the same—one's own actions needed to correspond with those of others so that a group expression and identity could emerge. Pursuing the limitations of my initial study revealed exciting areas for further investigation and insight. Hence, I realized how criticism helps a researcher achieve new insights into the phenomenon being studied.

Above all, during my research I found it comforting to note that qualitative research values self-reflection. I knew that any concerns that arose as I conducted my research would be welcomed, and expected, by other qualitative researchers; that sharing my concerns was part of the process and helpful; and that some uncertainty as one proceeds through the phenomenological research process is healthy and is in fact an indication that one is experiencing the necessary ambiguities inherent in conducting qualitative research.

6

A Phenomenological Investigation of "Good" Supervision Events

Vaughn E. Worthen, Brian W. McNeill

The learning and acquisition of counseling skills and the formation of a professional counselor identity are two of the most important functions of graduate training in counseling psychology, and psychotherapy supervision plays a central role in this learning. Although much effort is devoted to counseling and supervision activities, and theory building is in progress, little in the way of research has been conducted that examines the experience of "good" psychotherapy supervision events from the perspective of supervisees. What does the experience of good supervision consist of for supervisees? Are there any central factors that must be present for good supervision experiences to occur? Supervisees' experience of good psychotherapy supervision is essentially a question of personal meaning, and the phenomenological research method lends itself well to the investigation of personal meaning.

Phenomenological inquiry is very similar to the interviewing techniques central to the training of counseling psychologists. Thus, inquiry into the experience of good supervision events is a natural methodological extension of researchers' previous training experiences. Also, most supervisees have a very personal investment in supervision and developing their therapeutic skills. Therefore, they are apt to participate actively in describing their supervision experiences. The interview "dialogue" offers the opportunity for immediate clarification and further elaboration and probing. As new findings emerge, researchers can pursue those lines of inquiry, because the goal of the investigation is to understand the expe-

Vaughn E. Worthen & Brian W. McNeill. (1996). "A Phenomenological Investigation of 'Good' Supervision Events." *Journal of Counseling Psychology, 43,* 25–34. Copyright © 1996 by the American Psychological Association. Reprinted with permission.

rienced phenomenon as fully as possible. Knowledge is arrived at through an inductive process, leading from specific observations to the identification of general patterns (Patton, 1990). The essence of discovery-oriented research is the ability to see the depth and intricacies of the phenomenon within individual cases.

Past research has spent little time examining the experience of good psychotherapy supervision, in part because of the design characteristics of traditional research methodologies, which are not devised to ask questions about personal meaning. What has been lacking is the application of discovery-oriented research methodologies in the examination and description of supervision phenomena as a means of both testing the soundness of theory and discovering salient supervision components and processes that might contribute to theory building and effective practice (Borders, 1989; Holloway & Hosford, 1983; Stoltenberg, McNeill, & Creather, 1994). An in-depth understanding of what events constitute good psychotherapy supervision, as experienced by supervisees, is necessary if one is to fully comprehend the relevant and crucial aspects of supervision that contribute to the acquisition of counseling skills and the development of a professional identity.

Research on Good Psychotherapy Supervision

Past investigations have focused on the question of satisfaction with supervision, providing some indications that what constitutes good supervision varies according to the developmental level of trainees. Two general factors have been identified for positive supervision experiences: a good supervisory relationship and attention to the task of developing counseling skills. Good supervisory relationships consist of warmth, acceptance, respect, understanding, and trust (Hutt, Scott, & King, 1983; Martin, Goodyear, & Newton, 1987; Miller & Oetting, 1966), particularly for beginning trainees (Heppner & Roehlke, 1984). Good supervisors self-disclose (Black, 1988) and create an atmosphere of experimentation and allowance for mistakes (Allen, Szollos, & Williams, 1986; Hutt et al., 1983; Nelson, 1978). Beginning trainees prefer more attention devoted to developing intake skills (Heppner & Roehlke, 1984), didactic training in counseling (Worthington & Roehlke, 1979), and more time spent on developing self-awareness (Nelson, 1978). Intermediate trainees desire assistance with developing alternative conceptualization skills (for example, Heppner and Roehlke, 1984), more emphasis on personal development than technical skills, working within a cohesive theory, and clear communication about expectations (Allen et al., 1986). Advanced trainees prefer to examine more complex issues of personal development, transference–countertransference, parallel processes, and client and counselor resistance and defensiveness (McNeill & Worthen, 1989).

Supervision environment factors are also viewed as important in contributing to positive perceptions of supervision. Environmental discriminators of quality include longer duration of training, more weekly contact time, more frequent contacts per week, and the occurrence of good supervision experiences later in the training sequence (Allen et al., 1986). Nelson (1978) also found that trainees preferred supervisors who showed interest in supervision, had experience as a therapist, were conducting regular therapy, and possessed technical or theoretical knowledge.

What is apparent from the supervision literature is that few studies have specifically examined what is perceived as good supervision by supervisees beyond characteristics associated with general dependent measures of satisfaction with supervision determined on an a priori basis. Thus, the purpose of this investigation was to further explore the phenomenological experience of what elements or events constitute good supervision for trainees.

Method

Participants

Four women and four men of European American ethnicity were interviewed for this study. To ensure some variation in training experiences, we solicited and selected participants from three counseling psychology doctoral programs approved by the American Psychological Association (APA) and three APA-approved counseling center internship sites in the Midwest. Trainees ranged in age from twenty-three to fifty-four years, were in their third to seventh year of graduate education, had completed two to seventeen semesters of counseling experience, and had completed two to eight semesters of supervision resulting in levels of training that may be conceptualized as intermediate to advanced. Their supervisors were four men and four women with one to ten years of supervisory experience. Criteria for participant selection included willingness to participate in a tape-recorded interview and availability and willingness to participate in a follow-up interview if necessary, use of English as primary language, ability to articulate the experience of good supervision, and current counseling supervision in the practicum or internship. Participants were volunteers and were not paid for any part of their involvement in the research. All trainees who were invited to participate accepted the invitation.

Researchers

At the time of this investigation, Vaughn Worthen, a European-American, had completed his doctoral course work in counseling psychology, which included both didactic and experiential training in developmental conceptualizations of the supervision process, and was supervising doctoral trainees during his predoctoral internship. His current work includes ongoing provision of clinical services, as well as training and supervision of graduate students. He views supervision as consisting of the belief that supervisee needs vary as supervisees gain experience and that supervisory roles must be adjusted if both the supervision tasks and the supervisory relationship are to contribute to good supervision. Supervision helps a trainee become a better counselor; more broadly, it helps trainees form a counselor identity, and trust and anxiety are mitigating factors in good supervision.

Brian W. McNeill is of mixed Mexican American and European American ethnicity and has ten years of postdoctoral experience as a therapist, supervisor, and researcher investigating developmental models of clinical supervision.

Procedure

Interview. All interviews were conducted by Vaughn Worthen in person. Practicum-level trainees were interviewed approximately three-fourths of the way through their second supervised doctoral practicum experience. Two interns were interviewed in the middle of their second semester, and the other two were interviewed toward the end of the second semester, thus allowing trainees time to establish a supervisory relationship. Each participant was asked to read and sign an informed-consent form before being interviewed.

A research question was formulated to guide the interview. The initial statement made to participants was as follows: "Please describe for me as completely, clearly, and concretely as you can, an experience during this semester when you felt you received good psychotherapy supervision." The participant was then invited to elaborate on that comment, and the interviewer's role was to help facilitate the articulation of the good supervision description.

Adequate time was allowed so that interviews would not be constrained by an imposed time limit. No interview was more than an hour in length, and most averaged between forty-five and fifty minutes. Each interview was recorded with two tape recorders to ensure that the interview was taped adequately, thus avoiding lost data.

Participants were asked to clarify and elaborate phrases and words the researcher did not understand or in case of ambiguity or lack of clarity. The researcher attempted to maintain a focus on understanding the experience as it was being related by the participant. Examples of the interviewer's prompts for clarification and elaboration included, "Can you describe what you felt like?" "Can you recall what it was like for you as you came into that supervisory session and were getting ready to play this tape?" "And how did he show that understanding?" "How did you move to that broader level?" A strong attempt was made to make sure questions did not lead the interviewees toward specific or predetermined conclusions but, rather, led them to clarify and elaborate.

When the interviewer perceived that the experience had been fully articulated, the following question was asked: "Is there anything else that you would like to add that we haven't already addressed?" Any further descriptions were explored, and the interview was concluded.

Transcription. Tapes were transcribed verbatim and checked for accuracy by a second individual.

Transcript Analysis. Analysis of the transcribed interviews followed a modified pattern outlined by Giorgi (1985, 1989) and demonstrated by Wertz (1983, 1985). The essence of this pattern is to break down transcribed interviews into units that can be more easily analyzed. These units are called *meaning units*.

Each analysis consisted of examining the descriptions until patterns of good supervision could be discerned. After each individual experience had been analyzed, all individual experiences were examined to ascertain the essence of good supervision for all of the supervisees. Analysis of individual good supervision experiences followed a seven-step procedure. After completion of this phase of analysis, group analyses of the general meaning structure for supervisees were conducted in a four-step procedure. All analyses were performed by Vaughn Worthen under the immediate supervision of Brian W. McNeill. In addition, because the investigation was part of Vaughn Worthen's dissertation, input was provided by four other committee members, three of whom possessed extensive experience as supervisors and clinicians and one whose primary research focus is the application of qualitative research methods in education. In addition, a review of the analyses and interpretation of the results was provided by an external auditor well versed in both supervision and qualitative research. Any disagreements regarding analyses and interpretation were resolved through discussion and consensus between the two authors.

Individual Interviews: Developing a Situated Meaning Structure

Step 1: Obtaining a Sense of the Whole. Before the analysis was conducted, it was important to get a sense for the entire interview within its context. Each interview was listened to and read three or four times before analysis commenced.

Step 2: Identifying Meaning Units. This step consisted of identifying meaning units by listening to and reading the transcribed interview and identifying experienced shifts in meaning. Each shift in meaning was marked by a slash on the transcribed manuscript.

Step 3: Defining Relevant and Psychologically Explicit Meaning Units. At this point, meaning units were examined for relevancy to the investigation of good psychotherapy supervision. Irrelevant meaning units were discarded, as were some of the redundant meaning units that could be identified at this point. Each meaning unit was grammatically rephrased, if necessary, to more directly express the supervisee's meaning.

Step 4: Integration of Meaning Units. An important element of the analysis was to understand the temporal sequence of the events described in the interview, as suggested by Wertz (1983, 1985). Because an interview does not typically proceed along a linear thought process, it was important to organize interview data within a logical and contextual relationship. Meaning units were placed into a first-person narrative retelling of the good supervision experience.

Step 5: Articulating the Meaning Units. This step consisted of translating the participants' naive (that is, unanalyzed) description of their experience into psychologically relevant meanings bearing on their experience of good supervision. Thus, participant responses were examined with the intent of understanding expressed and implied meanings. These meanings were put into terminology that expressed the meanings in more direct psychological language. This process consisted of moving back and forth from data to meanings. Derived meanings were, in essence, tested against the raw interview data to determine whether they were supported by the data. This movement from concrete data to abstraction of meaning produced the articulate meanings.

Step 6: The Situated Meaning Structure. From the articulated meaning units arrived at through Step 5, derived meanings were integrated in a third-person narrative retelling of the events as expressed in more psychologically explicit language. The result was a meaningful description of the experience of good supervision for the individual supervisee. The term *situated* refers to meaning derived from the context of a specific situation or experience.

Step 7: The Essence of the Experience of Good Supervision. A final step in the individual analyses of the transcribed interviews consisted of refining the description into its most distilled and concise form. This was accomplished in the form of the following question: "What is absolutely essential for this experience of good psychotherapy supervision, for which if it were missing this would not represent the experience of good supervision?" This step in the analysis distanced the findings a bit from the context of the specific experience so as to distill the essential components of the experience. An example from one of our trainees illustrates this final step:

> Dave experiences a sense of discomfort with his personally defined therapeutic role. He then provides an implicit and ambiguous invitation to his supervisor in an effort to solicit understanding and assistance and avoid perceived criticism. He experiences genuine support, empathy, and validation from his supervisor, which facilitates a nondefensive perspective regarding experienced "unacceptable" feelings and the consequent development of a metaperspective. The relieving of discomfort and tension allows for new learning. This metaperspective is experienced as freeing and reinvigorates interest in original motivations for helping others but newly endows those original motivations with greater complexity. The horizon of therapeutic possibilities is expanded as Dave becomes forward looking with positive anticipation and planning for the next therapeutic contact with his client. The line between client responsibility and counselor facilitation is then redefined.

Group Analyses

After the individual interviews had been analyzed, an analysis and comparison of commonalities and differences between each of the interviews was performed. This procedure allowed general findings to emerge regarding the experiences of supervision for the supervisees. The analysis was conducted in four steps.

Step 1: Individual Events of Good Supervision. Step 1 consisted of examining all individual participant findings (Steps 6 and 7 of the preceding section) and then creating an inclusive list of events of each participant's meaning structure with his or her name beside the good supervision events. Thus, an exhaustive list of good supervision events was developed.

Step 2: Common Events of Good Supervision. Step 2 consisted of identifying and compiling a list of inclusive good supervision events shared in common by two or more participants with the participants' names identified for each element.

Step 3: Collective Events of Good Supervision. At this point, only those good supervision events held collectively by six or more of the participants were retained.

Step 4: General Meaning Structure for the Experience of Good Supervision. Those events that remained after Step 3 were used to generate a full narrative description of the general experience of good supervision for supervisees. A sequence of themes constituting good supervision events was then identified, and these themes were tied together in a temporal order of appearance.

Results

Good Supervision General Meaning Structure for Trainees

Good psychotherapy supervision unfolds from a level of confidence ranging from fluctuating to basic groundedness with an aversion to overt evaluation. There is at least an implied, and sometimes overtly expressed, desire for rewarding supervision from those who have a reported history of dissatisfaction with supervision. The therapeutic process is viewed on a continuum from some disillusionment to a fundamental sense of efficacy. With these elements in place, the supervisee experiences a disruption in the "usual" self-as-professional operation, with the concurrent feeling of anxiety-induced emotional arousal and an often opaquely perceived "needing." This is experienced as a state of inadequacy that is responded to from a level of global examination of therapeutic self-functioning up to a domain-specific problem focus. This state of disruption is pivotally addressed within a discernibly nonjudgmental, empathizing, supporting, and validating supervisory stance that acts to normalize the struggle. As a result, the supervisee feels a "freeing" that facilitates reduced self-protectiveness and increased receptivity to supervisory input. This sense of freeing allows for increased participation in supervision and fosters a nondefensive analysis of self and situation, as well as subsequent reexamination of therapeutic and professional assumptions, enabling the acquisition of a metaperspective from which a more comprehensive therapeutic pattern is revealed. Self-confidence is strengthened and endowed with greater complexity and stability. Consequently, the range of therapeutic conceptualizing and intervening is expanded. Positive anticipatory planning follows new awareness and incorporates new understandings, with an excitement to reengage actively again in the previous struggle. The supervisory alliance is energized and strengthened with an experienced invigoration and impetus for continued professional development.

Phases and Themes of Good Supervision Events

On the basis of the group analyses resulting in the general meaning structure for all of the trainees, the themes of good supervision events were viewed conceptually as involving four sequentially connected phases. The first phase was the *existential baseline,* or the context from which the events of good supervision emerged. *Setting the stage* was seen as a second phase, in which events leading up to good supervision were experienced. The third phase was labeled the *good supervision experience.* This was the pivotal phase in which the influence of supervisor and supervisee factors interacted to create within the supervisee a sense that something positive and eventful had occurred within supervision. The final phase was designated *outcomes of good supervision.* The effects of the good supervision experiences were manifested in this phase. Themes reflecting events identified in the general meaning structure for trainees during these four phases are depicted in Table 6.1 and discussed, along with illustrative examples, in more detail in the sections to follow.

Summary of Good Psychotherapy Supervision Events

Existential Baseline. A general sense of confidence for trainees prevailed, although more experienced supervisees appeared to have a greater grounding in their confidence. This confidence level is reflected in a statement by Kevin (all names are pseudonyms): "I was feeling like when I came out of my doctoral program, that I had a pretty good sense of how my theoretical orientation was working at the time with clients, basic attending skills, those types of things I was feeling pretty good with. But I felt like I was ready to move into a new realm, more in therapy and in supervision." Rebecca, another intern, expressed it this way: "I felt fairly competent in this situation but wanted to expand my view of what might be effective in this particular case."

Interestingly, three of the four practicum-level students made comments indicating some sense of demoralization or disillusionment with conducting therapy, as illustrated in the following comments: "I wasn't real happy; even my clients seemed all the same and I just wasn't really that into it" (Dave) and "[My interaction with the faculty] kind of made me feel, um, just really lost. I think, as a student and kind of lost about my abilities and the things I think are my strengths" (Colette). Interns, on the other hand, displayed no sense of demoralization or disillusionment and demonstrated a basic sense of efficacy in the counseling process.

Participants also reported an aversion to an overt evaluative stance by their supervisors. Moreover, most participants made reference to previous unrewarding supervision experiences. In relation to these experiences, there was also a hopeful desire for a qualitatively different supervisory relationship.

Themes for supervisees in the existential baseline phase directly influenced the way the following themes played themselves out in the other phases. It appears that the existential baseline acted as the ground on which the figure of later good supervision experiences emerged.

Table 6.1. Four Phases of a Good Supervision Experience for Advanced Supervisees:
The Supervisee's Perspective

Phase	Description
Existential baseline	Fluctuating to grounded level of confidence; aversion to overt evaluation; desire for rewarding supervision; previous unrewarding supervision; disillusionment to sense of efficacy with therapeutic process
Setting the stage	Sensed inadequacy consisting of disruption in the usual, anxiety-induced emotional arousal, and perceived needing; global to domain-specific response to sensed inadequacy
Good supervision experience	Supervisory relationship experienced as empathic, nonjudgmental, and validating, with encouragement to explore and experiment; struggle normalized; sense of freeing consisting of reduced self-protectiveness and receptivity to supervisory input; nondefensive analysis; reexamination of assumptions; acquisition of a metaperspective
Outcomes of good supervision	Strengthened confidence; refined professional identity; increased therapeutic perception; expanded ability to conceptualize and intervene; positive anticipation to reengage in the struggle; strengthened supervisory alliance

Setting the Stage. If it can be said that the existential baseline was the ground, then the next major theme, a sensed inadequacy, acted to separate the figure and ground and provide a focus for supervision. This theme was composed of three interrelated events consisting of disruption in the usual, anxiety-induced emotional arousal, and a perceived needing.

Disruption in the usual can be viewed as an event or experience that intrudes and provokes a disorder in what was the taken-for-granted operation of therapeutic or professional activities. This disruption acted as a focusing agent on an area of concern. The area of concern can be quite broad, consisting of such elements as a perceived deficit, a normal developmental professional task, a concern with the supervisory relationship, or enhancement or development of a new skill. An example of this disruption in the usual was demonstrated in the following comment by Dave: "It was just totally out of the realm of any kind of client experience I'd ever had before. Sometimes I'd been frustrated, or this or that, but it was in a working context. This I wanted to be over with. I didn't want this client."

Perhaps as a result of an observed difference in the level of groundedness in confidence or the sense of demoralization and disillusionment between practicum and intern participants, it appeared that three of the four practicum students made global responses to their sense of inadequacy. These global attributions included general questioning of their sense of efficacy as therapists. Interns, on the other hand, made more domain-specific responses to their sense of inadequacy. This domain-specific disruption in the usual is illustrated in the following two intern passages:

> *There was some kind of block in therapy. We reached a point where I felt like I was offering those things that were really necessary for us to move on and to continue a good working relationship, but she wasn't, I don't think matching my desire for her to experience that or to receive that. It was the first time I had ever worked with [a client] that had experienced incest.* (Kevin)
> *I had a sense of connecting with this person immediately, but not knowing whether the things that I normally do with a client were going to be as effective with this client or not, because I was not feeling sure of the culture or background.* (Rebecca)

Perhaps the motivation to address this disruption of the usual would be minimal unless the other two elements of sensed inadequacy—anxiety-induced emotional arousal and a perceived needing—were in attendance. Trainees reported feeling distress about the disruption, which activated and made them aware of a need that was sometimes experienced only opaquely. For example, Dave stated that "I went into supervision and I was disturbed by the reaction I'd had [emotional arousal]." He then elaborated: "And I didn't know what to do with it. I didn't have any kind of immediate answer or solution to it, with what I was going to do with my anger and what would I do with my client, what kind of process should go on, what changes should be made or anything. I was just really stuck with it [perceived needing]."

It appears that these three identified elements of sensed inadequacy need to be activated to set the stage for openness to supervisory input and new learning to occur. It also appears that these elements can be activated by naturally occurring events within the counseling or supervisory relationship or by the supervisor's strategic interventions. What is clear from this study is that this sensed inadequacy preceded the good supervision experience. It appears that interns are better able to direct the focus of supervision to address their sensed inadequacy and that they typically perceive this inadequacy as domain specific; practicum trainees feel a more global impact on their sense of inadequacy.

Good Supervision Experience. The most pivotal and crucial component of good supervision experiences that was clearly evident in every case studied was the quality of the supervisory relationship. All trainees described the supervisor as conveying an attitude that manifested empathy, a nonjudgmental stance toward them, a sense of validation or affirmation, and encouragement to explore and experiment. The sensed inadequacy discussed earlier set the stage for a learning experience. However, without a positive supervisory relationship that invited openness to learning, it is likely that learning from this anxiety-arousing experience would have been minimized. Supervisory relationship events and dynamics contributed to this supervision learning experience. According to Dave, "She kind of, empathized with, and said that she'd also felt some strong feelings towards her [the client] and could see why I had these emotions and why she did too." Tina's comment was similar: "Once I realized that he agreed with me, okay, or he showed that he could understand why I felt like I was giving Band-Aids. So he showed understanding." Colette's comments reflected similar relationship dynamics: "And what was so great, was that my supervisor was really affirming of and validating of my ability to speak clearly. I felt very much understood by her and I felt also like she appreciated those abilities that I had taken pride in the past and which I had felt, I just hadn't felt were being recognized at all, at any level."

It is likely that this kind of relationship can be developed only when concern about self and performance are minimized and anxiety is diminished, as the following comments by Jan illustrate: "Mary was just really great at kind of somehow calming me down," and "She just really gave me permission to think about things without pressuring me to do anything." Rebecca reported that "rather than launching into what I could do, I was first given that kind of step up by the supervisor and reassurance and it seemed to take off from there."

In many of the cases, it was hinted at or hypothesized that without this type of relationship being present, the supervisees would likely have undergone a different kind of experience. For example, Dave declared: "But if she'd given me a look of kind of like, 'you're angry,' I would have wanted to put the file away. I don't want to have that client. I would have had to, like I did the week before, not think about it." And Kevin stated: "When I talk about that process, when we play with these process pieces or when we would stop the tape at whatever times, that couldn't have happened, I don't think, if it didn't feel like a real collegial relationship, if I didn't feel like I was respected at a level that, I guess, I wanted to be respected at, or if I was going to move on as a professional."

These findings also suggest that the desire and need for a supportive supervisory relationship are ever present in supervision. Although all supervisees value and benefit from a supportive supervisory environment, this need is not necessarily expressed directly (Black, 1988).

Trainees believed that their supervisors helped normalize their "struggle." This was often accomplished by a personal self-disclosure from their supervisor. In this study, self-disclosure of the supervisor played a significant role in helping supervisees, especially those with less experience, reduce negative attributions of their behavior and decrease anxiety by allowing them to "see" into the supervisor's behavior and thinking, thus normalizing and tacitly relabeling "mistakes" as learning experiences. Dave's supervisor shared her reaction to his client, which was similar to Dave's own reaction, as well as disclosing a similar experience from her own training: "I think two things happened. The first, my supervisor helped me normalize what I was feeling and that it was OK as a therapist to be having [angry feelings]. . . . And she also disclosed her own experience of, I'm not sure whether she was in practicum or intern, where she had some countertransference."

Jan also described her supervisor as providing a normalizing experience: "I guess that was normalizing in a way, like this is OK, you're going to get through this. This is how it works, you know."

Participants also experienced a freeing, the next significant theme. Jan felt freed from her self-imposed restrictions, which were brought on by anxiety and fear, and felt a renewed energy to engage in the previously feared and burdensome tasks of completing a dissertation and beginning a job search. Kevin described the experience of freeing as helping him move beyond some of his self-imposed constraints regarding therapy. He reported being able to develop a deeper level of perception and understanding. In his words: "And working through this process with him, I experienced [a better understanding of what was going on in therapy]. And the way I experienced that, was that it was freeing. It was like I can move up now to the next level or a deeper level."

Dave also felt freed from his assumptions of overresponsibility for his client and thus could see how to intervene with his client differently: "I remember it was kind of freeing at the end. It was like, I'm going to throw this back on your lap, if you don't want to do it, that's OK."

The theme of freeing comprises two separate but related events. Reduced self-protectiveness was evident as supervisees felt supported and came to sense the supervisor's benevolent interest in promoting learning and development. As supervisees perceived less need for self-protectiveness, they concurrently experienced the second important element of the freeing experience, an increased receptivity to supervisory input. These findings are similar to Black's (1988) conclusion that reduced defensiveness and a strong learning alliance contribute to supervisees' perceptions of supervision effectiveness. A statement made by Dave illustrates these two themes at work: "What changed was, as soon as she like said 'Oh me too,' it let me have, it was like, now we can deal with it and talk about it." He further stated, "It kind of took the heat off, you know, is this my individual reaction?. . .So it really let me have this issue in supervision. I felt like it was OK to be talking about them." Mike showed a clear pattern of high self-protectiveness to begin with, followed by an increased responsiveness to his supervisor. Mike's initial guardedness is reflected by the following statement: "I felt a little bit vulnerable, that's probably due to it being my first quarter. I didn't know how supervision was going to go or if I was going to get picked apart. . .I felt like I needed to defend my orientation." As Mike's supervisor responded to this expression of defensiveness from him with a nondefensive acceptance, Mike felt a greater openness to listen and possibly learn from his supervisor: "Maybe that modeled something for me, I don't know, maybe his being willing to hear what I had to say, maybe it modeled, maybe I should consider what he has to say." Suffice it to say that when supervisees felt a sense of safety and support, there was increased ability to participate actively in supervision and receptiveness to supervisory input.

The preceding themes set the stage for the next three related themes: non-defensive analysis, reexamination of assumptions, and acquisition of a meta-perspective. Because supervision is concerned with the acquisition of skills and the development of a professional identity, it is important that supervisees be able to examine themselves as honestly as possible. As long as the supervisee feels a need to protect or defend himself or herself, the likelihood of honest introspection and examination of therapeutic activities and beliefs is minimized.

Nondefensive analysis occurred as supervisees felt safe in exploring and experimenting. Colette, a practicum trainee, originally felt an intense self-referent threat in her encounter with a faculty member. She felt misunderstood and invalidated. This intense self-referent, emotionally charged confusion dissipated as she experienced congruence between her self-perception and the understanding expressed by her supervisor. The experience became detached from its prior self-referent threat as it was given the status of "chalk it up to experience." In Kevin's case, he was able to examine his feelings more "objectively": "I could sense that I was wrestling with it in session, but, in a sense what we did was, we kind of put it in a box and I stepped back from it and I could just look at those feelings and experiences by stepping away from it and analyze it more objectively."

One trainee discussed this process as developing an "internal supervisor." This internal supervisor is reminiscent of the advanced stage of self-supervisor described by Littrell, Lee-Borden, and Lorenz (1979).

Outcomes of Good Supervision. There were six identifiable themes that constituted this phase. In each of the individual cases, there were many expressions regarding the effects of good supervision, but the six outlined subsequently were those consistently identified among the supervisees in this study.

Supervisees experienced both a strengthening and affirming of their confidence. Colette, who was questioning her ability to communicate effectively, remarked, "I would say the main thing for me is just that it really instilled self-confidence once again." And according to Rebecca: "What then developed in the session was, I felt like I relaxed, because I was being affirmed for what I had done so far was very natural and I was being given a reassurance that I was competent and that I had done a good job, and that then allowed me to kind of open the blinds a little bit more. . . . It was even more of an opening to the experience by me, by being given that kind of undergirding of feeling like I was competent."

In each of the cases, it appeared that there was an increased ability to see greater complexity in the issues being faced. The flip side of this theme was that, along with an increased ability to see complexity, there was a corresponding ability to make what was complex and confusing more coherent. It would be expected that a natural outcome of supervisees being able to develop a meta-perspective would be the ability to perceive therapeutic activities with an increased comprehensiveness and sophistication. Dave stated it this way: "I think that part of that was that I was still being manipulated. I hadn't been able to step back and look at what do I want to do, really what's my role. How do I fit into this picture to where I'm comfortable?"

Similarly, Mike reported: "It made me start thinking about what I was doing, instead of just doing it. It's like each time I do something, now I'm assessing whether that was effective, how was the timing on it and not only what is that person feeling, it's a much more complex process than beginning counselor, when you're just trying to figure how to respond to the affect and you don't see anything else or hear anything, you're just nervous."

The heart of psychotherapy supervision is the attempt to increase the supervisee's ability to work effectively with clients. Thus, the ability to conceptualize clients more fully, as well as to intervene successfully, is central to the task of supervision (that is, an expanded ability for therapeutic conceptualizing and intervening). What was interesting about this study was that participants did not focus on specific tangible skills. Predominantly, attention was centered on developing new, more refined abilities in conceptualizing clients or dealing with professional development situations. Although therapy outcome was not examined in this study, it appears that supervisees felt an increased ability to conceptualize client issues and intervene with a greater sense of efficacy. An excerpt from Kevin's transcript is illustrative: "And so I walked out of there with what I felt were a handful of things to try out and a real good sense that I'd had a valuable experience, that my repertoire was expanded. My understanding of myself, my understanding of therapy was broadened just a bit, in a real tangible way. . . . It really turned on lights."

With a new sense of understanding for either a therapeutic or a professional development issue, the participants acquired a positive anticipation to reengage in their previous struggle. Dave spoke of developing a "game plan" to return to his client to implement his new understanding. That same phrase was used by Bruce. "That's basically how we wound up that session, with a game plan." Both Kevin and Rebecca expressed an eagerness to return to their clients with their new understanding.

> I think for me I was really excited to get back and work with the client. I felt like I had picked up a lot of good information about myself, about what I thought with the client, certainly my relationship with her. I was just raring to get into the next session and continue this. (Kevin)
>
> And in a sense I was looking forward to going back into that counseling situation and seeing what I then could do, feeling freed up regarding the situation and dealing with the client. (Rebecca)

Although the focus was on professional development rather than therapy skills, there was still a planning to reengage in the struggle. Some of the language used to described the feelings of reengaging in the struggle suggested that trainees felt energized, focused, and ready to try out new strategies in dealing with what was previously believed to be challenging or difficult.

The good supervision events also had the effect of strengthening the supervisory alliance. Many of the trainees talked of other constructive experiences that transpired later in supervision because of the trust that had developed through this positive experience. One intern suggested that her good experience had been a tacit test of the supervisory relationship and preparatory for discussion of other more intense issues later.

The final theme was increased impetus for continued professional identity development. This theme was concerned with the supervisees' motivation. In this light, Dave made the following comment: "I basically said, 'Cool, now let's turn on my psychological thinking which brought me into this field, what I love to do.'" For Jan, this event included breaking through some of the "rigidity" that she had developed. As for Kevin, he related that this had the effect of opening up a whole new part of the therapeutic process: "It was kind of like adding an entirely new dimension and such an important dimension. And that was what was happening, just the general process of what was occurring between the client and I, and I don't think I really focused on that much before." Finally, as trainees perceived a need and desire for honing their professional identity, they experienced an increase in their commitment to supervision.

Discussion

The results of this phenomenological investigation provide an in-depth, detailed, and intricate picture of the experience of good supervision events from the perspective of the trainee that is often missing in investigations of the supervisory process obtained by more traditional quantitative methodologies. The finding of a distinct structure of good supervision comprising the salient themes and events occurring within the phases of an existential baseline, setting the stage, a good supervision experience, and the outcomes of good supervision help clarify the context of supervision as well as the anatomy of good supervision experiences. This particular structure of supervision has not been noted elsewhere in the literature to date and therefore adds significantly to an understanding regarding the process of good supervision.

Within this structure, many of the themes and events are also generally consistent with previous quantitative studies in terms of what constitutes good supervision. For example, events reflected positive aspects of the supervisory relationship, which include supervisor self-disclosure (Black, 1988) as experienced by participants in this study as a technique helpful in normalizing the struggle, a supervisory environment of experimentation and acceptance of mistakes and failures (for example, Allen et al., 1986; Hutt et al., 1983), task orientations specific to developmental level (Allen et al., 1986; Heppner and Roehlke, 1984), and expression of warmth, respect, support, acceptance, trust, and understanding by supervisors (Hutt et al., 1983; Martin et al., 1987).

In each of the eight transcripts examined, participants referred to the quality of the supervisory relationship as crucial and pivotal. Perhaps over the course of an entire semester of supervision, the supervisory relationship, although a significant factor in supervision, would not always play a predominant part in each session, and other issues might become more focal. However, it is likely that, in the course of addressing the variety of supervision issues, the supervisory relationship would continue to serve as the base of all good therapeutic and professional training, thus suggesting that the learning and acquisition of professional skills and identity may be delayed, hampered, or not fully developed outside the context of an effective supervisory relationship. Indeed, previous investigators have concluded that "didactic and structural aspects of supervision were not nearly as influential determinants of quality as clear communication and respect" (Allen et al., 1986, p. 95). In addition, Black (1988) has stated that "the largest and most structurally similar factor found in both effective and ineffective [supervision] was that of the supervisory relationship" (p. 167), describing such differences between supervisory relationships and supervision as correspondingly responsive and supportive versus insensitive and judgmental. It is perhaps these components that led Loganbill, Hardy, and Delworth (1982) to suggest that the supervisory relationship is essential in supervision in much the same manner as the counseling relationship is in psychotherapy. Thus, a more central role and examination of the supervisory relationship in theory building may be warranted.

However, a surprising aspect of this study was that six of the eight participants, in expressing a desire for a qualitatively different supervisory relationship, indicated that they had experienced some previous supervisory relationships as less than fulfilling. This result, along with Galante's (1988) finding that 47 percent of trainees reported that they had experienced at least one ineffective supervisory relationship, provides support for the notion that supervisors may need much more extensive training in supervisory models and processes exclusive of therapeutic training and experience to increase their effectiveness. However, future research needs to determine whether the nature of the supervisory relationship is such that supervisees have been genuinely disappointed or whether the developmental perspective of supervisees influences their retrospective view of supervision such that past supervision is seen as negligent when in fact, at the time it was received, it was viewed to be adequate. It is also possible that retrospective evaluations of previous supervision experiences may be biased by viewing present needs as being inadequately met in previous supervision relationships, especially in cases in which current supervision needs are being adequately attended to.

We found it particularly interesting that a disruption in the usual, with its attendant anxiety and perceived needing, operates so as to set the stage of good supervision and that this often overlooked event can provide some guidance in structuring supervisory interventions. For example, we may be posed to intervene more strategically as supervisors if we understand that when supervisees experience a disruption in the usual, it is a possible opening for new learning to occur and a positive supervisory experience to unfold. When it is determined that a supervisee is entrenched prematurely in certain therapeutic thinking patterns or activities, strategically evoking a disruption in the usual could be productive by providing a new challenge. "Catalytic" interventions (as described by Loganbill et al., 1982) designed to promote change and "get things moving" may evoke the disruption in the usual. In addition, those supervisees experiencing natural disruptions in the usual could be assisted to see the possibility for new and expanded learning opportunities arising from the disruption. However, it is possible that, if the usual becomes disrupted too frequently and the experience with counseling and supervision lacks sufficient continuity, a supervisee might not develop a coherent pattern to his or her therapeutic thinking and interventions.

The results of the present investigation are best viewed in the context of the developmental training level of the participants, which ranged from intermediate practicum level to the second semester of internship. In fact, some observed differences based on the trainees' general level of experience are consistent with developmental models of supervision (for example, Littrell et al., 1979; Loganbill et al., 1982; Stoltenberg & Delworth, 1987). These included differences between the practicum and intern trainees in levels of confidence, a respective disillusionment to a sense of efficacy with the counseling process, and a global versus specific response to sensed inadequacy. However, as noted by Stoltenberg and Delworth (1987), general experience level only roughly equates with developmental level. Indeed, in this investigation, a number of events of good supervision experienced by all trainees appeared to encompass aspects of both Level 2 and Level 3 supervisee issues as hypothesized in Stoltenberg and Delworth's integrated developmental model, and perhaps reflect the transition between these levels. Because these findings were not derived via hypotheses and dependent measures determined a priori, they complement and expand the growing quantitative literature supportive of developmental conceptualizations of the supervision process (Stoltenberg et al., 1994).

This investigation focused on the examination of an experience of good supervision from the perspective of supervisees. A different vision of good supervision might emerge if supervisors' perspectives were also investigated; differences in perceptions between supervisees and supervisors have been found in previous studies (Heppner & Roehlke, 1984; Krause & Allen, 1988; Worthington & Roehlke, 1979; Worthington & Stern, 1985). For example, what supervisors may view as a challenging, growth-producing intervention constituting good supervision (for example, a disruption of the usual) may be negatively viewed initially by trainees. It is also natural to assume that how supervisees perceive supervision will affect how they develop and function as emerging professionals. Therefore, it will be important in future studies to examine the link between the phenomenological experience of supervision for supervisees and the therapeutic process and outcomes that are related to those phenomenological experiences. In other words, when supervisees experience what they believe is good about supervision, do they become more effective in facilitating better therapy outcomes in their clients?

Readers may question the generalizability of the sample of participants in terms of lack of representativeness or small size. Thus, it is important to reaffirm that the intent of this phenomenological investigation was to describe and uncover the structures of personal meaning regarding good supervision events from the perspective of the participants. As a result, the structure of good supervision themes and events derived from the eight interviews is best understood as applying to the recalled experiences of the eight participants and may be used to view experiences of other supervisees. However, this structure is not necessarily generalizable to or predictive of all good experiences of supervision and may not be inclusive of all important events or elements of what may be considered good supervision.

Thus, in this study, we discovered components of good supervision that appeared to be uniform between the participants and constituted a "structure" of good supervision. It is evident that even though commonalities were found, each trainee had a unique experience that varied in some degree from those of other trainees. It is also evident that there is a richness to each individual's experience of good supervision that is difficult to capture through collective descriptions and identification of themes and events. These results suggest that there is no uniform formula that can be applied in supervision to ensure a good experience. Rather, it is important that supervisors demonstrate certain interpersonal qualities that will accompany their theoretical knowledge, practical interventions, and experience base. With the creation of a facilitative supervisory relationship, a supervisor will be attuned to opportunities to intervene strategically with trainees to meet their unique supervisory needs.

Acknowledgments

This investigation was conducted by Vaughn Worthen under the supervision of Brian W. McNeill as partial fulfillment of the requirements for the doctor of philosophy degree at the University of Kansas. We wish to extend our gratitude to Gary Price, Dennis Karpowitz, Diane McDermott, and Valerie Janesick for their valuable input as members of the dissertation committee. We would also like to extend appreciation to Aaron Jackson for his role as an external auditor of the present data and for his helpful comments and input. Illustrative examples of the steps in the individual and group analyses are available from Vaughn Worthen.

Correspondence concerning this article should be addressed to Vaughn Worthen, Counseling and Development Center, Brigham Young University, I49 SWKT, P.O. Box 25548, Provo, Utah 84602–5548.

References

Allen, G. J., Szollos, S. J., & Williams, B. E. (1986). Doctoral students' comparative evaluations of best and worst psychotherapy supervision. *Professional Psychology: Research and Practice, 17,* 91–99.

Black, B. (1988). Components of effective and ineffective psychotherapy supervision as perceived by supervisees with different levels of clinical experience (Doctoral dissertation, Columbia University, 1987). *Dissertation Abstracts International, 48,* 3105B.

Borders, L. D. (1989). A pragmatic agenda for developmental supervision research. *Counselor Education and Supervision, 29,* 16–24.

Galante, M. (1988). Trainees' and supervisors' perceptions of effective and ineffective supervisory relationships (Doctoral dissertation, Memphis State University, 1987). *Dissertation Abstracts International, 49,* 933B.

Giorgi, A. (1985). *Phenomenology and psychological research.* Pittsburgh, PA: Duquesne University Press.

Giorgi, A. (1989). One type of analysis of descriptive data: Procedures involved in following a scientific phenomenological method. *Methods, 1,* 39–61.

Heppner, P. P., & Roehlke, H. J. (1984). Differences among supervisees at different levels of training: Implications for a developmental model of supervision. *Journal of Counseling Psychology, 31,* 76–90.

Holloway, E. L., & Hosford, R. E. (1983). Toward developing a prescriptive technology of counselor supervision. *The Counseling Psychologist, 11,* 73–77.

Hutt, C. H., Scott, J., & King, M. (1983). A phenomenological study of supervisees' positive and negative experiences in supervision. *Psychotherapy: Theory, Research, and Practice, 20,* 118–123.

Krause, A. A., & Allen, G. J. (1988). Perceptions of counselor supervision: An examination of Stoltenberg's model from the perspectives of supervisor and supervisee. *Journal of Counseling Psychology, 35,* 77–80.

Littrell, J. M., Lee-Borden, N., & Lorenz, J. A. (1979). A developmental framework for counseling supervision. *Counselor Education and Supervision, 19,* 119–136.

Loganbill, C., Hardy, E., & Delworth, U. (1982). Supervision: A conceptual model. *The Counseling Psychologist, 10,* 3–42.

Martin, J. S., Goodyear, R. K., & Newton, F. B. (1987). Clinical supervision: An intensive case study. *Professional Psychology: Research and Practice, 18,* 225–235.

McNeill, B. W., & Worthen, V. (1989). The parallel process in psychotherapy supervision. *Professional Psychology: Research and Practice, 20,* 329–333.

Miller, C. D., & Oetting, E. R. (1966). Students react to supervision. *Counselor Education and Supervision, 6,* 73–74.

Nelson, G. L. (1978). Psychotherapy supervision from the trainee's point of view: A survey of preferences. *Professional Psychology, 9,* 539–550.

Patton, M. Q. (1990). *Qualitative evaluation and research methods* (2nd ed.). Newbury Park, CA: Sage.

Stoltenberg, C., & Delworth, U. (1987). *Supervising counselors and therapists: A developmental approach.* San Francisco: Jossey-Bass.

Stoltenberg, C. D., McNeill, B. W., & Creather, H. (1994). Changes in supervision as counselors and therapists gain experience: A review. *Professional Psychology: Research Practices, 25,* 416–449.

Wertz, F. J. (1983). From everyday psychological descriptions: Analyzing the moments of a qualitative data analysis. *Journal of Phenomenological Psychology, 14,* 197–242.

Wertz, F. J. (1985). Methods and findings in a phenomenological psychological study of a complex life event: Being criminally victimized. In A. Giorgi (Ed.), *Phenomenological and psychological research* (pp. 155–216). Pittsburgh, PA: Duquesne University Press.

Worthington, E. L., Jr., & Roehlke, H. (1979). Effective supervision as perceived by beginning counselors in training. *Journal of Counseling Psychology, 26,* 64–73.

Worthington, E. L., Jr., & Stern, A. (1985). Effects of supervisor and supervisee degree level and gender on the supervisory relationship. *Journal of Counseling Psychology, 32,* 252–262.

Phenomenological Research and the Making of Meaning

Vaughn E. Worthen
Brigham Young University, Provo, Utah

I was one of the first ever in our department to conduct a qualitative study, and the first to use a phenomenological method. I believe there were several key ingredients that helped me in my role as a novice investigator. First, I found a topic of interest that I had some personal investment in (I had experienced supervision, both good and bad), which sustained my curiosity during what turned out to be a long and challenging process. Second, I had a dissertation chair who provided encouragement, support, challenge, and ultimately faith in me and in the process. Third, I searched for and found a methodology that worked for me and would help me explore an experience that I wanted to understand better. I had to believe in the philosophy of science behind that methodology. Fourth, I had to identify appropriate co-investigators (subjects) who would be able effectively to articulate their experience and be representative of the experience I wanted to understand. Fifth, I needed a question that would keep me, the interviews, and the analysis focused. Sixth, I needed to believe in both the process and myself as being effective vehicles for eliciting and organizing the data. I had to allow time to immerse myself in the data and trust that the data would speak to me. I had to believe, especially in the early stages, that the parts would begin to come together into a meaningful whole. Seventh, I had to find a way to communicate and represent what I was finding to others and open myself to the critiques and questions that would invariably come.

I would now like to share a few critical issues from my experience as a phenomenological qualitative researcher.

Although qualitative research is well designed to examine "soft" data such as human experience, the methodology needs rigor. I spent quite a lot of time searching for a methodology that made sense for me, a methodology whose philosophy of science was consistent with my own view of human nature. I also wanted a methodology that would help me understand how to move from raw interviews to final knowledge statement in systematic transformations of the data. I found Giorgi's (1989) methodology did that for me.

Another critical element was preparation for conducting effective interviews, the source of the data. I read quite a lot about qualitative interviewing and found Kvale's (1983) article very helpful. Although I did not practice interviewing with someone, which in hindsight might have been helpful, I participated in mental preparation through imaginative rehearsal, picturing how to question and prompt co-investigators effectively. I also was very conscious of the problem of asking leading questions, which might bias the data, and prepared so that I might avoid these kinds of questions. I was acutely aware (in fact probably put off longer than necessary this phase of the research for fear of not conducting the interviews effectively) that whatever data were generated were dependent on the quality of the interviews I conducted. As I began the interviews, I experienced them as very interesting and quite rewarding.

The quality of the interview is determined by the relationship we establish with our co-investigators. (I should point out my use of the term co-investigator is purposeful, since I viewed us as both having interest and some investment in understanding this experience better.) This is a departure from quantitative methods. Objectivity is a highly valued stance in traditional quantitative research, since you do not want to bias the findings. In phenomenological research you are striving to access the experience within individuals. A trusting relationship, where both are committed to better understanding the experience being explored, allows for greater access to the richness of their experience. Some of my co-investigators reported that the interview was "enjoyable," "rewarding," "insightful," and almost therapeutic.

The analysis was very time consuming and plain hard work. It was hard to do the analysis in small doses. I found I was more productive when I would work in longer periods. I was filled at alternating times with confusion, doubt, illumination, and exhilaration. I found that my doubt diminished as I would take my initial findings and go back to the data to check or verify that the data supported the findings. Often I would end up reworking or revising my ideas to better fit the data. Language became a vital concern. I found myself spending time exploring the thesaurus and dictionary to try and capture the right kind of language to convey the concepts that were emerging. I attempted to avoid language that might have the baggage of other meanings. On reflection, I think I was only partially successful in that endeavor.

Validity was a big concern. You do not have the luxury of falling back on statistical numbers to back up your findings. You do not have an established significance level to tell you when you have found something meaningful. You look for meaning in the data and for its repetition and redundancy across cases. You see whether there are patterns to the data, and whether you can match the data with the emerging meaning and take the meaning and impose it back on the data to see whether it holds up. In phenomenological analysis you do not necessarily rely on the consensus of others who are looking at the same data, because you acknowledge that each might bring a legitimate but different perspective to the data. Thus, you may feel alone with your findings, since you are the ultimate authority on your perspective on the data. You demonstrate validity by showing that you collected your data in a thorough and authentic manner, were rigorous in your analysis, can explain alternative competing meanings, and can show through your steps of data transformation the path you took to develop your knowledge statement or findings. In some qualitative methods this is called an *audit trail.* If others can see the integrity of the process and the ability to explain competing findings you have demonstrated validity from a phenomenological perspective. Polkinghorne (1989) stated that the phenomenological use of the term *validity* is applied more as a general principle, that is, "as a conclusion that inspires confidence because the argument in support of it has been persuasive" (p. 57). For those who have had similar experiences, your findings should resonate with their own experience as a way of personal validation. In conjunction with this, I expected my greatest critics would be those steeped in quantitative methodologies, who would be looking for traditional measures of internal and external validity. Those I experienced as sometimes the harshest critics were other qualitative researchers who came from a different theoretical underpinning and believed that I had not conducted the analysis in the right way. In fairness, they also made some of the most significant contributions to strengthening the research.

Phenomenological methods can provide a useful tool for understanding human experience and meaning. There are other legitimate and useful research methods, both qualitative and quantitative. Phenomenological methods require a commitment to rigor and openness to learning, a respect for those who will participate as your co-investigators, and a sense of humility about the whole process. Enjoy the process as much as possible; develop a sense of wonder and awe for the phenomena you are investigating. Don't set out to change the world, just try to understand better the experience you are exploring. This method of inquiry can be very exhausting and hugely rewarding, ultimately adding meaningful understanding to the experience we call life.

References

Giorgi, A. (1989). One type of analysis of descriptive data: Procedures involved in following a scientific phenomenological method. *Methods, 1,* 39–61.

Kvale, S. (1983). The qualitative research interview: A phenomenological and a hermeneutical mode of understanding. *Journal of Phenomenological Psychology, 14,* 171–196.

Polkinghorne, D. E. (1989). Phenomenological research methods. In R. S. Valle and S. Halling (Eds.), *Existential-phenomenological perspectives in psychology: Exploring the breadth of human experience* (pp. 41–60). New York: Plenum Press.

Grounded Theory

Grounded theory first came to the attention of qualitative researchers with the publication in 1967 of Glaser and Strauss' book, *The Discovery of Grounded Theory*. As with other forms of qualitative research, grounded theory is "the study of experience from the standpoint of those who live it" (Charmaz, 2000, p. 522), the investigator is the primary instrument of data collection and analysis, and the mode of inquiry is inductive. The end product of a grounded theory study is the building of substantive theory—theory that emerges from or is "grounded" in the data. Theory is "inductively derived from the . . . phenomenon it represents. That is, discovered, developed, and provisionally verified through systematic data collection and analysis of data pertaining to that phenomenon. . . . One does not begin with a theory, then prove it. Rather, one begins with an area of study and what is relevant to that area is allowed to emerge" (Strauss and Corbin, 1990, p. 23). Substantive theory is not grand theory, but theory about some facet of professional practice, about real-world situations, about "slices of social life" (Charmaz, 2000, p. 522). This interest in theory generation rather than theory testing and the potential usefulness of substantive theory for practice can be found across many professional and applied fields.

In most grounded theory studies data come from interviews and observations. Glaser and Strauss (1967) explain that a wide variety of documentary materials, literature, and previous research are also potential sources of valuable data and entire studies can be conducted with just documents. They suggest searching for data-caches such as collections of letters, interviews, speeches, using fictional literature as a source of ideas, and in general, randomly browsing for any materials that might be helpful to the investigation. In a study by Pandit (1996), for example, a grounded theory of corporate turnaround was developed exclusively from existing literature and documents.

Data collection is guided by *theoretical sampling* in which "the analyst jointly collects, codes, and analyzes his [sic] data and decides what data to collect next and where to find them, in order to develop his theory as it emerges" (Glaser & Strauss, 1967, p. 45). An initial sample is chosen by its logical relevance to the research problem. As data collection and analysis proceed, "we likely find gaps in our data and holes in our theories. Then we go back to the field and collect delimited data to fill those conceptual gaps and holes—we conduct theoretical sampling" (Charmaz, 2000, p. 519). The sampling procedure may also include individuals, sites, events, and so on that are quite diverse. Comparing diverse groups quickly reveals the similarities and differences that give rise to theoretical categories and, in turn, the strength of these emerging categories is tested by collecting data from diverse groups.

The basic analysis procedure in grounded theory research is the *constant comparative method* of data analysis. Units of data deemed meaningful by the researcher are compared with each other in order to generate tentative categories and properties, the basic elements of a grounded theory. Through constantly comparing incident with incident, comparing incidents with emerging conceptual categories, and reducing similar categories into a smaller number of highly conceptual categories, an overall framework or substantive theory develops. As Strauss and Corbin (1990, p. 7) write, "categories are the 'cornerstones' of developing theory. They provide the means by which the theory can be integrated." This process is facilitated by coding (open, axial, and selective [Strauss & Corbin, 1990]) and the continual writing of memos recording any insights that arise in the course of data analysis and, in particular, connections that are seen between and among categories and properties.

Theory building also involves the identification of a *core category*—the main conceptual element through which all others are connected. Strauss (1987, p. 36) writes that the core category "must be *central,* that is, related to as many other categories and their properties as is possible, . . . must appear frequently in the data . . . and must develop the theory." The linking of categories and properties through hypotheses, or propositions, is also part of the process of developing grounded theory. The theory itself can be assessed on four criteria (Glaser & Strauss, 1967): *fitness*—the theory must be closely related to the reality of the substantive area of investigation; *understanding*—laypersons working in the substantive area should be able to understand and use the theory; *generality*—categories of the grounded theory "should not be so abstract as to lose their sensitizing aspect, but yet must be abstract enough to make . . . theory a general guide to multiconditional, everchanging daily situations" (p. 242); and *control*—the theory must offer enough robustness and clarity resulting in enough control "to make its application worthwhile" (p. 245). Glaser (1978, 1992) has since proposed that a grounded theory must *fit* the data, *work* in terms of a useful explanation, be *relevant* to actual problems, and be capable of being *modified* by future inquiry.

The two examples of grounded theory studies in this section illustrate several of the characteristics of grounded theory studies reviewed here. In Brott and Myers' (1999) study of professional school counselor identity, participants were selected to represent diverse perspectives, thus maximizing variation in the data gathered and making for a richer grounded theory. They also made use of the coding scheme proposed by Strauss and Corbin (1990), which includes open, axial, and selective coding. The theory consists of interrelated categories and properties centered around the core category of "blending of influences."

Jones and McEwen's (2000) study of women college students' sense of self or personal identity also employed a grounded theory approach. As with the above study, they sampled for maximum variation in racial and ethnic background, which resulted in diversity of religious affiliation. Using open ended interviews and analyzing the data by using Strauss and Corbin's (1990) coding scheme, they identified a core category and ten key categories which they interrelated in a "model of multiple dimensions of identity."

References

Charmaz, K. (2000). Grounded theory: objectivist and constructivist methods. In N. K. Denzin & Y. S. Lincoln (eds.), *Handbook of qualitative research.* (2nd ed.) (pp. 509–535). Thousand Oaks, Calif.: Sage.

Glaser, B. G. (1978). *Theoretical sensitivity.* Mill Valley, Calif.: Sociology Press.

Glaser, B. G. (1992). *Basics of grounded theory analysis: Emergence vs. forcing.* Mill Valley, Calif.: Sociology Press.

Glaser, B. G., & Strauss, A. L. (1967). *The discovery of grounded theory.* Chicago: Aldine.

Pandit, N. R. (1996). The creation of theory: A recent application of the grounded theory method." *The Qualitative Report,* 2(4), pp. 1–20 (on-line journal available on the World Wide Web at [http://www.nova.edu/ssss/QR/QR2–4/pandit.html]).

Strauss, A., & Corbin, J. (1990). *Basics of qualitative research: Grounded theory procedures and techniques.* (2nd ed.) Newbury Park, Calif.: Sage.

Strauss, A. L. (1987). *Qualitative analysis for social scientists.* Cambridge, England: Cambridge University Press.

7

Development of Professional School Counselor Identity

A Grounded Theory

Pamelia E. Brott, Jane E. Myers

Professional identity formation and development have been studied in numerous professions including teaching (Kuzmic, 1994), psychoanalysis (Rosenbloom, 1992), and psychology (Watts, 1987). What appears to be salient across these studies is a process of continual interplay between structural and attitudinal changes that result in a self-conceptualization as a type of professional. This self-conceptualization, which has been termed one's *professional identity,* serves as a frame of reference from which one carries out a professional role, makes significant professional decisions, and develops as a professional.

The literature on professional counselor development has identified similar processes involved in identity formation and development of counselors (Bruss & Kopala, 1993; Hogan, 1964; Loganbill, Hardy, & Delworth, 1982; Reising & Daniels, 1983; Skovholt & Ronnestad, 1992). The focus of previous research has been on counselors-in-training, with little attention paid to identity development during the working years beyond graduate school. Further, whether counselor identity development is identical for professionals in the various specialties of counseling, such as school counseling, has not been determined.

The counseling literature is saturated with studies and articles that examine the role and functions of school counselors (for example, Carroll, 1993; Helms & Ibrahim, 1983, 1985; Shertzer & Stone, 1963; Stanciak, 1995; Wrenn, 1957). In spite of the best efforts of professional associations, accrediting bodies, and training programs to define the profession of school counseling, studies cited in the literature indicate that the actual functions of counselors in the schools do not always reflect what have been identified as the best practices in school counseling

Pamelia E. Brott & Jane E. Myers. (1999). "Development of Professional School Counselor Identity: A Grounded Theory." *Professional School Counseling, 2,* (5), 339–348. Reprinted with permission.

(Hutchinson, Barrick, & Groves, 1986; Partin, 1993; Peer, 1985; Tennyson, Miller, Skovholt, & Williams, 1989). A major theme that is repeated throughout the literature related to the professionalization of school counseling relates to this dissonance or conflict between school counselor preparation and the realities of the work environment. How decisions are made in this context reflects one's self-conceptualization as a professional—one's professional identity.

The development of a professional school counselor identity thus serves as a frame of reference for carrying out work roles, making significant decisions, and developing as a professional. Unfortunately, there is a lack of available information on how this professional identity develops. By understanding the meaning-making framework in professional identity development, school counselors may be in a better position to determine their roles and functions for serving students and the school community. Further, counselor educators will be better able to provide training to students aspiring to become professional school counselors.

Because professional identity development is a process rather than an outcome—which begins in training and continues throughout one's career—it is best studied with emerging research paradigms (for example, qualitative methods). One such research paradigm is grounded theory (Glaser & Strauss, 1967; Strauss & Corbin, 1990). A grounded theory orientation allows theoretical categories to emerge from the data that explain how individuals continually process and respond to a problem. Data are gathered primarily through interviews and are analyzed inductively. The resulting theory is thus grounded in real-world patterns. A judgment can then be made about the adequacy of the research and the credibility of the newly developed theory.

A qualitative study was undertaken to propose a grounded theory that will contribute to an understanding of school counselors' professional identity development. Based on a review of the literature, the salient theme related to the professionalization of school counseling seemed to be one of conflict or, more specifically, conflict decisions. Given that conflict is inevitable, the process of conflict decisions may describe the development of an identity as school counselors manage professional conflicts and carry out their role as service providers to students. Therefore, six research questions were developed and addressed in the study to look at the process of conflict decisions.

Method

The qualitative research design included a sampling of school counselors who were selected to represent diverse perspectives. Data collection was through qualitative interviews using a structured, open-ended approach incorporating an interview guide (that is, research questions) as well as observations in the schools.

Participants

Ten school counselors from elementary and middle school settings in the United States ($n = 7$) and the Caribbean ($n = 3$) participated in this study. The participants included nine females and one male who identified their ethnic-cultural group as Caucasian/white (n = 5) or African American/Afro-Caribbean/black (n = 5). All ten counselors had a master's degree in counseling or a related field, or a professional studies certificate in counseling from a country other than the United States. Seven of the participants were certified by their state as school counselors. In addition, four of the counselors were National Certified Counselors (NCC), two were Licensed Professional Counselors (LPC), and three were counselors certified in another country. Their years of experience as a school counselor ranged from one to twenty-nine.

Researcher-Interviewer

The researcher-interviewer was a white female with a master's degree in counseling and was completing a doctorate in counseling and counselor education. Her qualifications include school counselor certification, National Certified Counselor, and Licensed Professional Counselor. Her fourteen years of experience as a school counselor included six years in the United States and eight years in the Caribbean.

There are, of course, several possible biases that can result from the research process when the researcher is also the interviewer, and these biases can affect the subsequent generalizability of the findings. Foremost is the possibility that the researcher would find what she was looking for through selective attention to details and selective interpretation of data. The fact that several doctoral faculty representing multiple disciplines participated in systematic and frequent reviews of the data and interpretations was intended to minimize researcher expectations as a possible source of error. Additional concerns are the possible selection of participants by the researcher to reflect preexisting biases and perceptions, and the unique perception and experiences of the school counselors that would lead them to respond in particular ways to the research questions. The selection of participants was intentional, as described above, and thus provided sufficient variety in experience, credentials, and other demographic variables to overcome the possibility of selection bias. The unique perceptions and experiences of the school counselors were actually a strength of the study rather than a limitation, in that their uniqueness contributed to the variety of perspectives and thus themes which emerged in the analysis of the data.

Interview Questions

Six research questions were developed to elicit the process of conflict decisions for school counselors. These questions evolved from a review of the literature, experiences of the principal investigator during fourteen years as a professional school counselor, and through Socratic dialogue with experts in school counseling, educational administration, measurement, and qualitative research design. Several iterations and revisions of the questions were developed and discussed with these experts, resulting in the following six research questions addressed in the study:

1. What factors determine the school counseling program?
2. Who is involved in determining the school counseling program?
3. How do school counselors make decisions about the school counseling program?

4. What issues of conflict with principals have been dealt with by school counselors?

5. What is the decision process used by school counselors when interacting with principals in professional conflict situations?

6. In what ways do conflict decisions reflect the role of school counselors?

Procedure

A purposeful sampling approach (Patton, 1990) was used to generate information-rich cases that illuminated the study and elucidated variation as well as significant common patterns within that variation. Data collection was through structured interviews using an open-ended approach with an interview guide as well as observations in the schools. The interviews lasted approximately one hour and were completed at each school counselor's respective work site. The questions included in the interview guide focused on the school counseling program and on the school counselor's perception of the issues and processes used in making professional decisions. The interviews were tape recorded with prior consent of the participants, and verbatim transcriptions were produced for data analysis. Each school counselor who participated also was asked to complete a brief paper-and-pencil assessment of demographic variables.

The researcher, as an active participant in data collection, was intent on understanding in detail how school counselors think and how they came to develop the perspectives they hold. The interview guide provided topic or subject areas within which the researcher explored, probed, and asked questions to elucidate and illuminate the subject area. Therefore, the researcher remained free to build a conversation within a particular subject area, word questions spontaneously, and establish a conversational style, albeit with the focus on a particular subject that had been predetermined. In addition to the interview and descriptive data, the researcher observed participants on two or three occasions for a total of two hours each in the respective school setting. Observations were recorded as field notes (Bogdan & Biklen,1992; Lofland, 1971; Patton, 1990). A narrative that was a composite of the descriptive questionnaires and participant observations provided a portrait of the school counselors who participated in the study.

A set of rigorous coding procedures (Strauss & Corbin, 1990) guided the analysis to develop theoretically informed interpretations of the data. Data analysis progressed through the stages of open, axial, and selective coding. Open coding identified and developed concepts in terms of their properties and dimensions. Axial coding put the data together in new ways by making connections between a category and its subcategories to develop several main categories. Finally, selective coding integrated the categories to form a grounded theory for the development of a professional school counselor identity.

Open Coding

The naming and categorizing of phenomena through a close examination of the data is referred to as open coding (Strauss & Corbin,1990). In taking apart an observation by a line, a sentence, or a paragraph of transcription, each discrete incident, idea, or event was given a name or code word that represented the concept underlying the observation. Creativity is an important element in analyzing the data; assigning code words was the first creative step in the data analysis. Code words were selected by the researcher to elicit new insights from the data. Examples of code words identified in this study include *assaying* (that is, trying), *conceptual* (that is, issues), *connection* (that is, relationship), and *discovery* (that is, realize). A total of 295 code words were identified in this study.

Grouping the code words around a particular concept in the data, called categorizing, reduced the number of code words with which to work. Once again the creative aspect of the data analysis was incorporated with the researcher naming categories as a basis of innovative theoretical formulations. For example, the code words *assaying, conceptual, connection,* and *discovery* were grouped around the category named *evolving* (that is, personal perspectives). A total of twelve categories were identified through open coding in the study.

Finally, categories from the open-coding process were written as code notes that are a type of memo. Memos were written and coding paradigms were created to analyze the data further by asking questions and making comparisons about the content of the interview. The purpose of questioning is to open up the data by thinking of the categories in terms of their properties and dimensions. The basic questions are who? when? where? what? how? how much? and why? Examples of the types of questions asked were, What are the properties (that is, attributes or characteristics) of the category? What are the dimensions (that is, frequency, duration, rate, timing) of the property along a continuum?

Axial Coding

Whereas open coding fractured the data, axial coding put the data back together in new ways by making connections between a category and its subcategories to develop several main categories (Strauss & Corbin, 1990). The resulting model denotes causal and intervening conditions, phenomena, contexts, action/interactional strategies, and consequences.

Selective Coding

The selective coding process integrated the categories to form a substantive theory (Strauss & Corbin, 1990). This theory describes an interrelated set of categories that emerged from the data through a constant comparative coding and analysis procedure. The identification of a core category, one that accounts for most of the variation in a pattern of behavior, was essential for the development of the theory. Once the core category was identified, the remaining categories could then be related to the core category as the conditions that led to the occurrence of the phenomenon and as the phases that represented the phenomenon.

Credibility of the Study

A qualitative study can be evaluated accurately only if the procedures are sufficiently explicit and the research standards (that is, scientific canons) are appropriate to the study (Strauss & Corbin, 1990). The credibility of the study was judged by both the adequacy of the research process and the adequacy of the empirical grounding of the research findings (Strauss & Corbin, 1990). The research process was guided by detailed procedures (for example, selection of participants, identifying categories) and conceptual relationships among categories. These conceptual relationships were formulated and tested by reexamining each interview through a comparative method to test the relationships. The resulting conceptual relationships among the categories included the following: (1) there is a reciprocal interplay within the process, (2) there is a fluid nature to the process as the conditions and decisions change, and (3) the phenomenon as a blending of influences is a dynamic process within the context, conditions, and phases for a counselor performing in the role.

The adequacy of the empirical grounding of the research findings addresses concepts, linkages, variation and specificity, conditions, creative interplay, and process. Concepts were generated from the data and systematically related. The conceptual linkages were presented as strategies and activities of counselors performing in their role. Variation and specificity were built into the theory as conditions for the process under study. Broader conditions that affect the process were seen as the settings within which the counselors were providing services. The theory described a dynamic process for the blending of influences involving phases and actions/interactions in response to prevailing conditions. The theoretical findings represented the creative interplay between the researcher and the data. Finally, the substantive theory was presented as a process.

Although the credibility of the study and the adequacy of the empirical grounding have been addressed from a qualitative viewpoint, a few comments regarding the limitations of the study should satisfy those readers more familiar with quantitative analysis. First, grounded theory is generalizable to the specific actions and interactions that pertain to a phenomenon and the resulting consequences. This study represents the theoretical perspectives of ten participants. Variations uncovered through additional research can be added as amendments to the original formulation. Second, reproducibility of the study may be questioned. Theory that deals with a social or psychological phenomenon is probably not reproducible because conditions cannot be exactly matched to the original study though many major conditions may be similar. However, given the same theoretical perspective of the original researcher and following the same general rules for data gathering and analysis in a similar set of conditions, another investigator should "reproduce" the same theoretical explanation about the given phenomenon. Should discrepancies arise, they are worked out through reexamination of the data and identification of the different conditions that may be operating in each case.

Results

The results of the coding procedures reflect the emergence of theoretical categories that explain how the participants continually processed the problem (that is, self-conceptualization of their role). These categories form the basis for a substantive theory, which describes an interrelated set of categories grounded in the data that emerged from the constant comparative coding and analysis procedures.

Eight theoretical categories emerged through the axial coding process that explained how the participants continually processed the problem (that is, self-conceptualization of the role). The eight theoretical categories included (1) accounts, (2) advocates, (3) defines, (4) intertwines, (5) manages, (6) rates, (7) responds, and (8) sustains.

The basic problem grounded in the data was the counselor's need for personal guidelines in carrying out the professional role. Personal guidelines referred to the self-conceptualization of the role as a school counselor. As revealed reviewing each story (that is, interview), counselors were faced with multiple influences, and each counselor found a way to intertwine or blend these influences. As a process, the core category was thus entitled "blending of influences." Using selective coding, each of the remaining theoretical categories was related to the core category as conditions (that is, events or incidents that led to the phenomenon) or phases (that is, strategies and activities of the process).

Performing in the role of a school counselor was the context for the blending-of-influences process. Performing was influenced by three conditions, namely experiences, other counselors, and essentials in a particular setting or context. Experiences were defined by one's length of service or years of experience as a school counselor and by one's knowledge of what had been done before (that is, legacy) and of the setting (that is, school community, counseling directives). Counselors were providing services to students in the school either as the only counselor or as one of two counselors. This condition was expressed in terms of time and responsibilities for the counselors. Essentials were defined as the needs or developmental issues of the students and the directives issued by the principal or the counseling supervisor. The conditions are summarized in Table 7.1.

The four phases in the blending of influences for school counselors performing in their role became structuring, interacting, distinguishing, and evolving. The phases are described in terms of strategies and activities. The phases for the blending of influences are summarized in Table 7.2.

Substantive Theory for the Blending of Influences

The problem grounded in the data of this research was to identify counselors' self-conceptualizations (that is, personal guidelines) that provide a meaning-making framework in carrying out the professional role of a school counselor. It was discovered that a process occurred as counselors were involved with professional interactions when performing their role in the context of elementary and middle school counseling. This process for performing in the role of a school counselor was identified as the blending of influences (that is, core category). The core category, blending of influences, and the major theoretical categories were linked through the conditions (Table 7.1) and phases (Table 7.2) that described

Table 7.1. Selective Coding: Conditions for Performing in the Role.

Condition	Facets	Examples
Experiences	Length of service	Novice or seasoned counselor
	Previous knowledge	What has been done before (i.e., legacy); knowing the setting (i.e., school community, counseling directives)
Counselors	Number of service providers	Exclusive service provider; work with one or more co-counselors
	Time and responsibility	Not having time as the only counselor; sharing of responsibilities with a co-counselor
Essentials	Developmental issues	Related to population being served
	Directives	Related to administrators' expectations of the counselor

Table 7.2. Selective Coding: The Strategies and Activities in the Phases for the Blending of Influences.

Phases	Strategies	Activities
Structuring	Defining	Implementing training received, knowing directives, recognizing home-base timbre, informing multiple publics
	Rating	Appraising structure, receiving rejoinder, evaluating self
Interacting	Managing	Maneuvering hindrances and obstructions, making judgments, identifying a strategy
	Responding	Recognizing realm of services, intervening information to multiple publics
Distinguishing	Advocating	Focusing on essentials to safeguard, counter, or broker
	Accounting	Asserting professional responsibility, performing approvingly
Evolving	Sustaining	Experiencing challenges, learning on the job, forming cognition
	Intertwining	Reflecting professional substance, tying together as tongue-and-groove, developing a guiding focus

how school counselors performed their role. Figure 7.1 presents the context, conditions, and phases that comprise the process for the blending of influences.

Conditions from which school counselors may be viewed include experience, number of service providers, and essentials or needs in the particular setting. A

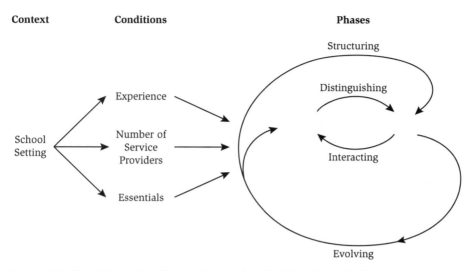

Context   **Conditions**   **Phases**

Figure 7.1. The Substantive Theory: Process for the Blending of Influences.

school counselor in a particular setting may be considered a novice or seasoned counselor based on years of experience. The counselor's experience contributed to his or her knowledge regarding the legacy of the setting and the timbre of the school. Within a particular setting, the counselor may be the exclusive service provider or may work with one or more co-counselors. Essentials or needs of a particular setting include the developmental issues related to the population being served and the directives related to administrators' expectations of the counselor. Given the dynamics when these conditions are intermixed, each school counselor can be viewed as a unique service provider entering the phases for the blending of influences.

School counselors, at the onset of their professional role, become involved in the structuring phase for the blending of influences using a structural or external perspective based on their graduate training. Counselors may move in and out of this phase as conditions of the role change (for example, experiences, different principal/co-counselor). This phase can be discerned through the counselors' description for determining the school counseling program (for example, "I was trained. . .," "our students need. . ."). As influences beyond the structural perspective surface, counselors enter the interacting phase.

Interactions with multiple publics are inherent to the role of the school counselor. The interacting phase initiates the personal or internal perspective of the self-conceptualization as counselors become involved with managing and responding to multiple influences. Whether viewed as challenges, hindrances, and/or obstructions, the counselors maneuver the multiple influences and make decisions regarding their role. Through the interacting phase, the personal guidelines emerge as a meaning-making framework from which decisions or judgments are enacted.

Counselors move in and out of the distinguishing phase based on their performance goals and perceptions. This phase is marked by the what and how of the influences. As early as the novice year, counselors determine the focus (that is, what) of their role performance and the perceptions (that is, how) of self and others in performing the role. This phase may be revisited numerous times as conditions in the role change.

The dynamic interplay of the structuring, interacting, and distinguishing phases is a precursor to the evolving phase. Sustaining a variety of experiences develops the personal perspective. The intertwining of the structural and personal perspectives weaves a guiding focus that is revealed through personal guidelines for carrying out the role of a school counselor. The evolving phase becomes a part of the interplay of the phases for blending of influences.

Describing the phases as a dynamic interplay represents the fluid nature of the process for the blending of influences. What is viewed as the consequences of the dynamic interplay of phases is presented as the self-conceptualization or identity of school counselors performing in the role. The identity also has a fluid nature as the conditions change and counselors become involved in the phases of the process. The identity is not viewed as a final outcome but rather as a consequence of the conditions and phases of the process.

Discussion

The purpose of this study was to generate a grounded theory of school counselors' professional identity development. The aims of the study were to explore and conceptualize school counselors' professional interactions as defining experiences in the development of a professional school counselor identity. The substantive theory generated from the study describes the context, conditions, and phases for a process identified as the blending of influences.

It appears as if the development of a professional identity does contribute to defining the role of school counselors, which in turn shapes the counseling programs and services provided to students. In providing appropriate services, school counselors are involved in making decisions that involve complex interactions. Managing interactions with multiple publics—which include administrators, teachers, and co-counselors—are particularly important. Further, managing interactions are one part of a larger process identified as the blending of influences. As was expected, the blending-of-influences process was conceptualized as a dynamic interplay of internal and external perspectives; however, the resulting personal guidelines were far more individualized than initially expected. This is important because the personal guidelines followed by counselors determine the school counseling program, hence the highly individualized personal guidelines result in diverse programs and services offered to students and the school community.

In determining the school counseling program, a process of transformation occurs as the school counselor moves from determining the program based on external (that is, structural) influences such as the graduate training received to an internal (that is, attitudinal) conceptualization of the role. As part of the transformation process, the school counselor recognizes the needs of students that may elicit challenges from multiple publics, which the school counselor must manage. Professional identity develops over time and is a part of an experiential and maturation process. Although the study revealed a similar process among the participants for developing a professional identity, involvement in the process was unique to each school counselor.

Findings from this study support what has been defined in the literature as professional socialization and development (for example, Hall, 1987; McGowen & Hart, 1990; Watts, 1987). The literature for a number of professions (for example, teachers, counseling psychologists) reports that professional growth and development begins during one's training for the profession, evolves during entry into the profession, and continues to develop as the practitioner identifies with the profession. This concept was true for the school counselors who participated in this study. The maturation process began with the structural perspective developed during one's graduate training and was moderated by experiences during entry into the profession. Further development occurred as each participant internalized the role, which resulted in counseling services that were determined by individualized personal guidelines. What was illuminating was the similarity of experiences among the participants and yet the dissimilarity of how these experiences were internalized into the self-conceptualization of the role among the participants. It was the personal or internal perspective as a self-conceptualization of the role that led the participants in the current study to develop new values, attitudes, and self-identity components portrayed through each individual's personal guidelines as a school counselor.

The substantive theory for the blending of influences presents a conceptualization of professional identity development for school counselors. Previous studies have presented professional identity development as a career spectrum model (Hall, 1987), a stage model (Skovholt & Ronnestad, 1992), and a tripartite model (Watts, 1987) of professional socialization. The current study presents professional identity development as a dynamic interplay of phases as school counselors become involved in a variety of strategies and activities when performing in the role. Further, the findings from this study support the literature that professional identity development is not a final outcome. The theory for the blending of influences conceptualizes professional identity development of school counselors as being responsive to a variety of influences and the importance placed on those influences by the individual counselor when performing in the role. The internalized self-conceptualization contributes to defining the role of school counselors who shape counseling programs and services provided to students and the school community.

The findings reveal that the professional identity of school counselors may mediate what and how services are delivered to the students and to the school community. The implications have relevance for the practice of school counseling as well as training and credentialing of school counselors.

The implications for practicing school counselors are seen in terms of professional multifaceted growth. The concept of personal guidelines is integral to the development of professional identity and thus to the counseling programs and services offered in our schools. In the future, personal guidelines may become the focus for assessing school counseling programs and services as well as school counselors' performance by asking questions such as, "How do individual school counselors assess their performance as providers of counseling services in schools as viewed through the blending-of-influences process?" The strategies and activities that delineate the phases of professional school counselor identity development may give rise to empirically measurable outcomes. These outcomes may be used as indicators for the level of excellence in school counseling programs.

The phases of the process have significant implications for both novice and seasoned school counselors. The study supports programs such as mentoring (for example, VanZandt & Perry, 1992) and academies (for example, Splete & Grisdale, 1992) that have been instituted to support practicing school counselors. Where these types of programs are not available, experiences that provide reflective opportunities can be a means of engaging in the process for the blending of influences. Such experiences include writing a journal, attending professional conferences, and networking with other counselors.

The importance of the interacting phase as counselors manage and respond to requests speaks to practitioners "picking their battles." School counselors' identities are formed by the decisions made when interacting with multiple publics, in particular principals and co-counselors. Requests for school counselors to perform administrative and/or clerical tasks will continue to be made if such administrative directives are held in the same esteem as administrative directives for counseling services. This condition will impact the blending process, with administrative and clerical tasks becoming integral influences that practitioners must address. In addition, interactions between co-counselors can provide opportunities for confrontation, arbitration, and collaboration that can be seen as an integral part of the process, resulting in appropriate programs and services to address the developmental needs of students.

Professional identity development is not a final outcome; rather it is an evolving perspective that spans a practitioner's professional career. The evolving phase needs to be as important to the seasoned counselor as it is to the novice counselor. Opportunities need to be made available to challenge the seasoned counselor to identify issues and plan strategies that address conditions that are constantly changing and that impact the blending-of-influences process. The issues faced by students in schools continue to change, and the practice of counseling continues to change as we learn more about meeting the needs of students. These changes are significant factors that have a bearing on the dynamic interplay of phases within the identity development process.

The structural (that is, external) perspective of professional identity development is formed during one's graduate training. The implications for training of school counselors are that counselors-in-training be prepared with a mindset that they will evolve and change in their professional role, that they will be made aware of the factors that impact their professional development, and that they will ultimately determine the counseling program and services offered in the school setting. The process of developing a professional identity, as defined in this study, made the participants increasingly aware of the differences between what they had learned in their training programs and the realities of the requirements of their position. This observation has implications for courses, seminars, and internships as part of pre-professional training for school counselors.

Courses within the training program should address not only the structuring of the school counseling program but also the importance of decision making in determining the program and services. Decisions involve interacting with multiple publics that become part of the fluid process for the blending of influences. Practicing school counselors as well as practicing principals would make excellent guest speakers in training courses to share examples of decisions and to stimulate discussions or, in the context of the present study, interactions.

An innovative approach to introducing the blending-of-influences process to counselors-in-training would be seminars with other educators-in-training (that is, principals, teachers). These seminars could provide an opportunity for participants to become involved with the interacting phase as each individual manages and responds to seminar topics related to issues in schools. In addition, seminars would provide a forum to discuss the services of the school counselor and to develop an understanding of the profession.

A review of the Council for Accreditation of Counseling and Related Educational Programs (CACREP) standards (1994) indicates a strong emphasis on the structural perspective of school counseling through specified curricular experiences that include a required internship experience. However, the standards do not provide the same structural guidelines for intensive supervision of the internship beyond the requirements for supervision of any counseling intern. Consideration should be given to developing guidelines for the supervision of internship experiences in school settings by both the on-site host and the university supervisors. For example, the host supervisor's responsibilities could include the supervision of the intern's experiences in group counseling, classroom guidance, and consultation with teachers and parents. This would complement the university supervisor's responsibilities that include the supervision of the intern's individual counseling experiences utilizing both individual and group supervision techniques. It is through the internship experience that a bridge between the training and the practice of school counseling can be provided; in other words, this is where students learn about the reality of school counseling.

Further exploration and conceptualization of this grounded theory through both qualitative and quantitative methods would be advantageous. Future research would be focused on testing and refining the theory through examining relationships within the theory, collecting data from multiple publics (that is, principals, teachers, co-counselors), and determining relationships between consequences of the process and the services provided to students.

In testing and refining the theory, the consequences of the process need to be explored and conceptualized. There are numerous possibilities for the consequences that may include decision styles, program services, and personal attachment/detachment. Once conceptualized, consequences can then be considered in relation to contexts, conditions, and phases in the blending-of-influences process.

There was an indication from this study of a professional maturation. This concept needs to be further explored. The development of identity across the professional life span would be an important contribution to the theory and would have implications for both practicing counselors and training programs.

Collecting data from multiple publics would be a view from the other side of the process. Qualitative studies involving principals and teachers would focus on the origins of their perceptions of school counseling and school counselors. Studies of co-counselors would provide a comparison between intentions and perceptions in the blending-of-influences process.

With the extensive literature on the role and function of school counselors, another study in this area certainly is not needed. However, a study to link the blending-of-influences process to programs and services could be enlightening. Searching for linkages among contexts, conditions, and phases that result in certain types of programs and services (for example, developmental, directive) may help determine whether it is the training or the person, or a particular blending of the training and the person, that is the critical ingredient for the blending-of-influences process.

In conclusion, the self-conceptualization of practitioners as a particular type of school counselor has been shown to be directly linked to the programs and services offered to students in schools. Clearly, the beneficiaries of the blending-of-influences process defined in this study are the students. Further research is needed to test and refine the theory across elementary, middle, and high school settings as a basis for improving the quality of school counseling services for students of all ages.

References

Bogdan, R., & Biklen, S. K. (1992). *Qualitative research for education: An introduction to theory and methods* (2nd ed.). Boston: Allyn & Bacon.

Bruss, K. V., & Kopala, M. (1993). Graduate school training in psychology: Its impact upon the development of professional identity. *Psychotherapy, 30,* 685–691.

Carroll, B. W. (1993). Perceived roles and preparation experiences of elementary counselors: Suggestions for change. *Elementary School Guidance and Counseling, 27,* 216–226.

Council for Accreditation of Counseling and Related Educational Programs. (1994). *CACREP accreditation standards and procedures manual.* Alexandria, VA: Author.

Glaser, B. G., & Strauss, A. (1967). *The discovery of grounded theory.* Chicago: Aldine.

Hall, D. T. (1987). Careers and socialization. *Journal of Management, 13,* 301–321.

Helms, B. J., & Ibrahim, F. A. (1983). A factor analytic study of parents' perceptions of the role and function of the secondary school counselor. *Measurement and Evaluation in Guidance, 16,* 100–106.

Helms, B. J., & Ibrahim, F. A. (1985). A comparison of counselor and parent perceptions of the role and function of the secondary school counselors. *The School Counselor, 32,* 266–274.

Hogan, R. A. (1964). Issues and approaches in supervision. *Psychotherapy, Theory, Research, and Practice, 1,* 139–141.

Hutchinson, R. L., Barrick, A. L., & Groves, M. (1986). Functions of secondary school counselors in the public schools: Ideal and actual. *The School Counselor, 34,* 87–91.

Kuzmic, J. (1994). A beginning teacher's search for meaning: Teacher socialization, organizational literacy, and empowerment. *Teaching and Teacher Education, 10,* 15–27.

Lofland, J. (1971). *Analyzing social settings.* Belmont, CA: Wadsworth.

Loganbill, C., Hardy, E., & Delworth, U. (1982). Supervision: A conceptual model. *Counseling Psychologist, 10,* 3–42.

McGowen, K. R., & Hart, L. E. (1990). Still different after all these years: Gender differences in professional identity formation. *Professional Psychology: Research and Practice, 21,* 118–123.

Partin, R. L. (1993). School counselors' time: Where does it go? *The School Counselor, 40,* 274–281.

Patton, M. Q. (1990). *Qualitative evaluation and research methods* (2nd ed.). Newbury Park, CA: Sage.

Peer, G. G. (1985). The status of secondary school guidance: A national survey. *The School Counselor, 32,* 181–189.

Reising, G. N., & Daniels, M. H. (1983). A study of Hogan's model of counselor development and supervision. *Journal of Counseling Psychology, 30,* 235–244.

Rosenbloom, S. (1992). The development of the work ego in the beginning analyst: Thoughts on identity formation of the psychoanalyst. *International Journal of Psycho-Analysis, 73,* 117–126.

Shertzer, B., & Stone, S. (1963). The school counselor and his publics: A problem in role definition. *Personnel and Guidance Journal, 41,* 687–693.

Skovholt, T. M., & Ronnestad, M. H. (1992). Themes in therapist and counselor development. *Journal of Counseling and Development, 70,* 505–515.

Splete, H. H., & Grisdale, G. A. (1992). The Oakland Counselor Academy: A professional development program for school counselors. *The School Counselor, 39,* 176–182.

Stanciak, L. A. (1995). Reforming the high school counselor's role: A look at developmental guidance. *NASSP Bulletin, 79,* 60–63.

Strauss, A., & Corbin, J. (1990). *Basics of qualitative research.* Newbury Park, CA: Sage.

Tennyson, W. W., Miller, G. D., Skovholt, T. M., & Williams, R. C. (1989). How they view their role: A survey of counselors in different secondary schools. *Journal of Counseling and Development, 67,* 399–403.

VanZandt, C. E., & Perry, N. S. (1992). Helping the rookie school counselor: A mentoring project. *The School Counselor, 39,* 158–163.

Watts, R. (1987). Development of professional identity in black clinical psychology students. *Professional Psychology: Research and Practice, 18,* 28–35.

Wrenn, C. G. (1957). Status and role of the school counselor. *Personnel and Guidance Journal, 36,* 175–183.

My Journey with Grounded Theory Research

Pamelia E. Brott
Virginia Polytechnic Institute and
State University, Blacksburg, Virginia

Research: a method to develop a knowledge base; a scientific endeavor to understand, support, or dispute what is known; a required component to obtain a Ph.D. Thus research is a method of discovery as a way to know the nature of the research problem and to uncover and understand what lies beneath a phenomenon about which little is yet known. A researcher can statistically analyze the data, or the researcher can allow the knowledge to emerge from the data. There are quantitative methods, and there are qualitative methods.

Qualitative research should not be entered into lightly; it should not be seen as a shortcut; it should not be viewed as a way to avoid quantitative methods. Instead, qualitative research should be entered into with a firm commitment; it should be seen as an in-depth, immersion experience into one's search for meaning; it should be viewed as a commitment to a qualitative method. It is a journey.

My journey with grounded theory has changed me in many ways. The theory is a reflection of me and of who I have become as a professional. Each time I present the theory and each time I use the knowledge I gained from this inquiry, I realize that I now live with qualitative inquiry ingrained in my cognitive and affective experiences.

I have seven suggestions for novice qualitative researchers who are embarking upon the grounded theory journey. I share these suggestions from the perspective that each suggestion would have assisted me in preparing for my journey. The suggestions deal with triangulation, flexibility, immersion, logistics, creativity, trust, and process.

In some ways, I fought against a qualitative approach to my dissertation. Quantitative methods seemed so cut-and-dry and provided a definitive means to an end for my Ph.D. Why would I embark on a qualitative method that could take several years to complete? Well, I could not find in the literature an answer to my question: How do school counselors develop a professional identity? Wisely, two of my committee members gently yet firmly guided me to my own realization that grounded theory would allow me to explore and find meaning to my question. These two faculty members were seasoned researchers and supported my personal development as a researcher.

In looking back on my first experience as a qualitative researcher involved with discovering a grounded theory, the shortest period in the process was completing the observations and interviews, and the longest period was the immersion process as I allowed the theory to emerge. My timeline consisted of three goals: (1) completing the observations and the interviews, (2) discovering an emergent theory, and (3) obtaining my Ph.D. I never allowed myself to hurry the process, although I did become impatient with myself as I reached numerable detours during the journey.

The immersion process engulfed my life for months, and it was an amazing experience. Hours would melt away, and the days and nights became indistinct. My inspirations were never planned; instead, they became new roads to explore. And I wrote everything down. Newsprint paper containing notes, ideas, and questions decorated the walls of my study throughout the process. Every time I entered the study, I entered my new world as a researcher.

I am not sure I was adequately prepared for the volume of data generated with grounded theory research. My advice on dealing with the logistics of grounded theory data includes the following:

1. After typing an interview transcription yourself, consider hiring a professional transcriptionist to word process all the taped interviews and observations. I cannot stress adequately the importance of typing each word yourself; however, it is a labor-intensive experience. For me, hiring a transcriptionist was a prudent investment. It allowed me to keep my focus as a researcher.

2. There are computer programs available to manage qualitative data (that is, interview and observation transcriptions). However, your handwritten analysis will, as a rule, be more detailed and complete than the computer analysis; the computer "sees" only what you have programmed it to look for in the words. My suggestion is to seek out computer programs to code the transcriptions and compare those results with your handwritten analysis. After comparing Nudist and Qualpro analysis with my handwritten analysis, I consciously made the decision to complete the open, axial, and selective coding procedures by hand. My in-depth study of the qualitative data through a handwritten analysis was critical to my understanding and the development of a grounded theory.

3. Keep at least two back-up copies of all the information stored on your computer. You never know when something untoward will happen (power surge, lightning strike, theft, and so on).

Besides discovering a grounded theory (that is, the development of professional school counselor identity), I also discovered my creative potential as a researcher. I developed numerous conceptual mapping techniques as I dealt with the coding process, and I then applied a conceptual mapping technique to tell each participant's story in the framework of the grounded theory. I have laminated the newsprint sheets and continue to use them in my presentations.

The unleashing of my creative potential led me to trust my intuitions. The faculty member who was chair of my dissertation committee continually asked me, "what does your gut tell you?" I needed, on the one hand, to learn to trust myself and, on the other hand, to continually submit my process to two of my committee members for review. There is always another question to explore.

Once you have proposed a grounded theory, you will realize that your journey has just begun. As I wrote the implications from the study, I became cognizant of the potential for my professional watermark. The implications have become my next steps in an ongoing process; the journey continues.

In summary, I offer the following seven suggestions based on my experiences as a qualitative researcher:

Suggestion 1: Enlist the support of competent researchers to guide you throughout the process.

Suggestion 2: Be flexible and do not let time be your master.

Suggestion 3: Immerse yourself in the process.

Suggestion 4: Deal with the logistics of the data you will generate.

Suggestion 5: Be creative in your discovery process.

Suggestion 6: Trust your instincts.

Suggestion 7: Remember, above all else, that grounded theory is a process, not a product.

8

A Conceptual Model of
Multiple Dimensions of Identity

Susan R. Jones, Marylu K. McEwen

Development of socially constructed identities has received increasing attention within literature and research in psychology and student affairs
within the last decade. Racial identity (for example, Cross, 1995; Helms,
1990, 1992, 1995), ethnic identity (Phinney, 1990, 1992), sexual identity (Cass,
1979; McCarn & Fassinger, 1996), and gender identity (Ossana, Helms, & Leonard,
1992; O'Neil, Egan, Owen, & Murry, 1993) have received primary focus. Yet most
developmental models and related research have addressed only a single dimension of identity, such as race or sexual orientation. Atkinson, Morten, and Sue
(1993), in their well-known Minority Identity Development model, do not specify
type of minority status (for example, race, gender, sexual orientation, or disability could apply) and also do not address how an individual may simultaneously
develop and embrace multiple minority statuses. Although research has frequently
considered differences according to gender, age, or other particular social conditions, the models and research have generally not addressed intersecting social
identities. In addition to racial, ethnic, sexual, and gender identities, college students may have other identity orientations, such as social class, religious, geographic or regional, and professional identities (McEwen, 1996).

Not only have researchers placed increasing emphasis upon identity development, but the number of identity development models has also increased. In terms
of models regarding multiple identities, the only frequently acknowledged model
is that of Reynolds and Pope (1991). However, Reynolds and Pope's model concerns primarily multiple oppressions (not identities in general) and possible ways

Susan R. Jones & Marylu K. McEwen. (2000). "A Conceptual Model of Multiple Dimensions of
Identity." *Journal of College Student Development, 41,* 405–413. Reprinted with permission.

that one can negotiate multiple oppressions. McEwen (1996) has proposed a theoretically driven model concerning development of multiple identities, but this model has not been empirically tested. A small number of studies have addressed multiple identities, and some theoretical and autobiographical essays speak to the experience of multiple identities (for example, Bridwell-Bowles, 1998; Espiritu, 1994; Moraga, 1998; Thompson & Tyagi, 1996). So although existing literature can inform discussions on multiple identities, no models specifically concerning multiple identities have been developed.

Reynolds and Pope (1991) drew attention to the importance of multiple identities through their discussion of multiple oppressions. They used several case studies to provide examples of how individuals might deal with their multiple oppressions and then extended Root's (1990) model on biracial identity development to multiple oppressions. Specifically, Reynolds and Pope (1991), in creating the Multidimensional Identity Model, suggested four possible ways for identity resolution for individuals belonging to more than one oppressed group. These four options were created from a matrix with two dimensions—the first concerns whether one embraces multiple oppressions or only one oppression, and the second concerns whether an individual actively or passively identifies with one or more oppressions. Thus, the four quadrants or options become

1. Identifying with only one aspect of self (for example, gender or sexual orientation or race) in a passive manner. That is, the aspect of self is assigned by others such as society, college student peers, or family.

2. Identifying with only one aspect of self that is determined by the individual. That is, the individual may identify as lesbian or Asian Pacific American or a woman without including other identities, particularly those that are oppressions.

3. Identifying with multiple aspects of self, but choosing to do so in a "segmented fashion" (Reynolds & Pope, 1991, p. 179), frequently only one at a time and determined more passively by the context rather than by the individual's own wishes. For example, in one setting the individual identifies as black, yet in another setting as gay.

4. The individual chooses to identify with the multiple aspects of self, especially multiple oppressions, and has both consciously chosen them and integrated them into his or her sense of self.

The value of Reynolds and Pope's (1991) work lies in their focus on the topic of multiple identities, their attention to the possible danger of considering an individual's identity development too narrowly by only using identity development models that address singular dimensions of one's identity, and their attention to identity resolution in the context of multiple oppressions. Yet in the decade since the publication of Reynolds and Pope's model, researchers have only minimally addressed multiple identities, contributing no application or testing of their model and little follow-up to their work.

McEwen (1996), drawing on her education in mathematics and physics, considered how such dimensions and developmental processes regarding multiple identities might be represented. She suggested that the interaction and intersection of multiple identity development could be viewed as a conical structure with varying radii and heights. The conical structure is similar to a helix. The increasing length and circumference of the cone represent the greater complexity of an individual's development as one's age, experiences, education, and reflection change. A two-dimensional cross section of the cone, similar to a circle or ellipse, would represent an individual's development at that particular point in time. Thus, an examination of many horizontal cross sections of the cone would provide a comprehensive picture of one's development at various points in time. These horizontal cross sections, however, would not provide any sense of one's developmental patterns over time.

On the other hand, vertical cross sections might incorporate only one or two dimensions of identity. However, a vertical cross section would suggest how an individual's identity in that particular dimension or dimensions has developed over the span of one's lifetime. A vertical "slice" would represent just one part of the picture of an individual at multiple points in time. Other kinds of cross sections of this conical representation could be considered. McEwen's model, through various cross sections, enables a portrayal of intersections or interactions among identity development dimensions or between multiple identities not seen in other models.

In addition, theoretical discussions by Deaux (1993), a social psychologist, relate to the conceptual model of multiple dimensions of identity presented here. She conceptualized identity as both defined internally by self and externally by others, which provides a foundation for understanding multiple identities. Other recent research (Ferguson, 1995; Finley, 1997; Kiely, 1997) underscored the importance of relative salience, sociocultural context, and overlapping identities. A strength in these studies lies in examining multiple identities; however, none provided a model of multiple identities or suggested a process by which multiple identities are developed and negotiated.

In an effort to extend existing work on multiple identities, the researchers attempted to advance a more complex understanding of identity and present a model of multiple dimensions of identity development. The model evolved from a qualitative study conducted at a large public university on the East Coast. Using the grounded theory approach of Glaser and Strauss (1967), the researchers explored the self-perceived identities and the multiple dimensions of identity from the perspective of women college students. The focus of the study was on students' understandings of their own identity and experiences of difference and of the influence of multiple dimensions of identity on an evolving sense of self.

Methodology

Participants

Participants were ten undergraduate women all enrolled at a large East Coast university and diverse in race, cultural background, and academic major. They ranged in age from twenty to twenty-four and were predominantly of junior or senior class standing. The racial and ethnic backgrounds of participants included five who were White, two who identified themselves as African American or Black, one woman who identified herself as African, one as Sri Lankan, and one as Asian Indian. A variety of religious affiliations were also represented: Jewish, Buddhist, Hindu, Catholic, Presbyterian, and Holiness Pentecostal.

Participants were drawn to the study using "purposeful sampling" (Patton, 1990), which emphasizes sampling for information-rich cases. The criterion for constructing the sample in this study was evidence of variation along identity dimensions such as race, culture, sexual orientation, and religion. An initial group of five participants was chosen from among those who responded to an invitation to take part in the study and who met sampling criteria for maximum variation and ability to participate. Consistent with grounded theory methodology and theoretical sampling (Strauss & Corbin, 1990), five participants were added as the study progressed. These participants were identified through snowball sampling strategies or through responses to invitations to participate extended at a campus leadership program. Sampling decisions were guided by initial data analysis, the opportunity for information-rich cases, and a commitment to a diverse sample. Saturation was achieved and sampling was ended when patterns and themes in the data emerged and a diverse sample had been accomplished.

Procedure

Data were collected through in-depth, open-ended interviews. The central purpose of the interviews was to engage in dialogue with participants to elicit their descriptions and perceptions of themselves and their understandings of identity development. This phenomenological approach emphasized the importance of providing a structure for participants to communicate their own understandings, perspectives, and attribution of meaning. Interviews were open-ended to permit and encourage participants' use of their own words in describing the internal and interpersonal processes by which they defined their identities and made sense of differences.

Three interviews were conducted with each participant. Interview protocols were developed in response to emerging patterns and themes for all participants as well as to pick up on experiences and perceptions particular to an individual. Initial questions were broad enough to create room for individual response and freedom. Subsequent interviews were more structured and focused specifically on particular identity dimensions identified in the previous interview. Interviews lasted between thirty and seventy-five minutes and all were audiotaped.

Several strategies to assure trustworthiness of findings were employed. These included member checking by providing participants an opportunity to read transcripts and check initial analysis, and the use of an inquiry auditor to verify the work by essentially conducting a parallel process of data analysis and comparing notes.

True to grounded theory methodology, data analysis was conducted using three levels of coding: open coding, axial coding, and selective coding. The first stage of coding involves breaking down data and beginning the process of categorization. Axial coding takes initial categories and makes further comparisons that describe relationships between categories. Using selective coding, saturation of categories is examined, which means that further analysis produces no new information or need for additional categories. In short, all the data are captured and described by key categories, and a core category emerges that tells the central story of all participants as a group. This core category then is used to develop an emerging theory and conceptual model that is considered grounded in the data and reflective of the lived experiences of all participants.

In this study, data analysis produced over two thousand concepts from raw data, seventy-one categories from initial comparison, ten key categories, and one core category (Jones, 1997). The conceptual model was developed to provide a visual representation of the findings from the study.

Results

Because the focus of this article is on the conceptual model developed from the findings, only a brief description of the ten key categories is included. More detailed descriptions may be found elsewhere (Jones, 1997). The key categories that emerged from analysis of data from the interviews with participants were (1) relative salience of identity dimensions in relation to difference; (2) the multiple ways in which race matters; (3) multiple layers of identity; (4) the braiding of gender with other dimensions; (5) the importance of cultural identifications and cultural values; (6) the influence of family and background experiences; (7) current experiences and situational factors; (8) relational, inclusive values and guiding personal beliefs; (9) career decisions and future planning; and (10) the search for identity. The key categories represent themes and constructs that are interrelated and when integrated define the core category.

The core category provides an integrative function by weaving together the key categories in a way that tells the central story of all the participants. In this study, the core category was defined as the contextual influences on the construction of identity. The contextual influences that emerged as significant included race, culture, gender, family, education, relationships with those different from oneself, and religion. The core category also reflects the finding that identity was defined and understood as having multiple intersecting dimensions. The particular salience of identity dimensions depended upon the contexts in which they were experienced. Therefore, both difference and privilege worked to mediate the connection with and salience of various identity dimensions (that is, race was not salient for white women; religion was very salient for Jewish women; culture was salient for the Asian Indian woman).

A Conceptual Model for Multiple Dimensions of Identity

The conceptual model presented here (see Figure 8.1) is intended to capture the essence of the core category as well as the identity stories of the participants. The model represents multiple dimensions of identity development for a diverse group of women college students. The model is a fluid and dynamic one, representing the ongoing construction of identities and the influence of changing contexts on the experience of identity development. Therefore, the model is illustrative of one person's identity construction at a particular time. The model is also drawn to depict the possibility of living comfortably with multiple identities, rather than simply describing multiple dimensions of identity.

At the center of multiple dimensions of identity is a core sense of self. This center, or core identity, is experienced as a personal identity, somewhat protected from view, which incorporates "valued personal attributes and characteristics" (Jones, 1997, p. 383). The core was frequently described by participants as their "inner identity" or "inside self" as contrasted with what they referred to as their "outside" identity or the "facts" of their identity. Outside identities were easily named by others and interpreted by the participants as less meaningful than the complexities of their inside identities, which they guarded and kept close to themselves and made less susceptible to outside influence. The words these women used to describe their core included intelligent, kind, a good friend, compassionate, independent. They resisted using terms that conveyed external definition and identity

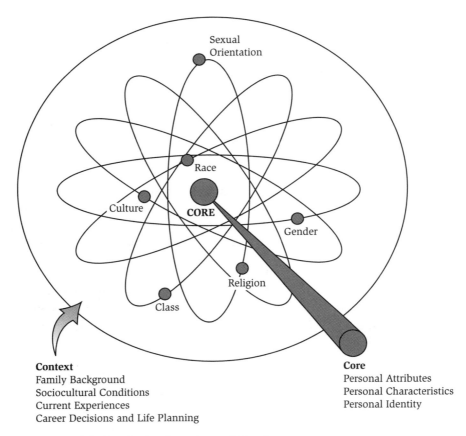

Context
Family Background
Sociocultural Conditions
Current Experiences
Career Decisions and Life Planning

Core
Personal Attributes
Personal Characteristics
Personal Identity

Figure 8.1. Model of Multiple Dimensions of Identity.

categories to describe their core sense of self. To these young women, labels lacked complexity, accuracy, and personal relevancy. They believed that labels rarely touched the core of an individual's sense of self. For them, individual identity was experienced and lived at far greater depth than such categories suggested or permitted. Surrounding the core, and at times integrally connected to the core, were what they experienced as more externally defined dimensions such as gender, race, culture, and religion.

The intersecting circles of identity in the model (see Figure 8.1) represent the significant identity dimensions and contextual influences identified by participants in this study. These dimensions were variously experienced and included race, culture, gender, sexual orientation, religion, and social class. The circles intersect with one another to demonstrate that no one dimension may be understood singularly; it can be understood only in relation to other dimensions. For example, for all the participants, gender was an identity dimension to which they related. However, the description of what being female meant to them was quickly connected with other dimensions (for example, Jewish woman, Black woman, lesbian, Indian woman). For those participants for whom culture was most salient, family and culture were inextricably connected.

The importance, or relative salience, of these identity dimensions is indicated by dots located on each of the identity dimension circles. The location of the dot and its proximity to the core represents the particular salience of that identity dimension to the individual at that time. For example, if culture is particularly salient to an individual, the placement of the dot on that dimension is closer to the core. If sexual orientation is not particularly salient to an individual at that point in time, the dot is farther away from the core. The model does, however, illustrate that various identity dimensions are present in each individual yet experienced in different ways as more or less salient. For example, race was found to be very salient for the Black women in the study and rarely salient for the White women. Similarly, culture was salient for the Asian Indian woman and religion for the Jewish women.

The intersecting circles and the various locations indicating salience of particular identity dimensions also represent that more than one identity dimension can be engaged by the individual at any one time. Identity dimensions then may be experienced simultaneously as well as more or less salient than other dimensions.

The context within which the individual experiences multiple dimensions of identity is represented by the larger circle that includes both the core and intersecting identity dimensions. These dimensions become more or less salient as they interact with contextual influences such as family background, sociocultural conditions, current life experiences, and career decisions and life planning. Participants perceived identity dimensions as both externally defined and internally experienced and also influenced by different contexts. When identities are imposed from the outside, dimensions are not seen as integral to core. However, when interacting with certain sociocultural conditions such as sexism and racism, identity dimensions may be scrutinized in a new way that resulted in participants' reflection and greater understanding of a particular dimension.

Influences of sociocultural conditions, family background, and current experiences cannot be underestimated in understanding how participants constructed and experienced their identities. The conceptual model presented in Figure 8.1 is drawn to illustrate the relationship of these factors to the identity development process. Salience of identity dimensions was rooted in internal awareness and external scrutiny (for example, race for black women), and lack of salience seemed prevalent among those more privileged identity dimensions (for example, sexual orientation for heterosexual women). These findings suggested that systems of privilege and inequality were least visible and understood by those who are most privileged by these systems. Thus, when difference was experienced, identity was shaped. When difference was not experienced, participants attributed these dimensions as relevant to others. Both privilege and difference mediated the connection with and relative salience of various dimensions of identity and shaped the connection to identity dimensions by the individual.

Discussion

Interest in understanding multiple identities emerges from a growing awareness of the nonsingular nature in which individual identities are constructed and self-perceived. Extending Erikson's (1980) description of identity, more recent research draws attention to the importance of considering the influences of dimensions such as race, culture, social class, and sexual orientation, as well as the need for examination of the sociocultural and sociopolitical contexts in which identities are constructed (Trickett, Watts, & Birman, 1994). The conceptual model of multiple dimensions of identity presented in Figure 8.1 is drawn from the words and understandings of a diverse group of women college students and depicts the complexities of identity development when multiple dimensions are considered. The model reflects an acknowledgment that different dimensions of identity will be more or less important for each individual given a range of contextual influences. It also presents identity development as a fluid and dynamic process rather than a more linear and static stage model.

The findings from this study and the resulting model reflect Deaux's (1993) conceptualizations of identities as both defined internally by self and externally by others. She suggested that "social and personal identity are fundamentally interrelated. Personal identity is defined, at least in part, by group memberships, and social categories are infused with personal meaning" (p. 5). More specifically, according to Deaux (1993): "*Social identities* are those roles [for example, parent] *or* membership categories [for example, Latino or Latina] that a person claims as representative. . . . *Personal identity* refers to those traits and behaviors [for example, kind or responsible] that the person finds self-descriptive, characteristics that are typically linked to one or more of the identity categories" (p. 6) Thus, the core identity in this conceptual model might be described as "personal identity" in Deaux's language, and the multiple identities (intersecting circles) characterize Deaux's "social identities." Further, and particularly important to this discussion of multiple identities, Deaux (1993) indicated that within the tradition of sociology, "multiple identities are assumed" (p. 5). An articulated assumption of multiple identities, however, does not seem to be the case within theories of student development.

Despite a complex discussion of identity development, Deaux (1993) provided no specific attention to how multiple identities are formed. Her research does, however, underscore the importance of the context in which social identities exist, distinctions between self-perceived inside self and outside identity, and the ongoing negotiations and relationships between one's personal and social identities that contribute to the experience of multiple identities. This model of multiple dimensions of identity goes beyond Deaux's work in suggesting how multiple identities develop and change.

Although Reynolds and Pope (1991) focused on multiple oppressions, their model suggests an expanded understanding of multiple identities and the idea of relative salience, as supported by the findings of this study. The model proposed here extends the work of Reynolds and Pope (1991) by contributing to an understanding of "the multidimensional nature of human identity" (p. 179) and providing a more integrative framework for understanding identity. Specifically, our conceptual model addresses multiple identities more broadly than multiple oppressions and provides a dynamic representation of the fit of the core self with other identities and the changing relative salience of particular dimensions of identity. Further, as Reynolds and Pope suggested through their examples, this model also incorporates the importance of contexts to how multiple identities are formed and shaped.

Finley (1997), in a qualitative study of six women with multiple minority statuses, used the Optimal Theory Applied to Identity Development model (Myers et al., 1991) and the Multidimensional Identity Model (Reynolds & Pope, 1991), and found that "multiple identities followed overlapping, interweaving spirals of development" (p. 3921B). Finley also underscored both the importance of environmental influences on identity development and the complexity of the process. This complexity is typically not represented in other models. The model of multiple dimensions of identity and Finley's findings share an understanding of the identity development process as dynamic, nonlinear, and complex.

This conceptual model complements and elaborates upon McEwen's (1996) emerging model of multiple identities by portraying how one's personal identity and other multiple identities might relate to any one point in time. Both this model and McEwen's model suggest the presence and interaction of multiple dimensions of identity. This conceptual model, however, shows how identity can be understood and experienced differently at different points in time, particularly in relation to one's personal identity and in terms of relative salience of each dimension. McEwen also suggested the importance of considering and representing the separate developmental processes of each individual's social identity over time.

The representation in the model of the relationship of the dots on the intersecting circles to the core identity suggests the evolving nature of identity and the changing salience of the various multiple identities. This aspect of the model that emerged from Jones's qualitative study (1997) also reflects Ferguson's (1995) findings in a quantitative study of the relationship of race, gender, sexual orientation, and self-esteem in 181 lesbians of African descent. Ferguson suggested that the women in her study "may be in a continual recycling process in which they retain ties with all three social identities and communities [lesbian, woman, and African American], but to greater or lesser degrees" (p. 4565A).

Kiely (1997), in a study of racial identity, womanist identity, and social class variables in Black (n = 173) and White (n = 163) women college students, found that students' incorporation of multiple aspects of their identity was more common among Black women than White women in her sample. Kiely's research supports the description in this conceptual model that the relative salience of multiple identities is influenced by those identities that are privileged and by those that are externally scrutinized.

The conceptual model for multiple dimensions of identity represents the researchers' attempt to capture the complexity of the identity development process. This model offers another option for thinking about multiple identities and the importance of contextual influences to the development of identity. The model does not portray a developmental process, although it incorporates the importance of the interaction and interface among one's multiple identities and hints at factors that contribute to the development of identity (for example, contextual influences). It does provide a developmental snapshot of the most salient dimensions of an individual's identity, how the individual experiences those dimensions, and directions for the individual's future growth and development.

This conceptual model suggests the importance of understanding the complexities of identity development. Student affairs educators must not presume what is most central to individuals, but must instead listen for how a person sees herself. This study underscores the importance of seeing students as they see themselves or as they reveal themselves to others. The participants in this study wanted to be understood as they understood themselves and as the totality of who they were, rather than be understood through externally imposed labels and by a singular dimension. Reynolds and Pope (1991) stated that the professional's responsibility is to conceptualize, "understand and facilitate this integration of [college students'] identity" (p. 179).

In addition, the results of this study suggest that educators have a responsibility to help students from majority identity statuses understand the implications of taken-for-granted identities. More specifically, student affairs educators can encourage students who are members of groups whose identity is not examined to consider these aspects of their identity. Similarly, educators must exercise caution in making assumptions about the relative salience of particular identity dimensions for students in traditionally marginalized groups.

The findings of this study suggest the importance of additional research on multiple identities and the development of models that depict this process. The model presented here has not been tested or widely applied. The inclusion of students' voices in this kind of research cannot be understated. Although this study was limited by a small sample, at one institution, of women who indicated an interest in talking about their identity development, the presence of diverse voices and identities contributed to the richness of the data and an understanding of the complexity of the process. Future research that explores this process and incorporates Deaux's suggestion that with "shifting contexts . . . people must continually work at their identities" (p. 10) will add greater clarity to understanding multiple identities. As one participant in the study articulated, the process of identity development when multiple dimensions are considered is an "ongoing journey of self-discovery."

References

Atkinson, D. R., Morten, G., & Sue, D. W. (1993). *Counseling American minorities: A cross-cultural perspective* (4th ed.). Dubuque, IA: Brown and Benchmark.

Bridwell-Bowles, L. (Ed.) (1998). *Identity matters: Rhetorics of difference.* Upper Saddle River, NJ: Prentice Hall.

Cass, V. C. (1979). Homosexual identity formation: A theoretical model. *Journal of Homosexuality, 4,* 219–235.

Cross, W. E., Jr. (1995). The psychology of Nigrescence: Revising the Cross model. In J. G. Ponterotto, J. M. Casas, L. A. Suzuki, & C. M. Alexander (Eds.), *Handbook of multicultural counseling* (pp. 93–122). Thousand Oaks, CA: Sage.

Deaux, K. (1993). Reconstructing social identity. *Personality and Social Psychology Bulletin, 19,* 4–12.

Erikson, E. H. (1980). *Identity and the life cycle.* New York: Norton (Original work published 1959).

Espiritu, Y. L. (1994). The intersection of race, ethnicity, and class. The multiple identities of second-generation Filipinos. *Identities: Global Studies in Culture and Power, 1,* 249–273.

Ferguson, A. D. (1995). The relationship between African-American lesbians' race, gender, and sexual orientation and self-esteem (Doctoral dissertation, University of Maryland, College Park, 1995). *Dissertation Abstracts International, 56,* 4565A.

Finley, H. C. (1997). Women with multiple identities: A qualitative search for patterns of identity development among complex differences (Doctoral dissertation, The Ohio State University, 1997). *Dissertation Abstracts International, 58,* 3921B.

Glaser, B., & Strauss, A. (1967). *The discovery of grounded theory: Strategies for qualitative research.* Chicago: Aldine.

Helms, J. E. (1990). Toward a model of white racial identity development. In J. E. Helms (Ed.), *Black and white racial identity: Theory, research, and practice* (pp. 49–66). New York: Greenwood Press.

Helms, J. E. (1992). *A race is a nice thing to have: A guide to being a white person, or understanding the white persons in your life.* Topeka, KS: Content Communications.

Helms, J. E. (1995). An update of Helms's white and people of color racial identity models. In J. G. Ponterotto, J. M. Casas, L. A. Suzuki, & C. M. Alexander (Eds.), *Handbook of multicultural counseling* (pp. 181–198). Thousand Oaks, CA: Sage.

Jones, S. R. (1997). Voices of identity and difference: A qualitative exploration of the multiple dimensions of identity development in women college students. *Journal of College Student Development, 38,* 376–386.

Kiely, L. J. (1997). An exploratory analysis of the relationship of racial identity, social class, and family influences on womanist identity development (Doctoral dissertation, University of Maryland, College Park, 1997). *Dissertation Abstracts International, 58,* 2086A.

McCarn, S. R., & Fassinger, R. E. (1996). Revisioning sexual minority identity formation: A new model of lesbian identity and its implications. *The Counseling Psychologist, 24,* 508–534.

McEwen, M. K. (1996). New perspectives on identity development. In S. R. Komives & D. B. Woodard, Jr. (Eds.), *Student services: A handbook for the profession* (3rd ed., pp. 188–217). San Francisco: Jossey-Bass.

Moraga, C. (1998). La güera. In M. L. Andersen & P. Hill Collins (Eds.), *Race, class and gender: An anthology* (pp. 26–33). Belmont, CA: Wadsworth.

Myers, L. J., Speight, S. L., Highlen, P. S., Cox, C. I., Reynolds, A. L., Adams, E. M., & Hanley, C. P. (1991). Identity development and worldview: Toward an optimal conceptualization. *Journal of Counseling and Development, 70,* 54–63.

O'Neil, J. M., Egan, J., Owen, S. V., & Murry, V. M. (1993). The Gender Role Journey Measure: Scale development and psychometric evaluation. *Sex Roles, 28,* 167–185.

Ossana, S. M., Helms, J. E., & Leonard, M. M. (1992). Do "womanist" identity attitudes influence college women's self-esteem and perceptions of environmental bias? *Journal of Counseling and Development, 70,* 402–408.

Patton, M. Q. (1990). *Qualitative evaluation and research methods* (2nd ed.). Newbury Park, CA: Sage.

Phinney, J. S. (1990). Ethnic identity in adolescents and adults: Review of research. *Psychological Bulletin, 108,* 499–514.

Phinney, J. S. (1992). The Multigroup Ethnic Identity Measure: A new scale for use with diverse groups. *Journal of Adolescent Research, 7,* 156–176.

Reynolds, A. L., & Pope, R. L. (1991). The complexities of diversity: Exploring multiple oppressions. *Journal of Counseling and Development, 70,* 174–180.

Root, M.P.P. (1990). Resolving "other" status: Identity development of biracial individuals. In L. S. Brown & M.P.P. Root (Eds.), *Complexity and diversity in feminist theory and therapy* (pp. 185–205). New York: Haworth Press.

Strauss, A., & Corbin, J. (1990). *Basics of qualitative research: Grounded theory procedures and techniques.* Newbury Park, CA: Sage.

Thompson, B., & Tyagi, S. (Eds.). (1996). *Names we call home: Autobiography on racial identity.* New York: Routledge.

Trickett, E. J., Watts, R. J., & Birman, D. (Eds.). (1994). *Human diversity: Perspectives on people in context.* San Francisco: Jossey-Bass.

Becoming Grounded in
Grounded Theory Methodology

Susan R. Jones
The Ohio State University, Columbus, Ohio

I am reaching for the words to describe the difference between
a common identity that has been imposed and the individual
identity any one of us will choose, once she gains that chance.
June Jordan (1985, p. 47)

This quote by June Jordan captures what I experienced as the core methodological challenge and opportunity of grounded theory methodology. Not coincidentally, it also illuminates a central theme in my research on identity development. In taking advantage of the clarity of a retrospective perspective, grounded theory methodology was the most appropriate for this study on the multiple dimensions of identity development because of the seamless blending of method and area of inquiry. How did I arrive at this particular qualitative methodology for my study? Intentional selection or fortuitous choice?

Because I was interested in how college women perceived their own identities, I wanted to preserve the individual voices and experiences of the women in my study while also generating theory about multiple dimensions of identity development. I embarked on a journey in search of the method that would provide structure to my research questions as well as preserve the integrity of the perspectives of those individuals participating in the study. I knew that when I finished this research I wanted the participants in the study to recognize themselves in what I wrote. To identify the appropriate methodology, I read a lot! I not only read about various qualitative methods and research designs, I also read a number of qualitative studies.

Two central elements of grounded theory led me to the decision that this was the appropriate methodology for my study. First, a grounded theory approach assures close proximity between theory and the experiences of those involved in the study. As the name implies, theory is grounded because it is anchored in the words, experiences, and meaning making of participants. Researchers do not begin with a theory that they set out to prove, but begin with an area of inquiry and then what is pertinent to that area emerges through data collection and a systematic analytic process (Strauss and Corbin, 1990). Second, the analytic process characteristic of grounded theory methodology can be understood as storytelling. What I mean by this is that the researcher begins with the individual stories of each participant in a study and then, through the analytic process, takes the story apart and puts it back together again in a way that tells the story of all the participants. This is the complex negotiation between the common story and the individual identities that comprise the story. The challenge in grounded theory is not to impose the common story (identity theory) but to enable that story to emerge from the perspectives of participants and truly reflect their individual and chosen story (identity as personal story).

The negotiation between the common and the individual was also apparent in sampling decisions. Because I was interested in the influence of multiple dimensions of identity on an evolving sense of self and participants' understandings of their own identity and experiences of difference, it seemed appropriate to create a "diverse" sample. What I learned through this process is that it is essential that the researcher be clear about what is meant by a "diverse sample" and why a diverse sample is important. Although a diverse sample in this study was theoretically driven, there were limits to what could be said from a study that included one African, one Sri Lankan, one Indian American, one lesbian, three Jewish women, one Hindu, two black women, and so on. It is important to be explicit about who is in the sample, but the goal of grounded theory methodology is not to make generalizations with one's findings. The strength of this methodology is in the depth of description and analysis that emerges from the data. To this end, it is important to bring to life the participants in the study for the reader, rather than simply describing them demographically and leaving them to stand alone as stick figures or "straw men" [sic] without the substance and richness their individual perspectives provide.

I found that the process of "bringing to life" the participants in the study depended upon my ability to reflect on my relationship with them and to listen well so that their stories truly unfolded. The first factor refers to an understanding of myself as a white researcher interested in the identities of those different from myself, and the need for me to constantly check my own positionality and standpoint in relation to understanding and conveying the identity stories of my participants through research. Related to this, I learned about the incredible importance of "listening eloquently," as Langston Hughes called it, to the words, experiences, and feelings of the participants so that their stories would truly unfold without my imposing one on them. This is very difficult to accomplish, as we are trained as researchers to "make meaning," describe, and analyze. I also learned to listen for what was not voiced by participants, which reflected the ways in which certain dimensions of identity had been silenced or been taken for granted.

At the beginning of the study, I identified a number of strategies to assure trust-worthiness of findings, the qualitative complement of reliability and validity. As the study progressed it became increasingly clear to me that participants were in essence telling me their life stories. These life stories were rich in what they revealed about the participants' particular sense of who they were and who they were to become. As the researcher, I developed a deep sense of obligation and responsibility to retell the stories in a way that made sense to each participant. I often reflected on a line from Toni Morrison's novel *Beloved* as I thought about my responsibility: "She is a friend of mind. She gather me . . . the pieces I am, she gather them and give them back to me all in the right order. It's good, you know, when you got a woman who is a friend of the mind" (Morrison, 1987, p. 272).

One of the strategies I used in my ongoing effort to serve the participants of this study as "a friend of the mind" was to write each participant a letter with an essay that was intended to capture the initial findings of the study. As such, each essay was grounded in what all the women in the study discussed, as well as their individual stories, experiences, and thoughts as they had expressed them to me. I asked each participant to provide me with feedback about how well the essay captured their thinking about their identities and what they had communicated to me. The response was overwhelming and unexpected. For almost every participant, reading the essay was an emotional experience. Several of them indicated that the essay was like a gift because it functioned as a mirror back to them. The participants delighted in telling their stories, but to see themselves in print was like returning their story to them. And for me as the researcher, this was the most authentic verification that, for these women, I had effectively navigated the difficult terrain of honoring both the common and the individual in telling their stories; that the theoretical and more abstract conceptualizations of the grounded theory still reflected, in a way participants recognized, their individual life stories and perceptions of the multiple dimensions of identity. This is the core challenge and opportunity of grounded theory methodology.

References

Jordan, J. (1985). *On call: Political essays.* Boston: South End Press.

Morrison, T. (1987). *Beloved.* New York: Knopf.

Strauss, A., & Corbin, J. (1990). *Basics of qualitative research: Grounded theory procedure and techniques.* Newbury Park, CA: Sage.

Case Study

Most of us have encountered case studies in our training as professionals and in our work in applied fields of practice. However, despite its prevalence in the literature, "the phrase 'case study'. . .is not used in any standard way" (Hammersley & Gomm, 2000, p. 1) and is often used interchangeably with other qualitative research terms. The fact that a lawyer, a social worker, a medical doctor, and even a detective can be involved in research on a "case" further clouds the issue as to what constitutes case study research. While some define case study research in terms of the process of doing a case study (Yin, 1994), or in terms of the end product, other scholars define the case in terms of the unit of analysis. As Stake (2000, p. 435) suggests, case study is less of a methodological choice than "a choice of what is to be studied." The "what" is a *bounded system* (Smith, 1978), a single entity, a unit around which there are boundaries. The case then has a finite quality about it either in terms of time (the evolution or history of a particular program), space (the case is located in a particular place), and/or components comprising the case (number of participants, for example). Stake (1995, p. 2) clarifies the bounded system as follows: "The case could be a child. It could be a classroom of children or a particular mobilization of professionals to study a childhood condition. The case is one among others. . . . An innovative program may be a case. All the schools in Sweden can be a case. But a relationship among schools, the reasons for innovative teaching, or the policies of school reform are less commonly considered a case. These topics are generalities rather than specifics. The case is a specific, complex, functioning thing."

While the study of a bounded system can include historical, quantitative as well as qualitative data, the focus on case studies in this volume is qualitative. Qualitative case studies share with other forms of qualitative research the search for meaning and understanding, the researcher as the primary instrument of data collection and analysis, an inductive investigative strategy, and the end product being richly descriptive. Of course defining a case study in terms of the unit of analysis, the bounded system, allows for any number of qualitative strategies to be combined with the case. Ethnography is one of the most common. Ethnographic case studies are studies focusing on the sociocultural interpretation of a particular cultural group; grounded theory can be built within a case, and people's stories could be presented as narrative case studies.

The process of conducting a case study begins with the selection of the "case." The selection is done purposefully, not randomly; that is, a particular person, site, program, process, community, or other bounded system is selected because it exhibits characteristics of interest to the researcher. The case might be unique or typical, representative of a common practice, or never before encountered. The selection depends upon what you want to learn and the significance that knowledge might have for extending theory or improving practice. Often, one must select samples within the case as for example when studying a large patient education program, a corporation, or a school. Who should be interviewed? When and which activities should be observed? Except for the selection of a "bounded system," qualitative case study researchers proceed in data collection and data analysis like other qualitative researchers. The findings of the investigation are written up as a comprehensive description of the case. And as Stake (2000) notes, there are a number of stylistic options for this case write-up including "how much to make the report a story," and "how much to compare with other cases" (p. 448).

Perhaps because a case study focuses on a single unit, a single instance, the issue of generalizability looms larger here than with other types of qualitative research. However, as several writers point out, much can be learned from a particular case (Merriam, 1998). Readers can learn vicariously from an encounter with the case through the researcher's narrative description (Stake, 2000). The colorful description in a case study can create an image—"a vivid portrait of excellent teaching, for example—can become a prototype that can be used in the education of teachers or for the appraisal of teaching" (Eisner, 1991, p. 1999). Further, Erickson (1986) argues that since the general lies in the particular, what we learn in a particular case can be transferred to similar situations. It is the reader, not the researcher, who determines what can apply to his or her context. Stake (2000, p. 442) explains how this knowledge transfer works: "Case researchers, like others, pass along to readers some of their personal meanings of events and relationship—and fail to pass along others. They know that the reader, too, will add and subtract, invent and shape—reconstructing the knowledge in ways that leave it. . .more likely to be personally useful."

There are two case studies included in this volume. Enomoto and Bair (1999) studied a comprehensive high school with a large multi-ethnic student body. The second selection (Hébert & Beardsley, 2001) is the study of a single child, "a gifted black child living in rural poverty." For each of these, the unit of analysis, or "bounded system," is clear—a particular child, a particular high school.

In both case studies the researchers became well acquainted with the community, conveying to the reader the general context of the lives of the students of interest. In Enomoto and Bair's study, we come to know the urban high school and the Arab immigrant students in particular; in Hébert's study we get a sense of the rural Southern community and the plight of Jermaine, a gifted black child. As readers, we can learn from these cases and perhaps transfer some of the knowledge gained to our own situations, our own practice.

References

Eisner, E. W. (1991). *The enlightened eye: Qualitative inquiry and the enhancement of educational practice*. Old Tappan, NJ: Macmillan.

Erickson, F. (1986). Qualitative methods in research on teaching. In M.C. Whittrock (Ed.), *Handbook of research on teaching*. (3rd ed.) Old Tappan, NJ: Macmillan.

Hammersley, M., & Gomm, R. (2000). Introduction. In M. Hammersley, R. Gomm, & P. Foster, (Eds.), *Case study method*. (pp. 1–16). Thousand Oaks, CA: Sage.

Merriam, S. B. (1998). *Qualitative research and case study applications in education*. (2nd ed.) San Francisco: Jossey-Bass.

Smith, L. M. (1978). An evolving logic of participant observation, educational ethnography and other case studies. In L. Shulman (Ed.), *Review of research in education*. Itasca, IL: Peacock.

Stake, R. E. (1995). *The art of case study research*. Thousand Oaks, CA: Sage.

Stake, R. E. (2000). Case studies. In N. K. Denzin, & Y. S. Lincoln (Eds.), *Handbook of qualitative research*. (2nd ed.) (pp. 435–454). Thousand Oaks, CA: Sage.

Yin, R. K. (1994). *Case study research: Design and methods*. (2nd ed.) Thousand Oaks, CA: Sage.

9

The Role of the School in the Assimilation of Immigrant Children

A Case Study of Arab Americans

Ernestine K. Enomoto, Mary Antony Bair

Since the beginning of the twentieth century, a major concern of American public education has been the assimilation and Americanization of immigrants. According to Tyack (1974), schooling was viewed as a socialization mechanism to integrate the diversity of first and second generation immigrant children into American society. From outward appearances, schools succeeded in converting the "daily arriving city-full of Russians, Turks, Austro-Hungarians, Sicilians, Greeks, Arabs, into good Americans" and creating a homogeneity of those ethnic newcomers (Tyack, 1974, p. 230). For the most part, educators believed that their school organization would reinforce American culture and were "confident that schooling could change the many into the one people, *e pluribus unum*" (Tyack, 1974, p. 232).

Over the course of the century, immigrants have come in greater numbers and from different countries, notably from Mexico, Southeast Asia, Central and South America, and the Caribbean (NCAS Research and Policy Report, 1988). According to Muller and Espenshade (1985), 60 percent of recent immigrants are between sixteen and forty-four years of age, with those of undocumented status even younger. Moreover, with immigrants settling in urban areas, rather than rural or suburban areas, public schools must accommodate increasing numbers of school-age immigrants.

In dealing with the racial and ethnic diversity among immigrants, there is tension between those educators who believe in schooling for assimilation and

Ernestine K. Enomoto & Mary Antony Bair. (1999). "The Role of the School in the Assimilation of Immigrant Children: A Case Study of Arab Americans." *International Journal of Curriculum and Instruction, 1*, 45–66. Reprinted with permission.

those who favor cultural pluralism. Assimilationists retain the notion of the "melting pot" where all ethnic minorities learn common language, cultural heritage, and set of values that are deemed American (Bloom, 1987; Hirsch, 1988; Ravitch, 1983). The move to legalize English as the country's official language gives evidence to the strength of this assimilationist perspective. Alternatively, cultural pluralists propose that ethnic minorities draw upon their cultural heritage in an American society viewed metaphorically as a "salad bowl" where the variety is presented rather than blended. "For example, a cultural pluralist believes that Blacks, Vietnamese, Irish, and Mexicans can retain the supporting benefits of their cultural group while considering themselves part of a larger American culture at the same time" (Bennett & LeCompte, 1990, p. 219). Educators who hold such a perspective seek to understand and accommodate, rather than remediate, the differences of minority students in order to create more culturally congruent classrooms (Au & Mason, 1981; McLaren, 1989; Van Ness, 1981).

In this sociological study, we explored this tension by examining the school's role in the assimilation process. Our intention was to be exploratory in our investigation, considering questions related to the assimilation and Americanization of immigrant children. How did a particular school transmit values, beliefs, and customs of American society? What was its social organization and structure? How were the teachers and administrators acting as socializing agents? By addressing these questions, we hoped to understand the nature and extent to which the school accommodated and assimilated its largely immigrant population. Our study focused on a large comprehensive high school, which reflected a multi-ethnic student population, largely from recently immigrated families. In this paper, we present a sociological framework, describe our method of investigation, and discuss our findings regarding how the school functions in assimilating its immigrant students.

Sociological Framework

For the purpose of our study, we utilized structural-functionalism and reproduction theories as the sociological framework in examining the structural aspects of school and its social transmission of the status quo. We chose to explore the role and function of school in transmitting the beliefs, values, attitudes, and norms from one generation to the next. In this way, we hoped to examine the tension between assimilation and accommodation of immigrant children.

Educational systems, from a functionalist perspective, are thought of as structures within a given society that facilitate the transmission of beliefs, values, attitudes and norms from one generation to the next (Dreeben, 1968; Durkheim, 1961; Parsons, 1959). As such, schools retain and perpetuate existing cultural values and norms of the society. Functionalists are not interested in questioning or changing the existing culture, rather there is a presumption that consensus exists on what beliefs and values should be transmitted through the school. When conflict over these occurs, adjustments and adaptations are made to regain balance and equilibrium.

Unlike the functionalists who endorse a common culture and consensus in beliefs and values within society, we were more skeptical of this notion and thus drew from the critical perspective of reproduction theory (Bernstein, 1970, 1977; Bourdieu & Passeron, 1977; Bowles & Gintis, 1976; Carnoy & Levin, 1985). In describing reproduction theory, Giroux (1983) states that schools act as reproduction agents in these ways: "First, schools provide different classes and social groups with the knowledge and skills they need to occupy their respective places in a labor force stratified by class, race, and gender. Second, schools are seen as reproductive in the cultural sense, functioning in part to distribute and legitimate forms of knowledge, values, language, and modes of style that constitute the dominant culture and its interests. Third, schools are viewed as part of a state apparatus that produced and legitimated the economic and ideological imperatives that underlie the state's political power" (p. 258).

From the reproduction theory perspective, we asked these kinds of questions: Whose interests were schools serving? Was the dominant class structure replicated through the schooling process? How did minority students fare as a result?

But equally critical of reproduction theory, we acknowledged that not all students are molded into class-stratified roles as theorized. In order to compensate for the overly deterministic nature of reproduction theory, we did the following: First, we noted individual response and resistance to socialization. Second, we also sought to incorporate the dynamics of social relationships within a school among students, teachers, and staff. Third, we examined educational alternatives that might suggest ways that the school was accommodating rather than assimilating or socializing its students.

Methodology

We selected a large four-year high school located in an industrial area adjacent to an urban metropolis in the midwestern United States. While this school might be considered an "inner city school" by its location and minority population, it was unique in that this student population comprised of students of Arabic or Middle Eastern origins, many of whom were recent immigrants.

We negotiated our entry into the school through university and school district contacts. Through several discussions with the principal, we obtained permission to conduct classroom observations with different subject area teachers during several of their periods in the school day. An initial meeting was arranged through the principal to meet the teachers who had volunteered to participate. There were four teachers in the following areas: special education, math, English, and social studies. We obtained their permission to visit their different class periods.

To gather data, we arranged to be nonparticipant observers in the classrooms. With two of us serving as principal investigators, we decided upon the strategy of sitting together in the classes. This was done as a means of securing greater reliability and validity in our observations.

Because courses were tracked according to ability groupings in the school (A-track = academic, B-track = general; C-track = remedial), we tried to observe

Table 9.1. Class Observations by Subject and Track.

Subject	Track A	Track B	Track C
English	1 English	3 English	
	1 ESL		
Math	6 Advanced geometry	2 Basic math	
Social studies	3 World civilizations		

classes that reflected the different curriculum tracks as well as different subject areas. Our ideal would have been to visit classes in English, math, and social studies in each track. However, we were not able to get all of the classes for each track. Table 9.1 notes the classes that we visited, giving the number of visits made and the course taught by subject area and track.

After two observation days, we developed a grid format (see Table 9.2) to systematize our observations and to note differences among the three tracks. In addition, we conducted observations during the lunch period, noting the groupings of students in the cafeteria and talking informally with the students and supervisory teachers. By sitting in the cafeteria, we found that students were willing to approach us and answer our questions about their school experiences and family background. For example, when requesting to take pictures of Arabic girls whose heads were covered by the traditional Muslim veils, we were able to solicit their comments about the religious practice of that head covering.

To clarify our observations and gain the teacher's perspective, we spoke with the classroom teachers following most observation periods. Informal conversations with teachers were held in the department teachers' lounges, thus giving us greater access to teachers other than those whom we initially observed in the classroom. Through these contacts we were able to gain access to other classrooms.

More formal interviews were held with the principal, the school's community liaison person (to be referred to as "liaison person"), a community minister, and the director of a local community center for Arabic immigrants (to be referred to as "community director"). These interviews provided us with the school administration and the community perspectives on Arabic students in the school.

Supplementary data were gathered through a variety of school publications—the curriculum guide, the student code of conduct, and the school's class schedule. Demographics and background information on the Arabic community were obtained from the community center agency and other education publications. Using different data sources, we aimed to triangulate our references to ensure greater data reliability.

Description of the Setting

The Community

An industrial suburb of a midwestern metropolis, this community is ethnically diverse and primarily working class. Its population is approximately 86,000 with

Table 9.2. Observation Grid.

	Track A	*Track B*	*Track C*
Composition: Class size	Varies	Largest size	Smallest size
Races	Mainly white	Greater percentage Arabic	ESL mostly Arabic
Gender	More boys than girls in all 3 tracks		
Mixed grade	Varies with course		
Content coverage	Adv. geometry covers twice as much as regular geometry	Adv. geometry covers twice as much as regular geometry	Pacing is individualized
Types of courses	Academics Gifted AP	General	Remedial, ESL Special ed.
Homework	Daily assignments	Occasional	Infrequent
Textbooks	Different content for different track		
Teacher expectations:	Greatest academic expectations		Least academic expectations
Grades given	Mostly A, B	Mostly C, D, E	Nongraded
Teacher-student interactions	Voluntary participation	More spirited than others	Remedial requires aides
Seating arrangements	Grouped by choice	Seating fixed	Varies
	Varies with class type as well		
Discipline-rules	Internalized Flexible	Reprimands frequently	Disciplinary actions taken
Student autonomy	Greatest autonomy		Least autonomy

more of the recent immigrants in the eastern area. Considered the "catch pot" of immigrants, this area consists mostly of immigrants from Arabic countries such as Lebanon, Syria, Iraq, and Yemen but also includes those from Armenia, Romania, and Poland. The western area tends to be upper middle class and generally white.

Noteworthy is that there are few African Americans despite the close proximity to an urban area where the concentration is largely African American. We were told that there had been a concerted effort by the leading industrialist to limit the integration of African Americans in this suburban community; thus few reside there.

Economically the community is dependent upon one major manufacturing industry. Due to a decline in production and a relocation to other suburban or off-shore areas, unemployment in this locale has risen over the past decade. However, there are many local businesses and a growing service sector (for example, fast food chains, hotels, and restaurants) that provide employment.

The Arabic Sub-Community

Arriving in the last quarter of the nineteenth century, the early Arabic immigrants were mostly Christian Syrians who were uneducated and poor. They provided cheap labor for the rail, auto, and steel industries in the greater metropolitan area. These immigrants were not interested in permanent settlement; rather they preferred to make money and return home. Consequently their assimilation into American society was limited and they remained in ethnic clusters (Alldredge, 1984). This pattern was characteristic until the end of World War II.

Immigrants arriving after that time came with intentions to settle. Coming from Arab countries such as Palestine, Iraq, Jordan, and Egypt, many were highly educated, were skilled professionals, and were no longer overwhelmingly Christian. After 1970, there was an increase in immigration due to the political conflicts in the Middle East. Between 1971 and 1975, there were, on the average, 10,430 immigrants entering the US and many more of them were young. By 1974, 35 percent of the immigrants were under nineteen years of age. "Since the pattern of Arab immigrant settlement has traditionally tended toward groupings rather than dispersal, this increase in youthful immigrants has significant implications for schools in those areas with large Arab populations" (Alldredge, 1984, p. 3).

At present there are approximately 200,000 Arab Americans in the greater metropolitan area (Ahmed & Gray, 1988). This population includes the third and fourth generation descendants of the earliest immigrants as well as very recent immigrants.

Most in the Arab community are predominantly working class with 90 percent employed in the automotive industry. There has been a recent movement into the service sector due to recession in the manufacturing industry. According to the community center director, the unemployment rate has never gone below 30 percent and is often greater than 50 percent, particularly in the eastern area of the community.

Thirty-three percent of the population speaks only Arabic and a third of these can read or write. Of the two-thirds who do speak English, 66 percent can neither read nor write the language. To further compound the situation, there is considerable diversity in the dialects spoken among Arabic speakers, which may differ significantly from classic Arabic.

Despite the fact that 60 percent of the community has been in this country for less than ten years, the Arabic community is politically active. An Arabic school board member and a local city councilman were recently elected for the first time in the community's history. In addition, Arabic citizens are becoming more vocal in asserting their rights. For instance, on our first visit to the community center, we were told that a group had gone to picket a local retail store for selling Halloween masks depicting Arab terrorists. Thus with the increasing political awareness and financial success of local Arabic businesses, the growing "weight and size of the Arabic sub-community" make it a more viable presence (Ahmed & Gray, 1988).

Observation High School

To retain the confidentiality of the school, we shall use the reference "Observation High School" throughout this paper.

One of three high schools in the community, Observation High serves the students in grades 9–12, enrolling approximately 1,800 students, 53 percent of whom are Arabic, a small percentage are Asians, and the remainder are white. There are only one or two African Americans in the school. The Arabic student body is composed mainly of Lebanese, some Yemeni, and others including those from Palestine, Syria, Egypt, Iraq, Kuwait, and Libya.

Teachers' comments on the "friendly" atmosphere characterize the ethos of the school. They complimented the students for their courteous and friendly manner. In our interactions with students in the school corridors, we too observed helpfulness to us. In addition, the principal described how the students show "compassion for the less fortunate" and reflect care and concern as denoted by programs such as Youth to End Starvation (YES), which has been in operation for the past twelve years. This school climate greatly contrasts the common notion of a blighted urban school with a large disadvantaged minority population.

Public education in the district has been supported by a manufacturing industry, which has contributed to the district spending for vocational education programs and the relatively low millage rate placed on taxpayers. The community's general fund millage is twenty-six mills as compared with thirty-five to thirty-six mills on average for other communities because of the financial support from industries in the area.

With an energetic principal who came on board four years ago, the school administrative leadership is relatively new. The principal encourages both teacher and student participation in school operations. She spoke of the teacher initiative to alter the annual Open House, turning it into a parent-teacher conference rather than the general session format that had been the tradition. Also teachers are involved in curriculum development through a curriculum council chaired by the principal. An example of student involvement was the implementation of a policy banning smoking in the school parking lot. The principal met with student leaders to ask that they suggest ways to enforce the policy. By actively involving the students, she was able to gain their support in implementing the policy successfully.

The school has maintained a positive relationship with the community through parent involvement and by promoting school support groups, such as an athletic booster organization and a band booster organization. In addition, there is a special position for an Arabic-speaking community liaison person to work on improving school-community relations. Over the past ten years, Observation High has grown to be the largest of the three high schools in the community in part due to the increase in immigration with people clustering close to their relatives in the eastern area. Also, families in this section tend to have larger families, unlike those living in the western area. Due to this differential growth pattern, feeder school boundary lines were changed and students were bussed to the western section to balance the high school enrollments. This will also mean that some Arabic-speaking students will be entering the other high schools.

Findings

The findings are reported under these categories: curriculum tracking, bilingual/ ESL program, special provisions made by the school, Arabic teachers on staff, Arab and American views on education, and student tensions.

Curriculum Tracking

A structural feature of Observation High is curriculum tracking, "the practice of dividing students into instructional groups on the criterion of assumed similarity in ability or attainment" (Oakes, 1985, p. ix). According to the school's curriculum guide 1989–1990, "students are divided into A, B, and C tracks according to ability, reading skill levels, and teacher recommendation" (p. 3). This practice was verified by the teachers who supported it as an effective way of dealing with the heterogeneous population and ensuring that every child was taught according to her or his ability and needs.

Although the school population is 53 percent Arabic-speaking, we were told that there were no appropriate ability measures to administer to students who did not speak English and often were illiterate in Arabic as well. Track placement was therefore done by an informal interview conducted either by a teacher or the liaison person. Immigrant students are invariably placed in the English as a Second Language (ESL) block for a maximum period of three terms, after which they are mainstreamed. With reading ability as a criterion for track placement, most students exiting the ESL block would enter the remedial track.

This was borne out by our observation that the majority of B-track (general) and C-track (remedial) students were of Arabic origin. Of the few Arabic students in the A-track (academic), we suspected these students to be second generation Arab Americans. Moreover, in the program for gifted students, out of fifty-five students enrolled, there were six Arabic students. We noted that there was the same number of Asians despite the much smaller number of Asians in the school as a whole.

We observed notable differences in the three tracks in the areas of class composition, content coverage, teacher expectation, and teacher-student interaction. (See Table 9.2, Observation Grid.) In terms of class composition, we found the largest class size in general track, which was made up of mostly Arabic students. There were more boys than girls in most classes.

As for content coverage, A-track classes covered twice as much material, had daily homework, and utilized more advanced textbooks. In the C-track, on the other hand, more basic textbooks were used and as one teacher told us, "due to the problem of absenteeism, I just teach the same thing thrice and hope that everyone gets it at least once." As teachers feel that C-track students will not do much homework, they tend not to assign any work outside the class period. It is not surprising that there is relatively less content coverage in the lower tracks.

In the area of teacher expectations, the A-track students were thought to be responsible and eager to learn. One teacher, for example, consulted the class on changing their test date. This type of negotiation, he said, would never be allowed in the C-track class where students were "lazy" and did not want to learn. If consulted, these students would "never want to take the test." Teachers had high expectations of A-track students and saw an academic future for them. In contrast, they felt that the C-track students would either join a family business or work in manufacturing. Most of the teachers we spoke with regarded having to teach C-track classes as punishment, calling those periods their worst classes and being reluctant to have us observe these groups.

Finally, in the area of teacher-student interaction, we observed the greatest amount of student autonomy and flexibility regarding class rules in the A-track. An example of this was the seating arrangements that were by personal choice in the A-track as contrasted with seating arrangements made by the teacher in B- and C-track classes. Another example was that the class conduct in the A-track was orderly, as student discipline was internalized. For C-track students, on the other hand, rules were constantly being issued and the teacher frequently reprimanded the class.

Bilingual/ESL Program

The English as a Second Language (ESL) program is geared toward students who are not native English speakers. In a maximum of three terms, students receive "instruction in English, Social Studies, and acculturation" before being placed in classes with native English speakers (curriculum guide, 1989–1990). The special bilingual math and science focused on learning vocabulary words and basic skills. It seemed unlikely that a nonnative speaker of English would enter anything other than a basic math course. Given that students were in the ESL program by virtue of their lack of knowledge of English, we wondered if, aside from their English proficiency, their different educational experiences and academic achievement were ever taken into account.

To develop a strong bilingual program is more complex than one would think. First, merely having an Arabic bilingual teacher or aide is not sufficient, as the student population consists of different Arabic nationalities speaking different dialects. For instance, we noted the difference between an urban multilingual Lebanese and a rural Yemeni, both immigrants whose mother tongue is Arabic but with vastly different social, cultural, and educational experiences. Second, the situation in bilingual classes is further exacerbated by the presence of other language minorities such as Romanian, Armenian, and so on. Third, there is disagreement over the efficacy of the presence of an Arabic bilingual staff. One teacher expressed the opinion that the presence of Arabic bilingual teachers and aids retards the language acquisition of Arabic students. They continue to speak

Arabic with their peers in school. That teacher believed that students of other nationalities who are forced to speak English would learn the language much faster.

The bilingual program was viewed rather unfavorably by those it did not serve. They regarded it as a provision of special favors to the Arabic students, without any equivalent favors for other students. In fact, the community center director talked about "an anti-bilingual campaign." We were led to suspect that due in part to this resentment, the number of bilingual teachers remained the same despite a substantial increase in the Arabic student population from 30 percent in 1980 to 53 percent by 1988 (see Table 9.3).

Special Provisions Made by the School

Apart from the bilingual program, other special provisions made by the school to accommodate its unique population were (1) a separate physical education (PE) class for girls, (2) the establishment of an Arab Club, and (3) the hiring of a liaison person to interact with the Arabic community.

The creation of a special PE class came about through the school's efforts to accommodate the religious restrictions of Arabic girls. The administration found that girls were opting out of coeducational PE classes because their religious upbringing did not permit wearing shorts and swim attire in front of boys. To solve this problem, the school met with the local Arabic religious leaders. It was decided that a separate girls-only PE class be offered as an alternative choice for completing the ninth grade PE requirement. This choice was availed of not only by Arabic girls but also girls from certain fundamentalist Christian groups.

The Arabic Club functions to introduce the school to Arabic culture and traditions and is reportedly attended by both Arabic and non-Arabic students. In addition, the school newsletter informs students of related Arabic activities as, for example, the annual Muslim Ramadan fasting period. We were also told that in an effort to draw the Arabic students into the "winter holiday celebration," a number of Arabic songs had been incorporated into the list of traditional carols to be sung.

A liaison person was hired by the school to facilitate the communication between the school and the community. He served as the advisor of the Arabic Club and gave occasional seminars to acquaint the teachers with Arabic culture. He was also responsible for communicating the school policies to the students, parents, and community. In order to accomplish this task, he translated the student handbook into Arabic. Given that half of the student body was of Arabic origin

Table 9.3. Bilingual Teacher Counts by Year.

Number of	1980	1988
Arabic student population	30%	53%
Bilingual teachers	2	2
ESL teachers	3	4
Aides	0	3

and many were recent immigrants, we wondered how effectively one person would be able to serve these students.

Arabic Teachers on Staff

Given the number of Arabic students, the school's long history of immigrant students, and the Arabic presence in the community, we were struck by the lack of Arabic teachers at Observation High. The number of bilingual teachers remained the same after eight years despite the increase of Arabic students. There were no Arabic counselors in any of the grade levels and no assistant principal of Arabic background.

According to the principal, this was due to two major factors. First, despite extensive advertising for teacher vacancies, there have not been sufficient numbers of qualified applicants. The principal felt that this was because top caliber Arabic students tended to go into professions like engineering and medicine, rather than teaching. Also, where women would make up the bulk of the teaching force, Arabic women are encouraged to marry early rather than pursue a career. A second factor contributing to the lack of Arabic teachers is the practice of teacher layoffs. When shifting enrollment and changes in curriculum occur, teachers with low seniority are the first to be laid off. Thus, Arabic teachers who were more recent hires would be laid off.

However, the principal made it clear that given two equally qualified candidates, she would give preference to the bilingual one. From our conversations with teachers, we gleaned that since the principal had assumed leadership at Observation High, she had made a concerted effort to select teachers with a sensitivity toward racial and cultural differences.

From the community director, we obtained a slightly different viewpoint. He felt that the school was complacent about the lack of Arabic teachers and administrators, and that it was content to maintain status quo. He noted that affirmative action policies were lacking and no *special* effort was made to increase the percentage of Arabic staff. He felt that a flexible recruiting procedure might be required to hire more Arabic teachers. Even though this might be unpopular, his suggestion was that such a procedure would be necessary if the special needs of the Arabic students are to be met.

Arab and American Views on Education

In our conversations with the teachers, the general impression was that the Arabic community had a negative attitude to education. Teachers commented (1) that the parents did not care to involve themselves in school activities, (2) that rather than encourage their children to do homework, parents wanted them to work as many as sixty hours per week in the family businesses, and (3) that students and their families had very low educational aspirations.

The Arabic view, called a "Third World view of education" by the liaison person, contrasted sharply with the one presented by the teachers. What the teachers regarded as "negative" was cultural difference in the expression of attitudes toward education. In the Middle East, we were told, the Arabic family has a very high regard for education, viewing the teacher as the authority and as infallible. Consequently, the parents are not expected to be involved with school affairs. This differs from the American view, where the regard for education (or mistrust of teacher competence) is expressed in active parent participation in school affairs.

Apart from parents not participating in school, teachers noted the numerous difficulties in communicating with Arabic parents. If parents did not speak English, any communication between them and the teacher would have to be mediated by an interpreter. Looking at it from the Arabic perspective, the problem lay with insufficient bilingual staff. The singular liaison person, who often functioned as the interpreter, could not possibly fulfill the needs of the many Arabic parents.

Teachers also felt that Arabic students were "impulsive" and consequently classroom discipline was a problem. A possible explanation of this behavior given by the liaison person was that of the recent immigrants, many had not attended any school in their native country. This meant that they had not been socialized into appropriate school behavior. For those who had attended Arabic schools, the pattern of socialization to which they were accustomed was very different from the American way. Discipline, especially for boys, often was in the form of corporal punishment. Accustomed to more authoritarian control, Arabic students quickly learned that in the United States, they will not be hit by their teachers, and the lack of severe punishment gives them more latitude to misbehave.

Teachers see Arabic students as being more dependent and requiring more direction than their American peers, a trait that in turn reflects students' lower ability. However, such a perception fails to take into account the cultural differences of the Arabic family. The strong family ties exert social control over the actions of the children. Used to having more supervision in instruction, Arabic children appear to be less independent and mature than the Americans.

Student Tensions

While there was little evidence of explicit conflict between white students and Arabic ones, student tensions did exist. For example, we noted racist graffiti in toilet stalls in several student restrooms. Asking about this, we were told that five years ago there had been more tension, with fights particularly between the "burned-out druggies" (white students who were known drug users) and Arabic students. Apparently the Arabic students treated the druggies with contempt. During one observation class, a physically well-developed Arabic student pointed to a white student and commented that "he's so small and skinny because he's a burnout."

An interesting aspect of the relationship between whites and Arabic students is the dating patterns. If Arabic girls date at all, they are under the supervision of a chaperone and might be restricted to dating only Arabic boys. White boys, we were told, often think that Arabic girls are not good enough for them. Arab boys, on the other hand, interact freely with white girls who are perceived as being more "open and friendly." If they do acquire a white girlfriend, it is considered a "good catch" or a "feather in his cap."

Another source of conflict among the students was between the second generation Arab Americans and the more recent immigrants. The latter were called "boaters," inferring that they had just come off the boat. Generally they were treated contemptuously by the others, who saw themselves as being Americanized. As Arab Americans, the newer immigrants often rejected their cultural past in order to assimilate and be accepted in the American society. They face the dilemma of living in two cultures—the American school, on the one hand, and the Arabic home, on the other. In dealing with this conflict, they try to adopt the customs of the new culture while retaining their old family traditions. This was reflected in the attire of some Arabic girls who cover their heads in the traditional Muslim way but dress in tight fitting jeans.

For the most part the Arabic student population was regarded collectively as being "Arabic." But our background reading (Alldredge, 1984; Zarrugh, 1984) made us aware of various groups of other nationalities present in the school and we raised questions about the interactions among them. Some teachers did mention a hierarchy among the different nationality groups. An example is in the contrast between Lebanese and Yemeni. Lebanese students tend to have more education and are more urbanized whereas Yemeni students, coming from a less-developed agrarian country, tend to have fewer educational experiences. There were also notable religious differences. Syrian immigrants might be Christian, as were the Caldeans residing in the greater metropolitan area who had experienced religious persecution by Moslems. The Caldeans, though of Middle Eastern origin, were offended when thought of as Arabic or Muslim. While these tensions were not apparent to us, we suspected that these cultural, nationality, and religious differences might affect relationships among the Arabic-speaking students.

Discussion

In undertaking a sociological study, we attempted to frame our observations within the school structure and organization by employing functionalist and reproduction theories as the framework. Our interest was not in how individual students were adapting but in how the school functioned as a system in the assimilation and accommodation of immigrant students. At the same time, in order to counter the criticism of an overly deterministic theory and draw upon the perspectives of the individuals within the school, we selected an observational methodology to examine the socialization process in a qualitative manner. We sought to affirm the "human agency" of the individuals within their specific social setting. Our aim was exploratory and we present the interpretation of our findings in hopes that it will suggest avenues for further research.

From the perspective of an American public school, Observation High is exemplary. The school ethos is "friendly and caring"; the administration demonstrates innovative leadership and encourages participatory democracy; the teachers believe in their students. As a multicultural, multi-ethnic school, it maintains a fine tradition and makes provision for its immigrant student population, as is evident by the special PE class, Arab Club, and hiring of a community liaison person.

At the same time, Observation High is typical of comprehensive high schools throughout the country. Large in size and heterogeneous in population, it maintains a differentiated curriculum, with students placed in tracks through teacher assessment. Often this assessment process is "informal," suggesting the arbitrary nature of this process. Since language proficiency is a key to assessment, it was not surprising to find that immigrant students were placed in the lower tracks.

Another feature of comprehensive high schools is the diversity of curriculum choice (Powell, Farrar, & Cohen, 1985). This practice attempts to provide something for everyone but gives little attention to providing students with proper guidance in making good choices. The criticism of the practice has been that students are left to make course choices on their own. With approximately three hundred students per counselor and only one Arabic-speaking community liaison person for roughly 950 Arabic students, students at Observation High were not adequately served in terms of educational guidance.

A third feature that is also consistent with schools having large minority student populations is the strong presence of a vocational educational program (Oakes, 1985). On the one hand, one might argue that located in an industrial community, this high school best serves the needs of its students by providing a strong vocational education program. However, if this were the case, why did the other two high schools in the community not have an equally strong program?

Our findings at Observation High support the reproduction theory assumption that the school reflects and maintains the social stratification present in society. First, in according some students an education that prepares them with restricted skills and knowledge, the school restricts the access immigrant students have to future opportunities; differential access thus reproduces the existing social order. Second, the school functions as an agent of cultural transmission that focuses on the development of habits, behavior, and patterns consistent with the dominant culture and interests. This socialization in Observation High was in essence a process of assimilation and Americanization, rather than one of inclusion and accommodation. Despite the high proportion of Arabic-speaking residents in the community and the high percentage of Arabic students in the school, we saw little evidence of the accommodation of Arabic culture in the school. There were limited provisions for immigrants, as evident in the small number of Arabic teachers and staff, the limited bilingual/ESL program, etc. Furthermore, the successful Arabic students in the school, as well as the Arabic teacher that we observed, were individuals who were considerably Americanized.

This is not to suggest that our findings of social stratification can be attributed to any deliberate experience of some students. "The inequities stem from the cultural context and systematic properties of the school rather than from the intentions of the adults within them" (Oakes, 1985, p. 212). In fact, we highly commend the school leadership and teaching staff at Observation High for their efforts to provide services to the Arabic-speaking students, for their cultural sensitivity, and for their commitment to a multi-ethnic, multicultural environment.

Conclusion and Recommendations

In conclusion, our findings suggest that the school "acts as a conduit for society," preserving the beliefs, values, attitudes, and norms of the existing society, with the immigrant student expected to adapt and adjust accordingly. Even with a "friendly and caring" school ethos and cultural sensitivity on the part of the administration and teachers, the accommodation of a cultural heritage different from the status quo is minimal. Special provisions were made in elective and nonacademic areas such as physical education, an extracurricular social club, and guidance, while the academic courses such as English, social studies, and math were differentiated by tracking. We conclude that the school's role continues to promote assimilation rather than accommodation of immigrants.

If Observation High seeks to move toward greater accommodation of its Arab American student population, we offer these recommendations. First, as research shows that differential curriculum through tracking and ability grouping contributes to magnifying social inequalities (Lee & Bryk, 1988; Oakes, 1985), we suggest that the school move toward greater inclusion and elimination of the tracking practice. However, we suspect that such a step might be too great a change from the status quo. As an intermediate step, the school could initiate a pilot study, perhaps of one subject area where all students are grouped together with the same textbooks and curriculum materials. Also, the school might consider using an Arabic language instrument for assessment and placement, instituting a standard assessment procedure as well. The school might promote classroom settings where student autonomy and greater flexibility are encouraged for all students regardless of language competency, grade level, or ability grouping.

Second, we recommend that Observation High define the aims and objectives of its bilingual/ESL program. If nonnative speakers are to become fluent in English, perhaps there should be more intensive English language training or more time in the program than only three terms. The school needs to address how different Arabic speakers as well as different language speakers would be encouraged in the program. Perhaps it might consider supporting a longitudinal study over the high school years for program evaluation purposes.

Third, all academic and nonacademic courses need to be examined in terms of their contribution toward social stratification. We note particularly the vocational education program which was present at Observation High and suggest a comparison be conducted of the three high schools in the district.

Fourth, while we commend the school's special provisions for its Arabic-speaking students, we suggest that more needs to be done to hire Arabic-speaking teachers, staff, and parent-school interpreters. At minimum, the school liaison person needs support to adequately serve the Arabic students there. The school might examine its hiring practices and criteria for teacher qualification. We suggest that there be further discussion on the discrepancy between the principal's view and the community director's view on the lack of Arabic teachers and staff.

Fifth, we encourage more dialogue between Arabic speakers and Americans on a host of topics: the education of children, expectations of teachers and administrators, student tensions, school-community relations, and so on. While individuals and groups such as the liaison person and the Arab Club might organize such activities, we would encourage the school administrator to endorse these events, thus acknowledging the importance of such discussion in public forums at the school.

Our study was an exploratory probe into the tension between assimilation and accommodation of immigrant children. While there has been much discourse about accommodating cultural pluralism, we found Observation High School to be more assimilationist in its orientation. Our recommendations are directed toward tipping the balance in the opposite direction. We affirm that we want all children, minority as well as majority, to have opportunities beyond their ethnic communities but not at the cost of their cultural heritage.

References

Ahmed, I., & Gray, N. A. (Ed.). (1988). *The Arab American family: A resource manual for human service providers.* Ypsilanti, MI: Eastern Michigan University.

Alldredge, E. (1984). *Raising Arab children in America.* Ann Arbor, MI: Arabic Language Bilingual Materials Development Center, University of Michigan School of Education.

Au, K. H., & Mason, J. (1981). Social organizational factors in learning to read: The balance of rights hypothesis. *Reading Research Quarterly, 17,* 139–152.

Bennett, K. P., & LeCompte, M. D. (1990). *The way schools work: A sociological analysis of education.* New York: Longman.

Bernstein, B. (1970). *Class, codes and control. Vol. I: Theoretical studies towards a sociology of language.* London, U.K.: Routledge & Kegan Paul.

Bernstein, B. (1977). *Class, codes and control.* Vol. II: *Towards a theory of educational transmission.* London, U.K.: Routledge & Kegan Paul.

Bloom, A. (1987). *The closing of the American mind.* New York: Simon and Schuster.

Bourdieu, P., & Passeron, J. (1977). *Reproduction in education, society and culture.* London, U.K.: Sage.

Bowles, S., & Gintis, H. (1976). *Schooling in capitalistic America.* New York: Basic Books.

Carnoy, M., & Levin, H. M. (1985). *Schooling and work in the democratic state.* Stanford, CA: Stanford University Press.

Dreeben, R. (1968). *On what is learned in school.* Reading, MA: Addison-Wesley.

Durkheim, E. (1961). *Moral education: A study in the theory and application of the sociology of education.* E. K. Wilson & H. Schnurer (Trans.), E. K. Wilson (Ed.). Glencoe, IL: Free Press.

Giroux, J. (1983). Theories of reproduction and resistance in the new sociology of education: A critical analysis. *Harvard Educational Review, 53*(3), 257–293.

Hirsch, E. D. (1988). *Cultural literacy: What every American needs to know.* New York: Vintage Books.

Lee, V. E., & Bryk, A. S. (1988). Curriculum tracking and mediating the social distribution of high school achievement. *Sociology of Education, 61*(2), 78–94.

McLaren, P. (1989). *Life in schools.* New York: Longman.

Muller, T., & Espenshade, T. (1985). *The fourth wave.* Washington, D.C.: The Urban Institute Press.

NCAS Research and Policy Report. (1988). *New voices: Immigrant students in U.S. public schools.* Boston: National Coalition of Advocates for Students. (Library of Congress No. 88–60962).

Oakes, J. (1985). *Keeping track.* New Haven, CT: Yale University Press.

Parsons, T. (1959). The school class as a social system: Some of its functions in American society. *Harvard Educational Review, 29,* 297–319.

Powell, A. G., Farrar, E., & Cohen, D. K. (1985). *The shopping mall high school: Winners and losers in the educational marketplace.* Boston: Houghton Mifflin.

Ravitch, D. (1983). *The troubled crusade: American education 1945–1980.* New York: Basic Books.

Tyack, D. B. (1974). *The one best system.* Cambridge, MA: Harvard University Press.

Van Ness, H. (1981). Social control and social organization in an Alaskan Athabaskan classroom: A microethnography of getting ready for reading. In H. Trueba, G. P. Gutherie, & K. H. Au (Eds.), *Culture and the bilingual classroom* (pp. 120–138). Rowley, MA: Newbury House.

Zarrugh, L. (1984). *Arab immigrant children and bilingual education: A preliminary inquiry.* Ann Arbor, MI: Arabic Language Bilingual Materials Development Center, University of Michigan School of Education.

Reflections of
Our Own Inner Lives

Ernestine K. Enomoto, University of Hawaii, Manoa
Mary Antony Bair, Grand Valley State University,
Grand Rapids, Michigan

In her book, *Social Science and the Self,* Susan Krieger writes of the psychological journey involved in doing qualitative research. She argues against the view that the researcher's subjectivity contaminates the work and needs to be minimized and controlled when doing social science research. Krieger advocates that this view be changed. "I think we ought to develop our different individual perspectives more fully in social science, and we ought to acknowledge, more honestly than we do, the extent to which our studies are reflections of our own inner lives" (Krieger, 1991, p. 1).

We shared Krieger's view when we did this study of how educational organizations socialize young people. Our personal interest directed the inquiry toward young people who were like ourselves—women, minorities, and immigrants. One of us, Ernestine, is a third-generation Asian American woman; the other, Mary, is a recent immigrant from Delhi, India, for whom the issue of assimilation is a very real one. We frequently spoke about how young immigrants were educated and socialized in the context of middle-class, white America. What were their experiences in school? What were they learning about themselves and their society? Having this personal interest in the topic, we were motivated to pursue the study.

Fortunately, we were in close proximity to a site that was especially suited to this research. Located in an industrial suburb, adjacent to a metropolitan area, the eastern section of the community was primarily working class and ethnically diverse, including a large Arabic population. The children residing here attended a four-year high school, "Observation High School," where the majority (53 percent) were of Arabic origin, mainly from Lebanon but also from Yemen, Palestine, Syria, Egypt, Iraq, Kuwait, and Libya. How were these young people socialized and assimilated in American ways? With that general question, we began our inquiry.

We gained access to the school through personal and professional contacts. One of our university faculty members had done considerable work in the community. Well informed and highly respected, he provided us the initial entry into the field. Not only did he introduce us to key individuals, he also took us on our first trip to the area, describing the section and identifying various community groups. He introduced us to the curriculum coordinator for the school district, who in turn was a friend of the principal. These individuals aided our entry into Observation High and assisted us in securing the necessary permission to conduct our study. Selection of subjects thus resulted from a sort of "snowballing," with each participant naming the next one.

Despite the easy access to the high school, we faced numerous challenges. First, neither of us was familiar with the Arab American community and we had little knowledge of the differences among the Arabic subcultures. For example, we learned that the Christian Syrians were most assimilated and least likely to relate to Muslims from their homeland. Had we had more background in the history and culture of the diverse groups, we might have been more insightful into the schooling that was taking place. Reflecting on our own transitions to life in the Midwest and the importance of family and community, we sought community contacts. We were introduced to a pastor who served the Arab American community, and through him we gained additional information, visited a feeder school, and met the Arab community center director. With more time to conduct the research, we might have interviewed family members to gain their perspective on student acculturation.

A second challenge was the limited number of teachers who were willing to have us observe and visit their classrooms. The principal had put out a call for volunteers and there were only four willing takers. However, our sustained presence in the school helped us gain other teacher volunteers. We often went to school early, stayed back after observations to talk with the teachers, and spent time "chatting" in the teachers' lounge. As a result, we were invited to more classrooms and could broaden the scope of our observations.

Our lack of skill in doing qualitative research was a third challenge for us. At the time, we were graduate students in a doctoral program that emphasized only quantitative research methods. We lacked the necessary preparation and skill but proceeded to let the research question direct our method. We learned from reading about qualitative methods, sought advice from faculty, and most important, learned by doing the fieldwork.

Beginning with a general question about the schooling of immigrant children, we proceeded by visiting the school and sitting in classrooms, the teacher's lounge, and the student cafeteria. We wrote down everything—even noting the graffiti on the bathroom walls. Although this process can lead to the collection of large amounts of irrelevant data, we made sure that data collection and analysis occurred simultaneously, one phase informing the other. After some preliminary work, we were able to devise a grid to collect data more systematically. We continued to refine our data collection by asking validating kinds of questions about what we observed and by speaking with students, teachers, counselors, and administrators. We collected supplemental documentation and general material on the Arab American community. Thus, our research study emerged, evolving as we proceeded.

Another vital step was documenting the events and organizing the data collected on a daily basis. After each visit to Observation High, we typed up notes from classroom and school observations. Together we would review, edit, and revise these field notes. The regular practice was important because handwritten notes scribbled on scraps of paper made little sense after two or three days, and the numerous classroom visits blurred together, making it difficult to recall who said what in what class. The difficulty of this practice was making the time to do it, especially after a long day in the field.

The team approach worked well for us both in conducting data collection and analysis. As co-principal investigators, we decided from the outset to observe and interview together. The benefit of this strategy was that we were able to check what we were seeing and validate data collected. However, the limitation was that we were not able to cover as many classes or interview as many individuals. Nevertheless, we felt that collaborating in this way strengthened our investigation and facilitated the writing of the study. We also enjoyed the sharing and reflections that came from the investigation.

Had we to do this over again, we would do so eagerly. The research question enabled us to inquire into issues that were personally meaningful to us. The qualitative method allowed for an exploratory approach to pursue the subject in a systematic yet flexible manner. Our teaming together made for hours of enjoyable pondering about the meaning of our school observations.

Reference

Krieger, S. (1991). *Social science and the self: Personal essays on an art form.* New Jersey: Rutgers University.

10

Jermaine

A Critical Case Study of a
Gifted Black Child Living in Rural Poverty

Thomas P. Hébert, Teresa M. Beardsley

As I traveled the silent rural highways of Alabama, I reflected on the special significance of kudzu. Having grown up near the rocky coast of Maine, I always imagine kudzu as a powerful tidal wave that overtakes the Southern countryside. Every spring in the South, the kudzu vine washes over the entire countryside, covering telephone poles, buildings, and all vegetation in its path. It blocks the sunlight from the tall pine trees and shrubs it covers, silently draining the life out of them. Though it appeared beautiful as it draped over the vegetation along the red clay roads I traveled that day, I was reminded of the choking qualities of this vegetation, and I thought about how this might reflect the rural isolation and poverty in the life of the gifted child I would come to know in my research. I approached this community as an ethnographic researcher to join a public school teacher named Teresa Beardsley and begin a three-year case study of her student, Jermaine, a gifted Black child living in rural poverty. During my travels, I pondered the question, As kudzu chokes life out of vegetation, does the isolation of an impoverished, rural environment have a similar effect on the creativity of a gifted child?

As I spent more time in the rural Alabama county, I continued to admire the beauty of the South; yet I grew to understand how an impoverished environment negatively affected children. Together, the data Teresa provided me on Jermaine's

Thomas P. Hébert and Teresa M. Beardsley. (2001). "Jermaine: A Critical Case Study of a Gifted Black Child Living in Rural Poverty." *Gifted Child Quarterly, 45*(2), 85–103.

creativity and the data I collected as a researcher interacting with him allowed me to explore the role environment plays in developing the gifts and talents of children.

Background

America's public schools are increasingly under attack. Beginning with *A Nation at Risk* (National Commission on Excellence in Education, 1983), numerous studies have identified serious problems in the education of our young people. These criticisms are not new to rural educators; Nachtigal (1992) noted, "Even before the turn of the century, educational leaders were concerned about the rural school problem" (p. 66). An unspoken perception exists in rural communities that people should settle for less in rural schools (Nachtigal, 1992). Herzog & Pittman (1995) reported that students in rural settings suffered from negative stereotypes because of their rural background and internalized antirural prejudices, and they "exhibited an inferiority complex about their origins" (p. 114). They found that students educated in rural communities attended poorly funded schools and experienced both a lack of quality facilities and limited educational programs, while their teachers struggled with limited access to cultural and information resources and university teacher training programs that did not adequately prepare them for specialized training for working in rural schools (Herzog & Pittman, 1995; Spicker, Southern, & Davis, 1987).

In addition, rural schools also face an exodus of intelligent young adults due to limited professional employment opportunities (Seal & Harmon, 1995; Spicker, 1992a; Stern, 1992). Young adults whose families have deep generational roots in rural communities often decide to leave not only because of a lack of opportunities but also because of inadequate health care and underfunded schools (Spicker, 1992b).

Although cognizant of serious problems facing rural schools, fewer researchers undertake studies in rural settings in this country than in urban or suburban settings. In addition, there is limited research on special populations of students in rural settings. Unfortunately, one population of students missing from much of the research literature on rural schools is gifted students. Consistent with other special populations in rural America, gifted students in rural communities face serious challenges. Spicker, Southern, and Davis (1987) highlighted major obstacles in providing for the special educational needs of rural gifted youngsters. They indicated that, within rural school districts, acceptance of the status quo and resistance to change made it difficult to initiate new programs for gifted students. Along with limited financial resources for programs perceived as benefiting a few students, rural schools were unable to provide adequate specialized teachers, counselors, school psychologists, and curriculum specialists to assist in providing appropriate services for high-ability youngsters. Finally, Spicker, Southern, and Davis (1987) indicated the rural belief in self-sufficiency and local control decreased the likelihood that school officials might see outside assistance from educational experts to address the needs of gifted students.

Poverty adds another layer of complexity to problems facing schools. According to a study conducted by the United States Department of Education (1993), children living in poverty faced the following obstacles: less access to formal learning opportunities, more serious physical and mental health problems, and more environmental barriers that affect their education. Dudenhefer (1994) highlighted the lack of research on rural, impoverished children, indicating "when researchers—or at least the principal sponsors of poverty research—think poverty, they think city, not town or country" (p. 4). Poverty is as much a serious problem in rural America as in urban America. Books (1997) indicated that although more than nine million people in rural areas of the United States lived in impoverished conditions, rural poverty is overshadowed by the media's fixation on issues of urban poverty, including drugs and violence.

Understanding the effects of poverty remains especially important when examining the life experiences of Black children, since they face a higher rate of poverty than children of any other racial or ethnic group in the United States (Sum & Fogg, 1991) and often live in conditions that may impede their school achievement (McLoyd, 1990). Ford (1996) noted that the poverty rates for Black families and children in this country have been high, both historically and currently. According to the 1990 federal census, over 55 percent of the rural poor, and nearly 97 percent of the rural Black poor, lived in the South (Dudenhefer, 1994). African American children in the South have borne a disproportionate share of the burden of poverty in America for decades. Though Black children in rural, impoverished environments face adverse conditions, Frasier (1987) cautioned us not to oversimplify the problem when she indicated that "there are too many examples of gifted adults who come from less advantaged backgrounds to make a tenable argument that culture, class, or environment are permanent obstacles to achievement" (p. 174). In examining diverse ethnic groups, both Frasier (1991) and Kitano (1991) identified within-group heterogeneity as prevalent as in the majority culture; therefore, socioeconomic status should not serve as a predictor of aptitude or academic achievement. Ford noted that "poverty is a circumstance, not a measure of inherent worth" (p. 72). Using the metaphor of "undiscovered diamonds," Baldwin (1987) encouraged educators to continue searching for the gifts and talents of Black children and urged policymakers to pursue increased research on gifted Black children in rural environments. Renzulli (1973) reminded policymakers over twenty-five years ago that gifted minority children in impoverished environments were being lost as he pointed out: "There can be little doubt that our nation's largest untapped source of human intelligence and creativity is found among the vast numbers of individuals in the lower socioeconomic levels. . .an invaluable natural resource is being wasted daily by a system of education that has shut its eyes and turned its back on [these children]" (p. 437).

Efforts to bring about change for these young people must be monumental when we consider "the great number of youngsters whose day-to-day school experience is nothing short of an educational and psychological disaster" (Renzulli, 1973, p. 439). Little research exists on gifted students in rural environments, and even less research has examined gifted Black students who live in impoverished, rural communities. This study attempts to add to the limited information on this population by examining the life experiences of a gifted Black child living in rural poverty. To do so, the following research questions guided the study: What relationships guide the behaviors, attitudes, and aspirations of a gifted Black child in an impoverished, rural environment? What factors influence the creativity of a gifted Black child in an impoverished, rural setting?

Theoretical Framework

Critical theory served as the framework for the study. The emergence of critical theory began in the 1920s with a group of German scholars collectively known as the Frankfurt School. These scholars focused on emerging theory, practice, and inquiry with a historically grounded understanding of contemporary social, political, and cultural issues. Since then, critical theorists have been influenced by the work of Habermas (1970, 1971, 1974, 1989), who believed human beings are unnecessarily oppressed by implicit cultural ideologies. Therefore, the goal of critical theory research is to make these unconscious belief systems explicit, thereby freeing individuals by providing alternatives through self-reflection and social action. Critical theorists work for social justice by constantly challenging and questioning societal values and practices (Crotty, 1998). Critical theorists undertake research with a concern for issues related to power and oppression. Critical inquiry "keeps the spotlight on power relationships within society so as to expose the forces of hegemony and injustice" (Crotty, 1998, p. 157). Themes addressed through critical inquiry include examining social institutions and highlighting historical problems of oppression and social struggles (Morrow & Brown, 1994). Although the ultimate goal of a totally free and just society may not be attainable, critical theorists believe that their research can at least improve contemporary societal conditions (Crotty, 1998). Merriam and Simpson (1995) noted that critical research "brings to focus the possibilities of how culture can sustain irrationality, unfulfilling lifestyles, and social injustice, revealing the degree to which certain ways of life within a culture are strategically organized to preserve the interests of some members of society at the expense of others" (p. 132).

In the present study, I used a critical theory framework to structure my examination of the environmental factors influencing the education of a gifted child. Incorporating a critical interpretive lens in the design of the study enabled me to explain how the ideology of an impoverished, rural community impacted his life. A critical inquiry approach was best suited for this study, for it is only through developing an understanding of the community's ideology that educators and policy makers will be able to determine appropriate methods of enabling gifted children in rural, impoverished communities to realize their potential.

Methodology

The primary goal of the study was to examine the life of a gifted Black child living in rural poverty and to understand how his rural environment influenced his academic achievement. To accomplish this goal, I chose a qualitative research design that integrated features of case study and critical ethnographic research. *Ethnography* refers to research that involves the description of a culture (LeCompte & Preissle, 1993). Merriam (1998) defined a qualitative case study as an "intensive, holistic description and analysis of a single entity, phenomenon, or social unit" (p. 27). Case studies provide researchers with an understanding of complex social phenomena while preserving the holistic and meaningful characteristics of everyday events (Yin, 1994). Case studies are a valuable tool for understanding human behavior in depth (Stake, 1995). Patton (1990) differentiated *critical cases* as "those that can make a point quite dramatically or are, for some reason, particularly important in the scheme of things" (p. 174). Patton noted that a clue to the existence of a critical case is the statement to the effect that "if it happens there, it will happen anywhere," or vice versa, "if it doesn't happen there, it won't happen anywhere" (p. 174). In this critical case study, Jermaine, a gifted Black child living in poverty, is the phenomenon under investigation, and the primary goal of this article is to focus on his experiences in his rural environment. The study was conducted in Pine Grove, Alabama, a community of approximately two hundred people situated in Milledge County.[1]

Data Collection

In this study, the data-collection process incorporated the following four distinct phases described below: (1) review of a portfolio and entry into a community, (2) three weeks of participant observation, (3) one-year correspondence with the child and his teacher, and (4) a final visit to the community and an in-depth interview with the child.

Phase One: Entry into the Community with the Help of a Gatekeeper. Jermaine was introduced to me during his third-grade school year. Teresa Beardsley was my student enrolled in a graduate gifted education degree program. As I came to know Teresa, I learned of Jermaine and her work with him. She explained that since having Jermaine as a student, she continued to provide after-school enrichment experiences for him and two other students. Teresa shared many intriguing stories of this highly creative Black child and helped me gain entry into the rural community in which she lived.

Teresa and her husband, James, had been living in Pine Grove, Alabama, since 1972, when they arrived in the community with Volunteers in Service to America (VISTA) following the civil rights movement. Although the civil rights movement had brought about significant changes in other areas of the South, when Teresa and James arrived in Milledge County they found a segregated society remained, with "Whites Only" signs hanging in the windows of local establishments. Following their work as VISTA volunteers, they were hired as teachers by the county school board and have remained there as dedicated rural educators. Since 1972, Teresa, James, and their two children have been the only Caucasian citizens in the rural, Black community of Pine Grove.

Teresa had maintained a portfolio of Jermaine's work in her first-grade classroom and continued to save examples of his creative writing and the art he produced during their continued after-school enrichment sessions. She shared those products with me and gave me the opportunity to examine the highly creative responses of this gifted young child. Personal documents such as Jermaine's portfolio of work provided rich, stable sources of information (Lincoln & Guba, 1985). My examination of this material was intended to assist me in developing a comprehensive understanding of the gifted young child under study.

Teresa helped me in gaining access to Jermaine and entry into the Pine Grove community. Having lived in Pine Grove for more than twenty years, she served as a key "informant" (Glesne & Peshkin, 1992, p. 34) in the study, an insider in the community who knew the individuals and the politics of the community and who could assist me in "traversing the often sensitive territory" (Glesne and Peshkin, p. 34) of the research setting. Following my review of Jermaine's portfolio, I arranged to visit Pine Grove and spent time traveling throughout Milledge County with Teresa. I toured the community of Pine Grove and several surrounding communities. I visited Pine Grove's schools and spent time in conversation with local citizens of this rural town. During my visits with the community members, several shared their perceptions of Pine Grove's children with me and expressed how their children had enjoyed having Teresa as their teacher.

Phase Two: Participant Observation. A local paper mill had provided philanthropic funding for a summer tutorial reading and science program for the children of Pine Grove for two years. The company recruited Teresa and James to coordinate the program each summer. During the three-week experience known as "Rocket Readers," local high school students worked as tutors with elementary school children by providing them with remedial drill activities to improve vocabulary and reading comprehension. In addition, James provided the youngsters with a curriculum unit on crustaceans to train them in scientific methodology. With parents and grandparents carpooling the children, approximately fifty youngsters arrived at a modest country church every morning for a four-hour academic program and some time for softball during a physical education period. Teresa and James explained that their rationale for providing the program each summer was to help children with reading and give them time to be together during the summer when they tended to become removed from each other, living many miles apart in isolated areas.

Teresa explained that during the previous year, Jermaine had attended the Rocket Readers program, and the experience had not been productive. Though they realized the tutorial sessions were inappropriate for him, Teresa and James encouraged Jermaine to attend the program simply for social interaction, thinking that Jermaine might benefit from seeing other children. Within a short time, Jermaine was bored and had become a discipline problem for his high school student tutor. The following summer, Teresa and I agreed that the Rocket Readers summer experience would be an ideal time for me to continue working with Jermaine in creative writing. Throughout the three-week summer experience, I traveled from my university community to Pine Grove and spent the mornings working with Jermaine on the front steps of the country church. I had an ideal opportunity to observe him with his peer group during the softball games, interview him regarding his life experiences, and provide him with time to pursue his writing craft.

Phase Three: Correspondence with Jermaine and Interviews with Informants. While working with Jermaine during the Rocket Readers program, I learned that the reading materials used with the children had been provided by outside educational consultants hired by the local paper mill to provide the reading curriculum. I noted that the paperback books used throughout the summer were worn copies of low-level children's literature. They featured simple vocabulary and rather mundane stories that were completely removed from the life experiences of African American children living in a rural, isolated community. I also realized that none of the books featured African American characters.

At the end of the three-week summer experience, graduation day would be held, and the children would receive a Rocket Readers T-shirt for having participated. Since Jermaine would not be receiving a T-shirt, I was prepared to provide him with his "graduation" present: a children's novel featuring African American youngsters. I explained to Jermaine that I wanted to continue working with him during the school year by corresponding with him. During his fourth-grade school year, I mailed children's novels each month and looked forward to hearing more about Jermaine's response to them. I selected Newbury-Award-winning novels, novels that featured African American children as main characters, and other reading material that I thought might appeal to Jermaine's creativity. Throughout that period, I regularly scheduled telephone conversations with Teresa regarding Jermaine's progress in school.

Phase Four: A Final Visit to Pine Grove and an Interview with Jermaine. The final phase of data collection consisted of a visit to Pine Grove during Jermaine's fifth-grade school year. I spent a day with Teresa and Jermaine, catching up on news of the community, and concluded the data collection with an in-depth interview with Jermaine.

Fieldwork Techniques. I used a variety of techniques for ethnographic data collection to elicit the insider's perceptions of reality. Fetterman (1989) emphasized the importance of field notes in ethnographic research, describing them as "the brick and mortar of an ethnographic structure" (p. 107). According to Fetterman (1989), field notes take on a variety of forms, including observations, speculations, cues, and lists. The field notes were transcribed daily at the conclusion of each day I visited Pine Grove. They formed an early stage of analysis during data collection and contained raw data necessary for more elaborate analyses in the study. The field notes were used as outlines of the interviews themselves, with the purpose of shaping subsequent interviews. In this study, tape recording did not substitute for direct field notes. Due to cross-cultural differences in dialect, I chose to record handwritten notes rather than tape record interviews. I determined that this less obtrusive strategy was a more culturally sensitive approach while working with Jermaine and the residents of Pine Grove.

I also used a variety of unobtrusive measures that supplemented observation and interview data and analysis. Fetterman (1989) defined *outcroppings* "as a portion of the bedrock that is visible on the surface, in other words, something that sticks out" (p. 68). For example, outcroppings in ethnographic research in an impoverished, rural community might include abandoned automobiles in the yards of Pine Grove residents, the citizens of the community seated in front of the country store, or the condition of the furniture in the vestibule of a small country church. As a researcher, I had to place these visible cues in a larger context, assess the information carefully, and not ignore it or take it for granted.

In this study, one example of an outcropping that became salient was the appearance of the television satellite dishes in the yards of the Pine Grove residents. The important role that satellite television programs played in the lives of children living in rural isolation gave me a better understanding of how important being connected to the world beyond Pine Grove through the satellite dish was to Jermaine and the development of his creativity.

In addition to examining outcroppings, photography was included in the data-collection process and was useful in documenting my observations. Photography enables an ethnographer to create a photographic record of specific behaviors. Collier and Collier (1986) noted that "the camera with its impartial vision has been, since its inception, a clarifier and a modifier of ecological and human understanding" (p. 8). Photography is a useful research tool, for the camera enables researchers to "see without fatigue [since] the last exposure is just as detailed as the first" (Collier & Collier, 1986, p. 9). Fetterman (1989) also indicated that photographs can serve as mnemonic devices for researchers. While researchers are involved with data analysis and writing of findings, photographs can jog their memory, allowing access to detail that they may otherwise have been unable to recall. Photographing prior to beginning a research study enables researchers to capture the culture being examined before developing a schema that may later cloud their interpretive lens after data collection has been completed.

Researcher's Journal. To further enhance data collection, I maintained a researcher's journal that included a record of my "experiences, ideas, fears, mistakes, confusions, breakthroughs, and problems" (Spradley, 1980, p. 71) that arose during fieldwork in Pine Grove. Fetterman (1989) noted that personal reflections such as these may also be included as data in the form of field notes. These diary-like reflections were not only cathartic, they also provided me with a record of my feelings, attitudes, and subjectivities during data collection. Later, during data analysis and writing, this record provided me with a context for understanding the observational field notes I had taken at the same stage of the data collection process. The record of my personal reflections allowed me to take into account how my personal reactions to my experiences in Pine Grove may have influenced my data collection.

Data Analysis

In case study research, data analysis consists of making a detailed description of the case and its context. In analyzing my data of Jermaine in the Pine Grove community, I followed the four procedures advocated by Stake (1995). I began "categorical aggregation" (p. 74) by searching for a collection of instances from the data, looking for issue-relevant meanings to emerge. I then examined single instances in my data and drew meaning from them without looking for multiple instances. Stake referred to this "direct interpretation" (p. 74) as a process of pulling the data apart and then putting them back together in more meaningful ways. I then worked to "establish patterns" (p. 78) and looked for any correspondence between two or more patterns or categories. Following this, I attempted to present my findings descriptively to facilitate my readers' forming "naturalistic generalizations" (p. 85), which are conclusions readers develop through vicarious experiences so well constructed that they feel as if the experience was their own. Therefore, in my data analysis process, the themes that emerged began with the analysis of my initial observations, were constantly refined throughout the data collection and analysis process, and continuously shaped the formation of categories (LeCompte & Preissle, 1993). To conclude my analyses, I developed generalizations about Jermaine's story in terms of patterns and how they compare and contrast with published literature on gifted students in rural communities.

To enhance the validity of the findings, I conducted intensive direct observations and interviews until data saturation occurred—when new information collected was redundant and did not offer any additional insights to elucidate further understanding (Bogdan & Biklen, 1998). I also provided a detailed description of how I conducted the investigation, the measures I took to ensure the accuracy of the observations, and the evidence on which the findings were grounded. In addition, I arranged to have fellow university researchers play the role of "devil's advocate" in reviewing my data analysis and the interpretation of my findings.

Context of the Study: Pine Grove, Alabama

Graue and Walsh (1998) defined context as "a culturally and historically situated place and time" (p. 9). The context of this study played an important role in understanding the way of life in Pine Grove and Jermaine's experiences. The study was conducted in Milledge County, Alabama. Historically significant events had taken place less than thirty miles away in Selma, Alabama. On March 7, 1965, over six hundred civil rights marchers were stopped at the Edmund Pettus Bridge in Selma, where state and local lawmen attacked them with billy clubs and tear gas and drove them back. Two days later, Martin Luther King led another symbolic march to the bridge. Later that month, over three thousand marchers walked from Selma to the state capital in Montgomery. Shortly after, President Johnson signed the Voting Rights Act of 1965. The memories of those events remained clear in the minds of residents of Pine Grove. Several community members had been with Dr. King and expressed how they hoped that children in Alabama appreciated "the gas they had to breathe" during those horrendous times in America's history.

The prevalent lifestyle in Milledge County for generations was rooted in a cotton plantation and sharecropper economy. This prosperous economy began to deteriorate with the invasion of the boll weevil following World War I. The cotton economy was further devastated by land erosion, the Great Depression, and the emergence of modern farming techniques. Timber growing and wood-pulp industries eventually replaced the fledgling cotton economy. During this time, a conversion from sharecropper to wage-hand farming also took place. Landless Black tenants were slowly eliminated as machines replaced the work of physical laborers and more cotton fields were cleared for timber growing.

According to the federal government's census, the estimated population of Milledge County in 1998 was 13,468. Noted as the poorest county in the state of Alabama, the per capita personal income reported was $10,759, with 45.2 percent of the county's population falling below the poverty level (Alabama Department of Archives and History, 1998). A journalist for the *Montgomery Advertiser* described the county as "one of the poorest parts of the country" (Benn, 1988, p. 1C) and indicated that the majority of people living in Milledge County were forced to rely on public assistance to survive. The McDonald Billings Company, a manufacturer of corrugated cardboard, is the only industry in Milledge County, employing only several Pine Grove residents. Residents of this rural community commute thirty to forty miles beyond the county lines to work in catfish-processing plants. Others are employed in the fast food restaurants in Selma.

Jermaine's Family and School

Jermaine is an ebony-skinned child with large brown eyes, a warm smile, and finely sculpted features. A small, slender child, he is animated and vivacious. Jermaine lives with his mother, his older brother and sister, and an aunt. According to his teachers, Jermaine and his sixteen-year-old sister, Tamara, are frequently left responsible for his elderly aunt, who is physically handicapped and mentally retarded. Residents in the community often noted Jermaine's mother's absence from the home. She is part of a group of Pine Grove residents who sit in front of an abandoned country store for long periods during the day and evening hours. Jermaine's older brother, Tyrell, also spends time in front of the store. Tyrell is a high school junior and receives services from the program for educably mentally retarded (EMR) students.

Jermaine attends the elementary school in Pine Grove, a prekindergarten through sixth grade facility serving 255 children. All students are African American, and 98 percent are eligible for a federally subsidized free-lunch program. The children are bussed from six small communities, all within twenty-five to thirty miles of Pine Grove and separated by rural highways. The school facility, a red-brick building constructed in the late 1940s, is in great disrepair, with rain leaking through the roof, dilapidated furniture, and equipment in need of repair. It consists of three classrooms and a modest lunchroom, with nine overcrowded mobile trailers housing classrooms behind the school. There is no media center, gymnasium, art room, or music facility. Special education classes and physical education classes share a classroom referred to as the "auditorium." The grounds surrounding the school consist of red clay, and no awnings cover the walkways between the main building and the portable classrooms. When it rains, the school is saturated with mud. A letter I received from Teresa one winter provided evidence of the difficulties faced by teachers in the school. She sounded discouraged when she wrote: "School is difficult this time of year. . .rain and mud seem constant, and my children slip and slide coming and going. Then there are SAT objectives. That's all we hear about, and apparently all we are expected to teach."

Administrators in Milledge County watch teachers closely. Schools throughout Milledge County have annually been on a list of school districts threatened to be taken over by the state department of education if achievement test scores do not increase substantially. Schools are designated "on alert," "under caution," or "clear" depending on the testing performance of students. Evidence that these conditions have existed historically in Milledge County was found in an investigative report published in 1967 by the National Education Association (NEA) Commission on Professional Rights and Responsibilities entitled *[Milledge] County: A Study of Social, Economic and Educational Bankruptcy.* The problems facing Milledge County schools also affect special education programs. Although the state legislature in Alabama mandated identification and programming for gifted students in 1972, Milledge County has not complied with the law since its inception.

Standardized testing in Pine Grove consists of the Stanford Achievement Tests conducted each spring. Throughout the three-year investigation, Jermaine's achievement scores ranged from the eighty-sixth to the ninety-ninth national percentiles in language arts and reading, with vocabulary and language expression ranked as his most prominent strengths. Jermaine's scores in math were in the average range. His Otis Lennon School Ability Test scores ranged from 118 to 120. According to Teresa and several of Jermaine's former teachers, when his test scores are compared with the above-average students in his class scoring in the fortieth to fiftieth percentiles, Jermaine's performance is considered remarkable. In addition, it is important to consider how the items on verbal IQ tests favor the acculturation experiences of urban children. For example, Jermaine has never experienced a modern shopping mall. As Spicker (1992a) noted, a child living in an isolated rural area who had never seen a shopping mall would be hard pressed to describe one. However, he may know more about snakes, fishing for catfish, or summer sunsets than most urban and suburban children his age. Unfortunately, questions involving shopping malls are more likely to appear on aptitude tests than questions that would be a better measure of a rural child's knowledge base.

Jermaine's Home

Pine Grove is a community in which pockets of homes are clustered at intervals along narrow, rural red clay roads. Jermaine's home is up a hill on a dirt road. The house is a cabin with a cinder block foundation. It is heated with a wood stove and cooled by opening windows and doors. In second grade, Jermaine included an entry in his creative writing folder that described an account of his typical morning routine before school and provided evidence of the impoverished conditions in which he lives:

5:30   Jermaine wakes up the family

Gets bathing pan, soap, and rag

Goes out to bathroom to get water

Puts water on heater and bathes

Finds some clothes, finds booksack and shoes

7:00   Jermaine goes to bus stop

Gets to school and waits for breakfast to get ready

Eats and talks until Mr. Jones tells us to go to class

Nestled in the woods, Jermaine's home is surrounded on three sides by trailers. According to the residents of Pine Grove, trailers are considered superior to houses since they come with central heat and air conditioning, furnishings, and appliances. In Jermaine's front yard sit a nonfunctioning automobile and a satellite dish. All of the surrounding residences have television service through a satellite.

Findings

A Struggle to Find a Place in the Community

According to Teresa and other residents, the small, rural community of Pine Grove determines a ranking for its members. Like many small towns, families in Pine Grove have roles according to their perceived place in the community. Jermaine's family falls into the lowest rank; they are considered outcasts and are largely ignored. They are often spoken of in derogatory terms and used as examples of how not to be. A distant cousin of the family explained, "I grew up knowing who to be like, and it sure wasn't them." The reason provided for this by most residents of the community interviewed was the "crazy" factor. Jermaine's handicapped aunt and older brother were mentioned. The whole family was marked as being inclined to odd or "crazy" behavior. The main generalizations that anyone could provide for this attitude was the presence of multiple family members with mental or physical handicaps. Another reason provided was the cemetery near the family property because "no one in their right mind" would live near a cemetery. Apparently, the stigma of the family has not been overcome, as Jermaine was recognized by the adult community as a "no-count bad child." The negative status of the family in the community was expressed in several phrases, but the general view was that Jermaine and his family were outside the normal population of the community.

The heart of this small, rural town is the church. In Pine Grove, the church serves as a vehicle for interaction, kinship, for the kind of time spent together that leads to understanding and tolerance. Few families can maintain significant status in the community without church affiliation. Jermaine's family does not attend church. No family relative or member of the community has ever taken Jermaine to church. The functions of the church and the support systems the church can offer have not served Jermaine.

Jermaine dismissed church attendance, indicating it was an intrusion on his television time. His older sister attributed a lack of church clothing and a lack of transportation as reasons for the family absence from Sunday services. Since church is more than a place of worship, services may last until the late afternoon; as Jermaine and his sister explained, "It takes too long." The result is that the community center focus is absent from the pattern of life in Jermaine's family.

Jermaine's lack of church experience became evident during his after-school enrichment sessions with several other students in Elizabeth's classroom. The holiday season was approaching, and Jermaine asked to hear the Christmas story. Teresa explained: "We read several versions of the Christmas story. Jermaine didn't know the story. Questions were flowing from him, which isn't unusual. Jermaine wanted to know the details. He concentrated on the three kings and on their travel and their place origin. He had rather quickly noticed the incongruity of the traditional telling of the Christmas story. Over the next several days he drafted a picture book. He wanted to be clear about things that he felt those around him already knew."

The Role of Family in Jermaine's Life

Although the majority of students in the Pine Grove school are poor, Jermaine knows that he has less than others. Teachers in Pine Grove reported that when Jermaine first arrived at the elementary school, his clothes were ill fitting, and on cold winter days he sometimes arrived at school in only a T-shirt and jeans. One teacher explained, "Jermaine knows that he is poor. Other kids have sneakers that cost $89. Some have sneakers that cost $189, but Jermaine's mom buys his sneakers at Bargaintown. 'Bargaintown Nikes' are spotted right away. Jermaine gets teased a lot."

Although Jermaine's situation may seem dismal, he is not discouraged. He is lively, humorous, and self-confident. The family disparaged by others remains very important to him. Jermaine attributes his keen sense of humor to his mother. He respects his mother but does not make demands of her. He is accustomed to the arrangement that she lives a life separate from his and is absent often. Jermaine's extended family is also important to him. Two of his mother's brothers, Walter and McKinley, are his favorites. They live in Detroit and come to Pine Grove regularly. Two vignettes from Jermaine's autobiography provide evidence of this fondness for his uncles:

Last Christmas, when I was little, Uncle Walter was there. He came for a visit.
He told my mom he had opened my presents to see what was in them, but I had

really done it. My Uncle Walter saved my butt just like he used to save my Uncle Carl's butt when they were kids. . . .Another time at Christmas when I was a little boy, Uncle Walter and Uncle McKinley were back home at my house.
It was Christmas morning, and when I got up, I walked in to see my presents. But I only saw my uncles. They were on the floor playing with cars. Those were my presents! So I ran over to them and we played all morning.

Jermaine's family functions almost as an outlet for his verbal abilities. He is a storyteller, and, like most storytellers, he does not limit himself strictly to facts. Not all his stories are true, but Jermaine's friends find them entertaining. Teresa reported that his peers were delighted with a story he wrote about his sister, Tamara. The following is a vignette from the story:

Early one morning, my mother wanted a glass of water. She told Tamara to go to the pump to get her some. Tamara was still asleep. She didn't get up, so my mother yelled at her. Tamara said she wanted to sleep. My mother went to get the shotgun and told her she better get up. Tamara was asleep, so my mother shot the gun. She shot a hole in the roof. Tamara jumped so fast she was pumping water before she saw that she didn't have a water glass in her hand!

Jermaine's Creativity

Teresa explained that the creative behaviors displayed by Jermaine during his early school experiences were not always appreciated by adults in his elementary school. Apparently, his family's reputation in the community extended into Jermaine's experience in school when he first arrived. The assistant principal referred to him as "that bad little boy I have to keep my eye on," while another teacher who had observed Jermaine during bus duty commented, "That boy is just too bad to handle." Teresa reported that in kindergarten, Jermaine was discovered hanging upside down in his chair while the teacher was presenting a lesson. When the teacher posed a question, Jermaine answered correctly and elaborated. The teacher announced to the class, "If you can do that and still give me the answers, then you can act like Jermaine." Fortunately, Jermaine's kindergarten experience was positive; however, Teresa became involved in many conversations with several of Jermaine's teachers who were not as appreciative of his high energy. Teresa noted that teachers appreciated his advanced vocabulary, but she found that she had to serve as an advocate for the creative young child whose classroom antics bewildered his teachers.

The portfolio of creative writing maintained by Teresa provided many fine examples of Jermaine's creativity. Jermaine's love of language and creative expression was evident in his work. As a first grader, he chose to write an autobiography during the after-school enrichment sessions. The following paragraph is the introductory paragraph of his autobiography:

I was tumbling through my mother's stomach—BOOM. . .BOOM. . .BOOM.
I came out crying. Everybody comes out crying. Someone was holding me, and I wanted my momma. I was named Germane after my granddaddy. He didn't have a nickname or a middle name, so I don't either. He was my momma's daddy.

Also included in the portfolio is a book authored by Jermaine entitled *Jermaine's World.* The book provides readers with a glimpse of Jermaine's view of himself. In his story, he is a hero using his calculating mind to solve problems. The following vignette provides evidence of Jermaine's view of his problem-solving creativity:

> I was leaving Jermaine's world. I needed to see my sister. It was soon to be her wedding. I wanted to stop her from marrying a jerk. I was riding my dragon through the hills. My dragon and I bumped into a gate. I wanted to show off my powers, so I burned the gate down with my powerful triton. We walked to where the gate had been. Suddenly, thousands of dragons arrived. They were breathing fire and smoke. I looked around. I knew we had to get out of there. I saddled up my dragon, grabbed my triton, and tried to escape. One of the dragons fired at my bottom. One fried my hair until I was bald. Another tried to claw me. I spoke out in my kingly voice, "What is this NONSENSE?!" A dragon said, "Who ARE you talking to?" "Who ARE YOU talking to? I am the most powerful king you will ever meet." "OH! NO! Fried king for supper tonight!" All the dragons were happy to hear that. "Fried! No, not fried," I said. "I would taste better boiled. And if you are going to boil me, you'll need water." The dragons turned and began to walk toward a pond several miles away. Dragons do not like to have water too close. It might put out their fire. It took them many hours to get to the pond. They walked so slowly because they were afraid. I turned south and went back to my world. I decided to never return. My dragon agreed with me. He was glad that none of the other dragons had noticed that he was toothless.

Another fine example of Jermaine's creativity follows. His first-grade story entitled "How the Sun Got Hot" included colorful, vivid illustrations that were expressive, detailed and depicted the emotions of his characters. The complete text of this story is provided below:

> Once upon a time, there lived a humongous sun and a smaller moon. They were very cold indeed. They lived in the dark, shivery sky. They kept warm by holding onto each other. One time, millions of years after time began, moon let go of sun, he was tired of holding onto his humongous friend. The sun fell from the sky. It fell to earth and landed in the hottest volcano there was. Moon tried to reach his friend, but he couldn't reach into the hot volcano. Moon cried. Thunder and rain came to earth. The enormous sun sank to the deepest part of the volcano. It turned so red from heat, it exploded from the volcano. The sun was on fire as it shot back into the sky. When the moon saw the sun coming home, he ran to his friend. Moon said, "SUN! What happened to you?" Sun said, "I fell into a warm place and now I won't ever be cold again." The moon had to move far away from the ball of fire that was his friend. And Moon missed holding his friend, Sun. Sometimes he still cries. When you hear thunder and feel rain, you will know that moon is crying for his lost friend.

In my work with Jermaine during the summer reading program, I spent mornings with him discussing ideas for additional creative stories he wanted to publish. I agreed to serve as his secretary, taking dictation as he tilted his head back, closed his eyes, and told his imaginative stories. In my work with him during those morning creative writing sessions, I learned how he obtained his creative ideas and infused them into his writing. At one point in a story in which he described a "virgin Black candle," he stopped in midsentence and said to me, "Do you want to know where I got that idea?" When I encouraged him to explain, he pointed out that he had seen a "virgin Black candle" in one of his favorite television shows on a satellite television station. Later that morning, he opened his eyes again and said, "That triton I just used. I got that idea from *Hocus Pocus*. It's one of my favorite shows." It was then I began to understand the significant role that the satellite dishes throughout Pine Grove played in the lives of children living in such rural isolation. Satellite television was for many the only connection to a world beyond their rural community, and for Jermaine, satellite television apparently served as a constant source of inspiration for his manuscripts.

I later realized that Jermaine was inspired in a variety of ways. Following my work with him that summer, I mailed him children's novels that I thought would appeal to him, corresponded with him, and continued to interview Teresa concerning his progress in fifth grade. I learned that his creative writing apparently was being inspired by the books I was mailing him. I had sent a copy of Todd Strasser's *Help! I'm Trapped in My Gym Teacher's Body,* an outlandish story about a young boy who undergoes a magical transformation and resides in the muscular physique of his physical education teacher while the gym teacher simultaneously becomes trapped in the youngster's body. Shortly after Jermaine received the book, Teresa reported that his fifth-grade teacher came to her classroom one afternoon after school and exclaimed, "I don't know where he gets all these ideas, but today, he wrote a story about a metamorphosis! Where could he be getting these words?" Apparently the rather whimsical story I had mailed him had served not only as the inspiration for a story but also as a vocabulary booster.

During our writing sessions on the front steps of the country church, we discussed the beauty of Pine Grove's countryside. We once became involved in a rather sophisticated discussion about the solitude and whether or not the quiet of country living would help a young child become more creative. He explained that the quiet of the countryside helped inspire his ideas, and through daydreaming he was able to foster his creative thinking process. Along with being inspired by the chirping of crickets and daydreaming about what a day in the life of a cricket would be like, Jermaine pointed out that his daydreams also took place at night as he pondered a sunset or watched the dazzling little glow of light from fireflies. He also indicated that daydreaming was an important part of every school day and may have served as a strategy for surviving the boredom he often experienced in school. He explained:

> Most of my day I spend daydreaming. In class, I daydream all the time. I think about my future plans for all the movie scripts I'm going to write when I become a movie producer. I just can't get over daydreaming. I read a book that explained it was normal for a kid my age to dream a lot. At night, when I'm not daydreaming, I like to go out and stare out at the dark and think. I call it my "thinking in the dark time." It's my nighttime inspiration. I like to think about some of the movies I've watched and think of ideas for movies I want to write someday.

Jermaine also noted that family members were often the inspiration for his manuscripts. He pointed out how his sister had been an important character in his dragon story. When I questioned Jermaine about his storytelling ability, he also pointed out the influence his family had on his creative abilities: "I think I get my storytelling from my granddaddy. He used to tell really good campfire stories. He always told funny stories about old people. Whenever we had family reunions and my uncles came down from Detroit and Boston, we would sit around a campfire for hours and listen to my granddaddy's stories."

Another source of inspiration for his story writing is Jermaine's fascination with animals. He is extremely knowledgeable about many animals that live in his rural environment. Numerous stories he dictated to me on the front steps of the church were stories about salamanders, catfish, and animals found in southern Alabama. The first story he crafted with me was entitled *The Odd Couple: Charley and Grant,* a clever tale about two baby iguanas who survive a severe winter blizzard together. He explained that although he spent hours watching satellite TV shows, he emphasized his favorite programs were *"National Geographic* shows on wildlife animals, and not *The Jerry Springer Show!"*

Teresa described one scenario in her first-grade classroom that highlighted Jermaine's early expertise on animals. She explained: "The children were invited, if they chose, to handle a small garden snake. Very few volunteered. Jermaine took the snake, the third child to even touch it, and began to talk about snakes. When he got to the part about vestigial legs, Shanika [a child in the class] was stunned. She stood up and told the rest of her classmates, 'Jermaine knows everything!' Shanika was impressed."

In a conversation with Jermaine about the books I had mailed him, I asked which book had been his favorite. He did not hesitate as he announced that *Phillip Hall Likes Me, I Reckon Maybe,* by Bette Greene, had really captivated him. Bette Greene's award-winning novel is about a gifted young Black female in rural Arkansas. The author provided her readers with a better understanding of the lives of Black children in the rural South along with typical elementary school boy-girl rivalries and some of the dilemmas posed by giftedness. Beth, the main character in the book, is an assertive young girl whose impetuosity sometimes gets her into trouble, and like Jermaine, she is an animal lover. Jermaine explained that he enjoyed the adventures of the main character, particularly the competition between Beth and her cow against Philip Hall in the county fair. Following the discussion of that novel, I asked Jermaine what type of books he would want me to continue mailing him, and he replied, "I really like those stories, but please send me some nonfiction books about animals!"

Extrafamilial Support

Along with emotional support from members of his extended family, Jermaine found support from people beyond his family. A school relationship with a classmate played an important role in Jermaine's life during his early years in school. Jermaine and Cedric became friends in kindergarten and were assigned to the same classroom from then on. Cedric was a popular boy who enjoyed Jermaine's sense of humor. Teresa explained the importance of their relationship and the effect it had on Jermaine's life:

> Cedric is the grandson of our school's cook. Cedric has connections. When he and Jermaine became friends, Jermaine began to have connections. Cedric's grandmother has always been empathetic to any child who enters the school cafeteria. When a child needs to be encouraged or "bragged on" or needs extra food on the tray, Sister Sophia is the one who provides. She became more familiar with Jermaine through his friendship with her grandson. She learned of specific accomplishments, and she praised him for a book he wrote or a good grade he earned. Cedric's mother, a teacher's aide, also became acquainted with Jermaine through her son. She described him as a "lost child" who was "just too sad for a little boy." She fixed his clothes when they needed a pin to hold them up or combed his hair when he needed it. She supported Jermaine. Eventually Jermaine asked Cedric if he could ride bus #3 and come home with him. Cedric asked and found that both his mother and grandmother were willing to have Jermaine as a guest. Jermaine began spending several weekends with the family. Sister Sophia mentioned that Jermaine was invited to spend Thanksgiving, so "he could get a good meal like everybody ought to have." The visits continued, and Jermaine began to receive a different view of himself.

Along with the support found in Sister Sophia's family, Jermaine also found support within Teresa's family. Teresa, James, and their children have been an important source of extrafamilial support for Jermaine since he was a student in Teresa's first-grade classroom. Jermaine visits Teresa's home occasionally and will join her son for an afternoon of computer games on the family's computer and for bowls of ice cream. He enjoys sharing his creative writing with Teresa's daughter. This family has appreciated and celebrated Jermaine's creativity since he was young and have called attention to his gifts and talents. Teresa has served as a strong advocate for Jermaine throughout his elementary school career, struggling hard during his primary grade years to get other teachers to understand his behavior and appreciate his special abilities. Jermaine feels strongly about his special relationship with "Miss Teresa," as he explained, "I don't know what I'd do without Miss Teresa. She's always there to help me. She helps me get my work right. Whenever I have a problem, I know that I can go to her, and she'll help me solve it."

Theresa and her husband have remained in Milledge County since their days volunteering for VISTA. Frustrated with the lack of progress in their school district for over twenty-five years, they continue to maintain a realistic view of the situation, constantly hopeful that the conditions in Pine Grove will improve. Teresa continues to provide enrichment experiences to talented children after her teaching day has ended. She continues to work with her colleagues to help them understand the needs of children like Jermaine, providing in-service training during staff development days. James is known beyond the county as a scavenger for used science and computer equipment for the Pine Grove school. Two humble individuals, these dedicated teachers remain passionate about their work with children in their rural, impoverished community. This passion was evidenced in an interview with James, as he explained:

> Occasionally you see a child like Jermaine, and he gives you so much hope. You know that you play an important role in shaping that youngster's experience and exposing him to a world beyond Pine Grove. You know that if you help him to achieve in school and provide him with the tools he needs to get accepted into a college, he'll leave here. So few ever return, since there's nothing here for them. Knowing that the community may never benefit from their talents and abilities is a difficult thing to have to accept, but that doesn't stop you from doing all you can to help them achieve a better life. You chip away at a big problem one child at a time, and you just hope and pray that you're making a difference.

During Jermaine's fifth-grade school year, another significant source of extra-familial support evolved when Mr. Cooper, a gentleman from Detroit, Michigan, returned home to Pine Grove to retire. Upon arrival, he decided he needed something to occupy his time, so he formed athletic teams for the children in the community to compete against teams from surrounding towns. Along with the athletic program, he organized a Boy Scout troop. Jermaine became involved with a number of sports and scouting. Coach Cooper has played an important role for Jermaine. He recognized Jermaine's intelligence and selected him as the quarterback for the new football team. Jermaine explained the coach's rationale for selecting him for such a prestigious position: "Coach Cooper saw that I really knew my plays, and I knew how to call them. That's what it takes to be a quarterback. Coach said he chose me to play quarterback because I'm smart and fast. Because I'm the quarterback, I'm getting new respect. A lot of kids who didn't used to like me now wave to me in school and say, 'What's up?'"

The Emergence of Jermaine's Self-Identity

In the three-year period during which I collected data on Jermaine, evidence of an emerging self-identity was noted. The young child known for hanging upside down in his chair behaved differently by fifth grade. Jermaine's belief in self had appeared in his creative writing; however, his fifth-grade school year seemed significant for him in a number of ways. Along with an emerging reputation as the community's elementary school quarterback, Jermaine's school year was positively influenced by the books he received in the mail. The children's novels did more than serve as inspiration for his creative writing. According to Teresa, when Jermaine finished the books, he shared them with Jerome, Lamont, and Niesa, his three new best friends who were grouped with him in the highest fifth-grade reading group. They were seen proudly carrying the books out to daily recess. Jermaine's small personal library was valued by his new peer group, and apparently he was becoming more highly regarded.

Along with enjoying new books together, Jermaine's friends collaborated with him in partnerships for the fifth-grade science fair, winning first place together in the countywide competition. He and his three best friends were also successful in earning another award for a Black History Month project in their school. Jermaine and his three friends designed a timeline of the life of Harriet Tubman to accompany a historical biography about the famous historical figure. Continuous success as a team helped Jermaine maintain healthy relationships with other children who appreciated his intelligence and creativity.

Another important factor that made a difference for Jermaine during fifth grade was the school district's decision to implement a school uniform. According to Teresa, early in Jermaine's school career, he was viewed as the child in ill-fitting clothes with a constant habit of holding his pants up with one hand while the other hand was free for whatever task he was attempting. During his fifth-grade year, the uniform became a socioeconomic equalizer that allowed Jermaine to arrive at school looking like everyone else. Teresa described the impact on him: "The talk of Pine Grove is the implementation of a school uniform. The uniform consists of khaki pants and a hunter green polo shirt and "tie-up Sunday dress shoes." They are being sold by stores in Selma, and everyone ends up with the same quality. Jermaine's uncles have paid for his. They are a real equalizer here, and they've really helped in creating a sense of community. This has really helped Jermaine this year. Fifth graders are so much more aware of brand-name clothing."

Jermaine has begun to find a place for himself in the community and has found a small group of students who appreciate his creativity and with whom he can compete academically. With the exception of a B in math, Jermaine achieved straight A's in fifth grade. The appreciation of his creativity and the community respect for his new role as quarterback has helped redefine Jermaine's self-identity. As a ten-year-old, he is constructing a strong sense of self, with a new confidence that is apparent in a number of ways.

Jermaine noted that problems typically associated with more urban communities were beginning to creep into his rural community. According to him, gangs were beginning to form in the county's middle and senior high schools, and he appeared worried. This concern was evidenced when he commented, "There's a lot going on in the country nowadays. There are gangbangers and kids are doin' smoke. There are kids in the middle school with blades. Even here in Pine Grove, young brothers need to get off the streets and get jobs."

Jermaine assured me he wanted nothing to do with gang culture. He sees himself as a ten-year-old who is perfectly comfortable being a fifth grader. He sees no need to rush the process of becoming more worldly or sophisticated before his time. He described an experience at a birthday party that highlighted his desire to remain naive for a while longer. "I went to a birthday party a few weeks ago. So many of the kids were talking about having boyfriends and girlfriends. They were playing games, kissing games. Tongue-suckin' kissin'. I talk to a girl like a friend. I just want to play games, and not that tongue-suckin' stuff! My mom says that stuff will affect your life."

Rather than become a teenager before his time, Jermaine appears happy being ten. He sees himself as a good person with special talents and is feeling positive about his abilities that are now valued by his peers. Jermaine's emerging self-identity and the positive view he has of himself was also evidenced in a story he crafted as part of a fifth-grade essay contest sponsored by the county teachers' association. The guidelines for students in the third- through sixth-grade category were to write a creative essay about themselves tackling problems of crime and misguided youth in Milledge County. In his essay, Jermaine decided to address a community problem by transforming himself into a super-hero. The introduction to his essay, entitled "The Adventures of Turbo Man," reads as follows:

> I live two lives. The first one is when I am Courtney Davis, a well-respected lawyer. My other life is as Turbo Man. That is my name when I help people who are in trouble. I wear a red suit of hard steel. I can bend metal with my bare hands and see through walls with my supersonic eyes. I have turbo disks on my arms that can knock out evil characters, and I drive a Turbomobile.

In this manuscript, Turbo Man's adventure concludes with Jermaine's character capturing a kidnapper and returning his community to safety.

In my work with Jermaine, I questioned him as to what he saw as his greatest strengths, and he quickly responded with "my creativity and my ability to write stories" and "my talent as a football quarterback." When asked to think about filling a time capsule for posterity with ten items that would best represent him, he included his primary-grade creative writing books entitled *Jermaine's World* and *How the Sun Got Hot,* further evidence of his pride in his ability as a creative writer.

Teresa reflected on a favorite memory of Jermaine. He was in an after-school enrichment session in her classroom. She described how he opened a conversation by saying, "You know what the real meaning of life is? It is to care about each other." Teresa explained that after this profound statement, he decided to read by himself. His only follow-up comment was that "he did not hear it on TV." What is apparent is that Jermaine wants to be cared about and wants others to care for each other.

Along with an empathy for others, Jermaine has a solid sense of ethics. He described an incident at school in which a jar of pennies being collected by students for a fund-raising project was stolen. He found this upsetting and could not understand how young people could steal from one another. He shook his head and expressed his concern for his community. The young man who was troubled by the school crime dreams of becoming a lawyer one day, but explained that his legal career may serve as his second profession, as he intended to first spend several years working as a Hollywood film producer.

Discussion and Implications

The Role of the Extended Family

If kudzu symbolizes the effects of rural poverty and isolation in the life of creative youngsters, then what could serve as a weed killer in fighting off the effects of this life-choking vine? In this study, filling the role of "weed killer" in helping to combat the kudzu were members of Jermaine's extended family who supported him. His relationships with his uncles were significant to him. Mentioned throughout the three-year study, Uncle Walter and Uncle McKinley gave him emotional support and were there for him via long-distance financial support, as evidenced in their purchase of Jermaine's school uniform in fifth grade. Also noted was his pride at having inherited his storytelling talents from his grandfather. Jermaine's relationship with his uncles highlights a distinguishing feature of the African American family. Nobles (1997) indicated that the traditional African American family is a "unique cultural form enjoying its own inherent resources" (p. 88). Comprising several individual households, the extended family is visible in the lives of its children and provides needed emotional support for its members. Walker and colleagues (Walker, Taylor, McElroy, Phillip, & Wilson, 1995) indicated that the Black extended family served as a "stress absorbing system" (p. 30) and helped develop positive self-esteem within all of its members. Sudarkasa (1997) maintained that Black families were "some of the most flexible, adaptive, and inclusive institutions in America" (p. 39) that provided nurturance for the children and support for adults.

Extrafamilial Support

The findings in this critical case study of Jermaine highlight the importance of strong emotional support and understanding from adults who understand and value creativity in young children. Teresa's appreciation for Jermaine's creative abilities at an early age and her advocacy for him as a student made a significant difference. Teresa struggled for years to develop an understanding within the faculty that giftedness was a multifaceted construct and a child's ability to think creatively was something to be celebrated. The child who teachers initially perceived as a problem child eventually was appreciated by more teachers in Pine Grove, as well as by his peers. Teresa and her family also provided Jermaine with friendship, hospitality, and a receptive audience for sharing his creative ideas.

In addition to the support Jermaine received from Teresa, other adults beyond his family provided support in a number of ways. Sister Sophia, the school's lunchroom chef, and her daughter, who provided time for Jermaine to spend with his friend Cedric, were also significant sources of emotional support early in his elementary school experience. The child perceived by the community as a "bad little boy" was understood by this family, and they provided nurturance they regarded as basic. Coach Cooper also appeared to serve as a significant "weed killer" in fighting off the kudzu in Jermaine's experiences. By selecting Jermaine as the football team's quarterback, he did much to elevate Jermaine's status in the community. Coach Cooper's recognition of Jermaine's ability to think quickly appeared to have helped Jermaine develop a positive view of himself. With a stronger sense of self, Jermaine's creativity could continue to flourish. This finding supports what urban researchers Heath and McLaughlin (1993) and Hébert and Reis (1999) found in studies of urban youth, in which supportive relationships with significant adults helped nurture resilience and shaped a belief in self within culturally diverse teenagers.

Nurturing Creativity

Two additional "weed killers" that were important in Jermaine's experience were the satellite television stations beamed into Jermaine's home and the collection of children's literature he received through the mail, enjoyed, and shared with his friends. These connections with a world beyond his isolated, rural community provided Jermaine with exposure to new ideas and new ways of thinking and served as an important source of new information about one of his childhood passions, wildlife. The information Jermaine was able to absorb through television viewing and reading from his new collection of books eventually was infused into his creative writing, helped strengthen his vocabulary, and allowed his creativity to flourish.

Although Jermaine's exposure to satellite television may have supported his creativity, we must also critically consider the negative impact television may have on children in communities such as Pine Grove. Realizing that nearly 99 percent of all American households have at least one television set (Abelman, 1992), Jermaine's experience with satellite television in his impoverished, rural community should not surprise us. Abelman described television as "the great cultural denominator, the one environmental factor that all children have in common" (p. 18), and noted that parents should consider it "a potentially positive and negative force in children's lives" (p. 18). Through his critical inquiry of the television industry, Williams (1974) noted that while television may be educational, it may also undermine intellect and critical thought, creating generations of passive individuals. Jermaine was exceptional in that his creativity was nurtured, rather than stifled, by his television viewing. However, we are reminded of the important conclusions drawn by Gray (1995) regarding the portrayal of Blacks on television programs: "Black representations in commercial network television are situated within the existing material and institutional hierarchies of privilege and power. . .television representations of blackness work largely to legitimate and secure the terms of the dominant cultural and social order by circulating within and remaining structured by them" (p. 10).

Since this medium was Jermaine's primary source for learning about the world outside his community, his impressions of life beyond Pine Grove may have been very distorted. When Jermaine watches television, does he ever see anyone like himself portrayed? No. More likely, he sees middle-class Black characters in situation comedies or urban Black youths portrayed unfavorably in dramas, both of which reinforce social stratification and social disharmony, as well as legitimate the status quo of White dominance (Spigner, 1991; Tait & Perry, 1994). For this reason, African American children in isolated, rural communities bombarded with racially stereotyped messages delivered through culturally insensitive television programs may eventually question their self-worth and their ability to achieve success in life.

The need that children in Pine Grove had for intellectual stimulation through satellite television and enriched educational materials calls attention to a serious problem facing schools in isolated areas. This finding supports what Descy (1992) proposed in linking rural schools to universities and other school districts via interactive technology. Interactive television would allow students in isolated, impoverished areas to take advantage of unique educational opportunities. In order to compete in an increasingly technological society, students from communities such as Pine Grove will need the same knowledge and skills as young people in suburban and urban communities. Since it is not always possible to take students to where educational opportunities may be available, such opportunities must be taken to students and teachers. If an interactive technology system is to be established in an impoverished area such as Pine Grove, a collaborative effort may have to evolve between the industrial community and the public schools. Given the impoverished conditions evidenced in Pine Grove and the philanthropic efforts of the local paper mill in Milledge County, the McDonald Billings Corporation might serve as a source of financial support for such efforts.

Although interactive technology may assist educators in addressing the needs of students in isolated, rural areas, we need to realize that rural isolation may benefit some children in some ways. It may be surprising that the quiet solitude of the rural environment in which Jermaine lived appeared to help nurture Jermaine's creativity. This quiet solitude essentially was another "weed killer." Although isolated, Jermaine found that his quiet surroundings gave him high-quality thinking time and inspiration for his creative writing. This finding suggests that educators need to examine rural life and realize that for those who are born and raised in a rural culture, the cultural qualities of their experiences are to be appreciated and respected. Kearney (1991a) noted the importance of this appreciation for rural life in the experiences of gifted children living in isolated, rural communities. She suggested that "to support the optimal development of these children without asking them to deny or denigrate the culture which has produced them requires an appreciation of the cultural foundations of rural life, and a willingness to use the strengths of the culture itself to support the child's development" (p. 16).

Jermaine's appreciation for rural solitude and his evening thinking time are important in highlighting a significant issue to consider when educating gifted students in rural, isolated areas. Gifted students growing up in such areas may actually enjoy some advantages. Jermaine's love of animals and his use of nighttime quiet for creative thinking may have helped him build an important knowledge base as he developed his creativity. What we have seen with Jermaine's experience is consistent with what Kearney (1991b) suggested when she noted that rural gifted children may "share the benefits of nature as a science laboratory, quiet places in which to reflect, and an independence and autonomy not always available to their city cousins—elements which can support the inner dynamics of a creative and intellectual life" (p. 16).

Creative Positives

Regardless of the kudzu-like rural impoverished conditions in which Jermaine lived, his creativity continued to flourish. In reviewing Jermaine's experience, it becomes apparent that a number of his personal characteristics as a creatively gifted youngster were similar to those mentioned in the literature. The findings of this study regarding Jermaine's creative abilities support Torrance's (1969) research in which he identified eighteen creative positives, characteristics that occurred to a high degree and with high frequency among economically disadvantaged African American children. In the case study of Jermaine, evidence of the following eight creative positives identified by Torrance exist: an ability to express feelings and emotions, articulateness in role-playing and storytelling, enjoyment and ability in visual art, expressive speech, responsiveness to the kinesthetic, a sense of humor, richness of imagery in informal language, and originality of ideas in problem solving.

Following five years of research with African American children, Torrance (1977) called attention to a number of critical issues. He noted that attention should be given to those kinds of giftedness that are valued by the particular culture to which a person belongs. He suggested that creative positives should be used in designing learning experiences. In addition, Torrance emphasized that learning activities should be planned and executed so as to help culturally different children cope with and grow out of any feelings of alienation by developing pride in their strengths and providing opportunities for sharing their creative strengths with others.

Emerging Self-Identity

The findings of the study regarding Jermaine's emerging self-identity allow us to generalize to theories regarding self-concept. Self-concept refers in general terms to the image we hold of ourselves. Byrne (1984) defined it as "our attitudes, feelings, and knowledge about our abilities, skills, appearance, and social acceptability" (p. 429). The literature on self-concept provides a number of multidimensional models as an approach to understanding self-concept. In these models, self-concept is depicted as a set of independent dimensions. Harter (1983) identified several aspects of self-concept: school competence, athletic competence, social acceptance, physical appearance, and behavior or conduct. Winne and Marx (1981) proposed a model of self-concept with four dimensions: academic, social, physical, and emotional. In this study, the findings revealed that Jermaine had an emerging belief in self that could best be described as a "multilayered embedded identity" (Heath & McLaughlin, 1993, p. 7). Jermaine saw himself as a combination of the following: scholar, creative thinker, athlete, and ethical young man. The various facets of his embedded identity are consistent with the facets of the self-concept proposed in the above multidimensional models. When considering how an emerging self-identity develops, most theorists acknowledge that both internal and external forces affect self-concept (Hogue & Renzulli, 1991). For example, individuals evaluate their performance against the expectations they hold for themselves, as well as the opinions expressed externally by parents, significant adults, and peers.

External influences on self-concept formation may include social comparisons whereby individuals use the reactions of significant others in their environment to assess their competence. One salient aspect of this social comparison issue has to do with the impact that the larger environment has on affecting self-concept. Marsh (1990) has proposed the big-fish–little-pond effect to explain that young people's perceptions of their self-worth regarding their performance in school is partially dependent upon the average level of performance displayed in their school or class. This is an important issue when considering the effects of gifted students attending rural, impoverished schools where students may not see the value of education. Given the level of competition Jermaine found in Pine Grove, he was a "big fish in a small pond." Should Jermaine leave Pine Grove, the factors that nurtured his creativity and reinforced his emerging self-identity, the "weed killers combating the kudzu," will be especially important if he is to remain successful following his high school graduation in Milledge County. A supportive family, significant adults who provide extrafamilial support, and perhaps his involvement in athletics and extracurricular activities may enable him to succeed in his rural setting and prepare him to compete as "a small fish in a big pond."

Resilience

Jermaine's life story serves as an example of a child overcoming chronic adversity through resilience. According to Rutter (1987), *resilience* is the term used to describe "the positive role of individual differences in people's response to stress and adversity" (p. 316). The literature on resilient individuals indicates that resilient children are those who, despite severe hardships and the presence of at-risk factors, develop characteristics and coping skills that enable them to succeed in life (McMillan & Reed, 1994). They appear to develop stable, healthy personalities and are able to recover from or adapt to life's adversities (Werner, 1984).

Jermaine's situation was consistent with the high-risk children Werner and Smith (1982) followed in a longitudinal study. These researchers concluded that children who thrived under adverse conditions had at least one person, such as a neighbor or teacher, who provided them with consistent emotional support. Resilient youth mentioned educators who took a personal interest in them as critical to their success. McMillan and Reed (1994) and Rhodes (1994) also reported that resilient students sought out professionals who had respect for them as people, listened to them, took them seriously, and provided them with encouragement. Masten and Garmezy (1990) found children who faced chronic adversity fared better when they had a positive relationship with a competent adult, were good problem solvers, were engaging to other people, and had areas of competence and perceived efficacy valued by self and society.

The significance of the relationships between Jermaine and Teresa, Sister Sophia, and Coach Cooper indicates the powerful impact mentors may have on gifted young children living in rural, impoverished environments. Torrance, Goff, and Satterfield (1998) proposed multicultural mentoring strategies appropriate for nurturing the talents of young people from economically disadvantaged environments. An ongoing relationship with a caring adult or mentor has tremendous potential for changing a child's life. Rural school systems may want to consider implementing such mentor programs in which students from surrounding college or university campuses travel to isolated areas and assist public school educators in fostering the talents of children in these environments. For example, a community such as Pine Grove would benefit greatly from a linkage with African American Greek honor societies at nearby colleges or universities. College students in such organizations often are required to become involved in outreach projects, and such an effort could easily be facilitated through a school administrator.

One interesting question emerging from this study is whether there is a connection between the resilience evidenced in Jermaine's experience and his creativity. Are creative children who face chronic adversity in their environments more likely to develop resilience because of their creativity? The literature addressing this issue is limited. In a six-year research study with the United States Air Force, Torrance (1957) examined the psychology of survival within combat aircrews and identified the following seven skills that were necessary in overcoming adverse conditions: inventiveness, creativity, imagination, originality, flexibility, decision-making ability, and courage. Researchers interested in discovering whether a connection exists between resilience and creativity may want to consider pursuing additional research in order to assist children living in impoverished conditions.

Racial Discrimination

The life experiences of Jermaine highlight many significant issues in addressing the needs of gifted students in rural settings. In discovering Jermaine and investigating the community in which he lived, I have called attention to a significant issue in this country. The impoverished conditions uncovered in Pine Grove, Alabama, resemble what Renzulli (1973) described as an "educational and psychological disaster" (p. 439). Although Jermaine has managed to survive in this community, we cannot overlook the fact that other children are "wasted daily by a system of education that has shut its eyes and turned its back on [them]" (Renzulli, 1973, p. 451). We must ask ourselves these questions: How many other children like Jermaine have gone unnoticed in similar communities? How many lives have been wasted? For how many more generations must this problem exist in our country?

What is happening in impoverished communities like Pine Grove, Alabama, is nothing short of educational genocide. No predominantly White school district in Alabama is faced with such impoverished conditions. We must remind ourselves of the events that took place in Selma, Alabama, in 1965 and ask ourselves several serious questions. When will Martin Luther King's message be understood? Why are we turning our backs on African American children in public schools? Why have we allowed social conditions such as those found in Pine Grove to exist? Haynes and Comer (1990) have eloquently provided us with their thoughts on these issues, and it is now time for us to respond: "Black children are heirs to the effects of the bigotry and racial prejudice that have guided national policy prior to the 1960s and that have resurfaced during the 1980s. To protect Black children and ensure [that] their rights as American citizens have been protected, an effective national policy that addresses racial prejudice in all forms must be developed. In particular, policies that divide local school systems racially, so that there are schools for Blacks that are substandard and schools for Whites that are superior, must be changed" (p. 105).

Implications for Future Research

This critical case study highlights a need to continue examining the life experiences of gifted Black children living in rural, impoverished communities in various parts of this country. The study needs to be replicated with gifted African American youngsters in different geographical regions. In addition, critical case studies should also examine the experiences of gifted young females in rural settings. Studies of other culturally diverse populations living in rural isolation would also add to our understanding. Researchers should also consider investigating the phenomenon through a longitudinal approach. This critical case study of Jermaine represents the beginning of such a longitudinal effort in order to broaden our understanding of the role that environment plays in nurturing giftedness and creativity.

Summary

Jermaine's story should serve as a cogent reminder to educators across this country that children who show potential for exceptional performance are present in every segment of society. Jermaine has spoken for children living in rural poverty by sharing his life story and his aspirations for the future with us. Whether the future remains bright for Jermaine and other gifted Black children will greatly depend on educational policymakers and the efforts of educators working to assure a better tomorrow for Jermaine and others like him.

Acknowledgments

We are grateful to the participants of this investigation who kindly shared their life experiences. We extend deep thanks to Dr. E. Paul Torrance, Dr. Mary Frasier, and Dr. Tarek Grantham for their insightful comments on earlier drafts of this manuscript. We also thank Kristie Speirs Neumeister for her editorial support and helpful suggestions. Research for this manuscript was supported by a grant from the University of Alabama Research Grants Committee. Grantees undertaking such projects are encouraged to express freely their professional judgment. This manuscript does not necessarily represent positions or policies of the University of Alabama and no official endorsement should be inferred.

Note

1. With the exception of Teresa and her husband James, the names of the people and places within Alabama were changed to protect the identity of the participants involved.

References

Abelman, R. (1992). *Some children under some conditions: TV and the high potential kid* (Research Monograph No. 9206). Storrs, CT: National Research Center on the Gifted and Talented, University of Connecticut.

Alabama Department of Archives and History [On line] (1998). Available Internet address: [www.asc.edu/archives/populate/[milledge].html].

Baldwin, A. Y. (1987). Undiscovered diamonds: The minority gifted child. *Journal for the Education of the Gifted, 10,* 271–285.

Benn, A. (1988, November 11). Quilting bee cooperative diminishing. *The Montgomery Advertiser,* pp. 1C–2C.

Bogdan, R. C., & Biklen, S. K. (1998). *Qualitative research in education: An introduction to theory and methods* (3rd ed.). Boston: Allyn and Bacon.

Books, S. (1997). The other poor: Rural poverty and education. *Educational Foundations, 11,* 73–85.

Byrne, B. M. (1984). The general-academic self-concept nomological network: A review of construct validation research. *Review of Educational Research, 54,* 427–456.

Collier, J., & Collier, M. (1986). *Visual anthropology: Photography as a research method.* Albuquerque, NM: University of New Mexico Press.

Crotty, M. (1998). *The foundations of social research.* Thousand Oaks, CA: Sage.

Descy, D. E. (1992). On the air in rural Minnesota. *Educational Horizons, 70,* 84–87.

Dudenhefer, P. (1994). Poverty in the United States. *Rural Sociologist, 14,* 4–25.

Edelman, M. W. (1985). The sea is so wide and my boat is so small: Problems facing black children today. In H. P. Fetterman, D. M. (1989). *Ethnography: Step by step.* Newbury Park, CA: Sage.

Fetterman, D. H. (1989). *Ethnography: Step by Step.* Newbury Park, CA: Sage.

Ford, D. Y. (1996). *Reversing underachievement among gifted black students: Promising practices and programs.* New York: Teachers College Press.

Frasier, M. M. (1987). The identification of gifted black students: Developing new perspectives. *Journal for the Education of the Gifted, 10,* 155–180.

Frasier, M. M. (1991). Disadvantaged and culturally diverse gifted students. *Journal for the Education of the Gifted, 14,* 235–245.

Glesne, C., & Peshkin, A. (1992). *Becoming qualitative researchers: An introduction.* White Plains, NY: Longman.

Graue, M. E., & Walsh, D. J. (1998). *Studying children in context: Theories, methods, and ethics.* Thousand Oaks, CA: Sage.

Gray, H. (1995). *Watching race: Television and the struggle for "blackness."* Minneapolis, MN: University of Minnesota Press.

Habermas, J. (1970). *Toward a rational society.* Boston: Beacon Press.

Habermas, J. (1971). *Knowledge and human interests.* Boston: Beacon Press.

Habermas, J. (1974). *Theory and practice.* Boston: Beacon Press.

Habermas, J. (1989). *On the logic of the social sciences.* Cambridge, MA: MIT Press.

Harter, S. (1983). Developmental perspectives on the self-system. In P. H. Mussen (Series Ed.) & E. M. Hetherington (Vol. Ed.), *Handbook of child psychology: Vol. 4. Socialization, personality, and social development.* (4th ed.; pp. 275–385). New York: Wiley.

Haynes, N. M., & Comer, J. P. (1990). Helping black children succeed: The significance of some social factors. In K. Lomotey (Ed.), *Going to school: The African American experience* (pp. 103–112). Albany, NY: State University of New York Press.

Heath, S. B., & McLaughlin, M. W. (1993). *Identity and inner-city youth: Beyond ethnicity and gender.* New York: Teachers College Press.

Hébert, T. P., & Reis, S. M. (1999). Culturally diverse high-achieving students in an urban high school. *Urban Education, 34,* 428–457.

Herzog, M. J., & Pittman, R. (1995). Home, family, and community: Ingredients in the rural education equation. *Phi Delta Kappan, 77,* 113–118.

Hogue, R. D., & Renzulli, J. S. (1991). *Self-concept and the gifted child* (Research Monograph No. 9104). Storrs, CT: National Research Center on the Gifted and Talented, University of Connecticut.

Kearney, K. (1991a, July). Highly gifted children in isolated rural areas (Part I). *Understanding Our Gifted, 3*(6), 16.

Kearney, K. (1991b, September). Highly gifted children in isolated rural areas (Part II). *Understanding Our Gifted, 4*(1), 16.

Kitano, M. (1991). A multicultural educational perspective on serving the culturally diverse gifted. *Journal for the Education of the Gifted, 15,* 4–19.

LeCompte, M. D., & Preissle, J. (1993). *Ethnography and qualitative design in educational research.* New York: Academic Press.

Lincoln, Y., & Guba, E. (1985). *Naturalistic inquiry.* Beverly Hills, CA: Sage.

Marsh, H. W. (1990). Influences of internal and external frames of reference on the formation of math and English self-concepts. *Journal of Educational Psychology, 82,* 107–116.

Masten, A. S., & Garmezy, N. (1990). Resilience and development: Contributions from the study of children who overcome adversity. *Development and Psychopathology, 2,* 425–444.

McLoyd, V. C. (1990). The impact of economic hardship on black families and children: Psychological distress, parenting, and socioemotional development. *Child Development, 61,* 311–346.

McMillan, J. H., & Reed, D. F. (1994, January/February). At-risk students and resiliency: Factors contributing to academic success. *The Clearing House, 67,* 137–140.

Merriam, S. B. (1998). *Qualitative research and case study applications in education.* San Francisco: Jossey-Bass.

Merriam, S. B., & Simpson, E. L. (1995). *A guide to research for educators and trainers of adults.* Malabar, FL: Krieger.

Morrow, R. A., & Brown, D. D. (1994). *Critical theory and methodology.* Thousand Oaks, CA: Sage.

Nachtigal, P. N. (1992). Rural schooling: Obsolete or harbinger of the future? *Educational Horizons, 70,* 66–70.

National Commission on Excellence in Education. (1983). *A nation at risk: The imperative of educational reform.* Washington, DC: U.S. Government Printing Office.

National Education Association Commission on Professional Rights and Responsibilities. (1967). *[Milledge] County: A study of social, economic, and educational bankruptcy.* Washington, DC: Author.

Nobles, W. W. (1997). African American family life: An instrument of culture. In H. P. McAdoo (Ed.), *Black families* (3rd ed.; pp. 83–93). Thousand Oaks, CA: Sage.

Patton, M. Q. (1990). *Qualitative evaluation and research methods.* Newbury Park, CA: Sage.

Renzulli, J. S. (1973). Talent potential in minority group students. *Exceptional Children, 39,* 437–444.

Rhodes, J. E. (1994). Older and wiser: Mentoring relationships in childhood and adolescence. *The Journal of Primary Prevention, 14,* 187–196.

Rutter, M. (1987). Psychosocial resilience and protective mechanisms. *American Journal of Orthopsychiatry, 57,* 316–331.

Seal, K. R., & Harmon, H. L. (1995). Realities of rural school reform. *Phi Delta Kappan, 77*(2), 119–120, 122–124.

Spicker, H. (1992a). Innovation in rural and small-town schools. *Educational Horizons, 70*(2), 50.

Spicker, H. (1992b). Identifying and enriching rural gifted children. *Educational Horizons, 70*(2), 60–65.

Spicker, H., Southern, T., & Davis, B. (1987). The rural gifted child. *Gifted Child Quarterly, 31,* 155–157.

Spigner, C. (1991). Black impressions of people-of-color: A functionalist approach to film imagery. *Western Journal of Black Studies, 15,* 69–78.

Spradley, J. P. (1980). *Participant observation.* New York: Holt, Rinehart, and Winston.

Stake, R. E. (1995). *The art of case study research.* Thousand Oaks, CA: Sage.

Stern, J. D. (1992). How demographic trends for the eighties affect rural and small-town schools. *Educational Horizons, 70*(2), 71–77.

Sudarkasa, N. (1997). African American families and family values. In H. P. McAdoo (Ed.), *Black families* (3rd ed.; pp. 9–40). Thousand Oaks, CA: Sage.

Sum, A. N., & Fogg, W. N. (1991). The adolescent poor and the transition to early adulthood. In P. Edelman & J. Ladner (Eds.), *Adolescence and poverty: Challenge for the 90s* (pp. 37–110). Washington, DC: Center for National Policy Press.

Tait, A. A., & Perry, R. L. (1994). African Americans in television: An Afrocentrist analysis. *Western Journal of Black Studies, 18,* 195–200.

Torrance, E. P. (1957). *Surviving emergencies and extreme conditions: A summary of six years of research.* Unpublished manuscript prepared at the Personnel Research Center at Lackland Air Force Base, Lackland, TX.

Torrance, E. P. (1969). Creative positives of disadvantaged children and youth. *Gifted Child Quarterly, 13,* 71–81.

Torrance, E. P. (1977). *Discovery and nurturance of giftedness in the culturally different.* Reston, VA: Council for Exceptional Children.

Torrance, E. P., Goff, K., & Satterfield, N. (1998). *Multicultural mentoring of the gifted and talented*. Waco, TX: Prufrock Press.

U.S. Department of Education. (1993). *National excellence: A case for developing America's talent*. Washington, DC: Office of Educational Research and Improvement.

Walker, K., Taylor, E., McElroy, A., Phillip, D., & Wilson, M. N. (1995). Familial and ecological correlates of self-esteem in African American children. In M. N. Wilson (Ed.), *African American family life: Its structural and ecological aspects* (pp. 23–33). San Francisco: Jossey-Bass.

Werner, E. E. (1984). Resilient children. *Young Children, 40*(1), 68–72.

Werner, E. E., & Smith, R. S. (1982). *Vulnerable but invincible: A study of resilient children*. New York: McGraw-Hill.

Williams, R. (1974). *Television: Technology and cultural form*. London: Fontana.

Winne, P. H., & Marx, R. W. (1981, April). *Convergent and discriminant validity in self-concept measurement*. Paper presented at the annual conference of the American Educational Research Association, Los Angeles, CA.

Yin, R. K. (1994). *Case study research: Designs and methods* (2nd ed.). Thousand Oaks, CA: Sage.

Reflections on My Research Experience with Jermaine and His Community

Thomas P. Hébert
University of Georgia, Athens

As I reflect on my experience working with Jermaine, I realize I learned a number of important lessons that may be helpful to a beginning qualitative researcher. Since I knew Jermaine's world was much different from my own, my concerns as a researcher revolved around my need to be accepted and trusted by him and his community. In establishing this trust, I found that Teresa Beardsley, my gatekeeper, emerged as a critical player. I also learned to be sensitive to the differences in my culture and the culture of Pine Grove by tailoring my personal appearance and my research tools so they were more appropriate for this rural, impoverished setting. In addition, I discovered ways to "go native" that also helped establish trust.

During my first visit to Pine Grove, I discovered how critical Teresa would become as my gatekeeper. Realizing how important it was for me to visit the community of Pine Grove before beginning the study, I spent one day with Teresa traveling through rural Milledge County in her family's van. Though she had described the impoverished conditions the people of Pine Grove were living in and the isolation experienced in that part of Alabama, I did not comprehend what she described until I experienced it first-hand. As we traveled red-clay country roads and passed by small clusters of mobile homes she referred to as "communities," I felt as though I had traveled back in time. I never imagined that people in the United States continued to live in such conditions.

Teresa introduced me to members of the community, from women working in their flower gardens to elderly regulars sitting in the front of the country store. When she introduced me to these significant citizens of Pine Grove, I immediately realized that I would have difficulty understanding the dialect of the people. After each visit with an elderly person, Teresa and I would hop back into her van, and I would be forced to have her translate portions of the conversations I had not understood. I knew that Teresa was more than simply a gatekeeper in helping me enter the community; she would be an important collaborator in the research process. Without her, meeting these significant figures in the community would have been a challenge, and I would not have been able to understand the nuances of their language.

Teresa also introduced me to my participant—Jermaine. Her presence during my initial meeting with Jermaine helped us begin to establish a comfortable relationship with one another. She arranged to have Jermaine join us for my tour of Milledge County. From his vantage point in the backseat of Teresa's van, Jermaine was able to "check out" this stranger whom Teresa had talked about, this gentleman from a place called the "university" who claimed to be interested in him and the creative stories he was known to have written.

That first day spent with Teresa and Jermaine also helped me realize the importance of being respectful of the culture of an impoverished rural community. As I traveled back to my university community that evening, I had time to think about how I might dress, the equipment I would use in data collection, and how I might participate within the community to earn their respect and trust. I decided I would need to be careful not to dress inappropriately as I collected data in Pine Grove. I chose to wear khaki pants or jeans and T-shirts or modest sport shirts, making a point to leave my professional clothing at home. As a White male researcher in Pine Grove and a "stranger," I did not want to advertise the fact that I was different from the people of the community.

I also decided that I would be viewed as far more respectful of the community if I did not use fancy technological equipment. Given that people in this rural village did not have indoor plumbing, I decided that a portable tape recorder might be viewed as something too flashy. I chose to carry a simple stenographer's pad and pencils with me instead. In addition, my early conversations with the elderly community members helped me foresee the difficulty I would encounter in attempting to transcribe tape recorded interviews, not being able to comprehend the dialect in this rural community. I decided that field notes would become far more critical in this study, and I would be able to depend on Teresa to interpret any of the language I could not comprehend.

I also chose not to use sophisticated camera equipment in shooting pictures of the community and the scenes of activity in the Rocket Readers summer program. I made a point to shoot photographs unobtrusively from my car. In capturing scenes of the country store that served as the hub of activity in the rural village, I was careful to shoot them from a distance so that the local townspeople who spent their day in front of the store would not view my visits to Pine Grove as an invasion of their privacy.

I discovered that another effective way to build trust with the members of this community was to "go native" by rolling up my sleeves and volunteering to help in any way I could. I assisted Teresa, her husband, and the staff of the Rocket Readers Program with everything from moving furniture to straightening out the classroom to sweeping the floor to helping supervise recess. My willingness to become involved in the operation of the summer program led to my acceptance as an outsider. It was also helpful for me to stay afterward and help with clean-up so I could debrief the events of the day with Teresa and ask questions of her and James regarding anything I had not understood, rather than interrupt them while they were involved in their work with the children. These conversations provided me with more useful data that allowed me to better understand the culture, the community, and the child I was studying.

Along with learning methods of developing trusting relationships with my informants, I also learned the importance of allowing time for reflection during the data collection experience. I traveled one hundred miles from my university community to Pine Grove each day. The four hours in the car during my round-trip journey provided me with quality "incubation time" to process through my thinking regarding the data I had collected that day. During these trips, I had the opportunity to tape record reminders to myself regarding questions that I might have forgotten to ask Teresa and questions I had for Jermaine, reflections on the experiences of the day, and, even more important, a record of the emotions I was experiencing as I worked with a child living in such impoverished conditions.

During my travels, I would regularly pull aside and stop along the Alabama highways to sit in my car and jot diagrams in my field notes that enabled me to better analyze my ongoing data. It was often during my long journey to and from Pine Grove that I would suddenly remember an event that occurred or a conversation I had experienced and had not been able to document it in my field note pad earlier. My time in the car allowed me to fill in the gaps in my field notes and flesh out the data of that day. I could also formulate questions to pursue the following day. Without this time for reflection, the quality of the data would have suffered. In addition to facilitating data collection, this time for reflection also provided me the opportunity to sort through my emotions as I left to return to the high-powered university community, complete with its libraries, shopping malls, and gourmet restaurants, a culture so far removed from the realities of Pine Grove.

Establishing trust with Jermaine and the people of Pine Grove did not happen quickly. As a researcher I learned to be patient and consider multiple ways of earning their respect. Eventually, as I traveled daily to Pine Grove, many residents would spot my Volkswagen approaching and would send a friendly wave in my direction. Those waves were an indication that Teresa's friend from out of town had gained their respect. Throughout my experience in this rural village, my respect for the people of Pine Grove and their hardships kept me committed to my goal of making certain their voices were heard.

Ethnography

An ethnographic study is one that focuses on human society with the goal of describing and interpreting the *culture* of a group. Historically associated with the field of anthropology, ethnography has come to refer to both the method (how the researcher conducts the study) and the product (a cultural description of human social life). This dual use of the term has led to some confusion in what is called ethnography; that is, the mere use of data-gathering techniques associated with ethnography does not result in an ethnography unless there is a cultural interpretation of those data. "Ethnographies re-create for the reader the shared beliefs, practices, artifacts, folk knowledge, and behavior of some group" (LeCompte & Preissle, 1993, p. 42).

Culture, the cornerstone of ethnography, has been studied from a number of perspectives. One common approach is to view culture as the knowledge people have acquired that in turn structures their worldview and their behavior. Working from this framework, the researcher would be interested in describing what people do, what they know, and what things people make and use. Another approach is to see culture as embodied in the signs, symbols, and language or the semiotics of culture. Here the research would focus more on understanding the meaning and importance of what is said and what is taken for granted. A more recent approach called "critical" ethnography "accounts for the historical, social, and economical situations. Critical ethnographers realize the strictures caused by these situations and their value-laden agendas. Critical ethnographers see themselves as blue-collar 'cultural workers' (Giroux, 1992) attempting to broaden the political dimensions of cultural work while undermining existing oppressive systems" (Fontana & Frey, 1994, p. 369).

An ethnographic study involves extensive fieldwork wherein one becomes intimately familiar with the group being studied. As Van Maanen (1982, pp. 103–104) notes: "The result of ethnographic inquiry is cultural description. It is, however, a description of the sort that can emerge only from a lengthy period of intimate study and residence in a given social setting. It calls for the language spoken in that setting, first-hand participation in some of the activities that take place there, and, most critically, a deep reliance on intensive work with a few informants drawn from the setting."

Immersion in the site as a participant observer is the primary method of data collection for ethnography. Interviews, formal and informal, and the analysis of documents, records, and artifacts also constitute the data set along with a field-worker's diary of each day's happenings, personal feelings, ideas, impressions, or insights with regard to those events. This diary becomes a source of data and allows researchers to trace their own development and biases throughout the course of the investigation.

At the heart of an ethnography is "thick description"—a term popularized by Geertz (1973). "Culture," he writes, "is not a power, something to which social events, behaviors, institutions, or processes can be causally attributed; it is a context, something within which they can be intelligibly—that is, *thickly*—described" (p. 14). The write-up of an ethnography is more than description, however. While ethnographers want to convey the meanings participants make of their lives, they do so with some interpretation on their part (Wolcott, 1999). A recent award-winning ethnography by Fadiman (1997) illustrates the power of "thick" description in a study of a Hmong child in the U.S. whose medical condition brought about the collision of two cultures' views of medicine and healing. The study also conveys the intensive and sustained immersion in the setting, the extensive data gathering necessary to produce a *cultural* interpretation of the phenomenon.

Ethnographers arrive at the cultural interpretation of their data through various data analysis strategies. Anthropologists sometimes make use of preexisting category schemes to organize and analyze their data. For example, one might use Murdock's *Outline of Cultural Materials* (1982) with its list of nearly eighty categories related to social and cultural behaviors and characteristics. Lofland and Lofland (1995) also suggest categories and subcategories for organizing aspects of society. The four broadest ones are the economy; demographics; "basic situations of human life," including family, education, and health care; and the environment, both "natural" and "built" (p. 104). For ethnographies in education and other applied fields, the classification scheme is likely to be derived from the data themselves. This is called the "emic" perspective, that of the insider to the culture, versus the "etic," that of the researcher or outsider. If the topics or variables within the scheme are seen to be interrelated, a typology may be created. Whatever the origin of the organizing concepts or themes, some sort of organization of the data is needed to convey to the reader the sociocultural patterns characteristic of the group under study. It is not enough, then, to describe the cultural practices of a group; the researcher also depicts his or her understanding of the cultural meaning of the phenomenon.

There are two selections in this volume that are ethnographies. The first, by Correll (1995), is an ethnography of an electronic bar. In this study of a lesbian community created in cyberspace, Correll employs an ethnomethodological perspective in framing her questions and in collecting and analyzing the data. This perspective is particularly interested in how members of a society build their "reality" through talk and interaction. Her study was thus guided by three questions: How do patrons reach consensus? How is the community maintained? And how does this notion of shared reality lead to certain actions of the members? An interesting overlaying question in this study is the extent to which reality and fantasy are blurred in this virtual environment.

The second study, by Krenske and McKay (2000), is of the culture of a heavy metal music club. However, with its focus on the gendered structures of power in the culture of this club, it could be described as a critical ethnographic case study. The authors identify their feminist and postmodern perspectives, perspectives that led to their "theorized ethnography of a HM subculture." Their ethnography is indeed both critical and feminist with regard to the power structures in this particular subculture.

References

Fadiman, A. (1997). *The spirit catches you and you fall down.* New York: Farrar, Straus and Giroux.

Fontana, A., & Frey, J. H. (1994). Interviewing: The art of science. In N. K. Denzin, & Y. S. Lincoln, (Eds.), *Handbook of qualitative research* (pp. 361–376). Thousand Oaks, CA: Sage.

Geertz, C. (1973). *The interpretation of cultures: Selected essays.* New York: Basic Books.

Husserl, E. (1970). *The crisis of European sciences and transcendental phenomenology.* Evanston, IL: North University Press.

LeCompte, M. D., & Preissle, J., with Tesch, R. (1993). *Ethnography and qualitative design in educational research.* (2nd ed.) Orlando, FL: Academic Press.

Lofland, J., & Lofland, L. H. (1995). *Analyzing social settings: A guide to qualitative observation and analysis.* (3rd ed.) Belmont, CA: Wadsworth.

Murdock, G. P., & others. (1982). *Outline of cultural materials.* (5th ed.), New Haven, CT: Human Relations Area Files.

Van Maanen, J. (1982). Fieldwork on the beat. In J. Van Maanen, J. M. Dabbs, & R. R. Faulkner (Eds.), *Varieties of qualitative research* (pp. 103–151). Beverly Hills, CA: Sage.

Wolcott, H. (1999). *Ethnography: A way of seeing.* Walnut Creek, CA: Altamira Press.

11

The Ethnography of an Electronic Bar

The Lesbian Café

Shelley J. Correll

With computers linked through phone lines, people all over the world can communicate with each other quickly and cheaply. Currently, there are about forty-five thousand computer bulletin board systems (BBSs) and about eighty million users in the United States (Osborne, 1993). These computer bulletin boards serve many different purposes. Some are mainly informational, such as Gaycomm's BBS, which provides AIDS treatment information (Osborne, 1993). Others, such as ECHO, host "conferences" on topics ranging from movies to Buddhism to aging (Katz, 1993). A great number of BBSs are social, such as the SeniorNet BBS linking six thousand senior citizens. This board hosts a Wednesday night cocktail party from 6 P.M. to midnight. The founder of SeniorNet said that it is a painless manner in which to socialize and that it is especially helpful for those who are reluctant to venture out by themselves such as widows, widowers, and disabled persons. Intimate relationships have been established through the SeniorNet service, with at least one couple getting married (Ansberry, 1993). Finally, a number of the bulletin boards are sexually explicit, such as Horny Harry's Dirty Words BBS (Katz, 1993). The social and sexual bulletin boards are especially popular with the gay and lesbian community. According to Osborne (1993) of the *Advocate,* bulletin boards and chat lines allow users to cruise anonymously with the purpose of meeting people with whom one can have sexually explicit conversation. Anonymity is important because many people use BBSs to try out behavior that they consider to be deviant. Osborne describes the experiences

Shelley J. Correll (1995). "The Ethnography of an Electronic Bar: The Lesbian Café." *Journal of Contemporary Enthography, 24*(3), 270–298. Copyright © 1995 by Sage Publications, Inc. Reprinted by permission of Sage Publications, Inc.

of a forty-eight-year-old married heterosexual who says that BBSs provided a way in which he could anonymously explore areas of human sexuality with which he was unfamiliar in the privacy of his own home, without entering adult bookstores or viewing adult movies. The purpose of this article is to describe an electronic lesbian bar, the Lesbian Café (LC), and examine how a community can be created and sustained through interactions restricted to computer screens.

Communities created and sustained solely through interaction via computer are relatively new. In fact, traditional definitions of community, by making reference to physical location, would not allow computer bulletin boards to be considered communities. Sociological studies of communities often make a distinction between *community* and *the community*. On one hand, Bernard (1973) claims that three characteristics are usually agreed on as a minimum for what makes a *community:* locale, common ties, and social interaction. *The community,* on the other hand, is characterized not by locale but by factors such as a high degree of personal intimacy, moral commitment, and social cohesion. Bernard concedes, however, that the very concept of community may not be viable in the future as space becomes less important due to changes in communication and transportation technology. In her review of research on lesbian communities, for example, Krieger (1982, p. 92) uses a broader definition of community as "the range of social groups in which the lesbian individual may feel a sense of camaraderie with other lesbians, a sense of support, shared understanding, shared vision, shared sense of self 'as a lesbian,' vis-à-vis the outside world." She further indicates that not all lesbian communities are located in specific geographic areas; some exist "only in spirit." In other words, what she terms *community* is more in line with what Bernard (1973) would call *the community.* However, her review exclusively includes studies of geographically located communities such as lesbian bars.

Lesbian communities have been described in the literature as serving the competing functions of enhancing one's sense of self and threatening individual identity. These communities often provide a haven or a retreat from a hostile outside world. At the same time, the lesbian community shares a problem with many minority communities: the desire to achieve group solidarity is at odds with goals of individuality (Krieger, 1982). From the 1930s to the present, bars have been a central institution in the lesbian community. They serve the roles of "teaching gays the meaning of what a 'homosexual' is" and providing a place where lesbians can "be together and feel somewhat okay" (Davis, Kennedy, & Michelson, 1981, p. 22). The establishment of intimate relationships is another function of the lesbian community. A recent popular press article found that lesbian sex clubs, designed solely for the purpose of making sexual contacts, are rising in popularity (Roxxie, 1993). Thus a lesbian community serves many functions, including the creation of a positive lesbian identity and the opportunity to establish intimate relationships. At the same time, the community demands from its members a high degree of conformity that limits individualism in an effort to maintain high group solidarity.

The studies of lesbian communities, and even the voluminous literature on communities of other types, share the common characteristic of focusing on communities that exist in specific locales (Krieger, 1982; Bernard, 1973). This study expands the definition of community by providing a sociological analysis of the LC, a lesbian community constructed in cyberspace.

Theoretical Framework

Interactionist and ethnomethodological perspectives are used to frame this study. Specifically, the works of Goffman (1959, 1974, 1981) and Garfinkel (1967) are used to elucidate how a community can be created and sustained electronically. Finally, the distinction between reality and fantasy is considered.

In understanding how a community can be created electronically, both the physical setting and the atmosphere of the community must be examined. The LC is patterned after a bar and described as being a "friendly space that welcomes all lesbians." Creating such an environment via computer requires careful manipulation of the setting in a manner reminiscent of Goffman's (1959) theoretical metaphor, which he first introduced in *The Presentation of Self in Everyday Life.* In this work, Goffman contends that in constructing the definition of a situation, individuals engage in "performances" through which each person presents herself or himself as a person with certain characteristics. These performances involve the creation of a "front" that includes emotions, appearance, manner, and physical or "stage props." Through these fronts, people present "idealizations" of identity that reflect the values of their society or community. Idealizations, therefore, restrict individual expression in the interest of group solidarity. Patrons at the LC have considerable leeway in creating their individual fronts because they cannot be seen or heard in the traditional sense. Likewise, the setting can be manipulated more freely than it can in everyday life due to the nonmaterial character. However, some expressions, such as emotional ones, are more difficult to convey via a computer.

Goffman's (1959) concept of "team" is also relevant in understanding how the atmosphere of a "friendly place that welcomes all lesbians" can be created and sustained. The term "team" is used to describe individuals who work together to project a particular definition of a situation. In so doing, team members often move between what Goffman calls a "front region" and a "back region." In the front region, performances are presented for the benefit of audiences. In the back region, team members relax. Behavior here is more informal, and the goal becomes maintaining solidarity and high morale among team members. Goffman states that a basic problem of all team performances is maintaining a particular definition in front of audiences. To accomplish this goal, members will often engage in morale-boosting activities such as making fun of the audience, joking with each other, and talking informally when backstage. On stage, however, control has to be maintained. Control is achieved by using subtle communications among team members that the audience will not understand. Of particular importance in understanding how the atmosphere of this community is created and sustained are Goffman's notions concerning the maintenance of solidarity through informal backstage behavior and subtle frontstage communication.

In addition to manipulating individual and group fronts, talk is important for sustaining the community created. In *Forms of Talk,* Goffman (1981) argues for the importance of talk in focusing interactions or giving actors a "footing" for conversation. Even though talk and meaning can be manipulated, Goffman demonstrates that such manipulation is normatively and ritually regulated to produce a sense of shared reality. This shared reality serves to focus future interactions. In this study, the role of talk in focusing interactions, and thereby sustaining the community, is examined.

How members of a group come to share a sense of common reality is of primary concern to ethnomethodology. In comparison to the creation and maintenance of a sense of reality, the content of that reality is irrelevant. Garfinkel (1967) contends that the primary technique actors use to construct a sense of an orderly world is verbal description. In his breaching experiments, he would disrupt a situation and thereby force actors to actively reconstruct reality. By so doing, the methods used to create a sense of reality could be identified.

This study, which examines an *explicit* construction of reality, provides a unique way of observing the methods actors use in creating, maintaining, and changing the appearance of an orderly social world. Of interest in this study are the following. First, in what ways do patrons reach consensus about the setting of the café? Second, what role does a shared sense of reality serve in maintaining the community? Third, in what way does the notion of a shared reality compel certain actions on the part of members? Finally, as the LC is fundamentally a shared fantasy, the distinction between what is "real" and what is not must be addressed.

In *Frame Analysis,* Goffman (1974) contends that people construct "strips of activity" by marking the boundaries of a setting or event, distinguishing it from surrounding activity. Primary frameworks are those that are embedded in the "real natural and social world" and are, therefore, taken for granted. However, primary frames are often modified by a process of "keying" whereby actors transform the primary frame into something patterned on the primary frame but substantially different. According to Goffman, primary frameworks are seen by people as more real than keyings. However, Chayko (1993) recently argued that technologies such as virtual reality are blurring the distinction between real and keyed experiences.

Of particular importance to this study are the following. First, how do patrons of the café decide what is real and what is not within the keyed frame of the LC? Second, to what extent does computer interaction blur the usual distinction between reality and fantasy?

The Computer as a Communication Medium

Computer bulletin boards are a unique communication medium. Unlike face-to-face communication, there are no facial expressions or other forms of body language to add meaning to verbal statements. Even with media such as the telephone or citizen band radio, which are more limiting than face-to-face interactions, voices and tone inflections can be hard, and these often allow for determining gender, ethnicity, and/or mood. However, like face-to-face communication, computer communication is accomplished quickly, and many people can participate in an interaction simultaneously.

The interaction between people via computers is completely limited to what can be typed and displayed on a computer screen. This limitation requires people to be very creative in conversing. Computer bulletin boards use a standard computer keyboard with no special graphics capabilities. A great effort has to be made to convey even the most obvious emotions such as anger or humor. For example, if people want to indicate that they are smiling during a conversation, they will use the keyboard to draw a smiling face. However, the keys that are available on a standard keyboard only allow for the construction of a *sideways* smiling face by using the colon key followed by the closed parenthesis key:). Even gender, ethnicity, age, and physical appearance have to be explicitly announced if they are to be known. While somewhat similar to letter writing, computer communication can easily be read by many people simultaneously and is considerably faster.

The three main methods of communication that exist on BBSs are public posting, electronic mail (e-mail), and live chat. Live chat allows users to communicate in "real time." In other words, letters, words, and sentences appear on the screen immediately as they are typed. Communication via e-mail or public post, on the other hand, is delayed. In both, a user will type a complete note and then "send" it. In the case of e-mail, the note is sent, uncensored, to the particular person or persons to whom it is addressed. This method of communicating is highly similar to letter writing except that e-mail messages are delivered in seconds. By comparison, public posts are, as the name suggests, public. A complete message is sent to a system operator whose job is to read the notes, censor them if they are judged offensive, and display them for public reading. Depending on the volumes of notes being sent, messages can be posted in seconds or up to an hour later. While users can address a post to a particular person, everyone who is logged on to the BBS can read the note and respond. In this form of communication, there is no prohibition against "eavesdropping." Another interesting feature of this type of communication is that public posts are saved for weeks so that a person who logs on can read all the conversation that has taken place over the past few weeks. In much the same manner as at a party, several conversations are usually occurring at one time. When a user posts a new note, a new conversation begins. It is common at the LC for ten to twenty notes, or conversations, to be posted at any one time, with each receiving eighty or ninety replies over a two- or three-day period. While many conversations are occurring simultaneously, users are often involved in most of them. This situation is analogous to going into a social setting and being able to hear and participate in all the conversations that are occurring.

One advantage of communicating with either posts or e-mail is that conversation can be carefully crafted before being transmitted, allowing for considerable control over the front presented. Although letter writing offers the same advantage, computer communication is quicker and often involves more people.

Methods

The data in this study were collected over a three-month period during the early 1990s through an ethnographic study of a particular BBS called the Lesbian Café. I use the real name of this BBS due to the descriptive nature of the name and because the nature of the bulletin board provides for anonymity. The LC is one of hundreds of bulletin boards on a large, popular on-line computer system that offers members many services such as travel tips, encyclopedias, national news, and bulletin board access.

Data collection was carried out through participant observation as well as through group and individual interviews. As a member of this on-line service, I had full access to the LC. First, I contacted the founder of the LC via private e-mail to ask for her approval of my study. At the same time, I posted a public note on the café BBS describing my study and asking for volunteers to be interviewed. Each week, I posted a new note describing my study so that patrons knew they were being "observed." Seven women responded to my initial request for interviews, and I interviewed them via e-mail in an informal and exploratory manner. A semistructured interview with the founder of the LC was then carried out over the telephone. As I read daily notes at the LC, I would occasionally post public notes asking the patrons to explain various actions or conversations to me. In such instances, I received numerous replies from a variety of patrons, including both regular and newer patrons. After one month, I conducted five more semistructured interviews via private e-mail with people I had observed to be regular patrons at the LC. These interviews focused on communication styles and the process of becoming a regular patron.

Finally, I triangulated my interview data by interviewing eight of the patrons in person. Approximately one month into the study, a woman posted a note asking patrons to pick a location where everyone could meet in person. Atlanta, Georgia, was chosen as a central location because the women were from all parts of the eastern and southern United States. Having received permission to join the group in Atlanta, I conducted two interview sessions with four patrons in each. By interviewing the respondents in person, I was able to observe the styles of interaction and the interpersonal relationships between the women when face to face and compare them to their relationships and interactions on the computer. I also was able to compare what occurred at the LC to what occurred when our entire group went to a real lesbian bar in Atlanta.

Because most of the "observations" for this study were read from the computer screen, the quotes in the following sections are taken from the actual notes, or posts, unless stated otherwise. Further, in quoting posts, I have retained their authors' abbreviations, unique spelling of words, and the use of upper- and lowercase letters. Determining the gender of patrons proved problematic. In e-mail interviews, I asked patrons to state their gender. Although it is possible that some patrons' responses were not truthful, follow-up interviews on the phone or in person indicated that regular patrons and newbies (described later) were exclusively female. Although none of the bashers (also described later) ever agreed to be interviewed via telephone, all stated in public posts and/or through e-mail that they were male.

Findings

Creating the Appearance of the Lesbian Café

The LC was clearly created to resemble a bar. The original café was founded by a woman, TJ, who created a new topic on the BBS menu that she called the Lesbian Café. In her original note (from which I paraphrase and quote), TJ described the bar using features that everyone would recognize as a bar. There was the bar itself, highly polished so that she could slide drinks down to her patrons. The pool table was to be a gathering place, but "no one is to knock the balls off the table." She added a fireplace and a hot tub, making this bar "a place more grand than any lesbian bar that actually exists." According to TJ, women quickly "found" the café and liked it. One of the first regular patrons explained to me in an e-mail interview that she searched through the bulletin board index until she found the word "lesbian." She found a couple of lesbian bulletin boards but preferred the café because the women seemed more friendly. She also describes being fascinated with the "bar fantasy." The posts of the first patrons include frequent reference to the fixtures described by TJ in her first post. In fact, every new note from the first few weeks mentions either the bar, the pool table, the hot tub, or the fireplace. As the café became more established, a ritual for "entering" it emerged. Each time a patron reenters the café, she orders a drink by posting a note asking the bartender (whoever it might be that day) for a specific drink. This behavior announces her presence and indicates that she is familiar with the café. Next, she places herself in a specific location in the bar. For example, one woman writes, "I am going to warm up by the fire." Another comments, "Anyone care to join me for a game of pool?" When I asked one of the original patrons why she always ordered a drink on arriving at the café, she replied rhetorically. "Don't people always order a drink when they arrive at a bar?" In an environment with very little ritual to guide behavior, these women follow that associated with real bars. By posting notes stating that they are ordering drinks, placing wagers over the pool table, and holding intimate conversations next to the fire, a common sense of reality is created on which future interactions can build.

Whereas one woman created the LC through her initial verbal description, the setting evolves as patrons discuss new features of the bar or fail to discuss old ones. For example, one day a patron mentioned in a public post that she was sitting in the rocking chair by the fireplace. Never before had a rocking chair been part of the features of the café. After a few days, however, as this patron continued to describe herself as sitting in the rocking chair, other patrons began to associate the rocking chair with "Sara" and accepted it as a part of the décor. In conversation, other patrons mentioned the rocking chair, as in this post: "I wonder where Sara has been, the rocking chair has been empty for the past few days."

A green bean bag chair was created in a similar manner and quickly became the coveted spot for early arrivers. Patrons would enter the café, read the notes posted thus far that day, and determine whether anyone was sitting in the green bean bag. If it was found to be empty, a patron would occupy it by posting a note such as this one: "I'm over here in the bean bag, waiting for all the ladies to arrive . . . . where is everyone???" After a few weeks, however, because no one mentioned the bean bag anymore, it no longer existed. Instead, the place where it used to lie, next to the fireplace, was occupied by the rocking chair. When I posted a note asking what happened to the bean bag, I received numerous replies ranging from a newer member who had "never seen a bean bag around here" to the regular patron who stated, "that old thing was such a mess—I put it in the attic." Never before had an attic been mentioned, but that reply triggered a conversation about cleaning the attic. Clearly, the verbal descriptions of patrons are used to construct a sense of reality.

It is interesting to note that once the LC had existed as a BBS for about one month, many regular patrons began to take the setting for granted. Occasionally, they would post notes without ordering drinks or making reference to some feature of the bar. Conversation could take place about a football game or a political event for several notes without anyone mentioning the setting. However, if the conversation began to wane, someone would immediately offer to buy drinks or play pool. In other words, the sense of a common reality was used by patrons much like physical settings are used by co-present conversationalists—as a source of mutually relevant topics (Maynard & Zimmerman, 1984).

Although the setting of the LC was created to resemble a bar, there are some notable differences between it and real bars. First, the café is always "open," with many women regularly "dropping by" for a cup of coffee on the way to work. It is interesting not only that a bar would be open in the morning but also that patrons would order coffee at a bar. As the beverages being ordered are not being consumed in a literal sense, there seems no reason why alcohol could not be ordered earlier in the day, especially if one is *pretending* to be in a bar. In other words, why not pretend that it is night? Similarly, all parties take place at night. So although the bar might be a fantasy, patrons adhere to real time.

In addition, most of the regulars indicated in interviews that they do not frequent real bars. For many, this is because they live in areas that have no bars. Others, however, described not liking the bar scene, "where the games are for real." When the group met in Atlanta, I was struck by how much more at ease these women were in the morning talking over coffee than they were at a real bar at night. Indeed, when we went to a real bar, all of the women were ready to leave long before it closed, even though the same women would still have been logged onto their computers had they been at home. As I questioned them about this observation, the women told me that they are not comfortable in bars. The café "is more about making friends and talking and playing with each other," one woman explained. Why, then, was the café created to resemble a bar? For many lesbians, bars are the only place where they have been around groups of other lesbians. As Krieger (1982) and Davis, Kennedy, and Michelson (1981) note, bars have long been a central institution in the lesbian and gay community.

Café patrons have carefully constructed the appearance of the café through verbal description. The setting serves the purposes of providing topics for interaction and creating a sense of shared reality. In line with the ethnomethodological perspective, the nature of the reality is less important than is the consensus over it. For example, whether a green bean bag or a rocking chair occupies the space next to the fire is less important than is the belief that patrons are occupying the same space. Members must include references to the café's appearance in their everyday conversation. If the features of the bar are not discussed, then patrons do not share a common reality and the café itself may cease to exist.

Functions of the Lesbian Café

The LC's primary function is to serve as a lesbian community for people lacking a community in their geographic areas or for those who are unable, for various reasons, to be visible members of existing geographic communities. Although a few regular patrons of the LC are from larger cities, the majority of the patrons I interviewed live in places too small to have lesbian bars, bookstores, or community centers. The café, then, serves as a surrogate community. As a community, it provides what many patrons describe as a sense of family. As one patron explained in an e-mail interview, "We are all able to be ourselves here and not worry about fitting in."

Indeed, the patrons do seem to share a strong bond. When the founder of the café was fighting a child custody case, she posted a note describing her problems. She got dozens of responses that were obviously meant to cheer her up. One patron, who is a lawyer, offered her legal advice; a therapist suggested ways of dealing with her stress; and people called her on the phone and sent her cards. She remarked that the café was "more of a family than she had ever had."

As a community, the café is also a place to be around one's own kind. As Paula commented during an interview that took place using e-mail, "I like this [the café] because I can meet other womyn who live the same lifestyle as me and I can be myself and share my love for Pam openly. We only know one other lesbian couple in Alabama, I wish there was a place like this here!"

The women at the café also described the importance of being around other lesbians, as one woman remarked during a phone interview. "Because of the pressures from family and friends, I lead a very straight life. The LC is the only place I can really feel 'at home.' For me the LC is an outlet. Somewhere I can go to get out of my reality."

For this woman, as well as for others who are not openly lesbian, the LC is a safe outlet. Going to a real bar means taking the chance of being seen and, therefore, threatening one's straight cover. Conversely, going to an electronic bar affords far fewer risks. One can "leave" the bar by flipping a switch. In addition, for women who have not, or at least have not yet, labeled themselves as lesbian, the LC offers an anonymous peek into the lesbian lifestyle. Indeed, Osborne (1993) describes the ability to experience different aspects of human sexuality as one of the reasons for the popularity of computer bulletin boards in the gay community.

Further, the café provides a place for recreation and meeting new friends. Theme parties, such as the Super Bowl party, are being planned constantly.

Planning for the Super Bowl party took more than a week as women posted notes placing wagers on the game and describing decorations and drinks. During the actual game, many of the women were logged onto their computer discussing plays, griping about referees' calls, cheering, and complaining. Cheering was accomplished by typing in all caps and, in some cases, by using the keyboard to graphically construct images of footballs, helmets, and the like. The game and the party continued to be the topic of conversation for the next few days.

Meeting friends is another important function of the café. As one patron commented during an e-mail interview, "I've made more friends here in less than a month than I do anywhere else." Another added, "The bar may be a fantasy, but the friends we make are as real as any anywhere." It is interesting to note that when I interviewed women in person, on the phone, or via e-mail, they were quick to acknowledge that the bar was a fantasy—an admission never made in a public post. However, by sharing this fantasy, they felt that they gained something real from the encounter. Additionally, the fantasy was repeatedly described as fun. By bracketing the world of the café, a reality is created. While the reality of the café may be different from the "paramount reality" (Schutz, 1970) of the "working world," the LC both is influenced by the paramount reality of real-world bars and has its own real elements. Friendships, for example, are formed in the LC but exist outside of it. Such fuzzy boundaries between reality and fantasy suggested, as Chayko (1993) does, that reality itself may need to be reconceptualized.

Perhaps the most obvious function of the café to the newcomer is the accessibility of women with whom one can flirt. The flirting at the café is described as being "all for fun," but often it is quite suggestive, as can be seen by the following post. The woman, identified as "Cunnie," posted a note stating that she had been out cutting the grass and that now she was packing to go out of town. I have included the next two notes as they appeared on the computer screen.

> cunnie . . . you mean "you" cut the grass today . . . be still my heart!! noway . . . heehee . . . funny . . . me going out of town tonight too . . . say . . . I'll see ya there! wink!! hehee . . . I travel light too . . . so . . . come over here and cut my "grass" . . . heheee
>   Jennie . . . trim this . . . < > . . . wink!!
>
> Jennie,
> Crack me up, trim this < >, rather kiss it with the blade of my tongue . . . oh my!
>   Pack light,
>   Darla . . .

Because both of these women are "coupled," as they put it, they are careful to make sure that they indicate to everyone reading these notes that their flirting is not to be taken seriously. Jennie's "heehee" is used to depict laughter. The word "wink" often represents a playful attitude. Darla, who also is called Cunnie, acknowledges Jennie's playful intent with her comment, "Crack me up." Nonetheless, the flirting is sexually graphic. By using the metaphor of cutting grass with the blade of one's tongue, these women are able to joke about oral sex in a way that regular patrons of the café will recognize but the censors of the computer network are likely to miss. Much of the flirting is done with metaphors that refer to various parts of the female anatomy. Caves and trees are used to represent the genital region, and mountains are used to indicate breasts. The symbol < > seen in these posts is also used frequently to refer to the genital region. These metaphors allow patrons to manage sexual talk without having their notes "zapped" (returned to sender unposted). Indeed, the ability to flirt in this manner is one way of differentiating regular patrons from newcomers.

A limited amount of flirting is done with more serious intent, as can be seen in the following set of notes.

> Stacy . . .
>   well, actually . . . I was wishing for a bit more . . . like . . .
>   . . having you . . .
>   . . . here in my arms . . .
>   . . . for as long as I could keep you . . .
>   *Brenda*
>   < smile >
>
> Brenda . . .
>   That's funny . . . < smile >
>   I was wishing the same thing, myself . . .
>   Stacey
>   < kiss . . . . . . > !

Notice that the language used is less sexual and more romantic: "having you . . . here in my arms . . . for as long as I could keep you." These two women, during recent weeks, have spent the majority of their time "talking" either to each other or to other patrons about each other. In an attempt to establish a romantic mood, they have used the word " < smile > " instead of the playful " < wink > " found in other notes. The excessive use of dots, as in " < kiss . . . . . . > ,"! is intended to represent a long-held kiss. By manipulating words and symbols, a very different mood is created from that of the playful flirtations in the previous posts.

Finally, the café serves as an information center to keep lesbians posted on news from around the nation that influences lesbians and gays. For example, during the political controversy surrounding the issue of gays in the military, one patron posted the names and phone numbers of the most important politicians to be called in the nation's capital. She urged everyone to "protect our brothers and sisters currently in the armed forces and those who may want to join . . . . Please."

This electronic community, therefore, serves many of the same functions as do geographic communities. It provides a place to make friends and establish more intimate relationships. Additionally, it is a place to gather for recreation, for advice, and to "be around one's own kind."

Effects of the Medium on Communication

Establishing relationships through an electronic medium can be both liberating and limiting. In either event, new issues arise that are unique to this form of communication. Many patrons describe the freedom that such a limited medium provides. One respondent remarked that she likes the lack of emphasis on physical appearance: "It seems better to get to know what really makes a person, her thoughts and beliefs, and not be so concerned with race and age and looks and all."

For a person who is shy, communicating by computer is easier primarily due to the ability to carefully construct and edit one's comments before they are "heard" by anyone else. One patron, Melanie, commented during an interview carried out through e-mail, "For shy people like me, the café is better than a regular bar. It's easier to communicate this way. Besides the games here are fun and not hurtful like it usually is in the regular bar."

Having observed Melanie at the café, I would not have described her as shy. She posts frequently and is often quite flirtatious. Indeed, many café patrons have told her that she does not seem shy. In person, however, Melanie is very reserved. The first day of the café patrons' trip to Atlanta, another person in the group commented that "Melanie did not seem to be enjoying herself." Someone else remarked, "Everyone is pretty much what I would expect, except Melanie." To which another woman responded, "Remember, she said she was shy; I guess she is." It took two days in Atlanta before Melanie began to be at ease with the group. When I asked her about why she was more shy in person, she remarked, "I've never been good at meeting people. On the computer, it's easier. I don't have to worry about what people think. Maybe it's because I don't really know them."

In a Goffmanian sense, computer relationships are easier because fronts and idealizations are more controllable. Goffman contends that an individual presents herself or himself as a person with certain characteristics. If a person desired to be more outgoing, on the computer that front would be easier to create. Emotions and appearance can be well thought out before they are presented to others.

Patrons also describe the advantage of being able to flirt without being taken seriously. Most of the women at the LC are, as they put it, coupled. Their partners do not feel threatened by flirting on the computer but would not understand the same flirting behavior if it took place in a real bar.

The computer can also be a limiting communication medium. As described earlier, emotions are hard to convey. BBS users have developed whole dictionaries of abbreviations to represent emotions, such as < VBG > for very big grin. One would use this abbreviation if she were making a comment in a joking manner that, without this marking, could be misconstrued as serious or rude. For example, Melanie commented one Sunday morning that she was going to sit on the porch and read the newspaper. Lori replied, "have fun relaxing on the porch and don't tax your brain too much with those comics < VBG > ."

Common facial expressions, such as a wink or a smile, are often stated after one's name, as was shown in the previously mentioned notes. Winks are used frequently at the café either to indicate a secret shared between two people or to convey a playfully flirtatious mood. Others try to depict emotions graphically by constructing facial features such as the sideways smile described earlier. In a situation where one would laugh at a comment made by someone else, café patrons type "heehee" to indicate laughter. Anger or frustration is conveyed by yelling, which means typing in all caps. Other emotions are stated with "tails" following the patron's name such as "Katie . . . lonely." The respondents in this study agreed that these crude attempts at conveying emotions are often inadequate. As Jennifer put it in an e-mail interview, "I do feel limited in the sense that I want to reach out and touch some of these people, or see their eyes while conversing, but I can't." Paula, in response to a particularly steamy note from Sharon, expressed her frustration with the computer through both her words and by typing in all uppercase letters: "I CAN'T STAND THIS FANTASY ANYMORE . . . JUMP THRU THE MONITOR AND COME TO ME . . . . I WANT YOU NOW!!!!!!!!!"

A few people have attempted to establish intimate relationships via the computer. For them, the limitations of this medium have been even more evident. In an interview, one woman told me that if her relationship with Paula were going to "make it," they would have to see each other. Another relayed the frustration of wanting to look into someone's eyes and seeing only the screen.

A final limitation is the censoring of sexually explicit notes. Many LC patrons complain that their roles have been zapped. However, private e-mail is uncensored, and so patrons often "leave the bar" for the privacy of e-mail to carry out their sexually explicit conversations.

In addition to carrying out sexually explicit conversations, e-mail is used by regular patrons for a variety of other reasons. If one patron wants to tell another "the way it really is," she will resort to e-mail. For example, during the Atlanta trip, a few personality conflicts arose. On returning home, the trip dominated conversation at the LC, but no mention was made of any unpleasant incident. However, several regular patrons told me that the regulars who did not go to Atlanta quickly began to e-mail those who did to "get the real scoop." In a Goffmanian sense, the public boards can be viewed as frontstage and e-mail as backstage. The behavior on the public boards has to be polite so that the appearance of this lesbian community is consistent with how the members describe it: friendly and family-like. Further, while frontstage, the patrons must continue to pretend that they are in a bar so that the created reality seems real. Backstage, in e-mail, the conversation is more informal and less polite. Patrons do not pretend to be in a bar, but they do express their suspicions to each other concerning others at the café.

Finally, many regulars e-mail each other on a daily basis "just to say hello." Members of this computer network pay for each e-mail message sent after they exceed a certain number. Several women I interviewed commented on the large amount of money they spent on e-mail each month. In a bar where drinks are free, this is one of the only ways available to indicate that a relationship is valuable enough to warrant spending money on it.

Typology of Lesbian Café Patrons

So far, this article has focused on the regular patrons who frequent the LC. Whereas regulars make up the majority of the patrons on any given day at the café, they are even more highly visible than their number would indicate because they post more frequently than do other patrons. In actuality, there are four types of patrons usually present at the café: regulars, newbies, lurkers, and bashers. Whereas the regulars do not call themselves regulars, the other three terms are used frequently by regulars to describe other types of patrons. People in these four groups can be differentiated primarily by their communication patterns. The regulars are discussed first because two of the other types of patrons, newbies and lurkers, are often en route to becoming regular patrons.

Regulars. Regulars are characterized primarily by their smooth conversational style. They are well aware of the norms regarding posting at the café and do not violate them. For example, they type in lowercase letters so as not to appear to be shouting. They post notes *to* people so that they are not just spouting comments out for anyone who will listen. Regulars know who the other regulars are, and they know many details about others' lives. They use this knowledge to personalize conversation, as is shown in this note posted by a regular patron early one morning when no one else appeared to be logged on.

> . . . so like am I just sitting here talking to myself???? Sure sounds like it. Mags lov . . . are you still stoned? hehee . . . looks like Sweet P is STILL at the store . . . cunnie has gone to Cleveland for her review . . . a review on sex . . . hehee . . . kris is still sipping her VAT of coffee . . . kd is still making muffins . . . so like where is everybody else . . . suzi lov . . . get out of bed will ya . . . so like everybody talk to me . . . carla

They further personalize conversation and convey emotion by using uppercase letters occasionally for emphasis and by constructing pictures using the letters and symbols on the computer keyboard. Additionally, most regulars add tails after their names to convey emotion. Regulars are also well aware of the fact that the café is a fantasy *bar;* in conversation, they refer to the features of the bar, such as the pool table or hot tub, and thus demonstrate an awareness of the setting. Many regulars have developed a personality through some sort of trademark in posting. For example, one regular (called Kris in the previous note) always starts the day at the café by making a pot of gourmet coffee. Every morning, she posts a note stating what the flavor of the day is. Other regulars expect this of her and come to the café for coffee and morning conversation. Others are known to be flirtatious or shy through the type of notes that they post. Some have a trademark drink that they always order. By counting the number of different people who post in a given day, it appears that regulars comprise about 50 percent of the crowd at the LC. Regulars are important because they, like the features of the bar itself, are part of the reality that patrons share. These patrons include two other types who may eventually become regulars: newbies and lurkers.

Newbies. Newbies are characterized by an awkward conversational style. Many stumble into the café by accident and are unsure as to what they have found. Often their posts have no relevancy to any current conversation. Some will honestly say, as one newbie did, "I'm new here, what am I supposed to do?" Regulars will quickly respond to this type of post, explaining that the café is a friendly place where one can talk about anything she wishes. Some newbies will make the mistake of typing with their CapsLock key on. This obvious posting violation clearly labels the person as a newbie. Regulars will gently reprimand in a manner such as the following: "There are only a few people here, there is no need to shout." The newbie is then put in the position of having to apologize for her inappropriate behavior. One newbie responded to being corrected for typing in all caps as follows: "sorry about the caps . . . i guess you can't play the game unless you know the rules."

As the newbie attempts to fit in, she will begin to mimic regular behavior such as ordering drinks or posting sexually suggestive notes. First attempts, however, are usually clumsy. For example, the sexual posts of newbies are often too direct, as they do not know how to use the subtle metaphors of flirting. Another mistake commonly made by newbies is to respond to a sexual note addressed to someone else or to jump in on a sexual conversation uninvited. Finally, newbies are often unintentionally rude. As newbies are unaware of how to use graphics, tails on their names, uppercase letters, and abbreviations to convey emotion, their joking comments will often be taken as rude.

The response by the regulars to the inappropriate behavior of a newbie can range from ignoring the newbie to attacking her verbally. If the newbie posts in a manner that is too sexual, the regulars will often treat her with suspicion. This behavior is especially likely if the newbie has an androgynous name. Treating someone with suspicion may involve using public posts to question the newbie about her background. Additionally, regulars contact each other via private e-mail to share their suspicions. Any sexual posts made by the newbie will be ignored; her note will receive no replies. These negative sanctions are important because they teach the newbie the rules of posting. The newbie then responds to sanctions and suspicions by answering any questions asked and by apologizing for inappropriate behavior. It is interesting that newbies I interviewed were not angry about the suspicious treatment they received. As the newbie continues to post, her posts become more polished, containing fewer mistakes and fitting into the existing conversations better. As she makes mistakes, she will be corrected, but more gently, as the regulars come to know and trust her. This process of posting, receiving negative sanctions, and posting again in a more polished fashion continues as the newbie learns the rules at the café. Eventually, she moves into the confidence-gaining stage where she develops her own trademarks, establishes a new level of trust, and creates her own personality traits. For example, the newbie may become known for always ordering a particular drink or using creative tails after her name. She may establish a certain way of conveying emotion by using graphics that she creates on the computer. She may begin to initiate sexual talk and get responses (a sign of trust). Eventually, she will be treated as a person whom the regulars know. For example, when Kris was a newbie, she became known as an excessive coffee drinker. As the regulars began to trust her, they would consistently mention her coffee drinking. Through this gesture, a bond was formed that helped her become a regular. Eventually, the confidence-gaining stage leads to becoming a regular. Based on the number of notes posted, newbies account for about 30 percent of the patrons at the café.

Lurkers. Lurkers converse very little, but when they do it is in a very tentative manner. Lurkers are so called because those who now post often admit to having spent much time first observing the café's activities. In other words, they are logged onto the LC, reading posts but not replying or posting their own notes. Some regulars, who were at one time lurkers, stated that they lurked for weeks, others for months, before posting their first notes. Whereas many people undoubtedly lurk and never post a note, those who wish to become involved use the observation period to learn who the regulars are and how to post. They see the newbies make mistakes and learn from the negative sanctions the newbies receive. They notice the regulars' trademarks and styles. They learn the regulars' names. Only after a lurker has learned enough about the LC to gain confidence will she tentatively post a note. Her first post is humble. As one lurker put it, "I usually just watch, but I wanted to introduce myself." This type of post is very different from the brash style of a newbie. The regulars' response to the lurker post is almost always to welcome her and invite her to post more. Usually, the regulars will take turns encouraging the lurker to join in on conversations. They will let her know that "this is a friendly place." Because the lurker shows the proper deference to the regulars when she first posts, she immediately gains respect from them. Further, she does not make typical newbie mistakes because she had been watching and has learned the norms and the structure of the café. After being invited to post more, some lurkers return to lurking. Others reply in a noticeably polite manner to the invitation to post. Some lurkers thank the regulars for welcoming them, and others comment on how friendly the café is, showing that they are aware of the atmosphere of the café. As this polite conversation goes back and forth, the lurker demonstrates that she knows the rules and the regulars. It is very rare to see a lurker make a mistake. Once the lurker has made the decision to quit lurking, she moves into the confidence-gaining stage described earlier. For her, movement through this stage is quicker than it is for the newbie because she has given a great deal of thought, during her lurker phase, to what her computer personality would be like if she were to post. Indeed, in a very deliberate manner, she has constructed her front. As she posts more frequently, her projected personality becomes obvious and she is recognized and referred to by the regulars. It is interesting to note that when lurkers become regulars, they are usually the type of regulars who do not engage in the highly graphic sexual talk. For them, the café is much more than a place to meet women sexually; it is a carefully crafted community that they have consciously chosen to join. The percentage of lurkers at the café is difficult to determine because many lurkers do not post even though they are "at the LC." In my observations, I have found that about 20 percent of the people who post in a given day were previously lurkers.

Bashers. The final group of patrons at the café are the bashers. By counting the number of different people who post notes over a period of time at the café, it seems that bashers account for less than 1 percent of all people at the café. Their hostile style of communication, however, makes their presence important. Bashers are people who log onto the LC BBS to harass the lesbian clientele. Some bashers are easy to identify because they use male names and make hostile comments about lesbians, such as the person who stated, "you people are sick!" Other bashers post under female names. When posting in this manner, bashers' notes can resemble those of newbies; in other words, their posts are awkward. It is for this reason that newbies are often treated suspiciously at first. However, the former newbies that I interviewed understood the suspicious treatment; bashers do not. Bashers respond to being treated suspiciously by posting hostile notes. The regulars and newbies gang up to verbally assault, or "flame," the bashers. This behavior often leads to bashers' becoming even more insulting. The conflict escalates until regulars convince their fellow patrons to ignore the bashers, as was done in this post: "ladies . . . he isn't worth our time . . . ignore the creep and he will go away." Often bashers will continue to post a few more inflammatory notes before they "go away." Once the basher has ceased posting notes, the regulars congratulate each other on defending the café, as is shown in the following two notes between two regulars. Susie says to Sylvia, "let me get you a clean shirt . . . my bloody nose made a mess out of yours . . . thanks for the help." Sylvia replies, "ya, but not as big a mess as you made out of his face."

Finally, some bashers come to the café apparently assuming that lesbians are bisexual. In the following note, Steve is clearly looking for bisexual women in his geographic area. He writes, "Any Ohio bi fems for me and my girlfriend to talk to? I'm not a kid or a prankster. We're just curious." LC patrons found this note offensive for two reasons. First, the lesbian café is often described as being strictly for women. During my observation, every patron using a male name who posted a note in the café, even if friendly, was asked to leave. Second, café patrons do not post notes attempting to meet people in their geographic areas. As one woman told me, "this place is bigger than that!" One regular responded to Steve's post indicating her anger by the use of uppercase letters: "NO!!! . . . please . . . Lesbians DO NOT SLEEP WITH MEN!!!!! . . . you are in the wrong place!"

Bashers usually do not last at the café for more than one day, but they are talked about for several days after their departure. Their presence is important in that it serves to unite the lesbian patrons against a common "enemy" and, thereby, strengthen the community. This finding is consistent with the writings of Coser (1956), who first described conflict as promoting integration based on solidarity. As one patron commented, "bashers remind us that there is no safe retreat from the heterosexual world." As is the case in many minority communities, this "us versus them" mentality serves to strengthen the community. Bashers also highlight the intrinsic difficulties faced in constructing a special place using a publicly accessible medium.

Discussion and Conclusion

This study illustrates how an electronic community can be constructed and sustained through interactions restricted to the computer screen. The setting of an electronic community is created through verbal descriptions of the type of space that patrons can recognize and those they desire. In other words, the appearance of the LC is influenced by both the medium of construction, the computer, and the past experiences of patrons in real bars. The café's appearance is important in that it provides a sense of common reality for all the members of the LC. Daily conversation serves to strengthen the reality shared by regulars and to inform newcomers of the nature of the place they have entered.

The findings presented here are important for several reasons. On a practical level, the ability to create communities electronically is significant because communities have been shown to have a positive effect in the establishment of self-concepts. Therapeutic activities aimed at improving a person's self-concept through the creation of electronic communities could be especially beneficial to those who are restricted in their ability to participate in geographic communities.

Additionally, this study has examined the benefits and limitations of the computer as a medium for establishing relationships. Whereas Jedlicka (1980, 1981), Ansberry (1993), and Osborne (1993) suggest that the computer can be useful in establishing intimate relationships, this study indicates that there is a limit as to how intimate a relationship can become without face-to-face contact. However, for people who are shy, disabled, or insecure about their appearance, this medium provides a positive environment for meeting people and fostering positive impressions.

This study also suggests some more general theoretical lessons. Although findings support some of the main tenets of interactionist and ethnomethodological theory, at the same time they call into question the distinction between reality and fantasy and challenge the traditional notion of community. Indeed, the members of this microcosmic society explicitly do what Goffman suggests people implicitly do in everyday life: they mobilize their expressions to present themselves as certain types of people. The setting is keyed to the primary frame of a real bar, and the bar fantasy is sustained through daily interactions among members. While individual patrons clearly craft and present their own fronts in a very Goffmanesque manner, patrons collectively stage a team performance that creates the image of a friendly place welcoming all lesbians. Maintaining such an atmosphere requires careful manipulation of frontstage and backstage behavior. Frontstage, public posts are noticeably polite, and new members are welcomed. Backstage, in the world of e-mail, suspicions are shared and conversation is less polite. The backstage region serves to increase the solidarity of the group by allowing regular members more sincere contact with each other. However, the atmosphere of the café is seen by patrons to be real rather than a cynical facade. Patrons willingly describe the bar as fantasy but adamantly insist that the friendliness of the place is real.

Interview data in this study suggest that members believe that they are sharing the same type of space when they are logged onto the LC. The descriptions members give of the physical layout and the atmosphere of the café are remarkably similar. Sharing a common view of the setting is important in that it focuses future interactions and gives members a sense of sharing the same space. While the LC community existed throughout this study and beyond it, most bulletin boards on this computer network have shorter lives. One explanation could be that these groups failed to create a sense of common reality for members to share and were, therefore, unable to survive. At the same time, the setting compels members to act in certain ways to maintain a shared sense of reality. It is interesting to note that what is being described as a sense of reality might better be called a shared fantasy. One significant aspect of this study is that it demonstrates how technologies such as this one can blur the distinction between reality and fantasy. As Chayko (1993) argued in her study of virtual reality, perhaps the definition of "real" experience needs to be reworked.

Nonetheless, the *sense* of common reality serves to maintain a community that carries out many of the same functions as do geographically anchored communities. The patrons who come to the café regularly do so to be around their own kind of people and thereby validate their identities as lesbian. Within this community, bashers provide a source of conflict that serves to increase community solidarity. That the LC serves many of the same functions and has many of the same features as do geographic communities challenges traditional definitions of community. Bernard (1973) suggests that the concept of community might lose its viability as locale disappears. Rather than disappearing, perhaps the notion of locale is only being reformulated. This study has demonstrated that a locale need not be confined to a specific geographic location but can instead be created and maintained in cyberspace.

Acknowledgments

Special thanks to Joseph Kotarba for his assistance in all aspects of this study. Thanks also to Janet Chafetz and the anonymous reviewers for their helpful suggestions on earlier drafts of this article.

References

Ansberry, C. (1993). Love affairs bloom amid bits and bytes of home computers. *Wall Street Journal*, February 12, A1.

Bernard, J. (1973). *The sociology of community.* Glenview, IL: Scott, Foresman.

Chayko, M. (1993). What is real in the age of virtual reality? "Reframing" frame analysis for a technological world. *Symbolic Interaction,* (16), 171–181.

Coser, L. A. (1956). *The functions of social conflict.* London: Free Press of Glencoe.

Davis, M., Kennedy, L., & Michelson, A. (1981). *Buffalo lesbian bars, 1940–1960.* Paper presented at the Berkshire Conference on Women's History, Vassar College, June.

Garfinkel, H. (1967). *Studies in ethnomethodology.* Englewood Cliffs, NJ: Prentice Hall.

Goffman, E. (1959). *The presentation of self in everyday life.* Garden City, NY: Anchor Books.

Goffman, E. (1974). *Frame analysis: An essay on the organization of experience.* Cambridge, MA: Harvard University Press.

Goffman, E. (1981). *Forms of talk.* Philadelphia: University of Pennsylvania Press.

Jedlicka, D. (1980). Formal mate selection networks in the United States. *Family Relations,* (29), 199–203.

Jedlicka, D. (1981). Automated go-betweens: Mate selection of tomorrow? *Family Relations,* (30), 373–376.

Katz, J. (1993). The news: Bulletin boards: News from cyberspace. *Rolling Stone,* 15 April, 35–36, 77.

Krieger, S. (1982). Lesbian identity and community. *Signs: Journal of Women in Culture and Society,* (8), 91–108.

Maynard, D. & Zimmerman, D. H. (1984). Topical talk, ritual and the social organization of relationships. *Social Psychology Quarterly.* 47:301–316.

Osborne, D. (1993). On-line with the FBI. *The Advocate,* 6 April, 44–46.

Roxxie. (1993). Sister act: The ups and downs of lesbian sex clubs. *The Advocate,* January 12, 63–64.

Schutz, A. (1970). Transcendences and multiple realities. In H. R. Wagner (Ed.), *On phenomenology and social relations* (pp. 245–262). Chicago: University of Chicago Press.

Reflections of a Novice Researcher

Shelley J. Correll
University of Wisconsin, Madison

My study of the Lesbian Café began as a class project for a graduate class on qualitative research methods at the University of Houston. As a requirement of this class, all students chose a group to study. We applied the methods we learned to studying our chosen groups, had weekly meetings about our projects, and ultimately wrote papers about our findings. In looking back, it seems that two factors led me to choose the Lesbian Café for study. First, I had just purchased my first computer modem and I was intrigued by electronic communication. This was in the early 1990s, before most people were connected by e-mail and before Internet browsers made the Internet easily accessible to most computer users. Instead of using browsers, some computer users joined on-line computer services such as Prodigy® or CompuServe.® These services gave members easy e-mail access to other members of the same service and allowed members access to computer bulletin boards like the one described in the study. People who were not members of a specific on-line service did not have access to the bulletin boards of that service. From a technical standpoint, then, the study is dated. However, this was the beginning of what has obviously become a very common form of communication, and I was intrigued by how this form of communication might lead to the creation of different kinds of community.

The second factor that led me to choose the Lesbian Café for study was my apprehension over doing this kind of research. I had never done a study like this. What if the group did not want me there? What if my questions and observations angered the group members? In worrying about these things while also playing with my new modem, I realized that the Lesbian Café was a group that I could observe discreetly and that I could interview members electronically, thereby reducing some of my anxieties about meeting face-to-face. Even if the group had refused to give me access, this rejection would have been cushioned by occurring electronically. The medium of communication therefore afforded me many of the same advantages as it provided to members of the Lesbian Café.

Although I was well supervised by the professor teaching the course, Joseph Kotarba, I was truly a research novice when I began this study. Additionally, studying a group that exists in cyberspace was relatively novel. The combined newness of me to the process and this type of group to ethnographic methods put me in largely uncharted territory. Although this newness is one of the strengths of the study, it also certainly meant that some of the substantive and methodological decisions I made about issues such as how to focus the study and how to collect and analyze the data were more emergent than planned.

My decision to study the Lesbian Café was serendipitous—a result of enrolling in a class on qualitative research methods at the same time I acquired a computer modem. I suppose one would normally have a substantive interest and then select one's sample. There may have been better groups to study if I truly had started with a more abstract interest in electronic communication and community, but I was intrigued by *this* group. What specifically intrigued me about them only became clear after hours of observing them and after sharing those observations with my classmates in our weekly meetings. In this regard, being new to this kind of research was probably an advantage: I was able to observe without having many preconceived ideas about what I would see.

Many of my decisions about data collection had to be modified over the course of conducting the study. In class, we were given guidelines about how to collect data through observing participants and conducting interviews. We took a grounded theoretical approach wherein we observed the group, conducted unstructured interviews with members of the group individually, revised our impressions of the setting, conducted a semistructured interview with a "leader" of the group, revised our impressions again, conducted group interviews, and so forth.

As a newcomer to this type of study, I was very grateful for these guidelines. Without them, I would not have had the confidence to do the study. However, it quickly became apparent that I had to be flexible in applying the guidelines to my study. It was not clear, for example, who the leader of the Lesbian Café was. Interview techniques do not readily apply to e-mail interviews, and e-mail was the only way some patrons of the Lesbian Café felt safe in communicating with me. When the opportunity arose to meet some of the regular members of the Lesbian Café in person, I jumped at the chance, even though this was not a source of data I had initially planned to collect. (Since members were geographically located all over the United States, I had not thought it would be possible to interview them in person.) At the time, I thought that my need for flexibility was the result of the somewhat unusual group I had chosen to study. However, I now think the more general lesson is that guidelines are just that—they are not rigid sets of rules to be applied to any setting.

Qualitative research has the potential to produce rich data that deepen our understanding of the interplay between real people, processes, and settings. The comments provided by the researchers whose works appear in this book contain many suggestions and considerations about how to conduct qualitative research. These "experience-tales" can provide you with confidence as you begin to conduct your own research and can give you some general ideas about how to proceed. However, these tales are likely to raise as many questions as they provide answers. This is as it should be. Qualitative research realizes its potential when researchers immerse themselves in a setting and struggle to figure out the best way to understand it.

My own suggestions for how to engage in that struggle are modest: stave off the tendency to draw conclusions prematurely and be flexible and adaptive. I also found it extremely helpful to be a part of a group working on qualitative research projects. Not only did the group members provide me with suggestions and insights, they also drew me out of the field for a time and allowed me to go back in with new eyes. Qualitative research *is* often a struggle, but allowing oneself to participate in that struggle can result in a study—indeed, even in a class project—that deepens understanding of some aspect of social life.

12

"Hard and Heavy"

Gender and Power in a
Heavy Metal Music Subculture

Leigh Krenske, Jim McKay

The future of rock belongs to women.
—The late Kurt Cobain, lead singer with grunge rock band *Nirvana*

It was like my dress was being torn off me, people were putting their fingers inside me and grabbing my breasts really hard. . .and I had a big smile on my face pretending it wasn't happening. I can't compare it to rape, because it isn't the same. But in a way it was. I was raped by an audience—figuratively, literally, and yet, was I asking for it?
—Courtney Love, Cobain's widow and grunge rocker, explaining why stage-diving inspired her to compose the song "Asking for It"

T his article uses a social constructionist perspective to analyze gendered structures of power in a heavy metal (HM) music youth subculture. According to most social constructionists, gender relations and identities are not the "natural" outcome of biology or the product of "appropriate" sex-role socialization, but rather institutionalized *practices* that all of us "do" (West & Zimmerman, 1987). Given that men control the most powerful social institutions and their values are more highly esteemed than women's, then women must continually "do" gender under disadvantaged conditions. Kandiyoti (1988, p. 286) uses the term "patriarchal bargains" to refer to the fluid and tension-ridden ways in which both men and women "accommodate and acquiesce" to preexisting gendered structures and meanings within which women generally "bargain from a weaker position."

Leigh Krenske and Jim McKay, (2000). "Hard and Heavy: Gender and Power in a Heavy Metal Music Subculture."*Gender, Place, and Culture, 7*(3), 287–304. http://www.tandf.co.uk/journals
Reprinted by permission of Taylor & Francis Ltd.

Our perspective relies heavily on the explicitly pro-feminist work of Connell (1987, 1990, 1992, 1993, 1995, 1998), who has provided a useful theoretical framework for studying structures of labor, cathexis, and power in specific *gender regimes* (for example, families, education, the military, work, religion). Connell argues that gender regimes are characterized by a combination of physical and economic coercion and hegemony. The latter concept refers to "the cultural dynamic by which a group claims and sustains a leading position in social life" (Connell, 1995, p. 77). Thus, he uses the term "hegemonic masculinity" to denote the "culturally idealized form of masculine character," which stresses "the connecting of masculinity to toughness and competitiveness," the "subordination of women," and "the marginalization of gay men" (Connell, 1990, pp. 83, 94). Depending on the context, other men (for example, gay men, men of color, working-class men) occupy a subordinate or marginal status in relation to the institutionalized exemplars of masculinity such as sports stars (Connell, 1995, pp. 76–81; 1998). Connell stresses that the reproduction of hegemonic masculinities is not based simply on sheer numbers and the crude imposition of a dominant ideology—it rests on consent and complicity rather than conspiracy and numerical superiority: "the hegemonic form of masculinity is generally not the only form, and often is not the most common form. Hegemony is a question of relations and cultural domination, not of head counts" (Connell, 1993, p. 610). "The public face of hegemonic masculinity is not necessarily what powerful men are, but what sustains their power and what large numbers of men are motivated to support. The notion of 'hegemony' generally implies a large measure of consent. Few men are Bogarts or Stallones, but many collaborate in sustaining those images" (Connell, 1987, p. 184).

Another key feature of gender regimes is the complex and contradictory articulations both within and between what Connell terms "hegemonic," "subordinated," and "marginalized" masculinities on the one hand, and "emphasized femininity" on the other. According to Connell (1987, pp. 183–184), emphasized femininity is the accommodation of women to "the interests and desires of men" and "women's compliance with this subordination," while other forms of femininity "are defined by complex strategic combinations of resistance and cooperation." Connell submits that there is "a kind of 'fit' between hegemonic masculinity and emphasized femininity," in that "hegemonic masculinity must embody a successful collective strategy in relation to women" (1987, pp. 185–186). Within Connell's framework, gendered relations of power are neither static nor uncontested: "The authority of men is not spread in an even blanket across every department of social life" (1987, p. 109). Thus, some men and women do struggle against the oppressive structures that constrain their everyday practices. However, dissenters have to contend both with men who derive what Connell (1995, p. 79) calls the "patriarchal dividend" from the subordination of women in general in society, as well as women who complicitly sustain the emphasized mode of femininity that helps to reproduce gender inequalities. Connell stresses that these elaborate gender formations interact in multifarious and uneven ways with other social divisions (for example, class, ethnicity, race, age). In short, we do not just "do gender," we also "do difference" (West & Fenstermaker, 1995).

In aligning ourselves with Connell's version of social constructionism, we take up a broadly poststructuralist emphasis on decentering and deconstructing hegemonic definitions of language, rationality, equality, subjectivity, truth, and objectivity, which we consider to be crucial to wider feminist critiques of "malestream" knowledge. But we also concur with those feminists who have noted that an unbridled acceptance of these ideas can easily slide into a "postfeminist" scenario in which "women" (and "men") cease to exist as a category (Franklin et al., 1991; Modleski, 1991; Bordo, 1992; Ebert, 1992–1993; Jackson, 1992; McRobbie, 1994). So although we focus on intertextual and intergeneric dimensions of HM's discursive practices, we argue that all social texts, identities, and practices are always in some way *relatively* anchored by structuring forces such as class, gender, race, and ethnicity. The "anchor points" in this case, we suggest, are Connell's concepts of "hegemonic masculinity" and "emphasized femininity."

Walser (1990, p. 168) states that "popular music's politics are most effective in the realm of gender and sexuality, where pleasure, dance, the body, romance, power, and subjectivity all meet with an affective charge." In this context, the first goal of this article is to demonstrate how Connell's scheme can help researchers identify gendered structures of power in youth subcultures like HM music. We do so through a theorized ethnography of a HM subculture, which complements existing historical, theoretical, and textual analyses of HM music (Gross, 1990; Straw, 1990; Walser, 1990, 1993; Weinstein, 1991; Hinds & Wall, 1992; Arnett, 1993; Binder, 1993; Pfeil, 1995). Our second goal is to show that although Connell's theoretical framework is useful for investigating gender relations and identities in the HM scene, his concept of emphasized femininity needs further elaboration in order to account for internal hierarchies *among* women. Before introducing the research site and our field methods, we describe the main features of the HM scene.

The Heavy Metal Music Scene

Dominant Codes and Signifying Practices

In her analysis of women in rock music, Sawchuck (1989) invokes de Lauretis' term "the trap of representation coherence" in order to caution scholars against collapsing heterogeneous cultural formations into a monolithic entity. This caveat is apposite in exploring the genealogy of HM. When HM emerged in Britain and North America in the late 1960s, it manifested strong elements of acid/psychedelic rock, which was then in decline. Despite retaining many psychedelic motifs, HM has embraced myriad musical and visual styles (for example, classical, glam, grunge, funk, rock, R & B, and punk) since its inception and constitutes a highly elaborate genre. For instance, much to the dismay of some fans, the archetypal HM band, *Metallica,* recently performed publicly and then recorded an album with the San Francisco Symphony Orchestra. As with youth subcultures in general, the dress code of the HM scene is a bricolage of styles. HM performers and fans have synthesized elements from the middle-class hippie counter-culture (for example, long hair) with ingredients of working-class subcultures. The biker style and S & M regalia (also used by punks) have had a major influence on the HM "look." Fans usually wear a picture T-shirt of their favorite band with jeans when going to concerts, and many performers and fans sport tattoos.

HM concerts usually involve *moshing* and *stage-diving.* The former is a sort of group dance that takes place in front of the stage, an area that is also known as the "mosh pit." Moshing is sometimes referred to as "slamming," although there is a subtle difference between the two, in that the latter entails particularly forceful body movements. Moshers jump and press toward each other in a type of collective bodily skirmish. Stage-diving involves a Superman-like "flying leap" into the upwardly-stretched arms of "catchers" in the pit. The activity is usually done head-first, with legs raised slightly in order to avoid hitting people in the head with the customary heavy boots. The successful mosh pit has a definite etiquette and requires a strategic balance among the (predominantly male) participants' bodies. The tasks in the mosh pit are frequently distributed in terms of somatotype, with the catchers usually being strong and tall and divers tending to be ectomorphic. A tight mosh pit is preferred, because chances of being dropped are lessened. These activities, which often leave the exponents kicked, bruised, and exhausted, are read by band members as a form of audience appreciation.

The Heavy Metal Sound

HM's distinctive sound is embodied in the genre's name. It is characterized by the use of "simplistic, very rudimentary harmonies and melodies [with an] endless repetition of simple [power] chords with extremely short progressions" (Denski & Sholle, 1992, p. 43). Loudness is a mark of competency, with the thunderous sounds of concerts giving the receiver the energy to respond with physical and emotional vigor. Sound is experienced through the body: "the music can be felt, not only metaphorically, but literally, particularly in the listener's chest" (Weinstein, 1991, p. 145).

The lyrics of HM span a continuum of possibilities, largely based on the (un)-holy trinity of sex, drugs, and rock 'n' roll (see Table 12.1). However, the sentimental notions of romance often found in pop music, and less frequently in rock music, are virtually absent from HM. References to sex are typically of a lustful nature, for the pleasure of men, and without commitment. For instance, the lead singer of the popular HM group *Guns 'N Roses* uses the moniker Axl Rose, which is an anagram for oral sex. The more "intellectual" and "political" lyrics (usually about rebellion) are likely to have been written within an alternative sub-genre. Enunciation of lyrics is secondary to intonation and expression, which are used to generate the appearance of power and control. The various intonations are enhanced by the particular types of body movements of a performer; gestures often relay the general thrust of lyrics, which are also summed up in key phrases (or choruses) and made more comprehensible via repetition.

Table 12.1. Examples of Common Themes in Heavy Metal Music
(Including Mainstream and Alternative HM Bands)

Heavy Metal Theme	Band Name	Song Title
Teenage rebellion	Alice Cooper	"Department of Youth"
	Motley Crue	"Smokin' in the Boys Room"
Death and the macabre	Cannibal Corpse	"Blood, Pus & Gastric Juices"
		"Skull Full of Maggots"
Depression	Rollins Band	"Low Self Opinion"
Odes to the genre itself	Judas Priest	"Rock Hard Ride Free"
	Rainbow	"Long Live Rock 'n' Roll"
Sexual exploits of men	Red Hot Chili Peppers	"Sir Psycho Sexy"
	Def Leppard	"Make Love Like a Man"
Oral sex	Kill	"Lick It Up"
	The Hard Ons	"Suck 'N' Swallow"
Drugs	Alice in Chains	"Drug of Choice"
	Saxon	"Drink Till You Puke"
	Black Sabbath	"Sweet Leaf"
Devil worship	Witchryche	"Ceremony"
The love of God	Blood Good	"Spirit with You"
Political statements	Sepultura	"Propaganda"
State of society	Suicidal Tendencies	"Institutionalized"
Humor	Scatterbrain	"Don't Call Me Dude"
Optimism	Bon Jovi	"You Gotta Have Faith"
Hedonism	Motorhead	"Ace of Spades"

Gender, Sexuality, and Power

*This music is not played from the head, it's played from
here [touches his heart] and here [ditto his groin].*
—Klaus Meine of HM band *Scorpions,* cited in Drozdowski (1990, p. 48)

HM's predominantly young, white, male performers and distinctive signifying practices mark it as an aggressively heterosexist formation. HM lyrics, artwork, language, bodily practices, and dress generally valorize hegemonic masculinity and denigrate women and gay men. For example, ridiculing some HM as "soft cock" frequently occurs when a particular genre is not considered "masculine enough." Much of the imagery of HM is resonant with men's power, typically articulated through technology, men's bodies, the voyeuristic male gaze of the sexually objectified female body, or the threat of violence.

Like the larger youth music setting, HM women artists tend to be marginalized or trivialized, with the few who do manage to infiltrate the scene "succeeding" by conforming to masculinist scripts. Some women have attempted to overcome their subordinate status by instituting alternative genres. A good example is *Riot Grrrl*, which evolved out of the American underground punk scene, and included "oppositional" bands such as *Babes in Toyland, Bikini Kill, Bratmobile, Huggy Bear,* and *Spitboy* (http://garnet.berkeley.edu/ ~ annaleen/riot.grrls.html). *Riot Grrrl* concerts often prohibit men, a prohibition that results in accusations of lesbianism (Williams, 1993). However, as one member of a *Riot Grrrl* band stated, "It is a refreshing change to play at a gig where there is no stage-diving, no slamming, and no women are being pushed around or groped" (France, 1993, p. 27). Yet the presence of all-women bands does not necessarily subvert the ascendant masculine codes, since women performers find it difficult to transcend the status of sex object. Moreover, they frequently personify Connell's concept of emphasized femininity and even sometimes manifest misogynous and violent tendencies (Gottlieb & Wald, 1994). The following letter to a HM magazine encapsulates some of the heterosexist and homophobic elements of the scene:

> MOSH ON: I've had it with the weak motherfuckers who stand in mosh pits like they're pulling their cocks to a porno. I was destroying my body at [a concert] when the screams of some dumbfuck told me to stop elbowing and bumping into him. My response was brief. "If you can't handle it in the pit and you're not going to mosh, get the fuck out!" This poof was in the middle of the pit with his arms crossed, staring into space. I warn all weak posers—if you are not gonna mosh in *my* pit, stay the fuck out! (*Hot Metal,* July, 1993, p. 31)

The Research Context

Situating Club Thrash

The empirical study was based on Club Thrash in the central business district of Brisbane, the state capital of Queensland, Australia. As part of "the north" or "deep north," Queenslanders inhabit a region that Australians generally equate with inferiority. In addition to being located in a northern area, Queensland's otherness has also been articulated in terms of its outback landscape, frontier or "hillbilly" mentality, racist treatment of indigenous people and indentured workers, relatively decentralized population, rural-based economy, and nearly three decades of postwar rule by an authoritarian-populist government. Civic boosters and the tourist industry regularly tout Queensland as "the California of Australia" and Brisbane as its Los Angeles. But in his recent *World Tour of Australia* video, comedian Billy Connolly invoked another frequently used description that he thought was more apposite: "the Alabama of Australia." Popular media representations of Queenslandness tend to reflect and reinforce regional and masculine stereotypes—what Morris (in Turner, 1992, p. 651) has termed the "dreaded tradition in Australia. . . of men, sport, and beer." For example, Queenslanders' success in the conspicuously masculine sport of rugby league has been an important site where the media has constructed myths about the state's allegedly rugged regional character in order to rebut attributions of its cultural backwardness by contemptuous southerners (McKay & Middlemiss, 1995).

Although Brisbane is large enough to attract entertainers of international caliber, its musical profile has generally been lower than that of larger southern state capitals like Melbourne and Sydney. At the time of the study, Club Thrash was the only venue in Brisbane that played live HM music. The heterogeneity of both the patrons and the music of Club Thrash can be explained by the relatively small population of Brisbane, the absence of a critical mass that can support distinctive HM subcultures, and the city's generally conservative culture. The depressed condition of the local economy has also made opening nightclubs a risk enterprise, so entrepreneurs are loath to offer alternatives to the conventional blues, jazz, rock, and country bands that predominate in most venues. In fact, the club where the study took place subsequently went bankrupt.

The type of music played at Club Thrash was a pastiche of speed, thrash, and alternative HM. Dim lighting was used to create a gloomy atmosphere for patrons, most of whom were Anglo-Celtic men aged between eighteen and twenty-four. The venue was often quite hot and had a distinctive smell—a conglomeration of sweat, tobacco and marijuana smoke, alcohol, and stale cleaning agents. Using illicit drugs, which was an integral part of the subculture, was facilitated by the dark lighting. The general ambiance was similar to the music that was constantly playing: *heavy.*

Research Methods[1]

A feminist framework underpinned the project. Men were included in the study, because the subordinate status of women in a given gender regime cannot be understood unless the relational aspects between men and women are examined. As Haraway (1997, p. 28) puts it: "Gender is always a relationship, not a performed category of beings or a possession that one can have. Gender does not pertain more to women than to men. Gender is the relation between variously constituted categories of men and women (and variously arrayed tropes), differentiated by nation, generation, class, lineage, color, and much else."

One of the central tenets of feminist inquiry is to replace the "view from above" with a "view from below" (Mies, 1983, p. 123). In this context, Smith (1987) identifies the importance of explicating and inserting the researcher's "embodied self" within the texts of sociological research. This stylistic gesture effectively grounds the reader in the subjective reality of the writer and the ways in which research may be affected because of such subjectivities. Smith calls this procedure the "standpoint of the viewpoint."

Adopting an ethnographic approach, one of the coauthors (Leigh) spent over forty hours observing interactions at the club during the period from July to November 1993. Preparation for the fieldwork included becoming familiar with the HM scene by reading relevant popular magazines and local entertainment guides, listening to a local FM radio program, and examining semiotic structures in various HM lyrics, posters, and album and CD covers. Relevant magazines (for example, *Metal Masters* and *Hot Metal*) and local entertainment guides (*Time Off* and *Rave*) were analyzed in order to identify dominant semiotic codes in HM music. Five hours of pilot work were then completed at the club in order to identify what correspondence, if any, there was between these semiotic codes and social interactions at the venue. It quickly became apparent that although individuals had their own practical understandings of the club's subculture, a number of distinctive codes were swiftly identifiable, especially through modes of dress, body decorations, and corporeal practices. These codes are presented in Tables 12.2 and 12.3. It was relatively easy to characterize "Metalheads," "Metal Wenches," and "Glam Chicks," since these were the terms that most participants used to describe members of these groups. Three peripheral groups were not as easily identifiable by the participants, so the "etic" categories of "Fanatics," "Cool Dudes," and "Hardcore Bohemians" were eventually used to describe them. It should be noted that some individuals evinced two or more codes, while others did not fit precisely into any of them. Definite intra- and intergender differences did appear, however, and generalizations were possible, which were significant in relation to data collection as well as its analysis. For instance, among the male participants, the Metalheads were clearly hegemonic over the subaltern Fanatics, Cool Dudes, and Hardcore Bohemians. These preliminary codes were subsequently refined through further participant-observation and in-depth interviews with ten participants.

In the club, most of my time was spent observing participants' interactions occurring in response to the performances of bands (for example, moshing and stage-diving). During intermissions, however, I endeavored to speak to as many people as possible. This usually resulted in musical "small talk," often articulated through the participants' drug-induced haze. In spite of this, such conversations were sometimes the prologue to some valuable data. Field notes were written at the venue in a pocket-sized journal. Contrary to a widely advocated procedure (Lofland, 1971), the toilet was not used for note-taking, because the line-up to use them was usually too long.

My background (young and Anglo) resembled the characteristics of most of the people who participate in HM music subcultures, which was an advantage in establishing an affinity with participants. Furthermore, although tertiary-educated, my working-class and rural background helped consolidate rapport with respondents. The considerable size of the audience and its dynamic nature from week to week meant that my status as researcher was largely unknown. However, my reasons for being at the club were given to all persons I approached. Thus, I believe my assimilation into the scene was successful and relatively unobtrusive (Stoddart, 1986).

An ethnographic encounter is not simply a matter of observing and noting. It creates a particular reality that reflects the situation and biographies of both researcher and researched (Emerson, 1987). An ethnography, therefore, is an artifact that is derived from a multiplicity of participants' realities. My view of the research site was greatly influenced by my sexed corporeality. While engaged in participant observation, I repeatedly encountered the same forms of

Table 12.2. Profile of Male Codes at Club Thrash.

Male Codes	Dress Code	Somatotype	General Mode of Participation
Metalhead	Simple combination of black jeans and picture T-shirt; sometimes has an iconic tattoo; fetishizes long hair as a status symbol	Usually mesomorphic, sometimes overweight	Enters club with male friends or Metal Wench; drinks at the bar, very seldom moshes or stage-dives; occasionally uses marijuana; often intimidates women
Fanatic	Shorts sometimes worn and shirt may be taken off because of the heat; short hair	Usually ectomorphic	Totally dedicated to moshing and stage-diving; favors alcohol and speed cocktail, sometimes uses LSD; occasionally uses marijuana
Cool Dude	Black jeans and leather jacket; long hair—often tied back	Usually ectomorphic	Sometimes enters club alone; usually drinks alone at the bar or mixing desk; seldom moshes or stage-dives, sometimes plays pool; occasionally uses marijuana
Hardcore Bohemian	Unkempt bricolage of hippie and punk (torn jeans, sometimes cut off at the knee and worn-out T-shirt or flannelette shirt); sometimes has body piercing; often has heavy, black tribal tattoos; short hair or dreadlocks	Usually ectomorphic; sometimes emaciated	Often involved in the fringes of the local art and music scenes; uses various drugs (heroin, LSD, marijuana); seldom moshes or stage-dives; often plays pool

male intimidation and feelings of vulnerability experienced by other women at the scene. For instance, irrespective of whether I was alone or with other people (male or female), I was habitually harassed whilst walking to and from the club. At times, movement within the institution of the street was particularly unpleasant and reaching the research site was often a relief.

Table 12.3. Profile of Female Codes at Club Thrash.

Female Codes	Dress Code	Somatotype	General Mode of Participation
Metal Wench	Simple combination of black jeans and picture T-shirt; little or no make-up; long, straight hair—sections may be bleached or colored	Usually mesomorphic; sometimes overweight	Female equivalent of the Metalhead; incorporates masculine codes of participation; young Wenches occasionally mosh and stage-dive
Glam Chick	Overtly sexual clothes that accentuate body shape (e.g., short, tight skirt; revealing top; high leather boots; highly "made-up"); long, teased or curly hair	Usually ectomorphic, or well-toned and meso-morphic	Usually gains access and status through attachment to a Metalhead or Cool Dude; occasionally moshes; never stage-dives
Hardcore Bohemian	Bricolage of hippie and punk (e.g., long, flowing skirt with short top in order to expose pierced navel); often have a pierced nose and mouth; often wear tribal jewelry and have "tattooed" armbands; short hair, dreadlocks, or long, straight hair with sections shaved off	Usually ectomorphic; sometimes emaciated	Often involved in the fringes of the local art and music scene; uses various drugs (e.g., heroin, LSD, mari-juana); occasionally moshes and stage-dives; often plays pool

My embodied self also affected the type of people that I was able to contact at the research site. Entering and being accepted into the research site required the adoption of appropriate dress and behavior codes (Spradley, 1980). I adopted a version of the Hardcore Bohemian dress code, which, within the terms of the HM scene, reflected my mode of participation and my body type. This decision had important consequences, since certain codes clashed with others. For instance, attempts to recruit Glam Chicks for interviews were constantly thwarted, because of their disdain for the pierced bodies characteristic of Hardcore Bohemians. I did not adopt the dress code of the Glam Chicks in an attempt to infiltrate their sub-set, because this would have been inconsistent with my own corporeality and, therefore, detrimental to my overall position, or sense of "authenticity," within the research site. Thus, all comments made about Glam Chicks are based on my observations and other participants' accounts of them. Contact with men, especially Metalheads, was also very difficult, because most interpreted my attempts to initiate conversations as a "come-on." Nevertheless, it was still possible to gain insights into the gender regime of the club from the particular position I adopted.

Participant observation allows the researcher to come to grips with some of the interactions transpiring at any particular site. However, if researchers do not ground observations in the experiences of the participants, they run the risk of imposing a fictional "reality" onto the field (Minichiello et al., 1990). Furthermore, the activities that were observed at the research site constituted only part of the subcultural activities. In order to bridge the gap between my own observations and the "realities" of the informants, a number of in-depth interviews were conducted. Minichiello et al. (1990, p. 87) describe in-depth interviewing in the following manner: "In-depth interviewing is conversation with a specific purpose—a conversation between researcher and informant focusing on the informant's perception of the self, life, and experience, and expressed in his or her own words. It is the means by which the researcher gains access to, and subsequently understands, the private interpretations of social reality that individuals hold."

Concurrent with the participant-observation, ten people were interviewed in order to examine participants' identities and perceptions of the research site. An effort was made to include at least one person from each of the main groups that were apparent at the research site. The female toilet provided a fertile ground for making connections and gaining rapport with women, so I often introduced myself to the small groups of women who congregated and talked both inside and outside it. Except for women who did not live in Brisbane, all of those approached in this manner agreed to participate and gave me their telephone numbers for future contact. I also offered my own telephone number in an effort to foster mutual trust. Five women were contacted using this procedure and another was contacted via a colleague. Making contact with men was exceedingly difficult. Both the context and my corporeally inscribed gender meant that talking to men on my own initiative was frequently interpreted as a sexual advance or regarded with suspicion. A good deal of my contact with men was spent negotiating this heterosexist regime and establishing a sense of legitimacy. In the end, I was able to interview four men. Two were contacted at the club through conversations initiated about the performing bands, I met one through a mutual friend during a game of pool, and I approached another one on campus after recognizing him as a regular at the club.

After obtaining the telephone numbers of possible respondents, I called to arrange a formal interview. All but two of the interviews were held in public places, such as art galleries, parks, and libraries. These locations were chosen because I felt uncomfortable about going to the homes of men I did not know, while some of the women were hesitant about inviting me into their homes.

The remaining interviews were conducted in homes—one in my own and one in the home of the interviewee.

Before each interview began, respondents were given a brief outline of my research question and its methodological and analytical framework. The interviews focused on the participants' views of the interactions within the club and its affiliated subculture, their reasons for liking HM music, and discussion about bodies, as well as gathering demographic and biographical details. Interviews lasted between forty-five minutes and a little over two hours.

Analysis of the data was continuous and sequential (Becker, 1970). The practice of moving between theory and data, with each modifying the other, was maintained throughout the whole research process, resulting in a question-observation-question research cycle (Spradley, 1980), whereby the collection of further data was directed by the data preceding it (Becker, 1970). After data collection was finalized, field notes and transcribed interviews were coded using codes based on both their manifest and latent content (Minichiello et al., 1990) and their relevance to Connell's theoretical framework.

Analysis and Discussion

Gender, Power, and Space

The territorial dynamics of the club illustrated both how space is gendered and gender, sex, and sexuality are spaced (Bell et al., 1994, pp. 31–32). Women who attended the club entered a social space that was "hard and heavy"—both symbolically and materially. In articulating their anxieties, women often made comments that exemplified Rose's (1993, p. 146) thesis of how the "threatening male look" intensifies women's consciousness of being gazed at and occupying spaces. Even Wenches, generally the most assertive group of women, were apprehensive about the ambiance: "when you walk into the room all you see is guys wearing black with long hair. Some of them are quite big and you just walk in and go, 'Oh shit, where are all my friends?' Just that first look around the place can be very intimidating" (Caroline, 20, Metal Wench).

Women increased their social space either by relying on male partners or friends or by forming groups of at least two women when going out. Women's precarious position and dependence on men was demonstrated by the following conversation:

LEIGH: Do you find that many men come here to pick up women?

DONNA: One just tried to pick me up five minutes ago.

LEIGH: What did you do?

DONNA: I told him I was here with my boyfriend, and he said that it didn't matter—we could have a threesome!

LEIGH: What did you say to that?

DONNA: Nothing. I just moved really close to my boyfriend and put my arm around him. (Donna, 20, Metal Wench)

Spatial arrangements changed during the evening. Early in the night before the bands began to play (about 10 P.M.), people tended to meet and talk, play pool, and drink in a relatively diffuse pattern. As the evening progressed, more people entered the club and an atmosphere of anticipation developed prior to the band's performance. A highly gendered spatial arrangement emerged, with various groups gravitating toward particular spaces where they "staked out" their territory: Metalheads and Metal Wenches positioned themselves at the bar; Fanatics moved toward the stage with the expectation of forming a mosh pit or creating opportunities to stage-dive; the Cool Dudes lingered on the second level or in front of the mixing desk; and the Glam Chicks and Hardcore Bohemians tended to circulate throughout the club.

Metalheads were extremely territorial, spending most of the night in a group in front of the bar on the lower floor. By herding together, Metalheads strengthened their "ownership" of space and effectively built a wall of intimidation that other patrons had to penetrate if they wanted to go to the bar: "I avoid the bar . . . I don't drink that much anyway . . . I go upstairs if I ever want to buy a drink. The people there are much more relaxed" (Michelle, 22, Hardcore Bohemian).

These social dynamics confined women spatially and created feelings of vulnerability. Any woman standing alone was a prime target for sexual harassment. Although extreme, the following incident illustrates the kind of harassment to which women were subjected: "There was this guy who carried rats around with him. He kept pet rats, and like he—it's pretty disgusting—but he stuck his tongue in the rat's rude bits, and he then came up and stuck his tongue down my throat. . .I went to the bathroom and just scrubbed my mouth until it bled—it just disgusted me" (Shirley, 22, Metal Wench).

The technique of taking up space was also used by the all-male bouncers, who "accidentally on purpose" bumped into people as they patrolled the crowd. Tensions sometimes developed when the etiquette of the mosh pit and stage-diving was breached. On several occasions tension occurred when some Metalheads approached the stage for a closer view of the band. By remaining steadfast—and, more important, physically *unchallenged*—in the middle of the mosh pit, they effectively broke a code of participation. It should be noted, however, that no major fights were witnessed during the four months of participant-observation, and any incipient conflict was quickly terminated by the bouncers. For the most part, the overall spatial order of the club was not contested, and the very fact that the various subsets maintained distinctive terrains suggests they were conscious of the hierarchy: "[Cool Dudes] are actually small-framed. . .pretty skinny. . .they are well aware of it and they are not going to hide it from anyone else. They don't go round starting trouble purely because they wouldn't be taken seriously anyway. They are going to be beaten up, so what does it matter" (Shirley, 22, Metal Wench)?

Despite these internal divisions among men, structures of power were defined almost totally on their terms: "[Women] can't go to a night club and do what they want. . .it is not what the guys are there for. They would move on, I think, and find another place to hang out. . .the club really does have the tendency to be a guy's world. . .I mean, it is not benefiting an understanding of women or anything like that" (Andrew, 24, Hardcore Bohemian).

Gender, Power, and Corporeality

Band members (almost all of whom were young white men) were expected to display their authenticity via particular bodily aesthetics and practices. As concerts progressed, audiences expected that performers' long hair would mat and their clothes dampen as they exerted themselves. Lead singers who did not sweat profusely were viewed as having given a "phony" performance. The few women who performed were seldom taken seriously. For instance, Rosa claimed that audiences perceived her performances to be inauthentic, because of her dress code (a hybrid of Hardcore Bohemian and Glam Chick) and the intimation that she was just a front for male musicians: "These people don't know me—right, but I am accused of being a bauble, because I front an all-male band. I am called a bimbo because of the clothes that I wear. A lot of women hate me in the scene."

Gendered differences in the use of corporeal space were particularly evident in moshing and stage-diving. First, men usually constituted at least 95 percent of the participants, while women were either absent or occupied the periphery. Second, men and women used their corporeal spaces differently. Men generally moved freely through the pit and stage-dived with little or no constraint:

LEIGH: Do you think stage-diving is something that you have to learn to do?

ANDREW: Nah, you just get up there and do it. It's a totally ordinary
   activity.

Both moshing and stage-diving rested on elements of violence and male bonding that made it difficult for women to participate in any substantive fashion, because status was achieved by demonstrating bravado and inflicting pain on one's body:

I think that the only criteria of being a stage-diver is that you can't do a half-hearted jump. You have to jump in such a way that if nobody catches you, you hit the deck really quite hard. (David, 24, Hardcore Bohemian)

You actually do it until you drop—we used to do it until we practically had heart attacks. . . after you're panting and sweating and wet right through, you think to yourself, I should have stopped three songs ago, before I got this black eye or strained my wrist or something, but it is just not really a concern. . .[it's]. . . maybe what you'd experience if you were working in a chain-gang—digging a hole together. You're all in there together and there is a feeling of being together, and doing it to excess, pushing yourself to the limit. (Peter, 24, Fanatic)

On the other hand, women's movements were usually fearful and hesitant, with women almost always confined to the periphery of the pit and tending to react to the vigorously moving bodies of men rather than slamming into others: "I have noticed that even when girls are in the pit, they don't really get into moshing as much as the guys. . .they are moshing to themselves" (Caroline).

Few women stage-dived and those who did hardly ever used their bodies confidently. When women were asked why so few of them stage-dived, their principal response was related to anxiety about pain. Women who dived usually approached the stage in a timid and ambivalent fashion and had to be repeatedly coaxed and reassured by the catchers. According to Michelle: "The guys just throw themselves into it a bit more, whereas women will sort of sedately jump back in or fall in or whatever. The guys will just throw themselves out there."

However, a few women reported a sensation of liberation after stage-diving successfully: "Occasionally you see the girls get up, the ones wearing jeans and shirt and no shoes—they will do a big full-on [jump], if not better than the guys. . .You see them get out of the pit and their eyes are just bulging—especially the ones who have done it for the first time" (Shirley).

When asked why she stage-dived, Shirley said: "Total adrenaline rush. It's just the closest thing that you can get, apart from skydiving and things like that—just the thrill of jumping into the unknown. You don't know what you are going to get once you hit the people, whether they are going to let you go or hit the floor."

Women like Shirley, who moshed and stage-dived, were considered to be "one of the boys": "I have chipped a few teeth and gotten black eyes from doing stage-diving and stuff. . .It is kind of a status thing, coming out of a gig with a bloody lip; you go, "Yeah, look what I got." The more damage you do, the more fun it is—everyone just laughs at each other. It is no big deal to get a black eye, it's only a bruise. Bloody nose? Big deal, it will stop. . .you just learn to accept it, it is fun to do."

In summary, women who moshed and stage-dived "successfully" were incorporated into the male-defined ethos of the subculture. On the one hand, this had the potential to free women from their restricted corporeal and spatial experiences. On the other hand, the damage that they did to their bodies was very real and hardly "liberating" at all.

Gender, Power, and Sexuality

Any prospect of women overcoming their subordinate status was negated by an internal hierarchy that revolved around rivalry for men's attention. Like women in motorcycle gangs (Hopper & Moore, 1990), Metal Wenches admired men who acted tough. Thus, their emphasized femininity was oriented toward complying with Metalheads' standards so that they could "relate to men on their level." This was usually done by adopting the Metalheads' codes of participation (for example, attempting to match their copious consumption of alcohol and demonstrating an "authentic" appreciation of HM music). Consequently, Wenches believed that they were the most "authentic" women in the scene. Wenches' bodies were normally concealed underneath an androgynous mode of dress and, therefore, not sexualized to the same extent as the Glam Chick or the female Hardcore Bohemian. Wenches perceived Glam Chicks, whose emphasized femininity was based primarily on looks, as the main threat to their power base: "You can really tell instantly, because [Glam Chicks] are there one weekend and the next they are not. They show up with a member of a band and it's like, 'Yeah, we know what you are on about.' That's all they are out to do—sleep with a band member. This is how a lot of girls that I know get status in the metal scene—they sleep with the band members. . .they are not really the metal chicks, 'cause the metal chicks are more down-to-earth and aren't into stuff like that" (Shirley).

The following comment by Shirley illustrates both some key differences in demeanor between Wenches and Glam Chicks and how such distinctions were interleaved with men's power: "You are there to have a bit of a bash around, be violent—not violent—but be bashed around a bit in a fun sense. [Glam Chicks] stand back and if you touch them or anything like that—spill your drink on them or blow smoke in their faces—they go off their brains. They get their big boyfriends to come down and. . .beat your boyfriend, and it's, 'Hey, he had nothing to do with it!'"

Because Wenches attempted to conform to Metalheads' ideals, they denied that there was any sexism in HM, despite its manifestly misogynist overtones:

LEIGH: Do you ever get offended by some of the Death Metal lyrics— when they sing about slicing up women after fucking them, because that is all they are good for?

SHIRLEY: No, no. . .it is just more extreme in form, more aggressive, not beating around the bush. . .it gets straight to the point. I don't take offense to the stuff.

Regardless of her personality, a Glam Chick was invariably positioned in terms of her appearance and alluring sexuality. Caroline described a Glam Chick as "someone who can wear the shortest dress or tightest jeans, the littlest vest, or something like that." Other terms used to describe Glam Chicks were "metal slag," "metal slut," "bimbo," and "groupie." According to Peter, Glam Chicks "always come across as being really ignorant. . .usually we would reclassify them as 'try-hards.'"

Female Hardcore Bohemians occupied a different position, set apart from the conflict between Metal Wenches and Glam Chicks. Associated with male Hardcore Bohemians, they were not viewed as competing for the attention of Metalheads, Fanatics, or Cool Dudes. They sometimes parodied emphasized femininity by wearing revealing clothes (for example, exposing pierced navels).

The heterosexual regime evident in the club was linked to homophobia, as the following exchange illustrates:

LEIGH: It is pretty heterosexual?

CAROLINE: Definitely. Oh god! If there was a gay person there, they would be dead.

LEIGH: You have never heard of a gay person being in there at all?

CAROLINE: No, even if they were, they would have to be thick to admit it. Everything is like, "faggot," "poofter," "kill that poofter."

Homophobia swiftly surfaced when the conventions of the mosh pit were encroached upon or misunderstood: Peter stated, "If any guys were [feeling a man's body in sexual manner] there would be hell to pay!" However, lesbians affiliated with the Hardcore Bohemian subset were occasionally apparent: "It seems that the lesbian thing is more accepted in the scene. . .it is probably more of a man thing as well, because a lot of the men that I have spoken to, their ideal fantasy is having sex with two lesbians. . .which is probably why they are accepted" (Caroline).

Contrary to expectations, women seldom cited apprehension about how men might treat their bodies as a reason for not moshing or stage-diving. However, the anonymous fondling of women stage-divers was acknowledged by men:

LEIGH: How much of an opportunity do you have to actually touch women?

PETER: Heaps. . .like you just see these hands, not so much catching but groping. It is quite common.

Unlike the women interviewees, men believed that "groping hands" would be the foremost explanation as to why women would not stage-dive.

LEIGH: Why do you think that not many women stage-dive?

DAVID: Because a lot of those guys would be copping quite a bit of a feel when they dived.

The difference between men's and women's explanations of why women did not stage-dive points to men's objectified and sexualized view of women's bodies. Moreover, the fact that women did not find "groping hands" terribly problematic suggests compliance with the male definitions of the HM scene.

In summary, both the forceful corporeal practices of men and the highly gendered structures of power in Club Thrash meant that women perpetually "did" gender on men's terms. Women's access to, and experiences of, the subculture were determined by unequal relationships with men—women "participated" in male-defined terms or not at all. To borrow a phrase from Allen (1990, p. 34), such strategies reproduce a gender regime that is based on "males judging their own value in terms of competitive performance against other males, and females judging their own value in terms of the degree to which they are valued by males."

CONCLUSIONS

The most frequent reason that women gave for gravitating toward the HM scene was a desire to escape stifling adolescent situations. For instance, women who had grown up in rural areas of Queensland often spoke of the "small town mentality" that they had endured. Some indicated that they had been frustrated during adolescence at seeing boys visit the "bright lights" or "big smoke" while they stayed at home: "When I was younger. . .I used to watch all my male friends go and see all these bands that I wanted to see, while I had to stay at home" (Michelle).

Caroline recalled:

> I would have to sneak out every Friday night. I would go over to a friend's house and her parents would drive us out to the bus stop. . .So we would catch the bus [to Brisbane] and stay up late and then catch the first bus back in the morning. And then her mum would come and pick us up—she was really cool. . . I just knew when I was growing up that all my friends at high school would stay in that stinking town in the middle of nowhere. They would marry the same people they went to school with, they would have babies and they would get fat. This was not going to be my life story.

Thus, most of the women in the study were involved in classic "escape attempts" (Cohen & Taylor, 1976) from the oppressive conditions of everyday life. Furthermore, both male and female HM fans often reiterated the generic HM discourse that they were engaged in rebellious activities in an "authentic" setting. However, this romantic conviction sits uneasily with the highly commodified nature of the HM scene at large, and the ways in which it reinforces conventional patterns of hegemonic masculinity and emphasized femininity. Consequently, women drawn to the HM scene to escape one oppressive context merely inserted themselves into another.

In returning to the two goals of this article, we can say that Connell's scheme is useful in assisting researchers to identify gendered structures of power in youth subcultures like HM. Connell's emphasis on the necessity of understanding the elaborate and contradictory interplay both within and between men and women in any given gender regime was borne out by this study. For instance, there was a clear hierarchy among men: Metalheads were clearly hegemonic, while Fanatics, Cool Dudes, and Hardcore Bohemians were subordinate and/or marginalized. Despite this internal hierarchy of masculinities, it was the men who took up most of the space, intimidated women, and valorized bravado and pain in stage-diving. Even the subordinated and marginalized men obtained both individual and collective benefits (the "patriarchal dividend") from socially constructed definitions of their bodily superiority over women.

We also found support for Connell's thesis that emphasized femininity is manifest in terms of how women generally have to accommodate men's values, as nearly all of the women in the study had a peripheral or incorporated status in most activities, and the Glam Chicks were sexually objectified. The most telling indicators of women's subordinate status were that (1) although some *individual* women held some power, this was always over other women, (2) when individual women did have power over men it was always exercised via a male friend or boyfriend in a defensive or reactive situation, and (3) women never exercised any collective power over men. However, a serendipitous outcome of our study was the array of competing femininities evident in Club Thrash, as it was clear that Metal Wenches, Glam Chicks, and Hardcore Bohemians had different statuses. So, just as Connell (1993, p. 603) has urged researchers to think of "multiple masculinities" in "multiple cultures," we suggest that it is also necessary to consider the hierarchy of feminine codes operating in particular settings and how these articulate with the arrangement of masculine codes. Finally, Connell's emphasis on the obdurate *structures* that underpin gender regimes was also firmly illustrated. Without advocating notions of a conspiracy among men or that women were cultural dopes, the HM texts, narratives, identities, and corporeal practices in this study constituted a complex and contradictory gendered regime of power that literally kept women "in their place."

The focus on a single HM music club necessarily limits the scope of the analysis advanced in this article. However, it could usefully be developed through comparative studies of similar venues and different subcultural HM scenes. Although the field researcher's embodied gender enabled the development of rapport with women in all groups except the Glam Chicks, it simultaneously restricted access to some men, particularly Metalheads. Therefore, male investigators could augment the research by providing complementary perspectives that "study up" the gender order (Connell, 1992). Another possible direction of future research would be to apply Connell's framework to other musical genres and settings in youth subcultures.

Acknowledgment

We would like to thank David Rowe, Liz Bondi, and four anonymous referees for their helpful comments on earlier drafts of this article.

Note

1. After completing pilot ethnographic work for this study, Leigh collaborated with Jim in order to theorize the results in a way that was sensitive to her site. Leigh then used the theoretical framework as a guide for the main phase of data collection. Jim took the main responsibility for writing up the project in full consultation with Leigh. The order of our names is meant to signify that Leigh instigated the project and collected all the primary data.

References

Allen, J. (1990). The wild ones: the disavowal of *men* in criminology. In R. Graycar (Ed.), *Dissenting opinions: Feminist explorations in law and society.* Sydney, Australia: Allen and Unwin.

Arnett, J. (1993). Three profiles of heavy metal fans: A taste for sensation and a subculture of alienation. *Qualitative Sociology, 16,* 423–443.

Becker, H. S. (1970). Problems of inference and proof in participant observation. In W. Filstead (Ed.), *Qualitative methodology: Firsthand involvement with the social world.* Chicago, IL: Markham.

Bell, D., Binnie, J., Cream, J., & Valentine, G. (1994). All hyped up and no place to go. *Gender, Place and Culture, 1,* 31–47.

Binder, A. (1993). Constructing racial rhetoric: Media depictions of harm in heavy metal and rap music. *American Sociological Review, 58,* 753–767.

Bordo, S. (1992). Review essay: Postmodern subjects, postmodern bodies. *Feminist Studies, 18,* 159–175.

Cohen, S., & Taylor, L. (1976). *Escape attempts: The theory and practice of everyday life.* London: Allen Lane.

Connell, R. W. (1987). *Gender and power.* Sydney, Australia: Allen and Unwin.

Connell, R. W. (1990). An iron man: The body and some contradictions of hegemonic masculinity. In M. Messner & D. Sabo (Eds.), *Sport, men, and the gender order: Critical feminist perspectives.* Champaign, IL: Human Kinetics Press.

Connell, R. W. (1992). Drumming up the wrong tree. *Tikkun, 7,* 31–36.

Connell, R. W. (1993). The big picture: Changing masculinities in the perspective of recent world history. *Theory and Society, 22,* 597–623.

Connell, R. W. (1995). *Masculinities.* Sydney, Australia: Allen and Unwin.

Connell, R. W. (1998). Studying Australian masculinities. *Journal of Interdisciplinary Gender Studies, 3,* 1–8.

Denski, S., & Sholle, D. (1992). Metal men and glamour boys: Gender performance in heavy metal. In S. Craig (Ed.), *Men and masculinity and the media.* Newbury Park, CA: Sage.

Drozdowski, T. (1990). Monsters of guitar. *Metal Musician,* April, p. 49.

Ebert, T. (1992–1993). Ludic feminism, the body, performance, and labor: Bringing *materialism* back into feminist cultural studies. *Cultural Critique, 23,* 5–50.

Emerson, R. (1987). Four ways to improve the craft of fieldwork. *Journal of Contemporary Ethnography, 6,* 69–89.

France, K. (1993). Grrrls at war. *Rolling Stone,* September, p. 27.

Franklin, S., Lury, C., & Stacey, J. (Eds.) (1991). *Off-centre: Feminism and cultural studies.* London: Harper Collins.

Gottlieb, J., & Wald, G. (1994). Smells like teen spirit: Riot grrls, revolution and women in independent rock. In A. Ross & T. Rose (Eds.), *Microphone friends: Youth music and youth culture.* New York: Routledge.

Gross, R. (1990). Heavy metal music: A new subculture in American society. *Journal of Popular Culture, 24,* 119–130.

Haraway, Donna. (1997). *Modest_Witness@Second_Millenium.FemaleMan©_Meets_OncoMouse': Feminism meets technoscience.* New York: Routledge.

Hinds, E., & Wall, J. (1992). The devil sings the *blues:* Heavy metal, gothic *fiction* and "postmodern" discourse. *Journal of Popular Culture, 26,* 151–164.

Hopper, C., & Moore, J. (1990). Women in outlaw motorcycle gangs. *Journal of Contemporary Ethnography, 18,* 363–387.

Jackson, S. (1992). The amazing deconstructing woman. *Trouble & Strife, 25,* 25–31.

Kandiyoti, D. (1988). Bargaining with patriarchy. *Gender and Society, 2,* 274–290.

Lofland, J. (1971). *Analyzing Social Settings.* Belmont, CA: Wadsworth.

McKay, J., & Middlemiss, I. (1995). "Mate against mate, state against state": A case study of media constructions of hegemoric masculinity in Australian sport. *Masculinities, 3*(3), 38–47.

McRobbie, A. (1994). *Postmodernism and popular culture.* London: Routledge.

Mies, M. (1983). Towards a methodology for feminist research. In G. Bowles & R. Duelli-Klein (Eds.), *Theories of women's studies.* London: Routledge and Kegan Paul.

Minichiello, V., Aroni, R., Timewell, E., & Alexander, L. (1990). *In-depth interviewing: Researching people.* Melbourne, Australia: Longman Cheshire.

Modleski, T. (1991). *Feminism without women: Culture and criticism in a "postfeminist" age.* London: Routledge.

Pfeil, F. (1995). *White guys: Studies in postmodern domination and difference.* London: Verso.

[riot.grrls.html.http://garnet.berkeley.edu/ ~ annaleen/riot.grrls.html].

Rose, G. (1993). *Feminism and geography: The limits of geographical knowledge.* Oxford: Polity Press.

Sawchuck, K. A. (1989). Toward a feminist analysis of "women in rock music": Patti Smith's "Gloria." *Atlantis, 14*(2), 44–54.

Smith, D. (1987). *The everyday world as problematic.* Toronto: University of Toronto Press.

Spradley, J. (1980). *Participant observation.* New York: Holt, Rinehart and Winston.

Stoddart, K. (1986). The presentation of everyday life: Some textual strategies for "adequate ethnography." *Urban Life, 15,* 103–121.

Straw, W. (1990). Characterizing rock music culture: The case of heavy metal. In S. Frith & A. Goodwin (Eds.), *On record.* New York: Pantheon.

Turner, G. (1992). "It works for me": British cultural studies, Australian cultural studies and Australian film. In L. Grossberg, C. Nelson, & P. Treichler (Eds.), *Cultural studies.* London: Routledge.

Walser, R. (1990). Forging masculinity: Heavy-metal sounds and images of gender. In S. Frith & A. Goodwin (Eds.), *On record.* New York: Pantheon.

Walser, R. (1993). *Running with the devil: Power, gender, and madness in heavy metal music.* Hanover, MA: Wesleyan University Press.

Weinstein, D. (1991). *Heavy metal: A cultural sociology.* New York: Lexington.

West, C., & Fenstermaker, S. (1995). Doing difference. *Gender and Society, 9,* 8–37.

West, C., & Zimmerman, D. (1987). Doing gender. *Gender and Society, 1,* 125–151.

Williams, G. (1993). Every girl is a violgrrrl. *Search,* July, p. 3.

"You're Researching What?"
The Importance of Self in Ethnographic Research

Leigh Krenske
University of Queensland, Australia

The position of researcher in a theorized ethnography is a highly complex one. Ethnographers are responsible for participating in, narrating, and analyzing the interactions that occur within a particular social space, in a manner that is sensitive to the meanings created by the participants. Adding to this complexity is the researcher's embodied self, which affects all stages of the research process. While researching the heavy metal (HM) music subculture, my own personal biography and embodied self influenced the research process in a number of ways. To illustrate this, I will focus in the following discussion on how the presentation of my own self as a subcultural participant and researcher was negotiated during the various stages of the study. Ostensibly, this will highlight some of the challenges that were encountered during the research process, which included choosing a research question, gaining authenticity within the scene, and moving between data collection and data analysis.

Finding a Research Question

The overall choice of my research question was largely determined by my own personal biography and a particular opportunity that presented itself during the stages of project formulation. In quite fortuitous circumstances I was invited to watch a long-term friend perform as lead singer in a newly formed HM band. The desire to support my friend and an active interest in music motivated me to accept the invitation and "cross my name off the door." Although previous experiences of different subcultures and music played at live venues equipped me with a certain range of expectations, I was not fully prepared for what actually transpired. As the night progressed, an unfamiliar social space slowly began to emerge—and there in the middle of it all was my friend, charging the stage with a powerful presence and fierce energy. I was confronted completely by the woman under the spotlight, who was no longer the friend I normally recognized but an exotic persona transformed by the cultural inscription of HM codes. The crowd that stretched out before her also made an impression. The scene was dominated by men in black T-shirts, people with long hair, smoking and drinking beer. Movement and activity was prescribed and maintained. It seemed that everyone but me knew their place. The decision to go to the venue alone also emphasized my position as an "outsider," so that by the end of the night a series of questions played in my mind: Who are these people? Why did I feel uncomfortable? Where were all the women? And what happened to my friend?

The formulation of these types of questions did not occur in an intellectual vacuum. They were inspired by the events that occurred during that night and reflected a sociological background highly informed by feminist theory and a personal interest in subcultures. These questions formed the basis of my research agenda and inspired the decision to produce a theorized ethnography about the HM subculture.

Developing "Authenticity"

The nature of my research question meant that the choice of research methods used to collect data was relatively straightforward. Apart from the fact that the use of participant observation and in-depth interviews has a long tradition within the field of subcultural theory and research, participant observation is particularly appropriate when research involves the recognition of nonverbal behavior. Furthermore, the use of qualitative research methods meant adopting methodological procedures that record direct experience. This was an important consideration, since it gave voice to both male and female participants.

The effective use of qualitative methods for my research, however, required developing rapport with interview respondents and gaining a sense of authenticity within the scene. As mentioned in the article "Hard and Heavy," this was accomplished by immersing myself in the music and media associated with HM, which led to a familiarization with HM codes. An understanding of the codes resulted in the ability to ask pertinent questions during interviews and an appreciation of how to interact within the scene without drawing attention to myself. The personal adoption of Hardcore Bohemian dress codes also meant that my own inscribed corporeality was modified, which consequently affected my interactions at the club and the type of people I was able to contact. Ironically, however, the social dynamics within the scene meant that, as a woman, I was never going to develop a true sense of "authenticity." Indeed, much of the valuable time afforded to me by respondents (especially male) was probably more out of respect for my role as researcher than subcultural participant. The way in which authenticity is gained within the research site has important consequences for the type and quality of data collected and eventually analyzed.

Moving between Data Collection and Data Analysis

In order to provide some form of explanatory analysis, an ethnographer is responsible for moving beyond the everyday interpretative meanings held by the participants of their research site. This is usually achieved through the implementation of a theoretical framework and creates a different researcher-participant relationship. Occasionally, the different responsibilities associated with the various roles assumed during my research on the HM music subculture came into conflict. On the basis of Connell's theory for example, my research found that women exhibited behavior that reinforced patterns of emphasized femininity. As a feminist, however, it was difficult to concede that the structures of power evident within the subculture meant that women participated on terms defined by men and did not find escape or refuge. The acknowledgment of women's subordinate position was especially pertinent given that female participants were not especially concerned with this aspect of subcultural participation.

Another point of conflict occurred with the decision to use archetypes in the study. This was done in order to profile the codes of participation apparent at the research site. However, the emphasis placed on creating identities of difference by some of the participants within the subculture meant that they were adverse to categorization and labels. This essentially meant that the use of archetypes—which risks the accusation of reductionism and static representation—somewhat contradicted the values evident within the subculture. Despite the limitations of archetypal classification, it is hoped that readers of the article understand that participants' interaction with the codes of HM is multilayered and continuous. The use of archetypes was implemented purely because of their ability to provide valuable reference points for discussion and analysis.

At the End

The reflective comments outlined above illustrate some of the ways in which my own subjective self affected my research on the HM music subculture. My personal biography and embodied self played a significant role in the development of a research question, limited my interactions within the subculture, and moderated the conclusions drawn during data analysis. Without wanting to undermine the importance of research participants and respondents—without which there would be no research site—I believe that the explication of the researcher's self is an integral component in the research process. This gesture acknowledges that research is always accomplished through the subjective medium of the researcher and that all social research projects represent the creation of another cultural artifact. The detached, unobtrusive, and objective research strategies that sociologists had once advocated are not possible. For this reason, the identification of the researcher's self within research texts acts to improve validity by demonstrating how data collection and data analysis may have been affected by the researcher's subjective reality.

Narrative Analysis

Life narratives, or narrative analysis of lives, is a form of qualitative research growing in popularity. Narratives are first-person accounts of experiences that are in story format having a beginning, middle, and end. Other terms for these stories of experience are biography, life history, oral history, auto-ethnography, and autobiography. Although informed by a myriad of disciplines and theoretical perspectives, "most scholars . . . concur that all forms of narrative share the fundamental interest in making sense of experience, the interest in constructing and communicating meaning" (Chase, 1995, p. 1). The same story for example, could reveal how culture shapes understanding, how developmental change affects personal identity (Rossiter, 1999), how language structures the meaning of experience. But the recognition that stories are powerful tools for understanding is not limited to the world of research. Storytelling has found its way into therapy, education, and even the workplace. Durrance (1997, p. 26), for example, writes that "the story is our oldest, proven motivational tool, and it's now being used in corporations large and small to motivate and educate employees and to consolidate corporate culture. . . . A story . . . carries the shared culture, beliefs, and history of a group. Moreover, it is a means of experiencing our lives."

The story is a basic communicative and meaning-making device pervasive in human experience; it is no wonder that stories have moved center stage as a source of understanding of the human condition. First-person accounts of experience form the narrative "text" of this research approach. Whether the account is in the form of autobiography, life history, interview, journal, letters, or other materials that we collect "as we compose our lives" (Clandinin & Connelly, 1994, p. 420), the text is analyzed via the techniques of a particular discipline or perspective.

There are several methodological approaches to dealing with the narrative. Each approach examines, in some way, how the story is constructed, what linguistic tools are used, and the cultural context of the story. Biographical, psychological, and linguistic approaches are the most common. In Denzin's (1989) biographical approach, the story is analyzed in terms of the importance and influence of gender and race, family of origin, life events and turning point experiences, and other persons in the participant's life. The psychological approach concentrates more on the personal, including thoughts and motivations. This approach "emphasizes inductive processes, contextualized knowledge, and human intention. . . . [It] is holistic in that it acknowledges the cognitive, affective, and motivational dimensions of meaning making. It also takes into account the biological and environmental influences on development" (Rossiter, 1999, p. 78). For example, Gramling et al.'s (1996) story of Tess, a woman with AIDS, is from a psychological perspective. Tess's story reveals not only how she interpreted her life, the meaning she found, but how she managed to cope with her condition in today's health care system. A linguistic approach, or what Gee (1991, 1999) calls discourse analysis, focuses on the language of the story or the spoken text, and also attends to the speaker's intonation, pitch, and pauses. He offers eighteen questions by which one can build the analysis. Finally, Labov's (1982) linguistic approach analyzes the structure of the narrative. Here, one summarizes the substance of the narrative and identifies the events and their sequence of occurrence, the meaning of the actions, and the resolution, or what finally happens.

The growing popularity of narrative as a means of accessing human action and experience has been accompanied by discussions as to how to best tell people's stories, the role of the researcher in the process, and how trustworthy these narratives are in terms of validity and reliability. In a thoughtful discussion of these points, Mishler (1995, p. 117) reminds us that "we do not *find* stories; we *make* stories." In fact, "we retell our respondents' accounts through our analytic redescriptions. We, too, are storytellers and through our concepts and methods— our research strategies, data samples, transcription procedures, specifications of narrative units and structures, and interpretive perspectives—we construct the story and its meaning. In this sense *the* story is always coauthored, either directly in the process of an interviewer eliciting an account or indirectly through our representing and thus transforming others' texts and discourses" (pp. 117–118).

There are two narrative studies in this section. The fact that each reflects a different theoretical orientation underscores the variety of narrative analysis as a qualitative methodology. In the first selection, Bloom's research is framed by feminist postmodernism wherein the goal is "to expose both the workings of the master script in women's narratives and women's subversions of it" and understand better the notion of a nonunitary self. She recounts Olivia's story of confronting sexism in the workplace, a story that has two versions, suggesting that the self is indeed not a single, unified, construction but a "being in process."

The second selection is Johnson-Bailey's story of Cathy, a Black woman who returned to college as an adult. Writing from a Black feminist perspective, Johnson-Bailey constructs Cathy's story to reveal how the intersection of race, class, and gender defined her experiences as a reentry nursing student. Johnson-Bailey's reflection on this research examines the issues related to reconstructing and interpreting these women's stories.

References

Chase, S. E. (1995). Taking narrative seriously: Consequences for method and theory in interview studies. In R. Josselson & A. Lieblich (Eds.), *Interpreting experience: The narrative study of lives* (pp. 1–26). Thousand Oaks, CA: Sage.

Clandinin, D. J., & Connelly, F. M. (1994). Personal experience methods. In N. K. Denzin & Y. S. Lincoln (Eds.), *Handbook of qualitative research* (pp. 413–427). Thousand Oaks, CA: Sage.

Denzin, N. K. (1989). *Interpretive biography.* Newbury Park, CA: Sage.

Durrance, B. (1997, February). Stories at work. *Training & Development,* pp. 25–29.

Gee, J. P. (1991). A linguistic approach to narrative. *Journal of Narrative and Life History, 1*(1), 15–39.

Gee, J. P. (1999). *An introduction to discourse analysis: Theory and method.* London: Routledge.

Gramling, L., Boyle, J. S., McCain, N., Ferrell, J., Hodnicki, D., & Muller, R. (1996). Reconstructing a woman's experiences with AIDS. *Family Community Health, 19*(3), 49–56.

Labov, W. (1982). Speech actions and reactions in personal narrative. In D. Tannen (Ed.), *Analyzing discourse: Text and talk* (pp. 354–396). Washington, DC: Georgetown University Press.

Mishler, E. G. (1995). Models of narrative analysis: A typology. *Journal of Narrative and Life History, 5*(2), 87–123.

Rossiter, M. (1999). Understanding adult development as narrative. In M. C. Clark & R. S. Caffarella (Eds.), *An update on adult development theory: New ways of thinking about the life course.* New Directions for Adult and Continuing Education, no. 84, San Francisco: Jossey-Bass.

13

Stories of One's Own

Nonunitary Subjectivity in Narrative Representation

Leslie Rebecca Bloom

In her delightfully thought-provoking article, "The Laugh of the Medusa," Hélène Cixous (1975/1976) proclaims that because women's biological differences from men render them invisible by logocentric systems of patriarchy, they must explode male discourse by speaking and writing in a language of their own. In this article, I want to suggest that one way that feminist qualitative researchers take up this language of their own is in their rejection of the humanist understanding of subjectivity as unchangeable, or unitary, in favor of an interpretation of subjectivity as always in the process of being produced, or nonunitary (Ferguson, 1993; Flax, 1993; Henriques, Hollway, Urwin, Venn, & Walkerdine, 1984; S. Smith, 1993). What I hope to illustrate is the way that narrative interpretations of subjectivity as nonunitary generate alternative understandings of the self.

Subjectivity has and continues to be a much discussed concept in qualitative methodology (Barone, 1992; Eisner, 1992; Guba, 1990; Jansen & Peshkin, 1992; Phillips, 1990; Roman & Apple, 1990). These discussions typically focus on the subjectivity of the researcher in the conduct of research. Further, despite considerable rethinking of the role of subjectivity over the last thirty years, these discussions still assume a subjectivity that is unitary. Because these discussions have shaped my understanding of subjectivity and are the historical and theoretical groundings from which my qualitative research practices both emerge and depart, I would like to take a few minutes to review, albeit superficially, the historical discourses surrounding the use of the term *subjectivity* in qualitative methodology.

As Denzin and Lincoln (1994) explain, in both what they called the "traditional period" and "modernist phase" of qualitative research, there was an attempt to emulate scientific inquiry. Consequently, subjectivity was relentlessly positioned in opposition to objectivity, narrowly defined as personal interests and values, and considered a nemesis of scientific validity. According to John K. Smith (1993), under this legacy of empiricism, "to criticize people for being subjective is to criticize them for the failure to maintain a proper detachment from their own particular emotions, values, and/or personal preferences" (p. 30). Thus the regulative ideal of good qualitative research behavior was the repression, or the appearance of repression, of subjectivity.

From about 1970 to 1986, in a period called *blurred genres,* qualitative researchers attempted to distance themselves from these scientific norms and to connect more with the humanities and humanistic conceptions of subjectivity (Denzin & Lincoln, 1994; Geertz, 1983). Subjectivity then attained a more nuanced definition as "the conscious and unconscious thoughts and emotions of the individual, her sense of herself and her ways of understanding her relation to the world" (Weedon, 1987, p. 32). Therefore, rather than trying to exorcise subjectivity from their hearts, minds, and texts, qualitative researchers instead attempted to analyze their subjectivities as interesting, inescapable components of an inquiry process. However, empiricism's grip being what it is, we also find in this genre attempts to systematically account for, manage, and even tame subjectivity (Peshkin, 1988). Both Schwandt (1994) and Heshusius (1994) rightly criticize this systematizing impulse as a failure to reject the opposition of subjectivity and objectivity, resulting in an objectification of the subjective experience and the continued pretense of distancing the knower from the known.

In what Denzin and Lincoln (1994) termed the "fourth moment" of qualitative research, which is generally characterized as the crisis of representation, subjectivity is inextricably linked with self-reflexivity and positionality. To be self-reflexive is equated with "coming clean" as a researcher about how race, class, gender, religion, and personal/social values influence the researcher's understanding of the power dynamics of the research setting, the phenomena under study, and the researcher-respondent relationship. Although self-reflexivity may well go beyond the systematic accounting and taming of subjectivity, as Marcus (1994) observes, "this kind of reflexive location of oneself, while potentially a practice of key importance, all too often becomes a gesture that is enforced by politically correct convention" (p. 572).

Perhaps more similar than they are different, both systematically accounting for subjectivity and reflexively locating oneself may result in the use of subjectivity in static, reductive, and self-justifying ways, rather than as complex problems that increase our curiosity about the ways that identity and subjectivity are actively produced both in the lives of researchers and respondents and in the field as part of the research process. These conceptions of subjectivity are, additionally, dissatisfying to me because of their tendency to focus almost exclusively on the researcher and her or his subjectivity. Although I heartily believe in the importance of self-reflexivity for a researcher and applaud those whose critiques take us beyond the limitations of researcher subjectivity and self-reflexivity as described above (Heshusius, 1994; Probyn, 1993; Roman, 1993; Visweswaran, 1994), in this article I want to suggest first that we are in need of a more complex understanding of the concept of subjectivity and, second, that we must have a more active engagement with analyzing subjectivity in our interpretive work.

Feminism and Subjectivity

Considering these questions of subjectivity, feminist postmodern theorists challenge the humanist assumption of a unitary subjectivity in which people are thought to have "an essence at the heart of the individual which is unique, fixed and coherent and which makes her what she *is*" (Weedon, 1987, p. 32). Such claims for the existence of a unique, fixed, and coherent self in humanist ideology deny the possibilities of changes in subjectivity over time; mask the critical roles that language, social interactions, and pivotal experiences play in the production and transformation of subjectivity; and ignore gender as a social position that influences the formation of subjectivity.

In contrast, feminist postmodern theory maintains that subjectivity is always active and in the process of production, or nonunitary. It is "an ongoing process of engagement in social and discursive practices. . .a continuous process of production and transformation [and]. . .a 'doing' rather than a being" (Robinson, 1991, p. 11). Subjectivity—particularly women's subjectivity—is also thought to be continually fragmenting from daily experiences living with the pervasive hierarchical, patriarchal structuring of sexual difference through which women learn to internalize negative and conflicted ideas about what it means to live as a woman.

Traditional humanist and masculinist notions about human identity would lead us to believe that fragmentation and change in subjectivity mean that a person is unstable or weak, lacking a necessary unified self. Rejecting this notion of the unified self, some postmodern feminists (Bloom & Munro, 1995; Braidotti, 1991; Davies, 1992; Hollway, 1989; Jacobs, Munro, & Adams, 1995; Richardson, 1994; Walkerdine, 1990) argue that an understanding of subjectivity as nonunitary and fragmented is a move toward a more positive acceptance of the complexities of human identity—especially female identity. To accept that subjectivity is fragmented, however, is not to "promote endless fragmentation and a reified multiplicity," for as Sidonie Smith (1993, p. 156) argues, this would be counterproductive to the narrative project. Smith's caution is well noted, for claiming nonunitary subjectivity and its fragmentation should not signify a loss of self but rather an alternative view of the self located historically in language, produced in everyday gendered and cultural experiences, and expressed in writing and speaking. It is for these reasons that exploring nonunitary subjectivity in women's lives is critical to feminist research and epistemology.

Therefore, in this article, my concern is not with taming my subjectivity, accounting for it, or reflexively contemplating it; rather, I am concerned both with understanding how nonunitary subjectivity is produced and how we can interpret it in narrative self-representations.[1] Toward these ends, I analyze two versions of a story told to me by Olivia, a respondent in my study of feminist methodology and women's personal narratives. Through close interpretations of these two versions, I demonstrate how subjectivity is manifested in her narratives and how her narrative self-representation as nonunitary in her second version subverts humanist and patriarchal modes of discourse. I also illustrate how narrative research that focuses on nonunitary subjectivity creates a context in which respondents are not bound by unitary self-representations and, therefore, have the opportunity for greater self-knowledge from the experience of being a respondent.

Personal Narratives

"The story is not all mine nor told by me alone. Indeed, I am not sure whose story it is; you can judge better. But it is all one, and if at moments the facts seem to alter with an altered voice, why then you can choose the fact you like best; yet none of them is false, and it is all one story" (Le Guin, 1985, p. 317).

When I met Olivia in 1991, she was a second-year assistant professor. A White woman who grew up in a midwestern working-class family, Olivia had previously been a middle and high school English teacher. After completing a Ph.D. in organizational management, she became a director of curriculum in a school corporation. Olivia's story, as told here, however, begins in 1988 when she was in her early thirties and working in a high-level management position at a Fortune 500 company in a large city after leaving her position as director of curriculum.

When we met, I was a graduate student beginning my dissertation. My goals for the dissertation were to implement and critique feminist methodology by conducting a life-history study of feminist teachers; I also wanted to critique various theories of narrative interpretation within the framework of analyzing the life-history narratives of these teachers (Bloom, 1993). When I met Olivia, we discovered that we shared commitments to feminist pedagogy and interests in qualitative methodology. She then expressed an interest in becoming a respondent in my study. My fieldwork with Olivia took place over an eighteen-month period during which time I conducted life-history interviews, observed her teaching, and, through discussions with her, generated interpretations of her narratives and critiques of the process of doing feminist methodology. On a chilly fall day in October of 1991 during one of our early life-history interviews, Olivia told me about an incident that happened during her last year in the corporation.

> Not too much earlier, I had just gotten rid of one of the biggest sexual perverts who was involved in all kinds of sexual harassment at the organization. He was a senior executive. And I went after him. And I got him fired. And it was very empowering. Just having experiences like that where I was a force to be reckoned with in the city and people knew me. It felt so good to be able to change

the image of women in management, you know? To open doors for other women. I hired three other women in management, and it felt good to be there to present a different point of view than what those men would have heard had I not been there. And I felt empowered because of that.

In accord with Harding's (1987) assertion that one of the most important contributions of feminist methodology is that it answers questions women have about their own lives, I gave Olivia copies of the transcripts of her personal narratives so that she could suggest further avenues for us to explore or return to in our interviews. Reading the above story in the transcripts several months after she narrated it, Olivia wondered why she had so many omissions and places where she felt that she had attempted to represent herself as, in her words, "a feminist icon." This realization was disturbing for her: "I had recalled the good part of several stories and failed to mention the less satisfying sides of these stories. In part this made me feel dishonest. I thought hard about that. I did not remember editing these stories in the telling, and I wondered why these stories emerged and not the less satisfying ones."

A few months after Olivia shared this impression of her transcripts with me, we agreed that it would be helpful for her to retell the above story, this time filling in the omissions. Olivia decided that she would prefer having the time to write in private about her experiences, rather than narrate a second version of the story to me. This process of writing, filling in the omissions, and allowing the "less satisfying" events to surface was painful for Olivia; it overwhelmed her with the memories of events that she had "failed to mention" when she narrated the story. The following is her written second version of the story.[2]

> My original story does not reflect how very wearing and disappointing the entire process had been. . . .This man on several occasions, put poor, single women who worked for him in the position of having to refuse his sexual advances in his office. . . .If they did not fight his advances, they remained at the main facility working for him; however, if they failed to respond to his advances they were soon transferred to a. . .remote facility and not granted overtime or promotions critical to many of these women who were single parents. For four days I listened to the stories these women had to tell. I comforted them through the tears and pain that these memories evoked. Why had this happened to them, they asked me? In our conversations they fought both paralyzing fears of losing their jobs, and personal humiliation and embarrassment for making the choices they made to keep them. Their stories drew me in. . . .What could they do? They felt powerless.
>
> Through pained expression, one woman asked me why we, management, had waited so long to do something. Didn't we know what was happening?. . . I felt ashamed and angered. I felt ashamed because I hadn't acted on my earlier discomfort with this man's treatment of women, and I felt angered because I allowed male colleagues to dissuade me from my concerns about his behavior. "That's just Joe," they would say, "he's harmless." But I knew better. I didn't know just how serious this situation had become, but I did know that his behaviors were unacceptable. It took an anonymous letter from a despondent Black woman detailing the racism, sexism, and sexual harassment that she had experienced. . .to wake me and others up to the seriousness of the situation.

> At the conclusion of the investigation, I wrote the report and in a meeting with the executive management team, I insisted that the man be dismissed. . . . I was assured by the CEO and the VP that this would happen. I learned later, however, that the VP [who was supposed to fire him]. . .asked Smith to turn in his resignation and gave him a consulting contract with an affiliate company. I was stunned. When I confronted the VP. . .he dismissed the entire investigation and stated matter of factly, "these are the things that happen when men and women work together." I was furious.
>
> To this day I am not comfortable knowing that Joe Smith moved on to another company. . .but there are also times when my thoughts are warmed by memories of those women thanking me for "getting rid of Joe Smith." They knew only that Joe Smith was gone. And that was good enough for them.

Olivia's question about why some stories emerge and why less satisfying ones do not get told is also a complex and persistent question for qualitative inquirers. We may respond by acknowledging that a respondent tells certain stories and not others because of the focus of the research and the intersubjective dynamics of a specific research relationship. Further, we may respond that, because respondents are often invested in representing themselves in particular ways, they will tell some stories rather than others and will tell these stories in particular ways. Although I think these responses illuminate critical aspects of fieldwork and storytelling, they do not encourage us to interrogate narrative representations and to examine how nonunitary subjectivity in the respondent's life produces and shapes her narratives.

A focus on interpreting nonunitary subjectivity, however, highlights the need for us to question the unitary self-representation of the first version and to interrogate how this unitary subjectivity was/is produced. My interpretations of Olivia's stories take us into the worlds of feminist literary theory, Sartre's (1960/1963) methods of interpreting biography, and Ellsworth and Miller's (in press) concept of "working difference," each of which will be discussed later in this article.[3]

Unitary Subjectivity and the Narrative Genre: Narrating and Interpreting the Feminist Icon

In the first version of the story, Olivia positions[4] herself, as she says, as a feminist icon. Because this is her primary mode of self-representation in that account, we can only read in it the voice of a unitary or coherent subjectivity. Such positioning creates a paradox that further limits Olivia's ability to represent herself: she wants to narrate a feminist tale in which she is the empowered feminist; however, by positioning herself in this way, she falls prey to reproducing masculinist and humanist ideologies. Moi (1985) explains that these ideologies rest on the implicit assumption of the "seamlessly unified self" that is part of the "phallic logic" that likes to see itself as "gloriously autonomous. . .banish[ing] from itself all conflict, contradiction and ambiguity" (p. 8). This mode of self-representation is a trap that de Lauretis (1987) warns women to avoid when they use the narrative genre as a means of self-expression. De Lauretis explains that when women create narratives, they often unconsciously reproduce patriarchal ideologies because these ideologies work like master scripts or master narratives on the individual subject, regardless of sex.[5] De Lauretis's fear is that women's use of the narrative genre may therefore reproduce structures of domination rather than liberate women from cultural silence.

S. Smith (1987) is also suspicious of narrative genres and the workings of master narratives on women. Taking up an argument similar to that of de Lauretis (1987), she contends that women's relationships to autobiographical narratives have always been troublesome because the genre is constructed according to ideologies of male selfhood that usually posit women as the incomplete man or the essentialized other.[6] Smith's misgiving about autobiographical narratives is based in part on the belief that "since traditional autobiography has functioned as one of those forms and languages that sustain sexual difference, the woman who writes autobiography is doubly estranged when she enters the autobiographical contract" (1987, p. 49). Therefore, although autobiographical narratives signal a woman's choice "to leave behind cultural silence" for the public arena, "she can speak with authority only insofar as she tells a story that her audience will read. Responding to the generic expectations of significance in life stories, she looks towards a narrative that will resonate with privileged cultural fictions of male selfhood" (S. Smith, 1987, p. 52).

Whereas a feminist action such as the one described by Olivia is certainly not a cultural fiction of male selfhood, the unitary representation of the self-as-hero is. For that reason, we may be able to read Olivia's first story as a retelling of the classical tale of the hero's conquering journey (Campbell, 1949), a master narrative of male success. She describes the hero (herself) who leaves the world (of female prescriptive roles) for the underworld (male-dominated corporate America) where she encounters evil (the sexual harassment of women) and an evil doer (the sexual pervert), and she slays the powerful evil doer (gets the senior executive fired) and emerges victorious (she is a force to be reckoned with in the city), bringing with her gifts to society (managerial jobs for women).

How then can women speak autobiographically while resisting these modes of narrative that promote a coherent representation of the self? DuPlessis (1985) suggests that if women want to subvert and rewrite master narratives rather than reproduce them, they need to change the conventional patterns of narrative closure by "writing beyond the ending" (p. 4). Narratives that write beyond the ending refuse "happily ever after" endings and, most important, reject the tradition of masking the conflicts women face living under patriarchy. In fact, DuPlessis advises that women make the conflicts that emerge from their marginalized status and their rebellions against marginalization central to their stories. The narrative thus becomes a site where "subtexts and repressed discourses can throw up one last flare of meaning" (DuPlessis, 1985, p. 3).

Along similar lines, Heilbrun (1988) and Christian (1985) suggest that in writing or telling their lives, women often describe their feelings, experiences, hopes, and identities in ways that live up to conventional patriarchal notions of being female made available to them by master narratives, as in the femme fatales and ideal mothers or matrons. Influenced both by racism and sexism, African American women writers may further limit the narrative-subjective roles of women to downtrodden victims (Christian, 1985; Collins, 1991). Therefore, as Heilbrun argues, for women's subjectivities to be fully narrativized, they must speak of the vast range of experiences and emotions they have and reject regulating patriarchal definitions of being female.

Seen through the lens of these feminist critiques, Olivia's first version of the story leaves the master narrative intact: despite its female heroine and feminist theme, she reproduces the masculine self of myth and autobiography in which unitary subjectivity, heroic action, and autonomy are foundational. Olivia does not make her internal conflicts central, as DuPlessis (1985) argues is necessary in feminist narratives, and she does not represent a full range of emotions and identities that Heilbrun (1988) and Christian (1985) propose is necessary for women's subjectivities to be written more fully into narratives.

This analysis would seem to suggest that the unitary representation of subjectivity in this first version emerged from Olivia's need to create a coherent self in which she was acting in the narrative as the feminist heroine. The analysis also demonstrates the point raised earlier that the traditional narrative genre facilitates this effort to reduce the complexities of subjectivity. The question that remains unanswered, however, is why this unitary self-representation was desirable to Olivia—a question that leads us to explore earlier life experiences to understand how fragmented subjectivity may have already created a need for Olivia to frame her self-representation in this unitary way at that particular time.

Progressive/Regressive Reading of a Life

In his autobiographical project, Sartre (1960/1963) asserts that "man [sic] is characterized above all by his going beyond a situation, and by what he succeeds in making of what he has been made" (p. 91). In other words, Sartre believes that individuals can go beyond given situations and act against the limitations or prohibitions that are hegemonically and objectively constructed but that are subjectively felt. This belief is the grounding for his progressive-regressive method, an analytic tool that Sartre claims can be used to make sense of a person's life (see also Barry, 1990; Denzin, 1989; Jackson, 1989; Pinar, 1974).

Sartre (1960/1963) explains that an individual life "develops in spirals; it passes again and again by the same points but at different levels of integration and complexity" (p. 106). The progressive-regressive method is used to analyze the pivotal points or experiences on an individual's life spiral by considering them in light of an analysis of previous related experiences. In the progressive or forward movement, the interpretation emphasizes the individual's experiences as a journey of becoming. The regressive or backward movement is a reflection "that takes one back among the objects, people, places, and events" of earlier times (Jackson, 1989, p. 162). Thus, by examining the same points of intersection in the life spiral, it is possible to locate examples of how the individual challenges, resists, learns from, or even surpasses her or his conditioning, thereby manifesting what Sartre calls *positive praxis.*

Sartre's method is a powerful heuristic for not only locating positive praxis but also for locating places on a life's spiral where subjectivity fragments due to personal conflicts.[7] What follows, therefore, is an interpretation of two earlier points of conflict that Olivia narrated; I examine them using the feminist icon story as the present point on her life spiral and read backward, reflectively, from that present point, gaining insight from that backward reading.[8]

The Early Battle Against Sexism

Olivia narrated a memory of an event that occurred when she was eleven or twelve years old—in about 1966.[9] Olivia recalled an evening when she rebelled against always having to do the dishes after dinner when her brother was free to go outside and play. She told her father that her brother should help with the dishes, explaining that it was unfair that she always had to do indoor chores when he got to his chores outside, which she would prefer. To this, her father responded: "'You just get over there and do the dishes,' or something to that effect." Obeying him, Olivia watched her brother riding his bike outside: "He was riding around—I was drying dishes at the door—and every time he'd go by he'd stick his tongue out at me: 'See! See!' I remember I was drying this knife and when he went past I just sliced open the screen. And my reaction was 'Oh, I don't believe I did that!'"

In the backward reading of a life, Sartre (1960/1963) suggests that we can see patterns emerge in a spiral that lead to the present. Therefore, it is possible to interpret this story as both a moment in which Olivia first rebelled against gendered prohibitions and a moment of conflict in which her subjectivity was fragmented. Outraged by the limitation placed on her by her father and by the taunting of her brother, Olivia's actions—her verbal challenge to her father and her slashing of the screen—can be characterized as attempts to overcome the limitations placed on her both as an individual and as a female. This characterization is particularly salient if we read her actions in light of Sartre's point that prohibitions are always felt individually and subjectively but become objective or influential in changing the life's status quo when the individual participates in a positive praxis to overcome these prohibitions. I believe that Sartre's example and analysis of such praxis is worth considering here because it demonstrates how an oppressed individual's actions against prohibitions contribute to moving both history and the individual to new patterns:

> A member of the ground crew at an air base on the outskirts of London took a plane and, with no experience as a pilot, flew it across the Channel. He is colored [sic]; he is prevented from becoming a member of the flying personnel. This prohibition becomes for him a *subjective* impoverishment, but he immediately goes beyond the subjective to the objective. This denied future reflects to him the fate of his "race" and the racism of the English. The *general* revolt on the part of colored men against colonialists is expressed *in him* by his particular

refusal of this prohibition. He affirms that a future *possible for Whites* is *possible for everyone.* This political position, of which he doubtless has no clear awareness, he lives as a personal obsession [italics in original]. (Sartre, 1960/1963, pp. 95–96)

If we consider Sartre's (1960/1963) emphasis on the internalized subjective that becomes objective even when the individual has no clear awareness of what he or she is doing, it is possible to go beyond the tempting but limited reading of Olivia's screen slashing as an act of symbolic castration or tongue cutting to a more enabling feminist reading, one that recognizes that her individual acts of rebellion (verbally challenging her father and slashing the screen) held the seeds for her later individual rebellions toward a different and better future for herself and for women more generally. It also offers a way of reading her screen slashing not only as a physical response of her anger but as a symbolic manifestation of her will to be independent of such prohibitions. This point becomes even more apparent if we retell Olivia's story using the framework of Sartre's description of the Afro French man:

An adolescent daughter in a working class family in a small midwestern town took a knife and, with no experience as a feminist activist, slashed a screen in anger at the male members of her family. She is female; she is prevented from becoming a member of the male order or community. This prohibition becomes for her a subjective impoverishment, but she immediately goes beyond the subjective to the objective. This denied future reflects to her the fate ascribed to her by gender and the sexism of the society. The general revolt on the part of women against males is expressed in her by her particular refusal of this prohibition. She affirms that a future possible for men is possible for everyone. This political position, of which she doubtless has no clear awareness, she lives as a personal obsession.

Recasting Olivia's childhood story following Sartre (1960/1963) demonstrates that individual actions do provide insight into the larger contexts of material realities that govern people's lives. Olivia's actions also illustrate that an individual has the ability to resist and rebel against prohibiting material conditions. The finesse with which one enacts rebellions, of course, increases with experience.

In the screen-slashing story, then, may be seen the grounds for Olivia's first version of the sexual harassment story—her desire to work against the limitations placed on girls and women by patriarchal society, especially limitations pertaining to work (girls do dishes and vacuum; boys do outside chores) and to their relations with men (a girl puts up with her brother's teasing; women put up with a boss's sexual harassment). Further, and most important, in this story we can recognize the profound conflict she faced knowing that whereas such prohibitions were wrong, challenging the authority of her father was considered more wrong, and in her particular situation, even dangerous.[10] It is in such conflicts that subjectivity fragments and becomes recreated.

Given this early beginning of rebellion and the resulting fragmentation of subjectivity, when we return to the present reading of the feminist icon story, we can understand that Olivia had a great deal invested in representing herself coherently as a feminist. Further, the first version may reveal Olivia's ongoing desire to assert her own voice (empowerment) to dispel the voice of her father (patriarchal authority) in her life.

Owning One's Own Life

The second excerpt in which conflict was central that I want to examine as part of the backward reading of Olivia's life is a journal reflection on her experiences of leaving her corporate job and moving to the university community with her husband, Marc. A university professor, Marc was offered a new position some distance from Olivia's office. Deciding that they did not want a commuting marriage and that Olivia, although conflicted about it, would enjoy returning to academia, they negotiated for a teaching position for her, as well. Although her position was not initially tenure-track, the department that hired Olivia was enthusiastic about her educational background and work experiences, and the department chairperson told her that she would be a prime candidate for the next tenure-track position that came open in the department. However, coming in as she did such that it was Marc who was courted was a difficult transition for Olivia, and in her first year in the university community, she felt lonely and missed her corporate life in the city. The following is an edited excerpt from her journal, written in January 1990, about six months after she and Marc began their lives at the university.

> About The City, an opportunity, and Being a Shadow—Since our move here, I have felt so very out of place. . . .I long to escape to the familiarity of the city. . . and the sense of owning one's own life. I have always owned my own life. Why do I feel that I do not own my own life here? Why do I feel that I am a shadow and not a person? A shadow of a woman I used to be. A shadow that people cannot see.
> "Are you going to [the conference]?" Will asked Marc as we sipped wine on a lazy Friday afternoon. "We both are," Marc said, attempting to include me in the event. But Will could not see me. Will could not see shadows. He could only see Marc. Marc is a person.

In this journal entry, we glimpse the results of Olivia's transition to a world where she felt that she was defined more by her marriage than by who she was as a separate, professional person. As she later told me, she felt that the person she was in the city was "so incredibly different" from who she was in the academic community because "it was like I had joined his world and I had no world of my own." For any woman who values a room or world of her own, experiencing its loss is painful. As Olivia expresses it, she lost not only a valued world but her own self, as well. I believe that it is in such statements, in which respondents themselves remark on the profound effects of change on their senses of self, that we can most readily discern the fragmenting of subjectivity and call into question the validity of the seamless, coherent self.

Olivia's journal excerpt is important because it illustrates the effects that difficult decisions had on her subjectivity and the way that she represents herself as a result of her fragmenting subjectivity. What it tells us about subjectivity is that even as women become more able to make choices in conflicted situations, there are still constraints on the way that we make decisions about our lives, constraints that further fragment subjectivity. This problem is made clear when Olivia admits that upon reflection about the decision to move, she realized that "somehow it was more important that I wouldn't do something that *he* would regret rather than if I made a decision and *I* would regret it."

That Olivia narrated the feminist icon version while she was feeling intense sadness and alienation suggests that it is during these times of subjectivity's fragmentation that we may have the largest investment in representing ourselves cohesively. Olivia's later analysis was that telling the feminist icon story was "less messy" because of what it left out and was also easier, because at that time the memory of her delay in intervening (described in the second version) was "intolerable" for her to think about.

Nonunitary Subjectivity and Subverting the Narrative Genre: Narrating-Interpreting the Complex Self

Considering that Olivia told the first version of the story before we had gotten to know each other very well, it is more than understandable that she would not have wanted to share what was "intolerable" or "messy" with me. Yet in the second version, shared many months later, we see a strikingly different self-representation.

Let me begin by reading the second version through the lens of feminist narratology. Most apparent to me is that Olivia no longer represents herself as having a unitary and nonconflicted subjectivity; she is more fully narrativized because she represents an array of emotions and diverse depictions of her interactions with others. She no longer uses such phrases as, "I was a force," "it was empowering," and "it felt good to be there." Instead, she uses such words as "wearing," "disappointing," "ashamed," "angered," "stunned," and "furious." Olivia also explains that she was drawn in by women's stories, gave comfort to women, and received comfort back from them by their thanks, thus allowing us to know her as a caring person. No longer invested in representing herself as a feminist icon, her wider range of emotional representation and conflicted presence narrativize Olivia as a more complex person.

The second version also has a larger cast of characters. Olivia did not, as the first version implies, single-handedly get the man fired. It was a team effort, and in the retelling, she acknowledges that it was both the women who painfully told their stories, risking their jobs to do so, and the men on her management team who all contributed to the case finally being made against Joe. This is a critical component of the retelling, for it shifts the image of Olivia as a solitary feminist icon to an image of a woman who is fully engaged in a community, thus reminding us that subjectivity is produced in the process of interactions with others.

Having allowed herself a more full self-representation, Olivia is also able to make her internal conflicts central to the narrated story. The major conflict that emerges concerns her decision to comply with management and her male colleagues to not take action against Joe when the sexual harassments were first reported. This conflict illustrates the difficult position Olivia was in as she attempted to balance her alliance with patriarchal management with her alliance with the other women. In both alliances, Olivia was positioned as insider and outsider: in management but not one of the guys; a woman but not one of the women whose jobs were so vulnerable. Olivia later explained further that dealing with the men meant that she had to call upon especially tactful means of expression to keep them on her side so that she could remain an ally to the women. These conflicted subject positions must have made her decision about how to handle the situation extremely painful. I therefore want to examine them closely as conflicted points on her life spiral to further understand how nonunitary subjectivity is produced and represented.

Ellsworth and Miller (in press) suggest that one way to make sense of subjectivity is to examine what they call the "strategic fixing and unfixing of subject positions" or working difference based on "situated responsiveness." *Situated responsiveness* refers to the idea that responses to particular situations are never generic but are specific to the complexities of the situation. It also suggests that individuals may call upon different strategies to respond to given situations (Hollway, 1989). *Working difference* refers to "the possibility of engaging with and responding to the fluidity and malleability of identities and difference, of refusing fixed and static categories of sameness or permanent otherness" (Ellsworth and Miller, in press; see also Probyn, 1993). Through actively working difference, an individual engages in strategic fixing and unfixing of subject positions in which, given a particular situation such as the management decision that Olivia was called upon to make, a person has available multiple ways to respond to that situation. Because there is no one definitive way to respond to a situation, people may avoid responding or feel doubt and alienation about their decisions. As Anzaldua (1987) maintains, the alienation that women feel in this patriarchal culture makes it difficult for women—especially women of color—to respond: "The ability to respond is what is meant by responsibility, yet our cultures take away our ability to act. . . . We do not engage fully. We do not make full use of our faculties. We abnegate. And there in front of us is the crossroads and choice: to feel a victim where someone else is in control and therefore responsible and to blame. . .or to feel strong, and, for the most part, in control" (p. 20).

Women's multiple subject positions in the world do make it difficult to respond, but the complexities of situations also compel us to speak from between the boundaries of these subject positions. Speaking from the boundaries means that the defining lines between subject positions often become blurred and ambiguous. Again, whereas humanist conceptions of the self would imply that the blurring of subject positions diminishes the coherence of an individual, the feminist-postmodernist conception of nonunitary subjectivity interprets the boundary speaking as both a positive aspect of human identity and a positive praxis. When these "uppity voices of informants" do speak from the boundaries, they resound with a powerful challenge to humanist discourses of self and other (Fine, 1994, p. 78).

With the concepts of fixing and unfixing and situated responsiveness in mind, I want to examine several configurations of Olivia's subject positions in the second version to understand her responses to the dilemma and the implications that these subject positions had for her subjectivity at that time. The interrelated subject positions that I identify include her place in management, her role as a woman, her social status, and her racial identity as White.

As stated above, we see that Olivia was variously positioned in the second version of the story. First, she strategically fixed her position in management by using the pronoun *we* when referring to management. However, this position became unfixed when she described the male colleagues who dissuaded her from being concerned about Joe's behavior. Her position was unfixed because it was no longer the inclusive *we* but *they* and *she*. With this unfixing, she simultaneously became fixed in the margins of management, a place where, as a woman, she may have been all along, according to some of her male colleagues. Therefore, when she said that she "did not know just how serious this situation had become," her voice emanated from her subject position in management, a position that may have made these women less visible to her initially, but when she added that she "did know that his behaviors were unacceptable," she was speaking from her marginalized subject position as a woman who acknowledged the experiences of these women. Thus, in this sentence ("I didn't know just how serious this situation had become but I did know that his behaviors were unacceptable"), we hear her conflicted and alienated voice from between the boundaries of multiple subject positions.

Olivia's subject position as a woman is further fixed and unfixed in relation to the unequal power she had compared with the other women whom she described in her story. At the risk of being repetitious, I need to start again from her strategic fixing of herself as a woman in management. This fixing is more overtly represented in the first version wherein she says that it "felt good to change the image of women in management, you know?" In the second version, rather than fixing her position as a feminist-managerial woman, she fixed herself more as a woman in the feminine role of the listener and comforter. It was Olivia (not her male colleagues) who "listened to the stories these women had to tell." It was she who "comforted them through the tears and pain that these memories evoked." It was she who had to answer their questions of "why this had happened to them." Although the image of Olivia responding to these women helped fix the image of her as also a woman, it simultaneously unfixed the stable representation of her as a woman because she did not share their gendered experiences of harassment. She was not one of them; she was management—and according to Olivia, that is how they saw her, which was painful to her. Unlike them, she had not had to "[fight] both paralyzing fears of losing [her] job. . .and personal humiliation and embarrassment for making the choices [she] made to keep [it]." It was not Olivia who felt powerless: they felt powerless. In relation to some of the men on her management team, she was marginalized and somewhat less empowered; but more critically, in relation to the women whose stories she heard, her management job placed her in a position of power that made her marginalized from them, as well. In the borderland, Olivia's relationship to these women was both precarious and ambiguous.

Another aspect of Olivia's subject position involves her unequal social class status in relation to the women whose stories she heard. She described them as poor, single women for whom overtime or promotions were critical because many of these women were single parents. For many people like Olivia who grew up in working-class families, the American dream of upward mobility was central; for women, it was often a dream deferred or dropped as they took their places in marriages and families. If Olivia had not gone beyond the material conditions of her childhood and attained a Ph.D., she may well have been one of the women who was afraid to lose her job and who was therefore vulnerable to a man like Joe. Indeed, Olivia, in a journal entry in which she compared her life experiences with those of her secretary, who continually experienced tragedies, Olivia acknowledged that she felt overprivileged.

Finally, White racial identity also plays a role in the strategic fixing and unfixing of Olivia's subject position in the second version as evidenced in the statement that "it took an anonymous letter from a despondent Black woman detailing the racism, sexism, and sexual harassment that she had experienced" to wake Olivia and others up to the seriousness of the situation. As Morrison (1992) maintains, the presence of an African American population today, like the slave population it is descended from, allows the White population to reflect on its own (privileged) position in the world by offering itself as that which White is not: powerless, enslaved, and poor. Through these distinctions between Black/White, enslaved/free, wealthy/poor, and so forth, Whites can know/produce who they are. In other words, it is in the context of the opposite other that Whiteness is constructed (see also Frankenberg, 1993; Feagin & Vera, 1995).

In light of Morrison's (1992) argument, how might the letter from a despondent Black woman have contributed to fixing and unfixing Olivia's subject position? One explanation might be that the letter from the Black woman fixed Olivia's subject position as White, reminding her of the privilege afforded to Whites in this society. Just as her secretary's problems made her feel overprivileged, this letter may have reminded her of how Blacks as "racialized others" are denied certain rights. With her own sense of otherness increasing as her subject positions fragmented her subjectivity, Olivia may have felt particularly sensitive to this woman's marginalized status in the company, her triply oppressed position due to racism, class elitism, and sexism.

These sites of fixed and unfixed subject positions destabilize subjectivity by making us question and examine who we are. For Olivia, her desire to make changes in the corporation based on her feminist and antiracist values, her intense need to be independent, and her ambition to be successful in management all created conflict and contributed to the reconstructing and fragmenting of her subjectivity. The specific decisions she made based on these often-competing desires leave her feeling conflicted to this day; however, they simultaneously contribute to her ability to act and engage more fully (Anzaldua, 1987) and to participate in positive praxis (Sartre, 1960/1963).

Olivia's retelling reminds us that to interpret fragmented subjectivity as a weakness or flaw would mean being blind to the energy and personal insight that such fragmenting can engender in an individual like Olivia. Although personal insight does not take away the pain of a disturbing event in one's life, it does allow the event to become meaningful and not a continued source of bitterness that may destructively stabilize subjectivity. By understanding the potential of nonunitary subjectivity, we can read it not as a weakness but as a strength and even, within the context of feminist work, as an alternative feminist discourse. It is a strength because giving up the myth of unified subjectivity allows respect for the complexity of subjectivity and the validation of conflict as a source through which women become strong and learn to speak their own experiences. Olivia's retelling also helps deconstruct the masculinist master narrative and gives us a tentative ending that is more in keeping with lived experience. As Heilbrun (1988) affirms, "endings. . .are for romance or for daydreams, but not for life" (p. 130).

Thus the cauldron of feelings expressed in the second narrative speaks of a female subjectivity that was masked by the essentialized masculinist subjectivity narrated in the first version. In the first version of the story, Olivia says that she is a force to be reckoned with. In the second version, although she does not say it, her narrative self-representation conveys that she really is a force to be reckoned with because she has taken her place in a feminist discourse that allows her stories of her own.

Conclusion

Like the many twentieth-century women novelists who make a project of examining narrative as gendered and who offer readers alternative narrative closures, researchers working on personal experience narratives must make a project of examining the conflicts of people's lives and writing against closure and unitary representation of subjectivity. Although initially conceived as a feminist project, I believe that if our qualitative research is going to challenge the status quo, both women and men who narrate their stories must be encouraged to examine their own narrative constructions, to critically interpret their self-representations, and to retell their stories as Olivia did, attempting to better articulate and understand their complex, ever-changing subjectivities. Although no story or self-representation will ever or should ever be understood as complete or final, this strategy may motivate stories and representations that explode the "happily ever after" romance myth of women's lives and the "I did it my way" autonomy myth of men's lives. Because unitary subjectivity fictionalizes and reduces male selfhood as well as female selfhood, a narrative project that encourages examination of nonunitary subjectivity through the analysis of self-representation and multiple storytelling would benefit qualitative research that seeks alternatives to current conceptions of masculinity and femininity and the dismantling of patriarchy.

Therefore, DuPlessis's (1985) and Heilbrun's (1988) arguments taken in the larger context of qualitative research are powerful: if our stories are ideologically grounded in patriarchal perceptions of what it means to live a life, and if we do not attempt to subvert the master narratives by bringing to the surface the complex and diverse realities of people's feelings and experiences, we perpetuate damaging humanistic/patriarchal norms. For women, this may especially result in our never learning to see ourselves outside of masculinist ideologies, and thus we will never gain strength from our own complex nonunitary subjectivities.

A research process, such as the one described here, that consciously focuses on nonunitary subjectivity, self-representation, and multiple storytelling has the potential to generate greater opportunities for respondents to learn about themselves because they work with the researcher actively to understand how their subjectivities fragment, change, and become transformed.[11] This strategy might encourage respondents to replace desire for positive self-representation with proactive efforts to use the research process to understand themselves better.[12] The fieldwork, then, creates a context that emphasizes deeper reflection on lived experience. But perhaps Olivia's articulation of what she gained from the process of examining her own self-representations and narrative constructions best explains the benefits of such a strategy. As she explains, despite the pain and confusion she experienced in rethinking and retelling her stories, she felt that it led to "self-revelation and illumination." I take her words to mean that although it is difficult to give up the idea of unitary subjectivity and its manifestations of iconic self-representations in narratives, having stories of our own makes it worthwhile.

Acknowledgments

I extend special appreciation to Olivia for her generous participation in my research. Thanks to Barbara Duffelmeyer, Jeffrey Kuzmic, and Petra Munro for thoughtful critiques and editorial assistance on earlier drafts of this article, and to the *Qualitative Inquiry* reviewers and editors whose recommendations for revisions were most helpful.

Notes

1. By self-representation, I mean the simultaneous unconscious and conscious strategic depictions of one's self, which I take to be viable means through which to interpret the production of subjectivity.

2. Because the written story is quite long and explicit, I have edited from it some of the details, especially those that describe locations of work sites.

3. The following interpretations of Olivia's narratives are grounded in the interpretive theories I employ and my own life experiences and, as such, privilege my voice and interpretive stance. Wherever possible, I also provide Olivia's analyses of her own narratives.

4. The terms *subjectivity* and *subject position* are often used interchangeably. In this article, I try to distinguish between them. Subject position refers to sociocultural

categories, such as ethnicity, religion, class, gender, sexual orientation. As individuals, we can choose to accept and use them, subvert them, or resist them. They are socially constructed, unstable categories; however, they profoundly influence our subjectivity because of the importance of language and social interactions in the production of subjectivity.

5. Jean-François Lyotard, Louis Althusser, Terry Eagleton, and Frederick Jameson also discuss that narrative conventions work on individual narratives like scripts. They similarly argue that dominant ideologies are represented, produced, and re-worked unconsciously in the texts and stories individuals write and tell (see, for example, Jameson, 1981). They do not, however, make central the workings of gender in the narrative script.

6. In this article, I use the terms *narrative* and *personal narratives* to mean the life-history data I collected in my interviews with Olivia. Although autobiographical, fictional, and personal narrative texts are not the same genre, they share enough similarities to make autobiographical/literary theory relevant for interpreting personal narratives.

7. Walkerdine (1990) similarly suggests that the most interesting sites for locating subjectivity and gaining understanding of how subjectivity becomes fragmented are those situations of personal conflict.

8. In the longer version of this interpretation (Bloom, 1993), I provide additional backward-forward readings and more extensive interpretations of the narratives. However, given the space limitations here, I provide fewer examples and abbreviated analyses with the hope that my points are nonetheless adequately supported and demonstrated.

9. Clandinin and Connelly (1994) raise the problematic issue of the use of childhood memories as part of our research texts. They rightly ask, Whose voice is being heard? If an "adult [is] interpreting the childhood experience," they ask, is it the voice of the adult or the child that we hear? They would argue that unaided by texts from childhood or corroborating memories, the narrative "expresses a current voice rather than a historical voice" (p. 424). In other words, we use childhood memories with the understanding that what is at stake is not the truth-fulness of a childhood memory but the meaning the memory has for the adult narrating it. For Olivia, the memory of this conflicted event is a critical aspect of her sense of self and has an important place in her life history narratives.

10. Olivia's father suffered from a severe heart condition and Olivia had learned that it was necessary to avoid making him angry lest it bring on a fatal heart attack.

11. Returning to the discussion of researcher subjectivity, I might also suggest that re-searchers who make central to their work the difficult task of analyzing their own subjectivities and their intersubjective fieldwork relationships use this strategy to examine both their self-representations as researchers and their research stories.

12. Whereas qualitative researchers rightly place great emphasis on "member check-ing" with respondents, this often results in no more than perfunctory readings of already-interpreted data, verification of quotations, or respondents' making sure that they have been represented fairly or, in some cases, in ideal ways. I am there-fore suggesting that fieldwork include the ongoing process of respondents' care-fully reading (or listening to the interview tapes or whatever is appropriate to

the specific situation) their transcripts (or other forms of narrative data) and discussing or interpreting them with us. Although some—perhaps many—respondents will not desire this kind of interaction, those who do may benefit far more from the process of being a respondent.

References

Anzaldua, G. (1987). *Borderlands/la frontera: The new mestiza.* San Francisco: Spinsters, Aunt Lute.

Barone, T. (1992). On the demise of subjectivity in educational inquiry. *Curriculum Inquiry, 22,* 25–38.

Barry, K. (1990). The new historical syntheses: Women's biography. *Journal of Women's History, 1,* 75–105.

Bloom, L. R. (1993). *"Shot through with streams of songs": Explorations of interpretive research methodology.* Unpublished doctoral dissertation, Indiana University, Bloomington.

Bloom, L. R. (in press). "Locked in uneasy sisterhood": Reflections on feminist research. *Anthropology and Education Quarterly, 26*(3), 245–263.

Bloom, L. R., & Munro, P. (1995). Conflicts of selves: Non-unitary subjectivity in women administrators' life history narratives. In A. Hatch & R. Wisniewski (Eds.), *Life history and narrative* (pp. 99–112). London: Falmer.

Braidotti, R. (1991). *Patterns of dissonance: A study of women in contemporary philosophy* (E. Guild, Trans.). New York: Routledge.

Campbell, J. (1949). *The hero with a thousand faces* (2nd ed.). Princeton, NJ: Princeton University Press.

Christian, B. (1985). Trajectories of self-definition: Placing contemporary Afro-American women's fiction. In M. Pryse & H. J. Spillers (Eds.), *Conjuring: Black women, fiction, and literary tradition.* Bloomington: Indiana University Press.

Cixous, H. (1976, Summer). The laugh of the Medusa (K. Cohen & P. Cohen, Trans.). *Signs: Journal of women in culture and society, 1,* 875–899. (Original work published 1975)

Clandinin, D. J., & Connelly, F. M. (1994). Personal experience methods. In N. K. Denzin & Y. S. Lincoln (Eds.), *Handbook of qualitative research* (pp. 413–427). Thousand Oaks, CA: Sage.

Collins, P. H. (1991). *Black feminist thought: Knowledge, consciousness, and the politics of empowerment.* New York: Routledge.

Davies, B. (1992). Women's subjectivity and feminist stories. In C. Ellis & M. G. Flaherty (Eds.), *Investigating subjectivity: Research on lived experience* (pp. 53–76). Newbury Park, CA: Sage.

de Lauretis, T. (1987). *Technologies of gender: Essays on theory, film, and fiction.* Bloomington: Indiana University Press.

Denzin, N. K. (1989). *Interpretive biography.* Newbury Park, CA: Sage.

Denzin, N. K., & Lincoln, Y. S. (1994). Introduction: Entering the field of qualitative research. In N. K. Denzin & Y. S. Lincoln (Eds.), *Handbook of qualitative research* (pp. 1–17). Thousand Oaks, CA: Sage.

DuPlessis, R. B. (1985). *Writing beyond the ending: Narrative strategies of twentieth-century women writers.* Bloomington: Indiana University Press.

Eisner, E. W. (1992). Objectivity and educational research. *Curriculum Inquiry, 22,* 9–15.

Ellsworth, E., & Miller, J. L. (in press). "Working difference in education." *Curriculum Inquiry.*

Feagin, J. R., & Vera, H. (1995). *White racism: The basics.* New York: Routledge.

Ferguson, K. E. (1993). *The man question: Visions of subjectivity in feminist theory.* Berkeley: University of California Press.

Fine, M. (1994). Working the hyphens: Reinventing self and other in qualitative research. In N. K. Denzin & Y. S. Lincoln (Eds.), *Handbook of qualitative research* (pp. 70–82). Thousand Oaks, CA: Sage.

Flax, J. (1993). Multiples: On the contemporary politics of subjectivity. *Human Studies, 16,* 33–49.

Frankenberg, R. (1993). *White women, race matters: The social construction of whiteness.* Minneapolis: University of Minnesota Press.

Geertz, C. (1983). *Local knowledge: Further essays in interpretive methodology.* New York: Basic Books.

Guba, E. G. (1990). Subjectivity and objectivity. In E. W. Eisner & A. Peshkin (Eds.), *Qualitative inquiry in education: The continuing debate* (pp. 74–91). New York: Teachers College Press.

Harding, S. (1987). *Feminism and methodology.* Bloomington: Indiana University Press.

Heilbrun, C. (1988). *Writing a woman's life.* New York: Norton.

Henriques, J., Hollway, W., Urwin, C., Venn, C., & Walkerdine, V. (1984). *Changing the subject: Psychology, social regulations and subjectivity.* New York: Methuen.

Heshusius, L. (1994). Freeing ourselves from objectivity: Managing subjectivity or turning toward a participatory mode of consciousness? *Educational Researcher, 23*(3), 15–22.

Hollway, W. (1989). *Subjectivity and method in psychology: Gender, meaning and science.* Newbury Park, CA: Sage.

Jackson, M. (1989). *Paths toward a clearing: Radical empiricism and ethnographic inquiry.* Bloomington: Indiana University Press.

Jacobs, M., Munro, P., & Adams, N. (1995). Palimpsest: (Re)reading women's lives. *Qualitative Inquiry, 1,* 327–345.

Jameson, F. (1981). *The political unconscious: Narrative as a socially symbolic act.* Ithaca, NY: Cornell University Press.

Jansen, G., & Peshkin, A. (1992). Subjectivity in qualitative research. In M. D. LeCompte, W. K. Millroy, & J. Preissle (Eds.), *The handbook of qualitative research in education* (pp. 681–725). San Diego, CA: Academic Press.

Le Guin, U. K. (1985). The left hand of darkness. In *Ursula K. Le Guin: Five complete novels* (pp. 311–491). New York: Avenel.

Marcus, G. (1994). What comes (just) after "post"? The case of ethnography. In N. K. Denzin & Y. S. Lincoln (Eds.), *Handbook of qualitative research* (pp. 563–574). Thousand Oaks, CA: Sage.

Moi, T. (1985). *Textual/sexual politics: Feminist literary theory.* London: Routledge.

Morrison, T. (1992). *Playing in the dark: Whiteness and the literary imagination.* Cambridge, MA: Harvard University Press.

Peshkin, A. (1988). In search of subjectivity—One's own. *Educational Researcher, 17*(8), 17–22.

Phillips, D. C. (1990). Subjectivity and objectivity: An objective inquiry. In E. W. Eisner & A. Peshkin (Eds.), *Qualitative inquiry in education: The continuing debate* (pp. 19–37). New York: Teachers College Press.

Pinar, W. (1974). Currere: Toward reconceptualization. In J. Jelinek (Ed.), *Basic problems in modern education* (pp. 147–171). Tempe: Arizona State University.

Probyn, E. (1993). *Sexing the self: Gendered positions in cultural studies.* New York: Routledge.

Richardson, L. (1994). Writing: A method of inquiry. In N. K. Denzin & Y. S. Lincoln (Eds.), *Handbook of qualitative research* (pp. 516–529). Thousand Oaks, CA: Sage.

Robinson, S. (1991). *Engendering the subject: Gender and self-representation in contemporary women's fiction.* New York: State University of New York Press.

Roman, L. G. (1993). Double exposure: The politics of feminist materialist ethnography. *Educational Theory, 43,* 279–308.

Roman, L. G., & Apple, M. W. (1990). Is naturalism a move away from positivism? Materialist and feminist approaches to subjectivity in ethnographic research. In E. W. Eisner & A. Peshkin (Eds.), *Qualitative inquiry in education: The continuing debate* (pp. 38–73). New York: Teachers College Press.

Sartre, J. P. (1963). *Search for a method.* (H. E. Barnes, Trans.). New York: Vintage Books. (Original work published 1960)

Schwandt, T. A. (1994). Constructivist, interpretivist approaches to human inquiry. In N. K. Denzin & Y. S. Lincoln (Eds.), *Handbook of qualitative research* (pp. 118–137). Thousand Oaks, CA: Sage.

Smith, J. K. (1993). *After the demise of empiricism: The problem of judging social and educational inquiry.* Norwood, NJ: Ablex.

Smith, S. (1987). *A poetics of women's autobiography: Marginality and the fictions of self-representation.* Bloomington: Indiana University Press.

Smith, S. (1993). *Subjectivity, identity, and the body: Women's autobiographical practices in the twentieth century.* Bloomington: Indiana University Press.

Visweswaran, K. (1994). *Fictions of feminist ethnography.* Minneapolis: University of Minnesota Press.

Walkerdine, V. (1990). *Schoolgirl fictions.* London: Verso.

Weedon, C. (1987). *Feminist practice and poststructuralist theory.* Oxford: Basil Blackwell.

From Self to Society:
Reflections on the Power of Narrative Inquiry

Leslie Rebecca Bloom
Iowa State University, Ames, Iowa

Reading "Stories of One's Own: Nonunitary Subjectivity in Narrative Representation" as preparation for writing this reflection reminded me of how strongly I believe that narrative research is an important and necessary form of social science and educational research. Although my work has been and continues to be on women's narratives, in this commentary I want to discuss narrative research as a methodology that can be used by all researchers who have "liberatory" hopes for their research.

What Is Narrative Research?

Narrative research, as a strand of qualitative research, focuses on the "self" for data collection and data analysis. There are three central theoretical goals that structure the narrative research approach. First, narrative research is concerned with using individual lives as the primary source of data. Second, it is concerned with using narratives of the "self" as a location from which the researcher can generate social critique and advocacy. Third, narrative research is concerned with deconstructing the "self" as a humanist conception, allowing for nonunitary conceptions of the self. While not all narrative researchers would agree with these three theoretical goals, those of us who are committed to feminist and/or postmodern approaches to research tend to agree that these goals structure how we collect and interpret narrative data.

Personal Narratives as Data

Feminist researchers have been particularly adamant about the importance of using women's narratives as primary sources of data. Women's narratives are understood to serve as a corrective to centuries of adrocentric narratives that demean or negate women's experiences in society. Hence, there are political, moral, and epistemological reasons for feminist scholars to collect and interpret women's narratives. However, as "Stories of One's Own" demonstrates, it is not simply the *content* of a narrative that is critical narrative research; rather, it is the interplay between the narrative that is told and the *structure* of the telling that is critical. Because narrative truth is always elusive, as postmodernism staunchly asserts, it is necessary to explore the narrative content as a constructed tale, one in which the narrator has a personal investment in how she represents herself. Even when a story is retold, as Olivia retold hers, and even if a story is told again and again, we cannot assume that each telling gets us closer to a final truth about an event or a life. Lives are too messy, too complex, and too deeply lived at an interior level for the narrator to ever tell it all, and the narrator's desires for particular kinds of self-representation are too deeply felt to be abandoned.

Therefore, in narrative research, what is important to understand is how each narrative offers a means for the narrator to construct herself through the act of narrating self stories. The task of the narrative researcher, then, is to make sense of the telling rather than the tale. This is done both by recording and interpreting how an individual has lived and made meaning about her life and by creating an interpretive text that explicates how and why individuals construct stories about themselves to serve particular purposes and fulfill particular needs brought on by one's social positions and personal desires.

Personal Narratives as Social Critique

Narrative research is also important for how it helps us construct social critique. We start from the individual at the center of the research, but the focus does not rest there. Rather, the individual is understood as a social being whose experiences are mediated by and in turn mediate the social world in which she lives. Carefully interpreted narratives can illuminate how, in an individual life, different dominant ideologies and power relations in society are maintained, reproduced, or subverted. When we examine society through the lens of the individual, we can better understand society and resist its hegemonic tendencies. Studies of narratives, when used to construct social critique, also help us construct social action at both personal and collective levels. The task for the narrative researcher, therefore, is to be dually conscious of the individual and the societal-cultural contexts in which the individual experiences and interprets her life.

Deconstructing the Humanist "Self"

One of my goals in writing "Stories of One's Own" was to explicate a theory of nonunitary subjectivity and then demonstrate how it can be used as an interpretive lens for narrative data. In the article, I suggest that nonunitary subjectivity is an empowering interpretive theory, both because it encourages researchers to generate alternative and more complex understandings of those who are studied, and because it helps respondents understand and interpret their lives in more forgiving and thoughtful ways. Theorizing the "self" as nonunitary, especially when combined with social critique, is particularly powerful for how it illuminates the ways that social norms, dominant ideologies, and power relations call upon the individual to respond in very situated ways to daily life. While not all researchers will find the idea of nonunitary subjectivity as compelling as feminists have, given that it diminishes the ability of both the researcher and the respondents to assert absolute explications or to make definitive claims, I think that what we give up in certainty, we get back in richer interpretations.

Fieldwork Challenges in Narrative Research

Narrative research, like any research with human participants, is always challenging. The challenges change with each research subject, because each intersubjective relationship raises specific issues; new challenges arise with each research project, because each research site has its own problematics that must be addressed; and finally, some challenges remain the same across each project and intersubjective relationship, because they originate in the mind and heart of the researcher.

One of the biggest personal challenges for me in doing narrative research is the feeling that the interview process often feels like I am invading a respondent's privacy. I find it difficult to ask probing questions to get beyond superficial self stories and I am uncomfortable when my questions open wounds through seemingly innocent questions. The research relationship exacerbates this, because it places respondents in a position to feel obligated to answer any and all questions and puts researchers in a position to get "deep" data, even if it means prying. When I disclosed to Olivia my feelings of discomfort about asking personal questions, our conversation led to the agreement that she could ask me questions about my life as well, so that the "prying" was two-sided, thus mitigating some of my discomfort (Bloom, 1998).

My recent research project has particularly illuminated for me how challenges in narrative research are both personal and contextual. I have been collecting personal narratives from women who are attending welfare-to-work programs. Because these women are in the social service system, they are continually being interrogated by government workers. They are asked deeply personal questions about their homes, their children, their extended families, their personal relationships, their child rearing practices, and their finances. Often, the responses to these questions are used to create psychological profiles that may be used against them when applying for much-needed cash assistance. My understanding of this contextual challenge, once acknowledged, was a catalyst for me to ask myself how my research questions similarly negate their privacy rights, and how my being "official," albeit in a very different capacity, means that I contribute to this surveillance of the women for whom my research is intended to help, not hurt. Reflection on this challenge has helped me greatly in my interviews and in developing my fieldwork relationships, leading me to find new ways to collect personal narratives without creating a sense of requirement for the women to respond, and helping me to not feel the awkwardness of prying and probing.

Suggestions for Novice Researchers

I have two suggestions that I would like to offer to novice researchers based on my own experiences: maintain humility and be ethically responsive to the research. First, maintaining humility means not taking ourselves or our research so seriously that we forget that those we research have other, more important things going on in their lives. While we as researchers often put our work at the center of our lives, as we struggle with deadlines and career goals, the research must be secondary to the positive relationships we build in our fieldwork, and our desires to get data should never jeopardize these relationships. We should always be gracious and grateful to those we research. Second, research requires us to act in ethical ways. Ethics begins with the conception of the research project and ends with how we represent and share with others what we have learned. In between, ethics should drive our fieldwork conduct, our theory choices for interpretation, and our conscientious attention to self-reflexivity. While qualitative researchers have general guidelines for ethical conduct, it is still the responsibility of each researcher to be continually aware of specific ethical problems that arise in each project and to respond not simply in ethical ways but in ethically situated ways.

Narrative research is rewarding and personally fulfilling. It has given me the opportunity to get to know some very wonderful women, and it has shown me new ways to think about my own life and experiences. When done with integrity, I believe that narrative research leaves us and, I hope, our respondents forever changed in the best possible ways.

Reference

Bloom, L. R. (1998). *Under the sign of hope: Narrative interpretation and feminist methodology.* Albany, NY: State University of New York Press.

14

Cathy

The Wrong Side of the Tank

Juanita Johnson-Bailey

Cathy is a petite thirty-nine-year-old Black woman who exudes joy. She lives in a cramped two bedroom apartment with her five-year-old daughter and eleven-year-old son. Her "place" is located in a cul de sac in Bird City, a government housing project so nicknamed because the streets have names such as Wren, Dove, and Crane. With quick, energetic, and constant movements, her smile, which is wide and sincere, accompanies constant gestures and intense eye contact.

When I arrived to pick her up on a Saturday afternoon in February, Cathy was dressed in pale blue sweat pants, an outdated frayed orange and yellow plaid wool coat that was two sizes too small, and a fluorescent yellow skull cap that covered her eyebrows and ears. Her bizarre dress belied her sharp wit and brilliant conversational style. Cathy's positive attitude seemed to ignore her desolate surroundings and this zest carried over to her conversations about school.

Despite a history of good grades in elementary and high school, she was hesitant to enter college. In her early thirties, Cathy says she feels old when she's at school. High school coincided with the beginning of integration and Cathy vividly remembers being ridiculed by White teachers and students. She has residual feelings of inadequacy that she attributes to those traumatic times. It took much encouragement by a friend who was also enrolled in college to convince Cathy to take a chance on herself. This girlfriend persuaded her by constantly reminding her of how smart Cathy had been when they were in school together.

Juanita Johnson-Bailey. (2000). "Cathy: The Wrong Side of the Tank." In *Sistahs in College: Making a Way Out of No Way*. Malabar, FL: Krieger. Reprinted with permission.

Cathy has been enrolled in a nursing program at a community college for a year. Although she is an honors student, she recently decided to change her major to elementary education because she believes that the nursing program is unfair to Blacks and because she does not want to "endure" the program.

Framing her adult schooling were memories of childhood experiences. She mentioned her initial experiences often as she grappled to discuss how school was fitting into her adult life. Although Cathy maintained that the disturbing events that occurred in her grade school and high school years were not connected to the present, it seemed more a wishful thought than a reality in which she believed.

Unequally Separate

I lived through the era of segregation. So I remember too well how much it influenced me, especially in the way I feel about my school days. In the early grades, I had no idea that there were differences between the way Blacks and Whites lived. But things were happening in my community and in home life. Back then the newspaper had a "colored" section. It seemed that all the news in the colored section was bad. Not that we didn't have our own clubs and organizations, but then hard things were happening in the world. I also remember my mother taking me four blocks away from where she was spending her money, to go to the "colored only" restroom. Yet we were lucky. I watched TV and I know that elsewhere people were dying.

In our city we had a mayor who placed a 6:00 P.M. curfew on the city. It was supposedly for White and Black neighborhoods, but it was racial. He purchased a tank and rode around in Black neighborhoods only. It was his intention to intimidate people. I was a little girl, around nine years old, but I remember him riding through our neighborhood when I was playing in the yard with a friend. Even though we were just children, the police told us to get back on the porch. But it was warm and we were playing in the yard the way children are supposed to play on warm summer days.

In spite of all of this, school was still fun. Achieving is the most fun I've ever had—being able to learn new things. My most pleasant memory of school was being involved in a little small play where I was Miriam of the Biblical story of Moses. My mother couldn't come because she had to work, but my father, who never lived with us, agreed to come. I felt kind of special. But in subsequent years, my father and I have never been really close.

I worked hard in the early part of school. During high school I had spring fever—hormonal uproar. I let a few subjects slide. Overall I finished with a 2.3. It wasn't that I couldn't do it. I just got lazy, rebellious, carefree. It was almost over. Why work?

Cathy's age puts her in the unique position of having been a product of both segregated and newly integrated school environments. Like many Black reentry women in their thirties and forties, she recalls her days of inequality with fondness because in this sheltered world she felt safe and smart. The days of difference were difficult for her and served as a marker for her educational and life narrative. Her statements about this period are terse and pain-ridden.

Some teachers would talk to you in such tones. The words did not matter. They would talk down to you. It was as if they knew that your background was lacking—your parents were uneducated and you were ignorant. But that wasn't the case. I remember how difficult it was to look in the teacher's eyes and ask a question. I feared asking a dumb question. When I did ask a question, it was out of sheer necessity, and I'd hear, "Well, you should know this," or "Why are you asking me this?" The kids would snicker and the teacher would not answer. And my ego would slouch even further.

I witnessed a lot of rifts between classmates. Once one of my Black friends chased a White girl all around the room. I could see the fear in both girls' eyes. I guess everyone was feeling a certain amount of pain. I know Black people were hurting long before King ever talked to the world about all the injustices. When the schools integrated, the kids, Black and White alike, came with harsh feelings and severe hostilities that grown people encouraged.

In addition to the period being painful, Cathy thinks that the disparity of her schooling was evident. According to her, the new, formerly all-White schools had equipment and books of which she had never seen the likes.

My schools did not prepare me adequately even though I maintained good grades. It was hard for me. When the schools integrated the White kids who came from "more equal" institutions did better. It appeared easier for them. Yet I believe that attending all-Black public schools was a good experience in a way because it gave me a sense of identity. I didn't feel different.

Often when discussing decisions made in youth, there seems to be regret in Cathy's voice. The same seems true for so many reentry women. Phrases like, "If I only had known then what I know now," or "Hindsight is twenty-twenty, but real life vision is blurry," are common refrains. The thirties and forties are not only years for reflecting on what you could have done differently, but seemingly for women these years are times for finishing or beginning tasks that can still be accomplished.

Revisiting Math and Science Demons
When I was in high school, I had the opportunity to go to Upward Bound. But no. I could kick myself now for thinking, "No. I don't want to go. I'm working. I'm working making nothing." Then came children, marriage, and divorce. Now I want to secure more of a future for my children. I've missed so many opportunities. I want to do better and obtaining a higher level of education will be my ticket.

Making the final decision to go to school was hard and I didn't make it alone. I was influenced by a friend that I kept running into at the laundromat. She said, "Cathy you were so smart. Did you go to school?" And I would say, "Nah." And she would tell me about the local community college and tell me that I should go. Every time I'd see her, she'd tell me this. She'd hound me about going back to school. And it got so that I stopped going to the laundromat.

When I made the decision to go to college, I was so afraid. The counselor will tell you the many times I called her at home and said, "Uh, uh, uh, I can't do this." She would say, "Yes you can." I was coming up with all types of excuses.

I was afraid. The fear of failure. It's been too long. I won't fit. I kept going back and forth. When I finally made the decision to go, I think it was the best decision I could have made. I was staying at home. I was on the system—Welfare. I had low self-esteem. I'd had good jobs in the past. I didn't want to sling hamburgers. And so I said, "Well, let me see how I can use this system to help myself so that I can get off Welfare."

The school sent me an application to complete for the minority Summer Enrichment Program. I didn't just send it back in the mail. I completed it, signed it, and took it out there the same day. But I didn't get in. There were no more spaces. I was crushed. They were trying to gear it toward the traditional student. I said to myself, "I'm the one who needs the little extra boost, the incentive, and the help." And so every other day I would call the counselor for the program. They [the school officials] had never seen my face, but they knew me well. I was so determined to get out there. I would call every other day and say, "Do you have a space available—maybe somebody is sick—maybe somebody decided to go somewhere else." And so finally, maybe about a week before the class was supposed to start, they sent me a letter. I got in. Later I found out that no one dropped. They had fifty slots open and they made it 51 because the secretary said listen, "You have got to get this Cathy in here, into this class."

Cathy has dealt with many rejections in her lifetime. It didn't embarrass her to let the school officials know how much she wanted to gain admission into their program. According to her, the worst that could happen would be that they'd just keep saying no. Past ordeals had taught her tenacity. She felt that she had nothing to lose and everything to gain. A wealth of life experiences from which to draw solace and guidance is one factor that sets reentry women students apart from younger women students.

I was so happy to get in. It was fantastic. I said, "Thank God," because I knew I needed it. I needed that summer program. I didn't know if my nerves could last until September. This would be something to get me re-acquainted with school.

I did things in that program that I had never done before. We went to museums and we got a chance to go to the Martin Luther King Center. It was real. We went on a tour of his house. I saw Coretta Scott King. I never had the money to go to those places.

After the summer program I wanted to bail out. The counselor said, "No, you're not. Not as many times as you bugged us. You are staying in." And so everything worked out.

My life since I came back to school has been a roller coaster ride. At first I felt a sense of intimidation, not knowing if I could measure up. There were a lot of insecurities. The first day there I looked around. I always sit up front in the middle of the T. And I could feel their eyes. That's my inferiority complex. I felt like everyone was looking at me like, "What is she doing?" I was the oldest. They used to call me mother, the mother hen. I had this feeling from the kids that I didn't belong. Then they started seeing that I was the one who was the first to ask questions. I was the one, you know, who was bringing in the homework and just really trying, trying, to do my best. I guess my age had its benefits. I was serious cause I had been through a lot of things. Age worked to my advantage. Before it was over with, I had won their respect. It was a good feeling.

During her second week of school, Cathy's car stopped working and she could not afford to repair it or to buy a new one. But she was already hooked on school and did not let her transportation problems deter her. She started commuting by bus.

> *I will never forget this one incident. I had missed the bus 'cause it would come so early. I had to get up—the children and everything. I just missed the bus. I was determined to get to school. My class was at 10:00 in the morning. It was 8:00 A.M. so I decided to walk. I said from where I live to the college is no problem until I started walking. It was raining and I fell. I got soaked. I looked back. I could see my house. I looked the other way and I couldn't see the college. But I was determined to go. I had to go. I walked up the street, slish, slosh, slish, slosh. I didn't want to miss, not just 'cause I had to walk. I wasn't sick. The children weren't sick and I didn't want to miss school. I was determined to get there. I had to get there. My hair shriveled. It's a good eight miles. It costs about $4.00 to get there in a cab.*

Cathy made it to school that day and every day thereafter. She talks readily of good times and negative experiences. Overall, it was harder than she imagined and more empowering than she expected.

> *There have been some hilarious times when I've had to stop and laugh at myself. I've shied away from math like many women. I eventually took the hard math course, the one designed to prepare me for nursing. There was one problem that still tickles me. The workbook said Ms. Doe has been prescribed 0.5 milliliter of a drug and your solution stock is 100 percent. How do you dilute it? I said to myself, Oops! This lady is dead. It had been so long since I took math that I just didn't get it. Though I was frightened, I learned to master it. Things did start coming back to me and I made an A in the class. It's a different type of math, doing equations, quadrants, linears. So I said, "Let me get some remediation," even though I had been exempted from development studies because I made a passing score on my college preparatory exam. You have to take the college preparatory exam if you have been out of school for over ten years or longer or if you have never been to college. You have to pass the exam's three parts. Taking extra courses just to make sure you understand seems like a common thing for older students to do. We want to be sure we can keep up. I have one friend who goes to school out here. She is taking some developmental studies, not because she wasn't exempted. She feels that she just needs to better prepare herself.*

When asked to describe school, Cathy said it was like a roller coaster ride, full of ups and downs. Here are some moments that she identifies as memorable ones on her reentry ride.

> *In my first year at the college I was nominated by my English 101 teacher for the honors program. And that first day I was the only little Black woman in there and the oldest again. And I called my counselor that night and said, "I'm leaving this." I felt like I had the weight of the rest of the Blacks at the college on my shoulders. I'm the only Black in the class. That old inferiority complex had me*

asking, Can I do this? I was afraid to fail. I would rather bail. I was so intimidated. Let me tell you what I discovered. Those kids in those classes don't know anymore than you do. If they are in the class it's for the same reason I'm there. Someone nominated them just like they nominated me. Still I felt it was all on me. I pulled a B out of the class. It felt good when I was one of the participants to walk up on the honors stage.

Some things do get me down. I was in a sociology class and the students were talking about Welfare recipients and homeless people. I didn't know that real people felt that way about people like me. You see people on talk shows saying cruel things about how poor and homeless people are in their circumstances because they prefer those conditions. Who wants to be homeless? To me that is ludicrous. I tried to respond in class. Then they asked me questions like, "Why don't they go on birth control and stop having babies? We're taxpayers." Apparently they don't know that things sometimes don't happen the way people plan. No one plans to be poor.

On one of my very first days of class, an instructor said, "Open your book to chapter four. If you don't know the first three chapters then you don't need to be in this class." It had been such a long time since I dealt with algebra. I skimmed through the three chapters. And the first chapter was OK, but when I saw those algebraic equations, I said, "Oh man I don't know this." The teacher was taking the class so fast. It was hard for me to learn it that fast. I didn't understand it like I should have. I withdrew and took remedial math for a refresher. Later I made an A for that course. The next time I take a math course I'll be more prepared.

I didn't feel prepared for anatomy and physiology either. It was a two-part class—lab and lecture. Everyone has problems with it unless you have the background for it. This course is the money maker for the college since it has such a large failure rate. Everyone knows that a third of the students in each class don't complete the course and the majority of those who remain won't make a passing grade. The average student has to take it three times in order to pass. Mostly the people who do well have private school backgrounds where they took anatomy and physiology in high school.

I didn't understand all the chemistry. I didn't take chemistry in high school. And so I got a lot of self-help books. Maybe I needed more books and more time. But for whatever reason I didn't get it. Instead of slowing down, the class sped up. I didn't feel mentally ready. I couldn't absorb that much. It took me so long just to understand one chapter. Mainly it was the terminology, the medical language. I had to look up every few words because I wanted to know what they meant and I wanted to be able to pronounce them. It slowed me down. It was very difficult.

I tried to talk to the teacher. He told me that there was no substitute for three or four hours of studying per day. At first I thought he was being smart. Then I thought about it. He was making all kinds of assumptions about me. Now I hadn't been studying that much because I can't study at home. It's so comfortable there and then there are the dishes. There is food. There's the telephone. I come to school early in the morning to study and study anywhere else that I find quiet. My schedule makes it hard to have four straight hours. Maybe he was telling the truth. I am deficient.

Of course the teacher didn't seem at all interested in me. He assumed that I was not studying adequately. He dismissed me. I tried to ask him if he felt that I should take remedial courses. But he said that we were just touching the surface.

But everything I saw was a chemical formula. The molecular structures looked foreign. And I didn't understand about conservation and reduction. I could see the definition but I didn't understand about adding and removing the water.

There is a test coming up and the teacher told me to wait until after the test to decide about staying in the class. I made a 70 on the first test and he thought that it was a good grade. I didn't think it was acceptable. Of course I'd take that over an F. But there was no leeway.

The counselor wanted me to hang in there. I gave it serious thought and decided to pull out. It's not the first time I've done that. But each time that I have made that decision it has worked best for me. I dropped a psychology course because my teacher was in another world. And when I took it from a different instructor I made an A. Well, I had a feeling, intuition, something inside, a knowledge within myself. I knew I didn't understand the test. I have no regrets. I dropped the class because I didn't feel prepared. Even though I made a 70 on the test, it was like walking along a ledge. I didn't even take the second test. Actually there were two tests on the same day, the regular test and the lab exam. The class test was going to cover twelve chapters. A lot of students took the second test and failed it miserably. And everyone I talked to asked me had I dropped the course. If they didn't fail the lecture, they failed the lab part.

Cathy dropped the course. She said that she had to follow her heart. Respecting your inner voice seems to be a common trait among the reentry women.

Maybe I would be better qualified in elementary education. A girlfriend told me that I looked like a teacher. It shocked me. She said that she would let me teach any of her six children but that if she saw me in her hospital room as a nurse she said she'd have to ring for help. I've had the opportunity to tutor a fellow classmate and I was uplifted. I had a sense of pride and satisfaction in helping others learn. I've always taught, whether it's working with my children at home or working with neighbors. There are other nursing programs. But I have transportation problems. I'm not closing the door on it. I want to get better prepared— to take biology and chemistry. I don't want a week to learn 206 bones inside and out. It may take me longer. I would rather be qualified. Black women have to be 105 percent qualified anyway in order to succeed in the long run.

There have been really good experiences. I had a poem published in the school magazine. It was hard for me to conceive that something that I had written was good enough to be seen by anyone else. I went on to write short stories and then essays. I won first place in a Minority Student Enrichment Program. You know, the one that I begged to get into. Now after a year, I feel more confident about trying new things.

The new confidence in the school setting is fragile. Yet it is encased in an adult's understanding that school is a business. There are rules and ways of succeeding. Cathy quickly applies previously learned life lessons to this environment.

The first day of class before the bell, I go to meet the instructor to find out their office hours. It's not necessarily brown nosing but to try to get an impression of them. Hopefully, it gives them a positive impression of me. It's also a good opportunity to ask questions about the class. I've gotten insider information this way—

about books and about any additional aids I might need to buy. I don't hesitate to ask for help.

I get to class early. I look on my left and say, "Hello, my name is Cathy. What's your name? And if you don't mind could we exchange numbers." I made it a rule of thumb to do this in every class.

Riding the Roller Coaster

My children are so proud of me. I often hear them tell their friends, "You know that my Mama goes to college." A lot of mothers around the neighborhood, for whatever reason, don't do anything. Now more and more mothers are going back to school. Some went back, I guess, because they saw me and realized that anyone could do it. Now there's a lot of media attention being given to women on Welfare who go back to school. The Housing Authority, who manages the housing project where I live, promotes entrepreneurship, GED completion programs, and community college programs. First it was a neighbor who went to the community school. Then I enrolled. Now there are two more women from my area who have started classes.

I think maybe I'm becoming a role model. The woman that I ride with just started school. She's a little older and she was very concerned. She was intimidated and overwhelmed by the amount of information and the new life that she was experiencing. Looking at her was like looking at a frightened chicken running around. I had to stop her and unruffle her feathers. She had actually started talking about dropping out of school. I told her, "You just got in. You're not going anywhere."

Cathy's pride in succeeding is short-lived. According to her it's always something. Every time she thinks it's smooth sailing something happens. Her greatest joy in school, enrolling in an honor's program, was clouded in controversy.

When I went to sign up for my first honors class, I was so proud. Not many students get this opportunity, especially Blacks. You get selected for these classes by having high standardized test scores or you have to be recommended by a professor. I had been recommended by my English teacher and it was a big deal for me. So there I was standing in the honors line. I was aware that I was the only Black and that I was surrounded by blue-eyed, blonde-haired young girls, cheerleader types. And just as this realization hit me a professor who was supervising the line came and stood next to me, looked directly at me, and announced that if there was anyone in the honors line that was not invited into the program, they should move to the other line. Well I didn't move. As I approached the registration desk, he took his place at the table. I watched him intensely after he made the announcement. He did the paperwork for several young women in front of me without question. When it was my turn, he asked, "Were you invited into the honors program? Do you have an invitation letter from a faculty member?" As I pulled the letter from my purse he processed my papers, placing the honors sticker on my registration card. He refused to look at my letter. I insisted. For that one moment it felt good. But it ticked me off. And it made we wonder again about everything.

I'd like to think that it's not as bad as it used to be when I was a little girl. I know individuals have their old gripes and prejudices on both sides, Blacks and Whites. But there have been several teachers, and I can't prove it, but there are advisors at my school that advise and treat Black students differently. Many are advised right out of school during their first quarter. They are told to take full loads, three and four courses. A lot of these people have been out of school for a while—twenty years or more—and they are easily discouraged because this is a brand new experience. A lot of them are the first ones in their family to attend college, just like me. And so we advise each other. We have to stick together because Black flight is occurring at my school. Black students are leaving in significant numbers. The numbers are getting smaller and smaller.

I'm a very different student now than when I first entered. The counselor at my college has taught me to hang in there. I'm more confident, committed, determined, very serious. Even though some people say you should never say never, there comes a time when you realize that you have potential and that you are only allotted so many days on this earth. I know this. I have already waited too long.

Cathy, like the majority of women of color and poor women who return to college, attends a community college. This point of entry has a higher dropout rate than traditional four-year institutions, but one advantage to attending a community college is that there are often remedial programs and more flexible class schedules. Such benefits are important to Cathy because she has been out of school so long that many terms and behaviors that are commonplace to traditional-age students are foreign to her. Playing catch-up is particularly important in the sciences and mathematics for many returning women students. In addition, Cathy's single parent status necessitated that she have some flexibility in when she attended classes.

Cathy's description of school as a roller coaster ride is indicative of the events she described as her day-to-day school life. But she smiles through it all and says that she just won't quit. This sense of "now or never" seems particular to women who are finally in school after a delay. The ability to take the good with the bad and to keep it all in perspective is a benefit of the wisdom that comes with experience. For Cathy, it seems to be an advantage that is buckling her safely into that roller coaster seat.

Dancing Between the Swords: My Foray into Constructing Narratives

Juanita Johnson-Bailey
University of Georgia, Athens

The imaginary sword dancer of my dreams is reconstructed from muddled flashes from old Aladdin and Scheherazade movies. She is a woman spinning around and waving multicolored scarves as on-lookers brandish sabers that synchronously determine the boundaries of her dance and challenge the expertise of her art. The dancer is smiling, the audience is mesmerized, the blades are sharp and dangerous, and she is twirling effortlessly between the pointed parameters. The performer ends the fun-filled night by spinning a story that further captivates the audience. This complex analogy from my dreams seems akin to narrative analysis in that constructing a narrative is a joyous balancing act among the data, the methodology, the story, the participant, and the researcher: the metaphorical swords. In the end a wonderful narrative is told, and the researcher, the symbolic dancer, has negotiated difficult steps to arrive at this finale.

The culmination of this narrative dance is Cathy's story, "The Wrong Side of the Tank." To collect the data and tell Cathy's tale, I followed the traditional format of interviewing the participant by using semistructured questions. However, in the collection of data it was necessary always to remember that a narrative analysis methodology dictates that the story remain the central focus. In addition, it was significant that I was interviewing an African American woman whose cultural group membership meant that she had inherited a rich oral tradition. Therefore, my interviewing resembled a dialogic process, since Black women have a traditional Afrocentric view that emphasizes oral tradition, dialogue, and communal structure (Collins, 1990). Accordingly, they filter knowledge claims based on the credibility of the person disseminating the knowledge, thus making awareness of the person transmitting the information essential to the process. So in talking with Cathy, we traded stories of our educational sojourns while the tape recorder captured our talks. The transcription for Cathy's three-hour interview, the field notes, and file memos became the data that would be used to construct the final narrative.

To organize the narrative in a way that preserves the essence of the story, I searched for tools that honored meaning and voice as the most important components of the narrative. Since stories are the way that people communicate and the way in which we construct sense in our lives, it is vital that the participant's intended meaning be maintained. In an effort to keep the idea of meaning primary, I used data analysis tools that concentrated on preserving voice and the specific and personalized sense contained in the data. The process of developing the narratives began by summarizing what I perceived as the highlights of the respondent's life, thereby generating categories. In analyzing Cathy's words as text, my questions were ignored and emphasis was placed on her responses. This procedure emphasized the voice of the person being interviewed. By removing the questions from the body of the transcript the text resembled a cohesive first-person statement, and at this point the oral narrative looked like a written autobiographical account. The new transcript, *sans* questions, was coded according to the major themes and the data pertaining to each theme were grouped and analyzed.

Next the narrative was analyzed by using three approaches. The first was a process of narrative analysis that employed Alexander's (1988) procedure of letting the data reveal itself by using his *principal identifiers of salience,* such as omission, frequency, and emphasis. This pragmatic process allows the researcher to sort through the data's "network of rules designed to call attention to importance. The sifting has a twofold purpose: (a) to reduce the data to manageable proportions, and (b) to break the conscious communication intent of the content" (Alexander, 1988, p. 268).

A second method used was Denzin's (1989) autobiographical analysis, which attends to such matters as subtle shifts in the life narrative, biographic markers (important life events), omissions (obvious gaps in the story), and epiphanies (verbalized insights into the meaning of life circumstances). Denzin explains how such elements characteristically occur in most stories. He also discusses the vantage points from which stories are situated—the cultural, ideological, and historical contexts—and the purposes and reasons stories are shared.

As a third method to my narrative analysis process I used a culturally specific linguistic approach. Since this narrative was obtained from a Black woman, I assumed that she would have a cultural locus outside of what is termed the "dominant" culture. So in addition to Denzin's (1989) and Alexander's approaches (1988), I used a culturally unique narrative analysis tool. Culture, "a shared organization of ideas that includes the intellectual, moral, and aesthetic standards prevalent in a community and the meanings of communicative actions" (LeVine, 1984, p. 67), gave measure and meaning to Black women's lives as Black women are defined by their communities (Etter-Lewis, 1991). A culturally distinctive analysis paid attention to the special ways Black women communicate, recognizing techniques such as signifying (repetition of words and revision of phrasing to emphasize meaning) and the use of Black English to show strong emotion (Etter-Lewis, 1991).

Cathy: The Wrong Side of the Tank

Using the three-part system described, I attempted to weave Cathy's educational narrative. The various themes that occurred in her data also doubled as subheadings that highlighted changes in direction within the story. To honor the scholarly audience for which I write and the academic forum in which I publish, it is requisite to give background information and to place Cathy, as a subject, in relation to other research. I accomplished this by using bridges of analysis throughout the text. These passages, which are set apart from the italicized narrative, provide contextual data and transitions for the story. Here is an example of an analytic bridge that simultaneously introduces Cathy's story within the story of pleading to get into her community college while also situating her circumstance within the larger body of literature on nontraditional women students: "Cathy has dealt with many rejections in her lifetime. It didn't embarrass her to let the school official know how much she wanted to gain admission into their program. According to her, the worst that could happen would be that they'd just keep saying no. Past ordeals had taught her tenacity. She felt that she had nothing to lose and everything to gain. A wealth of life experiences from which to draw solace and guidance is one factor that sets reentry women students apart from younger women students" (Johnson-Bailey, 2000, p. 21).

Overall in the academic arena, disenfranchised groups, which include women, women of color, and poor people, are "othered" in the telling of their stories (hooks, 1999; Johnson-Bailey, in press; Patai, 1991; Scott, 1999). As a woman of color, it was especially important that I not replicate this experience. Since the flexible and responsive methodology of narrative analysis allows for power disparities to be addressed, an essential part of this method for me involves asking the participants to read, react, and approve the constructed narrative, as one way of attempting to manage and present another's story (Johnson-Bailey, 1999).

In further assessing the ethical issues of this process, it has to be recognized that my voice—as the one presenting—is ever present. The nonitalicized text in a way is my dialogue with the story, my voice whispering directions, signaling changes in focus, and inserting opinions and synopsis from the literature as a type of "truth" or backdrop to the story. This omnipotent being has the power of the pen, and this seemingly innocuous format of telling a story—which is gaining widespread acceptance in academia for its apparent accessibility both for researchers and consumers—is wrought with issues of power. Who owns the story? What happens when there is disagreement on interpretations? What are the ethical boundaries in telling the story? How are those boundaries negotiated when within-group membership makes loyalty an issue? These are the concerns that come back to haunt me when I'm the dancer trying to keep her balance amidst the swords of data, methodology, participants, narratives, and my researcher's perspective.

References

Alexander, I. E. (1988). Personality, psychological assessment, and psychobiography. In D. P. McAdams & R. L. Ochberg (Eds.), *Psychobiography and life narratives* (pp. 265–294). Durham, NC: Duke University Press.

Collins, P. H. (1990). *Black feminist thought: Knowledge, consciousness, and the politics of empowerment.* New York: Routledge.

Denzin, N. (1989). *Interpretive biography.* Newbury Park, CA: Sage.

Etter-Lewis, G. (1991). Black women's life stories: Reclaiming self in narrative texts. In S. Gluck & D. Patai (Eds.), *Women's words: The feminist practice of oral history* (pp. 43–58). New York: Routledge.

hooks, b. (1999). Eating the other: Desire and resistance. In S. Hesse-Bier, C. Gilmartin, & R. Lydenberg (Eds.), *Feminist approaches to theory and methodology: An interdisciplinary reader* (pp. 179–194). New York: Oxford University Press.

Johnson-Bailey, J. (1999). The ties that bind and the shackles that separate: Race, gender, class, and color in a research process. *Qualitative Studies in Education, 12*(6), 659–670.

Johnson-Bailey, J. (2000). *Sistahs in college: Making a way out of no way.* Malabar, FL: Krieger.

Johnson-Bailey, J. (in press). Enjoining positionality and power in narrative work: Balancing contentious and modulating forces. In K. B. deMarrais & S. D. Lapin (Eds.), *Perspectives and approaches for research in education and the social sciences.* Mahwah, NJ: Erlbaum.

LeVine, R. (1984). Properties of culture: An ethnographic view. In R. Shweder & R. LeVine (Eds.), *Culture theory: Essays in mind, theory, and emotion* (pp. 67–87). Cambridge: Cambridge University Press.

Patai, D. (1991). U.S. academics and third world women: Is ethical research possible? In S. B. Gluck & D. Patai (Eds.), *Women's words: The feminist practice of oral history* (pp. 137–154). New York: Routledge.

Scott, J. (1999). The evidence of experience. In S. Hesse-Biber, C. Gilmartin, & R. Lydenberg (Eds.), *Feminist approaches to theory and methodology: An interdisciplinary reader* (pp. 79–99). New York: Oxford University Press.

Critical Research

The majority of qualitative research studies undertaken in applied fields of study such as management, allied health, social work, and education are interpretive; that is, the goal of the research is to understand the phenomenon and the meaning it has for the participants. What is commonly known as critical social science research takes a different stance. In critical inquiry the goal is to critique and challenge, to transform and empower. Crotty (1998, p. 113) writes that "it is a contrast between a research that seeks merely to understand and a research that challenges . . . between a research that reads the situation in terms of interaction and community and a research that reads it in terms of conflict and oppression . . . between a research that accepts the *status quo* and a research that seeks to bring about change."

Critical research has its roots in several traditions, and, as currently practiced, encompasses a variety of approaches. Early influences include Marx's analysis of socioeconomic conditions and class structures, Habermas's notions of technical, practical, and emancipatory knowledge, and Freire's transformative and emancipatory education. French feminists and Russian socioliguists also "find their way into the reference lists of contemporary critical researchers" (Kincheloe & McLaren, 1994, p. 139). Marx (1967, p. 212) himself wrote that at the heart of critical inquiry is "relentless criticism for all existing conditions, relentless in the sense that the criticism is not afraid of its findings and just as little afraid of conflict with the powers that be."

Those who engage in critical research frame their research questions in terms of power—who has it, how it's negotiated, what structures in society reinforce the current distribution of power, and so on. It is also assumed that people unconsciously accept things the way they are, and in so doing, reinforce the status quo.

Others may act in seemingly self-destructive or counterproductive ways in resisting the status quo. Power in combination with hegemonic social structures results in the marginalization and oppression of those without power. Oppression takes many forms and cannot be ferreted out without attention to its many manifestations. Ellsworth's (1989) well-known study of her attempt to implement a critical, emancipatory pedagogy in her classroom found "that key assumptions, goals, and pedagogical practices fundamental to the . . . critical pedagogy—namely, 'empowerment,' 'student voice,' 'dialogue,' and even the term 'critical'—are repressive myths that perpetuate relations of domination" (p. 298). She discovered that she and her students were ill equipped to handle the unequal power relations in the classroom, even as they studied oppression related to racism. There was "resentment that other oppressions (sexism, heterosexism, fat oppression, classism, anti-Semitism) were being marginalized in the name of addressing racism" (p. 316). In fact, critical theory itself has been called oppressive, "reproducing a culture of silence" due to its "technical jargon, obscure references, and ambiguous phrasing" (Pietrykowski, 1996, p. 84).

Critical research often consists of analysis of text (by *text* is meant written accounts as well as other forms of communication such as film, dance, drama, and so on) to reveal the assumptions underlying the text, assumptions about the world and the way things are, such that certain interests are reinforced. These certain interests are "privileged" above all others; other interests are marginalized or oppressed. The researcher's main goal is to be "critical," to uncover and challenge the assumptions and social structures that oppress.

Critical research often intersects with other forms of inquiry. For example, a critical ethnography is interested in more than the cultural interpretation of human interaction; it also takes into account the historical, economic, and political structures that have impact on the culture. Critical ethnographers attempt "to broaden the political dimensions of cultural work while undermining existing oppressive systems" (Fontana & Frey, 1994, p. 369).

Some critical research is informed by feminist theory. Here, issues of power and oppression are studied in terms of gender; the politicizing of women's experience is central in critical feminist research. As Crotty (1998, p. 182) observes, feminists bring to research "an abiding sense of oppression in a man-made world. For some, this may be little more than an awareness that the playing field they are on is far from level and they need to even things up. For others, the injustice is more profound and severe. They perceive the need for very radical change in culture and society. . . .Feminist research is always a struggle, then, at least to reduce, if not to eliminate, the injustices and unfreedom that women experience." Several articles in this collection are framed by feminist theory, including those by Pillow, Tisdell, and Johnson-Bailey. Krenske and McKay's "'Hard and Heavy': Gender and Power in a Heavy Metal Music Subculture," in this volume, is an ethnography informed by both critical and feminist theory.

A third type of research that is intended to address human inequality is participatory research. Participatory, or participatory action research, focuses on the political empowerment of people through participant involvement in the design and implementation of a research project. Collective action as a result of the investigation is a crucial component of this type of research. Thus, individuals engage in research in this mode to better understand the subtle and overt manifestations of oppression, and that understanding leads to more control of their lives through collective action.

There are two examples of critical research in this section. The first, by Burbules (1986), is a critical analysis of the children's book, *Tootle.* In this textual analysis, Burbules reveals how the seemingly innocent story of a baby locomotive learning to be an adult locomotive can be read as a parable of schooling, work, and adulthood—and how the oppressive structures of class and gender are reinforced in our society.

Sandlin's (2000) study is of the consumer education texts used in adult literacy programs. Working from a critical theory perspective, Sandlin found that the hidden curriculum of the texts reinforces current class inequalities by placing blame for financial failure on the individual, ignoring the larger social, political, and economic contexts.

References

Crotty, M. (1998). *The foundations of social research: Meaning and perspective in the research process.* Thousand Oaks, CA: Sage.

Ellsworth, E. (1989). Why doesn't this feel empowering? Working through the repressive myths of critical pedagogy. *Harvard Educational Review, 59*(3), 297–324.

Fontana, A. & Frey, J. H. (1994). Interviewing: The art of science. In N. K. Denzin & Y. S. Lincoln, (Eds.), *Handbook of qualitative research* (pp. 361–376). Thousand Oaks, CA: Sage.

Kincheloe, J. L., & McLaren, P. L. (1994). Rethinking critical theory and qualitative research. In N. K. Denzin & Y. S. Lincoln (Eds.), *Handbook of qualitative research.* (pp. 138–157). Thousand Oaks, CA: Sage.

Marx, K. (1967). *Writings of the young Marx on philosophy and society.* (L. D. Easton & K. H. Guddat, Eds., Trans.). New York: Anchor Books.

Pietrykowski, B. (1996). Knowledge and power in adult education: Beyond Freire and Habermas. *Adult Education Quarterly, 46*(2), 82–97.

15

Tootle

A Parable of Schooling and Destiny

Nicholas C. Burbules

In 1945 Gertrude Crampton wrote a children's book called *Tootle*, and forty years later the book is still in print (Crampton, 1945). Countless children have read and been read to from this book. What is *Tootle* about? Why was it written? Why has it remained popular for so long? This essay suggests some answers to these questions. My more general purpose is to demonstrate a style of critical textual analysis that can be useful in analyzing other cultural artifacts in order to reveal their ideological content and implicit normative commitments.[1]

In critical educational studies "ideology" and "hegemony" have become standard categories (see, for example, Apple, 1979; Giroux, 1981; Anyon, 1979). But both Marxist and neopositivist conceptions of ideology have often suffered from the premise that ideologies are demonstrably "false" and propagandistic, leading to the conclusion that the way to fight them is to juxtapose their misrepresentations with a "true" account of society. This approach underestimates the descriptive and explanatory power that ideologies can have and assumes the existence of an alternative "scientific" standpoint from which ideologies can be criticized.

As I have argued elsewhere, we should understand ideology on the model of a literary text: as a portrayal of social and political life that is suggestive, poetic, and nonliteral; as telling *a* truth if not *the* truth (Burbules, 1983). In my view, the process of ideology analysis and ideology critique is akin to literary criticism; it includes an attempt to hold a portrayal accountable to social reality while recognizing that ideologies that capture the popular imagination, however partial or biased, must be granted a degree of coherence and plausibility. By discussing *Tootle,* I will demonstrate this approach.

My responsibility as an interpreter is to justify my claims about what the story means by reference to textual elements that can be seen by others; for this reason I include excerpts from the text of the story in this essay. I will try to relate some of these elements to each other in ways that make sense. Alternative interpretations are, of course, possible: it is the nature of interpretation to select and emphasize certain features as significantly related to each other. Thus, any particular interpretation is simply one stage in an ongoing dialogue among readers, mediated by a common text. Because I am treating the text as ideological, I also have an additional responsibility, namely, critique. Where the text implicitly assumes certain social circumstances that can be raised to question; where it colors certain conditions with an evaluative shade, or makes outright judgments about them; and where it distorts, misrepresents, or offers a partial, incomplete version of social events, it can be subject to criticism. This criticism is usually not so simple as saying that the text is "false," nor so straightforward as saying that the text presents "immoral" values. Rather, one must show that the text, while usefully illuminating some concerns, does so at the expense of assuming or ignoring other significant problems, or that the text does not admit its own value stance. In the present case I will argue that *Tootle* presents an account of schooling, work, and being an adult in a capitalist society that cheerfully endorses some of the most repressive aspects of the process by which schools restrict the impulses and aspirations of children—primarily by class and secondarily by gender.

One might raise the following objection: "But this is just a *children's* book." Indeed, children's books usually have a convincing tone of innocence. And few if any children would derive most of the interpretations I will offer. This objection, however, misses several crucial points. First, it is difficult if not impossible to discover what children actually understand from a text, for two reasons. Children cannot reliably report either the conscious or unconscious effects of the story; moreover, it is impossible to know what elements of the story, repeated over and over, will be remembered later in adulthood when they may be indirectly recalled and interpreted in an entirely new way (see Bettelheim, 1976). Second, the book's effect on children is only part of the story. Publishing children's literature is a profit-making venture, and such books are generally purchased by adults (parents and teachers). For example, the quality appeal of "A Little Golden Book," such as *Tootle,* and many of its textual references (such as to the "Mayor Himself," with his ruddy nose and green coattails, clearly a parody of Irish politicians), are directed at an adult audience. Often books are purchased by adults because *they* find the books clever and interesting; children are the subsidiary consumers of the product, and with repetition the biases and interests of the adult may be transferred to the child.[2] Third, an undue focus on the functional effects of an ideological text distracts us from an equally important issue: *what we can learn about ourselves and our culture by examining the kinds of books we produce for our children to read.* Deriving the normative presuppositions that inform an educational text and give it consistency and meaning is important in understanding the world-views of educators and the set of assumptions about education that typify our society.

In addition, one may argue that the author "could not have intended" the range of interpretations and implications discussed here. Again, this objection misses the point. While Crampton's intentions may be of biographical interest, they are not necessarily the best key to understanding what is actually in her book. Once a text passes from its author to a reader, it takes on a life of its own; what interpretations the text will plausibly bear are legitimate whether or not the author intended them. The author's intentions are in no way a constraint on the reader's interpretive prerogatives (see, for example, Foucault, 1979). Authors frequently acknowledge that they benefit from readers' interpretations of their texts and learn things about the texts (and about themselves) that they had not seen before.[3] This point is worth stressing in the context of educational studies, since so much of critical educational research (for example, much of the work done on the "hidden curriculum") has foundered on the question of imputing motives or intentions to educators, when the very point should be to reveal activities, or the consequences of activities, that teachers emphatically *do not* intend (Phillips, 1981; Burbules, 1981). These observations are particularly pertinent to this book, because *Tootle* is a story *about* education. It reveals certain assumptions about teaching and learning as well as definite educational priorities. Whether Crampton herself recognized or consciously intended these assumptions and priorities is for my purposes beside the point.

Synopsis of *Tootle*

On its surface, the story line of *Tootle* is simple.[4] Tootle is a young locomotive in the town of Lower Trainswitch. He goes to school with other locomotives to learn to become a grown-up engine. The ideal of success is the New York-Chicago Flyer, a big train who gets to go very fast and makes a loud "ToooOoooot" instead of a "gay little Tootle."

The young locomotives must learn many, many rules to become "good trains," but their teacher Bill tells them that the most important rule is to Stay on the Rails No Matter What. This rule is repeated frequently in the text. Tootle tries very hard to follow all the rules, even the rule to Stop for a Red Flag Waving (although "there is nothing a locomotive hates more than stopping").

One day a "Dreadful Thing" happens. Tootle sees a black horse who challenges him to a race. Tootle speeds along, but when the tracks make a Great Curve, he must choose between staying on the rails or continuing the race. Tootle jumps off the tracks and races alongside the horse.

The race ends in a tie, and Tootle stays to talk with his new friend. He is happy. But later he realizes that he has broken a very important rule, and he resolves to work hard in the future. Yet he succumbs the next day when he sees the meadow full of lovely buttercups. He has heard that he can tell if he likes butter by holding a buttercup under his chin. He is strongly tempted and eventually jumps off the rails, dancing in the meadow and crying "What fun!"

Later that evening, the Chief Oiler finds grass between Tootle's wheels and reports this to Bill, who says sternly that Tootle must learn the rule about Staying on the Rails No Matter What.

On the third day, Tootle again plays in the meadow, watching a frog and making a daisy chain. He says into a rain barrel "Toot," and the booming echo that returns makes him feel like Flyer already. Day after day, Tootle continues to play in the meadow, chasing butterflies and frolicking among the hollyhocks.

Then one day the Mayor Himself sees Tootle, and he and Bill formulate a strategy to get Tootle back on track.

On the following day, all the villagers hide in the meadow, each holding a red flag. Tootle comes happily down the tracks and hops into the field, thinking what a beautiful day it is. But suddenly he sees a red flag poking up. He stops and thinks "I'll go another way." But as he turns he sees another red flag, then another, then another. The meadow is full of red flags and he is very frustrated. Just as he is about to cry, he sees Bill on the tracks, holding a green flag. Tootle goes over to him and says, "This is the place for me. There is nothing but red flags for locomotives that get off their tracks." All the townspeople cheer "Hurray for Tootle the Flyer."

Today Tootle is indeed a Flyer, and he always passes on the advice to younger locomotives, "Stay on the Rails No Matter What."

Themes

Three general themes are immediately apparent from a reading of this text. First, the story tells children what schools are for: they are for learning rules and learning to become an adult. Second, the story stresses the inviolate character of certain rules, and the bitter consequences of disobedience. Third, the story offers a portrait of adulthood and the world of adult work, of what it means to grow up and become a responsible member of society. I will elaborate these themes in some detail and extract some of the ideological content of the story; undoubtedly, readers will find still other interpretations that have eluded me.[5]

Rules

Without question the central concern of the story is the importance of rules. Rules are cited at least thirty-two times in twenty pages of text, with the prime rule, "Stay on the Rails No Matter What," cited fourteen times alone. A striking double-page illustration at the start of the story shows Bill surrounded by wide-eyed students, pointing to this injunction written large on a blackboard and holding up a cautionary finger—or perhaps indicating that the rule is of primary importance. Rules Are Always Capitalized, giving them the Appearance of Authoritative Truth. Furthermore, they are typically stated in unequivocal, inviolate terms: "no matter what"; "never, never"; "no locomotive ever, ever"; and so on. Rules are presented as absolute injunctions, not human-made conventions.

And yet nowhere are these rules ever justified; in fact they are never called "rules," but rather "lessons"—that is, not norms, but *facts.* Certainly there are reasons involving safety, convenience, and efficiency that underlie some of these rules, but the story does not discuss any. On the contrary, the rules are alluded to as common sense, as beyond question—that is, as hegemonic: they are often preceded by the phrase "of course." Because these rules, especially Staying on the Rails No Matter What and Stopping for a Red Flag Waving, are assumed to be indisputable and inviolate, they must be obeyed *without question:* they are taught by indoctrination rather than by reasoned persuasion. Thus children are presented with a particular message about what schools are for and what learning is all about; furthermore, the author reveals *her* strategy of instruction, which is illustrated in the very approach she takes in this book.

One paradox of the story, however, is that while "not one of the engines. . . would even think of getting off the rails," and while a successful engine must get a perfect score (100 A +) in Staying on the Rails, Tootle does otherwise. This implies that the inviolate character of the rules is exaggerated. In fact, there seem to be two kinds of rules: those dealing with safety (such as Stopping for a Red Flag) and those dealing with propriety (such as those concerned with making appropriate sounds)—which would require two utterly different sorts of justification, if justification were offered. Further, the first type is inviolate in a way that the second type need not be, since the text implies that for the sake of the first (Stopping for a Red Flag), a locomotive may violate the second (Not Spilling the Soup). Finally, while Staying on the Rails is, one might say, an instance of the first sort of rule, the story treats it entirely as an instance of the second—and this point is crucial for the moral of the story, since it infuses a criterion of appropriate behavior with the urgency of a rule of safety and survival.

For while no locomotive *ever* fails to Stop for a Red Flag, the engines are told they must get 100 A + in Staying on the Rails—a quantitative measure that itself implies the possibility, even the likelihood, of deviance. In fact, when Tootle is "sent to practice Staying on the Rails," it is clear that this is an unpleasant task, that is, a kind of punishment. "Staying on the Rails," of course, is an allegory: communicating, first, that there is a single, unidirectional, preordained path to success that the child is expected to pursue and, second, that obedience regardless of personal desires is the key to success. Moreover, it functions as a metarule that enjoins conformity by "following rules" (in one sense, following rails *means* following rules). Only a child who unconditionally accepts and obeys this "most important" rule can become a Flyer—the symbol of adulthood and achievement.

Identity and Role

It is striking in this story that all characters except Bill are nameless, identified only by their occupation: in Lower Trainswitch people *are* what they *do.* This feature illustrates well Louis Althusser's claim that ideologies "hail" subjects, identifying them in their relation to each other (Althusser, 1971). For example, the Chief Oiler has a definite relation to the First, Second, and Third Assistant Oilers. This is especially true for Tootle. Tootle is not simply an anthropomorphized engine. He is emphatically a child: wide-eyed, diminutive, and immature. He is called a "baby," and no child likes to be called that. His very name reminds us of the cute but ineffectual sound he and all young engines make: "But the best they can do is a gay little Tootle." He is an archetypal young locomotive, and by implication an archetypal child.

Tootle has no positive peer group among the engines. While illustrations occasionally show engines clustered in groups and even speaking with one another, nowhere in the text does Tootle interact with other baby locomotives. Peer relations and friendships are virtually ignored; where they are mentioned, it is because they are troublesome. Isolated, Tootle is entirely dependent on Bill's or the townspeople's approval, or disapproval—which, as we will see, is highly conditional. The one exception to this pattern occurs when Tootle leaves the rails to race with the horse. Fearful that "everyone at school will laugh at me," he races with the horse and finds it a "nice" experience: "The race ended in a tie. Both Tootle and the black horse were happy. They stood on the banks of the river and talked." But the text tells us that this was a Dreadful Thing. Tootle's concern for peer approval, on the one hand, and his attempt to form an independent peer relation, on the other, get him into trouble.

Tootle's specialness is highlighted by the fact that he alone of all the young engines is given a name. He is labeled from the first day as "the finest baby. . . since old 600" and acknowledged as having the potential to become a Flyer. This "halo effect" may explain why he can deviate from the rules (he does not get 100 A + in Staying on The Rails No Matter What) and still become a Flyer. Bill uses the prospect of becoming a Flyer as leverage to get Tootle to accept his structure of discipline; eventually, Tootle internalizes this ideal and applies it to himself.

This leads us to ask what "engine-ness" and "Flyer-ness" are. Being a locomotive is identified with two kinds of behavior: those concerning motion, especially speed, and those concerning sound. Little engines "love to go fast" and make noise. But they must learn to control these impulses, to constrain them in appropriate ways. A Flyer gets to go very fast (Two-Miles-a-Minute), but even a Flyer must Stay on the Rails, Stop for Red Flags, Not Spill the Soup, and so on. To be a young engine, like Tootle, is to be defined by immaturity and inadequacy: he is a short, stubby engine, not a long, sleek Flyer (clearly highlighted by the illustrations in the book); he "Tootles" but can't "Toot"; and he is an old-fashioned engine with cowcatcher and coal car, not a modern locomotive.

Moreover, Tootle is a machine and not a human being (although he does exhibit some anthropomorphic characteristics). It is essential to the symbolism of the book that Bill, the Mayor Himself, and other humans retain a status to which Tootle can *never* gain access. He can become a Flyer, but he can never become Mayor. At the end, when Tootle passes along the rule about Staying on the Rails to the next generation of engines, this is labeled "advice." He is not a *teacher*, as

Bill is, nor can he be. There are roles a youngster is suited for, which, with hard work, can be attained, but however successful one becomes at that role, there are other roles for which one is never destined. Growing up involves coming to recognize and accept this fact.

School

Tootle presents a very definite portrait of what school is and what it is for. "Lower Trainswitch has a fine school for engines," we are told; the "lessons" it teaches are cited as evidence of this. School is where you go to learn lessons that encompass only technical skills and rules of appropriate conduct. One learns to acquire habits, not to form relationships or acquire knowledge, reason, or autonomy. Moreover, a particular conception of teaching and learning is modeled here. Teaching is based on repetition: cite the rules as often as possible and stress how important they are without giving any reasons for their importance. Learning means listening and remembering. This learning can be quantifiably measured and compared. Where memorization of the rules is insufficient and misconduct occurs, as when Tootle leaves the tracks, a further strategy is employed: paired-associate conditioning. Link the pleasurable stimulus of the field with the aversive stimulus of the red flags, and the field will cease to be pleasurable. As I noted earlier, Crampton not only illustrates these methods in her story, but actively employs them. This book is *about* teaching and learning, but it is also a teaching device itself, relying on repetition (for example, citing one rule alone fourteen times) and emotional manipulation (for example, calling Tootle's romp in the meadow a Dreadful Thing when it clearly is not).

The teacher, Bill, is kindly and benign, but his affection is conditional: "he will not be angry if. . ." implies that he *will* be angry under other conditions. Actually, the story juxtaposes that assertion with the observation: "But they will never, never be good trains unless they get 100 A + in Staying on the Rails No Matter What." In other words, Bill *implies* that he will be angry under certain circumstances and *asserts* that under such circumstances the little engines will be failures. This happens often in the story: the teacher's personal judgment is subtly transposed into a prediction about the student's life chances. Bill's judgments are not the source of failure; it is the engine who fails.

Finally, school seems a dreary sort of place. One can enjoy one's tasks up to a point but not to excess. Enjoyment, in any event, is not what school is for. School is where one "works hard" at one's lessons. To be happy, one must play "hooky," yet the consequences of this are severe. Isolated from one's peers and fearful of their judgments, one is dependent on the conditional affection and approval of an authority who is continually shaping one's experiences with his or her own purposes in mind. This is the picture of school Crampton paints for her readers.

Adulthood

Here, as in the case of school, the story portrays what a child should expect from a later set of experiences. From the very beginning, inadequate childhood is juxtaposed with accomplished adulthood. Every little engine wants to grow up. Unfortunately, according to Crampton, along with adulthood comes sadness; the "long, sad, *ToooOoooot*" of the big locomotives is contrasted with the "gay little *Tootle*" of the young. Nevertheless, being a Flyer is unquestionably better than being a "baby" locomotive. And human adults in this story are universally more knowledgeable, wiser, and more clever than Tootle. They can detect his indiscretions and manipulate him without his knowledge.

What is adult is necessarily good. The path to adulthood is the path of rule-following, of foregoing childish pleasures, of acquiring self-control, and of abandoning play for the sake of satisfaction in one's work. Happiness beyond the rails is dysfunctional and "silly"; what matters is pride and success. Tootle often exhibits a childish petulance and impatience, as when he utters his expletive, "Oh, Whistle!" Such emotionality must be outgrown. As noted before, Tootle must also forego childish friendships: the life of the Flyer is solitary and independent. Adulthood, we are told, requires that we learn to accept sadness and do even the things we most hate (such as Stopping for a Red Flag).

Work

If the young must give up childish joys and pleasures, it is to acquire the more mature satisfactions of adult work—those derived from responsibly carrying out one's duties and obediently following the rules that define competent performance. Work is somewhat compulsive: locomotives love to hurry and hate to stop. The two features of "engine-ness"—sound and motion—are allowed expression, but in a controlled and disciplined manner: "Tootle," but not too loud; go fast, but Don't Spill the Soup. . .and Always Stop for Red Flags. We also see this portrait of work in the Day Watchman, who clearly takes pride in doing his job well (bridling when it is suggested there might be grass on the tracks) even though his job—"watching the tracks all day"—is pointedly boring.

Failure or success, in work as in school, is a personal matter. Characters in the story are defined by their occupations, and each person is accountable for a specific task. There is a hierarchical division of labor among the different characters: Bill is clearly more important than the Day Watchman, who doesn't even get to play checkers; the Chief Oiler is clearly superior to the First, Second, and Third Assistant Oilers; the Mayor Himself is clearly the final authority, since no one truly believes that Tootle has left the tracks until the Mayor Himself confirms it. When the time comes to play a trick on Tootle, Bill devises the plan, and the various Oilers do the "hard work"—the hammering, sawing, and so forth—a classic division of conception from execution of work tasks. As mentioned earlier, this specialization and stratification have special reference to Tootle: as a machine he is clearly subordinate to all humans in the story.

Society

In explicit and implicit ways, *Tootle* presents a definite picture of society. First, society is meritocratic: hard work gets you ahead. . .*if* you have the talent. Tootle, judged early to have special promise as a locomotive, receives special attention and special treatment: he breaks the second most inviolate rule, hardly earning a 100 A + , but still he can become a Flyer. Because he is labeled as promising *he is not allowed to fail;* the entire town turns out to help him get back on the proper course. "Stubby," an ordinary little locomotive no one bothered to write a book about, might have been kicked out of school for a similar infraction.

Second, the social system is clearly a class system. For both humans and engines, there are positions of special authority and privilege. As noted earlier, this is clear in the relations among Bill, the Mayor Himself, and the various functionaries of the railroad, as well as in the clear superiority of the Flyer to other types of locomotives. In fact, *Tootle* is a parable about schooling and working-class destiny. Begin with the location: "Lower" Trainswitch—a far cry from the elite New York–Chicago route of the Flyer. This is the humble origin Tootle seeks to escape, but it also defines the limits of his possibilities. Tootle is on a "track" that has a respectable terminus, but limited opportunities otherwise. If Tootle acquires the appropriate technical skills and the requisite self-restraint, he can become a proficient locomotive, maybe even a Flyer. But for all its sleek efficiency, the Flyer is still just pulling a train. In the same way, working-class students in society face career ladders with definite constraints. Schools assign students to various "tracks" which foster self-fulfilling prophecies by offering students skills, attitudes, and modes of behavior that help them acquire certain jobs while effectively excluding them from others (see, for example, Bowles & Gintis, 1976).

Third, Tootle is subject to the decisions and judgments of others, notably *humans.* Society works because responsible authorities make decisions and because everyone else follows rules. The authoritative nature of teachers ("But Bill said. . .") and public officials (the Mayor's unimpeachable testimony on Tootle's misconduct) is not questioned. On two occasions—when Tootle "Tootles" too loudly and when he leaves the rails—the Mayor Himself intervenes to resolve the conflict. When the Mayor Himself gets involved, we know that the problem has become truly serious. Fortunately, the conflicts are never fundamental; all difficulties arise in the context of a given framework of commonly accepted values and are due solely to the shortcomings of individuals, and of individual *engines,* not humans.

Here the State (in the person of the Mayor) appears to be impartial and benign, just as concerned for Tootle's welfare as for the townspeople's. The conspiracy to get Tootle back on the tracks is well-intentioned and the surveillance via informants who secretly keep an eye on Tootle is for his own good. But there is another way to view the extraordinary solidarity with which all humans band together to get Tootle back on the tracks. He is, after all, a servant to their benefit; trains are for the convenience and luxury of humans. The townspeople, Bill, and the Mayor Himself must remind Tootle that he is an engine, not a human; a child, not an adult; a rule-follower, not a free agent; a worker, not a decision maker. They must see to it that he stays in his place without question, that he doesn't presume to choose his own course or destiny. It is only when Tootle returns to the rails that they cheer and hail him as "Tootle the Flyer," which rewards him for conforming to their desires. Following this line of interpretation, the surveillance, conspiracy, and manipulation are decidedly partisan, benefiting Tootle only in a narrowly circumscribed way.

The absolute difference in kind between machines and humans in the story highlights more sharply what are actually differences of degree, in two separate cases. On the one hand, the locomotives, as children, are subject to the judgments, decisions, and benign manipulations of all humans, as adults. It is only by becoming adult engines that the locomotives can gain any kind of independence or esteem. On the other hand, the locomotives, as workers, are in the service of all humans, and even a Flyer remains in this subordinate class. In both cases, the dichotomous characterization of Tootle's relationship to humans, who decide important features of his destiny and who possess a status to which he can never aspire, makes his subordinate role (whether as child to adult, or as worker to creative authority) seem more natural and inevitable than it actually is. The fact that both messages are operating simultaneously means that Tootle is confronted with a double bind: he can derive some of the benefits of adulthood (such as being looked up to by young engines), but only at the expense of accepting the restrictive definition of adulthood and adult work defined for him by others.

Nature

This story clearly values technology over nature. Gleaming locomotives are praised; horses, butterflies, and hollyhocks are regarded as trivial and silly at best, as dire temptations and distractions at worst. The horse symbolizes wild and uncontrolled nature—precisely what Tootle must deny himself.

The story takes on a difficult task, however, in trying to convince us that Tootle's play in the idyllic meadow is a "Dreadful Thing," deviant and dangerously inappropriate. Indeed, all the illustrations show his innocent happiness, which the text confirms. What the meadow offers Tootle is a chance to play with other creatures, including the horse, in relations untainted by comparative judgments and rules. Labeled a potential Flyer, he fears the scorn of his peers if he loses the race to the horse, but when the race ends in a tie Tootle realizes that both he and the horse can be happy. Competition can be for fun, and not merely because future ambitions weigh in the balance. The meadow offers the possibility of play and noninstrumental and egalitarian relations, where Tootle can be happy *as a child* and not as a potential adult. This is juxtaposed with the world of the roundhouse, the tracks, the ambition to become a Flyer, and the attendant values of technology and efficiency. I would suggest that the meadow, the earth, and the animals of nature embody values that Tootle must forego if he is to succeed in the stereotypically masculine world of technology, competition, and "Flyer-ness." His sensitive, emotional, and relational qualities are not relevant to his work and in this story actually impede it; in the world of Tootle, it is clear which must give way.

Sin

Why is it bad that Tootle leaves the tracks? Because it is against the rules. Justification for those rules could be offered in terms of safety, efficiency, and so forth, but the story offers no such justification. The commentary and symbolism the story employs invite a very different sort of answer. There are five occasions on which Tootle's departure from the tracks is detailed.

First, he races the black horse. The race itself is not the Dreadful Thing; it is good that Tootle wants to compete and win—it is a sign of "Flyer-ness." Unfortunately, the Great Curve in the tracks leads him away from his desires, and he must choose between pleasure and responsibility. He chooses pleasure, leaves the rails, and races with the horse. The race ends in a breathless tie, and they talk, resting together by the bank of a river. Giving in to temptation is the Dreadful Thing. But desiring pleasure, and the infantile allusions to sexual relations, are in no way negative except that they are labeled as such. Indoctrinated with certain rules, Tootle feels guilt, and as a consequence redoubles his effort in his lessons, but in Tootling, not in Staying on the Rails!

Second, Tootle sees a field of buttercups. He doesn't mean to leave the rails, but the insistent rhythm of his wheels compels him to do it. Whether or not one sees the race with the horse as a kind of sexual congress and the urging rhythmic wheels as an expression of physical desire, it is plausible that the temptation to self-indulgence and the concurrent remorse that Tootle feels derive at least part of their symbolic energy from latent sexual tensions.

Tootle's bodily nature is treated differently in another part of this adventure. Tootle wishes to hold a buttercup under his searchlight to see whether he likes butter. Because locomotives don't eat butter, and because he must use a searchlight since he has no chin, his cry, "I do like butter! I do!" is strange; it implicitly reaffirms that Tootle is *not* a human, and that it is illusory for him to pretend to be one. Every time Tootle crosses the barrier of appropriate "engine-like" behavior and acts too much like a human or like an adult, it is in the context of doing something "silly" or "dreadful."

On the third occasion, Tootle finds a rain barrel and speaks into it. The booming "TOOT" that resounds suggests to him a new potency and maturity that are, again, illusory. Tootle thinks he sounds like a Flyer but he is not a Flyer yet, and he will not be until Bill and the townspeople so anoint him. His emerging sexual identity and growing independence from social conventions and judgments may be psychically liberating, but at the expense of any "reality checks." Tootle is not ready to make decisions for himself. Having been indoctrinated to accept a dichotomous and rule-governed view of childhood versus adulthood and of play/pleasure versus work/responsibility, he is unable to integrate these into a cohesive identity.

On the fourth occasion, Tootle plays with the butterflies and wishes he could fly as they do. As he has left the tracks for the meadow, he dreams of leaving the earth itself for the air. But this he cannot possibly do. In terms of the story, these four adventures reveal a progressive delusion reaching alarming proportions and a diminishing sense of responsibility. With each escapade, Tootle feels less remorse and exhibits less ability to integrate the facets of his personality. Pointedly, this visit to the meadow, and Tootle's pleasure, are contrasted with the "hard work" the Oilers are carrying out at that very moment.

Why is it bad that Tootle leaves the tracks? What is at stake is Tootle's obedience to the rules formulated for him by Bill and the others. What he threatens to do is to choose his own peer group, become independent of Bill and all adults/humans, and choose adventure and pleasure over respectability and diligence. Another paradox of the story is that while it shows him consistently happy in such experiences, it must create a sense of inappropriateness so that the reader will approve of Tootle's manipulation back into conformity with the rules. The illustrations emphasize the foolishness of his pretense and the progressive outrageousness of his conduct (we see him eventually with a daisy chain around his "neck"). The "proper" interpretation of these images, however, depends on the audience's acceptance of the same dichotomies that Tootle is meant to embrace—those between technology and nature, childhood and adulthood, work and play, and so on—dichotomies that the book itself establishes and reinforces. Given different premises, Tootle's plight could be viewed as tragic or heroic rather than comic.

Here again a parallel exists between what happens to Tootle and what happens to his readers. As Paul Willis has pointed out, student resistance is always partial and ambiguous: while some rules may be challenged, other, often deeper rules are so taken for granted that the actual effect of rebellion may be to reaffirm working-class destinies (Willis, 1977). For the reader, the commonsense nature of certain beliefs—that locomotives obviously should stay on the tracks, for example—ensures that Tootle's behavior will be interpreted in the "proper" way: of course he must return to the rails, no matter what. For Tootle as well, his acceptance of certain fundamental and commonsense assumptions provides the basis for eventually being manipulated into compliance with appropriate beliefs and behaviors during his fifth, and final, adventure.

Redemption

Because this is a children's book, it must have a "happy" ending. Conflict must be resolved, error must be corrected, and personal differences must be bridged. Tootle has transgressed the rules of Lower Trainswitch. He has presumed freedoms that are not his to sample, and he has succumbed to the temptation of sensual pleasures. But the failure is his alone; the norms governing this societal microcosm are right and proper. Hence the problem is simply one of inducing him to conform to such norms in the expected manner. For talented Tootle, mistakes are forgivable so long as he repents, returns to the path of righteousness, and reaffirms the commandments he has transgressed.

Tootle, thinking "What a beautiful day" as he plays in the meadow, suddenly encounters a Red Flag Waving from behind a bush. The flag has no functional meaning in this context, but for an unquestioning and ultimately obedient young engine that does not matter, since the rule had never been justified by a functional purpose in the first place. A red flag *always* means stop. Turning away, Tootle encounters another red flag, and another, and another. Because Tootle accepts this fundamental rule, he can be manipulated toward obedience to the others. As noted above, this dynamic is akin to the one that leads students to challenge one aspect of school rules, such as dress codes, while accepting other, more fundamental rules that have more to do with governing their lives, such as grading policies. It also reminds us that for students who meet the important criteria, a range of toleration usually exists for failing to meet those that are less important.

A simple point must be stressed here: *Tootle doesn't know that townspeople are behind the red flags.* He might resent it if he knew, and reject not the meadow but the community that is intruding on and spoiling his fun. The very efficacy of inviolate rules depends on their being abstracted from any social context or set of conventions—they just *are.* Just as Tootle does not see the people behind the flags, he does not see the human interests behind the rules he must obey.

Tootle complains: "This meadow is full of red flags. How can I have any fun?" Tootle rejects the meadow only because of the nuisance caused by the red flags, which are extraneous to it. The field is no longer fun for him. In other words, Tootle undergoes no real character development or maturation as a result of this "lesson." He merely finds the meadow no longer attractive, while it is, in fact, as pleasurable as it ever was. The strategy pursued by the townspeople creates in Tootle a distorted and inaccurate perception of the world for the purpose of manipulating him back into conformity with their desires and expectations.

Their strategy is classic behaviorist aversion therapy. The text explicitly links the highly aversive red flags (there is "nothing a locomotive hates more than Stopping for a Red Flag") with the buttercups, the daisies, the blue bird, the rain barrel—all things that have given Tootle pleasure.[6] "Why did I think this meadow was such a fine place?" Tootle moans. What is even more tragic than the way Tootle's pleasures have been robbed from him is that Crampton is using this strategy with her readers as well. A child who identifies with Tootle will despair along with him; whereas earlier in the story, illustrations portrayed Tootle frolicking in the meadow, at this point, they show him weeping. It appears that the child's desire for a happy ending can be satisfied only when Tootle learns to follow the rules.

This "happy ending" is insidious. Tootle looks up from the meadow and sees Bill with a green flag, standing on the tracks. This links his joy and relief at seeing the flag with returning to the rails and Bill. Here again we see paired-associated conditioning. The gratitude he feels for Bill reinforces Bill's legitimacy as a teacher. What we know, and what Tootle does not, is that Bill is as much responsible for those horrible red flags as for the green one. This seemingly benign old gentleman is actually conniving and scheming, albeit for Tootle's "own good"; he is given credit for the good he accomplishes but no blame for the unhappiness he causes in the process.

The townspeople cheer for Tootle. He receives strong positive reinforcement for conforming to their wishes. He has finally internalized the Protestant ethic of deferred gratification, hard work, and an achievement orientation. But he has not learned to integrate the various aspects of his personality; nor has he learned to control his desires and express them appropriately—he has merely submerged them under a set of rules, imposed from without, that cause him to reject those desires out of hand. The moral of the story—*There is nothing but red flags for locomotives that get off the tracks*—tells only a partial truth. While it is true that deviance elicits strong disapproval, the story does not examine the social genesis of that response or question the interests that lie behind it.

Bill, the Mayor, the Oilers, and everyone else in town can visit the meadow at their leisure. But Tootle has no leisure. Humans can even close up shop and leave work when it is important enough to them (for example, to get Tootle back on the tracks). But when Tootle leaves his work it is a Dreadful Thing. Adults of a certain class decide when work is necessary, what type of work it will be, and by whom it will be done. What was the Mayor doing out in the meadow on the day he found Tootle? Was he working?

Tootle learns his place. By restricting his ambitions to accord with his "class" origins, he becomes a successful Flyer. By foregoing the pleasures of the meadow and repressing his desire for peer relations, he becomes an independent and hard-working adult. By eschewing certain feelings and impulses, he becomes narrowly "masculine." By internalizing the rules that have been created for him by others, he becomes accomplished and even an agent of reproduction himself, passing on to later generations the advice that "most of all, Stay on the Rails No Matter What," because for him obedience to that rule has been the key to success and because he has experienced the bitter consequences of disobedience.

Conclusion

Tootle presents a remarkably detailed and complex educational ideology. While not monolithic in its message, or always consistent in its imagery or symbolism, it does portray a definite picture of social life. In this essay I have tried to draw out some of the assumptions and values that characterize its social worldview. By considering how those assumptions and values underlie a seemingly simple and innocent text, we may be better able to recognize them at work in other educational contexts.

The ideology expressed in *Tootle* is relatively coherent, and it is not difficult to see its plausibility and appeal. It is a "true" story insofar as it describes certain realities. As Tootle says, there *will* be red flags for those who leave the tracks. But in revealing some aspects of social life, it conceals others. It is true that there are certain rules for success in school and success in the world of adult work, but the story does not discuss where those rules come from or how they can be justified, if at all. It is true that the acceptance of discipline and the repression of certain desires are necessary for success by some standards, but the story does not ask at what cost. It is true that children from certain class backgrounds have limited opportunities, and that for most of them being "realistic" means accepting those limits, but the story does not consider how or why our society has been set up that way.

In this story, Crampton describes some real features of childhood, adulthood, schooling, and work as they exist in our society, but she presents them as inevitable, or good, while ignoring alternative conceptions of them. Enduring ideologies depend less on blatant falsehoods than on accurate but partial representations—as various theorists have noted, ideologies are notable for what they do *not* discuss (Eagleton, 1976). They depend for plausibility on repetition and on becoming part of the commonsense, taken-for-granted, "of course" level of daily life.

Furthermore, enduring ideologies represent the world in a way people find reassuring (Geertz, 1973; see his discussion of "strain theories"). Reviewing the main themes of *Tootle*, one discovers a general outlook that can satisfy some very real needs for self-justification on the part of educators and parents and that can provide children with a simplified view of life, school, and their destinies as adults. The generally rosy picture that Crampton presents assumes that even where there is frustration, unhappiness, and failure, it is for the sake of eventual "success"—as if there were not any serious disagreement about what that means.

Tootle portrays a world in which children and the adults responsible for them have very definite roles and obligations toward one another. Children depend upon adults for judgments on whether or not they are performing properly or well. Where children fail to meet these expectations, the source of error is easy to pinpoint: success and failure are individual matters, and the child needs to try harder. Typically, children fail by acting upon immature desires and habits; they must try to stop being "babies" who do "silly" or "dreadful" things. Children want and need direction from adult authorities; as much as they may "hate" to carry out their responsibilities, it is unquestionably in their interests to do so. These responsibilities and expectations can be formulated as simple and inviolate rules that are absolute, not accidental—facts, not mere conventions. Follow the rules, and your life will work out well. The paradigm of all rules is to Stay on the Rails No Matter What. This rule assumes a unitary, preordained path to success for each child. Its terminus is known and obviously desirable. The only difficulty occurs when children do not stay on this path. Deviation is treated differently for different children, however, because the truly promising child's deviation can be redeemed by redoubled effort and by eventual internalization of the rule. The greatest success accrues to the one who falls from grace, repents, returns to the flock, and with the fervor of a convert impresses the message upon succeeding generations.

School is where lessons are learned, where inadequate children (babies) become responsible and accomplished adults. These lessons cover technical skills and standards of appropriate conduct and are immutable—learning to obey rules is essential to success at one's work in the classroom and in adult life and to good citizenship in the community. The lessons do nothing to promote questioning, reasoning, or character development. Teachers are kindly and benign; what they do is always for the child's welfare. The burden of proof is not on the teacher's judgment but on the child's performance: teachers do not fail children—children fail themselves. Teachers are the source of more good than harm, and no thought is given to the problem that doing "good" for some students may necessarily entail doing harm to them or to others. Where learning or behavioral problems exist, there are technical solutions that directly address and remedy the difficulty. Some of these techniques may be misleading, deceptive, or manipulative, such as assigning tasks without explanation of justification; using rewards and punishments to elicit desired student behaviors; relying on personal allegiances in order to motivate students to perform certain tasks; presenting incomplete, inconsistent, or inaccurate accounts of the world in order to make it uncontroversial and palatable; or avoiding conflict by presuming that consensus exists about the methods and ends of education. These approaches are appealing because they simplify the school day for the teacher and for the student. An educational approach that calls into question the above goals and methods would vastly complicate the tasks of teachers and students in the classroom, making their activities and relations to one another much more problematic, controversial, and provisional.

The educational ideology represented in *Tootle* suggests that children are not ready to be autonomous. Their attempts at independent judgment, sensual investigation, and peer-group formation are at best naive; at worst they interfere with the important task of becoming responsible and productive adults. Becoming an adult, especially for children of working-class backgrounds, means learning self-control and self-denial; it means foregoing childish pleasure; it means accepting tasks and constraints that one may hate; it means suppressing certain emotions and desires; it means abandoning play and learning to work in a compulsive manner; and it means accepting without question the discipline of externally imposed rules. In exchange, an adult receives the satisfactions of a job well done, social approval (rather than social rejection), and the admiration of the next generation of ambitious youth. For the talented who work hard, extraordinary success is possible. But everyone must learn to occupy some place in the hierarchical scheme of things, subordinate to some, superior to others; this locus is a given, decided by wiser heads than ours. Where conflicts arise, an impartial and beneficent State intervenes, implementing and preserving a framework of common values and interests about which there is putatively no disagreement.

This is a picture that can convince teachers that their intentions are invariably good and that their basic endeavor can be unambiguously defined. Moreover, it can reassure students that the path to adulthood and success is simple and linear. Neither side has much stake in examining very closely why the Great Curve of the rails leads inexorably away from many of the warmest and most vibrant impulses of childhood, or what is lost to those who do Stay on the Rails, No Matter What.

Acknowledgments

I wish to acknowledge the students who contributed to the development of ideas presented herein. They were (at Stanford University) Tomas da Silva, Beatriz Fisher, Carol Keller, Margot Kempers, Brian Lord, Bill Magier, and Thom Thresher, and (at the University of Utah) Tom Callister, Andrew Kliman, Hal Molitor, Tom Pederson, Suzanne Rice, Mohammad Siahpush, and Laurence Thompson. Also, earlier drafts of this essay were read by Ann Cuthbertson, Andrew Gitlin, and Suzanne Wade; their suggestions, and the comments of the editors of the *Harvard Educational Review,* led to substantial improvements in the paper.

Notes

1. I was first introduced to *Tootle* by Henry M. Levin several years ago. The idea for this essay grew out of two seminars on ideology and education that I have taught recently; my exchanges with Levin and with students in those classes greatly informed my understanding of *Tootle.*

2. Roland Barthes, among others, stresses the role of repetition in the effect of ideologies; see his *The Pleasure of the Text* (1975), pp. 40, 42. Barthes's work is the primary inspiration for this essay, which is in the style of his essays in *Mythologies* (1972), *The Eiffel Tower* (1979), and his masterpiece of textual analysis, *S/Z* (1974).

3. For example, John Updike's assertion that he was "more than once startled, many times enlightened" by the insights of a reviewer of one of his books (1980, p. 23).

4. For the original text of *Tootle*, see Crampton (1945). This version of my essay does not include the original text of the children's book *Tootle,* on which it is based. Although permission was granted to republish the story in the original version, which appeared in the *Harvard Educational Review,* the publishers of the book would not approve reprinting it here. I have included a brief summary of the narrative instead—otherwise the original essay is unchanged.

5. I am aware of the limits of discussing a children's text without putting the illustrations before you; I will try to describe visual references where relevant.

6. A slightly different literary treatment of this technique can be found in Anthony Burgess, *A Clockwork Orange* (1962, pp. 114–115).

References

Althusser, L. (1971). Ideology and ideological state apparatuses. In *Lenin and philosophy* (pp. 173–174). New York: Monthly Review Press.

Anyon, J. (1979). Ideology and United States history textbooks. *Harvard Educational Review, 49,* 361–386.

Apple, M. (1979). *Ideology and curriculum.* Boston: Routledge & Kegan Paul.

Barthes, R. (1972). *Mythologies.* New York: Hill & Wang.

Barthes, R. (1974). *S/Z.* New York: Hill & Wang.

Barthes, R. (1975). *The pleasure of the text.* New York: Hill & Wang.

Barthes, R. (1979). *The Eiffel Tower.* New York: Hill & Wang.

Bettelheim, B. (1976). *The uses of enchantment.* New York: Random House.

Bowles, S., & Gintis, H. (1976). *Schooling in capitalist America.* New York: Basic Books.

Burbules, N. C. (1981). Who hides the hidden curriculum? In C.J.B. Macmillan (Ed.), *Philosophy of education, 1980,* (pp. 281–291). Normal, IL: Philosophy of Education Society.

Burbules, N. C. (1983). Ideology and radical educational research. Dissertation, Stanford University, Palo Alto, CA.

Burgess, A. (1962). *A clockwork orange.* New York: Norton.

Crampton, G., with pictures by T. Gergely. (1945). *Tootle.* New York: A Golden Book; Racine, WI: Western Publishing.

Eagleton, T. (1976). *Marxism and literary criticism.* Berkeley, CA: University of California Press.

Foucault, M. (1979). What is an author? In J. Harari (Ed.), *Textual strategies* (pp. 141–160). Ithaca, NY: Cornell University Press.

Geertz, C. (1973). Ideology as a cultural system. In *The interpretation of cultures.* New York: Basic Books.

Giroux, H. (1981). *Ideology, culture, and the process of schooling.* Philadelphia: Temple University Press.

Phillips, D. C. (1981). Why the hidden curriculum is hidden. In C.J.B. Macmillan (Ed.), *Philosophy of education, 1980,* (pp. 274–280). Normal, IL: Philosophy of Education Society.

Updike, J. (1980, 25 Sept.). *New York Review of Books,* p. 23.

Willis, P. E. (1977). *Learning to labor* (pp. 125–127, 145–159). Westmead, England: Saxon House.

Tootle *Revisited:*
Fifteen Years Down the Track

Nicholas C. Burbules
University of Illinois, Urbana-Champaign

I had not reread this essay for several years, and looking at it again for this reflection piece opened unexpected memories and pleasures. For one thing, I saw in it glimmerings of ideas that I only returned to years later (thinking that I was thinking them for the first time).

I also remember the enormous pleasure I had in writing this piece. It was my first Big Publication, but it was also my first academic essay in which I felt I was writing in my own voice: passionate, ironic, and with an ear toward the nice turn of phrase—the closing sentence for example. I have always been a big fan of good closing sentences, ones that close off one investigation, but also open up and suggest new ones.

For the purpose of this book, I want to reflect on five aspects of this project that may be of interest and relevance to scholars attempting similar kinds of investigation.

First, as mentioned in the footnotes, Hank Levin first held up this book in one of my graduate school seminars and made the basic point that really drove the essay—that *Tootle* could be read as a story about class destiny. Later I used the book as a reading and class project for two seminars I taught as a new professor, and students in both classes wrote some wonderfully sharp and revealing analyses. But when it came time for me to write my own piece, it was impossible to keep straight exactly what others first told me, what I told them, or what I later figured out for myself. It was a bit of a crisis for me, because I did not want to plagiarize anyone's ideas; but simply crediting them in the footnotes or acknowledgments did not seem adequate either. Without doubt, I wrote every word of the paper, but I could not escape the nagging sense that I should have listed fifteen or twenty co-authors.

Today I would worry about this less, not because plagiarism is any less of an issue, but because I am more accepting now of the inevitably dialogical nature of nearly all that we think of as "our" ideas and accordingly more suspicious of claims to pure originality. I would not recommend to any writer the reappropriation of other people's ideas without a conscientious effort at attribution and acknowledgment, but I would urge on all of us a certain lessening of anxiety that it might happen without our realizing it. It *often* happens without our realizing it, and the greatest benefit of admitting this is that it will prepare us for the inevitable instances when we see what we think of as "our" ideas suddenly appearing without attribution in the writings or statements of other people.

Second, I am pretty proud of this essay as an exemplar of a certain kind of scholarship based on a close, critical, textual interpretation. I happen to believe that this general approach is, if anything, even more important today as the range of multimedia influences (television, movies, video, music, computer games, and so forth) are taking on an even greater significance in the formation of young people's ideas, values, and attitudes. *Educational* scholars need to attend more to these noninstitutionalized forms of cultural reproduction, and this kind of writing has proven very effective in the hands of what today we call "cultural studies" scholars.

I am also glad that I didn't spend a great deal of time in this essay trying to justify the approach or make explicit exactly what I was trying to do. I just did it. I think this is a good piece of advice to scholars also: I often read or hear papers full of so much throat-clearing and foundation-laying that I impatiently wait for the "real" stuff, which is often less than promised. I believed in 1986, and I still do, that you *show* the advantages of a certain approach, method, or theory—not by arguing for it at length, but by putting it to work and showing through the results that it was beneficial. That stance is a reflection of my species of pragmatism, I suppose.

One other thought about style is that, rereading the essay today, I was struck by how "hypertextual" it was—a term I didn't have at the time. Partly this is because I had (and have) a tendency to repeat myself in writing; I saw several instances where I returned to the same point from a different point of view or different route of access. But the nature of my argument was such that several key points (for example Tootle's dual identity as a nonhuman machine and as a nonadult child) were relevant to several different aspects of the argument. As a result, I found the essay to be peppered with phrases like, "As discussed previously." A hypertextual version of this essay could have dealt with that cross-referencing in a different way.

Third, I can reveal today that this essay was almost never published at all, due to a copyright dispute with the original publisher of *Tootle.* As I mentioned in the opening of the essay, I had a strong commitment to including the text of the story in the piece so that (1) the reader could check my interpretation against the original text and (2) the reader might arrive at his or her own independent interpretations of the essay, which could reinforce, or conflict with, my own. I believed then, and still believe, that too much of what is broadly called "qualitative" research asks the reader to place a great deal of trust in the author to deal forthrightly with the "data" (whatever they are) and not merely to draw from them selectively to fit a prearranged scheme. I was insistent on not doing that.

Today, we have the technology that makes it much easier for researchers of all types to make their raw data available to readers (for example, through a Web site); and the increasing importance of on-line publishing means that essays can be linked directly to that data. In practice, however, many scholars seem to be quite possessive of their raw data. While this is understandable, it does deprive their readers of an indispensable method of cross-checking the validity of their analyses.

The problem with *Tootle* was that we were concerned that the Little Golden Book publishers would want to read the essay before agreeing to allow the text to appear in it—and since my analysis of the book was pretty scathing, we, frankly, hoped they wouldn't. The editors of *Harvard Educational Review* dealt with this problem, and fortunately it was resolved.

For this version, republished here, we could no longer gain the publisher's permission, and once again this nearly jeopardized publication. A compromise was reached that allowed me to paraphrase the original—but this is less than satisfying because it does not give you the complete text to read and interpret for yourself. Hence I urge you to get a copy of the book or refer to the original *Harvard Educational Review* version (1986, number 56, volume 3), if you are interested in seeing the full text of *Tootle*.

Fourth, as is clear by my own "throat-clearing and foundation-laying" in the essay, I was troubled by the anticipated reader responses that "this doesn't prove anything," "it's just a kid's book," and so on. I think that the key move here was to shift the discussion away from the issue of whether kids reading the book would understand it in any of these ways, or whether Gertrude Crampton intended for them to, for these are murky issues that would require an entirely different sort of examination. I think the essay was on stronger ground saying that these textual interpretations tell us something about *us,* our societal norms and expectations, our unspoken assumptions, our popular culture. There will never be an independent confirmation or proof of such matters except that the interpretation speaks to people and opens up a process of reflection. No one should expect to "prove" anything in matters of interpretation.

Still, I have to tell you that as I wrote the piece, and even rereading it today, I was sure I was "right"—that the patterns and relationships I traced were in some sense "in" the text and not just imposed on it by my preconceptions. Given the surface innocence of *Tootle* and its relative brevity, it does portray a remarkably complex, subtle, and coherent set of messages, overlapping and reinforcing one another.

One last issue I had in writing this analysis was how far to "push it." As I tiptoed around the edge of themes of infantile sexuality, masturbation, and phallic imagery (which would have been helped if readers had the illustrations to look at), I was continually aware of how far I could go before I would get the response of, "Oh, come *on.*" Another author might not have pushed it as far as

I did; others would have gone further—is the story about Tootle and the black horse about a prohibition against homosexuality? against miscegenation? In such cases the only answer can be "look at the text."

Finally, rereading the essay after so long, I am struck by how angry it was. The tone is even-tempered, considered, suitably academic—and yet the person I was when I wrote this was truly outraged and offended by the theft of childhood perpetrated by *Tootle*. It was with real shock and disappointment that I delved further and further into the iconography and messages of this book. I felt that I was *discovering* something, deep and sinister, and certainly not making it up. That was very much part of the mood during the 1970s and early 1980s in critical educational research (for instance, the early work on the "hidden curriculum"): the sense of turning over the shiny, happy message of what American schooling was supposed to be about, and seeing the dark and disturbing contradictions it concealed.

16

The Politics of Consumer Education Materials Used in Adult Literacy Classrooms

Jennifer A. Sandlin

For the past thirty years, beginning in the 1970s with the Adult Performance Level Project, life skills education and, more specifically, consumer education have been considered viable and important parts of adult literacy education (Lankshear, 1993; Levine, 1986; Office of Technology Assessment, 1993). Throughout this period, many adult literacy programs and textbook publishers responded to research and theory that stressed the importance of providing instruction that is grounded in the everyday life contexts or functional contexts of adult learners. In many cases, this move toward creating contextualized learning resulted in adult literacy classrooms and texts offering basic skills instruction embedded in the contexts of consumer life and centered around specific real-life tasks such as unit pricing and household budgeting. Other texts and programs elevated consumer education to a higher priority and focused on consumer education not as a means to learn basic skills but as an end in itself.

Consumer education in adult literacy contexts that appears either embedded in basic skills instruction or as an end in itself focuses on teaching technical skills that create savvy and knowledgeable consumers (Fingeret, 1992) with the implicit assumption or ideology that through teaching better money-handling behaviors, literacy teachers or programs can solve the financial problems of adult literacy learners and help them achieve individual social mobility. This assumption supports the idea that consumer problems lie with individual consumers. A more critical approach sees the problem not primarily as an inability to handle money wisely but as a problem of resource scarcity in an increasingly unstable economic

---

Jennifer A. Sandlin. (2000). "The Politics of Consumer Education Materials Used in Adult Literacy Classrooms." *Adult Education Quarterly, 50*(4), 289–307. Reprinted with permission.

climate. Research that questions the fundamental individual-deficit assumption present in dominant discourses of consumer education has been lacking. There is a need, then, to question this assumption and examine consumer education from a sociopolitical perspective, taking into account the ways in which the dominant discourses of the economic, social, and political systems in which this education is embedded are reflected within it and help shape it and also the economic, social, and political contexts that surround the adult learners who are the recipients of this education.

Researchers in the kindergarten through twelfth-grade educational contexts that operate out of critical social frameworks have increasingly situated schooling within its social, political, and economic contexts through questioning what types of knowledge are taught in schools and how schools come to reflect only certain knowledge and values (Apple, 1990). This research has revealed that "schools are political sites" that help shape and control "discourse, meaning, and subjectivities" (Giroux, 1983, p. 46) and that education always operates in someone's interests. Critical educational researchers have argued that schools help reproduce inequalities in the following two main ways: through the overt or formal curriculum and through the hidden curriculum, that is, "the unstated norms, values, and beliefs that are transmitted to learners through the underlying structure of meaning in both the formal content as well as the social relations of school and classroom life" (Giroux & Penna, 1979, p. 22). Recently, researchers have argued that schools are sites of ideological contestation (Apple, 1995) in which learners and teachers accommodate, shape, and resist dominant discourses. Critical pedagogy advocates seek to create counterhegemonic narratives in school that make "explicit the socially constructed character of knowledge" (Lankshear, Peters, & Knobel, 1996, p. 150).

One specific area in which critical researchers have examined hidden curricula has been textbooks. Critical researchers focus on the text as a political object and seek to illuminate its connection to social inequalities. Although several different aspects of textbooks are studied by critical educational researchers in the kindergarten through twelfth-grade setting, in this study I focused on the ideological content and form of textbooks used in adult literacy classrooms. Apple and Christian-Smith (1991), drawing on the ideas of Williams, argue that it is important to study textbooks in and of themselves because texts embody the selective tradition; that is, texts present particular views of the world that contribute to the maintenance of inequalities. They state that texts, in both their content and form, contain "someone's vision of legitimate knowledge and culture" (Apple & Christian-Smith, 1991, p. 3). The legitimate knowledge contained in textbooks "all too often. . .does not include the historical experiences and cultural expressions of labor, women, people of color, and others who have been denied power" (Apple & Christian-Smith, 1991, pp. 6–7).

Although a handful of researchers in the field of adult literacy education have begun to examine the relationships between classroom life and larger social, political, and economic contexts and have specifically focused on the hidden curriculum in adult literacy textbooks (Auerbach & Burgess, 1985; Coles, 1977;

Lankshear, 1987, 1993; Quigley, 1997; Quigley & Holsinger, 1993; Venema, 1995), more work needs to be done in this area. If, as Apple (1991) argues, there is a lack of understanding of the politics surrounding the textbook in kindergarten through twelfth-grade settings (in which numerous studies of texts and their uses have been conducted), it is even more true in adult literacy education, where relatively few studies have addressed these issues. This is surprising and alarming because adult literacy education is undoubtedly repeating the same processes of reproduction that occur within elementary and secondary schools (Keddie, 1980) and because textbook use overwhelmingly dominates instructional practices in adult literacy education classrooms, where learners often work alone in mass-produced curriculum workbooks (Mezirow, Darkenwald, & Knox, 1975; Quigley, 1997; Solorzano, 1993). Furthermore, there has been virtually no research that has examined the hidden curriculum specifically with regard to consumer education materials that are used in adult literacy classrooms. The purpose of this study, then, was to examine the hidden curricula of consumer education texts used in adult literacy classrooms. Specifically, I sought to determine how these texts portray adult literacy learners as consumers and the consumer market in which adult literacy learners operate.

Method

Using a qualitative content analysis, I examined sixteen lessons about consumer issues that were contained in five adult literacy workbooks that I obtained from a local adult literacy classroom (see Appendix: Textbooks Used in This Analysis at the end of this article). This adult basic education class was part of a small, state-funded local adult literacy program housed in a community center in a small town approximately forty-five minutes from a major metropolitan area. One full-time teacher and one part-time teacher's assistant taught in this class, which averaged five to ten learners on any given night. The class centered around individual workbook instruction, although learners occasionally worked with computer software packages and participated in group activities and discussions.

Workbooks like the ones I selected are the major type of textbook used in adult literacy programs. The texts I chose are published by two of the most popular or widely used publishing companies: Steck-Vaughn and Contemporary. I chose to examine lessons that focused on issues dealing with money, shopping, or some other aspect of consumer practice. I included reading texts that contained lessons about money use in addition to one text that was solely devoted to consumer education. The textbook that was totally devoted to consumer issues contained eight lessons of at least ten pages each. The four reading texts contained five short (one-page) lessons about consumer issues and three long (more than thirteen pages) lessons about consumer issues.

The theoretical framework for this study, which was grounded in critical theory and the critical sociology of school knowledge, shaped the research questions I asked and also drove my analysis. I started with the assumption that textbooks are not neutral but instead privilege certain viewpoints and knowledge over others. Textbooks do not simply contain neutral facts but, rather, take political stances with ideological consequences (Luke, 1995). Therefore, it is important to take a critical look at textbooks because curricula contain a certain vision of the world and how it should be (Apple & Christian-Smith, 1991).

What I attempted to do in my analysis of the textbooks was to identify and map out the worldviews or ideologies promoted or naturalized in the texts. When analyzing the textbooks, I used a method of content analysis that I drew from various sources. First, I followed a strategy that is based in Marxist literary criticism. This strategy consists of paying attention to the following three issues: content, form, and "absences or omissions in the text with respect to alternative points of view" (Wilson, 1991, p. 67). Eagleton (1976) discusses the notion of silence in a text to explain why it is important to look at not only what is contained in a text but also what is missing. He explains that "a work is tied to ideology not so much by what it says as by what it does not say. It is in the significant silences of text, in its gaps and absences, that the presence of ideology can be most positively felt" (p. 34).

I was also influenced by Potter and Wetherell's (1994) idea that researchers should examine "texts as social practices" (p. 48). That is, I was after "the answers to social or sociological questions rather than to linguistic ones" (p. 48). Potter and Wetherell also suggest that content analysis should involve questioning a text's taken-for-granted ideals or stories. Finally, for practical guidelines, I drew from Mayring's approach to content analysis (Mayring, 1983, cited in Flick, 1998). Following this approach, I first defined the material to be examined and then defined the direction of analysis. This includes determining what one actually wants to ask of the text (based on a guiding theoretical perspective) and then developing research questions. Based on the theoretical framework I detailed in the preceding sections, the questions that guided this analysis were the following: *What types of consumer information are the texts teaching and how? What assumptions do they make about their readers and the marketplace?* After extracting relevant passages from the texts, I coded them as themes emerged, and I interpreted them with reference to whether the texts ultimately reinforce or contradict the current status quo of inequality in the United States.

Findings and Discussion

Analysis of the consumer education texts centered around the following three aspects of the texts: lesson content, lesson form, and textbook ideology. Findings from each area will be presented and discussed in this section.

Lesson Content and Form

The five books in the sample contain a total of sixteen lessons about consumer issues. Of these sixteen lessons, eleven are long lessons, chapters, or units (ten or more pages of text), all with subheadings and multiple activities contained in them. The remaining five lessons are each one page in length and consist of one or two simple exercises each. Every long activity and two of the short activities from the reading workbooks are about using credit. Two of the short activities are about writing checks and deposit slips, and one is about reading a menu. In the textbook devoted solely to consumer lessons, the topics include using banking services, a checking account, and credit and interest; planning a budget; paying bills; being a "smart shopper"; buying insurance; and buying a car. Every lesson in the consumer book also contains a life-skills workshop at the end of the lesson chapter. In addition, two of the long lessons end with a life-skills page, and three of the short lessons are called "Life Skills." These life-skills lessons or workshops typically show a picture of some real-world item such as a check, deposit slip, or credit card application form; demonstrate how to fill it out; and then ask the reader to fill out a blank one that is also supplied, usually with information that is provided for the learner.

Each of the longer lessons in the reading texts presents at least a small amount of consumer advocacy information. In the first lesson, this information consists of what a credit counselor is and how to check a credit record to ensure that it contains accurate information. The second lesson that addresses consumer advocacy warns that, sometimes, business people who want customers to buy on credit will give them "the run around" (Beers, Beech, McCarthy, Dauzat, & Dauzat, 1987, p. 10). Finally, the third lesson, in *New Beginnings in Reading, Book Seven* (Tivenan, 1991), presents the stories of some people who have had both good and bad experiences with credit, thus encouraging the learner to think about the positive and negative aspects of using credit. For instance, one fictional character in this lesson writes the following: "I ripped all my credit cards up. I spent $2,000 by using them. I would just buy whatever I wanted. I almost forgot that I had to pay. But then the bills started coming in. I did not have the money to pay them. I had to get another job. I am never going to go through that again" (Tivenan, 1991, p. 19).

The consumer education lessons in these workbooks contain a variety of different activities and exercises. The lessons typically open with a reading passage to introduce a topic and give learners suggestions about what to think about as they read. For instance, one lesson, titled "Using Banking Services," encourages the learner to think about the following questions: "Why would you want to have a savings account or a checking account? How do you open a savings account or a checking account? How do you choose a bank?" (Bernstein, 1994, p. 5). At the end of the lessons or interspersed between reading passages are activities with questions designed to determine if learners are remembering what they are reading, check comprehension or vocabulary, or review math or language skills. These activities consist of fill-in-the-blank questions, questions requiring longer (sentence length) answers, sentence completion exercises, crossword puzzles, circle-the-answer questions, and vocabulary-matching activities. Also included in these activities are thinking-and-writing activities in which learners are given a statement and asked to think and write about it on the five blank lines given, and fill-in-the-bubble questions in which learners are given a question and three or four possible answers and are asked to "bubble-in" a circle next to the correct answer.

Of the more than one hundred different tasks that learners are asked to complete in these lessons, more than 80 percent consist of questions for which the correct answers are already provided in some way. The forms of these questions vary: some are fill-in-the-blank questions in which the learner is supposed to choose words from a list that is provided, some are vocabulary word-and-definition matching questions, and some are comprehension questions in which the learner is supposed to look in the story to find the correct answer to a question. However, there are also a handful of questions that ask the learner to create more original knowledge. The majority of these types of activities give learners ideas about what to think about as they read. Other questions of this type ask learners what they think about certain topics and urge them to express themselves in writing. For example, at the end of a lesson titled "Paying Bills" is the following thinking-and-writing scenario: "Imagine that you did not allow enough money in your budget to pay your electric bill and your phone bill. It is now very hard for you to pay these bills. You do not want to lose these services. In your journal explain how you would handle these problems" (Bernstein, 1994, p. 53). For these questions, there are no right or wrong answers provided or suggested.

Most of the topics covered in the texts fall into the category of technical skills. Much of the information in the lessons focuses on practical matters such as how to pay bills, plan a budget, apply for credit, and write a check. This focus on technical skills reveals that the texts view literacy as a skill or task and thus take a particular political stance toward the creation of knowledge and the position of the learner—mainly that knowledge creation lies outside of the learner and that learners must passively react to rather than change social situations. Fingeret (1992) states that there are four different types of literacy distinguished from each other by the way each perceives knowledge and the learner. The first follows a banking (Freire, 1970/1993) or a deficit model of education and views literacy as a discrete technical skill. This view sees literacy as "a set of discrete skills that exist regardless of context" (Fingeret, 1992, p. 5). The second view sees literacy as a task; that is, it sees literacy as "the ability to apply skills independently and successfully to accomplish specific tasks" (Fingeret, 1992, p. 5). Fingeret (1992) argues that this view "does not take into account the situation in which someone does the task"; rather, the "ability to do the task is considered stable across situations and requires only individual skills achievement" (pp. 5–6). Fingeret and Drennon (1997) state that "viewing literacy as skills or literacy as tasks separates adults from their knowledge about the world and defines literacy as a process of getting the meaning from the texts rather than as constructing meaning through interaction with texts and the social world" (p. 62). The content in the consumer education lessons that focuses on how to do certain tasks, which constitutes the major type of content in the texts, would fall within these first two realms of literacy.

Fingeret (1992) states that a third type of literacy takes a more contextual approach and views literacy as social and cultural practices. Viewing literacy as practices entails seeing that "literacy cannot be separated from the system of ideas in a specific setting" and that people "use literacy within their social and cultural contexts to manipulate the system, trying to get their needs met" (Fingeret & Drennon, 1997, p. 62). What this view does not do, however, is challenge the status quo or problematize situations learners may find themselves in; it instead "accepts the meanings in situations as nonproblematic" (Fingeret and Drennon, 1997, p. 62). The last view of literacy problematizes meanings and views literacy as critical reflection and action. When one views literacy this way, he or she makes "the context an explicit subject of analysis and reflection and proposes that it is possible to act to change the situation itself" (Fingeret & Drennon, 1997, p. 63).

A few of the lessons contain content, such as consumer advocacy information, that goes beyond technical skills and thus moves in the direction of viewing literacy as social practices or as critical reflection and action. These lessons move beyond viewing literacy as technical skills because they invite the reader to question the world around them. However, just how critical a consumer these consumer advocacy lessons are attempting to create can be questioned. Although encouraging questioning is certainly commendable, it can also be argued that the texts encourage questioning only inside a taken-for-granted, naturalized, capitalist consumerist system. No attempt is made to encourage the fundamental questioning of consumption as a way of life. I will discuss this idea further in the next section.

The forms of the lessons and activities, which mainly focus on small, discrete tasks and on questions with answers that are provided, complement the focus in the content on technical skills. The majority of the questions provide the correct answers for the learners, and relatively few questions ask the reader to create new or original knowledge. This focus on the learner finding the one correct answer promotes the idea that knowledge lies outside of the learner. It also gives the message that there is, indeed, one way to think about things, or one right answer, and diminishes the power of the learner to negotiate what is correct. As previously discussed, there are also a handful of questions that ask the learner to create more original knowledge, and these questions promote a more active role for the literacy participants and position learners in a more active, creative role with regard to knowledge creation. Because these questions do not provide right or wrong answers, they seem to promote a more authentic and active reading and knowledge-creating experience.

Ideologies Within the Materials

Two major themes, each containing subthemes or categories, emerged with regard to ideologies in these textbooks. The first, which I call "half-wit consumers," concerns assumptions about the learners who are using the texts. The second, which, after Marcuse (1966), Coles (1977), and Quigley and Holsinger (1993), I call "happy consciousness," concerns assumptions about society and about the market system in which learners exist.

Half-Wit Consumers. The first major theme captures the general attitude that these texts convey about the people assumed to be reading them. Although not every lesson includes this attitude, in general, both the content and the forms of the majority of lessons assume that learners have had little experience with the real-world skills presented in the lessons, and they also assume that without proper guidance, learners will spend more than they have, go into debt, and make unwise consumer decisions.

Consumers without histories. The first major category in this larger theme reflects the conveyed view that the adult learners engaged in the texts are not fully complex adult human beings with histories, life experiences, or knowledge. The content of most of the lessons, all of which are written expressly for an adult audience, is very basic and starts with the assumption that learners know very little about very simple consumer topics and situations—topics that most adults are already familiar with and situations in which most adults have negotiated in their everyday lives. This kind of content seems to be more appropriate for grade-school children who are learning for the first time about the everyday consumer experiences of life. For instance, one text explains the concept of a budget in a way that assumes that the learners do not already budget their money and that they do not know the difference between a *need* and a *want*. "You use your income to pay your expenses. You have two kinds of expenses. They are your needs and your wants. You need food, clothes, and a home. Your wants help you to enjoy life. You may want to go out to eat. You may want to go to concerts and movies. Your budget helps you plan how to spend and save your money. Your budget includes all of your needs. It includes some of the things you want. Your budget can also help you save some money each month" (Bernstein, 1994, p. 37).

Another lesson states the following: "Comparison shopping can help you save money. To comparison shop you compare prices. . . .For example, one brand of orange juice may cost less than another. You may want to buy the cheaper brand" (Bernstein, 1994, p. 57). Finally, another lesson states that "it is not always a good idea to buy things on credit. Sometimes credit charges are too high. Sometimes people buy things that they cannot pay for" (Tivenan, 1991, p. 26).

Contrary to the authors' assumptions, much research that has explored how consumers with low levels of reading and/or low incomes navigate and negotiate the economic worlds around them has concluded that these consumers already possess a great deal of consumer information, can successfully navigate in the consumer world, and can make careful decisions about how to spend their limited money (Edin & Lein, 1996, 1997; Jarrett, 1994; Mogelonsky, 1994; Newton, 1977; Roberts, 1991). Although it is too simplistic to equate adult literacy learners with low-income people, it is true that many learners who participate in adult literacy programs work for low wages or do not work at all (Kim & Collins, 1997; U.S. Bureau of the Census, 1998), so findings from such research with low-income adults can be applied to many adult literacy learners.

For instance, in an article on how people with low incomes make consumer decisions, Newton (1977) uses ethnographic data to support her argument that despite mainstream assumptions that the culture of poverty creates consumers with certain irrational consumer values, "poor people do perceive and act in accordance with marginal costs and returns—that they make the most of what they have" (p. 58). Newton found evidence of "individual, family, and neighborhood adaptations to economic stress" (p. 59) among her participants and, as a result, concluded that "the poor are not in need of programs designed to increase their efficiency; what they need are more resources" (p. 50). Newton's findings resonate with preliminary findings from a research study I am currently conducting. In this study, the adult learners I have interviewed about their consumer behaviors have demonstrated that they are quite knowledgeable about consumer issues, think a great deal about how they spend their money, and have come up with ways to successfully stretch their dollars.

Consumers without control. The second subcategory addresses another assumption that is prevalent in these books: the adult learners reading the texts have insatiable consumer appetites. This theme is especially clear in many of the lessons on credit in which it is implied that if adult learners obtain a credit card, they are likely to overspend and get in trouble if they are not careful. This assumption is clear in the following passage:

> Buy now and pay later is what credit is all about. Credit allows you to buy things you need even though you don't have the money to pay for them right now. Buying everything from cars to clothes on credit has become a popular way of life in America. "Incredible!" you say. "Where do I sign up?" Slow down. Think first. Remember that credit isn't an invitation to rush out and buy everything you always wanted. Credit carries certain duties with it. Before you get yourself into debt, let's read the fine print and see how credit really works. (Beech & McCarthy, 1990, p. 84)

The following dialogue from *New Beginnings in Reading, Book Seven* (Tivenan, 1991, p. 15) also promotes this idea:

MAN: I just got a credit card from a credit company.

WOMAN: Why did you get a credit card?

MAN: I got a credit card so I could charge all the things I want.

WOMAN: What will you charge?

MAN: I am going to get a car. Then I will go to the store and buy lots of clothes.

WOMAN: But how will you pay for a car and the clothes?

MAN: Oh, I never thought of that! You mean I have to pay for everything I charge?

WOMAN: He never thought of that!

A final example comes from *Reading for Today, Book Five* (Beers et al., 1987, p. 3). In a story about two people shopping for furniture, the text states the following: "Star and Ray wanted to forget about saving money when they saw the furniture they wanted. They liked it so much that they did not want to think about cost. But they could not afford all the furniture at once. Can they buy it a little at a time?"

Consumers in need of discipline. An additional assumption of the authors that goes hand in hand with the idea that adult learners are consumers without control is the idea that the adult learners using the texts are more like children than adults. It is assumed that these childlike adults need to be told exactly what to do so that they will not get into trouble. Many of the reading passages in the texts give advice or admonishment to learners about making sure they behave properly with regard to money. For instance, one text admonishes that "when you plan your budget, think about the bills you need to pay. Then set aside money for these bills. Keep the money for paying bills in a savings account or in a checking account. You can move money from your savings account into your checking account when you need to pay bills" (Bernstein, 1994, p. 46).

In another passage, this same book warns learners to "use credit carefully. Never borrow more money than you can repay. It is against the law to borrow money and not repay it" (Bernstein, 1994, p. 46).

Again, research has concluded that these assumptions do not hold. For instance, such findings emerged from a survey of consumers conducted by the Opinion Research Corporation (Mogelonsky, 1994). This study asked adults how interested they were in obtaining information on the products and services they purchase and found that adults with the lowest incomes were the most likely group of consumers to seek such advice "despite their lower education levels" (Mogelonsky, 1994, p. 14). In addition, consumers without high school diplomas sought product information more often than those with college degrees. Mogelonsky's (1994) study and Newton's (1977) ethnographic research belie the assumptions made by the authors of the consumer education texts about the learners reading the texts. Also, Caskey (1994) states strongly that "despite the widespread notion that lower-income households tend to be more shortsighted and wasteful in their spending behavior, this has not been demonstrated in statistical studies" (p. 82). Caskey also shares anecdotal evidence from workers he interviewed at not-for-profit credit counseling agencies who work with low-income families. These workers said that "budgeting mistakes are responsible for only a small part of their clients' economic problems" (p. 83). Instead, "the level and instability of their clients' incomes were far more important factors" (p. 83).

Happy Consciousness. The second major ideology in the texts concerns assumptions about society and the market system in which learners exist. Freire (1970/ 1993) states that elites in a society promote myths in popular consciousness that help keep the oppressed in their place and that are "indispensable to the preservation of the status quo" (p. 120). Typical myths, for example, include the myth of "the oppressive order is a 'free society'" and "the myth of the industriousness of the oppressors and the laziness and dishonesty of the oppressed" (pp. 120–121). Myths such as these work to create what Quigley and Holsinger (1993), after Marcuse (1966), call "happy consciousness." Happy consciousness exists when "the established social system is considered rational and . . . is understood . . . to provide people with satisfying lives" (p. 25). Quigley and Holsinger further explain that happy consciousness is "reflected in a blind acceptance of the order of things" and is "the complete absence of critical thought" (p. 25).

I identified three such myths in the textbook lessons with regard to their presentation of the consumer world. These myths, which I will next present, work to create a sense of happy consciousness in the texts and, therefore, work to preserve the status quo. In general, the textbook lessons exhibit this theme of happy consciousness through their unquestioning acceptance of consumer culture and their inaccurate portrayal of the market system as it is currently constituted. In the world of the textbooks (in which it is taken as a given that people are consumers and our consumer culture is a natural and good thing), consumers have fair and equal access to a wide range of reasonably priced financial services and consumer goods, and lending institutions are compassionate, benevolent, and helpful. This worldview naturalizes consumer culture and thus leaves consumer education to the task of creating informed consumers, but only informed within the given parameters of our current system.

Consuming is natural and good. Perhaps the most pervasive myth that is promoted by these textbooks is the idea that the consumer economy we live in is natural. Each and every lesson—indeed, the texts in their entirety—promotes this idea through the very teaching of consumer education as something that adults should use to better fit into the consumer world around them. Consumer education is not offered or promoted as a tool that adults could use to question or change society. This ideology has been found in other analyses of consumer education texts or programs (Grahame, 1985; Griffith & Cervero, 1977; Lankshear, 1993; Ozanne & Murray, 1995). Grahame (1985) states, in the magazine *Consumer Reports,* that "the legitimacy of the marketplace as an instrument of satisfaction remains largely unquestioned" and that there is a "failure to probe implicit normative claims" (p. 166). Ozanne and Murray (1995) state that *Consumer Reports* "assumes participation in a consumer culture" and "does not encourage reflection on the origins of this culture and which groups in society benefit from this system" (p. 521).

These statements also apply to the texts I examined. Learners are invited to learn how to comparison shop or learn how to fill out a bank form. They are not, however, allowed to question the value placed on consumption in our culture or encouraged to think of a way of life in which human relations, for instance, are elevated above consumer goods. The texts' version of consumer education focuses on improving decision making among consumers, which works to "recreate the existing system by more firmly entrenching people into their primary role in life as consumers" (Ozanne & Murray, 1995, p. 521). Far from being a natural activity, consumerism requires "socialization, education, and effort" (Ozanne & Murray, 1995, p. 522) and thus stems not from the world of nature but from culture. Anything that has been created can be recreated differently, but this idea, and the active agents it would promote, is missing from the world of the texts, a world in which "the message is a call to adapt to the given and to be assisted: not to be active, critical, or to seek to know and transform" (Lankshear, 1993, p. 105).

Equal access for all. The second myth that the texts promote is the idea that consumers have fair and equal access to a wide range of financial services, including banks, checking accounts, savings accounts, and credit cards. Most of the lessons that discuss such financial services explain how they work and do not question whether the learner even has access to them; the assumption that they do is taken as a given. For instance, one text discusses the many services that banks provide and encourages learners to shop around for a bank that is convenient and that provides the best services for the best price. In doing so, this text tacitly assumes that the bank actually provides these options to everyone. The text states the following: "Look for a bank that pays higher interest on savings accounts. You also want a bank that charges less money for other services. What else do you look for when you choose a bank? You may want a bank that is near your home or your job. You may want a bank that is open on Saturdays. . . . Banks provide many different services. These services help you save and borrow money. They allow you to write checks and protect important papers. Visit banks to learn about the services that can help you" (Bernstein, 1994, pp. 9–10).

Another lesson describes different checking accounts and asks the reader to decide which bank account would be the best for him or her.

> You can choose the kind of checking account you use. Think about the number of checks you may write each month. If you will write many checks, you may need to keep a large balance in your account. A free checking account would be good for you. You do not pay a fee for this kind of account if you keep a minimum balance in your checking account at all times. . . . If you will not write many checks, you may not need to keep a large balance in your account. So you may want a budget checking account. (Bernstein, 1994, p. 17)

These passages do not realistically portray the options available to many lower-income consumers and entirely disregard the growing "fringe banking" market that low-income consumers are increasingly being forced into. In the first passage, by focusing on the idea that banks exist to provide services, this text obscures the fact that banks operate on a profit motive—a fact that limits the financial options of many adult learners with low incomes. The second passage makes the tacit assumption that whether one will keep a large balance in a checking account is largely a matter of choice, not something determined by one's economic situation. It also assumes that not only do all consumers have access to a checking account but they also have the luxury of making a choice between different kinds of accounts.

Contrary to the author's tacit assumption that everyone has access to banking services, access to these services is not equally distributed throughout all income groups. Caskey (1994) estimates that about 11.5 million households in 1989 did not have bank accounts. These are mainly concentrated among lower-income households and households headed by non-Whites, the young, and the less educated (Caskey, 1994). Even fewer lower-income households have savings accounts (Caskey, 1994). As a result of the shrinking mainstream market for financial services available to many low-income consumers and the increasing economic stability of these same households, many of these consumers have been increasingly forced into using alternative or fringe banking services. Fringe banking businesses, which include pawn shops, check-cashing outlets, rent-to-own stores, finance companies, used-car dealers, high-interest mortgage lenders, and other alternative forms of credit, have burgeoned in the past few years. Hudson (1996) estimates that perhaps sixty million consumers who are "virtually shut out by banks and other conventional merchants" use these various fringe banking businesses (p. 1). These fringe businesses charge a great deal more for financial services than the traditional businesses that are frequented by middle-class consumers. Yet although fringe banking continues to grow the authors of these texts completely ignore this sector of the economy and instead provide examples from mainstream checking, banking, and credit, which unrealistically present the kinds of fees associated with many of the financial services available to low-income consumers.

Another aspect of fairness that the texts fail to address is the issue of racial and gender discrimination in financial institutions. Many of the texts that discuss credit, loans, and credit cards imply that most anyone who has a job can receive loans. Although some of the lessons do mention that without a few factors, such as a steady job and good credit, a person may be turned down, in general they promote the idea that it is fairly easy to get credit and loans. For instance, one lesson states the following: "How can you get a credit card? You must be eighteen years old. First, fill out a credit card application. The Life Skills Workshop on page 32 shows you how to do this. After you have filled out the application, mail it to the address on the form. Then wait a few weeks. During that time the credit card company will check the information on your application. The company wants to be sure you will be able to pay your credit card bills" (Bernstein, 1994, p. 28).

Another lesson states that "credit is not too hard to get. You have to pay all of your bills on time" (Tivenan, 1991, p. 16). The following is stated later in this same lesson: "Most people can get credit if they have good jobs. Having money in savings also helps. The best way to get credit is to pay all of your bills on time. Sometimes a company will ask you if you want a credit card. But most people must ask the company for a card. You can write to a credit card company if you want its card" (Tivenan, 1991, p. 26).

These texts imply that it is fairly easy to get credit if one has a good job and a good past credit history. No other factors are mentioned that might impede someone from getting credit or a loan—factors such as a borrower's race, ethnicity, or gender. These lessons, then, ignore the racism and sexism that is present in the credit and loan businesses. They fail to acknowledge that a significant percentage of people who apply for loans and credit are denied, and they ignore the fact that minorities are more likely than Whites to be denied loans by banks (Ayres, 1991; Campen, 1996; Folbre, 1995). For instance, a study conducted in 1993 by the Federal Reserve Bank of Boston established "beyond a reasonable doubt that banks discriminate along racial lines when making mortgage loans" (Campen, 1996, p. 100).

The market is benevolent. One final way that many of the lessons promote the happy consciousness idea is by implying that lending institutions are benevolent, understanding, and eager to help people who have gotten behind in their payments. For instance, one text states the following: "Ten years ago, after Fred Johnson enlisted in the military, he had trouble meeting his credit obligations. His father was in the hospital with a severe injury, and Fred faced huge hospital and doctor bills. Fortunately, Fred didn't try to conceal the problem. He notified his creditors right away. He told them why he was having financial problems. The creditors understood Fred's situation. They were willing to let Fred adapt his payment plan so he could meet his obligations" (Beech & McCarthy, 1990, p. 91).

Another lesson in the same textbook states the following:

> Fred's past problems won't hurt the Johnsons' chances of getting that washer. The Johnsons got a car loan two years ago, despite Fred's previous credit history. They've paid off the car, which is further evidence that they are now a good credit risk. . . . Like Fred Johnson, most people have money problems at some time. Often these problems can be solved. You may be able to pay off your debts, or you might get a job that pays more money. Lenders know that just because you once had problems, you aren't always going to be a bad credit risk. (Beech & McCarthy, 1990, p. 91)

Finally, the following example comes from Contemporary's *New Beginnings in Reading, Book Seven* (Tivenan, 1991):

> Sometimes a person cannot pay off all his or her bills at once. By writing a letter to the companies or stores where money is owed, a person can sometimes maintain good credit. Read the letters that these . . . people have written. Then write one of your own.

Mr. Filt
AA Credit Card Company
22 Easy Street
Motherly, NJ

Dear Mr. Filt,

I am writing about my bill of $500. I am unable to pay all of the bill right now. But I can send $75 a week.

Al Japlin

Mr. Mixer
The Art Store
106 Friendly Street
Motherly, NJ

Dear Mr. Mixer,

I know that I owe The Art Store $200. I have been sick, and I will not be able to go back to work for a long time. Could you take the picture and the sculpture back? I will still try to pay you something. But I don't know when.

Jill Anderson

These lessons assume that lenders are willing to cooperate with customers and leave out the harsh realities of repossessed goods, foreclosed homes, and ruined credit records that prevent people from obtaining bank accounts and future credit, events that are well documented by consumer researchers and advocates (see, for example, Hudson, 1996).

However, not all of the lessons promote the idea that businesses and the consumer market always help the consumer. Most of the lessons at least mention that some people who are bad credit risks can be turned down. This shows at least a slight attempt to portray reality; hence, this represents a slight crack in the overall ideology of happy consciousness. But for the most part, even in the few lessons in which characters encounter money problems, the situations are resolved in favor of the characters. Thus, even these lessons leave the reader with a happily-ever-after feeling, which is a characteristic of happy consciousness. For instance, two lessons present stories about a couple who are in the process of looking for furniture. These stories portray the consumers as smart and critical and portray the salespeople as tricky and untrustworthy. In these two stories, the consumers are active, question authority, and do not assume that they are being treated fairly. But although these stories question business practices and expose the exploitation that some businesses participate in, in the end the stories are cheerily resolved and have happy endings. This can be seen in the following excerpt:

> Star and Ray looked some more. They didn't find any furniture that day. It took two months before they once again saw some bedroom furniture they wanted. It was at the Holiday Home Furniture Company. By then they had saved a little more money, and they could afford to put more money down. They could pay a bit more every month, so the bill would be paid sooner. "I feel much better about this," said Star. "We are buying from a store with a good name, and we will be paying bills we can afford. I think we got a fine bedroom set, too." (Beers et al., 1987, p. 11)

But in this story, the learner is being taught a more informed and educated way of navigating through the consumer world and a better way of making consumer decisions. This kind of consumer is the goal of traditional consumer education (Ozanne & Murray, 1995). In this story, the critical consumer is one whose resistance has been incorporated into the economic system. This moment of critical consumer education has thus "become appropriated by the dominant system" (Ozanne & Murray, 1995, p. 521). Truly critical consumers might do what these texts do not allow: they might form "a different relationship to the marketplace in which they identify unquestioned assumptions and challenge the status of existing structures as natural" (Ozanne & Murray, 1995, p. 522).

Conclusion

The results of this study show that these consumer education textbooks operate to reproduce class inequality in this country through promoting ideologies that ignore larger social, political, and economic contexts; that unquestioningly accept the present system or naturalize the status quo; and that place blame for economic troubles on the inadequacies of individuals. These lessons exhibit disrespectful, unwarranted, and insulting assumptions about adult literacy learners, and they also fail to address or they misrepresent many fundamental injustices of our economic and social system that create negative economic situations for adult literacy learners.

These lessons tacitly encourage the idea that if consumers learn enough about how to manage their money, they will have happy and successful lives, while also promoting the myths of meritocracy and equality of opportunity. Although there are certainly cases in which hard work and perseverance lead to financial success, these cases are the exceptions, not the rule, in our society, and they should not be promoted as the sole answer to individuals' financial troubles. The fact is that income inequality is built into a hierarchically organized capitalist society such as ours, and only a "complete transformation of the mode of production could eliminate income inequality in currently capitalist societies" (Edwards, Reich, & Weisskopf, 1986, p. 215).

Education that focuses on helping people with low incomes simply manage their money better and that does not address structural problems inherent in our market system places the blame for personal economic situations wholly on the individual and ignores the structural system that creates these economic situations in the first place. If adult literacy education continues to adopt a deficit perspective and deny harsh economic and social realities, we are doing a disservice to learners and are contributing to the oppression of the learners in our programs. This study is one attempt to expose the misguided assumptions and ideologies being taught in consumer education materials in hopes that adult literacy educators can begin to envision a more critical practice of adult literacy education.

Appendix: Textbooks Used in This Analysis

Beech, L. W., & McCarthy, T. (1989). *Reading for tomorrow, book one.* Austin, TX: Steck-Vaughn.

Beech, L. W., & McCarthy, T. (1990). *Reading for tomorrow, book two.* Austin, TX: Steck-Vaughn.

Beers, J., Beech, L. W., McCarthy, T., Dauzat, J. A., & Dauzat, S. (1987). *Reading for today, book five.* Austin, TX: Steck-Vaughn.

Bernstein, V. (1994). *Life skills for today's world: Money and consumers.* Austin, TX: Steck-Vaughn.

Tivenan, B. (1991). *New beginnings in reading, book seven.* Chicago: Contemporary.

References

Apple, M. (1990). *Ideology and curriculum* (2nd ed.). New York: Routledge.

Apple, M. W. (1991). The culture and commerce of the textbook. In M. W. Apple & L. K. Christian-Smith (Eds.), *The politics of the textbook* (pp. 22–40). New York: Routledge.

Apple, M. W. (1995). *Education and power* (2nd ed.). New York: Routledge.

Apple, M. W., & Christian-Smith, L. K. (1991). The politics of the textbook. In M. W. Apple & L. K. Christian-Smith (Eds.), *The politics of the textbook* (pp. 1–21). New York: Routledge.

Auerbach, E. R., & Burgess, D. (1985). The hidden curriculum of survival ESL. *TESOL Quarterly, 19*(3), 475–495.

Ayres, I. (1991). Fair driving: Gender and race discrimination in retail car negotiations. *Harvard Law Review, 104*(4), 817–872.

Beech, L. W., & McCarthy, T. (1989). *Reading for tomorrow, book one.* Austin, TX: Steck-Vaughn.

Beech, L. W., & McCarthy, T. (1990). *Reading for tomorrow, book two.* Austin, TX: Steck-Vaughn.

Beers, J., Beech, L. W., McCarthy, T., Dauzat, J. A., & Dauzat, S. (1987). *Reading for today, book five.* Austin, TX: Steck-Vaughn.

Bernstein, V. (1994). *Life skills for today's world: Money and consumers.* Austin, TX: Steck-Vaughn.

Campen, J. (1996). Lending insights: Hard proof that banks discriminate. In Dollars and Sense Collective (Ed.), *Real world micro* (6th ed., pp. 100–103). Somerville, MA: Dollars and Sense.

Caskey, J. P. (1994). *Fringe banking: Check-cashing outlets, pawnshops, and the poor.* New York: Russell Sage.

Coles, G. S. (1977). Dick and Jane grow up: Ideology in adult basic education readers. *Urban Education, 12,* 37–54.

Eagleton, T. (1976). *Marxism and literary criticism.* Berkeley: University of California Press.

Edin, K., & Lein, L. (1996). Work, welfare, and single mothers' economic survival strategies. *American Sociological Review, 61,* 253–266.

Edin, K., & Lein, L. (1997). *Making ends meet: How single mothers survive welfare and low-wage work.* New York: Russell Sage.

Edwards, R. C., Reich, M., & Weisskopf, T. E. (1986). *The capitalist system* (3rd ed.). Englewood Cliffs, NJ: Prentice Hall.

Fingeret, H. A. (1992). *Adult literacy education: Current and future directions: An update.* Columbus, OH: ERIC Clearinghouse on Adult, Career, and Vocational Education.

Fingeret, H. A., & Drennon, C. (1997). *Literacy for life: Adult learners, new practices.* New York: Teachers College Press.

Flick, U. (1998). *An introduction to qualitative research.* London: Sage.

Folbre, N., with the Center for Popular Economics. (1995). *The new field guide to the U.S. economy.* New York: The New Press.

Freire, P. (1993). *Pedagogy of the oppressed.* New York: Continuum. (Original work published 1970)

Giroux, H. A. (1983). *Theory and resistance in education: A pedagogy for the opposition.* South Hadley, MA: Bergin and Garvey.

Giroux, H. A., & Penna, A. N. (1979). Social education in the classroom: The dynamics of the hidden curriculum. *Theory and Research in Social Education, 7*(1), 21–42.

Grahame, P. (1985). Criticalness, pragmatics, and everyday life: Consumer literacy as critical practice. In J. Forester (Ed.), *Critical theory and public life* (pp. 147–174). Cambridge, MA: MIT Press.

Griffith, W. S., & Cervero, R. M. (1977). The adult performance level program: A serious and deliberate examination. *Adult Education, 27*(4), 209–224.

Hudson, M. (Ed.). (1996). *Merchants of misery.* Monroe, ME: Common Courage Press.

Jarrett, R. L. (1994). Living poor: Family life among single parent, African-American women. *Social Problems, 41*(1), 30–49.

Keddie, N. (1980). Adult education: An ideology of individualism. In J. L. Thompson (Ed.), *Adult education for a change* (pp. 45–64). London: Hutchinson.

Kim, K., & Collins, M. (1997). *Participation in basic skills education: 1994–95* (NCES Report No. 97–325). Washington, DC: U.S. Department of Education, Office of Educational Research and Improvement.

Lankshear, C. (1987). *Literacy, schooling and revolution.* New York: The Falmer Press.

Lankshear, C. (1993). Functional literacy from a Freirean point of view. In P. McLaren & P. Leonard (Eds.), *Paulo Freire: A critical encounter* (pp. 90–118). New York: Routledge.

Lankshear, C., Peters, M., & Knobel, M. (1996). Critical pedagogy and cyberspace. In H. Giroux, C. Lankshear, P. McLaren, & M. Peters (Eds.), *Counternarratives: Cultural studies and critical pedagogies in postmodern spaces* (pp. 149–188). New York: Routledge.

Levine, K. (1986). *The social context of literacy.* London: Routledge Kegan Paul.

Luke, A. (1995). When basic skills and information processing just aren't enough: Rethinking reading in new times. *Teachers College Record, 97*(1), 95–115.

Marcuse, H. (1966). *One-dimensional man: Studies in the ideology of advanced industrial society.* Boston: Beacon.

Mezirow, J., Darkenwald, G. G., & Knox, A. B. (1975). *Last gamble on education: Dynamics of adult basic education.* Washington, DC: Adult Education Association of the USA.

Mogelonsky, M. (1994, July). Poor and unschooled, but a smart shopper. *American Demographics,* pp. 14–15.

Newton, J. M. (1977). Economic rationality of the poor. *Human Organization, 36*(1), 50–61.

Office of Technology Assessment, U.S. Congress. (1993). *Adult literacy and new technologies: Tools for a lifetime* (Report No. OTA-SET-550). Washington, DC: Government Printing Office.

Ozanne, J. L., & Murray, J. B. (1995). Uniting critical theory and public policy to create the reflexively defiant consumer. *American Behavioral Scientist, 38,* 516–525.

Potter, J., & Wetherell, M. (1994). Analyzing discourse. In A. Bryman & R. G. Burgess (Eds.), *Analyzing qualitative data* (pp. 47–66). London: Routledge.

Quigley, B. A. (1997). *Rethinking literacy education.* San Francisco: Jossey-Bass.

Quigley, B. A., & Holsinger, E. (1993). "Happy consciousness": Ideology and hidden curricula in literacy education. *Adult Education Quarterly, 44,* 17–33.

Roberts, S. D. (1991). Effects of sudden income loss on consumption and related aspects of life: A study of unemployed steel workers. *Research in Consumer Behavior, 5,* 181–214.

Solorzano, R. W. (1993). *Reducing illiteracy: Review of effective practices in adult literacy programs* (Report No. RR-93–15). Princeton, NJ: Educational Testing Service.

Tivenan, B. (1991). *New beginnings in reading, book seven.* Chicago: Contemporary.

U.S. Bureau of the Census. (1998). *1998 Statistical abstract of the United States* [Online]. Available: [http://www.census.gov/prod/3/98pubs/98statab/cc98stab.htm]

Venema, M. S. (1995). Help! (Not-so-good materials for learning to read). *Women's Education des Femmes, 11*(3), 11–14.

Wilson, A. L. (1991). Epistemological foundations of American adult education, 1934 to 1989: A study of knowledge and interests. *Dissertation Abstracts International, 52,* 06A:2047.

Structure and Subjectivity:
Reflections on Critical Research

Jennifer A. Sandlin
Texas Center for Adult Literacy and Learning, College Station, TX

The defining feature of critical research is that it critiques and challenges unequal distributions of power within social, economic, and political systems. In this reflection piece I will address this and several other important aspects of critical research and discuss some of the challenges that arose for me during the research project discussed in the preceding article.

I will begin by relating how I became interested in this research project. I often have found that critical research projects have their roots in personal experiences that cause researchers to question oppressive practices or taken-for-granted ideas. This was certainly the case for me in this research on consumer texts. For several years I was a volunteer literacy tutor and worked with women who wanted to increase their English and basic reading skills. During tutoring sessions, conversations often turned to economic matters and learners talked with me about the difficulties they faced trying to survive on limited incomes. Learners also shared the many strategies they used to stretch their dollars, budget their money, and meet their financial responsibilities. I was impressed with how these learners learned to navigate this difficult economic terrain.

How learners described themselves as consumers was often in conflict with the simplistic portrayals in many of the textbooks I saw being used in different literacy classrooms. I began looking more closely at these texts and started seeing disturbing and insulting assumptions about learners as consumers, and depictions of economic systems that obscured how disadvantaged people are negatively affected by those systems. I was led by these experiences to a desire to conduct research that would document and call into question the often misleading assumptions of these consumer education texts.

Critical research is not defined by a particular set of methods but means to use a critical theoretical perspective to guide the choice of project, shape the research questions, help decide what data to collect and from whom, and aid in the analysis and interpretation of data. A critical study using qualitative methods differs from a mainstream qualitative study in that the research questions and data collection set out to make the workings of societal power visible. Critical researchers place their research within wider social structures and engage in an analysis and critique of these structures of power, whereas some other forms of qualitative research are mainly concerned with actors' subjective meanings. Critical researchers argue that qualitative approaches seeking only to interpret data fail to address power and power relations because they ignore social, economic, and political structures. The meanings individuals make of their social situations are indeed important to critical methodology, but critical research also places specific meanings, experiences, and practices into wider social structures in an attempt to dig beneath surface appearances.

In this particular project I was interested in exploring and interpreting messages in consumer education curriculum textbooks, which drove me to choose a qualitative research design. A similar project could have been done with quantitative methods, and, indeed, has been. Quigley and Holsinger (1993) conducted a quantitative content analysis of literacy textbooks with similar results. Despite methodological differences, both of these research projects are critical because the data were collected and interpreted within a critical social theory framework.

Because a major theme of critical research is power structures in society, critical research challenges researchers to learn about the social structures that shape and influence the research context and determine how these structures manifest in their data. In this project, in order to discuss consumer economic texts used in adult literacy programs in a critical way, I had to learn about the economic system in the United States, especially about those aspects of the system with a negative impact on the lives of poor people. One strategy I used in my analysis was to compare the consumer "reality" of the textbook lessons with the reality of the economic system of the United States and expose the contradictions. Because this was a crucial part of my analysis, I had to be extremely clear about what is reality for the disadvantaged in the United States. I investigated banking discrimination, "fringe banks," and the credit system by using a variety of data and research—including both qualitative and quantitative—in order to place the lessons into a wider social context and show the disconnect between the texts and economic reality.

Another important aspect of critical research is the explicitly ideological approach it takes. In order to do this research you have to take a strong stand on issues, exposing injustices and naming them for what they are. This presented a challenge during this research project, and I still struggle with this issue. I experience conflict when I feel passionately about an issue but find writing passionately about it difficult. I think some of this difficulty comes from being raised as a woman in the southern United States, where we are taught to be polite and nonconfrontational. Some of it also stems from being schooled in an educational system where I was taught to write in the third person, distance myself from my writing, and aim for neutrality and dispassionate prose. Only after writing that way for years did I encounter the model advocated by critical researchers, where an integral part of the research itself involves declaring biases, writing from a particular point of view, and "defining the enemy" (Newman, 1994). I felt in some ways I had to learn (and am still learning) to write again. I am still struggling to find my voice after it has been buried for so long.

Finally, besides simply critiquing social structures and power relationships, I believe that critical research should point to positive possibilities and articulate a better, more just, vision of the world. This creates quite a challenge for critical researchers because presenting alternatives is much harder than simply critiquing what exists. I think this is an often neglected responsibility of taking a critical stance and a challenge that I did not embrace in this research project. In this article I did not address how the texts could be better, or how they could be used in a more critical way, although this research did prompt me to begin thinking through these issues after the project was completed. If I were to conduct this research again I might try adding an action piece in which I worked with learners and teachers to create texts addressing issues of economic inequality and exploring life situations of learners.

It has been several years since I completed this research project. During those years I conducted another piece of critical research for my dissertation and encountered many of the same issues and challenges that I discussed in this reflection. Because critical research challenges social inequalities and addresses power structures, it is certainly never the "easiest" kind of research to engage in. It is exciting work, though, and an important part of a larger ongoing project of building a more democratic society—work I know I will continue to pursue.

References

Newman, M. (1994). *Defining the enemy: Adult education in social action.* Sydney: Stewart Victor.

Quigley, B. A., & Holsinger, E. (1993). "Happy consciousness": Ideology and hidden curricula in literacy education. *Adult Education Quarterly, 44*(1), 17–33.

Postmodern Research

P ostmodern research deviates significantly from the largely interpretive stance of qualitative research featured in this volume. Nevertheless, a postmodern theoretical perspective is infusing and challenging the more traditional forms of qualitative research. It is thus important to have some understanding of what constitutes postmodern research. *Postmodernism* is a broad term encompassing a number of theoretical positions and interrelated concepts such as deconstructionism and poststructuralism that are too numerous to cover in this short introduction. Readers interested in the variety of positions and nuanced differences among philosophers espousing these positions can consult Alvesson and Skoldberg (2000) and Crotty (1998) for fuller discussions. Lather's (1992, p. 90) perspective is adopted here, where she defines *"postmodern* to mean the larger cultural shifts of a post-industrial, post-colonial era and *poststructural* to mean the working out of those shifts within the arenas of academic theory."

A postmodern world is one where the rationality, scientific method, and certainties of the modern world no longer hold. According to postmodernists, explanations for the way things are in the world are nothing but "myths or 'grand narratives,' rhetorically colored, dominant discourses that should be replaced by microhistories—local, always provisory and limited stories" (Alvesson & Skoldberg, 2000, p. 148). In the postmodern world everything is "contested." What has been or is considered true, real, or right can be questioned; and there are multiple interpretations of the same phenomenon depending on where one is standing. There are no absolutes, no single theoretical framework for examining social and political issues. While critical theory and feminist theory have been used in conjunction with postmodern studies, even their goal of overcoming oppression can be questioned because this goal represents a "logic" that "does not tolerate difference" (Pietrykowski, 1996, p. 90).

Postmodernists celebrate diversity among people, ideas, and institutions. By accepting the diversity and plurality of the world, no one element is privileged or more powerful than another. Such a perspective allows "spaces for . . . hitherto oppressed and marginalised groups such as women, Blacks, gays, and ethnic minorities to find a voice, to articulate their own 'subjugated' knowledges and to empower themselves in a variety of different ways and according to their own specific agendas" (Usher, Bryant, & Johnston, 1997, p. 22).

"Most postmodernists do not talk about methodology" (Alvesson & Skoldberg, 2000, p. 184), and the "literature provides only the vaguest indication of what ideals of multiple voices mean concretely in empirical studies" (p. 185). Indeed, it would be congruent with this worldview to *not* come up with a singular approach to doing research. Instead, postmodern research is highly experimental, playful, and creative, and no two postmodern studies look alike. Nevertheless, the literature does suggest certain characteristics of postmodern qualitative research, which are of course themselves "contested." The following suggested characteristics are from Alvesson and Skoldberg (2000):

- *Pluralism.* Multiple voices and multiple selves are tenets of postmodernism and should be represented in research. In practice, this means looking at a phenomenon from various perspectives, providing space for different voices "not only or mainly the dominant, but also and especially the marginal" (p. 187).

- *A well-grounded process of exclusion.* Since not all voices can be included in a research report, researchers must "have a well-thought-out pluralism and a balanced multiplicity" (p. 188), being aware of what is left out or excluded from the representation.

- *Cautious processes of interacting with empirical material.* While being conscious of multiple voices and what is being excluded, the researcher must also use theoretical perspectives to guide interpretation.

- *Avoidance of "totalizing" theory.* By this is meant that "a chosen interpretation" needs to be confronted "with other interpretations." Through this process "text and understanding are opened up" (p. 191).

- *Authorship and linguistic sensitivity.* In the write-up of a postmodern study, attention is paid to how the authoritative voice of the researcher can be subdued to allow for multiple voices to be heard. There is also greater sensitivity to language and language usage, which can "become the object of study in their own right, rather than merely a medium for understanding what lies beyond language" (p. 193).

- *Research and the micropolitics of the text.* Since "the research text is always, in some sense, about authority and consequently about power" (p. 194), the choices made in what is represented and how it is represented are political and need to be recognized as such. A particular representation by necessity privileges some voices over others.

Currently postmodern researchers are experimenting with various data analysis techniques, including genealogy, archaeology, rhizoanalysis, and deconstruction. The best known of these is deconstruction in which taken-for-granted binary oppositions in text (such as male/female, private/public) are "deconstructed," that is, reversed, displaced, taken apart to reveal the assumptions about relationships and power. As Lather (1992, p. 96) points out, "the goal of deconstruction is to keep things in process, to disrupt, to keep the system in play, to set up procedures to continuously demystify the realities we create, to fight the tendency for our categories to congeal." Postmodern researchers are also experimenting with various forms of representation. Lather and Smithies' (1997) book is a good example of a postmodern text that allows for multiple voices to be heard. Transcriptions of group sessions for an intact support group for women living with HIV-AIDS can be viewed and read from the top of the page, and memo-writing, field notes, and so forth of the researchers can be read on the bottom half of the page. Poetry and artwork are also included throughout the book. The reader can choose where to enter the text and how to proceed in reading it.

There are two postmodern selections in this volume. Pillow's (1997) postmodern study of pregnant teens is also informed by critical and feminist theory. Here she focuses on the sheer physicality of the pregnant body, "deconstructing" and thus exposing how culture and politics have regulated the experience for the girls as well as the programs designed to assist them. In the second selection, St. Pierre (1997) deconstructs the notion of "data," finding that emotional, dream, sensual, and response data, though not often used in qualitative research, were relevant to her study of older, White, Southern women of her hometown.

References

Alvesson, M., & Skoldberg, K. (2000). *Reflexive methodology: New vistas for qualitative research.* London: Sage.

Crotty, M. (1998). *The foundations of social research: Meaning and perspective in the research process.* Thousand Oaks, CA: Sage.

Lather, P. (1992). Critical frames in educational research: Feminist and post-structural perspectives. *Theory into Practice,* Spring, *31*(2), 87–99.

Lather, P., & Smithies, C. (1997). *Troubling the angels: Women living with HIV/AIDS.* Boulder, CO: Westview.

Pietrykowski, B. (1996). Knowledge and power in adult education: Beyond Freire and Habermas. *Adult Education Quarterly, 46*(2), 82–97.

Usher, R., Bryant, I., & Johnston, R. (1997). *Adult education and the postmodern challenge: Learning beyond the limits.* New York: Routledge.

17

Exposed Methodology

The Body as a Deconstructive Practice

Wanda S. Pillow

*She had the two courages: that of going to the sources, to the foreign
parts of the self. That of torturing, to herself, almost without self,
without denying the going. She slipped out of the self, she had that
severity, that violent patience, she went out . . . by laying bare the
senses, it requires unclothing sight all the way down to naked sight.*
—H. Cixous (1994, p. 91)

Bodies are essential to accounts of power and critiques of knowledge.
—E. Grosz (1995, p. 32)

The body has gained both attention and importance, not only in feminist and postmodern theories, but more broadly in social theory as a place from which to theorize, analyze, practice, and critically reconsider the construction and reproduction of knowledge, power, class, and culture. Michel Foucault's reformulation of the social body and feminist accounts of the gendered body have proliferated discussions concerning the absent (Moore, 1994); regulated, inscribed, and docile (Foucault, 1974/1990); gendered (Butler, 1990, 1993; Diprose, 1994; Gaskell, 1992; Moore, 1994); classed (Allison, 1994; Davis, 1981); raced (hooks, 1990; Trinh, 1989; Walker, 1995); and sexed (Diprose, 1994; Grosz & Probyn, 1995) body. Recent works in ethnography have explored and critiqued the use and representation of the body in methodological practices and analyses (Moore, 1994; Visweswaran, 1994).

Wanda S. Pillow. (1997). "Exposed Methodology: The Body as a Deconstructive Practice." *International Journal of Qualitative Studies in Education, 10*(3), 349–363. Reprinted with permission of Taylor & Francis, Ltd., http://www.tandf.co.uk.

This paper draws upon these previous works to consider how paying attention to the body, literally and figuratively, can inform and disrupt methodological practices. How does paying attention to bodies change what we look at, how we look, what we ask, and what we choose to represent? I found myself immersed in these questions and their problematics three years ago when I began a research project on teenage pregnancy programs. I entered field settings filled with critical, postmodern, feminist, and qualitative research theories and practices yet found myself unprepared for the utter *physicality* of my research experiences.

During my research, I spent almost every day in classrooms with young women whose bodies were continually changing and changed—pre- and post-pregnancy swelling, stretching, widening, lactating. Our bodies provided a place and space from which we talked, shared experiences, and gained confidences. As I attempted to write stories and representations of the girls,[1] I repeatedly turned and returned to the body—to our bodies. Henrietta Moore (1994) states that feminist scholars have been "struggling with the question of how or to what degree women might be the same or similar without being identical. What is it, if anything, that we share?" (p. 1). What seemed shared, common with difference, across the girls and myself, were our bodies, their reproductive capacities, and the interests of such by the state in those capacities.

However, the stories I heard from the girls, the observations I had made, were varied and complex, and I did not wish to simplify them by claiming some essentialized identity related to our female bodies. Yet I did not want to, and indeed could not, ignore the body in this research. I began to question what it would mean to pay attention to bodies, in this case, in an arena where teenage girls' bodies are simultaneously stereotyped, proliferated, ignored, and silenced. How could I, as a woman studying young women who were pregnant, use the flux of our own bodies as a site of deconstruction[2] toward an understanding of the paradox of how social structures and modes of representation simultaneously "form and *deform*" women (de Lauretis, 1984, p. 51)? What kinds of strategies and commitments might a move toward the body make possible or hinder?

Elizabeth Grosz (1995) delineates what she terms "two broad kinds of approaches to theorizing the body"—one, "inscriptive," a Nietzchian, Foucauldian notion of the social body upon which "social law, morality, and values are inscribed" (p. 33). The second is the "lived body," which references the "lived experience of the body, the body's internal or psychic inscription" (p. 33). Grosz suggests that, while we are becoming adept at naming the inscriptive details of the body, we tend to shy away from the messiness of the corporal body—the lived experiences. Grosz (1995) states: "If the notion of a radical and irreducible *difference* is to be understood with respect to subjectivity, the specific modes of corporeality of bodies in their variety must be acknowledged" (p. 32).

There is, however, little research on the lived experience—the specific physicality of the teen pregnant body (Burdell, 1993, 1995; Lesko, 1990, 1991, 1995; Pillow, 1994; Tolman, 1992, 1994). Therefore, in this paper I explore what is exposed when I pay attention to the *messiness* of bodies that exceed the boundaries of what we think we know about young women who are pregnant. After an overview of the specific corporeality of the pregnant body, I present two stories (in)formed by a specific attention to bodies. The first story considers what gets exposed when we pay attention to how teen girls experience and use their pregnant bodies as sites of resistance specifically around issues of sex, pleasure, and power. The second story exposes the literal impact of space and architecture on teen girls' bodies and the ways this affects issues of self-representation, teacher pedagogy, and program implementation. I conclude by reflecting upon what these stories tell us and how the body worked in the telling of these stories.

Exposing the Pregnant Body

Bodies are not new to feminist theory. Feminist theory has used the specificity of the woman's body to challenge the separation of theory from experience under what has come to be known as the caveat, "the personal is political." The "personal is political" highlights how the practices, representations, and knowledge of the female body are not simply innate, natural occurrences, but are *political*—that is, contrived, monitored, controlled, and moralized by a social system in which the female body as a collective has not had much say.

The body, particularly the female body, is at best a curious and conflictual site to "go from"—a site of paradoxical social attention and avoidance. Our bodies are sites of humanist prescription, places from which binaries are structured, forming polemical categories that define them: "inside-outside, subject-object, surface-depth" (Grosz, 1995, p. 33). Grosz (1995) states that "bodies speak, without necessarily talking, because they are coded with and as signs. They speak social codes. They become intextuated, narrativitized; simultaneously, social codes, laws, norms, and ideals become incarnated" (p. 35). These social codes we live by are complex and conditional and are further coded, often without acknowledgment, by issues of gender, race, class, physical characteristics, and sexual identity.

The pregnant female body further confounds and conflates our social codes and norms. "The significance of the maternal body differs from the public body in that it is *the site of the reproduction of the social body*" (Diprose, 1994, p. 25). Tamsin Wilton (1995) states that it is "precisely because of their ability to mother that women's bodies (and their political and social selves) have been so rigidly controlled within all patriarchal political systems" (p. 182). Even in a "normal" pregnancy, what the mother does with her body—what she eats, where she goes, how and when—is open to public scrutiny. She, the mother, is a "legitimate target for moral concern" (Diprose, 1994, p. 26) and thus "subject to very direct state control" (Wilton, 1995, p. 183).

Pregnancy further interrupts accepted and assumed demarcations of the body and self. Questions of what is woman and fetus, woman and society, and where the locus of decision making and control lies during pregnancy have resulted in moral, ethical, and legal debates surrounding issues of birth control, abortion, and surrogacy (Diprose, 1994). Pregnancy confounds our notions of where one body ends and another begins and interrupts assumptions of a single self (Young, 1990, p. 163). Because pregnancy exists and exhibits itself in a fluctuating, changing state, it is unclear where the pregnant body ends and the world begins (Young, 1990, p. 116).

Teen pregnancy offers further complications and excessiveness to the already complicated issue of the state and reproduction. Teen pregnancy operates outside the norm of legitimate reproduction, marking it as a site of moral concern and state control. Teen pregnancy presents itself as a paradox to the state. While giving birth is the obligation of the female citizen, the state also has controlling interests in who gives birth. Articles promoting fear of a "browning of America" (Bane, 1986; Center for Population Options, 1990) feed into the concerns of the public over who gives birth, proliferating the idea that "reproduction is most certainly the obligation (and hence the right) of White, middle-class, able-bodied women" (Wilton, 1995, p. 183). Teen pregnancy presents the paradox of young women fulfilling their reproductive responsibilities, but not in the way the state wishes (Cusick, 1989).

The paradoxical issues surrounding teen pregnancy make it difficult to even define what teen pregnancy is. Is teen pregnancy primarily a problem of "morality, fertility, or poverty" (Lawson & Rhode, 1993, p. 1)? At what age is a woman a teen parent? Are you a teen parent when you are eighteen or nineteen years of age or only if you are in public school? Is teen pregnancy as a social problem defined as only pregnancies that are carried to full term or does it include all teen pregnancies, including those that are terminated by a miscarriage or an abortion? Are you a teen parent if you are married or middle class?

Correspondingly, teen pregnancy intervention and prevention programs present conflictual messages to the girls they target. On the one hand, a major purpose of teen pregnancy programs seems aimed at helping pregnant teens be good mothers, and such programs include topics related to child development, health care, enrichment, household management, and responsibility (Pillow, 1994). On the other hand, these programs have the goal of preparing young mothers[3] to be independent (that is, not on welfare) and thus concentrate upon job skills and enforce many "tough love" requirements in the interests of teaching the girls to take responsibility[4] (Lesko, 1990, 1991; Pillow, 1994). These goals—good mother and fiscal provider—and the actions they require are often conflictual and even polemical.[5]

Consistent across teen pregnancy programs, however, is an avoidance of engagement with the specific physicality of the pregnant female body. Teen pregnancy programs ignore the body outside of linear, taxonomical lists of expected changes and corresponding, acceptable required actions (Burdell, 1995). Teen pregnancy programs thus promote and assume a clear separation of teen girls' pregnant bodies and their selves as woman, mother, student, provider. Teen pregnancy research avidly avoids mentioning teen girls' bodies—ignoring and silencing what Nancy Lesko (1995) terms "the leaky needs" of pregnant teen girls. Research and policy aim at controlling the behavior of the teen girl's body while remaining silent about the changes and needs of the female body.

Yet even as pregnant teen girls' bodies are silenced or even removed from some settings,[6] our society maintains a voyeuristic fascination with the sexualization of the female body, evidenced in our media, advertising, fashion, cultural practices, and myths. Research and popular media articles on teen pregnancy replicate this phenomenon by displaying visuals depicting the contrast of the young teen girl's face with her swollen belly. Such images feed our fascination and incite a moralistic response without ever acknowledging the sexual physicality of teen pregnancy (Burdell, 1995; Lesko, 1990). Ironically, teen pregnancy research and policy simultaneously ignore and proliferate the teen pregnant body (Pillow, 1997). What is made possible, then, by paying attention to the coded bodies of teen girls who are pregnant? How do the girls themselves enact, resist, and live with the increased interest and control that their pregnant bodies incite in others?

Exposure I: Sex, Pleasure, and Power

While the state, policy, and research arenas may avoid the pregnant body, the teen girls I talked with, in a study conducted during 1992–1994 (Pillow, 1994), certainly could not ignore their bodies. To the contrary, I found girls who talked openly and loudly about their bodies, sex, pleasure, and their feelings on being pregnant "schoolgirls." I was drawn to these *unruly* (Rowe, 1995) girls with their strong voices and their display of confidence in their bodies; however, I did not want to simply script the vocal girls' voices as victory narratives and ignore or script the "silent" girls as suffering from low self-esteem as most teen pregnancy research does.

By paying attention to bodies, I began to observe how the girls used their bodies—their changing bodies—as sites of resistance. The girls were working toward and resisting the terms of their lives as well as the requirements of the teen pregnancy program in which they participated. Whether verbally or nonverbally, I observed the girls gain an awareness of the power their bodies had over the behavior and attitude of the adults with whom they worked. For example, many girls found that adults were "uncomfortable" with their pregnant teen body and would use that fact to their advantage. One girl stated, "I could always get out of that teacher's class. He could not look at me without staring at my stomach. He could not get over it, y'know, he just couldn't handle me being pregnant."

One way to have power over adults, to resist, was to talk about what was forbidden or to make obvious what adults did not want to acknowledge. This was clear around issues of sex and sexuality. The program guide for the teen pregnancy program I observed had defined units to discuss sexual activity and assumed the teen girls would be silent in this process, reinforcing the gendered stereotypes of women, particularly young women, that to voice and take control of their sexual lives is not appropriate. However, during a discussion of birth control options, one girl interrupted with, "Well it's not like I don't know what

I'm doing, I do and I get tired of people acting like I don't. So I had sex—I got pregnant. I'm dealing with it. Y'know at some point you've gotta have sex—this isn't like the sixties—you can't wait anymore, or maybe you don't want to. But it's hard for girls to get birth control and most of the boys won't. At least while I'm pregnant, I won't have to worry about getting pregnant!"

This young woman's comments—that a teen girl was aware of the choices and consequences of being sexually active, that she spoke of pleasure, and that she may remain sexually active during her pregnancy—exceeded the boundaries of what the teen pregnancy program (and in this case the teacher) was designed or prepared to address.[7] Often such comments would later be described to me as "immature" or "flippant" by the teachers—they were not to be taken seriously, except to the extent these comments spoke to how deep the girl's problem was. The girls' "silences" were coded as acquiescence and appropriate, responsible behavior, whereas their verbal participation was often coded as irresponsibility. In this way, presentations on birth control options that ignored factors that many women find objectionable about birth control and contribute to their nonuse— limited access, limited choice, changes in body, the idea that you are "bad" if you plan ahead for sexual activity, interruption of pleasure, and the ways to handle birth control with a guy who may not go along with it—can legitimately be continued with minimal involvement from the girls.

Fine (1988) states that precisely because young females' discourses of desire only usually occur in marginalized settings, young teens are learning that what they, as females, feel, think, or desire is not pertinent or important enough to be discussed in a "legitimized" setting. In this way a female discourse of desire becomes an object of regulation. However, in classrooms during discussions of sex and birth control I observed silence both as repression and resistance. It was easy to characterize girls' silences—their lack of discussion about their own sexuality—as repression. In this way "silence is pathologized as absence" (Walkerdine, 1990, p. 35). But I also came to identify girls' silences as resistance,[8] resistance to a teacher's regulatory discourse, resistance to what was being left unsaid in the presentation of the lesson.

For example, after observing a teacher-presented lesson on the girls taking responsibility for their sexual activity, during which the class had remained mostly silent and noncommittal, a girl remarked to me and her friends: "What is that teacher talking about when she says just say 'no' to sex. What if I don't wanna say 'no!' But they'll never talk about that with us—they look down their noses at you, like you're bad. Whatta she know anyway—she's wound so tight she looks like she hasn't had any in over a year!"

Nowhere were the girls' voices stronger, more independent, and more resistant than when they were talking about their school experiences. Repeatedly I heard the girls talk about how they felt they had been treated unfairly in their schools. They voiced a strong desire to learn, but because they did not "fit," they felt they were often ignored or put aside. They felt they had not been given opportunities or chances, and they were not afraid to state this fact to teachers, principals, and administrators. One girl stated: "I made him nervous . . . I stuck my pregnant stomach out at him and said if I'm gonna be in someone's class, I expect to learn something. They were harassing me for about five weeks, telling me I wasn't smart enough to go to day and night school and creating problems for me. I say you're here to help me to understand—that's what you're paid for. If you can't help me then I'm gettin' out."

Another girl, a middle-class, White, attractive, honor roll student was a tuition-paying student at a high school out of her district when she became pregnant. "He called me into his office, and he said I hear you are pregnant. And I say 'yeah,' so what. He says we don't have pregnant girls in this school—how it was bad for the school's reputation and would give other girls ideas. I said give me that slip right now; I'm signing and getting out of here."

"Kelley" transferred from her high school with its good reputation to "Parkside," an alternative school for students experiencing learning or behavior problems, because, "No other high school would let me in." She said she never felt like she fit in at Parkside—"it's not challenging; it's boring." Kelley had been on a college preparation track and felt Parkside was ill-suited to her academic needs, as it focused on minimal graduation requirements and passing proficiency tests. She and her mother and the teen pregnancy teacher spent two months petitioning and moving through paper work so that she could receive a variety of advanced placement courses either through home tutoring, night courses, or additional courses after her baby was born.

After the birth of her baby girl, Kelley thus shuttled across counties to attend her "old" school for academics and Parkside for her family life courses. For Kelley this was a hard-won battle. Although she felt like she had lost her fight to attend her school while she was pregnant because "he [the principal] couldn't handle seeing my pregnant body in his school,"[9] she remained determined to attend her school after the birth of her baby, to show the school, in her words, "that having a baby didn't take away your brains." She had to repeatedly petition the administration at her home school to attend classes and functions at her school, and the decision about whether she could attend graduation and receive her diploma was not finalized until one week before graduation.[10]

Kelley was very proud of graduating "on time" and "with my class" even after the birth of her baby. She brought her graduating class sweatshirt into Parkside and showed her name on it to everyone in the school. Kelley found herself making friendships and alliances with girls at Parkside who "I never would even have talked to before," stating "we're going through the same things, with our bodies, with our schools." These friendships were also reciprocated. Kelley had received the respect of fellow students at Parkside across marked differences of race and class because, as one girl said, "she wore 'em down. She know now what it's like to have to fight for everything you want for your life. We all have a lot of feelings for Kelley; she deserved to graduate with her old school." Kelley commented on and summarized the events in her life over the past year by stating simply: "I never thought anyone would ever treat me this way."

Exposure II: Physically Exceeding Boundaries

What happens when pregnant schoolgirls can no longer fit into the traditional student desk? Where do school administrators decide to place the teen pregnancy classroom in their school? How visible is the teen pregnancy classroom in the school setting? While these questions may appear simplistic and pragmatic, I believe they are questions that are vital to understanding and analyzing the lives of teen pregnant girls in schools. How do the bodies of teen girls fit into their schools? How is it that teen pregnancy and thus the teen girl's body come to be an issue to be regulated and contained?

I did not visit teen pregnancy classroom sites with these issues in mind. It was only after several visits to suburban classroom settings when I felt myself continually being led "downstairs," "around the corner," or "down and back to the left" that I began to question a classroom's physical and embodied positioning in the school as speaking and having an impact on a larger discourse about teen girls who are pregnant within schools. Scheurich (1995) describes Foucault's notion of governmentality, of regulatory practices, as "a kind of governmental rationality" that is concerned with "an insatiable management of social spaces, social practices, and forms" (p. 20). I began to view teen pregnancy classrooms as spaces that were the recipients of this "insatiable management."

Architecture operates as a form of disciplinary power that is exercised in its invisibility. We tend not to turn our gaze on spatial and structural practices—except, for example, the "natural" character and design of a school building. Weedon (1987) defines "spaces as the site for a range of possible forms of subjectivity" (p. 34) through which we define "our sense of ourselves" (p. 21). Thus the following analysis also seeks to undo the traditional mind-body split that is prevalent in modernist discourse and stories of education. Ann Game (1991) writes that she is interested in "practices of space" in terms of the "practices a place makes possible, or closes off" (p. 83). Particularly, I am interested in how practices of surveillance, self-surveillance, and regulatory practices are reinforced through architectural discourses and how these spatial practices are written onto the bodies of students and teachers. How, then, did teen pregnancy classrooms produce their own "insatiable management" of teachers' and girls' bodies?

As I visited classroom sites, I began to notice differences in classroom location, size, accessibility, and physical set-up of the rooms. I identified two main classroom styles: first, traditional classrooms and second, home economics classrooms. The seven teen pregnancy classrooms situated in traditional classroom settings shared several features, including their location and (in)visibility in their schools. These classrooms were all located down- or upstairs off the beaten path of main hallways. Five of the classrooms were approximately half the size of normal classrooms, and none of the seven classrooms was identified as a teen pregnancy classroom. In other words, a visitor to the school would not be able to identify the presence of a teen pregnancy classroom in the building without help.

Indeed, in six of the schools I visited, I was led to the teen pregnancy classrooms because I was told, "you will not be able to find it on your own." In two of the buildings, students working in the office who were asked to take me to the teen pregnancy classroom did not know where it was, and in one building a student and I wandered a corridor as the student said "I know it [the classroom] is here somewhere."

A teacher described the invisibility and obscurity of the teen pregnancy classroom in this way: "We have to keep it very quiet that we are here. I am not allowed to hang a banner or flier up saying this is a GOALS[11] classroom. Some of the teachers do not even know I am here. I cannot go into other classes and talk about GOALS—so the girls really have to find me."

Another teacher stated: "The fear is that if we are too visible, that the community will get upset—kids will go home talking to their parents about the pregnant girls in their school and the parents will call the principal. This hasn't occurred yet, but the principal is very clear that he does not want this to happen. So I keep it pretty quiet. That makes it hard because I don't feel like I really belong to this building."

When asked how this invisibility affects the implementation of the teen pregnancy program, the teachers responded in a similar manner: "Well, you just do what you have to do. I still feel like what I'm doing is important, and I make the agency contacts and help the girls as much as I can. But, yeah, I think I am probably missing some girls because they do not know that help is available to them in the school.

Another teacher states: "You have to start out with a low profile; then when your principal, other teachers, and school board see results, you'll get support. It is difficult, though, because there is always the idea that GOALS is endorsing teen pregnancy by making it too easy for them [the girls]."

While the teachers discussed the placement and invisibility of their classrooms as having an impact on implementation in terms of numbers of students they served (a fact supported by other research; see Burdell, 1995), they did not mention the placement and invisibility of their classrooms as affecting program and curriculum implementation. However, the second similarity found in these seven sites, in addition to issues of location and visibility in the school at large, concerns issues of implementation that situate the physical classroom environments as important to the kinds of discourses occurring in the classrooms. Traditional classroom environments evoked similar pedagogy and also similar *body* discourses.

The seven traditional classroom sites operated with very traditional teacher–student relationships. The students sat in desks in rows, while the teachers stood at the front of the room and taught. The teachers in these classrooms tended to be the teachers who "followed the APRG [the program guide] closely" and developed their discourse and relations with the girls based on the suggestions in the program guide. For example, the teachers in these classrooms, although situated in middle-class suburban communities, were more likely to describe teen parents (girls) as[12] "hard luck kids. They are just hard luck kids. They haven't had very much go right in their life, and they've made a mistake which is now going to affect another innocent life. You have to try to help them deal with their mistakes in a mature and responsible way."

The pregnant girls at these sites were "good" girls who had made a mistake. When adults—teachers, administrators, parents—in these communities face the need to develop programs for teen girls who are pregnant, they do so with a sense of alarm. Comments such as "we have good girls here" and "this has never been a problem here before" incite a cause for alarm and practices of containment. Lesko (1995) finds that school districts, limited by the political rhetoric of the New Right and its focus on "family values," respond to the "specific needs" of school-aged mothers with neglect and invisibility. The needs of teen mothers are excessive, "leaky," "overflowing the current boundaries that attempt to contain them in the realm of 'just economic' or 'just family' issues" (Burdell, 1995, p. 190).

The pregnant girls in these settings also *seemed* to embody a similar contained view on teen pregnancy. They spoke more often of their own pregnancies as "mistakes" and were quick to classify other girls' pregnancies as "definitely a mistake." Lesko (1990) found that girls in teen pregnancy programs speak a type of reformation talk—what Lesko calls "rites of redemption" (p. 125). This discourse of redemption was also typified by the girls in the traditional classroom settings: "I made a mistake and did some things I should not have done. I know that now. And now I need to learn how to take care of my baby and be a responsible parent and get a job, and, yeah, this program will help me do that."

These discourses were embodied through the teachers' interactions with the students and the students' regulation of their own bodies in school. Seldom did the girls at these sites interact actively together in the classroom—exchanging stories or friendly gossip. In fact, I observed only one instance of this behavior over a series of sixty visits to these classrooms. While the teachers showed warmth and jocularity with their students, there was little physical interaction. The girls also regulated their own bodies in these classrooms. While girls' bodies became relaxed in the home economics classrooms, the girls in traditional classroom settings remained proper and stiff even as they tried to fit into traditional desks, which by their second trimester often became difficult to sit in and were certainly uncomfortable. By their last trimester, many of the girls had to sit on the edge of the desk seat and turn sideways to fit within the confines of the desk space.

The contrast of the girls' emerging pregnancies and the confines of the traditional classroom was not discussed in these classrooms. Sometimes, as a girl attempted to fit into a desk and made a grunt or a comment, wry smiles would pass around the room, and others stared until she was "comfortable," but there were no verbal complaints. The teacher and girls seemed to expect that the girls should adapt to their environment even if it did not suit their changing bodies. A couple of girls explained this adaptation in the following way:

> *You're just not supposed to complain in this school or act like you should be treated different because you are pregnant.*

But they treat us like we're different and you get watched twice as closely. Mrs. ___ [their teacher] says we have to set a good example, that some people think we should not even be in school.

Yeah, it's like we shouldn't be here so you just get watched a lot, and you can't make any mistakes or let anyone know you feel sick—not when you're pregnant.

I can't wait to get home at the end of the day and relax on my couch. I think I will do home schooling for my last month—it's just too hard to be here.

While in school, these girls knew they were being watched, regulated, and expected to perform in ways that show their gratitude to be at school and demonstrate redemption for their mistakes. These girls realized they had engaged in a contract, albeit an unwritten one, with their schools that allowed them to stay in school and stay on track with their classes only if they behaved in certain ways.[13] As one girl stated: "It's like when you're pregnant and in school, you have to be quiet or people think you're bad. They act like something is wrong with you anyway, and you can forget about being in clubs or anything—they won't let you. It's like you have to pay for your mistake, and you better do it quietly or only say the things he [the principal] wants you to say."

In contrast, the three teen pregnancy classrooms that were housed in home economics rooms provided stories of bodies and practices different from the stories described above. The home economics rooms, although they varied in size, were situated in the main floors of their schools on a main hallway. Two of the rooms had doors opening onto two main hallways. Thus, the rooms were visible and often served as "stop-in" spots or "resting" places. These rooms had banners hanging on windows or doors acknowledging the presence of the teen pregnancy program in the building, and inside the rooms hung announcements and pictures of recent births.

The rooms were certainly more comfortable than traditional classrooms with chairs separate from large tables. Two of the rooms had couches. One room had playpens, although it did not provide on-site child care.[14] The addition of stoves, refrigerators, sinks, end tables, lamps, and rugs provided a more homey if often crowded feeling to the rooms. The teachers in these classrooms were more likely to "do my own thing" in implementing the teen pregnancy program and were less likely to say that the girls in their classes had made "mistakes." Rather, these teachers described the girls they worked with as in the following: "They got in trouble, and society tells them [the girls] that they're the ones who have to deal with it. They just don't get a break so I try to help them make it against everything else." This particular teacher also said: "Well, I don't think they are necessarily bad. I don't think they have thought very clearly—and part of it is they get so wrapped up in boys. But now they have to stop and think of themselves and their babies, and they need help to do that."

The teachers in these settings were observed to engage in different pedagogical strategies to increase student participation, and the formal line between teacher and student was much less rigidly drawn. Group discussions, popular culture (for example, rap, pop music, or videos), and games were used to introduce topics of relationships, gender roles, sex, and birth control. Every time I observed in these settings I witnessed student/student and student/teacher interactions that were friendly and informal. It was in these settings, often during "informal" times, that I heard stories of independence and "discourses of desire" (Fine, 1988, p. 48). The girls in these rooms looked forward to their times together and shared information with each other about pregnancy, boyfriends, sex, birth control, and their own sexuality. Often the teachers would let these conversations continue, interjecting only to correct misinformation or provide further information.

The most emphatic difference noted in these classroom settings, however, was the differences in bodies in the rooms. As described previously, the girls in the traditional classrooms remained "proper" in their classrooms and had to work to adapt their changing bodies to the limits of the classroom environment. The girls in the home economics classrooms claimed this space as their own—they spewed textbooks and note books on the tables, draped sweaters and coats on the chairs, drew on the chalkboards, admired baby pictures on the walls, and relaxed their bodies onto sofas or into chairs, putting their feet up or heads down.

Here was a space where the pregnant teen could be pregnant. Here she could put feet up, complain about nausea or swollen ankles, and get sympathy, a soda cracker, or a foot rub. Here girls loosened pants that were too tight, massaged abdomens and backs, and compared "stomachs" to "see who's biggest." Here girls shared stories and secrets. Here girls stayed in school until their ninth month and after, often sharing frank and explicit ideas on sex, sexuality, labor, and childbirth: "You all are laughing at me, and I know this sounds gross, but the nurse was telling me to do it, and I wanted to have my baby—so I'm in the room rubbing my nipples like not to get off or something, but it can help you have your baby 'cause it makes you have, what is it?"

Here the teacher intervened and answered "contractions" and confirmed to the other girls who were looking skeptical that the girl was right. And the girl continued: "You wait—you'll be so ready to have your baby you'll do anything. 'Tanya' be twisting her nipples off by eight months!"

This discussion exceeded the boundaries of what the program guide suggests should be included in the curriculum, and I never observed such a conversation in the traditional classroom settings.[15] This teacher allowed many conversations like this to occur, and she felt that "the girls know what they need to know about and this way gives the girls important information on pleasure and childbirth in a way they can hear it." This ease and relaxation of bodies did not mean that there were not "lessons" presented and regulatory practices in place. The teachers in these classrooms still monitored their students' diets and home lives and still had clear goals of helping the students in their programs. As described, however, these lessons took place through alternative formats and discussions and often followed the lead of the girls themselves.

"Relaxed" bodies also did not mean more easily regulated bodies. The girls in these classrooms spoke the strongest stories of independence and evoked the strongest messages of self-esteem. The girls acknowledged the importance of the classrooms in their lives in the following ways: "I can't wait to get in here and see everyone and just relax." "It's about the only place in the school where I feel comfortable—where you can just let it all hang out." "It's [the teen pregnancy room] where I come if I'm feeling depressed or sick or something—just to get away and feel okay about myself or get a hug." "I'm glad we don't have guys in our class. It's the only time you can get away from them teasing us and pulling on you and stuff. Sometimes we have to close our doors to keep 'em out too."

Thus, the teen pregnancy classes housed in home economics rooms demonstrated that space regulates practices and bodies in very different ways than in the traditional classroom setting. In the home economics classrooms, the girls reacted in more relaxed bodies and coveted their space to do so. A combination of teacher attitude and school setting provided a space where teen pregnant girls' bodies were allowed to be excessive, proliferative, leaky, and openly pregnant. These settings also provided more space for counter voices of independence and "discourses of desire" not heard in other team pregnancy classrooms.

Concluding with Bodies and Exposures

For this research, paying attention to bodies methodologically highlights the fact that there is a physicality obvious in teen pregnancy that has for the most part been avoided. Working in a research arena that is already overexposed, such as teen pregnancy, the body as site of deconstructive practice can work to make explicit what is both overexposed and obscured elsewhere. Both of the exposures presented point to the inability of our theories, practices, and programs to deal with certain bodies, in this case, the pregnant teen body.

While school-based teen pregnancy programs assume that a separation of school and the body can be regulated and sustained (Burdell, 1995), the girls in this research demonstrated the body is not so easily separable, nor do they desire it to be. The first exposure points to how teen girls use the tension, the uncomfortableness their changing, pregnant bodies invoke in others as a site of resistance. Paying attention to the bodies of teen girls who are pregnant and how they negotiate their bodies interrupts a simplistic telling of representation and resistance. Can teen girls' silence in their teen pregnancy classrooms be simply written as acquiescence or repressive practice? This research suggests it cannot. McNay (1994) points out that such a "(re)formulation of power does not deny the phenomenon of repression, but it does deny its theoretical primacy" (p. 91).

In this case, paying attention to the body methodologically seeks to acknowledge how teen girls who are pregnant take on the repressive discourse of the teen pregnancy program and speak it back, tracing how they use their bodies to this end. This move toward the body is not about celebrating what is marginalized, but an engagement in a move that interrupts a simplistic telling or a goddess worshipping of the body, moving instead toward what Elizabeth Grosz (1995) describes as "more an enjoyment of the unsettling effects that rethinking bodies implies for those knowledges that have devoted so much conscious and unconscious effort to sweeping away all traces of the specificity, the corporeality, of their own processes of production and representation" (p. 2).

Turning the gaze upon the teen pregnancy program itself, holding a teen pregnancy program accountable for its corporeality, raises many questions and exposes alternative interpretations. A view from the body sees teen pregnant girls' interruptions, silences, or unruliness as not simply irresponsible behavior, but as interruptive, *embodied* forms of resistance. The second exposure further explores how the *invisibility and locatedness* of teen pregnancy programs may affect the implementation of these programs. How does spatial management of teen pregnancy classrooms regulate and/or contain the bodies of teachers and girls?

Paying attention to the body and embodied practices necessitates specific and particular attention to the body as a site of information and practice, regulation, power, and resistance. Tracing the body, its practices and exposures, is particularly important in regard to the study of gendered social issues such as teen pregnancy. Brian Fay (1987) points out that "oppression leaves its traces not just in people's minds, but in their muscles and skeletons as well" (p. 146). In other words, bodies bear the marks of our culture, practices, and policies.

I have proposed a deconstructive reading of the body that calls for attention to the body deconstructively, not to build new formulations but to open possibilities for further strategies. Donna Haraway (1988) describes the view from the body as "always complex, contradictory, structuring" (p. 585). While my own research experiences have demonstrated that attention to bodies in practice and theory is complex and at times uncomfortable (see Pillow, 1996b), I view this complexity as desirous in working toward social justice. Working with the complexity of our bodies—their messiness and "leakiness"—allows thinking beyond our current boundaries, exposes what we may be too uncomfortable to portray, and works to make what is obscured explicit.

Notes

1. I use the term *girls* here and throughout this paper to refer to the females aged thirteen to seventeen who were a part of a study I conducted during 1992–1994 (Pillow, 1994). *Girls* was the preferred term they used among themselves, and I have come to consider how the term *girls* captures the tension between their lives as girls and lives as women.

2. I am alluding here to what I see as a critical difference between reflective and deconstructive practices in ethnography. Visweswaran (1994) differentiates the two by stating that while reflexivity "says that we must confront our own processes of interpretation," deconstruction "says we must confront the plays of power in our processes of interpretation" (p. 79). See Pillow (1996b) for a discussion of the body as a site of reflective and deconstructive practice.

3. While public interest has lately been focused upon the fathers of teen pregnancies, intervention programs remain focused upon the teen mother. Although the traditional married, two-parent family may be presented as a model, it is expected that

teen mothers, in most cases, will bear full physical, developmental, and fiscal responsibility for their children.

4. Many teen pregnancy intervention programs begin with the assumption that the girls have made a mistake and must learn to make better, rational decisions in their lives. Girls who are teen parents are already viewed as having made irresponsible decisions and thus must demonstrate and prove their ability to engage in responsible decision making. Thus, programs that require girls to return to school one month after childbirth, make their own child care arrangements, excuse only three absences a year for sick children, expect girls to schedule doctor appointments for their children after school hours, and demonstrate that they are actively searching for employment justify these requirements as in the best interests of the girls (Burdell, 1995; Pillow, 1994). However, many of these practices seem more aimed at the best interests of the state, and Nancy Lesko (1990), in fact, refers to these practices as "rites of redemption" (p. 125).

5. Combining mothering and work is something that is difficult for any mother, regardless of age, and certainly is compounded by single-parent status and socioeconomic class. In essence, we are asking teen parents to overcome society's own conflictual and stereotypical messages about single mothers and to do so in a responsible fashion. I have often wondered how I and the other single parents I know would hold up under the scrutiny, standards, and judgment of the teen parent programs I have studied.

6. Most programs for teen girls who are pregnant operate in separate classrooms, buildings, or campuses away from the rest of the public school setting.

7. Ironically, most teen pregnancy programs enforce and promote an asexual, neutral approach toward young women's sexuality, ignoring the fact that they have obviously already been and may continue to be sexually active (Pillow, 1994).

8. I do not want to encourage a simplistic definition of resistance (see Haney, 1996, for a discussion of the complexities of resistance between girls and the state) but rather to focus on how I observed girls in the teen pregnancy program become aware of the way in which their pregnant bodies were both assumed resistant and how the girls came to use this phenomenon to incite further resistance. In addition, with the stories presented here I am not attempting to situate a case of girls versus the program, where the girls are "right," but to provide a forum for a discussion of girls' bodies and resistance. I have explored and discussed elsewhere the complexities of telling teen girls' stories of resistance, where the forms of resistance may occur in ways that resist a critical or feminist telling and are stories that are uncomfortable to tell (Pillow, 1994, 1996a, 1996b).

9. Kelly also discussed that while her mother, the teen pregnancy teacher, and herself were working to arrange a continuation of her advanced placement classes, she "took pleasure" in going to every meeting "myself, with my pregnant body, so that they [the school administration] would have to deal with the fact that 'yes,' I was pregnant and that I was still a student at their school."

10. Kelley received support from the students at her old school. Against administrative wishes the Senior Class included Kelley's name on a sweatshirt with signatures of the "Class of 1992." The administration threatened not to let the seniors sell the sweatshirt and then later said the sweatshirt could not be worn on the school grounds—a decision which was later revoked.

11. Pseudonym for the teen pregnancy program I studied.

12. It is important to note here that the goal is not to critique these discourses or say they are "wrong"—the teachers I talked with are dedicated, caring professionals whom I developed much respect for—but to situate and attempt to understand what impact the regulatory function of architecture may have on the discourse spoken and embodied in these classrooms.

13. Similar to Fine's (1988) work on school drop-outs, this research raises questions about who teen pregnancy programs serve and, perhaps more important, who they do want and do not want to serve. Several girls at these sites told me that they had friends who had opted not to enroll in the teen pregnancy program "because of the way you're treated in school." While the teen pregnancy program I researched claimed a high graduation rate of its students, by my closest estimations, the program served less than 35 percent of the teen pregnancies in the state. Burdell (1995), in a review of related literature, had similar findings: programs tend to target "specific segments of students and ignore the rest" (p. 185).

14. Child care was not provided at any of the settings I observed and not condoned by the state teen pregnancy program. Girls in the suburban schools were particularly discouraged from bringing their babies to school for any reason, as it was, in one teacher's view, "an inappropriate thing to do—this is a high school—a place to learn with your mind not to show off what you made with your body."

15. As discussed above, this is not to say that this type of conversation did not occur in the traditional school settings, only that these conversations were regulated out of the official space of the teen pregnancy classrooms I observed.

References

Allison, D. (1994). *Skin: Talking about sex, class and literature*. Ithaca, NY: Firebrand Books.

Bane, M. (1986). Household composition and poverty. In S. H. Danziger & D. H. Weinberg (Eds.), *Fighting poverty: What works and what doesn't* (pp. 209–231). Cambridge, MA: Harvard University Press.

Burdell, P. A. (1993). *Becoming a mother in high school: The life histories of five young women*. Unpublished doctoral dissertation, University of Wisconsin-Madison, Madison, WI.

Burdell, P. A. (1995). Teen mothers in high school: Tracking their curriculum. *Review of Research in Education, 21*(3), 163–208.

Butler, J. (1990). *Gender trouble: feminism and the subversion of identity*. New York: Routledge.

Butler, J. (1993). *Bodies that matter: on the discursive limits of "sex."* New York: Routledge.

Center for Population Options. (1990). *Teenage pregnancy and too early childbearing: Public costs, personal consequences* (6th ed.). Washington, DC: Center for Population Options.

Cixous, H. (1994). *The Helene Cixous reader* (S. Sellers, Ed.). London: Routledge.

Cusick, T. (1989). Sexism and early parenting: Cause and effect? *Peabody Journal of Education, 8*(4), 113–131.

Davis, A. Y. (1981). *Women, race, and class.* New York: Vintage Books.

de Lauretis, T. (1984). *Alice doesn't: Feminism, semiotics, cinema.* London: Macmillan.

Diprose, R. (1994). *The bodies of women: ethics, embodiment and sexual difference.* London: Routledge.

Fay, B. (1987). *Critical social science.* Ithaca, NY: Cornell University Press.

Fine, M. (1988). Sexuality, schooling and adolescent females: The missing discourse of desire. *Harvard Educational Review, 58,* 29–53.

Foucault, M. (1990). *The history of sexuality: An introduction: Vol. I.* New York: Vintage Books. (Original work published 1974).

Game, A. (1991). *Undoing the social: Towards a deconstructive sociology.* Toronto: University of Toronto Press.

Gaskell, J. (1992). *Gender matters from school to work.* Philadelphia, PA: Open University Press.

Grosz, E. (1995). *Space, time, and perversion.* London: Routledge.

Grosz, E., & Probyn, E. (Eds.). (1995). *Sexy bodies: The strange carnalities of feminism.* London: Routledge.

Haney, L. (1996). Homeboys, babies, men in suits: The state and the reproduction of male dominance. *American Sociological Review, 61*(10), 759–778.

Haraway, D. J. (1988). Situated knowledges: The science question in feminism and the privilege of the partial perspective. *Feminist Studies, 14*(3), 575–599.

hooks, b. (1990). *Yearning: Race, gender, and cultural politics.* Boston, MA: South End Press.

Lawson, A., & Rhode, D. L. (Eds.). (1993). *The politics of pregnancy: Adolescent sexuality and public policy.* New Haven: Yale University Press.

Lesko, N. (1990). Curriculum differentiation as social redemption: The case of school-aged mothers. In R. Page & L. Valli (Eds.), *Curriculum differentiation: Interpretive studies in U.S. secondary schools* (pp. 113–136). Albany, NY: State University of New York Press.

Lesko, N. (1991). Implausible endings: Teenage mothers and fictions of school success. In N. B. Wyner (Ed.), *Current perspectives on the culture of schools* (pp. 45–64). Brookline, MA: Brookline Books.

Lesko, N. (1995). The "leaky needs" of school-aged mothers: An examination of U.S. programs and policies. *Curriculum Inquiry.*

McNay, L. (1994). *Foucault: a critical introduction.* Cambridge, MA: Polity Press.

Moore, H. L. (1994). *A passion for difference.* Bloomington, IN: Indiana University Press.

Pillow, W. (1994). *Policy discourse and teenage pregnancy: The making of mothers.* Unpublished doctoral dissertation, Ohio State University, Columbus, OH.

Pillow, W. (April, 1996a). *Embodied analysis: Unthinking teen pregnancy.* Paper presented at the annual meeting of the American Educational Research Association, New York, NY.

Pillow, W. (April, 1996b). *Reflexivity as discomfort.* Paper presented at the annual meeting of the American Educational Research Association, New York, NY.

Pillow, W. S. (1997). Decentering silences, troubling irony: Teen pregnancy's challenge to policy analysis. In C. Marshall (Ed.), *Feminist critical policy analysis I: A primary and secondary schooling perspective.* London: Falmer Press.

Rowe, K. (1995). *The unruly woman: Gender and the genres of laughter.* Austin, TX: University of Texas Press.

Scheurich, J. J. (1995). Policy archaeology: A new policy studies methodology. *Journal of Policy Studies, 9*(4), 297–316.

Tolman, D. L. (1992). *Voicing the body: A psychological study of adolescent girls' sexual desire.* Unpublished doctoral dissertation, Harvard University, Cambridge, MA.

Tolman, D. L. (1994). Doing desire: Adolescent girls' struggles for/with sexuality. *Gender and Society, 8*(3), 324–342.

Trinh, T. M. (1989). *Woman, native, other: Writing post-coloniality and feminism.* Bloomington, IN: Indiana University Press.

Visweswaran, K. (1994). *Fictions of feminist ethnography.* Minneapolis, MN: University of Minnesota Press.

Walker, R. (Ed.). (1995). *To be real.* New York: Anchor Books.

Walkerdine, V. (1990). *Schoolgirl fictions.* London: Verso.

Weedon, C. (1987). *Feminist practice and poststructuralist theory.* Cambridge: Basil Blackwell.

Wilton, T. (1995). *Lesbian studies: Setting an agenda.* London: Routledge.

Young, I. M. (1990). *Throwing like a girl and other essays in feminist philosophy and social theory.* Bloomington, IN: Indiana University Press.

Looking Back to Move Forward: Reflections on How I Did Research Impacts What I Know Now

Wanda S. Pillow
University of North Carolina, Greensboro

Rereading "Exposed Methodology" takes me back to the "field," back to school sites, back to the girls I came to know and whose children now are ages eight to ten, back to the heady days of graduate school, and back to the newness of doing qualitative research. These are strong memories and lead me to pull out field note journals, transcripts of interviews, and my dissertation from which the article "Exposed Methodology" emerged. I wonder how some of the "girls" I became close to during my research are doing—by this point I am no longer in contact with any of "my subjects." But I am also a bit shaken in my rereadings to find how much of my life history is also in these research documents. In these pages, I find reflections on who I was as a researcher, graduate student, woman, mother, and writer; my passions, beliefs, insecurities, and doubts stare out at me on every page along with quotes from favorite authors, telephone numbers, grocery store and to-do lists, and the more than occasional doodle of one my children mixed in throughout and often right over my field notes. I am reminded of how intense the experiences of doing long-term qualitative research is, how the doing of this work becomes integrated intimately into and with your life.

As a teacher of qualitative methodology courses, I attempt to convey to students how the doing and the writing up of their research will consume their lives; now I have gained a renewed appreciation for this fact. As researchers I think we often feel as prepared as can be to do the methods of our research—observations, interviews, field notes, journal entries—while we typically do not feel prepared to do what comes *after* fieldwork, the work of analysis and writing. There are no protocols to tell us how to analyze and write—we are simply and impossibly faced with a sea of data collection, thus the cry and fear in the phrase, "I am drowning in my data!" I have even worked with some students who try to extend data collection because of the "What do I do now?" fear they feel when data collection is coming to an end. I do not want to draw clear lines here between the fields of research and writing, as I think they occur simultaneously. However, there is a point when data collection in the field does end, and then we are faced with our data and ourselves, a daunting prospect.

I think first after data collection you have to learn to be alone again, but you do not want to be too alone. This is the time, if you have not already done so, to form or join a writing group. The structure, support, and companionship are vital. At this point, you have to immerse yourself in your data; listen to it, read it, touch it, play with it, copy it, write on it, color code it, over and over again. Keep track of possible themes that arise from your data and titles for chapter headings or papers when they come to mind. Envision your written product— what will it look like, how will the data be displayed, where will you be in the text—and write down what you think. Begin writing, anything, and write every day. Read what motivates you and if you cannot write an original sentence of your own, "write" down all your favorite quotes from pieces that help you think (and keep a complete reference list so you do not have to search for where that great quote came from later).

Now you are working, but the work still feels overwhelming. Overwhelming not only because it is difficult for many of us to claim space for ourselves as writers, but also because of the relationships we often form, or feel we form, with our research subjects. "Exposed Methodology" was one of the first pieces I wrote out of my research, and I felt a great sense of responsibility in this piece to represent the girls well. Although it went through several drafts, including two versions presented at conferences, I see how much I tried to fit into one piece. Now I tell students, "do more with less"; I also try to follow that advice.

However, this piece has served me well and I am still asking questions about the paradox and irony of the presence and absence of body talk in teen pregnancy literature. This brings up two points I think are important about the role of theory in our work. First, it is important to acknowledge and identify that we all have theories we work out of. Indeed, the doing of qualitative research is based upon a belief that we can observe reality and know someone's story by talking to her. Certainly, the degree to whether or how we can do this has been debated. However, how you see the world, what you believe about the nature of truth, reality, voice, and identity will affect how you conduct your research and for what purposes, including the kinds of questions you ask, the kinds of data you collect, how you think about your data, and how you write up your data and present them to an audience.

Second, theory is not a container to pour yourself or your data into, it is a lens that you use because it works and because you cannot write or think without it. You may try on multiple theories, use them interchangeably, even promiscuously. The point is your theories should work for you. If they do not, discard them or retool them. I picked up feminist, poststructural, and race-based theories because I needed them to think through the paradoxes of teen mothers' lives. Looking back, I also see I needed this theory work myself. What is hinted at but left out of "Exposed Methodology" is how similar I found my life, as a single mother of two young children too close in age who used social welfare services, to the teen mothers I interviewed. I know that my status as a single mother gained me access and trust to many young women. They saw similarities between our lives often before I was ready to do so—we shared stories about juggling work, school, and child care and about dealing with bureaucracies. Perhaps because at that time the idea that being too close to your research was a liability was still prevalent, I kept these stories private. I am not calling for self-indulgent writing (that is why we keep research journals), but now I would discuss how my own status and identities affected my research.

Another change I wish I could make is a problematic I saw the first time I read the piece in print. Although I do not specify the race of the girls in the data vignettes, I do identify Kelley as a "middle class, White, attractive, honor roll student." This leaves readers with several possible readings, none of which are factual, that Kelley is attractive because she is White and smart, that the other girls are not attractive, or that the other girls in the article are all Black. By identifying Kelley's race and not specifically any of the other girls', I privilege present racial thinking, letting readers assume racialized identities for the other girls, and as teen pregnancy is typically assumed a "minority" problem, readers tell me they typically read "Black" for the other girls. I know why I voiced Kelley the way I did—she was always described by other girls in the teen pregnancy school, White and Black, as "White, attractive, and smart." I should have made clear why this occurred and how as Kelley's status as a middle-class, honor roll student did not protect her from being treated poorly by school personnel, her presence at the teen pregnancy school galvanized many of the girls to an awareness of injustice, not just for Kelley, but for all of them—a recognition that they were being treated differently and poorly because they were pregnant at the wrong time. However, my attempt to interrupt a racialized discourse of teen pregnancy backfired and can be read as perpetuating one. This nags at me, but it has certainly been a lesson from which I have learned. I would now discuss race and racialized discourses around teen pregnancy from the beginning, keeping in mind that if we do not write it we leave our readers to assume it, and that such absences often allow hegemonic privileges to perpetuate.

I always emphasize to my students "you will make mistakes" because they often hold tightly to what is right or wrong when it comes to their research. When we are working with human subjects we cannot help but be fallible, yet we often do our best thinking and writing from such "mistakes." This is why it is so important for qualitative researchers to talk with each other and show our "dirty laundry," so we can learn from each other and also learn that there is no such thing as the perfect research project or the perfect written piece. What we need to share more of and make evident is how we produce our works.

That said, I close with advice that has sustained me as a researcher, thinker, and writer. Do what you are passionate about. Use theory not because it is there but because you cannot think without it. Keep reading and keep the one to two books that most inspire you as a writer by your side during your research. Participate in a writing and support group—it is vital that you talk about your research and also share writing with your peers. This group will sustain you emotionally, theoretically, and physically, and check you when you need to be checked. Identify who you are as a writer—how do you write, when, where—and claim a status for yourself as a writer. Write what you are passionate about. And on occasion take the time to reflect on your writing, see where you have been, where you are going, and what you have learned, share it with others, and begin again.

18

Methodology in the Fold
and the Irruption of Transgressive Data

Elizabeth A. St. Pierre

As the effects of the crises of legitimization and representation disperse in a rhizomatic[1] fashion throughout the traditional disciplines produced by the epistemology of humanism, qualitative researchers in the social sciences who are fond of poststructural critiques search for strategies that might enable them to produce different knowledge and to produce knowledge differently. Many of us have begun to suspect that "the epistemological point of departure in philosophy is inadequate" (Butler, 1992, p. 8); that knowledge is contingent and bound up more with power than with truth (Foucault, 1980); that "the discourse of a non-empiricist knowledge barely exists as yet" (Belsey, 1993, p. 561); and, finally, that in education, at any rate, the "'state of emergency' in which we exist is not the exception but the rule" (Benjamin, 1950/1968, p. 257). As a result, we believe it is urgent that we rethink our understanding of both knowledge and its production in order to envision revitalized academic and public discourses to guide our teaching and learning.

This charge is grand and glorious but seems to proceed at a snail's pace as we tackle one at a time those transcendental signifiers we have been given to think about our world: science, method, validity, truth, power, rationality, objectivity, identity, sexuality, culture, history, democracy, and so forth. Our work is surely limited by our received understandings of such words, but we do have the option of placing these signifiers *sous rature*,[2] of using them even as we attempt to escape their meaning.

Elizabeth A. St. Pierre. (1997). "Methodology in the Fold and the Irruption of Transgressive Data." *International Journal of Qualitative Studies in Education, 10*(2), 175–189. Reprinted with permission of Taylor & Francis, Ltd., http://www.tandf.co.uk.

However, once we begin to be suspicious of the everyday language we take for granted—"our mother tongue" or our "language with a history" (Spivak, 1993, p. 69)—the world becomes shaky, indeed. We begin to see that nothing is innocent and that everything is dangerous. After all, language is the foundation upon which knowledge, the *logos,* rests; and if that foundation can be put under erasure, if meaning is not fixed in language, and if knowledge is therefore contingent, how can we proceed? How can we continue to live and work in a world where truth appears fleetingly and at once begins to decay?

Indeed, posthumanist critiques, such as deconstructive analyses, insist that we stand at the edge of the abyss—that fearful and terrible chaos created by the loss of transcendent meaning—and struggle with our loss. And if we still seem condemned to meaning, we may wonder whether it is possible to make a different kind of meaning as we survey this "site of failure" (Butler, 1993, p. 11), this "field of ruins" (Borinksi, cited in Benjamin, 1963/1977, p. 178). Rorty (1986) posits that "we only know the world and ourselves *under a description*" (p. 48) and perhaps "we just *happened on that description*" (p. 48). If we entertain the possibility that all might not be what we have been led to believe—that there might be worlds other than the one described by liberal humanism—then poststructural theories offer opportunities to investigate those worlds by opening up language for redeployment in revitalized social agendas. Butler (1993) summarizes this position by saying that we can "resignify the very terms that, having become unmoored from their grounds, are at once the remnants of that loss and the resources from which to articulate the future" (p. 11). This is very good news for many people.

Those who have been much burdened and even violated by the language and practice of humanism, those who have been locked in painful categories and trapped on the wrong side of vicious binaries, are delighted to adopt an affirmative position and throw off the burden of a life weighed down by the transcendence of "higher values" (Deleuze, 1962/1983, p. 185), values whose worth is not at all self-evident to them. They see nothing nihilistic or apolitical or irrational or relativistic or anarchistic or unethical about the task of resignification. In fact, they believe it would be nihilistic and unethical *not* to practice "a constant 'civil disobedience' within [their] constituted experience" (Rajchman, 1985, p. 6). They believe that people "are much freer than they feel, that people accept as truth, as evidence, some themes that have been built up at a certain moment during history, and that this so-called evidence can be criticized and destroyed" (Foucault, cited in Martin, 1982/1988, p. 10). They adopt the "joyful yet laborious strategy of rewriting the old language" (Spivak, 1974, p. xx) so that they may ask different questions and thus change the topic of the conversation entirely.

Resignification lends itself to a variety of approaches, including a "pessimistic activism" (Foucault, 1984, p. 343), a "non-stupid optimism" (Kushner, cited in Lather, 1995a, p. 3), and even "an audacious sense of hope" (West, 1995), and these approaches are shot through with ethical concerns, since ethics is no longer transcendental and clearly defined in advance for everyone in every situation. Rather, ethics explodes anew in every circumstance, demands a specific reinscription, and hounds praxis unmercifully. In a postmodern world, the individual's responsibility is much different in the world of liberal humanism. If the self is not given, if there is no core, essential self that remains the same throughout time, if subjectivity is constructed within relations that are situated within local discourse and cultural practice—both of which can be resisted to some extent—then "we have no excuse not to act" (Caputo, 1993, p. 4). We can no longer justify positions that are hurtful because "that's just the way it is (I am)."

The foundations may have crumbled, but we are obliged to continue. We are in play, working on the verge of intelligibility with no guarantee of liberation. We understand that we may never "'adequately' 'solve' the problems of being, truth, or subjectivity" (Flax, 1990, p. 193). On the contrary, we must learn to live in the middle of things, in the tension of conflict and confusion and possibility; and we must become adept at making do with the messiness of that condition and at finding agency within rather than assuming it in advance of the ambiguity of language and cultural practice. In addition, we must be on the lookout for each other as we negotiate meaning and create new descriptions of the world. We can never get off the hook by appealing to a transcendental Ethics. We are always on the hook, responsible, everywhere, all the time.

If we wish to engage in this risky poststructural practice of redescribing the world, where do we begin? Derrida (1967/1974) encourages us to begin, "*Wherever we are; in a text where we already believe ourselves to be*" (p. 162). However, given that we must use the language we have inherited even as we put it under erasure, how can we think differently? We can, perhaps, employ a device such as the metaphor to help us move toward the unthought. A metaphor reorients experience by helping us understand one thing in terms of another (Lakoff & Johnson, 1980). After humanism, however, the metaphor can no longer provide a structural, truthful coherency in the midst of confusion. Rather, it assists in a radical interpretation, in a "reading that *produces* rather than *protects*" (Spivak, 1974, p. lxxv).

What knowledge, then, might be produced if an educational researcher uses a metaphor to open up a received signifier of qualitative methodology that no longer seems adequate when "looking awry" (Zizek, 1991) at the world? This essay[3] represents an attempt to think differently about one word commonly used in research, *data.* By employing Deleuze's (1988/1993) image of the fold to trouble the received meaning of *data* in a study (St. Pierre, 1995) that uses Foucault's (1984/1986a) ethical analysis, care of the self, to examine the place of education among the arts of existence used by a group of older, White, Southern women in constructing their subjectivities, I have been able to shift my understanding of the research process to some extent and thus to think about different kinds of data that might produce different knowledge in qualitative research in education.

First, I briefly describe my research project and explain how foregrounding my own subjectivity in my study of others' subjectivities with the help of Deleuze's image of the fold enabled me to make intelligible the imbrication between the inside and outside of the research process. Second, I describe the different kinds of data I was able to theorize once I placed *data* under erasure: emotional data, dream data, and sensual data. Third, I identify the methods that I believe produced those kinds of data in my particular study. Fourth, I name and discuss another kind of data, *response data,* that I believe has been folded into the research process all along under several other signifiers, such as member checks and peer debriefing. Finally, I join a conversation recently begun that addresses the ethical and epistemological implications of foregrounding the fold of response data and of acknowledging its significance.

Troubling Subjectivity: Employing the Fold

I found myself pursuing deferred meanings of the signifier *data* as I wrote about my methodological practices in a research project, a combination of an interview study and an ethnography, that examines the construction of subjectivity in a group of older, White, Southern women who live in my hometown. I was an insider in this project, since I had grown up in the community I studied and had known many of my participants since I was a child. I was also an outsider who had left the community as a young woman of twenty-five to return from time to time to visit my family over another twenty-year period before my official research began.

Since my study focuses on the construction of the subjectivities of these others, it necessarily examines the construction of my own subjectivity that was folded into theirs in particularly fruitful and disturbing ways. After all, my participants, the older women of my hometown, had taught me how to be a woman, and I heard myself as I listened to them. I was like them but different too, for I had moved away from their community and had been reconstituted by other discourses and practices. I was both identity and difference, self and other, knower and known, researcher and researched. Foregrounding this doubling of subjectivity became crucial to my theorizing and my methodological practices. As I worked in this "collapse of identity" (Kondo, 1990, p. 17), I determined to pay attention to what this folded subjectivity might enable as I practiced qualitative research in a postmodern world.

I immediately encountered all sorts of problems, many of which dealt with issues of language and linearity. The disjunction between my praxis and the signifiers I had been given to represent it was not unbearably troublesome, however, until I began to labor in the thinking that writing produces. Indeed, it was only when I struggled to write a traditional description of my ethnographic practices, my fieldwork, and to insert those practices into the categories provided by the grid of traditional qualitative methodology—categories such as *data, method, peer debriefing,* and *member check*—that I experienced what Spivak (1993) calls "moments of bafflement" (p. 248). I realized that those categories do, as Foucault (1977) explains, "suppress the anarchy of difference, divide differences into zones, delimit their rights, and prescribe their task of specification" (p. 186). The categories, the words, simply did not work; and I knew that in order to continue writing and producing knowledge I had to find a different strategy of sense-making, one that might elude humanism's attempts to order what can never be contained. The risk of deconstruction is, after all, to "say yes to that which interrupts [our] project" (Spivak cited in Hutnyk, McQuire, and Papastergiadis, 1986/1990, p. 47). Thus, as the unthought and unnamed hovered near all the words I wrote, I determined to become a stranger in my own language and learn some of what it was hiding.

Escaping the mother tongue is not easy, so I decided to employ Deleuze's (1986/1988; 1988/1993) image, the fold, which he derived from Foucault (see Deleuze, 1986/1988), as a strategy to help me think differently. Deleuze (1986/1988) writes that the fold disrupts our notion of interiority, since it defines "the inside as the operation of the outside" (p. 97) by "treating the outside as an exact reversion, or 'membrane,' of the inside, reading the world as a texture of the intimate" (Badiou, 1994, p. 61). The fold's function is to "avoid distinction, opposition, fatal binarity" (Badiou, 1994, p. 54); thus, it breaks apart humanist dualisms such as inside/outside, self/other, identity/difference, and presence/absence. And "it is the individual who causes the outside to fold, thereby endowing itself with subjectivity, as it bends and folds the outside" (Boundas, 1994, p. 114). I believed, since I had such difficulty separating myself from my participants, that I was working within a fold and that that fold was constructing a subjectivity, my own, that enabled me to think differently. Like a fold, my subjectivity had no inside or outside; the boundary, the division, the violent binary partition was not there. "What always matters is folding, unfolding, refolding" (Deleuze, 1988/1993, p. 137). That image seemed to describe the "shifting boundary of otherness within identity" (Bhabha,1994, p. 51) that I had experienced in the field and that the practice of writing demanded be taken into account. And it is perhaps inevitable that a subjectivity that thinks and acts within such shifting boundaries will find that much else begins to shift as well.

Troubling Data

It is this shiftiness that has led me to my trouble with data and has enabled me to identify at least two problems with the signifier *data* as it is used in traditional qualitative research methodology. I must admit that it is difficult to describe these two problems in isolation, since all sorts of accompanying problems emerge as we reach the limits of the epistemology that grounds the humanist narrative of qualitative methodology. When we put a signifier such as *data* under erasure, the entire structure that includes it begins to fall apart, and clarity becomes impossible. Attempting to follow the rhizomatic disintegration of the narrative of knowledge production in qualitative research is more than one researcher can manage. Thus, I encourage readers to follow their own "lines of flight" (Deleuze & Parnet, 1977/1987, p. 125) based on their own work as they think about data with me in this discussion.

The first problem I address is the notion that data, whatever they are, must be translated into words so that they can be accounted for and interpreted. In their early work, Lincoln and Guba (1985) describe data as "the observational and interview notes accumulated in the field, documents and records, *unobtrusive traces* [italics added], and the like" (p. 333). Data are generally understood to be words, photographs, and other artifacts that are "*constructions* offered by or in the sources" (Lincoln and Guba, 1985, p. 332). Researchers collect data using methods such as observation, participation, and the interview. They are encouraged to immerse themselves in the field in order to collect rich data and produce "thick description" (Geertz, 1973). Van Maanen (1988) explains that "'Textualization' is Ricoeur's term for the process by which unwritten behavior[s] become fixed, atomized, and classified as data of a certain sort. Only in textualized form do data yield to analysis" (p. 95).

With this received understanding of data in mind, we believe we must translate whatever we think are data into language, code that language, then cut up pages of text in order to sort those coded data bits into categories (we do this either by hand or computer) and produce knowledge based on those categories, which, in the end, are simply words. We are very concerned that we have pieces of data, words, to support the knowledge we make. Yet how can language, which regularly falls apart, secure meaning and truth? How can language provide the evidentiary warrant for the production of knowledge in a postmodern world? In my study I knew that I had analyzed much data that had never been textualized into words on a page. Data that escaped language (perhaps those "unobtrusive traces" that Lincoln and Guba refer to above) exploded all over my study—data that were uncodable, excessive, out-of-control, out-of-category. But since I was obliged to work within the narrative of qualitative research methodology, I decided to try to identify and describe those data in order to demonstrate that the commonplace meaning of the category, data, no longer held. In effect, I put the signifier *data sous rature*. In doing so, I identified at least three nontraditional kinds of data— emotional data, dream data, and sensual data—and named another, response data, which I believe has been folded into our research projects all along under other signifiers such as member checks and peer debriefing. I am sure there are still other unidentified, unnamed data working in my study. Searching for those data is one of the seductive aspects of poststructural work. Redescribing the world, is, after all, a playful and joyful activity.

The second problem I encountered is the ruthlessly linear nature of the narrative of knowledge production in research methodology, which goes something like this: first, we employ methods, such as interviewing and participant-observation, which produce data; then we code, categorize, analyze, and interpret those data; finally, from that analysis and interpretation, we develop theories of knowledge. What happens, however, when this linear process is interrupted because the researcher enters this narrative in the middle?[4] For example, in my study, I first identified data and then, despite my disinclination to work in a humanist fashion, had to go backward to identify the method of data collection that I thought had produced the data and then go forward to learn how those data had produced knowledge.

Identifying the method of data collection was amusing, thought-provoking, and not too difficult; but I had no idea how to link some of the data with the knowledge that was produced. I surely did try to overlay the linear narrative of methodology on my practice, but it never fit. I still cannot find data bits that produced certain sentences. Indeed, I often felt that all the activities of the narrative—data collection, analysis, and interpretation—happened simultaneously, that everything happened at once. In protest, I wrote the following (St. Pierre, 1995) about my distaste for the requirement that I construct a linear story describing my methodology:

> This project has transgressed its legitimate bounds into the realm of the unnamed, and the requirement of this format to represent a clear, linear process of research which can be judged as worthy becomes violent, coercive, and distortive. Even though I have journaled ceaselessly during this research process, I can hardly remember what I thought on many working days or why I woke up one morning knowing I must next do this or that. This text appears to represent the real, but this inscription is a simulacrum, today's story, and the following attempt to unfold the methodological processes of this project is limited and partial and a bit absurd, like all attempts to capture the real. (p. 114)

Resistance to humanism's requirement that we simplify the complex may begin in frustration and even anger, but, as Spivak (cited in Rooney, 1989) reminds us, "deconstruction is not an exposure of error, certainly not other people's error. The critique in deconstruction, the serious critique in deconstruction, is the critique of something that is extremely useful, something without which we cannot do anything" (p. 129). She goes on to explain that deconstruction deals very seriously with a very familiar concept and that the aim of deconstruction is to examine a concept "with literal seriousness, so that it transforms itself" (Spivak cited in Rooney, 1989, p. 129). Since the concept, data, is so crucial to the research process and since my desire is that it transform itself so that we can use different methodology and different knowledge to describe the world, I intend to treat *data* with the utmost seriousness in the following discussion that describes data I consider to be transgressive: emotional data, dream data, sensual data, and response data.

Emotional Data

The first of these transgressive data, emotional data, was almost overwhelming at times. I found, indeed, that it was impossible for me to ignore the emotions that sometimes threatened to shut down my study. I talked with very old women near the end of their lives, women who have lost almost everything and struggle to make sense of that loss, women who work very hard at remaining good Christian women in the face of disaster after disaster. I also talked with women in their early sixties who are just coming into their own, women who are breaking all the rules, assuming public positions of power and making decisions among alternatives that were not available even a decade ago. I had no doubt but that my interpretation was influenced by emotional data, data that I could hardly textualize, code, categorize, and analyze. Are emotions data? Kleinman and Copp (1993) say that we should indeed count our emotions as data to be analyzed. In fact, Van Maanen, Manning, and Miller (1993) write that fieldwork is "yet another addition to our repertoire of ways to make ourselves uncomfortable," that "emotional labor is thus central to the trade," and that "we might be made somewhat more comfortable if less of our efforts were devoted to the avoidance, denial, and control of emotions and if more of our efforts were directed to the understanding, expression, and reporting of them" (p. viii). So my question became the following: if emotions are data, then what is the method that produces them? Surely, the method used to collect emotional data varies from study to study. However, I came to believe that my emotions were most often produced when, in a search for some kind of scandalous, rhizomatic validity,[5] I forced myself to theorize my own identity as I theorized my participants'. I wrote the following about my painful search for validity (St. Pierre, 1995):

> In the end, you must take me at my word, and whether and how you do that is undoubtedly beyond my control. I will give it my best, since I care immeasurably for the women of this study. I find my own validity when I write and cry and then write some more. As the bones of my soul break ground for my intellect, I push through into spaces of understanding I did not particularly want to occupy. Why do the tears come? My posture as academic researcher and writer is jolted and deflated and displaced by connections and thoughts and folds erased from awareness until they are worded. As I write and theorize the lives of my participants, I theorize my own, as Fay (1987) says we must. The outside folds inside and I am formed anew.
>
> My writing disturbs the fear which skulks among my own identity relays and flushes my attachments which furtively dodge analytical attention. In the thinking that writing produces, I wobble in the movie Trinh (1989) describes between other and not other; I am provoked into Butler's (1995) subversive citation; I am flayed by Spivak's (1992) wounding process of deidentification. This is deconstruction at its finest, most caustic and abyssal—my own displacement and irruption into difference—self-formation. (p. 114)

It was during this very emotional process of deconstruction that I found myself working much harder to understand my participants, respect their lives, examine my relationship with them, and question my interpretations. The examination of one's own frailty surely makes one more careful about the inscription of others'.

Lather (1995b) writes of a "situated/embodied" transgressive validity (p. 41) that emerged from her study of women with HIV-AIDS. With Lather, I began to understand that validity in my study must be situated within the construction of subjectivity—my own as well as my participants'—since that was the focus of my research. I also believe that it was this search for validity within self-formation that produced corrosive, painful emotional data. I therefore name the "desire for validity" a method of data collection in my research project. The effects of that rhizomatic and deconstructive method were ongoing and wrenching, and my obligation to take into account this method and the data it produced forced me to continue to theorize my own life and, in the process, to reconstitute my subjectivity.

Dream Data

There is another form of transgressive data produced throughout my study, dream data, that surely influenced my interpretation. I textualized these data only once, at the very beginning of my dissertation, but never deliberately analyzed them. Foucault (1984/1986b) calls the "space of our dreams . . . the space of our primary perception" (p. 23). If this is so, how can I discount dreams? Can I name dreaming a method of data collection and mine my extra-consciousness? Since my study examines my own subjectivity, which has always already been at least partially produced by dreams, it seems appropriate and even necessary to adopt the view that dreaming is a process of inquiry (see Durek, 1989; Mullen, 1994).[6]

A confrontation with dream data occurred as the deadline for beginning to write the representation of my research slipped farther into the past. I was deeply troubled by the charge to produce a text with an identifiable origin and a proper closure, since I knew there was no beginning or end of my project. I could not envision a text that reflected coherency, unity, equilibrium, and linearity, and I began to dream and dream—the same dream. Finally, I decided to begin by writing that dream, to display it but not to analyze it. The following is a portion of that dream data, which are supplementarity, excess, and overflow:

> I am uneasy about beginning. The Beginning promises the End, with the evidentiary warrant strategically propping up the weighty, tidy essay in the middle. I am suspicious of straight lines.
>
> Dissertations are about backgrounds, problems, positionings, literature reviews, methodologies, validities, conclusions, and even implications, for Heaven's sake— all constituting a carefully staged academic *fictio*, a construction approved by the authorities, a rite of passage into citationality, a normalizing function of the gaze of the institution. I would rather speak for a time about the book I wanted to write when I returned to Ohio after I interviewed all those southern women and studied their place but didn't because I had to save my energies for this overcoded dissertation. That book is lost forever. I cannot speak of it.
>
> But I dream smidgens of it in the early dark interiority of winter mornings. I see my old and new friends—my participants, my subjects—posed in their exquisite satin wedding gowns, smiling around the years at their daughters who smile back at them wearing the same gowns as they pose regally in pictures hung side-by-side on living room walls. I eavesdrop on the conversations between the lovely young women of the wedding photographs who tell each other stories of their lovers, who praise each other's children, who cross their ankles properly as they sit in the Sunday School circle of chairs, who stand beside each other in their good suits and sing the Clubwoman's Song at every Woman's Club meeting, who hold their sick husbands' hands as they die, who wear widows' weeds for a time and then are reborn into selves that are a bit shaky, more careful, and increasingly fragile and strong and even more lovely. The bones of their faces have sucked in time and exude it in whispers through delicately fragile skin. They say "I think," "I suppose," and "I guess," more often now. They qualify their new-found knowledge for your sake.

. . . This story never begins but has always been, and I slip into it over and over again in different places, and it is as if I too have always been there. As a dream . . . I listen eagerly for the snag, the loose thread in the conversation, that I can grab hold of and use for entry. But their southern voices are as fluid and vertiginous as time. I hear them laughing delightedly at some old story whose moral will answer my main research question, and I can't quite make it out. In my dream I begin to understand that I will never hear that answer, that I will only hear a phrase, a syllable, the beginning of a tune. That is all I can know.

That is why these enforced Beginnings leading to Ends give me the willies, the heebie jeebies, and make my head hurt with plot promises I don't particularly care to keep. I am pretty jumpy about all this orderliness. Do you understand?

(Lordy, Lord. Was that my dream or someone else's?)

My dreams, then, added a layer of complexity to my study, foregrounded problems I encountered, and reconstructed and reproduced data in representations that helped me think about data differently. Dreams refuse closure; they keep interpretation in play. I slipped into that dream world night after winter night, often desperate for meaning that eluded me, and sometimes for refuge from the demand for clarity. I talked with many of my participants in my dreams, and I interviewed one woman repeatedly. And I confess that I wonder sometimes about the dreams I have forgotten and fear that many important data are still unintelligible. Even though they were never officially accounted for, the dreams remembered and those deferred linger in some dislocated space of my text, producing dissonance, alterity, and confusion. My dreams enabled and legitimized a complexity of meaning that science prohibits.

Sensual Data

I believe that a third kind of data, sensual data, also became significant in my study and was produced by the very physical act of having lived in the community I studied when I was a child and a young woman. Ann Game (1991) writes about "living in a place that refuses the objectifying gaze; and what cannot be seen cannot be spoken either" (pp. 183–184). Jill Ker Conway (1989) writes, "It took a visit to England for me to understand how the Australian landscape actually formed the ground of my consciousness, shaped what I saw, and influenced the way a scene was organized in my mental imagery" (p. 198). If our understanding of the world has been and is influenced by the earth itself, then my question is whether we can ignore those effects on our bodies and, in turn, on our mental mappings? I don't believe we should, yet how do we account for the sensual effects of our responses, for example, to the soft rolling fertility of the stream-laden Piedmont, to a field of tobacco turning golden in hot September afternoons, to the sharp and musty scent of pines and azaleas growing in shady red clay, to a fitting angle of the sun to which our bodies happily turn, to the rhythm of southern September days so very different from the same days in Yankee country, to a bone-deep attachment to one landscape in particular, a "sweet spot" (Hiss, 1990, p. xiii), which is the literal ground of our knowing? Our bodies' peculiar angles of repose have much to do with what and how we know, and the knowing that is mapped beyond the mind-body trap produces lines of flight that remain uncoded.

A whole body of literature about *place attachment* is being researched and theorized (see, for example, Altman and Low, 1992; Blunt & Rose, 1994; Hiss, 1990; Massey, 1994), and perhaps we need to think about our physical as well as our theoretical grounding in our research projects. How are these physical and theoretical sites of knowing related and what are the effects of those relations? A researcher who studies her own growing-up place, as I did, may find that sexual data have long since mapped and fashioned in a subtle way her consciousness and extra-consciousness. Such sensual data add folds of situated richness that may only be accessible through something like "Walter Benjamin's attempts at 'revelation' or recovery of meanings sedimented in layers of language" (Fischer, 1986, pp. 194–195). I have only just begun to think about the sensual data that were always already present in my own study and now am curious about what their foregrounding might enable in others. It appears to me that there is much work to be done on the physicality of theorizing.

Folding and Refolding: The Irruption of Response Data

My understanding of emotional data, dream data, and sensual data seems to have emerged from a close analysis of barely intelligible transgressive data produced by my own subjectivity, and yet I hardly ever worked in isolation during my study. I was haunted by Spivak's (1993) warning that "what I cannot imagine stands guard over everything I must/can do, think, live" (p. 22). Research is so hard, and I knew I needed other people to help me think, since I feared I would commit some horrible and unforgivable blunder, disgrace myself in my own hometown, embarrass my mother who still lives there, and do irrevocable damage to the women I had grown to admire and love. If we believe that personal experience is a shaky basis for epistemology (Fuss, 1989, p. 17) and if we are increasingly suspicious of the "lone scholar" approach to knowledge construction (Hood, 1985), then perhaps we are obliged to bring the outside into our research projects. I deliberately sought the Other, many different others, at every stage of the research process, knowing that my very limited, partial, and situated position in the world was both productive and dangerous.

Spivak (1993) writes about the importance of breaking apart the investigator/audience binary by inviting the audience to be a coinvestigator (p. 22). I found that working in the fold disperses that self/other binary into a continuous tacking movement that finds no rest in a pause that is either self or other. As I positioned myself as a fold of the outside, I was able to foreground and legitimize my need for what I have begun to call *response data*.

Traditional qualitative methodology does provide a function for the Other in the research process through activities such as peer debriefing and member checks (see Lincoln & Guba, 1985, for descriptions). The purpose of both of these activities has been to lend credibility to qualitative research projects by bringing the outside—the outside chiefly in the form of members and peers—into the process, but only to a limited extent. The notion that there is some correct interpretation out there that the researcher can reproduce and that members and peers can recognize and verify, however, is suspect in postpositivist research.[7] Yet our members and peers do provide us with data that are often critical and that may even prompt us to significantly reconstruct our interpretation as we proceed. These data surely influence the production of knowledge, yet we hardly ever acknowledge them. How might our sense of inquiry shift if we began to focus on mapping responses and examining how they enable our mapping of the world?[8]

In any case, each researcher and each project will produce different possibilities for response and different kinds of response data. In my own study, I have collected response data from an official peer debriefer,[9] my dissertation committee members, members of writing groups at two different universities, my mentor, my mother, my aunt, my cousin, friends who are not academics, my informant who is a dear friend and almost-participant, members of seminar audiences, members of several conference presentation audiences, participants, nonparticipants who live in the community I studied who could have been participants, the women of my dreams, the authors I read whose texts respond to my questions, journal editors, journal referees, and so on. All these others move me out of the self-evidence of my work and into its absences, and give me the gift of different language and practice with which to trouble my commonsense understanding of the world. They help me move toward the unthought. I hope that the naming of this practice, the collection of response data, will be an incitement to discourse and that other researchers will address this disruptive, unplanned, uncontrollable, yet fruitful fold in their work so that we can begin to collect data about response data and study the transgressions they enable.

Unfolding into Ethics: The Responsible Audience

As I explained in the introduction to this essay, ethics is not abandoned in poststructural critiques but rather demands a specific reinscription. The simple task of troubling one signifier, data, has foregrounded an ethical relation—the relation between the researcher and those who provide response data—that generally escapes scrutiny. We certainly cannot define ethical practices for those outside the academy who provide us with response data. However, it seems to me that those of us in academe who are much concerned, as we should be, about the ethical practices of the academic researcher must begin to take a hard look at the ethical practices of the academic respondent. Such attention is critical, since researchers may be encouraged by their colleagues, particularly by respondents in positions of power, to revise methodological practices and to reconstruct texts in ways that do not reflect either their theoretical or ethical positions and, even more important, in ways that do not honor their participants.

I am thinking in particular about the debate that has been engaged around the issue of clarity in the representation of research. Those who find the differences enabled by a poststructural concern with language confusing and sometimes difficult to understand demand clarity. On the other hand, those who find difference hopeful and productive continue to trouble language. To this point, it appears that the demand for clarity has won out. However, an emerging body of literature (Britzman, 1995; Elam, 1994; hooks, 1990; Lather, 1996; Spivak cited in Danius & Jonsson, 1991/1993; Trinh, 1989) addresses the politics and ethics of clarity and accessibility. It should not be surprising that such a reaction formation has emerged in response to those who reject in the name of Ethics a complexity that refuses to simplify issues that many, in the name of ethics, believe should remain complex.

Those who try to problematize the language of humanism and its demand for instant and transparent understanding believe that the language of the *logos* has produced very real structures in the world that have been terribly brutal to many people. Posthumanists are thus suspicious of language; they tend to use it differently; and their work may not, on first reading, seem so clear. The problem, of course, is that poststructural discourses continue to use the words of humanism but to use them differently. For instance, even though I will continue to use the word *data,* its meaning has forever shifted for me and will continue to shift as I prod and poke at this foundational signifier on which knowledge rests. I will, in the future, undoubtedly write sentences using *data* that may not be too clear.

However, there is no going back to a time before poststructuralism when language was clear and transparent and innocent. As the breakdown of humanist language and practice accelerates, we will encounter difference at every turn: different theories that frame research, different research methodologies, and different representations of research. And these differences will surely require different language, experimental writing (Richardson, 1994), and perhaps "messy texts" (Marcus, 1994) that may be hard to understand but that require "a reading that is responsible to the text" (Spivak, 1994, p. 27). Lather (1996) writes that "reading without understanding is required if we are to go beyond the imaginary 'real' of history" and that, for some, "not being understood is an ethical imperative" (p. 528). There is much to consider in this debate, but the point is that neither a deliberate obfuscation nor the desire for clarity and accessibility is innocent; both are dangerous. As ethical readers of research and as ethical producers of response data, we might consider why we read and respond in the ways we do. This process is about theorizing our own lives, examining the frames with which we read the world, and moving toward an ongoing validity of response.

The ethics of those in the response position would seem to be about risking an engagement with the difference of the other, acknowledging the counterargument, and being open to the theory that we resist (Spivak, 1994). This positioning is about "moving from the critical phase into a more affirmative phase, into areas from where agencies of critique can come" (Spivak, cited in Danius & Jonsson, 1991/1993, p. 27). A charged engagement with alterity in the response relation then becomes a pedagogical and ethical moment of enormous importance in educational research. Teaching and learning become crucial in this place where language and theories ricochet and have the power to inscribe and reinscribe lives.

How can we offer responsible response to other researchers and their participants? I do not believe that an ethics of response can be defined for all situations. Rather, I suggest that ethics is invented within each relation as researcher and respondent negotiate sense-making by foregrounding their theoretical frameworks, by risking confusion, by determining to read harder when the text begins to seem inaccessible, and by being willing to attend to the absences in their own work that are made intelligible by the difference of the other.

In conclusion, I must admit that my troubles with language, in this case with the signifier *data*, have produced lines of flight I would never have imagined. Emotional data, dream data, and sensual data seem fairly tame compared with response data whose sprawling tendrils creep into and dehisce the staged unity of every research project. Troubling language can be big trouble, and I ask myself bell hooks' (1989) question, "do we have to go that deep?" (p. 1). Yet the charge to redescribe the world word by word is an endless if joyful task and, when weary and discouraged, I remember Spivak's (1993) reminder that even when "nothing seems displaced or cracked, what 'really happens' remains radically uncertain" (p. 145). To play in the possibilities of that space outside language that is opened up when words fall apart is my desire. Many such local, strategic subversions of self-evidence will be required if we are to reinvent education in a postmodern world.

Acknowledgments

I am very grateful for the thoughtful response data provided me on earlier drafts of this paper by Donna Alverman, Patti Lather, and the members of my writing group: Eurydice Bauer, Fenice Boyd, Michelle Commeyras, and Peg Graham.

Notes

1. Deleuze and Guattari (1980/1987) employ the image of the rhizome to describe a kind of adventitious multiplicity that is not rooted as are the roots of trees but which produces stems and filaments, like crabgrass, that penetrate what *is* rooted and put it to "strange new uses" (p. 15).

2. Gayatri Spivak (1974) explains in her "Preface" to Jacques Derrida's (1967/1974) *Of Grammatology* that there are some signifiers, such as truth, that we seem unable to do without. However, if we are to think differently, we must question the received meaning of such signifiers. Thus, we may choose to write *sous rature*, which Spivak (1974) translates as "'under erasure.' This is to write a word, cross it out, and then print both word and deletion. (Since the word is inaccurate, it is crossed out. Since it is necessary, it remains legible.)" (p. xiv). This task of troubling taken-for-granted signifiers is well under way with the work of other researchers with a poststructural bent, such as Patti Lather (1986, 1993, 1995b) and her work on validity and Jim Scheurich (1995) and his work on interviewing.

3. Portions of this paper were presented at the *Journal of Curriculum Theorizing* Conference in Monteagle, Tennessee, in September 1995, and at the American Educational Research Association Annual Meeting in New York City, New York, in April 1996.

4. Deleuze and Guattari (1980/1987) explain that rhizomes (see Note 1) have no beginnings or ends but are always in the middle. Beginnings and ends imply a linear movement, whereas working in the middle is about "coming and going rather than starting and finishing" (p. 25). They explain that "the middle is by no means an average; on the contrary, it is where things pick up speed. . . . *Between* things does not designate a localizable relation going from one thing to the other and back again, but a perpendicular direction, a transversal movement that sweeps one *and* the other away, a stream without a beginning or end that undermines its banks and picks up speed in the middle" (Deleuze and Guattari, 1980/1987, p. 25).

5. Patti Lather (1995b) describes rhizomatic validity as one that "unsettles from within," that "supplements and exceeds the stable and the permanent," that "works against constraints of authority via relay, multiple openings, networks, complexities of problematics," and "puts conventional discursive procedures under erasure" (p. 55). Lather's rhizomatic validity is derived from Deleuze and Guattari's (1980/1987) concept, the rhizome, whose "multiplicity cannot be overcoded" (p. 9). See Note 1.

6. Thanks to Noel Gough, who listened attentively to a version of this essay at the *Journal of Curriculum Theorizing* Conference in Monteagle, Tennessee, in September 1995, and generously pointed me to the work on dreams by Carol Mullen (1994).

7. Thanks to Laurel Richardson for helping me understand early on that member checking is about collecting more data rather than verifying that an interpretation is true. Our discussions in her class on qualitative methodology informed by poststructural critiques prompted me to think about all the other data we collect from other people during the course of our projects and to wonder how we account for it.

8. Patti Lather posed this question to me in an e-mail conversation (January 28, 1996) about response data.

9. Kate McCoy continues to be my chief peer debriefer and to model ethical response. Kate provided me with thoughtful response data about this paper that extends my research project as well as my relationship with my participants and, as always, provides me with provocative possibilities for self-formation.

References

Altman, I., & Low, S. M. (Eds.). (1992). *Place attachment*. New York: Plenum Press.

Badiou, A. (1994). *Gilles Deleuze. The fold: Leibniz and the baroque*. In C. V. Boundas & D. Olkowski (Eds.), *Gilles Deleuze and the theater of philosophy* (pp. 51–69). New York: Routledge.

Belsey, C. (1993). Towards cultural history. In J. Natoli & L. Hutcheon (Eds.), *A postmodern reader* (pp. 551–567). Albany, NY: State University of New York Press. (Reprinted from *Textual Practice*, 1989, *3*, 159–172).

Benjamin, W. (1968). Theses on the philosophy of history (H. Zohn, Trans.). In H. Arendt (Ed.), *Illuminations* (pp. 253–264). New York: Shocken Books. (Original work published 1950)

Benjamin, W. (1977). *The origin of German tragic drama* (J. Osborne, Trans.). New York: Verso. (Original work published 1963)

Bhabha, H. K. (1994). *The location of culture.* New York: Routledge.

Blunt, A., & Rose, G. (Eds.). (1994). *Writing women and space: Colonial and post-colonial geographies.* New York: Guilford Press.

Boundas, C. V. (1994). Deleuze: serialization and subject-formation. In C. V. Boundas & D. Olkowski (Eds.), *Gilles Deleuze and the theater of philosophy* (pp. 99–116). New York: Routledge.

Britzman, D. P. (1995). "The question of belief": Writing poststructural ethnography. *International Journal of Qualitative Studies in Education, 8,* 229–238.

Butler, J. (1992). Contingent foundations: Feminism and the question of "postmodernism." In J. Butler & J. W. Scott (Eds.), *Feminists theorize the political* (pp. 3–21). New York: Routledge.

Butler, J. (1993). Poststructuralism and postmarxism. *Diacritics, 23,* 3–11.

Butler, J. (1995). For a careful reading. In L. Nicholson (Ed.), *Feminist contentions: A philosophical exchange* (pp. 127–143). New York: Routledge.

Caputo, J. (1993). *Against ethics: Contributions to a poetics of obligation with constant reference to deconstruction.* Bloomington, IN: Indiana University Press.

Conway, J. K. (1989). *The road from Coorain.* New York: Vintage Books.

Danius, S., & Jonsson, S. (1993). [Interview with Gayatri Spivak]. *boundary 2, 2, 29,* 24–50. (Interview conducted 1991)

Deleuze, G. (1983). *Nietzsche and philosophy* (H. Tomlinson, Trans.). New York: Columbia University Press. (Original work published 1962)

Deleuze, G. (1988). *Foucault* (S. Hand, Trans.). Minneapolis, MN: University of Minnesota Press. (Original work published 1986)

Deleuze, G. (1993). *The fold: Leibniz and the baroque* (T. Conley, Trans.). Minneapolis, MN: University of Minnesota Press. (Original work published 1988)

Deleuze, G., & Guattari, F. (1987). Introduction: rhizome. In *A thousand plateaus: Capitalism and schizophrenia* (B. Massumi, Trans.) (pp. 3–25). Minneapolis, MN: University of Minnesota Press. (Original work published 1980)

Deleuze, G., & Parnet, C. (1987). *Dialogues.* (H. Tomlinson & B. Habberjam, Trans.). New York: Columbia University Press. (Original work published 1977)

Derrida, J. (1974). *Of grammatology.* (G. Spivak, Trans.). Baltimore: Johns Hopkins University Press. (Original work published 1967)

Durek, J. (1989). *Circle of stones: Woman's journey to herself.* San Diego: LuraMedia.

Elam, D. (1994). *Feminism and deconstruction: Ms. en abyme.* New York: Routledge.

Fay, B. (1987). *Critical social science: Liberation and its limits.* Ithaca: Cornell University Press.

Fischer, M.M.J. (1986). Ethnicity and post-modern arts of memory. In J. Clifford & G. E. Marcus (Eds.), *Writing culture: The poetics and politics of ethnography* (pp. 194–233). Berkeley, CA: University of California Press.

Flax, J. (1990). *Thinking fragments: Psychoanalysis, feminism, and postmodernism in the contemporary West.* Berkeley, CA: University of California Press.

Foucault, M. (1977). Theatrum philosophicum. In D. F. Bouchard (Ed.) (D. F. Bouchard & S. Simon, Trans.), *Language, counter-memory, practice: Selected essays and interviews* (pp. 165–196). Ithaca: Cornell University Press. (Reprinted from *Critique*, 1970, *282*, 885–908)

Foucault, M. (1980). *Power/knowledge: Selected interviews and other writings, 1972–1977*. (C. Gordon, Ed.). (C. Gordon, L. Marshall, J. Mepham, K. Soper, Trans.). New York: Pantheon Books.

Foucault, M. (1984). On the genealogy of ethics: An overview of work in progress. In P. Rabinow (Ed.), *The Foucault reader* (pp. 340–372). New York: Pantheon Books.

Foucault, M. (1986a). *History of sexuality, Volume 2: The care of the self.* (R. Hurley, Trans.). New York: Vintage Books. (Original work published 1984)

Foucault, M. (1986b). Of other spaces. (J. Miskowiec, Trans.). *Diacritics, 16*, 22–27. (Reprinted from *Architecture–Movement–Continuité*, 1984, March, no page numbers)

Fuss, D. (1989). *Essentially speaking: Feminism, nature and difference.* New York: Routledge.

Game, A. (1991). *Undoing the social: Towards a deconstructive sociology.* Toronto: University of Toronto Press.

Geertz, C. (1973). Thick description: Toward an interpretive theory of culture. In *The interpretation of culture* (pp. 3–30). New York: Basic Books.

Hiss, T. (1990). *The experience of place.* New York: Alfred A. Knopf.

Hood, J. C. (1985). The lone scholar myth. In M. F. Fox (Ed.), *Scholarly writing and publishing: Issues, problems and solutions* (pp. 111–125). Boulder, CO: Westview Press.

hooks, b. (1989). *Talking back: Thinking feminist, thinking black.* Boston: South End Press.

hooks, b. (1990). *Yearning: Race, gender, and cultural politics.* Boston: South End Press.

Hutnyk, S., McQuire, S., & Papastergiadis, N. (1990). Strategy, identity, writing. [Interview with G. C. Spivak]. In S. Harasym (Ed.), *The post-colonial critic: Interviews, strategies, dialogues* (pp. 35–49). New York: Routledge. (Interview conducted 1986) (Reprinted from Melbourne *Journal of Politics*, 1986/87, *18*)

Kleinman, S., & Copp, M. A. (1993). *Emotions and fieldwork.* Newbury Park, CA: Sage.

Kondo, D. (1990). *Crafting selves: Power, gender, and discourses of identity in a Japanese workplace.* Chicago: University of Chicago Press.

Lakoff, G., & Johnson, M. (1980). *Metaphors we live by.* Chicago: University of Chicago Press.

Lather, P. (1986). Issues of validity in openly ideological research: Between a rock and a soft place. *Interchange, 17*, 63–84.

Lather, P. (1993). Fertile obsession: Validity after poststructuralism. *The Sociological Quarterly, 34*, 673–693.

Lather, P. (1995a, October). *Naked methodology: Researching the lives of women with HIV/AIDS.* Paper presented at the Revisioning Women, Health and Healing: Feminist, Cultural and Technoscience Studies Perspectives Conference, San Francisco, CA.

Lather, P. (1995b). The validity of angels: Interpretive and textual strategies in researching the lives of women with HIV/AIDS. *Qualitative Inquiry, 9*, 41–68.

Lather, P. (1996). Troubling clarity: The politics of accessible language. *Harvard Education Review, 66,* 525–545.

Lincoln, Y. S., & Guba, E. G. (1985). *Naturalistic inquiry.* Newbury Park: Sage.

Marcus, G. E. (1994). What comes (just) after "post"?: The case of ethnography. In N. K. Denzin & Y. S. Lincoln (Eds.), *Handbook of qualitative research* (pp. 563–574). Thousand Oaks, CA: Sage.

Martin, R. (1988). Truth, power, self: An interview with Michel Foucault, October 25, 1982. In L. H. Martin, H. Gutman, & P. H. Hutton (Eds.), *Technologies of the self: a seminar with Michel Foucault* (pp. 7–15). Amherst, MA: University of Massachusetts Press.

Massey, D. (1994). *Space, place, and gender.* Minneapolis, MN: University of Minnesota Press.

Mullen, C. (1994). A narrative exploration of the self I dream. *Journal of Curriculum Studies, 26,* 253–263.

Rajchman, J. (1985). *Michel Foucault: The freedom of philosophy.* New York: Columbia University Press.

Richardson, L. (1994). Writing: A method of inquiry. In N. K. Denzin & Y. S. Lincoln (Eds.), *Handbook of qualitative research* (pp. 516–529). Thousand Oaks, CA: Sage.

Rooney, E. (1989). In a word: *Interview.* [Interview with G. C. Spivak]. *Differences: A journal of feminist cultural studies, 1,* 124–156.

Rorty, R. (1986). Foucault and epistemology. In D. C. Hoy (Ed.), *Foucault: A critical reader* (pp. 41–49). Cambridge, MA: Basil Blackwell.

Scheurich, J. J. (1995). A postmodernist critique of research interviewing. *International Journal of Qualitative Studies in Education, 8*(3), 239–252.

Spivak, G. C. (1974). Translator's preface. In J. Derrida, *Of grammatology* (G. Spivak, Trans.) (pp. ix–lxxxvii). Baltimore: Johns Hopkins University Press.

Spivak, G. C. (1992). Acting bits/identity talk. *Critical Inquiry, 18,* 770–803.

Spivak, G. C. (1993). *Outside in the teaching machine.* New York: Routledge.

Spivak, G. C. (1994). Responsibility. *boundary 2, 21,* 19–64.

St. Pierre, E. A. (1995). *Arts of existence: The construction of subjectivity in older, white southern women.* Unpublished doctoral dissertation, Ohio State University, Columbus, OH.

Trinh, M. T. (1989). *Women, native, other: Writing postcoloniality and feminism.* Bloomington, IN: Indiana University Press.

Van Maanen, J. (1988). *Tales of the field: On writing ethnography.* Chicago: University of Chicago Press.

Van Maanen, J., Manning, P. K., & Miller, M. L. (Eds.). (1993). Editors' introduction. In S. Kleinman & M. A. Copp, *Emotions and fieldwork* (pp. vii–viii). Newbury Park, CA: Sage.

West, C. (Speaker). (1995). *Race matters* (Lecture, February 24). Columbus, OH: Ohio State University.

Zizek, S. (1991). *Looking awry: An introduction to Jacques Lacan through popular culture.* Cambridge, MA: MIT Press.

Troubling the Categories of Qualitative Inquiry

Elizabeth A. St. Pierre
The University of Georgia, Athens

"Methodology in the Fold and the Irruption of Transgressive Data" illustrates how deconstruction can be used in a poststructural qualitative research project. Deconstruction is not only a poststructural method of analysis but also, in the larger sense, a philosophy that is generally attributed to Jacques Derrida (1974) by way of, at least, Heidegger and Nietzsche. It is a complex system of thought with a rich, almost thirty-year history that has been interpreted and used differently by scholars in a variety of disciplines who have found its possibilities for producing different knowledge and producing knowledge differently both seductive and useful.

Deconstruction allows a scholar/researcher to look awry at what seems commonsensical and normal. It is often used to disrupt the violent binaries that structure the language and practice of humanism that have very real, material effects on people's everyday lives. In simple terms, deconstruction operates to locate the violent hierarchy of the binary opposition (for example, male/female, Black/White, objective/subjective), to overthrow or reverse the hierarchy (to fight violence with violence), and then to displace the reversal, thus making room for "the irruptive emergence of a new concept, a concept which no longer allows itself to be understood in terms of the previous regime" (Derrida, cited in Spivak, 1974, p. lxxvii). In fact, what happens in deconstruction is a "general displacement of the system" (Derrida, 1971/1982, p. 329), a system that is never just linguistic but also nondiscursive and material.

The final point made in the preceding paragraph is very important because, with deconstruction, one does indeed move into a different discourse, a different way of doing and thinking that does not operate within humanist discourse, the ordered system of statements with its own particular rationality that permeates so thoroughly not only qualitative inquiry but Western thought in general

417

that it is almost invisible. Foucault (1971/1972) explains, however, in his archaeological analysis, another poststructural method, that each domain of knowledge is structured by certain assumptions that allow certain statements and not others to be made. Thus, the work of deconstruction is to make visible the underlying structures of whatever domain we are caught up in so that we can examine the kind of statements that are possible (and not possible), where those statements go, and what they do there. This involves a commitment "persistently to critique a structure that one cannot not (wish to) inhabit" (Spivak, 1993, p. 284).

Now deconstruction is not negative or apolitical as some think. Rather, it is affirmative in that it insists that we say "yes" to that which interrupts our projects—that we say "yes" to the political, for example, that interrupts theory. Deconstruction insists that we not gloss the incongruous, the paradoxical, the inconsistent, or the ambiguous but rather that we seek out such interruptions and focus on the breakdowns, the absences, the hidden internal contradictions, and the warring forces of signification that are operating in whatever text (I am using *text* here in the large sense) within which we are working.

In addition to troubling the binaries that lock us into certain ways of thinking and doing, deconstruction helps us critique "something that is extremely useful, something without which we can do nothing . . . and to take it with the utmost seriousness, with literal seriousness, so that it transforms itself" (Spivak, 1989, p. 129). In order to accomplish this task, deconstruction enables us to put certain concepts that are impossible yet necessary, concepts such as *truth* and *justice,* under erasure or *sous rature.* This means that we retain the concept (because it is necessary) even as we trouble it (because it is impossible) and open it up to reinscription. This is exactly what I did in the paper, "Methodology in the Fold." I took very seriously a very ordinary concept of qualitative inquiry, *data,* a concept that we certainly cannot do without, and opened it up to different possibilities. As a result, I will never again be able to think of *data* in the same way. Indeed, I am no longer sure I know what *data* "means," nor does what it "means" assume the importance it once did.

When I used deconstruction to think about methodology in my research project, when I moved into poststructural discourses—and Jane Flax (1990) writes that "postmodern discourses are all deconstructive in that they seek to distance us from and make us skeptical about beliefs concerning truth, knowledge, power, the self, and language that are often taken for granted within and serve as legitimation for contemporary Western culture" (p. 41)—when I made this shift, not only did the concepts of qualitative inquiry begin to fall apart, the entire structure fell apart. The foundations crumbled, and I had to proceed by the seat of my pants to rethink research each step of the way. But this is the task of poststructural qualitative researchers—to persistently critique received concepts and practices, including whatever new concepts emerge in the reinscription.

How do we begin this task? As Derrida (1967/1974) explains, we begin to practice deconstruction, "*Wherever we are*" (p. 162), in the middle of whatever project we are working on, in the middle of whatever seems so strange and squirrelly that we avoid talking about it with someone, in the spaces where the old concepts break down and simply aren't adequate to the task at hand. Clearly, we cannot ignore or give up the language and concepts of qualitative inquiry, concepts such as *data,* the *field, validity, interviewing.* We can, however, acknowledge that they have limits, since they have been defined in a certain way within a certain discourse and that they will necessarily be reinscribed differently within a different discourse.

What is important here is that we cannot ignore the link between epistemology and methodology. These concepts *cannot* have the same meaning or function in the same way in a poststructural research project as they do in a positivist or interpretivist or critical project. Indeed, in poststructuralism, we are less concerned with essentializing questions about what concepts *mean* than about how their meanings have come to be "true" and how that truth operates to produce the world, ourselves, and qualitative inquiry in a certain way.

The work of troubling various concepts of qualitative inquiry is well under way. Patti Lather (1993), for instance, has taken on *validity* with a vengeance; James Scheurich (1993) has taken on *interviewing*; and I have critiqued not only *data* but the *field* (St. Pierre, 1997). Poststructuralism is causing quite a stir in qualitative educational research, perhaps because it is so useful in "transforming conditions of impossibility into possibility" (Spivak, 1993, p. 5). If it continues to be taken up and used at the rate it has during the last ten years, qualitative inquiry may soon be unintelligible to itself.

References

Derrida, J. (1974). *Of grammatology* (G. C. Spivak, Trans.). Baltimore: Johns Hopkins University Press. (Original work published 1967)

Derrida, J. (1982). Signature, event, context. In *Margins of Philosophy* (A. Bass, Trans.) (pp. 307–330). Chicago: University of Chicago Press. (Original work published 1971)

Flax, J. (1990). Postmodernism and gender relations in feminist theory. In L. J. Nicholson (Ed.), *Feminism/Postmodernism* (pp. 39–62). New York: Routledge.

Foucault, M. (1972). *The archaeology of knowledge and the discourse on language* (A.M.S. Smith, Trans.). New York: Pantheon Books. (Original work published 1971)

Lather, P. (1993). Fertile obsession: Validity after poststructuralism. *Sociological Quarterly, 34*(4), 673–693.

Scheurich, J. J. (1993). The masks of validity: A deconstructive investigation. *International Journal of Qualitative Studies in Education, 9*(11), 49–60.

Spivak, G. C. (1974). Translator's preface. In J. Derrida, *Of Grammatology* (G. C. Spivak, Trans.) (pp. ix-xc). Baltimore: Johns Hopkins University Press.

Spivak, G. C. (1989). In a word: Interview. (E. Rooney, Interviewer). *Differences 1*(2), 124–156.

Spivak, G. C. (1993). *Outside in the teaching machine.* New York: Routledge.

St. Pierre, E. A. (1997). Nomadic inquiry in the smooth spaces of the field: A preface. *International Journal of Qualitative Studies in Education, 10*(3), 363–383.

19

Reflections on
Doing Qualitative Research

Sharan B. Merriam

The authors of the sixteen examples of qualitative research presented in this workbook were all asked to reflect upon some aspect of their experience doing this type of research. My guidelines to them were quite open-ended. They were invited to comment on *any* aspect of their experience conducting the research that interested them, emphasizing methodological issues in particular. And they did just that, sharing with us their insights, their "lessons learned," and their advice. Each reflection is unique and personal, but at the same time there is some commonality in their experiences and their advice to the rest of us. So, using their reflections as the database, and proceeding in good "qualitative" fashion, I have come up with the following general points about doing qualitative research.

First, all speak directly to, or reflect in their writing, a *genuine interest* in and engagement with the topic of their research. Several spoke of their "passionate" interest and commitment to the research. Tisdell found her research study on women's spirituality "a joy," one that "emerged out of my own passion and interests" and "concern for equity issues." Hébert drove two hundred miles roundtrip to his research site each day. Enomoto and Bair, who studied Arab immigrant children, revealed that "personal interest" directed their inquiry, as one is a third-generation Asian American and one is a recent immigrant from India. Sandlin wrote, "in order to do [critical] research you have to take a strong stand on issues, exposing injustices and naming them for what they are." Similarly, St. Pierre comments that doing research from a postmodern stance requires that we become committed "to practice deconstruction . . . in the middle of whatever project we are working on, in the middle of whatever seems so strange and squirrelly that we avoid talking about it with someone, in the spaces where the old concepts break down and simply aren't adequate to the task at hand." Investigating a topic that really engages you provides the motivation for getting you through the process. As Worthen notes of his experience, "I found a topic of interest that I had some personal investment in (I had experienced supervision, both good and bad), which sustained my curiosity during what turned out to be a long and challenging process." At times the process is all-consuming; without genuine interest to sustain you, it might be too easy to abandon the project in those intense moments.

Expect to learn about yourself is a second maxim I would draw from these reflections. The researcher as the primary instrument of data collection and analysis is a familiar characteristic of qualitative research. But knowing this at some abstract level is different from what happens in the actual experience of collecting and analyzing data. Tisdell, Krenske, Jones, Johnson-Bailey, Pillow and I all point out that one's positionality vis-à-vis the participants has both insider and outsider dimensions. Through reflecting on the process, we as researchers learn our strengths and weaknesses, our points of connection, and the boundaries of connecting with our participants. Sandlin remarks on the tension she experienced in doing critical research—research that requires a confrontational stance—when her Southern upbringing has taught her "to be polite and non-confrontational." Wolff goes a step further, commenting that the entire process in phenomenological research is itself "an embodied process." It is the "lived experience not only of the research participants but also that of the researcher." He gives an example of knowing when to end data gathering and begin analysis. The answer lies "inside the one who embodies the research process"—you "recognize" the moment, rather than making a rational decision.

There is yet another dimension to learning about yourself in qualitative research, and that is you are equally likely to be changed by the process. Brott's grounded theory study of counselor identity changed her "in many ways," including discovering her "creative potential as a researcher." In addition, the theory she came up with has come to be "a reflection of me and of who I have become as a professional." Pillow confides that in revisiting her study she is "a bit shaken . . . to find how much of my life history is also in these research documents." Burbules, whose article was published the longest ago of any in the collection, was surprised to find "looking at it [the article] again . . . opened unexpected memories and pleasures. For one thing, I saw in it glimmerings of ideas that I only returned to years later (thinking that I was thinking them for the first time)." Qualitative research cannot help but to have an impact on the researcher in often unanticipated ways.

A third lesson in these reflections is that *there is no substitute for experience*; that is, qualitative research cannot be learned from reading a book on the topic, talking to others, or even from reading the studies presented in this collection. The best we can get from methodology books and examples of qualitative studies are some suggestions or guidelines about how to proceed and what issues and concerns might arise in the process. Correll recalls that these guidelines helped her have the confidence to initiate her study, but that "it quickly became apparent . . . that I had to be flexible in applying the guidelines to my study." Mistakes will be made; some things will happen that we cannot anticipate, other things will work out serendipitously in spite of ourselves. It involves long periods of uncertainty. Brott equates the process to a long, hard journey with many challenges along the way. Wolff recognized that sharing concerns is part of the process, "and that some uncertainty as one proceeds through the phenomenological research process is healthy, and in fact an indication that one is experiencing the necessary ambiguities inherent in conducting qualitative research." Worthen recommends approaching the process with "a sense of humility," a theme underscored by Bloom, who writes that "maintaining humility means not taking ourselves or our research so seriously that we forget that those we research have other, more important things going on in their lives."

A major concern in all research is the validity, trustworthiness, or authenticity of the study. But like the process of data collection and analysis, the issues around rigor and trustworthiness are best understood once you become involved in the study. In qualitative research we learn how to deal with these issues through immersion in the process and through our actions and their unintended outcomes. For example, as part of her responsibility to her participants, Jones wrote each one a letter with an essay capturing the initial findings of the study. She recounts how "the response was overwhelming and unexpected. For almost every participant, reading the essay was an emotional experience. Several of them indicated that the essay was like a gift because it functioned as a mirror back to them . . . . to see themselves in print was like returning their story to them." For Jones, this response was an "authentic verification."

For Hébert and Krenske, authenticity had to do with their own role in the research process. Hébert "learned to be sensitive to the differences in my culture and the culture of Pine Grove by tailoring my personal appearance and research tools so they were more appropriate for this rural, impoverished setting." Krenske felt that to establish rapport within the Heavy Metal music subculture she had to immerse herself in the "music and media associated with HM" and adopt dress codes that allowed her to fit in with this community. However, she also recognizes the tradeoffs in terms of the type and quality of data collected as a result of her conformity to the situation. As a woman of color, Johnson-Bailey made a concerted effort not to disenfranchise her participants through the research process; indeed, she also asked "the participants to read, react, and approve the constructed narrative" of their educational experiences. When Tisdell uncovered the fact that she had misinterpreted an incident told to her by one of her participants, she became "far more vigilant about the importance of member checks," especially with those in her study most different from herself. Burbules, "troubled by the anticipated reader responses that 'this doesn't prove anything,'" came to terms with this concern by realizing that in interpretive research, "there will never be an independent confirmation or proof of such matters except that the interpretation speaks to people and opens up a process of reflection. No one should expect to 'prove' anything in matters of interpretation."

Thus, there is no substitute for actually engaging in a qualitative study, whether it be learning to collect better data through being authentic or having to handle the unanticipated encountered in the field. Correll captures this aspect of doing qualitative research by commenting that the most she can do is to make suggestions such as "stav[ing] off the tendency to draw conclusions prematurely and be[ing] flexible and adaptive." She summarizes, "Qualitative research realizes its potential when researchers immerse themselves in a setting and struggle to figure out the best way to understand it."

Finally, nearly everyone commented on *the value of other people* being brought into the research process. The inclusion of other people, hence other perspectives, is built into a formal research team, but "lone" researchers, as suggested by St. Pierre, can informally draw upon fellow students, friends, or colleagues for personal as well as technical support. And of course some feminist researchers and participatory action researchers involve participants as co-investigators or co-researchers. Reflections from the research teams of Merriam and Muhamad and Enomoto and Bair also suggest that the studies were definitely stronger and the process more enjoyable working as a team. Mazanah and I each brought different expertise to the study of older adulthood in Malaysia, and our respective insider/outsider statuses worked in combination to strengthen both data collection and analysis. Enomoto and Bair together interviewed and observed in the school and felt "the benefit of this strategy was that we were able to check what we were seeing and validate data collected. . . . We felt that collaborating in this way strengthened our investigation and facilitated the writing of the study. We also enjoyed the sharing and reflections that came from the investigation." They conclude with the comment that "our teaming together made for hours of enjoyable pondering about the meaning of our school observations."

Several mentioned the benefits of in-class or out-of-class support groups. Correll speaks of her experience as part of a student group working on qualitative research projects: "Not only did the group members provide me with suggestions and different insights, they also drew me out of the field for a time and allowed me to go back in with new eyes." Pillow suggests that after some data collection you form or join a writing group—"the structure, support, and companionship are vital." Others referred to advisors, mentors, even family members who helped the researchers to "think through" their experience.

In summary, all of these authors are telling us, first, that the nature of qualitative research is as much a social and psychological process as it is systematic inquiry. Because the process is a journey, if not a struggle, it is crucial to study a phenomenon that you are *really* curious about, that you care about, that you are passionate about. This interest will motivate and sustain you through the process. Second, the process will affect you; we learn a lot about ourselves as we design and carry out the study, write it up, and disseminate the results. Third, it is only in the doing of a qualitative study that we really learn what it means to be the primary instrument of data collection and analysis, how the design is really "emergent" and not predetermined, how questions of authenticity, validity, and reliability become dealt with, and how, as Bloom states, ethics underlies all of these concerns. Finally, it helps to have some companions along on the journey; other people not only strengthen a study but also provide the support to bring it to completion.

Name Index

Subject Index